Colonial Wrongs and Access to International Law

Morten Bergsmo, Wolfgang Kaleck and Kyaw Yin Hlaing (editors)

2020
Torkel Opsahl Academic EPublisher
Brussels

This and other publications in TOAEP's *Publication Series* may be openly accessed and downloaded through the web site http://www.toaep.org/, which uses Persistent URLs for all publications it makes available (such PURLs will not be changed). This publication was first published on 9 November 2020.

ISBNs: 978-82-8348-133-4 (print) and 978-82-8348-134-1 (e-book).

*Dedicated to those who will transmute
the legacies of colonial wrongs and slavery
into a wider, world-embracing solidarity and unity*

FOREWORD BY THE CO-EDITORS

This book is published during a year of unprecedented concern for our planet's forests. The fires in the Pacific rims of Australia and the United States are widely perceived as related to climate change. The fires in the Amazon are seen as reinforcing the root-causes of climate change. There are also alarming reports that remaining indigenous inhabitants in our Amazon rainforests are being placed under further existential pressure. Such pressure is not new. Indeed, extraction of valuable timber has been one of the forces motivating colonization, with subsequent mineral extraction through mining or agriculture. The photographs on the cover of this book remind us of the intense logging that occurred in Colonial Burma on the part of the Bombay Burmah Trading Corporation and other actors during British colonial rule. As you can see, the Corporation used elephants to bring logs to rivers for onward transport and export. The Corporation "owned over three-thousand elephants" in 1920 when the pictures were taken, which gives us an indication of the scale of teak extraction in Burma during colonialism.[1]

At the very end of this book, in the last paragraph of Chapter 18 ("Colonial Crime, Environmental Destruction and Indigenous Peoples: A Roadmap to Accountability and Protection"), Professor Joshua Castellino sets out an agenda to

> restore indigenous peoples to the centre of the critical fight for climate justice initially perpetrated by colonial rule that has left a lasting legacy of tort. Along the way, this lens, if adopted without bias, will also enable a review of the role of profiteers and their handmaidens in governance, including international lawyers currently venerated with respect, to the way that indigenous peoples often view them: as armed thieves who came in the dark, tricked their way to profit, used law to justify themselves, and devastated the people and planet.

---

[1]   Jonathan Saha, "Teak and Photography in Colonial Burma", *Colonizing Animals*, 23 March 2016 (blog post by Associate Professor Jonathan Sana (South Asian History), Department of History, Durham University).

i

We quote these words here at the outset because this anthology is in many ways about international lawyers and how they relate to colonialism, colonial wrongs and colonial grievances. One of the objectives of the project conference held in Yangon on 16-17 November 2019[2] – the papers of which are published in this book – was to bring together a group of international lawyers, in particular international criminal law experts, to reflect on how contemporary international criminal law relates to colonial wrongs broadly understood. It may be the first time that this wide range and variety of international criminal lawyers sat together and discussed colonial wrongs. Castellino tells us that 2019 is late in the day. Chapter 18 confirms, however, his belief that there is still time for international lawyers to become engaged with this important topic.

This means that most of the authors in this anthology are not experts on colonialism or post-colonialism as such. It is important that this issue not be left to 'specialists' only, but that mainstream lawyers – especially international criminal lawyers – become better informed and do not see this as an area reserved for historians, experts on Third World Approaches to International Law, or persons from former colonies.

That said, our focus on legal notions and classifications, on the persistent problem of double standards, should not make us lose perspective or impose agendas on partners and actors who live in post-colonial communities. Chapter 11 below offers a very clear warning:

> The focus of efforts to address colonial wrongs and the double standards of international law must be on measures which will help all peoples and promote sustainable peace. Promoting accountability and the legitimacy of international law are valid considerations, but are less important than the lives and well-being of the populations (of all kinds) living in former colonies.[3]

Keeping the focus on "measures which will help all peoples and promote sustainable peace" is not easy when lawyers start engaging in doctrinal upending. The monograph *Double Standards: International*

---

[2] For more information on the conference (with the concept note, abstracts, programme and links to films and podcasts of lectures at the conference), please go to https://www.cilrap.org/events/191116-17-yangon/. The conference and this anthology are part of a project financed by the Norwegian Ministry of Foreign Affairs as the sole donor.
[3] See Kyaw Yin Hlaing, "The Importance of Hearing Grievances Linked to Colonial Wrongs in Burma", Chapter 11 below.

Criminal Law and the West[4] was recommended reading for participants in the Yangon-conference to help focus on "the well-being of the populations (of all kinds)", rather than merely the legitimacy (or other) prospects of the international law discipline. Inspired by this monograph, the project concept paper – 'Myanmar, Colonial Aftermath, and Access to International Law'[5], reproduced as Chapter 7 below – zoomed in on the tension between the international law community's response to grievances based on practices in Colonial Burma prior to World War II (transfer of civilians into occupied or otherwise dominated territory), on the one hand, and contemporary practices elsewhere that are alleged to violate the same values, on the other. This way, Colonial Burma became a case in point to illustrate double normative standards.[6]

The concept paper's choice of norm or value – that is, harm caused by transfer of civilians into occupied or otherwise dominated territory – was never intended to elevate this specific international law prohibition above others, certainly not above the norms that protect human life and physical integrity, or to suggest that it should take centre stage in the discourse on colonial wrongs and access to international criminal law. Rather, it was selected because it is particularly relevant to Colonial Burma and contemporary armed conflict and violence in Myanmar. Although the Yangon-conference was "*not* about Rakhine or the contemporary situation in Myanmar", the conference was "held in Yangon because the situation in Myanmar is illustrative of problems that can arise if colonial grievances are long ignored by moderate actors and abused by other actors. The location highlights why the topic of the meeting is important", stated the conference programme[7] – fully cognizant that, "unless approached in a context-sensitive manner there is a risk that such discussions will strengthen the position of nationalists and be used to promote discriminatory policies

---

[4] Wolfgang Kaleck, *Double Standards: International Criminal Law and the West*, Torkel Opsahl Academic EPublisher, Brussels, 2015 (http://www.toaep.org/ps-pdf/26-kaleck).

[5] Morten Bergsmo, 'Myanmar, Colonial Aftermath, and Access to International Law', Torkel Opsahl Academic EPublisher, Brussels, 2019 (http://www.toaep.org/ops-pdf/9-bergsmo).

[6] In his lecture at the Yangon-conference, Morten Bergsmo discusses the concept of 'double normative standards', in particular in relation to 'norm internalisation', see https://www.cilrap.org/cilrap-film/191116-bergsmo/.

[7] The quoted words are taken from the Yangon-conference concept description which appears on pages 1 and 2 of the programme document at https://www.cilrap.org/events/191116-17-yangon/.

and agenda".[8] In this balancing act, we have not seen any such negative consequences, but rather a groundswell of constructive interest.

The concept paper first triggered a response from former British Ambassador Derek Tonkin on "Migration from Bengal to Arakan During British Rule 1826–1948" appearing as Chapter 8 of this anthology.[9] Then several participants at the Yangon-conference presented papers related to Colonial Burma. As a consequence, Part III of this anthology contains six chapters, including by Dr. Jacques P. Leider (Chapter 6) and professors Ryan Mitchell (Chapter 9) and Elisabeth Fyfe (Chapter 10). Interest continued to grow, so on 14 August 2020, the Centre for International Law Research and Policy (CILRAP) – the owner of the Torkel Opsahl Academic EPublisher – released a symposium 'On Myanmar' with 16 publications, including 14 new policy briefs covering geopolitical, historical and other aspects of the contemporary armed conflicts in Rakhine in Myanmar, with a number of authors from the region.[10] Colonial Burma grew from being a case in point at the outset of this project, to becoming an important case study.

But this "does *not* mean that past colonial practices of the United Kingdom are being singled out by the project",[11] far from it. Parts IV ("Other Former Colonial Territories") and V ("Indigenous Peoples) of this book contain seven chapters, including two focusing on the Great Lakes Region and the role of Belgium: Dr. Mutoy Mubiala's comprehensive Chapter 15 ("Addressing Colonial Wrong-Doing in the Great Lakes Region of Africa"), and Chapter 14 ("Possible Impediments to Justice for Colonial Crimes: A Belgian Perspective") by Christophe Marchand, Crépine Uwashema and Christophe Deprez. Part IV also includes chapters on China's 'century of humiliation' and its impact on how China sees international law by Professor LING Yan (Chapter 12, "On the Relevancy of Chinese Colonial Grievances to International Law"), and Chapter 13 ("Winds of Justice: Post-Colonial Opportunism and the Rise of the Khmer Rouge") by Dr. Kevin Crow on the role of China and the United States in

---

[8] See Dr. Kyaw Yin Hlaing, "The Importance of Hearing Grievances Linked to Colonial Wrongs in Burma", Chapter 11 below.

[9] It was first published on 6 December 2019 as Occasional Paper Series No. 10 (2019), Torkel Opsahl Academic EPublisher, Brussels, 2019 (https://www.toaep.org/ops-pdf/10-tonkin).

[10] For a synopsis of the symposium and links to the publications, see https://www.cilrap.org/myanmar/.

[11] Yangon-conference programme document, see *supra* note 2.

post-colonial Cambodia and how they contributed to the rise of the Khmer Rouge.

Prior to Castellino's above-quoted, thought-provoking Chapter 18, Part V offers two chapters on the treatment of indigenous populations in Canada and Norway: Chapter 16 ("Avoidance Techniques: Accounting for Canada's Colonial Crimes") by Dr. Asad Kiyani and Chapter 17 ("Past Wrongdoing Against Romani and Sámi in Norway and the Prism of Modern International Criminal Law and Human Rights") by Gunnar Ekeløve-Slydal. They describe how the protection of the law was not extended to members of indigenous peoples in Canada and Norway, but also that the law itself was discriminatory for long periods. This reinforces the importance of the emphasis on double standards that has guided the project and the work on the anthology. Fortunately, both countries have taken active steps to remedy negative consequences of their past practices, to come to terms with their own wrongdoing and reconcile with members of the groups concerned, in an effort to embrace all members of the nation.

In addition to the 13 case studies in Parts III, IV and V – most of which also contain discussions and insights of general value – Chapter 1[12] includes analysis of the role of Germany with regard to the former colony of Namibia. We would have liked to include more case studies and a more diverse group of authors, also for the obvious reasons referred to by Makau Mutua: "Attempts to craft a truly universal regime of rights, one that reflects the complexity and the diversity of all cultures, have generally been viewed with indifference or hostility by the official guardians of human rights".[13] If interest continues to grow, we will try to produce a second, expanded edition of the anthology that incorporates perspectives from more former colonies and colonial powers. We would also like to expand Part II: Legal Notions, which presently contains Chapter 4 ("On Subjugation and the Case of Burma") by YANG Ken, and Chapter 5 ("The Notion of Continuous or Continuing Crimes in International Criminal Law") by Matthias Neuner, who also discusses several specific potential continuous crimes, including transfer of civilians into occupied territory – both fascinating texts.

The title of the anthology refers to "access to international law". That may sound abstract at first glance. When you read Ambassador

---

[12] See Wolfgang Kaleck, "On Double Standards and Emerging European Custom on Accountability for Colonial Crimes", Chapter 1 below.

[13] Makau Mutua, "Critical Race Theory and International Law: The View of an Insider-Outsider", in *Villanova Law Review*, 2000, vol. 45.

Narinder Singh's foreword immediately following the present text, you will see why the problems of access to international law are very common even in the most resourceful of the former colonies. There has been an interest in 'access to justice' among international lawyers and diplomats for some time. This perspective has also permeated discussions on rule-of-law development and so-called 'positive complementarity' in the context of international criminal law. More recently, the point has been made that access to justice may remain elusive unless there is 'access to law'.[14] Ambassador Singh – and the co-editors of the anthology – suggest that we need to take a wider perspective yet, if we seek to understand the real problems of access to, and ownership in, international law today.[15]

In her foreword, Brigid Inder OBE eloquently places the anthology and the Yangon-conference in the wider context of the international criminal law and justice discourse. Chapter 1 reinforces this contextualization, and goes wider to place the book in the double standards and post-colonialism discourses. It sets an important part of the tone for the anthology as a whole. Chapter 2 ("Transitional Justice for Colonial Era Abuses and Legacies: African versus European Policy Priorities") by Dr. Hugo van der Merwe and Annah Moyo considers the extent to which colonial wrongs have found a place in transitional justice in Africa and in transitional justice policies of the African Union and the European Union. Chapter 3 ("Colonial Wrongs, Memory and Speech Along the Atrocity Spectrum") by Professor Gregory S. Gordon offers a synthetic reflection bridging the Yangon-conference and this anthology, with a Section 3.6. on hateful utterances and how they can lead to conflict and violence. Faithful to the invitation in the Yangon-conference programme – and its call for "a new tool that could be used to address [colonial] grievances, including ensuring the participation of relevant expertise in the listening to, analysing of, and otherwise engagement with the grievances through consultation or other processes"[16] – Gordon suggests "a kind of fusion between

---

[14] See Morten Bergsmo, "Decomposition Works in Our Favour", Policy Brief Series No. 114 (2020), Torkel Opsahl Academic EPublisher, Brussels, 2020 (http://www.toaep.org/pbs-pdf/114-bergsmo/), with references.

[15] Anthea Robert's *Is International Law International?* (Oxford University Press, 2017) was hailed as an eye-opener when it was published. But how new was its perspective to international lawyers in, for example, China, India, Indonesia, Iran or Nigeria? Was it perhaps perceived as new more by international lawyers in a relatively small number of Anglo-American countries or by individuals shaped by the discourse communities in those countries?

[16] Yangon-conference programme document, see *supra* note 2.

[his] atrocity spectrum framework and [the proposed] consultation process".[17]

> More specifically, in the period before persecution reaches critical mass, when 'salutary' speech may help stem mass violence, we should consider that discourse acknowledging colonial wrongs or mismanagement may constitute a type of salutary speech within my framework that could ease the friction and thereby help prevent commission of core international crimes. This opportunity to rely on 'salutary speech', in the form of discourse acknowledging colonial wrongs or mismanagement, can be the object of [the proposed] 'consultation process'. I am offering a conceptual temporal framework for when we can inject the 'consultation process' into a situation of potential atrocity and suggest how and to what extent it may be effective.[18]

The Centre for International Law Research and Policy (CILRAP) has announced that it is working on a follow-up conference in Yangon in 2021 on 'Religion and Hate Speech', which provides an opportunity to take Gordon's constructive proposal forward.

If we proceed to make a second edition of this volume, it would probably be desirable to include chapters on relevant aspects of colonial and post-colonial slavery. The trans-Atlantic trade in African slaves would be one pillar of this query, with responsibility shared among European slave traders, market facilitators on American soil, and Africans who enslaved fellow-Africans on a large scale.[19] Interestingly, some leaders of African enslaver-nations may have gone further than European counterparts in apologizing for the role played by their predecessors.[20] The bigger

---

[17]   See Gregory S. Gordon, "Colonial Wrongs, Memory and Speech Along the Atrocity Spectrum", Chapter 3 below.

[18]   *Ibid.*

[19]   See Professor Henry Louis Gates Jr., "Ending the Slavery Blame-Game", *The New York Times*, 22 April 2010:

The historians John Thornton and Linda Heywood of Boston University estimate that 90 percent of those shipped to the New World were enslaved by Africans and then sold to European traders. [...] there is very little discussion of the role Africans themselves played. And that role, it turns out, was a considerable one, especially for the slave-trading kingdoms of western and central Africa. These included the Akan of the kingdom of Asante in what is now Ghana, the Fon of Dahomey (now Benin), the Mbundu of Ndongo in modern Angola and the Kongo of today's Congo, among several others.

[20]   *Ibid.:*

But the culpability of American plantation owners neither erases nor supplants that of the African slavers. In recent years, some African leaders have become more comfortable dis-

pillar of the query, with obvious lingering consequences, is the systematic use of slaves to build the United States of America between 1619 and 1865, a staggering 246 years. There may not have been any use of slaves to create wealth in today's advanced economies as comprehensive as slavery in the United States during these 2.5 centuries.

African-Americans were brought to do the hard work of making the United States an agricultural nation, first to grow tobacco, then cotton:

> Enslaved workers felled trees by ax, burned the underbrush and leveled the earth for planting. "Whole forests were literally dragged out by the roots," John Parker, an enslaved worker, remembered. A lush, twisted mass of vegetation was replaced by a single crop. An origin of American money exerting its will on the earth, spoiling the environment for profit, is found in the cotton plantation. [...] As slave labour camps spread throughout the South, production surged. By 1831, the country was delivering nearly half the world's raw cotton crop, with 350 million pounds picked that year.[21]

Some of the most important figures in United States national self-representation – such as the Presidents George Washington, Thomas Jefferson and James Madison – owned and used high numbers of slaves. Their homes – and many other national monuments of United States identity – were built with the help of slaves. During the century following 1865, descendants of American slaves came to make up a sizeable portion of the manufacturing population in towns across the United States, including Baltimore, Chicago and Philadelphia. Many were brought to Oakland during World War II to produce armaments for the Pacific War. When globalization made it easier to outsource manufacturing jobs to lower-cost countries, thousands of families in such manufacturing hubs who descend from American slaves were in effect abandoned. Oakland, not many kilometres from Silicon Valley, suffers sustained unemployment and related social problems.

The broad impact of the 'Black Lives Matter' movement that started in 2013 shows how entrenched is the connection between the slave econ-

---

cussing this complicated past than African-Americans tend to be. In 1999, for instance, President Mathieu Kerekou of Benin astonished an all-black congregation in Baltimore by falling to his knees and begging African-Americans' forgiveness for the "shameful" and "abominable" role Africans played in the trade. Other African leaders, including Jerry Rawlings of Ghana, followed Mr. Kerekou's bold example.

[21] See Matthew Desmond, "In order to understand the brutality of American capitalism, you have to start on the plantation", *The New York Times Magazine*, 14 August 2019.

omy of the past and continuing structural discrimination and social exclusion of slave descendants. The important Resolution No. 56 of the General Assembly of the Commonwealth of Virginia – on the occasion of the 400th anniversary of the first permanent English settlement in Jamestown and the Americas – "recognize[s] the pain caused by the enslavement of generations of African Americans in Virginia, and call for reconciliation among all Virginians".[22] It seeks to make its recognition of "the stain of slavery and its legacy [...] visible to the nation and the world", and to "extend [its desire for, and determination to preserve, freedom] to people abroad".[23] In her address on 3 May 2007 to the Virginia General Assembly (whose origins go back to the House of Burgesses at Jamestown in 1619), Queen Elizabeth II also alluded to the wider impact of American slavery:

> Human progress rarely comes without cost. And those early years in Jamestown, when three great civilizations came together for the first time – Western European, Native American and African – released a train of events which continues to have a profound social impact, not only in the United States, but also in the United Kingdom and Europe.[24]

Perceptions in Europe and world-wide therefore matter. And the concern around the world is not so much a dis-owning of the colonial period between the arrival of the first slaves in Virginia in 1619 and the Declaration of Independence in 1776 – a period for which the United Kingdom and, in this case, Virginia would seem to share responsibility[25] – but a perceived dis-owning by better off Americans of their responsibility towards descendants of the slaves who built their country. If there is a widespread sense around the world that solidarity is struggling to rise above racial barriers in the United States, it will be difficult for the United States to successfully reclaim global moral leadership. As Brigid Inder OBE observes so incisively in general terms in her foreword: *"when solidarity rises above political, cultural or other affiliations, then we will have truly*

---

[22] Commonwealth of Virginia, General Assembly, House of Delegates, House Resolution No. 56, 22 February 2020 (on file with author).

[23] *Ibid.*

[24] Queen Elizabeth II, Address to a special joint session of the Virginia General Assembly, 3 May 2007 (available on C-SPAN's web site).

[25] Speaking of the relationship between the peoples of the United Kingdom and the United States, Queen Elizabeth II declared that it "is one of the most durable international collaborations anywhere in the world, at any time in history", see *ibid.*

established international justice as a powerful and transcendent global norm".[26]

It is against the general background of this insight that we have dedicated this book to "those who will transmute the legacies of colonial wrongs and slavery into a wider, world-embracing solidarity and unity". We believe that international criminal lawyers can play a role in this process, also as enablers or organisers of access to justice for people affected by (post-)colonial injustice, supporting their legal actions. We hope that this book can stimulate involvement.

We would like to thank the Norwegian Ministry of Foreign Affairs for its support to the project that has made this book possible. We also thank the Yangon-conference partners: China University of Political Science and Law (Beijing), Centre for Diversity and National Harmony (Yangon), the European Center for Constitutional and Human Rights (Berlin), the Institute for International Peace and Security Law (University of Cologne), and Maharishi Law School (New Delhi). Finally, we place on record our sincere appreciation to Mr. Subham Jain and Mr. Antonio Angotti of the Torkel Opsahl Academic EPublisher for their copy-editing and production assistance in the making of this book.

Morten Bergsmo
Wolfgang Kaleck
Kyaw Yin Hlaing
Co-Editors

---

[26] Italics added.

FOREWORD BY NARINDER SINGH

When the United Nations was established in 1945, approximately 750 million people, or about one-third of the world's population at that time, still lived under colonial rule. Decolonisation was taken up as a major objective of the United Nations ('UN'). Since then, 80 former colonies, including 11 trust territories, have achieved self-determination and have become part of the UN family.

These newly independent countries or the former colonies had no role in the development of international law previously. One main purpose of international law prior to 1945 was to justify the actions of colonial powers in conquering new territories, subjugating their peoples, and appropriating their resources and markets.

Even after attaining independence and being accepted as equal members of the international community, there are certain factors that limit the ability of these newly independent countries to influence the development of international law for their benefit.

The first constraint is the acceptance of the status quo. When a country becomes independent, it can choose under the law of state succession to begin life with a clean slate. It may choose to not apply the treaties entered into by the former colonial power on its behalf, but most countries would find that to be a difficult way to start life: to have no relations with any other state. So, they feel the need to continue with those treaties. In principle, they are accepting what was decided by the colonial power on their behalf in their relations with other countries. While declaring they will continue, many countries also declare that within a specified period they will review those treaties and then take a final view whether to continue with them or not.

All newly independent countries also aspire to join the UN as full members because that is seen as a very important recognition that they are part of the international community, and recognises the principle of sovereign equality of all its members and prohibits the threat or use of force against their territorial integrity and political independence. This also comes with certain obligations: they must be recognised by others as peace-loving and be in a position to fulfil their international commitments. Even to join the UN they must declare that they accept the commitments under international law. That is the international law which previously had led to their subjugation, one of the topics addressed in this volume.

On becoming UN members, the newly independent countries were focused on issues concerning colonial rule, which led to adoption by the UN General Assembly of important declarations on Granting of Independence to Colonial Countries and Peoples (1960); Permanent Sovereignty over Natural Resources (1962); and the Declaration on Principles of International Law concerning Friendly Relations and Co-operation among States (1970).

After becoming members of the international community, all States have the right to participate in the work of the UN. One objective of the UN General Assembly under the UN Charter is to work for the progressive development of international law and its codification. In other words, by definition, under the Charter all the newly independent countries that have become members of the UN have a role to play in the formation and development of international law and its codification.

What are the constraints that developing countries face in this regard? First of all, they lack experience in the conduct of international relations. Even where some measure of self-governance was given to the former colonies, they had no role in external relations, defence matters or certain other commerce matters. It was only and purely in domestic areas that the local governments would be given some limited authority, and even there they could be overruled by the viceroy or whoever was in charge. With their limited experience of government, they were completely new to the field of international relations. They neither had the knowledge of international law nor did they recognise the importance of acquiring the expertise and knowledge of international law.

Take the case of India. It became a member of the UN in 1945, as British India. We became independent in 1947, but it was only in 1957 that the Foreign Office set up its own legal division. For a full decade, our Foreign Office depended on one lawyer, a part-time legal adviser who was practicing law before the Indian Supreme Court (he had interned in the Legal Adviser's Office at the United Kingdom's Foreign and Commonwealth Office). This was the level of engagement with international law even for a very large country like India. Following the Bandung Asian Relations Conference, India and six other Asian countries (including Myanmar) joined together to establish the Asian Legal Consultative Committee, later expanded to include African members. In 1959, the Indian Society of International Law was set up to encourage study and research in international law.

It was only gradually that the importance of international law came to be accepted, and a full-fledged legal division was established. Even in doing that there are problems. Having set up a division for international law, you need to staff it with the right kind of legal advisors, and finding them is an even greater challenge. Seventy years after independence, there are still vacant posts in the legal division. Although the number of posts is currently larger than what it was in the beginning, we are still not able to find good candidates for all the posts which we managed to create after great difficulty. Convincing the Ministry of Finance and other divisions and ministries which have a say in the creation of new posts in government is itself a difficult task. Having gone through that process and having obtained approval for the requisite funds, we find ourselves unable to recruit the right candidates. We interviewed about 30 candidates in July 2019 for five posts, but could only recommend two candidates. One reason for this is that universities are not focusing enough on public international law, and students are also choosing areas which they think will be more lucrative for their private practice as lawyers (such as private law and international commercial arbitration). Sometimes when you ask young Indian lawyers about their area of practice, they would say international law, but upon closer questioning, you find that they are talking about arbitration. The only international angle is that they have travelled abroad for arbitration.

This lack of human resources affects the participation of the developing countries in international conferences where international law issues are considered. For example, in the Sixth (Legal) Committee of the UN General Assembly many countries have no representative present in the meetings, while some countries have a representative who covers the Legal Committee only on a part-time basis. He or she would be following the Human Rights Committee or something else, and occasionally come to the Legal Committee.

Another important factor that affects the participation of developing countries in international conferences is the lack of adequate financial resources. Most developing countries are unable to participate effectively in major international codification conferences, and even when they do, they are not able to participate on a regular basis. Their views are therefore not heard, or accounted for, or they are unable to influence the outcome of such conferences. The lack of continuous presence in the conference affects the ability of the delegates to understand the complexity of the issues under consideration. Therefore, although you are part of the process of international law-making, in practice the ability to influence the outcome is severely limited.

The UN General Assembly has the mandate under the UN Charter to contribute to the progressive development of international law and its codification. As part of this mandate, the UN General Assembly established the International Law Commission ('ILC'), which is a group of experts that makes recommendation to the Assembly on various topics, and on that basis, conventions can be adopted. This particular method of having a continuous dialogue with the Sixth Committee of the Assembly was adopted because the earlier efforts of the League of Nations – which had tried to have a codification conference based entirely on the works of academic experts – had not met with success. Every year, the ILC meets, the members adopt the reports on the progress made, and the Sixth Committee has an opportunity to debate the outcome of that ILC session. There is an ongoing dialogue. This process has resulted in a number of significant conventions. In fact, the ILC's work resulted in the first two conferences on the law of the sea where four conventions were adopted. The conventions on diplomatic and consular relations, the law of treaties, international rivers, state succession, and even the Rome Statute of the International Criminal Court are results of the work done by the ILC.

However, the ILC is not the only body which is developing international law. Even within the UN, the Third Committee deals with human rights matters and adopts human rights treaties. Then the UN General Assembly has also set up the UN Commission on International Trade Law ('UNCITRAL'). There are also separate processes such as independent diplomatic conferences like the third United Nations Conference on the Law of the Sea ('UNCLOS III') which resulted in the 1982 United Nations Convention on the Law of the Sea. We also have the specialised agencies of the UN, like the International Maritime Organization which has competence in the field of shipping, and the International Labour Organisation which has competence in the field of labour. Each of these agencies are also developing international law, and all these processes are also going on simultaneously. It is therefore a difficult task for the developing countries to participate in the work of all these law-making bodies and to effectively contribute to all of them. Sometimes the work in two bodies may overlap, and if you are not present in both bodies then you do not know how the outcome is going to affect you. This is another impediment for the developing countries to make any meaningful contribution to the development of international law.

Many of these conferences deal with highly technical issues such as the climate change. Then it is not only the international law experts who are needed, but they need backup in the form of technical experts who must be aware not only of what is being debated in the meetings, but also how the technical issues will affect their own countries. This requires significant research which is often lacking because they lack resources. Neither do they have timely awareness that this type of research will be needed in order for them to effectively participate and protect the interests of their countries. All these factors put additional pressures on the delegates from developing countries.

Let us take the example of UNCLOS III. This was a major codification conference in which all the newly developed countries participated. They did so with great expectations because this was a period when there were high expectations that the minerals from the sea would be the answer to the problems being faced at that time – the oil shortage, copper shortage, and the oil embargo which led to an increase in prices. The major impediment, of course, for the developing countries was that they lacked both technology and finances to engage in seabed mining themselves and so they hoped to do this through the convention. There were long, protracted negotiations, which went on for 10 years – two long sessions each year of about six weeks each. You can imagine the kind of efforts and resources which all delegations had to put into these negotiations. At the end, compromises were reached. The common heritage of mankind was recognised. It was recognised that the International Seabed Authority would be set-up, and that this authority would have a mining wing called the Enterprise which would carry out seabed mining from the profits of which the developing countries would also benefit. The convention was finally adopted in 1982, but it required 60 ratifications to enter into force and the ratification were slow in coming, particularly from the industrialised countries which were expected to contribute with funds and technology.

This led to great disappointment. The ratifications were finally achieved in 1996, but they came at a price. In 1993 States had to conclude another agreement which put on hold the provisions relating to seabed mining by the Enterprise. These provisions would be deferred for the time being until seabed mining becomes a reality and only then the convention entered into force. The United States, which wanted this postponement of the Enterprise, has still not come on board, even if other industrialised countries have joined the convention. Seabed mining is not a reality due to other factors, including the discovery of minerals on land, lack of price appreciation, and discovery of substitutes, such as optical fibre that has replaced copper for many purposes. This only shows that even when the developing countries were able to make an impact on the final outcome, it was a very limited impact. This kind of sustained effort is not possible for all developing countries to make in all the different areas of international law which are currently under negotiation.

In the climate change negotiations, the industrialised countries, which have caused the maximum amount of pollution of the earth, agreed to voluntary controls on emissions. But they have not fulfilled their commitments. Nevertheless, all the developing countries have been pressurised into a second round to agree to severe restrictions on their own emissions. This affects the pace of development in those countries, and even with these severe limitations, countries are still bound by obligations to work towards achieving the Millennium Development Goals, which we had already not able to meet by the earlier deadline, and which we are still struggling with.

Before ending my foreword, I would like to congratulate CILRAP for organizing this project on such an important subject, such as the extent to which contemporary international law addresses lingering consequences of colonial wrongs; the risks of double standards and related perceptions in affected populations; and legitimacy of international law. I look forward to the further programmes planned for the future. I also congratulate Morten Bergsmo for bringing together a galaxy of experts from various backgrounds and experiences who shared their knowledge, experiences and perspectives on these important issues, and also including a number of case studies from former colonies that highlight the wrongs and atrocities committed by the former colonial powers which, in the contemporary world, amount to grave crimes as defined by the Statute of the International Criminal Court.

Ambassador Narinder Singh
Formerly Legal Adviser, Ministry of External Affairs of India and Chairman, United Nations International Law Commission

FOREWORD BY BRIGID INDER OBE

I warmly congratulate CILRAP, especially its Director Morten Bergsmo and his team, along with their organizing partners, for conceptualizing this important project on "Colonial Wrongs, Double Standards, and Access to International Law". This project is the most recent example of CILRAP's aptitude and instinct for consistently creating thoughtful spaces for reflection and analysis of complicated and difficult issues.

It is always tempting when faced with seemingly intractable problems to respond with what is familiar or expected. Unfortunately, such impulses often lead to settling for short-term and sometimes simplistic solutions to multi-dimensional and complex challenges. This project and anthology, addressing colonial wrongs, double standards and access to international justice, embraces the deep complexities inherent to each of these issues and invites us to rethink our old responses and 'trusted' solutions.

In my opinion, this theme is one of the most courageous conversations ever undertaken by CILRAP and its partners because it is initiating a global debate within the international justice community about colonization and double standards with the potential to engage those formerly colonized, former colonial powers, as well as other parties. Whilst many countries have struggled and continue to grapple domestically with the ongoing impact of colonization and the inter-generational harms caused to nations and indigenous communities, there have been few attempts at hosting global conversations on these issues with the important exception of the World Conference on Racism, Racial Discrimination, Xenophobia and Related Intolerance held in 2001, where the effects of colonization were robustly aired and discussed.

At that time, several countries expressed their experience, anger and frustration regarding the historic and long-term harms caused by colonization, including: the loss of land and other natural resources; the loss of autonomy, self-determination, economic opportunities and power; and the loss of language, culture, sacred sites, heritage and spiritual expressions. Indeed, the Declaration of the World Conference explicitly recognizes that people of Asian descent, African descent, and indigenous peoples were not only victims of colonialism in the past but continue to be victims of its consequences today.[1] So, it is of little surprise that some of the ongoing effects of colonialism and its associated practices may overlap with the interests of the international justice sector with respect to the undertones of current conflicts, and therefore should be contemplated by this field.

As far as I am aware, this conference and the series of conversations to follow, is the first time such a debate has been launched within the international justice community and certainly since the creation of the International Criminal Court (ICC), with the jurisdiction to prosecute specific international crimes, several of which are typical of the kinds of acts which occurred within the commission of colonization. Crimes such as murder, forcible transfer of children from one ethnic or national group to another, displacement of the population, creating conditions of life calculated to bring about the physical destruction of a group, in whole or in part, readily come to mind.

This dialogue frames colonization as neither morally neutral nor simply a matter of historic fact of little relevance to modernity and today's technologically and economically globalized world. Rather, firstly, it seeks to create space to discuss colonial wrongs, including within the broader context of access to justice and accountability for the purpose of better contextualizing the current commission of international crimes and human rights violations.

Secondly, it acknowledges the sense of double standards experienced by some, particularly countries formerly colonized, who keenly observe the imbalance of the global expectation of accountability for actions now recognised as crimes under international law, without accountability for, or even acknowledgment of, similar or comparable historic acts which were not recognised as criminal conduct at the time they were committed, but were nevertheless experienced as harmful, wrong, and unjust by the communities affected.

Thirdly, this dialogue includes a clear invitation to explore what else is needed to recognize the multi-generational effects of a colonial past, and ultimately to reconcile and heal the profound sense of injustice, collective violation, and pain experienced by countries and communities colonized in past decades and earlier centuries.

---

[1]   United Nations, "Report of the World Conference Against Racism, Racial Discrimination Xenophobia and Related Intolerance", UN Doc. A/Conf.189/12, 8 September 2001, para. 14, p. 12 (https://www.legal-tools.org/doc/cli7ol/).

Everything that has ever happened in the life of a country is re-membered.[2]

It is reflected in stories and art, recorded in social narratives, encapsulated in songs and poetry, and memorialised in public statues. Even when certain events or entire people are written out of history and invisibilized in the public record, the memories of their experiences still exist. They are sewn into the social and cultural DNA of the victimised and perpetrator communities. They are embedded within the history of the land that witnessed the violence and bloodshed and whose resources were instrumentalized in the pursuit of domination.

Unacknowledged harm and historic wrongdoing appear to create an environment in which the development of human rights principles and accountability practices may be delayed or perhaps never properly take hold, making structural violence and discrimination normative.[3] In some contexts, this may give rise to a sense of collective insecurity and a perception of constant threat that can be utilised to justify the commission of ongoing atrocities if such acts can be explained or posited as necessary for group survival.[4]

Reflecting upon colonial wrongs does not diminish nor justify more recent atrocities, including those that are or could become the subject of national or international prosecutions. Rather, it is looking at these issues through a broader lens to better understand some of the drivers of these acts, thus adding greater nuance to legal remedies and potential prosecutions. It is also an opportunity to explore complementary models and processes within and beyond the justice sector necessary to address the perception of double standards and ultimately to facilitate the process of international healing.

Based on my upbringing in Aotearoa-New Zealand witnessing firsthand the inter-generational effects of colonization on Maori in my country, and drawing on my work in the gender equality, human rights and justice fields for over 30 years, I believe there is a deep global grief aching to be acknowledged with respect to the injustice of colonization and its associated violence. There is a collective yearning for opportunities to express the multiple long-term harms caused and created by these acts for which

---

[2] Adapted from an interview with Professor Stephan Harding, Schmacher College, 8 November 2019 (on file with the author).

[3] An historical discussion on these issues in the South African context can be found in Alex Boraine and Janet Levy, *The Healing of A Nation?*, Justice in Transition 1995.

[4] *Ibid.*

expressions of regret and remorse by those responsible could be sincerely offered. Such an exchange may usher in a process of healing and liberation both for those harmed as well as for those who feel and bear the burden of wrong-doing.

When I was the Executive Director of the Women's Initiatives for Gender Justice, we encountered these kinds of complexities in our country-based programmes in east, central and north Africa where the historic context of contemporary armed conflicts often had deep roots in the countries' past experiences of violence, including during their colonial and post-colonial eras. We learned that the reconciliation and truth telling desires of these communities were usually far greater than simply addressing the current conflict or the latest outbreak of violence. We grew to appreciate the sense of frustration experienced by some communities with respect to the perceived and actual limitations of the legal process including the jurisdictional parameters that determine the work of courts like the ICC. We came to recognise that for many, the desire for truth is untarnished by time, it neither diminishes nor wanes as the decades or centuries pass.

There is a hunger for truth telling beyond that which is verifiable or should be tested by evidence and adjudicated, as essential as that process is within formal accountability processes. But there is a desire for another kind of truth – one that is told through the voicing of harms and impact, and through the sharing of stories that are not linear and do not neatly fit within temporal jurisdiction requirements.

Truth telling liberates us from the past, as we perceive it and our past as we experienced it. Truth is sacred because it connects us to our pain, dreams, vulnerabilities, and freedom. Truth is healing because it propels us to see ourselves and others with both candour and perhaps, in time, compassion. Ultimately, the sharing of truth opens a pathway for reconciling past conflicts and co-creating a more peaceful future.

In the absence of truth, we create myths, which usually portray our perceived enemies as the worst version of humanity we can imagine, and ourselves as heroic and resilient human beings. That is why there can be no single or privileged perspectives in the pursuit of truth.

All sides in a conflict will be able to justify their use of violence and brutality towards the other. Each party will have its own collective stories of harm, loss and shame and without truth-telling successive generations will continue to be affected by the communal memories of violence and unresolved trauma.

It is a sign of our shared evolution that we have established a global expectation of accountability. The rule of law, although not quite universal, is a widely shared value and there is undeniably a growing global consciousness towards equality and justice.

It is right that we should expect and demand accountability in response to international crimes and mass violence. But it is important that we continue to perfect and finesse, perhaps with some urgency, our exercise of international justice and address what may be perceived as an appearance of selectivity in the crimes and situations to which the international community reacts and for which it demands justice, whilst at the same time it continues to demonstrate its preparedness to look the other way on other equally egregious situations and atrocities as affiliations are assessed and analysis adapted depending upon the identities of the alleged individual or state perpetrators and those of the perceived or actual victims.

When the demands for justice become consistent regardless of the originators of the crimes and the identity of the victims, when we grieve for anyone affected by mass violence based on the one criterion of our shared humanity, and when solidarity rises above political, cultural or other affiliations, then we will have truly established international justice as a powerful and transcendent global norm. More than that, we will have manifested U Thant's concept of planetary citizenship.[5]

It is a tall order, but reflecting upon colonial wrongs and double standards is exactly the kind of conversation needed as we seek ways to reconcile historic and current experiences of injustice.

Brigid Inder OBE
Advisor and Senior Consultant
Formerly, Executive Director, Women's Initiatives for Gender Justice;
Special Advisor on Gender to the ICC Prosecutor

---

[5] U Thant, *View from the UN*, David & Charles, London, 1977, p. 454.

TABLE OF CONTENTS

PART IV:
OTHER FORMER COLONIAL TERRITORIES

PART I:
CONTEXT

1

On Double Standards and Emerging European Custom on Accountability for Colonial Crimes

Wolfgang Kaleck[*]

1.1. Introduction

There is a need for criminal and human rights lawyers to position themselves *vis-à-vis* colonialism, and to explore the imperial and colonial history, including the history of law and the colonial dimensions of current political situations.

There are many valuable critiques from critical legal and decolonial scholars of the current practice of contemporary international criminal justice, including the recognition of frequent unequal application of the standards. But this critique should not put international criminal justice on hold, nor lead to excuses, legitimize post-colonial violence, or argue against accountability of powerful actors today.

The approach taken in this chapter is a different one: however imperfect international criminal proceedings might be, they provide both basic legal categories and fora to combine pragmatic concrete improvements in the possibility and delivery of transformative justice, alongside a more fundamental critique.

This chapter is overarching, addressing several questions: (1) what may we understand with the term 'colonial crime' (Section 1.2. below); (2) why the problem of double standards in international criminal justice should concern us today, and how the rhetoric of double standards has been politically instrumentalized and neutralized; (3) that legal remedies for colonial crimes have – notwithstanding all difficulties – been devel-

[*] **Wolfgang Kaleck** is the General Secretary of the European Center for Constitutional and Human Rights. This chapter is an edited and expanded version of his lecture at the CIL-RAP seminar 'Colonial Wrongs, Double Standards, and Access to International Law' in Yangon on 16–17 November 2019. The author thanks Morten Bergsmo, Joshua Castellino, Rieke Ernst, Judith Hackmack and Magdalena Kaffai for their support.

oped in recent years, and colonialism can be challenged in the legal field in different ways; and (4) some preliminary ideas for ways forward, also about the role lawyers and civil society actors can play.

> Can the Germans ever see black Ovaherero and Nama as their equals? How the Germans respond to the genocide of 1904-1908, as a state and a people, will answer that question.[1]

Seeking to develop a position on colonial wrongs and international (criminal) law is an approximation for what amounts to a late start to questions of historical accountability. The emphasis on criminal law derives from the focus of the November 2019 seminar in Yangon – on which this volume is based – although it is accepted that this may itself prove to be a barrier for more profound discussions of colonial wrongs. In addition, the chapter is written by a human rights and criminal law expert, not an expert in the study of colonialism or the different histories referenced in the chapter. It is written by a citizen of Germany, a former colonial state, an author who thinks that challenging colonialism should not be considered an exclusive task only for the former colonized societies, and definitely not a service for the 'wretched of the earth', but rather that it is in our own interest because we want to live in a society fully reconciled with its colonial past, not least to better inform contemporary racism and racist violence in former colonizing countries.

This inquiry calls for more conceptual discussions and further research, for example, as to whether the legal language, norms and practices are suitable to address colonial wrongs and, if yes, which attempt to conceptualize an appropriate temporal scope of the colonial and post-colonial wrongs we should address. The options available would include post-2002, when the Rome Statute of the International Criminal Court entered into force; post-1945 and the Nuremberg and Tokyo trials; post late-nineteenth and early-twentieth centuries, when at least a minimum standard of rights and humanitarian protections existed for a few world citizens; or the slave trade perhaps, and the destruction and exploitation of the population of the Caribbean or the Americas in the preceding times?

---

[1] Makau Mutua, "Reflections on the Genocide of the Ovaherero and Nama Peoples 115 Years Later", in Wolfgang Kaleck (ed.), *Namibia: Colonial Repercussions*, European Center for Constitutional and Human Rights ('ECCHR'), Berlin, 2019, pp. 20–21.

Also, what needs further clarification is how to conceptually address 'colonial wrongs'. At the outset, we need to question use of the term 'wrongs' which could be seen as diminutive when compared with 'colonial crimes' or the 'crime(s) of colonialism'. Another question that persists is whether we need a definition of what constitutes the crime of colonialism. Consideration needs to also be given to whether and why the umbrella term 'colonial crime' was not considered to fit under the category of today's international criminal law ('ICL'), especially for core international crimes. Further, it is important to understand how these efforts should be related to the present post-colonial injustice, including socio-economic structures of racism, economic exploitation, and present-day violence for which colonialism is frequently cited as one, if not *the* root cause?

Any comprehensive approach should be inter-disciplinary, involving other academic disciplines than law, as well as trans-disciplinary, considering other cultures, knowledge and practices. But it is also a genuine task for lawyers – a profession which could be justifiably accused of traditionally standing silently on the side of the oppressors, providing knowledge and skills to elites during the colonial period when western lawyers legitimized the colonial and imperial mission with their theories and arguments. In a recently published letter of the Washington Supreme Court it is rightly stated – in the context of 'Black Lives Matter' – in its final recourse:

> We must recognize that systemic racial injustice against black Americans is not an omnipresent specter that will inevitably persist. It is the collective product of each of our individual actions – every action, every day. It is only by carefully reflecting on our actions, taking individual responsibility for them, and constantly striving for better that we can address the shameful legacy we inherit. We call on every member of our legal community to reflect on this moment and ask ourselves how we may work together to eradicate racism.[2]

The decolonization of law would require that Western-based lawyers take equal responsibility to address the extent to which law can be an effective instrument to unravel the damage, or at the very least to determine legal accountability, while developing more tools and practical sup-

---

[2]   See Mike Scarcella, "'Our Moral Imperative': Washington State Justices Issue Open Letter Confronting Racial Injustice", *The National Law Journal*, 5 June 2020 (available on its web site).

port for affected societies, as argued below. The conceptual groundwork for decolonizing international law have been laid; it is now up to national and international lawyers to translate these into a meaningful decolonial practice within their legal systems. And it remains up to lawyers and activists to identify, challenge and demand changes in the law where it continues to be used for abuse of power and exploitation.

1.2. Colonial Crime

Needless to say, the analysis of colonialism, which has existed in different forms and has lasted centuries in different parts of the world, is too complex to leave to lawyers alone.

Moreover, it is important to stress that contemporary international lawyers have often stood out as apologists of the *status quo*, both in past and present debates. There are actually striking similarities between past and current discourses about colonialism. This tends to be overlooked by European scholars.[3] It is equally frequently overlooked that, also in the past, there were critical voices within legal scholarship on colonization[4] who failed to prevail in the discourse at the time.[5] The argument between Las Casas and Sepulveda on slavery demonstrates that more progressive voices like Las Casas could only moderate the excesses.

Over the last decades, a tradition arose from the Critical Legal Studies and Third World Approaches to International Law ('TWAIL'). Antony Anghie's study *Imperialism, Sovereignty and the Making of International Law* shows how public international law has been formed as an expression of colonial and imperial times. Legal concepts justifying colonialism, such as interpretations of what constituted *terra nullius*, no man's land (to enable its possession), in conjunction with what was often viewed as the 'civilizing mission', are critically assessed as establishing a 'topos' of the

---

[3] See, for example, Jörn Axel Kämmerer and Jörg Föh, "Das Völkerrecht als Instrument der Wiedergutmachung? Eine kritische Betrachtung am Beispiel des Herero-Aufstandes", in *Archiv des Völkerrechts (AVR)*, 2004, vol. 42, no. 3, pp. 294–328.

[4] Andrew Fitzmaurice, "Scepticism of the Civilizing Mission", in Martti Koskenniemi, Walter Rech and Manuel Jiménez Fonseca (eds.), *International Law and Empire: Historical Explorations*, 2017, pp. 359–384.

[5] For an overview, see Luigi Nuzzo, "Kolonialrecht", *Europäische Geschichte Online (EGO)*, Institut für Europäische Geschichte (IEG), Mainz, 14 July 2011, especially paras. 21–26 (available on its web site).

applicability of international law only among the so called 'civilized nations' and thus denying colonies protections emanating from law.[6]

The critique of the World Economic Order stated that, in general, with the limited say of independent post-colonial states and the interventionist politics of World Bank and International Monetary Fund ('IMF'), the Order generated systemic injustices with international law unable to mediate the burden of newly independent countries.[7] The role of international and transnational law in this has been analysed and discussed by legal scholars. In the 1970s, Third World countries proposed and advocated for a New International Economic Order ('NIEO') to replace the Bretton-Woods System, which was designed to benefit industrialized countries in the 'global north'. The new system was meant to promote global social and economic justice, especially with regards to the activities of multinational corporations and foreign property on national territories of developing countries, as well as with regards to international trade. Legal scholars in Africa and Asia attempted to use recognized principles of international law, such as sovereignty of states, to legitimize their claims under NIEO while seeking adaptation of international law, which had furthered colonial policies in serving the interest of developed countries.[8] The NIEO campaign was unsuccessful in implementing claims. Instead, the existing power structures were further strengthened and institutionalized, among others through the interventionist policies of the IMF and the World Bank, aggravating dependencies.

Another example of how international law is impairing the trajectory of developing countries is through the proliferation of arbitral tribunals, which decide commercial disputes between sovereign states and multinational corporations, applying transnational law that favours protection of foreign investment.[9]

Critical legal analysis of the role of international law in the causation and perpetuation of global social and economic injustices focus on a variety of issues. Martti Koskenniemi's critique of Eurocentrism in inter-

---

6   Antony Anghie, *Imperialism, Sovereignty, and the Making of International Law*, Cambridge University Press, 2005.

7   David Singh Grewal and Jedediah Purdy, "Law and Neoliberalism", in *Law and Contemporary Problems*, 2015, vol. 77, no. 4, p. 9.

8   Antony Anghie, "Legal Aspects of the New International Economic Order", in *Humanity Journal*, 2015, vol. 6, no. 1, p. 149.

9   *Ibid.*, p. 151.

national law,[10] and Anne Orford's analysis of the global food economy,[11] are two integral parts of this critical legal discourse. Orford links seemingly isolated fields of law like investment law and human rights to illustrate the relationship between social questions and market liberalization, which materializes in legal technicalities. When disputes are settled in favour of property interests by following an inner logic, questions of human health or the environment are sacrificed without providing a suggestion of who should deal with them up.[12] The example of food security shows that "the capacity to access adequate food is strikingly unevenly distributed, both within states and between states".[13]

The continuity of colonial paradigms such as the 'civilizing mission', which was invoked in the spirit of anti-communism, is equally striking. Important examples include Cold War interventions against democratically-elected progressive governments of Jacobo Arbenz in Guatemala 1954, Mohammad Mossadegh in Iran 1953, and Salvador Allende in Chile 1973; the new 'civilizing missions' calling for humanitarian intervention; the breath-taking proposals by parts of the environmental movement led by the World Wildlife Fund and others; and the furthering of colonial practice of protected areas (Fortress Conservation) over rain forests in the Amazon and Central Africa, even when this would displace indigenous communities who are best placed as custodians of the environment (compared to corporate interests integral to our colonial present).[14]

Critical Legal Theory and TWAIL play an important role in the decolonization of international (criminal) law, and encourage more concrete interventions. They encompass enduring critique of the longstanding focus of Western actors, including non-governmental organizations ('NGOs') that focus exclusively on political and civil rights, a tendency that has affirmed the development of international criminal law since the 1990s as

---

[10] Martti Koskenniemi, "Histories of International law: Dealing with Eurocentrism", in *Rechtsgeschichte: Zeitschrift des Max-Planck-Instituts für europäische Rechtsgeschichte*, 2011, vol. 19.

[11] Anne Orford, "Food Security, Free Trade, and the Battle for the State", in *Journal of International Law and International Relations*, 2015, vol. 11, no. 2.

[12] Taylor Woodcock, Antoine Duval and Dimitri Van Den Meerssche, "'I Want to Put the Social Question Back on the Table' – An Interview with Anne Orford", *OpinioJuris*, 27 November 2019 (available on its web site).

[13] Orford, 2015, p. 2, see above note 11.

[14] See Joshua Castellino, "Righting Colonial Era Wrongs in Land Rights", *place*, 9 April 2019 (available on its web site).

one of the most prominent fora to deal with human rights violations. Social and economic rights are ignored in the process, with negligible attempts made to hold economic entities such as corporations involved in
core crimes accountable. Far from a holistic analysis of the Nuremberg
prosecutions, especially in the follow-up trials, criminal prosecutions confirmed a fragmented view of situations, lacking discussion of the root
causes of the crimes. One might therefore assume that – though not at all
mainstream within the academic sphere – at least in this field, colonialism
was challenged in the past decades.

However, as important for the project of decolonization of international law as the aforementioned legal thinkers were, their thoughts have
not been adequately translated into concrete legal actions. Comprehensive
legal research has not yet been carried out, the documentation of such
crimes is far from complete, and where they exist, especially for the most
egregious colonial crimes, they are confined to libraries in the former colonial countries, with very little research dedicated to its legal analysis, a
defect which cannot be rectified there.

Before diving deeper into criminal law, some caveats should be
placed on record. The discussion about colonial crimes should be located
within a broader discussion about violations of rights based on the human
rights meta-narrative. The inter-temporal rule of law is of crucial importance because it concerns many different aspects of colonialism, such
as legal personality, statute of limitations, right to property, fairness, validity of contracts, crimes against humanity, and should therefore be analysed separately.

When discussing legal theory and practice with regards to challenging colonialism, it is notable that the criminal law discourses evolve
around grave crimes and episodes perpetrated during colonialism, including massacres, torture and crimes against humanity. The invasion, land
dispossession and oppression of the inhabitants of the colonies itself, daily
exercise of sovereignty and discrimination based on an ideology of superiority of the colonizers, are rarely discussed in criminal legal terms.

There is an obvious lack of legal research and debate, and there are
new criminal types that need to be considered. Even a comparison between current international criminal statutes and the scope of crimes
committed in the colonial context would provide much more potential for
legal interventions – beyond the prosecution of torture and mass killings.

Therefore, Joshua Castellino suggests[15] to analyse a number of categories of colonial wrongs – beyond episodic crimes during colonial rule (genocide, crimes against humanity, gross violations of human rights) – which could either fall under existing criminal types, give reason to establish new criminal types, or sanctions in other fields of law, namely:

- acquisition of title to territory (determination of *terra nullius*, extinguishing native title, intra-colonial negotiations, unequal or disingenuous treaties);

- systemic and widespread practices (denial of rights, systemic/specific discrimination, oppressive colonial practices, environmental destruction,[16] exploitation of natural resources, misappropriation of cultural artefacts, divide and rule);

- crimes based on relinquishing colonial title (favouring actors, [17] excluding actors, establishing preferential rights, transition arrangements, unequal logistic support);

- legacy crimes with contemporary resonance (construction of legal systems, majoritarian biases,[18] specific policies such as 'Fortress Conservation' and capital punishment);

- support for wrongful acts post-independence (biased technical co-operation, retention of preferential trading rights, unequal partnerships, maintenance of financial assets, maintenance of sovereign bases).

It appears that the latter practices, approaching colonization as a crime *sui generis*, are still perceived as something too inherent to modern history. Yet, as criminologists Marianne Nielsen and Linda M. Robyn correctly state, colonialism is "an ongoing process of invasion and oppres-

---

[15] Joshua Castellino, "Colonial Repercussions: The Nambian Case", on Akademie der Künste's *YouTube* channel, 29 November 2019.

[16] For example, racist segregation politics, as the German policy regarding the Hutu and Tutsi, were a root cause for present-day conflicts.

[17] The same questions could be asked about the role of European missionaries, whose effects continue to influence present-day activities of Evangelist churches against LGBT persons in Africa.

[18] As in the example of the phosphate mining conducted fist by the Germans and then Australia and New Zealand in Nauru, see International Court of Justice ('ICJ'), *Certain Phosphate Lands in Nauru (Nauru v. Australia)*, Judgment, 26 June 1992 (https://www.legal-tools.org/doc/7fff88/).

sion, a centuries-long crime, resulting in the destruction of lives, communities, cultures, human rights, and other grave social harms".[19] As such, it should not be exclusively left to historians to work through the colonial past of Europe and the United States.

It may be necessary to divide colonialization into components in order to process each segment of activity in criminal law terms.

In 2000, the United Nations ('UN') Sub-Commission on the Promotion and Protection of Human Rights asked the UN Secretary-General to name concrete facts in which colonialism was connected to crimes against humanity, and to identify a possible way of compensation and remembrance of its victims.[20] This process was later neglected, probably due to the fact that the following world conference on racism in Durban in 2001 only concluded with a clear terminology regarding slavery, but did not define colonialism as such as a crime *sui generis*. Despite attempts to generate serious discussion around colonial crime, the backroom politicization at the Durban Conference appeared to effectively stall rather than progress the discussion. The Sub-Commission maintained its focus on the theme, taking up the Secretary-General's idea again in 2002, requesting states to accept historical responsibility for colonialism and to initiate measures accordingly.[21]

Much later, in a resolution by the European Parliament on 26 March 2019, one can find the same category: "Colonialism as crime against humanity", but this has lacked further explanations and found no real traction in the European public. In the non-binding resolution, the Parliament called upon member states to admit to their historical responsibility for past injustice and crimes against humanity, like transatlantic slavery or European colonialism. Compared to current international law, this application of crimes against humanity seems rather vague.

---

[19] Marianne Nielsen and Linda M. Robyn, *Colonialism Is Crime*, Rutgers University Press, New Brunswick, NJ, 2019.

[20] Office of the High Commissioner for Human Rights ('OHCHR'), Sub-Commission on Human Rights, Mass and flagrant violations of human rights which constitute crimes against humanity, UN Doc. E/CN.4/SUB.2/DEC/2000/114, 18 August 2000 (https://www.legal-tools.org/doc/cat5xy/).

[21] OHCHR, Sub-Commission on Human Rights, Recognition of responsibility and reparation for massive and flagrant violations of human rights which constitute crimes against humanity and which took place during the period of slavery, colonialism and wars of conquest, UN Doc. E/CN.4/SUB.2/RES/2002/5, 12 August 2002 (https://www.legal-tools.org/doc/mbvzh6/).

The crime of forced disappearance demonstrates that the legal community can react to new forms of grave crimes in developing legal definitions and constructions, even if the crimes are complex (longer time period, various actors in different stages, different forms of contribution and accountability). In 2006, the International Convention for the Protection of All Persons from Enforced Disappearance was adopted by the UN General Assembly, requesting all member states to ensure that enforced disappearance constitutes an offence under its criminal law.[22] Many national criminal codes do not recognize forced disappearance as a crime *sui generis*. Nonetheless, it is possible to prosecute the perpetrators under these criminal codes, invoking crimes such as deprivation of liberty, assistance after the fact, obstruction of justice, failure to render assistance, or incitement of a subordinate to the commission of offences.[23] A similar approach to grasp colonization in (international) criminal law terms is thinkable. However, a deeper legal analysis and academic discourse into this idea is required.

Bearing that in mind, the following remarks cover a more restricted segment of the field, namely those crimes that have already transformed into positive international criminal law, especially the core international crimes. And to make it clear, we do not need to go back to 1492, but with regard to colonial crimes committed after 1945, meaning post-Nuremberg and post-Universal Declaration of Human Rights in 1948, where the sheer number and scale of war crimes and crimes against humanity orchestrated and justified by the colonial nations is quite shocking. This double standard persisted despite victory over the Nazis, the cry of 'never again' that underpins the foundation of the UN and the promise of national sovereignty and equality of all human beings and peoples as enshrined in the post-war order.

The struggles for independence in Indochina, Southeast Asia and Africa against colonial powers like Britain, France, Belgium, the Netherlands and Portugal was met by the colonial powers with tactics of counterinsurgency and colonial rule, including the bombing of civilian populations, forced displacement of parts of the population, and mass imprison-

---

[22] International Convention for the Protection of All Persons from Enforced Disappearance, 23 December 2010, Article 4 (https://www.legal-tools.org/doc/0d0674/).

[23] Bundestagsdrucksache 16/12592, p. 33.

---

ment and torture. Many of these acts qualify as war crimes; some also constitute crimes against humanity.[24]

Some striking examples could be mentioned. In 1944, 300 Senegalese *tirailleurs* who had fought for France in World War II were massacred by French forces in Thiaroye, Senegal, as they returned home from battle. They had demanded payment of salaries, settlements and discharge allowances owed to them. In Cameroon, French soldiers opened fire on a group of protesters in Douala in September 1945, killing up to a hundred of them. Similar events occurred in Morocco, Tunisia and British-occupied Ghana.[25]

A specific kind of warfare with devastating effects for the affected populations was employed in Madagascar, Malaya, Indochina, Algeria and Kenya, but these atrocities have been ignored by the hegemonic European accounts of history, and not considered for any legal recompense. War crimes were a common feature of colonial wars during this period of contested decolonization. The first armed insurgency in Africa during this period took place in Madagascar between 1947 and 1949. Between 15,000 and 20,000 rebels were involved in an uprising, which escalated into a brutal war involving mass killings and torture, and entire regions were ravaged by French troops in the course of counter-insurgency operations. In total 89,000 Madagascans lost their lives, many of them were refugees who died of hunger or disease.[26] In late November 1946, the French air force bombed the North Vietnamese port town of Haiphong following disagreements about customs duties, with around 6,000 people killed in the attack. Over the course of the war in Malaya, which lasted from 1948 to 1960, the British army, who fought against the Malayan National Liberation Army, engaged in the destruction of entire villages, mass shootings, and the widespread use of torture. The Dutch army waged a bloody war in

---

[24] Wolfgang Kaleck, *Double Standards: International Criminal Law and the West*, Torkel Opsahl Academic EPublisher, Brussels, 2015, p. 27 (https://www.legal-tools.org/doc/971c3c/); Fabian Klose, Dona Geyer (translator), *Human Rights in the Shadow of Colonial Violence: The Wars of Independence in Kenya and Algeria*, University of Pennsylvania Press, Philadelphia, 2013, p. 56.

[25] Fabian Klose, *Menschenrechte im Schatten kolonialer Gewalt: Die Dekolonisierungskriege in Kenia und Algerien 1945–1962*, Oldenbourg Wissenschaftsverlag, Munich, 2009, p. 73; Klose, 2013, p. 57, see above note 24; Rheinisches JournalistInnenbüro and Recherche International e.V. (eds.), "Unsere Opfer zählen nicht", in *Die Dritte Welt im 2. Weltkrieg*, Assoziation A, Berlin, 2005, pp. 62–295.

[26] Klose, 2009, see above note 25; Klose, 2013, pp. 57–74, see above note 24.

Indonesia from 1945 to 1949 to foil Indonesian independence that was declared on 17 August 1945. Between 80,000 and 100,000 Indonesians lost their lives in the war. British troops also waged war on European soil – in their fight against the Cypriot liberation movement, they engaged in collective punishment of the civilian population as well as systematic torture in internment camps.[27]

Another infamous example is the destructive campaign in Kenya, committed by the British army, which resulted in major depopulation of Kikuyu land.[28] Britain responded to the armed struggle of the political independence movement in Kenya – known as the Mau Mau uprising – with the internment of around 24,000 persons in camps for systematic interrogation involving abuse and torture, as well as with indiscriminate bombardments and forceful resettlements. Over the course of the conflict, 167 members of the British army lost their lives along with 1,819 Africans who were on the side of the British, while on the opposing side there were an estimated 20,000 to 100,000 Kikuyu deaths.[29]

In Algeria, the war of liberation of the *Front de Libération Nationale* (FLN) against France was contested by the latter with a brutal counter-insurgency policy which, like the British approach in Kenya, was to serve as a notorious example for counter-insurgency operations during the cold war. Entire regions were razed as villages were bombed and destroyed, and millions of Algerians were forcibly displaced into protected villages. Over 24,000 people were interrogated and roughly 3,000 of them died as a consequence of the torture they endured during questioning.[30]

There have never been serious efforts to investigate colonial crimes before national or international courts, nor to punish any of the surviving perpetrators, nor sanction the governments involved or to compensate the victims for the ongoing health problems triggered by the crimes.

---

[27] Klose, 2009, p. 78, see above note 25; Klose, 2013, p. 51, see above note 24.

[28] See Wunyabari O. Maloba, *Mau Mau and Kenya: An Analysis of a Peasant Revolt*, Indiana University Press, Bloomington, IN, 1998.

[29] Kaleck, 2015, p. 29, see above note 24; Klose, 2013, p. 61, see above note 24; Anthony Clayton, *Counter-Insurgency in Kenya: A Study of Military Operations Against the Mau Mau, 1952–1960*, Sunflower University Press, New York, 1984.

[30] Kaleck, 2015, p. 30, see above note 24; Rita Maran, *Torture. The Role of Ideology in the French-Algerian War*, Praeger, New York, NY, 1989.

1.3. Double Standards: International Criminal Law and the West[31]

It cannot reasonably be contested that there were double standards in international law in the past, in specific terms in the delineation of overseas territory as *terra nullius*, the use and validation of unequal treaties, and the process in which customary norms around traditional ownership were overridden.[32] Rather than a mere historical footnote, the double standards still permeate the current practice in international criminal law, namely when it comes to investigations and possible prosecutions against Western and powerful actors. One has therefore to understand the politics of law behind the decision whom to prosecute, when, and how for what.[33]

This conclusion is backed by the research of scholars such as William Schabas[34] and Maximo Langer. The latter's devastating statistics of international criminal proceedings are important. He counts 1,051 criminal proceedings in 15 years in Western Europe of which only 32 proceeded to trial, whereas the complaints directed against a variety of powerful actors such as China, Russia and the United States were never seriously prosecuted. Trials only involved suspects from Afghanistan, the Democratic Republic of the Congo, ex-Yugoslavia, and some old Nazi criminals. Langer rightly concluded that European states only exercise universal jurisdiction and prosecute in "low cost" cases, cases which are generally aligned with their political, economic and military interests and do not harm them.[35]

---

[31] My own book (Kaleck, 2015, see above note 24, which was translated into English from the original German version entitled *Mit zweierlei Maß: Der Westen und das Völkerstrafrecht*), was selected by the main organiser, CILRAP, as one of the *Leitmotif* for the research project of which this anthology forms part, so the following references are not intended as self-promotion.

[32] Joshua Castellino, "Referencing Boundaries: Why the World Needs the World Court", in *Wisconsin International Law Journal*, 2015, vol. 33, no. 3.

[33] This is not only the conclusion of my book, written in 2011, but also drawn from my own practical experiences as a lawyer, especially in the 1998 Argentinian Military Dictatorship cases, including the case of the disappeared trade unionists of Mercedes Benz and the 2004–2007 Rumsfeld-US Torture Universal Jurisdiction cases, in which the prosecutors were not willing, not considering, not even imagining the possibility of prosecution – until recently with my organisation, the European Center for Constitutional and Human Rights.

[34] William Schabas, *Unimaginable Atrocities: Justice, Politics and Rights at the War Crimes Tribunals*, Oxford University Press, 2012.

[35] Máximo Langer, "The Diplomacy of Universal Jurisdiction: The Political Branches and the Transnational Prosecution of International Crimes", in *American Journal of International Law*, 2011, vol. 105, no. 1.

A quick scan of different historical situations from Nazi Germany and Japan, the aforementioned colonial crimes, the Vietnam War, to military dictatorships in Argentina, Chile, to ex-Yugoslavia and Iraq, demonstrates that in many moments of history only some of the crimes that would today constitute core international crimes have been subject to investigations or trials, although more prosecution would and should have been possible under past and current laws. So the current lament about double standards should not surprise us – because powerful political, military and economic actors at all times dominate what is seen as a crime and what not, and which of these crimes deserve to be prosecuted.[36]

In any area of law, there remains a gap between the letter of the law and how that law is applied in practice. However, in the practice of international criminal law, the law is applied so irregularly as to undermine the very legitimacy of the law and its claims of universal applicability. Double standards constantly appear when pursuing prosecutions for grave violations of human rights. In practice, the assessment of whether to prosecute crimes under international law is almost always a political decision made in reference to the situation at hand, involving a great amount of both 'horizontal' and 'vertical selectivity'.

'Horizontal selectivity' is at play when grave crimes are committed in a number of similar situations throughout a given historical period, but only some of these are prosecuted as crimes in international law, while others are ignored. As we will see, raising this point often provokes vehement kneejerk objections.[37] These debates on the historical categorization of the discussed crimes should be borne in mind when recourse is had to legal definitions, which are not always helpful in the context of a broader discussion.

Prosecution for crimes under international law is also prone to 'vertical selectivity', which refers to the decision as to which of the individuals involved in a situation should be singled out for prosecution. Perpetrators of international crimes who hold high-level office, the so-called 'big fish', often manage to escape prosecution. The focus is often placed instead on lower-ranking soldiers and other less powerful individuals, who are selected to serve as scapegoats. Securing these kinds of convictions is a strategy often employed to appease national and international demands

---

[36] Kaleck, 2015, pp. 1–9, see above note 24.
[37] *Ibid.*, pp. 7–8.

for action while avoiding taking politically sensitive steps against major perpetrators.[38]

The inter-temporal rule dictates that only those criminal law standards can be applied which were valid at the time of the alleged conduct – exceptions like Nuremberg and Nazi crimes where *ex post* substantive and procedural rules have been established are, however, well justified. It often seems, especially to people from outside Europe, that the willingness to make exceptions to the inter-temporal rule was all too pertinent when it concerned European victims during World War II, but this dynamic is not considered relevant in viewing episodic crimes against humanity, war crimes or even genocide (leaving aside aggression) perpetrated during colonial rule, further strengthening the claim of double standards.

It is difficult to talk of unequal application when pointing to situations of different time-periods, with different laws in place, especially when comparing crimes committed before and after 2002 when the ICC's Statute entered into force. However, the discussion of accountability gaps is not foreclosed, because many past and present situations that do not fall within the jurisdiction of the ICC could nonetheless be investigated and sanctioned in some way, even bearing in mind the overall dogma of inter-temporality.[39]

Anne Orford describes the dilemma as follows:

> For many lawyers, however, the past should not, and indeed cannot, be forgotten. Law is a site not only for the creation of new obligations but also for the transmission of inherited obligations. Law is inherently genealogical, depending as it does upon the movement of concepts, languages and norms across time and even space. The past, far from being gone, is constantly being retrieved as a source or rationalisation of present obligation. For a lawyer, relating a concept to a history is not simply about making sense of something that is past and immutable as opposed to a law that is present and freely chosen. While some legal historians identify as histo-

---

[38] Probably the best example in recent history was President George W. Bush's tactic to point to "some rotten apples" amongst the field personnel from the night shift in Iraqi prison Abu Ghraib when the infamous pictures were published and caused a scandal in spring 2004.

[39] See Joshua Castellino, "The Doctrine of *Uti Possidetis* and Crystallisation of Modern Identity", in *German Yearbook of International Law*, 2001, vol. 43.

rians, and preach against the sin of anachronism, in a sense lawyers are and must be sinners in this sense. Law necessarily has to reckon with obligations that are not solely derived from the current rulers of a state – in that sense whatever the felt urgency of breaking with the past, the past persists in custom and precedent and legal tradition. The difficulty then lies in knowing (or perhaps choosing) which precedents should be invoked to make the present intelligible.[40]

According to Orford, anachronism is inherent to law. Ignoring anachronism can lead to problematic results, because present-day interpretation of the law itself according to past standards reintroduces these standards in present discourses and social structures, to which they no longer are appropriate. This can be seen in the court case against Germany in New York, as well as in the debate about the restitution of colonial artefacts. The German defendant in the New York Ovaherero case cited the International Court of Justice in support of their view on the doctrine of inter-temporality, stating:

Finally, it is supported by the consistent jurisprudence of the International Court of Justice (ICJ), stating that a question has "to be interpreted by reference to the law in force at that period".[41]

There are, however, ways out of this dilemma. Not least using the formula of the German legal philosopher Gustaf Radbruch, which he wanted to apply to the Nationalist Socialist period, and which was not very well-perceived by the representatives of the German justice system, whose personnel had started their careers during National Socialism and continued in their position also in the Federal Republic of Germany. Radbruch stated:

Where justice is not even strived for, where equality, which is the core of justice, is renounced in the process of legisla-

---

[40] Anne Orford, "The Past as Law or History: The Relevance of Imperialism for Modern International Law", in *New York University School of Law Institute for International Law and Justice Working Paper*, 2012, vol. 2, p. 6.

[41] ICJ, *Western Sahara*, Advisory Opinion, 16 October 1975, ICJ Reports 1975, p. 38, para. 79 (https://www.legal-tools.org/doc/512a2a/); ICJ, *Jurisdictional Immunities of the State (Germany v. Italy)*, Judgment, 3 February 2012, ICJ Reports 2012, p. 124, para. 58 ("the compatibility of an act with international law can be determined only by reference to the law in force at the time when the act occurred") (https://www.legal-tools.org/doc/674187/).

tion, there a statute is not just 'erroneous law', in fact is not of legal nature at all.[42]

At no point has it seriously been asked what would follow from applying this formula, with its strong focus on equality, on the openly racist statutes that were adopted in colonial times and that the German defense referred to in the case in New York.

Looking at the law not from a static, but from a dynamic perspective, what stands out is, for example, that the concept of the crime of genocide was adopted only after the Holocaust; that the prescription period for murder was abolished only in 1965, when claims in relation to the Nazi era were about to prescribe; that unexpected developments such as the unification of Germany can lead to a renewal of restitution claims that before were considered void; that in 2005, the UN General Assembly demanded that states decline from applying their national laws with regard to prescription in cases involving international crimes.[43]

With regards to the current debate, an ever-larger number, not only of TWAIL scholars, but also traditional scholars, acknowledge that the legal history of our colonial past has to be re-written.

Meanwhile, a less fundamental and more practically oriented alternative exists. The International Law Commission has pointed out:

> But the intertemporal principle does not entail that treaty provisions are to be interpreted as if frozen in time. The evolutionary interpretation of treaty provisions is permissible in certain cases, but this has nothing to do with the principle that a State can only be held responsible for breach of an obligation which was in force for that State at the time of its conduct.[44]

---

[42] Gustav Radbruch, *Gesetzliches Unrecht und übergesetzliches Recht*, Süddeutsche Juristen-Zeitung, 1946, vol. 1, no. 5, pp. 105–108 (translation by the author).

[43] Basic Principles and Guidelines on the Right to a Remedy and Reparation for Victims of Gross Violations of International Human Rights Law and Serious Violations of International Humanitarian Law, UN Doc. A/RES/60/147, paras. 8–9 (https://www.legal-tools.org/doc/bcf508/).

[44] Draft articles on Responsibility of States for Internationally Wrongful Acts, with commentaries, UN Doc. A/56/10, Article 28, commentary, para. 9 (https://www.legal-tools.org/doc/10e324/).

German legal scholar Matthias Goldmann, in his Declaration before the U.S. District Court of the Southern District of New York, emphasized the following:

> It is [...] time to take a fresh look at the international legal status of the Ovaherero and Nama peoples at the time. While the Defendant argues that the rules relating to intertemporality bind the Court to apply the rules of international law of the time, even if this were assumed to be true, the Court needs to verify the existence of these rules and their application correctly, based on a proper assessment of the facts, not on the ignorance and racist stereotypes of Western international lawyers of the colonial period. Under the rules of international law during the period in question, peoples and other entities – whether called states or not – enjoyed international legal personality when it consisted of a defined population occupying a specific territory and equipped with a mechanism for the exercise of power.[45]

In conclusion, there are many ways to legitimize how today's judicial and political actions categorize colonial crimes and its consequences, to sanction individuals where possible and states, to restitute and compensate, to investigate and search for the truth. Some might argue with Radbruch, others with TWAIL; some might, like the example above, interpret law in light of sources other than imperialist and colonial law of the time, especially non-European law of the time, or international criminal or human rights law. However, under such conditions, it should be allowed for colonizing states to refer to colonial law and base its actions – even without further reflections – on what Germany did in the Namibia court case.

The issue of double standards is not merely a perception that needs to be corrected, but it encompasses a genuine critique, and the failure to engage with it undermines the legitimacy of international criminal law. My main motive is not a prophylactic defense of international criminal law. However, when double standards are a reality of injustice, with serious material impacts such as lack of access to justice for many victims, impunity with lack of land and resources, poverty, and so on, it needs to be addressed rather than dismissed in a dogmatic manner.

---

[45] Matthias Goldmann, "The Ovaherero and Nama Peoples v. Germany - Declaration of Matthias Goldmann before the SDNY Court", *SSRN*, 25 April 2018, p. 18, paras. 43–44 (available on its web site).

On a broader level, unequal application of law has had a serious impact on the legitimacy of particular investigations or of specific courts as observed in the growing critique of the ICC, but it also impinges on acceptance of the salience of international criminal law and international law in general. This takes on added impetus when the unquestionable role of international law is factored into justifications of the illegitimate acquisition of overseas territory.

This influences not only on the macro but also on the micro level – for example, norm internalization, or as Morten Bergsmo described:

> Norm *inconsistency, exceptionalism, eclipses* or *neglect* may therefore have a disproportionate impact on relational norm implementation. This is why a practice of double normative standards – including legal standards or norms – can be so fundamentally disruptive to societal norm internalisation. This may be particularly relevant to normative clusters that are sought to be used as a 'gentle civiliser of mankind', as is the case with international law.[46]

Double standards are as much a reality of the past as in the present, with the pure facts not really disputed, while their interpretation is disputed, especially when the causes for these double standards and injustice are ignored. It seems clear, however, that those who aspire for legitimacy and equality as basic values of international criminal law need to be able to take up the mantle to challenge the impunity of powerful actors. This is not only a prod for those of us who pursue cases against powerful perpetrators,[47] but for the legal community as a whole and the general public.

Questions of legitimacy regarding court bias have been raised before various international tribunals with the so-called *tu quoque* ('you too') objection – that is, the complaint that the accusing party failed to act consistently in accordance to its own claims and had committed similar crimes.

The classic example of a *tu quoque* situation in a criminal context is the trial of Admiral Karl Dönitz as part of the proceedings against major war criminals in Nuremberg. Dönitz's defence lawyer, Otto Kranzbühler,

---

[46] Morten Bergsmo, "Double Standards and the Problem of Access to International Law", CILRAP Film, Yangon, 16 November 2019 (emphasis added) (https://www.cilrap.org/cilrap-film/191116-bergsmo/).

[47] See, for example, the Center for Constitutional Rights in New York or the Berlin-based European Center for Constitutional and Human Rights.

argued that a US Navy Admiral had given similar orders to those of Dönitz for comparable methods of submarine warfare. In doing so, Kranzbühler was not attempting to put forward the argument that the US was also guilty of war crimes in order to relativize the crimes and imply that the US was in no position to put his client on trial. Instead, he wanted to show that in pursuing these methods of warfare, both the US Navy and his client were acting within the boundaries of the law. His intention was to draw on the victor's code of practice as authority to interpret the relevant provisions of the laws of war to secure an acquittal for his client. Ultimately the court settled on a pragmatic solution, sentencing Dönitz to 10 years of imprisonment, but without adding any additional prison sentence for the charge relating to submarine warfare. Although the *tu quoque* objection was a useful defense strategy in this case, the court rejected the argument in the subsequent Nuremberg follow-up trial (*Rasse- und Siedlungshauptamt* – Race and Settlement Headquarters, 'RuSHA'). In the RuSHA trial, the defence argued that the killing of innocent civilians could not be tried as a war crime, since the Allies had also killed noncombatants in their bombing of German cities. The court stressed that a law does not become invalid simply because one of the legislators has itself acted in violation of that law.[48]

Since Nuremberg, the *tu quoque* argument has often been raised by accused parties on various sides of the political spectrum, for example by the leaders of the Algerian FLN, during the *Kupreškić* trial before the ex-Yugoslavia tribunal, or by Saddam Hussein at the Baghdad tribunal.[49]

A wider problem attached to such trials of prominent political leaders is that the relevant tribunals are – as international scholar Martti Koskenniemi puts it –lodged between the Scylla of impunity and the Charybdis of show trials.[50] Taking the trial of Slobodan Milošević before the ex-Yugoslavia tribunal as an example, Milošević's conviction would carry

---

[48] Kaleck, 2015, p. 14, see above note 24; Nicole A. Heise, "Deciding not to Decide: Nuremberg and the Ambiguous History of the *Tu Quoque* Defense", in *The Concord Review*, 2007, vol. 18, no. 2.

[49] Leaders of the Algerian FLN attempted to use this claim in their defence by pointing to atrocities committed by the French. The argument was also addressed – and ultimately rejected – by the ex-Yugoslavia tribunal in its Kupreškić decision. Saddam Hussein voiced similar arguments against the USA when an American-backed tribunal in Baghdad sentenced him to death.

[50] Martti Koskenniemi, "Between Impunity and Show Trials", in *Max Planck Yearbook of United Nations Law*, 2002, vol. 6, no. 1, p. 1.

less weight if he succeeded in demonstrating that he had been tried according to victor's justice, and he would be offered a platform to establish his performative version of the underlying historical events which would even be accompanied by an "aura of iconoclasm". As Koskenniemi sees it, this paradoxical result is something that tribunals of this kind must simply learn to accept.

When it comes to discussion on double standards in the current practice of ICL, it resembles the *tu quoque* debate of former days. The African bias of the ICC is at the centre of several controversies – rightly so – but if this critique is raised by persons who are themselves suspected of core international crimes, the answer to them should be the same as in the RuSHA trial: let us first talk about your contribution to those crimes because the law does not become invalid even if others who acted in violation of that law go unpunished. It is fundamentally important to defend the clearly defined standards of war crimes and crimes against humanity rather than to use the vague and political category of 'terrorism'.

1.4. Emerging European Custom on Accountability for Colonial Crimes?

Notwithstanding the many obstacles, there remain multiple ways to challenge colonialism and colonial crimes today beyond the discursive and academic challenges mentioned above. This section discusses some examples of litigation in concrete cases (Section 1.4.1.); the case of German colonial crimes in Namibia will be described in further detail (1.4.2.); and another area where legal interventions are needed, restitution of colonial artefacts, will be highlighted in Section 1.4.3. The thrust of this section argues for the fledgling emergence of a regional custom in Europe with regards to the treatment of colonial crimes.

1.4.1. Litigating Colonial Crimes in European Courts

In the 1990s and 2000s, efforts were undertaken through newly-formed coalitions of affected communities and individuals and lawyers to address litigation of post-World War II colonial crimes, with a view to seeking redress in court for human rights violations that occurred long ago, often without the support of political leaders of the affected countries.

The early limited attempts did not achieve any traction as demonstrated in the attempt to prosecute French state officials for crimes in Algeria. During the Algerian war for independence, secret service tactics were employed to pursue the cadres of the FLN by the French authorities. Over 24,000 people were interrogated and roughly 3,000 of them died as a consequence of the torture they endured during questioning.[51] Henri Alleg,[52] a French communist and journalist who was subjected to torture at the hands of French elite troops, made a criminal complaint denouncing the torture while on trial for crimes against the state. The proceedings concerning his case, as well as many other cases of torture, were not pursued. Following public admissions by both former generals of the Algerian army, Jacques Massu and Paul Aussaresses, that they had used systematic torture in Algeria, lawyers took renewed action in 2000 to initiate criminal proceedings. These efforts were thwarted by French amnesty laws. Only Aussaresses was fined with EUR 7,500 along with a dishonourable discharge from the army and the French Legion of Honour for having glorified war crimes.[53]

In September 2018, French President Emmanuel Macron formally acknowledged the culpability of French authorities in the torture of freedom fighter and anti-colonial activist Maurice Audin in Algiers in 1957. It was the first time that France acknowledged its use of state-authorized torture in the Algerian war for independence.[54] While Macron's apology offered to Audin's widow is highly insufficient in view of the severity of the crimes committed in a number of cases, it finally represents an important shift by French standards.[55]

The veterans of the Mau Mau uprising were more successful when they lodged a class-action suit in a London court in October 2006, seeking millions in compensation for the torture suffered in British internment camps. The British government initially argued that the liability for any compensatory payments had passed over to the Republic of Kenya with independence in 1963 – an argument the court rejected in 2011. When the matter returned to court in 2012, the British government argued that the

---

[51] Maran, 1989, see above note 30; Jim House and Neil Macmaster, *Paris 1961: Algerians, State Terror, and Memory*, Oxford University Press, 2009.

[52] See also his account on waterboarding that he suffered in French detention. Henri Alleg, *La Question*, Editions de Minuit, Paris, 1958.

[53] Klose, 2009, see above note 25; Klose, 2013, p. 3, see above note 24.

[54] Yasmeen Serhan, "Emmanuel Macron Tries – Slowly – To Reckon With France's Past", *The Atlantic*, 14 September 2018 (available on its web site).

[55] Angelique Chrisafis, "France admits systematic torture during Algeria war for first time", *The Guardian*, 13 September 2018 (available on its web site).

case was time barred, which was rejected by the court, noting that colonial powers had kept such precise records of their activities in Kenya that a fair trial was possible.[56] The case was ultimately settled out of court in June 2013 with Britain agreeing to pay a total of GBP 19.9 million (EUR 23.4 million) to 5,228 victims. A permanent memorial was also unveiled in Nairobi in September 2015, commemorating the victims of colonialism.

Another rare example of the application of criminal law to colonial crimes is still unfolding in Belgium at the time of writing this chapter.[57] In the summer of 2011, the family of Patrice Lumumba, Congo's first elected president, lodged a criminal complaint with the public prosecutor in Brussels against surviving former members of the Belgian military and ministries suspected of involvement in Lumumba's murder. An investigation was launched by the Federal Prosecutor's Office in December 2012, focused on eight surviving Belgian suspects.[58] In 2020, the case remains in the investigative phase and no formal indictment has been issued yet. As is the case with legal interventions dealing with crimes committed during colonial rule, time is an important issue not only with regards to the statute of limitations but also given the advanced age of the victims, their relatives and the suspects. In fact, the majority of the suspects in the Lumumba case have passed away since the initiation of the investigations.

The civil proceedings initiated in the Netherlands in 2009 by relatives of some of the estimated 431 victims, who were massacred by the Dutch army on 9 December 1947 in the Indonesian village of Rawagede, is an outstanding example of what litigation can achieve. None of the soldiers or officers involved in the massacre had ever been brought before a court. In September 2011, the Dutch court ruled that the statute of limitations for the executions could not be invoked for civil liability because the case concerned a "particularly exceptional situation". The court justified

---

[56] Caroline Elkins, "Alchemy of Evidence: Mau Mau, the British Empire, and the High Court of Justice", in *Journal of Imperial and Commonwealth History*, 2011, vol. 39, no. 5; a summary of the trial proceedings can be found on the web site of the law firm Leigh Day, which represented the Mau Mau claimants before the court.

[57] See Chapter 14 below by Crépine Uwashema *et al.*, "Possible Impediments to Justice for Colonial Crimes: A Belgian Perspective"; Leo Zeilig, *Patrice Lumumba: Africa's Lost Leader*, Haus Publishing, London, 2008; Ludo de Witte, *Regierungsauftrag Mord. Der Tod Lumumbas und die Kongo-Krise*, Forum Verlag Leipzig, Leipzig, 2001.

[58] Deutscher Bundestag, Wissenschaftliche Dienste, "Gerichtliche und außergerichtliche Möglichkeiten der Aufarbeitung kolonialen und rassistisch motivierten Unrechts", WD 2 - 3000 - 016/18, 8 March 2018, p. 8 ('German Parliament Report 2018').

this decision in light of the gravity of the committed crimes, and the immediate acknowledgement of the state of all the events as well as of their wrongfulness.[59] Yet, the applicability of the statute of limitations was only ruled unacceptable in relation to the widows of the executed men, but was applied in the case of subsequent generations as they were, according to the court, affected to a lesser extent.[60] In conclusion, the court awarded damages to the widows but did not specify the amount of the compensation – the claimants and the Dutch state then settled for the amount of EUR 20,000 per affected person.[61] In August 2013, ten widows of men who had been summarily executed on the island of Celebes obtained a settlement along similar lines.[62] In a further case, the District Court of The Hague in a 2015 interlocutory judgment, established that the Netherlands is liable for damages of the widows and children of victims of summary executions in the former Dutch East Indies. While the Dutch state settled in the case of the widows, it appealed the claims of the children of those killed in the massacres. The court of appeal rejected the application of the statute of limitations in the case of the children, correctly stating that language differences and social disadvantage had stood in the way of claims made against the Dutch state.[63] In March 2020, the claimants – including eight widows and three children of executed farmers – were awarded compensation.

While these judgements are a significant step towards justice for the relatives of those executed by the Dutch state in the former Dutch East Indies, they have not led to a meaningful shift in the conduct of the Dutch government towards its colonial past. The apologies expressed by the Dutch ambassador in Indonesia were limited to the "excesses committed

---

[59] Larissa van den Herik, "Addressing 'Colonial Crimes' through Reparations? Adjudicating Dutch Atrocities Committed in Indonesia", in *Journal of International Criminal Justice*, 2012, vol. 10, no. 3 p. 693; Netherlands, The Hague, District Court, Civil Law Section, Silan and ors (on behalf of Stichting Komite Utang Kehormatan Belanda) v. Netherlands, Trial Judgment, 14 September 2011, LJN: BS8793, para. 4.14 ('Rawagede Judgment').

[60] Van den Herik, 2012, p. 696, see above note 59; Rawagede Judgment, para. 4.17, see above note 59.

[61] German Parliament Report 2018, p. 12, see above note 58.

[62] Kathrine McGregor, "From National Sacrifice to Compensation Claims: Changing Indonesian Representation of the Westerling Massacres in South Sulawesi, 1946–47", in Bart Luttikhuis and A. Dirk Moses (eds.), *Colonial Counterinsurgency and Mass Violence: The Dutch Empire in Indonesia*, Routledge, Abingdon-on-Thames, 2014.

[63] Daniel Boffey, "Relatives of Dutch colonial victims in Indonesia to get day in court", *The Guardian*, 1 October 2019 (available on its web site).

---

by Dutch forces" between 1945 and 1949, and the special scheme for widows of the executed persons in this period was only aimed at those cases which are similar in nature and severity to those of Rawagedeh and Celebes.[64] Also, the appeal in the case of the children indicated the Dutch government's lack of remorse and ongoing denial. It shows that the Netherlands is still largely unwilling to address human rights abuses committed during their colonial rule – for example in 1904, when 5,621 Indonesian civilians were killed in the village of Kuta Rih – let alone readiness to properly apologize for the invasion and colonization of Indonesia as such. Yet, the small compensations and partial apologies have a great impact on the sense of justice of the affected people and their communities. It is now up to the Netherlands to fully address issues connected with their colonial rule through comprehensive reparations and apologies.

All examples described above go back to activities of affected families or communities, together with organized constituencies and outstanding lawyers. However, none of the self-acclaimed traditional human rights strategic litigation organizations were or are significantly active in this context, not to talk of broader efforts to link these isolated struggles. Also, none of these actions were initiated *proprio motu* by the prosecutorial authorities of the colonizing states.

1.4.2. Challenging Colonial Past: The Namibia Example

As a German lawyer who is – together with his organization – involved in the struggle for apology, acknowledgment and reparation, there are good reasons to point to the Namibian example of how to challenge a colonial past.[65] Namibia is also a suitable example of the potential as well as the limits of litigation and legal interventions.

The facts have never been comprehensively investigated by any official institution until now. Mainly historians from Namibia as well as from East and West Germany have, over the past decades, established a level of knowledge which leads to the following description.[66] During the *Kaiserreich*, from 1904 to 1908, the German imperial military forces (*Schutztruppe*) caused the death of tens of thousands of Ovaherero, Nama

---

[64] See Government of the Netherlands, "Special scheme for widows of victims of executions in the Dutch East Indies", 30 August 2013 (available on its web site).

[65] Kaleck, 2019, see above note 1.

[66] Jürgen Zimmerer and Joachim Zeller, *Völkermord in Deutsch-Südwestafrika: Der Kolonialkrieg (1904-1908) in Namibia und seine Folgen*, Ch. Links Verlag, Berlin, 2003.

and other communities in Namibia, formerly known as German South-west Africa. An estimated up to 80 percent of the Ovaherero and up to 50 percent of the Nama were killed, died by means of physical violence, held in concentration camps where conditions of malnutrition, starvation, and thirst were created. This conduct targeted against the Ovaherero and Nama peoples could be qualified as the first genocide of the twentieth century.

Apart from other obstacles, German colonial crimes could not be addressed during the South African occupation and the struggle for independence. After Namibia gained its independence in 1990, the genocide was challenged by civil society groups, above all the then-Paramount Chief of the Ovaherero, Kuaima Riruako and the Chairperson of Nama Genocide Technical Committee, Ida Hoffmann, and the Nama Traditional Leaders Association. Starting from 2001, the Herero filed several lawsuits based on the Alien Torts Statute in the US against Germany and several German private entities,[67] of which the last was dismissed in 2007.

Like in other European countries, the colonial past did not play a role in the German public discourse for a long time. The German relationship to colonialism in Namibia has been described as a state of "colonial amnesia", "overshadowed by the country's focus on other parts of its history".[68]

In 2004, on the occasion of the centenary of colonial crimes, a parliamentary motion concluded that the events from 1904–1908 establish a "special responsibility" for Germany, intended to be of political-moral nature. On a visit to Namibia in 2004, the Social Democratic Minister for Development Cooperation, Heidemarie Wieczorek-Zeul, spoke at Waterberg, the site where the genocide against the Ovaherero supposedly began:

> The atrocities committed at that time would today be termed genocide – and nowadays a General von Trotha would be prosecuted and convicted. We Germans accept our historical

---

[67] For details, see Business and Human Rights Resource Centre, "German cos. Lawsuit (by Hereros)", 18 February 2014 (available on its web site).

[68] Report of the Working Group on People of African Descent by the United Nations after a visit to Germany, UN Doc. A/HRC/36/60/Add.2, 15 August 2017, p. 7.

and moral responsibility and the guilt incurred by Germans at that time.[69]

However, this view was not only not shared by the German government, but the then-Foreign Minister, Joschka Fischer, made clear that Germany feared reparation claims in the context of World War II influences, which underpinned the German position that "there will be no apology with relevance for compensation".[70]

Since 2015, an inter-governmental dialogue has been held between Germany and Namibia,[71] following discussions about an acknowledgement of the Armenian genocide by the German Federal Parliament.[72] These negotiations deal with acknowledgment, apology and reparations for the genocide of the Ovaherero and Nama 1904–1908. They are led by two special envoys appointed by the two countries.

The participation of the organized communities of the Ovaherero and Nama as the targeted groups of the genocide is relevant both for the credibility and effectiveness of the negotiations. Representatives of Ovaherero and Nama who are not involved in the negotiations have made clear that they will not accept an agreement if they are not included in the discussion. From the outside, it seems that a possible agreement between Germany and Namibia could contain collective commemoration as well as material redress, not explicitly as reparation, but rather through targeted development projects.[73] All these potential remedies are already heavily

---

[69] Speech of Heidemarie Wieczorek-Zeul in Ohamakari in Namibia, "The atrocities committed would today be termed genocide", 14 August 2004 (Namibian embassy in Germany's web site).

[70] Reinhart Kößler, *Namibia and Germany: Negotiating the Past*, Verlag Westfälisches Dampfboot, Münster, 2015, p. 242, quoting an article in the *Namibische Allgemeine Zeitung* (AZ), 30 October 2003.

[71] Germany talks of an "intergovernmental dialogue on coming to terms with the past", see Federal Foreign Office, "Addressing Germany and Namibia's past and looking to the future", 1 July 2019 (available on its web site); and by Namibia as "deliberations on the 1904-1908 genocide", see New Era Staff Reporter, "Ngavirue appointed as special envoy on genocide", on *Boschaft der Republik Namibia in der Bundesrepublik Deutschland*, 5 November 2015 (available on its web site).

[72] Deutscher Bundestag, "Antrag der Fraktionen CDU/CSU, SPD und BÜNDNIS 90/DIE GRÜNEN: Erinnerung und Gedenken an den Völkermord an den Armeniern und anderen christlichen Minderheiten in den Jahren 1915 und 1916", 31 May 2016, Drucksache 18/8613.

[73] See Kae Matundu-Tjiparuro, "Genocide negotiations a 'window of opportunity' – Ngavirue", *New Era Live*, 25 March 2019 (available on its web site).

disputed, for example, the question of whose memories will be represented in any commemorative process, to the question of who will be reached by the measures intended to ameliorate the long-term effects of the genocide and the open land questions.[74]

In 2018 the High Commissioner for Human Rights of the United Nations, Michelle Bachelet, demanded that the "Ovaherero and Nama peoples are included in the negotiations between the Governments of Germany and Namibia following the apology by Germany for the genocide of these people".[75]

In September 2016, a legal opinion of the Research Service of the German Parliament was drafted regarding the qualification of the events under international law and related liability risks. This opinion denied, referring to the principle of inter-temporality, the illegality of the conduct under international law, stating the following: [76]

> The German Empire has in principle not violated international contract law through the suppression of the uprisings [...]. As for international customary law, it can be concluded in contrast that individuals already enjoyed a rudimentary protection in the beginning of the 20th century, dictated by the imperatives of humanity and civilization. However, the legal conviction of the community of international law at the time excluded the in their view "uncivilized" indigenous peoples also from this minimum protection.[77]

Several German officials emphasized on different occasions that the negotiations were not about legal, but political-moral questions, and that Germany was not inferring any legal, but only moral consequences from the acknowledgment. Compensation claims were void, as national courts

---

[74] See the special initiative launched after the visit of Heidemarie Wieczorek-Zeul to Namibia, which was regarded not to have had any concrete effect on site, Reinhart von Kößler and Henning Melber, *Völkermord - und was dann?: Die Politik deutsch-namibischer Vergangenheitsbearbeitung*, Brandes & Apsel, Frankfurt am Main, 2017, p. 53.

[75] Michelle Bachelet, "Letter by the High Commissioner to the Foreign Minister of the Federal Republic of Germany", 2 November 2018 (available on Office of the High Commissioner of Human Right's web site).

[76] Deutscher Bundestag, Wissenschaftliche Dienste, "Der Aufstand der Volksgruppen der Herero und Nama in Deutsch-Südwestafrika (1904-1908) Völkerrechtliche Implikationen und haftungsrechtliche Konsequenzen", WD 2 - 3000 - 112/16, 27 September 2016 ('German Parliament Report 2016').

[77] *Ibid.*, p. 16.

would not consider these claims admissible, and as there were no individual victims alive who could bring these claims, since compensation claims could not be inherited under German law.[78]

After years of talks and bilateral governmental negotiations, the Chiefs Vekuii Rukoro and David Frederick of Ovaherero and Nama peoples respectively, and other indigenous peoples, filed a lawsuit against the Federal Republic of Germany at the US District Court of the Southern District of New York in January 2017. In the lawsuit, the plaintiffs sought compensation for the colonial crimes.[79]

Germany rejected the claim, but later responded, for the first time in a courtroom, with a position on the events from 1904–1908. In a memorandum in support of the motion to dismiss, Germany's lawyers referred not only to state immunity and forum inconvenience, but other jurisdictional arguments related to limitations of the Alien Torts Statute.[80] It also commented on the case in substance. The argument followed the line provided in the opinion of the Research Service of the German Parliament and concluded:

> History cannot be rewritten, as far as its legal framework is concerned. Legal rules change as time goes by, but the law of the 21st century cannot be introduced back more than 110 years in history.[81]

In taking such a position, Germany is in effect re-enacting colonial statutes.

On 6 March 2019, the U.S District Court for the Southern District of New York dismissed the case based on lack of subject matter jurisdiction.[82] The plaintiffs appealed the decision of the District Court, with the appeal pending before the United States Court of Appeals for the Second

---

[78] *Ibid.*, p. 5.

[79] For more details, see Richard Dören and Alexander Wentker, "Jurisdictional Immunities in the New York Southern District Court? The Case of *Rukoro et al. v. Federal Republic of Germany*", *EJIL: Talk!*, 13 August 2018 (available on its web site).

[80] *Ibid.*

[81] United States District Court of the Southern District of New York, *Vekuii Rukoro et al. v. Federal Republic of Germany*, Defendant's Memorandum of Law in Support of Defendant's Motion to Dismiss, 13 March 2018, No. 17 CV 62-LTS.

[82] United States District Court of the Southern District of New York, *Vekuii Rukoro et al. v. Federal Republic of Germany*, Opinion and Order, 6 March 2019, No. 17 CV 62-LTS.

Circuit in New York.[83] The decision is considered as a confirmation by the German government, who writes on the web site of the Foreign Office:

> There is no legal basis for material claims against Germany by the state of Namibia or by individual Herero or Nama or representatives of these ethnic groups because of events from the colonial past. The talks therefore cannot address compensation payments or reparations.[84]

Different measures are publicly discussed, such as a programme for the especially affected areas, including vocational education, affordable living, health and electricity supply, as well as co-operation on a land reform. In addition, a common declaration was to be adopted by both parliaments, which would for the first time officially address the events as genocide. Finally, a foundation for a common memory culture is in discussion, "to also educate the Germans about the dark sides of the colonial history – a colonial history, which many today think, has never happened".[85] In June 2020 it was reported that President Hage Geingob rejected the latest German proposal of an apology and a payment of EUR 10 million.

As difficult as it is to resume a pending process, including in the context of a potential trial in New York, one can conclude that the whole issue would not be on the agenda of either government without the decades-long struggle of the affected communities at international and national levels. Civil society actors and academics support the process through academic and political publications, public events, and protests. Visits and public appearances of the Herero and Nama representatives in New York and Berlin, partly in traditional attire, gained much attraction. Some people argue that the fact that the Germans are negotiating with the government delegation of Namibia about the genocide is more than what many other colonial nations are doing. There was no attempt on behalf of both governments to act, before the organized communities of the Ovaherero and Nama initiated a civil lawsuit in the New York court in January

---

[83] United States Court of Appeals for the Second Circuit, *Vekuii Rukoro et al. v. Federal Republic of Germany*, No. 19-609 (ongoing).

[84] Federal Foreign Office, 2019, see above note 71.

[85] Ruprecht Polenz as quoted in Jan Sternberg, "Namibia: Bundestag plant Anerkennung des deutschen Völkermords", *Redaktionsnetzwerk Deutschland*, 28 November 2019 (available on its web site).

2017. The trial triggered the attention of mainstream media which contributed enormously to the political pressure on both governments.

However, the lawsuit has its limits, especially since the negative decision in the first instance no longer serves as a threat for the German government. One may argue that the New York case might not bring justice to the Namibian people, that it might not even be the right forum. However, without the ongoing pressure of the communities, supported by momentum created through the resolution on the Armenian genocide in the German parliament, and the lawsuit itself, Germany would not have been forced to re-open this historical chapter, and would have resisted any negotiation with Namibia. There are some serious actors within the German government who are – so far in theory – willing to apologize for and acknowledge the genocide. However, when it comes to the reparation question, all public declarations remain vague and, moreover, the process takes much longer than initially announced.

After an agreement between the two governments, any meaningful reconciliation process has to be dictated and orchestrated by the two governments. One of the main deficiencies of the inter-governmental dialogue is that the affected communities are not participating as communities, and therefore lack ownership over the implementation process, which calls for organization of a real dialogue between the two societies of Germany and Namibia.

1.4.3. Restitution of Colonial Artefacts: The Sarr/Savoy Report and the German Discussion

Some of the court cases mentioned above are criminal cases, some civil proceedings – but the legal qualifications, the inter-temporality and other questions discussed in the chapter resemble each other. In the Namibia example, the legal analysis and consequences play a role not only in the New York court case, but also in the public discussion in Namibia and Germany. Even more so, the qualification of the crimes as genocide is one of the most disputed topics in both countries. However, the ongoing discussion about the restitution of colonial artefacts should also be considered in the current context.

A look into the German Museum Association's Guidelines demonstrates why this topic should matter here as well:

> The current legal system – this applies to both German and
> international law – does not provide suitable instruments for

deciding ownership issues surrounding acquisitions from colonial contexts. Of course, it would be conceivable to create such legal instruments at both levels. However, it is very questionable whether the political will to enact such instruments exists.[86]

The conditions under which restitution is invoked are often neglected in legal discussions. This includes the violent character of colonization and the loss of cultural goods – not only of objects but also as (parts of) identity, history and culture – that are still exhibited in Western museums, based on legal and social norms created during colonialism, on imperialism and racism the structures of which sometimes still exist today. Restitutions of those art and cultural objects have to be seen as and become outdated in this context: they are, at the same time, a reaction to past violence and injustice, as well as a compensation for an ongoing loss. They stand and enjoy their legitimacy in the tension between colonial structures and post-colonial power imbalances.

International law does not provide definite answers in this regard. After national initiatives like the US Lieber Code, the Oxford Manual or the unratified Brussels Declaration from 1874, the first international framework of regulations concerning the protection of cultural objects in armed conflicts was in the Hague Land Warfare Code from 1899 and 1907. Its Martens Clause guaranteed the protection of the "principles of the law of nations, as they result from the usages established among civilized peoples, from the laws of humanity, and the dictates of the public conscience". The Code, on the other hand, also protects private property (Article 46), prohibits plundering (Article 47), and puts property of municipalities, that of institutions dedicated to religion, charity and education as well as arts and sciences, on the same level as private property (Article 56). The Code did not contain rules on restitution, but regulations concerning cultural goods and private property in armed conflict. As described above, according to European states' legal opinion, this Code should only be applied among European countries.

It is therefore proposed that international (criminal) law and the various human rights norms should be considered when discussing how to deal with historical facts today. Our current actions should not be ruled by

---

[86] Carola Thielecke and Michael Geißdorf, "Sammlungsgut aus Kolonialen Kontexten: Rechtliche Aspekte", in Deutscher Museumsbund e.V., *Leitfaden zum Umgang mit Sammlungsgut aus kolonialen Kontexten*, Deutscher Museumsbund e.V., Berlin, 2019.

references to the principle of inter-temporality, which states that the law should be applied which was valid when events occurred. The law in force back then, at least for the colonial powers, was – as rightly stated by post-colonial theorists – an imperial and colonial law that legitimized oppression and violence.

Some aspects are discussed in the report Felwine Sarr and Bénédicte Savoy delivered to French President Emmanuel Macron in 2019, which states:

> The effects and the legacy of this very sensitive history are numerous. They can be seen in a variety of ways on a global scale: economic inequality, political instability, humanitarian tragedies. Given this context, to speak of the restitution of African cultural heritage and works of art to Africa is to open merely one chapter in a much larger, and certainly much vaster, history. But perhaps this chapter can help to open up yet another one. Underneath this beauty mask, the questions around restitution also get at the crux of the problem: a system of appropriation and alienation—the colonial system – for which certain European Museums, unwillingly have become the public archives. However, thinking restitutions implies much more than a single exploration of the past: above all, it becomes a question of building bridges for future equitable relations. Guided by dialogue, polyphony, and exchange, the act or gesture of restitution should not be considered as a dangerous action of identitarian assignation or as the territorial separation or isolationism of cultural property. On the contrary, it could allow for the opening up of the signification of the objects and open a possibility for the "universal", with whom they are so often associated in Europe, to gain a wider relevance beyond the continent.[87]

Sarr and Savoy refer to one of the few museum collections that have been roughly catalogued and whose lists are, at the same time, publicly available, the Musée du Quai Branly. From their surely exemplary lists, it can be seen that most parts of the collection were acquired during colonial conquest and the established colonial rule. They rightly demand for the objects obtained during these military contexts to be returned. Not only those that were "acquired during direct warring conflict", but all

---

[87] Felwine Sarr and Bénédicte Savoy, "The Restitution of African Cultural Heritage: Toward a New Relational Ethics", 2018, p. 2.

those that due to the military context suggest an acquisition under "power imbalance and authority qua colonial armed violence".[88]

The implicit act of the gesture of restitution is very clearly the recognition of the illegitimacy of the property that one had previously claimed ownership of, no matter what the duration of time was then. As a consequence, the act of restitution attempts to put things back in order, into proper harmony. To openly speak of restitutions is to speak of justice, or a re-balancing, recognition, of restoration and reparation, but above all, it is a way to open a pathway toward establishing new cultural relations based on a new awareness of an ethical relation. Consequently, the questions that emerge from thinking about restitutions are far from being limited to only the juridical aspects and questions of legitimate ownership. The implications tied to the method of restitution are also of a political and symbolic order, if not also of a philosophical and relational order. Restitutions open up a profound reflection on history, memories, and the colonial past, concerning the history as well as the formation and development of Western museum collections. The question of restitution also bears on the different interpretations or conceptions of cultural heritage, of the museum, and their various modalities of the presentation of objects as well as their circulation and, in the end, the nature and quality of relations between people and nations.[89]

Thus, it is less a question of claiming financial compensation than a symbolic re-establishment through a demand for truth. Compensation here consists in offering to repair the relation. The restitution of objects (having become the nodes of a relation) also implies a fair and just historiographic work and a new relational ethics; by operating a symbolic redistribution, repairing the ties, and renewing them around reinvented relational modalities that are qualitatively improved.[90]

This discussion should not only be led by museum experts, but should include (criminal) lawyers – not to focus only on the legal aspects, but to contribute to it and clarify the normative ground and set of norms that would be applied to contemporary situations of the magnitude of colonial crimes.

---

[88] *Ibid.*, p. 100.
[89] *Ibid.*, p. 29.
[90] *Ibid.*, p. 40.

1.5. Ways Forward

The role of civil society actors and lawyers from the colonized as well as colonizing states has been discussed in the previous sections on legal struggles. They should not be spared from critique. Especially the Western human rights organizations are often absent when it comes to the colonial past and its consequences – that is, contemporary post-colonial injustice. Here, Makau Mutua's critique comes into play:

> Even the international law of human rights, arguably the most benign of all the areas of international law, seeks the universalization of Eurocentrism. The human rights corpus is driven by what I have called the savage-victim-savior metaphor, in which human rights is a grand narrative of an epochal contest that pits savages against victims and saviors. In this script of human rights, democracy and western liberalism are internationalized to save savage non-Western cultures from themselves to "alleviate" the suffering of victims, who are generally non-Western and non-Europeans.
>
> In the human rights idiom, the European West becomes the savior of helpless victims whose salvation lies only in the transformation of their savage cultures through the imposition of human rights. Attempts to craft a truly universal regime of rights, one that reflects the complexity and the diversity of all cultures, have generally been viewed with indifference or hostility by the official guardians of human rights.[91]

Tshepo Madlingozi criticizes the "transitional justice experts", in particular those who "legitimize their existence on the basis of speaking about and for victims". Moreover, for him, a leading member of South African Apartheid Victims Association – Khulumani, "the main point of encounter between the authoritative expert and the marginalized victim" is the, what he calls, "responsibility to the story", which "should mean more than being nice to victims". It should also "be about redistribution of resources and power. In exercising responsibility to the story experts need to dismantle trusteeship and reproduction of colonial relations".[92]

---

[91] Makau Mutua, "Critical Race Theory and International Law: The View of an Insider-Outsider", in *Villanova Law Review*, 2000, vol. 45.

[92] Tshepo Madlingozi, "On Transitional Justice Entrepreneurs and the Production of Victims", in *Journal of Human Rights Practice*, 2010, vol. 2, no. 2.

Both scholars link the biased attitude of Western human rights actors to their lack of understanding of colonial relations. In particular, their focus on political and civil rights is striking, as well their preference for criminal law, which is directed towards individuals and often is not dealing with the root causes of systematic and structural rights violations.

While this critique is still valid to a large extent, in the last decade many more human rights actors have used international criminal law to challenge crimes of Western actors and double standards, in particular US and UK torture in Afghanistan and Iraq, and the extraordinary renditions. Economic and social rights are on the agenda of bigger human rights entities. Business actors, including transnational corporations around the world, are sued by civil society actors in criminal and civil courts.[93] Even collective struggles for global social rights, such as the right to food or to water, are organized in countries like India or South Africa. The scene has become more diverse and globally dispersed the last two decades. Even the unequal power relations between North- and South-based organizations are more often discussed, especially the claim for co-operation as equal partners.

But there still many attitudes and taboos which fit the above-mentioned critique. Whereas several established international NGOs speak with and to power, the human rights networks in the West have difficulties confronting power. They often hide behind a technical, neutral legal and human rights discourse. Especially violations of the basic norms of (post-colonial) justice, the rights to land and to natural resources, are not challenged. The ideas behind the claims of the 1960s and 1970s NIEO are not taken up by litigators and advocates; they are not transformed into more fundamental litigation and advocacy.

Despite this sobering context, the use of international criminal law still provides tools and inspiration to challenge colonialism and colonial crimes. So far, only a few criminal lawyers and scholars, in the North as well as the South, seem interested in the struggles against colonial aftermaths. Communities have gained considerable transnational and international experience in addressing gross human rights violations since the mid-1990s, in the domestic sphere as well as before international tribunals, the ICC and in universal jurisdiction cases. There is much to learn from

---

[93] For an overview, see Business & Human Rights Resource Centre's web site.

the matured toolbox of transitional justice – notwithstanding the critiques of the concept.

The advantage of strong and independent judicial procedure is clear. It gives the whole process a certain legitimacy and trustworthiness. The less independent and fair mechanisms are – or when absent – those who have suffered wrongs and want to make claims have to find other ways: regional, transnational, international, or alternative forms such as opinion tribunals.

In order to defend the rights of marginalized communities in particular, and organize their access to law, an active and self-reflective civil society is required – inside and outside institutions, criticizing law, questioning bad law, calling for law reform, but, at the same time, exhausting all available remedies in creative manners through litigation, legal interventions and advocacy.

Under certain conditions criminal proceedings can play a useful role: they can serve as archive, foundation for the debate outside the courtroom (Nuremberg), as door opener, transmitter, facilitator, and so on. In particular, the different stages of criminal proceedings are interesting tools to be considered to address colonialism and colonial crimes:

- investigating the facts;
- establishing (procedural) truth;
- declaration of guilt verdict; and
- sanction.

However, the toolbox of transitional justice contains more diverse instruments than criminal proceedings, such as:

- investigative mechanism;
- truth trials;
- *ad hoc* missions;
- truth commissions or parliamentary inquiries;
- alternative sanctions;
- mediation; and
- apology, acknowledgment or reparation.

This list is not exclusive, and it is only to demonstrate the number of available tools that can be applied to colonial situations in more or less creative manners to contribute to social mobilization around truth seeking, reparation claims, and related objectives. They can cause disruption, and lend strength to efforts to de-colonize law.

Obviously, non-traditional legal interventions could include opinion tribunals in the tradition of the Russell Tribunals or co-operation with artists such as the theatre director Milo Rau. The latter's well-known project 'Congo Tribunal' combined research of post-colonial injustice and human rights violations with participatory sessions on Congo as well as in Germany, in the theatre and cinema context.

From my point of view, the use of international criminal law categories can serve as an analytical tool. The application of the core international crimes has an important symbolic effect, capable of challenging ongoing efforts to legitimize the colonizing 'civilizing mission' and only refer to select excesses when the talk is about violence.

Irrespective of that, more extensive studies could be realized by legal scholars, historians and political scientists that assess each individual situation of land grab, rape, repression and oppression of the population with regards to its legal qualification under present international criminal law, such as genocide, crime against humanity or war crimes. Such studies would, for the first time, make it clear that we are dealing with offences where their perception as a common history or shared heritage or colonial entanglement only covers the extent of guilt. Current post-colonial injustices should be studied also from a legal standpoint to consider all forms of reparation and restitution, including re-transfer of lands, access to natural resources, (odious) debts, and re-open the discussion about a fair global trading and financial system.

Once it has been acknowledged that the events at hand qualify as international crimes, it has to be asked what follows from this recognition. Due to the long time that has passed, accountability for the perpetrators in terms of a trial and conviction is no longer an option. In only a few cases – like the Belgium Lumumba investigations – are those responsible still alive. One should not forget, however, that the German justice system still puts quite old men in their 90s on trial for Nazi crimes. The public attention in these trials centres very much around the survivors and witness testimonies. Interestingly for cases of colonial crimes, the German justice system is harshly criticized for its complicity in the first decades after World War II, when it was much more imaginative in establishing near complete impunity for former Nazi elites who were considered important to the construction of a strong West German fortress against the Soviet bloc.

It does not follow from this that no type of accountability or reparation is possible in this type of situation. Instead of referring to the time passed, one has to seriously pose the question of which is the type of reaction and accountability that has to follow the established colonial wrong in such historical situation.

The recognition that wrongs amount to core international crimes points to another aspect that is well-established in international criminal law: dealing with these types of crimes cannot (only) be a matter of negotiations between states. What is at stake here is the history of communities, the experiences of individually affected persons and communities who have to appear as subjects and holders of rights in this debate.

Official statements on past wrongs, such as those against the Sámi and the Romani in Norway described in Chapter 17 below, uses rather unspecific terms, such as 'injustice', 'failed policies', or 'downplaying of the seriousness of the abuses'.

The heritage of (post-)colonial injustice deserves much more interest by legal scholars first, and then by the affected states and communities, to properly explore the broader field of potential legal interventions.

Makau Mutua asked: "can the Germans ever see black Ovaherero and Nama as their equals? How the Germans respond to the genocide of 1904–1908, as a state and a people, will answer that question". Germany and other European colonial powers did not accept black Africans as equal human beings during their colonial regimes. They slaughtered, tortured, raped and robbed, and legitimized their crimes by describing them as being part of the 'superior white race's civilizing mission'.

The current debate is not only about criminal law, but about the relationship between colonizers and the colonized; between profiteers of the relationships created by colonialism – including aspects of the existing system of property ownership – and those subject to them. The current problems facing humankind (in the age of the Anthropo-scene/Capitalo-scene) can only be solved by countries working together: consider the pandemic affecting the world at the time of writing, but also climate change, access to water, nutrition, environmental degradation, international peace and security, and other contemporary problems.

In view of what has been developed in the earlier sections of this chapter, political, moral-historical conclusions could be drawn for an appropriate reappraisal of colonialism. The law of the time – as well as the sense that wants to make this law applicable also today, decades later – constitutes an obstacle that has to be overcome by both jurists and non-jurists. New coalitions of lawyers, social movements, academics from other fields, and actors such as artists should be explored.

2

Transitional Justice for Colonial Era Abuses and Legacies: African versus European Policy Priorities

Hugo van der Merwe and Annah Moyo[*]

This chapter explores how transitional justice has been framed in a way that prioritizes certain aspects of past violence and conflict, and how this approach has been challenged by African role players to address broader transformative goals, particularly colonial era abuses and their social and economic legacies. It explores how transitional justice has evolved on the African continent in relation to the evolution of key international norms and the politics of transitional justice in various national contexts. These shifts have highlighted tensions between African and international justice agendas that have become concretized in the way that transitional justice policy frameworks have been articulated by the African Union and the European Union.

2.1. Introduction: Transitional Justice as a Contentious Field

Transitional justice was initially conceived as a process to deal with transitions from authoritarian rule to democracy in Latin America and Europe. The field emerged in the context of the end of the Cold War and was mainly framed within a liberal conception of democracy in contexts where colonialism was not part of the political landscape, for example in Spain, Portugal, Greece and Eastern Europe, or where it was a less immediate historical concern such as in South America.[1] Its more recent application to contexts of transition from war to peace, which has largely been the

---

[*] **Hugo van der Merwe** is the Director of Research, Knowledge and Learning, and **Annah Moyo** is the Advocacy Programme Manager at the Centre for the Study of Violence and Reconciliation (CSVR), South Africa. Dr. van der Merwe is Co-Editor in Chief of the *International Journal of Transitional Justice*.

[1] Ruti G. Teitel, "Transitional Justice Genealogy", in *Harvard Human Rights Journal*, 2003, vol. 16.

case in African transitional contexts, has seen these mechanisms being applied without sufficient consideration for these particular historical and geopolitical contexts, and particularly their very discernible colonial legacies. Furthermore, the expansion of transitional justice as an interdisciplinary field, beyond its previous narrow legalistic framing, has created more opportunities for transitional justice processes to also address the socio-economic dimensions of human rights abuses as well as the structural and systemic issues stemming from the colonial era inequalities and abuses.

Transitional justice can be conceptualised in a way that addresses the colonial abuses and its conventional tools may have specific application to these forms of abuses and legacies. However, the way that transitional justice has been framed and operationalised by policy makers, scholars and many human rights activists present a version of transitional justice that lacks political imagination. It has instead been presented by the mainstream as a set of technocratic tools that should be found in every regime-change toolbox. This narrow framing of particular models has dominated popular conceptions of transitional justice and shaped much of the 'common-sense' views on how to deal with the past. This has limited the value of transitional justice as a tool or conceptual framework for addressing more deep-seated social problems.

The question is whether transitional justice is fundamentally flawed through its original articulation during the post-Cold War period, where its goals and method were narrowly framed in terms of criminal accountability for those most directly responsible for state abuses of bodily integrity rights. Or can it be (and has it been) reformulated by some actors in a way that makes it useful in understanding and rectifying historical patterns of abuse and their legacies, particularly those of colonialism. Building on the example provided by Morten Bergsmo,[2] this chapter explores whether and how transitional justice can be used as a conceptual and policy framework for addressing colonial human rights abuses and legacies of colonial rule.

We seek to answer this question in practical terms with reference to the African experience of transitional justice over the last 25 years. We examine how transitional justice has been used as a concept that frames justice during times of transition as a particular agenda regarding which

---

[2] Morten Bergsmo, "Myanmar, Colonial Aftermath, and Access to International Law", Occasional Paper Series No. 9 (2019), Torkel Opsahl Academic EPublisher, Brussels, 2019 (https://www.legal-tools.org/doc/64a8fc/), reproduced in a version as Chapter 7 below.

rights should be prioritised, what kind of actors need to be held accountable, who is a victim, and as a narrowly conceived set of tools that should be utilised in such transitional contexts. We explore how these boundaries have been challenged and how they have evolved particularly in the African context over the last 25 years.

This chapter therefore seeks to highlight some of the shortcomings of mainstream transitional justice approaches when it comes to addressing the colonial era abuses and legacies, the narrow focus on civil and political rights, while marginalising considerations of economic, social and cultural dimensions of justice. These dimensions are key in addressing the structural inequalities and systemic patterns that have been entrenched and institutionalised in modern post-colonial societies. Similarly, transitional justice has been constricted by a narrow framing of justice in terms of geopolitical context, individualistic accountability, and time-bound processes and mechanisms. The chapter will critically analyse the conceptualization and application of transitional justice in various contexts, observing how these have transformed over the last 25 years.

Rather than a systematic analysis of African countries during this period, the chapter picks out some illustrative cases that we suggest demonstrate certain key trajectories and two critical policy frameworks that may be helpful in understanding the way competing conceptions of transitional justice play out across the African continent. To this end, the chapter draws on the experiences of various countries in Africa that have implemented transitional justice processes over this period to illustrate particular approaches and trends, and critically examines in more detail the two key policy frameworks that have emerged to guide funding allocation and technical support for the continent, namely the European Union's *Policy Framework on Support to Transitional Justice* and the *African Union's Transitional Justice Policy*.

2.2. Challenging the Orthodoxy of Transitional Justice

'Transitional justice' remains a contested and vaguely defined concept. Scholars have defined the terms 'transition' and 'justice' separately in an attempt to concretise and define the concept of transitional justice. Traditionally, the term 'transition' has been understood to indicate a shift from conflict or autocratic rule to a more liberal political democracy, or a "move from less to more democratic regimes".[3] This narrow, restricted framing of the term has been challenged by scholars especially in view of the fact that transitional justice is increasingly being applied in contexts that do not follow a liberal political transition such as Rwanda and Uganda, and in some cases, without any political transition, such as Kenya, Zimbabwe and Colombia.[4] The notion of 'justice' has also been a subject of intense study that has remained contested. Kelsen[5] defined justice as the "quality of a social order regulating the mutual relationship of men" and further highlighted four types of justice, namely distributive justice[6], which is also referred to as economic justice (or rather redistributive justice especially in the African context), procedural, retributive and restorative justice. Despite this broader popular understanding of justice, transitional justice policies have till recently adopted quite a restricted notion of justice that has prioritised retribution and restorative forms of justice. The United Nations defined transitional justice quite broadly as "the full range of processes and mechanisms associated with a society's attempts to come to terms with a legacy of large-scale past abuses, in order to ensure accountability, serve justice and achieve reconciliation".[7]

Transitional justice has at times been appropriated and put to use in justifying very narrow justice agendas. It has even been used to consolidate authoritarian regimes through framing justice in nationalistic terms and imposing hegemonic narratives. There are many aspects of transitional justice that are open to political manipulation. What concerns us in this particular debate though is the narrow framing of justice concerns during transition to: 1) focus on bodily integrity rights,[8] 2) individualising guilt,[9]

---

[3] Ruti G. Teitel, *Transitional Justice*, Oxford University Press, 2000, p. 5.

[4] Prosper Maguchu, *Transitional Justice and Socio-Economic Justice Rights in Zimbabwe*, Springer, The Hague, 2019, p. 7.

[5] Hans Kelsen, *What is Justice? Justice, Law and Politics in the Mirror of Science*, University of California Press, Berkeley, CA, 1957, p. 1.

[6] On the application of distributive justice in contexts of transition, see Morten Bergsmo, César Rodríguez-Garavito, Pablo Kalmanovitz and Maria Paula Saffon (eds.), *Distributive Justice in Transitions*, Torkel Opsahl Academic EPublisher, Brussels, 2010 (https://www.legal-tools.org/doc/17cc19/).

[7] The rule of law and transitional justice in conflict and post-conflict societies, UN Doc. S/2004/616, 23 August 2004.

[8] *Ibid.*, p. 1.

[9] Kamari Clarke, "Rethinking Africa through its Exclusions: The Politics of Naming Criminal Responsibility", in *Anthropological Quarterly*, 2010, vol. 83, no. 3.

3) focusing on the recent past,[10] and 4) prioritising judicial interventions.[11] Our concern is not that this approach leads to inappropriate interventions. The concern is that it frames justice in very narrow terms that limits our ability to imagine solutions that address structural and systemic violence, the role of institutions, more historic roots of conflict, and solutions that lie in the economic, political, social and cultural realms.

Ruben Carranza[12] sums up these concerns in the following reflection in relation to how this narrow framing creates blind spots for addressing other justice concerns:

> The prevailing assumption seems to be that truth commissions, human rights trials and reparations programs are meant to engage mainly, if not exclusively, with civil and political rights violations that involve either physical integrity or personal freedom, and not with violations of economic and social rights, including such crimes as large-scale corruption and despoliation. To a growing number of transitional justice advocates, particularly those who work in or come from impoverished post-conflict or post-dictatorship countries, this traditional view is inadequate. It ignores the experience of developing countries abused by dictators or warlords who have been both brutal and corrupt. It perpetuates an impunity gap by focusing on a narrow range of human rights violations while leaving accountability for economic crimes to ineffective domestic institutions or to a still evolving international legal system that deals with corruption.

If we frame transitional justice more broadly as ideals and tools to address past and ongoing injustices, we need to look more ambitiously at what transitional justice may accomplish. What concerns us about the recent popularised version of transitional justice is that it presents a limited vision of what such justice looks like. While it has helped in promoting particular forms of justice in various countries in ways that should be cel-

---

[10] Lars Waldorf, "Anticipating the Past: Transitional Justice and Socio-Economic Wrongs", in *Social and Legal Studies*, 2012, vol. 21, pp 171–173. See also Sam Szoke-Burke, "Not Only 'Context': Why Transitional Justice Programs Can No Longer Ignore Violations of Economic and Social Rights", in *Texas International Law Journal*, 2015, vol. 50, no. 3.

[11] Kieran McEvoy, "Beyond Legalism: Towards a Thicker Understanding of Transitional Justice", in *Journal of Law and Society*, 2007, vol. 34, no. 4.

[12] Ruben Carranza, "Plunder and Pain: Should Transitional Justice Engage with Corruption and Economic Crimes?", in *International Journal of Transitional Justice*, 2008, vol. 2, no. 3, p. 310.

ebrated, it has also blinded many to other injustices, or at least made them more complacent in accepting them as inevitable or as too big to solve.

Justice for civil and political rights is presented by current convention as the priority for post conflict justice. This focus of transitional justice somehow shifts from being a priority to being an end point in addressing the past. Providing solutions to some of society's past injustices should inspire us to further efforts to address other social problems. If done successfully, it should not leave us complacent, but rather provide a platform for more ambitious justice goals.

What was initially an exciting field of experimentation and innovation that sought creative solutions to addressing seemingly intractable problems (such as the continued power of the exiting elites) has become a body of conventional thought that has been institutionalised through norms, institutions and scholarly conventions.[13] Some have argued that the field has been captured by conservative actors that now bind transitional justice to liberal, capitalist, racist, Northern or Western agendas.

Conventional transitional justice approaches, particularly truth commissions, have been vigorously critiqued for their narrow *time frame* (post-colonial), narrow framing of the *types of abuses* they focus on (excluding socio-economic rights abuses), and *geographic limits* (national actors). These limitations have skewed transitional justice processes towards a more conservative orientation that leaves underlying structural inequalities unaddressed and historical grievances unresolved.

Battling against this narrow conventional notion of transitional justice, some practitioners and scholars have argued for an expanded notion of transitional justice which:

1) goes beyond narrow legalistic frameworks and retributive justice approaches, and engage with political, cultural and social processes of repair (such as truth commissions, reparations and rehabilitation programmes, vetting, institutional reforms, memorial projects and reconciliation rituals);[14]

---

[13] Kora Andrieu, "Transitional Justice: A New Discipline in Human Rights", on *SciencesPo Mass Violence and Resistance – Research Network*, 18 January 2010 (available on SciencesPo's web site).

[14] Lydia K. Bosire, "Overpromised, Underdelivered: Transitional Justice in Sub-Saharan Africa", in *Sur – Revista Internacional de Direitos Humanos*, 2006, vol. 3, no. 5.

2) seeks to go beyond legal truth regarding individual events and personal responsibility to provide a broader history of patterns, causes and consequences of violations;[15]

3) seeks to draw in range of voices into recounting events, particularly those of the victims and marginalised communities;[16]

4) seeks to create processes that are more inclusive and less state-centric, particularly in contexts where the state has become distrusted and state institutions are seen as biased and inaccessible;[17] and

5) seeks to engage with a broader transformative agenda that addresses structural foundations of discrimination, exclusion and marginalisation.[18]

Transitional justice has thus not been abandoned by activists and progressive scholars. Conventional approaches have, however, been treated with great scepticism, and transitional justice policy development and agenda-setting have become key political battle grounds.

We argue here that while this potential capture of transitional justice by local and global elites and interests is indeed a concern, various role players on the African continent have adopted transitional justice as a field that they believe can also serve other causes. In response to this critique, a number of institutions and organisations have started adopting more expansive approaches. The International Centre for Transitional Justice, introduced a comprehensive definition that supports the expanded notion of transitional justice that factors in the five elements listed above, by referring to transitional justice as

> a response to systematic or widespread violations of human rights. It seeks recognition for victims and promotion of possibilities for peace, reconciliation and democracy. Transitional justice is not a special form of justice but justice adapted to societies transforming themselves after a period of pervasive human rights abuse. In some cases, these trans-

---

[15] Lia Kent, 2016. "Transitional Justice in Law, History and Anthropology", in *Australian Feminist Law Journal*, 2016, vol. 42, no. 1.

[16] Makau Mutua, "What Is the Future of Transitional Justice?", in *International Journal of Transitional Justice*, 2015, vol. 9, no. 1, p. 5.

[17] *Ibid.*

[18] Wendy Lambourne, "Transitional Justice and Peacebuilding after Mass Violence", in *International Journal of Transitional Justice*, 2009, vol. 3, no. 1.

formations happen suddenly; in others, they may take place over many decades.[19]

Transitional justice thus remains a contested terrain that gets pulled in different directions depending on the local actors who engage with these policies and the global normative shifts that frame the political and legal landscape of these debates.

2.3. The Politics of Transitional Justice in Africa

The African continent has presented a particularly contentious arena for transitional justice. It was the location of the first truth commission (Uganda 1974), the most celebrated truth commission (South Africa 1995), the site of all the ICC trials by the time of writing,[20] and remains the location for numerous ongoing national trials, truth commissions, and other transitional justice processes.

This continental evolution of transitional justice has been shaped by various national and international actors. Until 2004, transitional justice remained a somewhat amorphous idea that only took on more concrete form particularly through its adoption by the United Nations. The UN definition of transitional justice as "the full range of processes and mechanisms associated with a society's attempts to come to terms with a legacy of large-scale past abuses, in order to ensure accountability, serve justice and achieve reconciliation"[21] was quite generic and all-inclusive. In practice, however, it took on a more rigid form of a set of tools with a specifically liberal human rights mindset.[22] Transitional justice has also been applied in certain contexts where national actors have not defined their actions as transitional justice or as a response to human rights abuses. As pointed out by scholars, it is not uncommon for states to undertake reparations programmes without the actual acknowledgment of, and taking legal

---

[19] "What is Transitional Justice", on *International Centre for Transitional Justice* (available on its web site) (cited in Andrieu, 2010, see above note 13).

[20] To date, the majority of ICC's indictments are in Africa – more specifically, in the following countries: Uganda, Central Africa Republic, Democratic Republic of Congo, Sudan, Republic of Kenya, Libya, Cote D'Ivoire and Mali, through referrals from governments and the UN Security Council and by the Prosecutor's investigations. For further reading, see Lydia A. Nkansah, "International Criminal Court in the Trenches of Africa", in *African Journal of International Criminal Justice*, 2014, vol. 1, no. 1.

[21] The rule of law and transitional justice in conflict and post-conflict societies, see above note 7.

[22] Andrieu, 2010, see above note 13.

responsibility for the human rights abuses and the crimes that were committed, and instead such programmes are undertaken under the guise of helping victims to move forward.[23]

This mindset of limiting transitional justice to something that is achievable in a particular timeframe and which can be managed through technical direction and support has shaped much of international engagement in African transitional justice. Where transitional justice was imposed by external actors, and funded almost exclusively by foreign donors, it often took on a minimalist form, a tick-box set of steps needed to be done to keep international donors and trading partners satisfied. The Democratic Republic of the Congo, Sierra Leone and Burundi provide some illustration of this internationally-imposed transitional justice approach. A number of scholars have pointed out the limitations of imposed forms of truth-telling and Western conceptions of justice in countries that have their own traditions of dealing with traumatic events.[24]

In some contexts, international intervention in transitional justice took on more ominous tones, where a narrow conception of justice was combined with a specific targeting of actors that raised suspicions among local actors of regime change agendas shaped by international political and economic concerns (Ivory Coast and Sudan).

In some situations, though, transitional justice has emerged through more locally-driven initiatives by the state or civil society. In places where a fairly a strong state (that can resist external justice agendas) has embraced transitional justice (or at least some of its tools), it has given it a particular local flavour that has much greater traction and integration with political and economic programmes, but also one that raises serious concerns about consolidating hegemonic narratives and limiting scope for diverse voices. Both Rwanda and Algeria have construed transitional justice processes that have helped support their post-conflict consolidation of national identity and legitimation of the state.[25]

---

[23] Clara Sandoval Villalba, *Transitional Justice: Key Concepts, Processes and Challenges*, Institute for Democracy and Conflict Resolution, University of Essex, 2011.

[24] See, for example, Gearoid Millar, "'Ah lef ma case fo God': Faith and Agency in Sierra Leone's Postwar Reconciliation", in *Peace and Conflict: Journal of Peace Psychology*, 2012, vol. 18, no. 2.

[25] On Rwanda, see Susan Thomson, "The Darker Side of Transitional Justice: The Power Dynamics Behind Rwanda's *Gacaca* Courts", in *Africa: Journal of the International African Institute*, 2011, vol. 81, no. 3. On Algeria, see Djamila Ould Khettab, "Algeria", Case

In other contexts, transitional justice has been a more openly contested and negotiated process. South Africa, Liberia and Kenya all had truth commissions (and other justice processes) that were subject to intense political debate involving a range of political and civil-society actors. The ultimate establishment of transitional justice mechanisms in these countries was a compromise between different agendas. These compromises also involved a precarious balance between narrow civil and political (bodily integrity) rights and broader social and economic rights, recent versus historical claims, and individual versus structural accountability. These compromises, many have argued, paved the way towards an ultimate consolidation of transitions without fundamental transformation of structural inequalities.[26]

The mix of local and international political actors involved in shaping transitional justice agendas have thus been increasingly critical in framing these approaches. The underlying politics of transitional justice has been foregrounded and the boundaries of its scope have been contested and renegotiated.

The conventional belief that transitional justice should have a narrow lens has, however, been increasingly questioned. Each truth commission that has been established in Africa seems to gradually open the window more widely to the inclusion of social and economic rights abuses, the legacies of colonial eras and the responsibilities of corporate and other international actors.

Especially in the light of the limits of judicial processes and legal frameworks, transitional justice promises a broader normative framework and set of tools to engage with this legacy. Where the law is not up to the task of narrating or judging the past, transitional justice processes have explored ways to establish an official record of the past, evoke moral outrage, and shape national and international narratives about events, reputations and discourses of victimhood and guilt.

---

study for Comparative Transitional Justice in Africa Project, Centre for the Study of Violence and Reconciliation, 2018.

[26] See for example, Richard Wilson, *The Politics of Truth and Reconciliation in South Africa: Legitimizing the Post-Apartheid State*, Cambridge University Press, 2001; Mahmood Mamdani, "Reconciliation without Justice", in *Southern African Political and Economic Monthly*, 1997, vol. 10, no. 6.

2.4. The Applicability of Transitional Justice to Colonial Era Abuses

The question of whether to engage with colonial era abuses is particularly apt in contexts where countries establish transitional justice processes for recent mass abuses and the causal factors for these abuses can be traced back to colonial era events, institutions and legislation. This link is supported by both individual country analyses[27] and by multi-country comparative studies. In a statistical study of the colonial legacy of 160 countries, Matthew Lange and Andrew Dawson found that "a history of colonial rule promotes either oppositional communal identities, communal divisions of labor, ethnic-based stratification, animosity between indigenous and non-indigenous populations, or some combination of the four".[28] Liberia's 2006 Truth and Reconciliation Commission pointed out in its 2009 report that the Liberian conflict has its "origins in the history and founding of the modern Liberian state".[29] However, this acknowledgement did not translate into substantive commitments to addressing the colonial era structural issues that enabled the conflict in Liberia. The Kenyan Truth, Justice and Reconciliation Commission documented the effect of colonialism on Kenyan communities and its role in the establishment of the Kenyan state, as well as the "legacies of impunity, land injustices, corruption, non-responsive justice systems, non-participatory governance and coercive state institutions used to further repression".[30]

It is thus quite bizarre that almost all these transitional justice policies and mechanisms have defined their starting point for their temporal mandate as some point during the post-colonial era. The reasons suggested for this are generally related to the feasibility of what can be accomplished within a limited timeframe, the jurisdictional reach of a mechanism (whether it can hold the colonial power accountable), the depend-

---

[27] See, for example, Hakeem Yusuf, "Colonialism and the Dilemmas of Transitional Justice in Nigeria", in *International Journal of Transitional Justice*, 2018, vol. 12, no. 2; Laryssa Chomiak, "Tunisia: The Colonial Legacy and Transitional Justice", in *Research Report*, Centre for the Study of Violence and Reconciliation, 2017.

[28] Matthew Lange and Andrew Dawson, "Dividing and Ruling the World? A Statistical Test of the Effects of Colonialism on Postcolonial Civil Violence", in *Social Forces*, 2009, vol. 88, no. 2.

[29] Truth and Reconciliation Commission of Liberia, "Final Report of the Truth and Reconciliation Commission of Liberia, Volume I: Findings and Determinations", 2009 ('Liberia TRC Final Report volume 1').

[30] Andrew Songa, "Transitional Justice in Kenya as a path to transformation", in *Research Report*, Centre for the Study of Violence and Reconciliation, 2018.

ence on oral testimony, or the significance of more recent events in communal memory and thus their prioritisation for justice and reconciliation efforts. While these are reasonable concerns that should be considered in terms of the challenges that can be expected in taking on a broader mandate, they are often simply presented as 'common sense' or 'realistic' goals that reduce transitional justice to a technical exercise rather than as engaging a broader historical justice agenda. There are thus clear practical considerations that make more historical engagement difficult, a limited mandate more efficient, and goals of such as criminal prosecutions impossible. However, when viewed in the context of complex social and political change-processes, this broader perspective of how transitional justice can contribute is critical.

More recently, a broader range of actors have engaged with transitional justice policy development both internationally and locally, which has challenged these boundaries and raised some optimism about transitional justice's relevancy for addressing colonial era abuses and legacies.

2.5. Normative Shifts in the Scope of Transitional Justice

More recent transitional justice processes have been pushed to address these concerns raised by local justice advocates, and have been facilitated by a more expansive approach adopted by the UN and other international actors. The local national politics of transitional justice has also played a role in framing a more transformative agenda for this transitional process. Both these dynamics (normative shifts and political contexts) need to be understood in order to make sense of how they interact to create new opportunities.

A normative shift has happened in framing the meaning and scope of transitional justice that can be seen in various transitional justice policies adopted by international and regional bodies. Most of these changes are not specifically geared towards addressing colonial-era abuses, but they do expand transitional justice's ambit in a way that makes these abuses fall more clearly within its scope.

2.5.1. Inclusion of Social and Economic Rights in Transitional Justice

The emergence of transitional justice in the context of the post-Cold War era (and the consequent dominance of the liberal political and economic model) framed its initial bias in relation to prioritising civil and political rights. Transitional justice did not initially encompass measures to address injustice for economic violations, instead, considerations of economic and social rights violations as well as structural injustices were only incorporated as background factors that helped explain the emergence of violations of civil and political rights.[31] The South African Truth and Reconciliation Commission ('South African TRC') cemented this model on which abuses to address, and how this accounting could happen. This model appeared to fit very nicely with a process that facilitated serious political transformation while leaving underlying local (that is, land and property ownership and income inequality) and global (trade relations and dependencies) structural injustices unchanged. While it may be unfair to blame the South African TRC for what it was not mandated to do, its widespread celebration on the international stage served to hype the value of this particular form of justice and this narrow conception of what should be prioritised during times of transition.[32]

While the South African model was one that was duplicated in many ways by other African countries, it was also questioned and challenged for not doing enough to address broader structural injustices. Civil society actors were particularly critical of the South African TRC for its narrow focus on civil and political rights such as politically motivated killings, torture and detention, while overlooking the need for measures to address the widespread socio-economic aspects of apartheid violations.[33] Many subsequent transitional justice processes thus sought to build on the lessons regarding its shortcomings, or at least apply some of its innovation to a more honest assessment of their own structural challenges.

Scholars have however continued to problematize the shift towards including socio-economic rights within the transitional justice fold.[34]

---

[31] Maguchu, 2019, p. 8, see above note 4.

[32] Alongside the Truth and Reconciliation Commission, the South African State also established a Land Claims Court, which had a much bigger budget, longer life span, and wider temporal focus, and which should be considered as part of the South African transitional justice model. Mainstream representations of transitional justice in South Africa, however, focus very narrowly on the Truth and Reconciliation Commission.

[33] Evelyne Schmid and Aoife Nolan, "'Do No Harm'? Exploring the Scope of Economic and Social Rights in Transitional Justice", in *International Journal of Transitional Justice*, 2014, vol. 8, no. 3.

[34] Lars Waldorf, "Anticipating the Past: Transitional Justice and Socio-Economic Wrongs", in *Social and Legal Studies*, 2012, vol. 21, no. 2, p. 171.

Schmid and Nolan[35] argue that part of the challenge arises from the failure in such analyses to distinguish between economic, social and cultural rights as enshrined in the International Covenant on Economic, Social and Cultural Rights, and the broader socio-economic and structural injustices. They point out that in determining "the desirability and feasibility of including a socio-economic dimension to transitional justice, the distinction between Economic and Social Rights and broader socio-economic issues often gets lost, with problematic implications for both opponents and proponents". Socio-economic rights are enshrined in the International Bill of Rights and their scope is settled in law through various international and regional human rights instruments and declarations, and they are defined as "those privileges that grant people access to certain basic needs that are necessary to lead a decent and dignified life", including resources, opportunities and services that people need in order to sustain a humane and decent life, such as food, shelter, land and access to education, clean water and work.[36] Economic, social and cultural rights are therefore binding on states.

Other socio-economic concerns underlying structural injustices have, however, not yet been well-defined, neither in theory nor practice, even though they are recognised as key causes of conflict and violence. Scholars have highlighted a number of issues that are regarded as socio-economic issues that can be linked to transitional justice, which include economic crimes, corruption, economic policies, odious debts, structural violence and human developmental issues.[37] Although the socio-economic dimensions of violations are gaining recognition and are being addressed through transitional justice, these continue to be framed around the economic, social and cultural rights, using the 'rights' language to frame their arguments even when these claims do not necessarily fit within the economic, social and cultural rights framework.[38] Schmid and Nolan[39] also point out the misconception of associating the inclusion of economic, social and cultural rights violations in transitional justice with addressing structural and systemic issues such as inequalities and exclusions that often constitute root causes of the conflict. They also problematize the ten-

---

[35] Schmid and Nolan, 2014, p. 364, see above note 33.

[36] Maguchu, 2019, p. 32, see above note 4.

[37] Ibid., p. 33.

[38] Schmid and Nolan, 2014, p. 371, see above note 33.

[39] Ibid., p. 372.

dency by transitional justice scholars and mechanisms, to relegate economic, social and cultural rights to background issues and magnifying the civil and political rights violations – within this misconception, economic, social and cultural rights are not viewed as past violations and therefore are not afforded special analysis on their own, but rather as secondary or contextual consequences of civil and political rights violations.[40]

The South African TRC is a case in point wherein the experiences of the majority of South Africans of apartheid and the daily violence of poverty were viewed as part of the contextual background to the violations of civil and political rights, and not as stand-alone, separate crimes and violations.[41] Notwithstanding the academic debates, a number of African truth commissions in particular, have shaped the practice of transitional justice by including economic, social and cultural rights violations as well as broader socio-economic issues in their investigations of what happened in the past. We thus see truth commissions in Sierra Leone (2002), Liberia (2006), and Kenya (2008) that were more directly tasked with addressing social and economic rights abuses in their mandates, reflecting shifting and expanding conventional wisdom about the feasibility of such endeavours.

The Sierra Leone TRC found that the widespread economic injustices existed before the conflict and were root causes of the conflict. Their report highlighted patterns of extensive economic crimes and further documented the role of companies that were found to be complicit in committing crimes in the diamond and timber industries, and concluded that "the central cause of the war was endemic greed, corruption and nepotism that deprived the nation of its dignity and reduced most people to a state of poverty".[42]

Liberia's TRC was mandated to specifically include investigations on socio-economic crimes. The Commission's 2009 report highlighted the following issues as primary root causes of the conflict: poverty, corruption, limited access to education, economic, social, civil and political inequalities; identity conflict and land tenure and distribution; the lack of reliable and appropriate mechanisms for the settlement of disputes; as well as the

---

[40] *Ibid.*, p. 376.

[41] *Ibid.*

[42] Kimberly Lanegran, "Justice for Economic Crimes? Kenya's Truth Commission", in *ASPJ Africa and Francophone*, 2015, vol. 6, no. 4.

duality of the Liberian political, social and legal systems which further polarised and exacerbated the disparities between Liberian peoples, the indigenous and settler Liberians.[43]

Kenya's Truth, Justice and Reconciliation Commission was tasked with a mandate to investigate alleged economic injustices following the 2008 post-election violence, particularly the misappropriation of land since Kenya's independence. The findings of the Commission included a volume covering the country's economic violations and injustices including land misappropriation which implicated some of the members of the government.[44]

The misconceptions highlighted by Schmid and Nolan above of relegating economic, social and cultural rights to the background, as context and root causes of conflict and authoritarian rule, shed light to some extent, on the disconnect between the deliberate investigations into economic, social and cultural rights violations in the three countries above, and the failure to take forward and address the economic, social and cultural rights violations through a follow-up process such as reparations or economic reforms.

Some strides have been made, however, towards concretising the inclusion of socio-economic rights and socio-economic issues, both as violations and as root causes of conflict within transitional justice discourse and policy. In March 2010, the United Nations Secretary-General released a *Guidance Note on the United Nations Approach to Transitional Justice*. Its principle 9 calls on the United Nations to "strive to ensure [that] transitional justice processes and mechanisms take account of the root causes of conflict and repressive rule, and address violations of all rights, including economic, social and cultural rights". And in a 2014 report on *Transitional justice and economic, social and cultural rights*, the Office of the High Commissioner for Human Rights acknowledges that "there has been no widespread move to include root causes and violations of economic, social and cultural rights in transitional justice processes".[45]

---

[43] Liberia TRC Final Report volume 1, see above note 29.

[44] Waldorf, 2012, see above note 10.

[45] United Nations Office of the High Commissioner for Human Rights, *Transitional Justice and Economic, Social and Cultural Rights*, United Nations Publication, New York, 2014, p. 1. Even this report only includes passing reference to these rights being abused by colonial powers as a relevant consideration in Timor-Leste, while not mentioning it in any of the other examined countries with colonial legacies.

The report points to the limitations in how transitional justice has been framed in relation to these rights, challenges the arguments used to counter their inclusion, and suggests ways that they can be incorporated more effectively in transitional justice processes.

In his maiden report, the UN first Special Rapporteur on Promoting Truth, Justice, Reparations and Guarantees of Non-recurrence aptly captured the evolving nature of transitional justice over the years, leading to the current articulation and application that encompasses economic, social and cultural rights violations:

> The measures of truth-seeking, justice initiatives, reparation and guarantees of non-recurrence emerged first as practices and experiences in post-authoritarian settings, such as the Latin American countries of the Southern Cone and, to a lesser extent, those in Central and Eastern Europe and South Africa.
>
> More recently, the measures defined under the mandate have been progressively transferred from their 'place of origin' in post-authoritarian settings, to post-conflict contexts and even to settings in which conflict is ongoing or to those in which there has been no transition to speak of. Moreover, a common feature of these recent transitions is the prominent role that claims relating to economic rights occupy in these transitions; claims against corruption and in favour of economic opportunities have been raised to a par in the regions with claims for the redress of violations of civil and political rights.[46]

The shifting role of the UN in supporting an expanded transitional justice scope that includes social and economic abuses was evident in its role in Tunisia. While local political interest in addressing the structural inequalities and economic abuses by the Ben Ali regime was a driving force in the transition, the key role of the UN in supporting a truth commission with an expansive mandate to address these abuses would not have been possible without the evolution of the transitional justice lens.[47]

---

[46] "Report of the Special Rapporteur on the Promotion of Truth, Justice, Reparation and Guarantees of Non-Recurrence", UN Doc. A/HRC/21/46, 9 August 2012.

[47] Another instructive example is Colombia, where the transitional justice framework was pushed to provide substantive relief for a very large displaced population. The inadequacy of such relief measures in the context of structural inequalities and systematic dispossession has however been noted. The commitment to more structural reforms that adequately

Scholars further argue that when transitional justice is viewed as an "inherently short-term, legalistic and corrective" strategy with a narrow focus on accountability for gross violations of civil and political rights", it runs the risk of becoming far removed from the needs of victims and societies.[48] When viewing transitional justice either from the perspective of victims of a range of conflicts, or in terms of the role it plays in preventing future conflict, the significance of addressing economic, social and cultural dimensions of abuses and injustices, both as root causes of the conflict and as significant violations emanating from the conflict, becomes more apparent. Narrow transitional justice processes risk entrenching impunity and thus the continuity of these dynamics into a post-conflict society, especially where socio-economic injustice (as highlighted in Tunisia, Liberia and Kenya) is at the centre of abusive state policies and drive popular resistance to the regime.

Given the highly politicised nature of transitional justice and the contentiousness of attempts to introduce measures that seek to uncover past abuses and introduce reforms, socio-economic measures are likely to receive serious pushback from economic elites who retain power post-transition. Expanding the reach of transitional justice into this arena is thus where it may face its fiercest resistance. Such an ambitious transformation agenda may create pushback that also puts other components at risk.

2.5.2. Temporal Frame Covered by Transitional Justice

The temporal frame of transitional justice has also shifted significantly over the last two decades. While the criminal justice focus of much of conventional transitional justice limits its scope to more recent cases (that is, cases where perpetrators are still alive, where the temporal reach of the law can still apply, and where forensic evidence may still be obtained), more expansive forms of transitional justice have discarded these limitations to take on more historical patterns of abuse. This has been particularly prominent within colonial settler societies such as Canada, Australia and New Zealand. This historical mandate has similarly been tackled in African transitional justice processes such as in Mauritius, where the leg-

---

address historical patterns of dispossession remains a concern. See Julia Zulvar, "Feasible Justice: Has Colombia over-promised and under-delivered reparations to its 8.6 million victims?", *Justiceinfo.net*, 12 June 2018 (available on its web site).

[48] Waldorf, 2012, see above note 10; Szoke-Burke, 2015, pp. 465 and 469, see above note 10.

acy of slavery and indentured labour was a key focus of its truth commission (2009).[49]

Other commissions have also taken an increased interest in the colonial roots of many of the abusive institutions, legislation, economic systems, and ongoing trade dependencies as key to understanding the root causes of the conflict and abuses. Many truth commissions, even when they do not seek to document colonial era violations, do scrutinise this period to understand the foundations of present problems.

The Tunisian truth commission is perhaps the most prominent (albeit not the most ambitious) example of this expanded temporal frame. Its mandate includes the period leading up to independence as this was a critical time in the evolution of the tensions between the key parties to the conflict, and one in which the colonial power had a direct hand.[50]

2.5.3. Geographic Reach of Transitional Justice

The geographic scope of transitional justice has also substantially grown over the last two decades. While national boundaries provide seemingly rational boundaries for the powers of investigations, judicial action, and institutional reforms, these objections have become increasingly spurious.

Even though the last 30 years have seen mainly conflicts within rather than between countries, the meaning of national boundaries have become less significant. Those responsible for abuses have commonly crossed borders with ease (to commit violations or escape justice), victims commonly flee across national borders to seek refuge from conflict, international actors (governments and corporations) have commonly been implicated in supporting local perpetrators, and international actors have shown an increased willingness to support justice initiatives outside their borders. Universal jurisdiction has also become a reality even if in a very selective manner.

One thus looks back with some surprise at the anachronistic South African TRC which had almost no regional mandate and very limited attempts to engage with violations outside its national borders despite the very violent and abusive role of the Apartheid State in waging war on its neighbours and their citizens.

---

[49] Rosabelle Boswell, "Can Justice be Achieved for Slave Descendants in Mauritius?", in *International Journal of Law, Crime and Justice*, 2014, vol. 42, no. 2.

[50] Chomiak, 2017, see above note 27.

Transitional justice in other countries took such geographic limitations much less seriously. Conflicts with a strong regional dimension (for
example, Sierra Leone) and countries with a large refugee diaspora (such
as Liberia) developed approaches to overcome this challenge.

The issue of international corporate perpetrators has also increasingly fallen within the scope of transitional justice. The South African
truth commission provided the initial foundation for a subsequent claim
lodged in the United States court system against international corporations
that provided support to the apartheid military and police.[51] The idea of
holding corporations accountable for their support to oppressive regimes
has increasingly been incorporated into transitional justice policies.

Tunisia again demonstrates how this expanded geographic reach
can result in a truth commission that calls for reparations from colonial
powers, and international agencies that had collaborated with oppressive
regimes.[52]

It is however often civil society rather than the state that pursues
such legal claims, particularly when this raises difficult political questions
between African countries and key donors or trade partners. In Kenya, for
example, it was civil society that supported victims who claimed reparations from the British government for torture during the Mau-Mau revolt.[53]

2.6. Political Shifts in the Scope of Transitional Justice

Alongside shifts in norms and discourses of transitional justice, there have
also been changes in the patterns of political engagement in national level
transitional justice debates. Transitional justice is a highly contested process where different parties seek to 'win the peace' by framing transitional
justice processes in a way that confirms their narrative of the conflict and
their vision of a future social order and national identity. Transitional justice is a very malleable process that has been used by authoritarian states
to consolidate their authority through marginalising opponents and creating an official truth, pursuing selective justice processes, and implement-

---

[51] Mia Swart, "Requiem for a Dream? The Impact of *Kiobel* on Apartheid Reparations in
South Africa", in *Journal of International Criminal Justice*, 2015, vol. 13, no. 2.

[52] Olfa Belhassine, "Tunisia's Truth Commission vs France, the IMF and World Bank", *Jus-
ticeinfo.net*, 3 September 2019 (available on its web site).

[53] Songa, 2018, see above note 30.

ing reparations in a way that rewards allies or buys compliance. While international norms (and intervention by regional and international actors) provide some limits on how much this process can be manipulated, the reach of transitional justice ultimately depends more on how far local political actors are willing and able to push this agenda.

The degree of accountability of recent human rights perpetrators in transitional justice processes is largely dependent on the power of these perpetrators in the new political dispensation. Similarly, the degree of accountability for colonial era abuses is dependent on the power relations between those actors who seek to expose and those who seek to marginalise these concerns. While the positions of political actors regarding accountability for recent human rights abuses are usually fairly apparent, the standpoint of different actors regarding colonial era abuses is much less clear.

National political shifts that characterise recent transitional justice processes have not seen radical transformations of governance and economic systems as was the case during the Cold War. Many peace agreements have served to reform governments and have not seen radical changes in constitutions or radical breaks with fundamental ideologies of past rule. Where new political actors do not want to challenge existing property systems (for example, colonial era land regimes) and economic relations (such as colonial era trade dependencies) they do not see any need in addressing these through transitional justice. Where these legacies are, however, questioned by political actors in the emergent political space, the boundaries of transitional justice have become more contested.

Recent political transitions illustrate this complex transitional justice politics regarding colonial culpability and how it has intersected with a shift in norms and approach by international actors. The case of Tunisia illustrates the role of workers and youth in the revolution and the prioritisation of their concerns in the transitional justice process. The brief rule by Islamist party also provided a window for addressing colonial accountability for establishing an oppressive hegemonic state. The transition was ignited by desperation regarding poverty and inequality, and anger about the economic exclusion, and repression of workers. The politics of transition justice are also demonstrated by the reversal of some of these achievements when elements of the previous regime regained political control and then limited the more ambitious aspects of the transitional justice programme.[54]

The Tunisia case illustrates the increased politicisation of transitional justice, which has challenged the technocratic approach that simply viewed it as a set of tools that could be applied irrespective of context. The inherent *politics of transitional justice* has increasingly become apparent.

The emergence of the principle of inclusion in transitional justice processes has also opened the door to a wider set of stakeholders who have seen value in transitional justice for addressing a broader set of rights. Gender justice advocates, landless people, refugees, trade unions, and others who previously viewed transitional justice as a narrow elite concern, have become interested in its potential for more radical uses. Some of these agendas incorporate in their approach the need to engage with the colonial era or challenge the inheritance from this era. The colonial erasure of gender and sexual identity and institutions that supported greater gender equality provide one illustration of how this expanded transitional justice framework may also open new avenues for transformative change.[55]

Where political actors question the ultimate goals assumed by technocrats of the transitional justice industry (for example, liberal democracy and international economic integration) or the tools for building a peaceful society (for example, rule of law and state-centric authority), the contours of the policy debate have become much more fluid and open ended.

The colonial legacy is one that contains numerous complex strands, and political actors choose which aspects of this legacy to challenge while simultaneously seeking to preserve other elements. In one country, for example, the colonial allocation of land rights might be challenged by the governing party, while at the same time it seeks to retain colonial era borders or norms regarding gender relations or security regulations. The colonial legacy is thus a very mixed bag that is not preserved or discarded by different actors, but are selectively challenged and upheld as sacred (or even re-appropriated as 'traditional').

---

[54] This was clearly demonstrated in the case of Kenya and Tunisia. See *ibid.*, and Chomiak, 2017, above note 27.

[55] See Thokozani Mbwana, "Transitional Justice and the Inclusion of LGBTQIA+ Rights", in *Policy Brief*, Centre for the Study of Violence and Reconciliation, 2020.

The focus on colonial legacies can be used as a smokescreen for trying to distract from more recent patterns of abuses or for seeking to distribute blame for ongoing suffering ('we are all to blame so nobody should be held accountable'). Zimbabwe provides a very strong illustration of this competition over the narrative of which colonial legacies should be removed, which past violations should be prioritised, who should be viewed as a victim and which perpetrators should be held responsible.[56] On the one hand, the state seeks to focus attention on the legacy of colonial era land expropriation and allocation and its continuing impact on poverty and inequality, while on the other hand, local human rights NGOs seek to draw attention to colonial era repressive laws and ongoing violations committed by the state against activists and political opponents. Both sides accuse the other of seeking to distract from (or even cover up abuses) committed in the past by prioritising particular concerns.

2.7. African versus European Frameworks for Transitional Justice

Both the political agendas and normative frameworks for engaging with colonial era abuses and legacies shape how the regional bodies in Africa (where these policies are implemented) and the European Union (who mainly fund these processes) seek to lay out the meaning of transitional justice. Understanding how they respectively seek to consolidate and shape the shifts in norms and political discourse at the regional level is very revealing.

Transitional justice has been viewed by many civil society and state actors on the African continent as a code word for regime change. For them, the concept was created by particular international actors as a cynical tool that can be used to disguise their attempts to promote a particular global agenda which ensures the compliance of South-based political elites. Rather than a clear set of principles that can be universally supported and impartially applied, it is viewed as an instrument with built-in biases regarding what it can be used for and who can use it.

While sharing the concern regarding the way transitional justice processes have been manipulated and used in targeted ways, African human rights activists were concerned that the baby would be thrown out

---

56 See Shastry Njeru, "Taking Transitional Justice to the People: Challenges for Civil Society in Zimbabwe", in Jasmina Branković and Hugo van der Merwe (eds.), *Advocating Transitional Justice in Africa: The Role of Civil Society*, Springer, Cham ZG, 2018.

with the bath water. There was thus a concerted initiative by African civil society organisations to use the concept and discourse of transitional justice in a way that made it more palatable and relevant to various African contexts.

Human rights advocates in civil society collaborated with the African Union over period of almost 10 years to develop a more integrated framework for transitional justice on the African continent, one that would incorporate national, regional and international conceptions and priorities for justice. In February 2019, the African Union ('AU') adopted a *Transitional Justice Policy* ('AUTJP')[57] which encourages that implementation of a range of transitional justice measures to deal with legacies of violent conflicts and systemic or gross violations of human and peoples' rights. While it does not directly suggest that these mechanisms engage with the crimes committed by colonial powers during that the periods of colonialization, it makes reference to transitional justice as a process that can assist societies "to come to terms with the traumas of slavery, *colonialism*, apartheid, systematic repression and civil wars".[58] It also calls on such processes to address the root causes of conflict, which has been interpreted by truth commissions to include colonial legacies. The recently launched *African Commission for Human and People's Rights Study on Transitional Justice* also specifically highlights that the "causes of these conflicts could often be traced back to the *structural violence of the colonial period*".[59]

In his preface to the AUTJP, the Commissioner for Political Affairs at the African Union Commission puts the colonial legacy in the forefront of his comments: "The history of Africa is characterized by different political upheavals, struggles for liberation and socio-economic transformations. These political struggles and transformations include, for instance, *the fight against colonialism*".[60]

---

[57] African Union, "Transitional Justice Policy", February 2019 (available on African Union's web site).

[58] *Ibid.*, paragraph 2.

[59] See African Commission on Human and People's Rights, "Study on Transitional Justice and Human and People's Rights in Africa", 2019 (available at the Commission's web site) (emphasis added).

[60] Minata Samate Cessouma, "Preface", in African Union, 2019, p. 6, see above note 57 (emphasis added).

The European Union's *Policy Framework on Support to Transitional Justice* (adopted in 2015) contains no mention of colonial era abuses or legacies, but it suggests that transitional justice processes should "aim to transform the society by identifying and dealing with root causes of conflict and violence that may reside in discrimination, marginalisation or violation of social, economic and cultural rights".[61]

Most revealing though in the EU's framework is that it is presented as guidelines for transitional justice in other countries. It is seemingly blind to the fact that its own members are implicated in past abuses and would need to account for and redress these abuses. Transitional justice is framed as something required in far removed, 'less civilised' societies, and the EU's role is simply to support countries to address these problems.

While containing many similar elements and principles, the two policy frameworks present quite contrasting conceptions of the reach and scope of transitional justice. The AUTJP places much greater emphasis on the need to address socio-economic rights abuses, structural injustices and redistributive justice challenges. While the EU policy sticks with the United Nations' generic definition of transitional justice, the AU presents a definition that directly frames the goals of transitional justice as including overcoming past inequalities and creating conditions for socio-economic transformation.[62]

The AUTJP also presents "redistributive (socio-economic) justice" as one of its key indicative elements of transitional justice which it suggests entails "measures designed to rectify structural inequalities, marginalization and exclusion for achieving social justice and equitable and inclusive development".[63]

The EU framework takes a more circumspect approach to addressing economic injustices and structural causes of violence. It frames transitional justice as part of an integrated approach involving, "the links between rule of law, peacebuilding, development and transitional justice. [...] The EU therefore supports transitional justice processes that are forward-looking, with the aim to transform the society by identifying and dealing

---

[61] European Union, "The EU's Policy Framework on Support to Transitional Justice", 2015, p. 12 (available on European Parliament's web site).

[62] African Union, 2019, p. 11, see above note 57.

[63] African Union, 2019, pp. 10, 22, see above note 57.

with root causes of conflict and violence that may reside in discrimination, marginalisation or violation of social, economic and cultural rights".[64]

The frameworks both contain the conventional mainstream elements of transitional justice. The EU however does not venture much beyond these limits, while the AU adopts a more expansive vision for what justice means in transitional contexts on the African continent.

In practice, EU funding and expertise have also tended towards advising that states focus on more narrow mandates (civil and political rights) and more recent periods of conflict. Where there have been initiatives to engage with colonial era abuses (for example, Kenya and Namibia) these have been treated as falling outside the EU's transitional justice engagement framework. Even the recently adopted German strategy to support transitional justice makes no mention of its responsibility for genocide in Namibia or other colonial legacies.[65]

These policy frameworks intersect at the national level where the AU and EU both seek to shape local transitional justice policies, legislation and mechanisms. Both the AU and EU provide advice and expert input for countries engaged in developing transitional justice policies. Even the AU expert support is largely, in turn, dependent on EU funding to African NGOs. Some countries that are directly dependent on external funding to support their transitional justice processes may well think twice about including the colonial abuses and legacies as a key focus for such processes.

2.8. Conclusion

Transitional justice has expanded significantly, both as a field of practice and as a field of academic research. The boundaries have been pushed beyond its focus on conventional comfort zone of civil and political rights in post-autocratic states, to encompassing various forms of injustice including socio-economic justice, and to finding resonance with applications to pre-transition periods where conflict is ongoing, in contexts where there is limited democratic reform and even in democratic states where

---

[64]   European Union, *The EU's Policy Framework on support to transitional justice*, 2015, p. 12, see above note 61, p. 12.

[65]   German Federal Government, "Inter-ministerial Strategy to Support Dealing with the Past and Reconciliation (Transitional Justice) in the Context of Preventing Crises, Resolving Conflicts and Building Peace", July 2019 (available on German Federal Foreign Office's web site).

there is peace and political stability. Moreover, it has grown in terms of its remit to encompass all forms of injustices and socio-economic rights. However, transitional justice remains a contested set of discourses, policies and norms, which has evolved both in relation to the contexts where it is applied and the actors who seek to shape social order and political identity in these societies. Some of these shifts, such as the range of abuses covered and it's temporal and geographic scope, make it more amenable to also addressing colonial era abuses and legacies.

The need to address colonial abuses and colonial legacies has been placed on the transitional justice agenda by civil society and post-colonial states. The legal norms and intervention tools have also gradually shifted to become more responsive to this glaring omission in the field. The politics of how this plays out in various countries is, however, dependent on the national and international dynamics of particular transitions. These politics present a range of different scenarios that reflect the complex way that colonial legacies remain entrenched in post-colonial societies.

Regional bodies have recognised the role they can play in consolidating and shifting norms and reframing the global discourse that provide the 'common sense' of how these historical legacies are addressed. These contrasting policy frameworks however demonstrate that there is still a deep divide between former colonies and former colonial powers in how they approach this challenge.

3

Colonial Wrongs, Memory and
Speech Along the Atrocity Spectrum

Gregory S. Gordon[*]

As the co-editors have explained in their foreword, this volume draws on papers prepared for the international conference 'Colonial Wrongs, Double Standards, and Access to International Law' held in Yangon on 16-17 November 2020. I had the great honour to provide the closing comments at that conference, as I have had the privilege of doing for other conferences organised by the Centre for International Law Research and Policy (CILRAP). Those conferences and the accompanying publications have had participants engage in fascinating and useful dialogues regarding issues of both substantive and procedural international criminal law ('ICL'), as well as ground-breaking explorations expanding or even creating new sub-disciplines. We have covered an incredible range of topics in these projects, including the philosophical foundations of ICL, power and the sociology of ICL, integrity in ICL, and quality control in international criminal investigations. Although, from a distance, we were reflective and critical of ICL at those colloquia, we still remained, in most of them, *within* the discipline, focused primarily on the discipline itself: its origins, its dimensions, its problems, and suggested solutions for those problems.

For the Yangon conference, we truly stepped outside the conventional confines of ICL analysis, breaking new ground from conceptual, policy and doctrinal perspectives. The linkages to ICL here are clear. But the focus on colonial wrongs within the framework of current ICL issues

---

[*] **Gregory S. Gordon** is Professor at the Faculty of Law of the Chinese University of Hong Kong, and a CILRAP Research Fellow. He is the author of the monograph *Atrocity Speech: Foundation, Fragmentation, Fruition*, Oxford University Press, 2017, the leading work on hate speech and international criminal law. He touches on hate speech among other topics in his CILRAP Conversation on World Order, CILRAP Film, Florence, 2 August 2020 (https://www.cilrap.org/cilrap-film/200802-gordon/). His lecture at the Yangon conference 16-17 November 2019 is available at CILRAP Film, Yangon, 17 November 2019 (https://www.cilrap.org/cilrap-film/191117-gordon/).

is novel in our field – and, I believe, will make a vital contribution to the development of post-conflict and transitional justice.

When I started to reflect on how I would begin this chapter, I was focused on scholarship and research in the field. But, inevitably, my thoughts turned to teaching. And what struck me as most relevant was the way in which I have traditionally treated ICL in the classroom. When teaching the subject, I always like to give hypotheticals to help illustrate the doctrinal and policy points via in-class discussion. And, for final examinations, I also create hypotheticals for students to analyse in writing.

And in reflecting on this, I had a startling realisation: reviewing my lecture notes and past examinations, I realized that every single hypothetical I have created involved a situation of international crimes whose origins could be traced to colonial wrongs or mismanagement. Those wrongs ranged from forcibly injecting new ethnic groups into an existing demographic composition, designating one group as 'overlords' over another group or groups to facilitate colonial administrative agendas, and the redrawing of borders to suit imperialist political or economic agendas in a region.

Clearly, the patterns incorporated into my atrocity class and test hypotheticals have constituted colonial mismanagement palimpsests. Whether it was the British bringing in Bangladeshi labourers into Myanmar, the Belgians deputizing Tutsis as their preferred administrators over Hutus in Rwanda, or, per the Sykes-Picot Agreement, the British and French creating artificial borders in the Middle East, without regard to the ethnic or religious realities on the ground, which has resulted in endless cycles of sectarian violence.

In essence, as we see in the case studies contained in this volume, when we arrive at the point of considering the application of ICL, there is always the proverbial big white elephant in the room that is never *substantively* discussed: colonial wrongs or mismanagement. These might be alluded to by way of setting the context and providing historical background. But they do not, I submit, factor into the spectrum of ICL processes beyond that.

The Yangon expert meeting suggested many ways in which they *could* – whether it be via crafting a *pre-atrocity* process of consultation, adjusting or modifying responsibility assessment mechanisms that complement the ICL process *during the criminal-responsibility-assessment phase*, or reconceptualising the origins of conflict or the gradations of fault during the *post-criminal-responsibility-assessment phase*. And, thus, CILRAP is breaking very important conceptual, doctrinal and policy ground in intellectually designing and convening the Yangon expert meeting and publishing this book in conjunction with that.

Of course, it must be stressed again that this important contribution, as I have described it so far, is within the field and context of ICL. And, as noted, that has been the focus of many CILRAP projects, especially in the broadly-based Quality Control Project with its several components. But let us not forget what 'CILRAP' stands for – the Centre for International Law Research and Policy – not the Centre for International *Criminal* Law Research and Policy. The point is that the organization's concerns extend to international law more broadly. So does the name of this volume, *Colonial Wrongs and Access to International Law*. And certainly, the topics covered in the Yangon expert meeting reflect that – our discussions encompassed human rights law, State responsibility, international humanitarian law, and *jus ad bellum*, among others. The proceedings were quite rich.

The conference's programme outline gives us a pretty good roadmap of how all of it was conceived and structured.[1] In "Double Standards and the Problem of Access to International Law", we had an excellent introduction to and overview of the subject of colonial wrongs and double standards with Morten Bergsmo reprising and building on his already influential concept paper "Myanmar, Colonial Aftermath, and Access to International Law", which appears as Chapter 7 below. We then had helpful follow-up presentations exploring some of the important themes introduced by Bergsmo: Shannon E. Fyfe's "The Transfer of Civilians as a Collective Harm (and Wrong)" and Devasheesh Bais and Narinder Singh's "Colonial Aftermath and the Need for an Effective International Legal Order".

Next followed a series of case studies: Mutoy Mubiala and Crépine Uwashema covered the Great Lakes Region; Jacques P. Leider, Kyaw Yin Hlaing and Ryan Mitchell explored Colonial Burma; LING Yan, CHAN H.S. Icarus and Claus Kreß considered cases in China and Japan; and

---

[1] The conference programme as well as audio-visual recordings and podcasts of conference presentations are available at https://www.cilrap.org/events/191116-17-yangon/, the designated project web page.

Gunnar Ekeløve-Slydal and Asad G. Kiyani looked at indigenous populations and Romani in Norway and Canada.

After the case studies, we had presentations on certain "Key Legal Notions". YANG Ken enlightened us on "The Doctrine of *Debellatio* or Subjugation: Its Past and Contemporary Relevancy". And Matthias Neuner tackled "The Notion of Continuous or Continuing International Crime".

In the final session "Agendas, Risks and Ways Forward", Hugo van der Merwe and Annah Yvonne Moyo examined "Transitional Justice Policy Priorities: African versus European Agendas". Wolfgang Kaleck presented his paper "Double Standards in International (Criminal) Law Past and Present: Thoughts on Ways Forward". And I concluded the conference, by providing some perspective on these presentations and my own original contribution on speech along the atrocity spectrum, which, I hope, was a fitting capstone to what I summarized.

This book follows a reordered structure, as explained by the co-editors in their foreword: Part I: Context, Part II: Legal Notions, Part III: Colonial Burma, Part IV: Other Former Colonial Territories, and Part V: Indigenous Peoples. In the following, I will share some perspectives on the presentations and deliberations at the Yangon conference, organised pursuant to yet another organizational structure based on Bergsmo's set of questions posed at the outset of the expert meeting's programme. His outline considered the following points: a) relevant patterns identified by the case studies; b) the extent to which contemporary international law addresses lingering consequences of colonial wrongs; c) the risks of double standards and related perceptions in affected populations; d) wider implications of such risks for the Third World Approaches to International Law movement and legitimacy of international law; e) whether traditional truth and reconciliation mechanisms are adequate to address lingering grievances linked to colonial wrongs; f) important elements for a new tool that could be used to address such grievances, including ensuring the participation of relevant expertise in the listening to, analysing of, and otherwise engagement with the grievances through consultation or other processes; and g) the relevance of legal notions such as subjugation, reoccupation and continuing core international crimes.

Combining and reshaping these points into the following criteria, I am able to present my reflections as follows: (1) the parameters of the 'colonial wrongs' problem; (2) patterns of colonial wrongs; (3) theoretical and policy insights into the 'colonial wrongs' problem; (4) legal issues related to the 'colonial wrongs' problem; and (5) mechanisms for solving the 'colonial wrongs' problem. Let us now proceed pursuant to these criteria.

3.1. The Parameters of the 'Colonial Wrongs' Problem

The Yangon conference began with Morten Bergsmo, who presented on "Double Standards and the Problem of Access to International Law". For a precise reading of his presentation, I refer you to the recording of his conference lecture[2] as well as Chapter 7 below. The following are some of the main points that I took away from his lecture.

Although, as the conference programme pointed out, the conference was *not* about Rakhine or the contemporary situation in Myanmar, it was held in Yangon because, as the programme notes, "the situation in Myanmar is illustrative of problems that can arise if colonial grievances are long ignored by moderate actors and abused by other actors". Collectively, I will refer to these "problems" as the 'Colonial Wrong Problem'. What are the elements of the 'Colonial Wrong Problem'? I submit there are four: (1) colonial practices that caused harms to indigenous peoples; (2) a current situation of alleged gross violation of human rights; (3) as a result of ignoring past colonial wrongs, polarization in the country where the alleged colonial wrongs and current human rights violations are taking place; and (4) creating fora for consideration of colonial wrongs (for example, not just traditional truth and reconciliation commissions).

Bergsmo then gave some examples of colonial wrongs, going beyond his concept paper and Chapter 7 below. He looked at the United States and slavery in North American colonial times, including the early capital-formation in Virginia based on cultivation of land of slaveholders such as the U.S. presidents Washington, Jefferson and Madison. He wondered whether we should also look at European nations other than the British in their American colonies who profited from slavery. Thus, he alluded to the role of Arabs who used African slaves extensively – and considered whether we should be examining them. He also suggested that fellow Africans who enslaved and sold slaves should perhaps also be the object of further scrutiny. Could we go too far in this regard? he queried.

---

2   I recommend the audio-visual recording of Bergsmo's 65-minute lecture, wherein he gently challenges international lawyers, see https://www.cilrap.org/cilrap-film/191116-bergsmo/.

The concern would be not merely the potential opening of a Pandora's Box, but also the difficulty of conducting a dispassionate inquiry into what essentially concerns the foundations of American self-representation and identity. This would include the rise of agriculture- and land-based capital accumulation of the class of 'planters' – among them several 'founding fathers' of the republic – and their trade and other ties to the United Kingdom. He suggested that a real discourse on the slave economy in the United States will need to be courageous and not beholden to successor power or interests.

Transfers of civilian populations represent an easy example of a colonial wrong that can help problematize our theme, and Bergsmo then discussed this as he does in his Chapter 7 below. Other chapters in this book, in particular by Matthias Neuner, Jacques P. Leider, Derek Tonkin, Shannon E. Fyfe and Kyaw Yin Hlaing, also discuss such colonial population transfers, so they are comprehensively addressed by this volume.

Finally, Bergsmo drew our attention to key legal concepts used to sustain colonial strategies, such as the notion of *debellatio* – conquering a people, eliminating its sovereignty and disposing of its territory. He showed that the notion was accepted by international law authorities such as Oppenheim and Schwarzenberg, more recently than we might tend to think.

Related to this, he also considered colonial rule and the phenomenon of 're-occupation'. Originally, in the case of colonial Burma, it was about colonial seizure of land and exercise of jurisdiction. Interestingly, after World War II, for purposes of quick resumption of control, the United Kingdom suddenly referred to the 're-occupation' of Burma, thus seeking to justify a civilian administration under the control of the armed forces, setting aside the pre-war constitutional order and administration in Burma. If Britain 're-occupied' Burma after World War II, had Burma in effect been under occupation or the equivalent during the entire colonial period? Had, to this end, the massive migration into colonial Burma essentially – and by admission – been a form of transfer of civilian population into 'occupied territory'?

In addition to discussing the types of colonial wrongs, Bergsmo also addressed ways to deal with them within the context of human rights abuses being alleged in a country with a legacy of colonial wrongs. This requires our evolving toward a kind of effective, positive complementarity. We need to avoid 'external actors' only pointing fingers and not seeking to help domestic accountability actors. Since the adoption in 2010 by States Parties of the International Criminal Court of a positive complementarity or capacity-development approach, it is necessary to be able to hold two thoughts at the same time: accountability advocacy, on the one hand, and discrete technical assistance to domestic accountability actors, on the other. If such a balance is achieved, there may be more progress on accountability and compliance, as well as less tension between the country in question and the international community. In some situations, such lowering of polarisation may also be helpful in ongoing peace processes. Finding ways to listen to colonial grievances and concerns to the effect that double normative standards are at work, may increase one's ability to contribute in such situations, as well as to explain the role that international law should play.

Narinder Singh and Devasheesh S. Bais presented on "Colonial Aftermath and the Need for an Effective International Legal Order".[3] Devasheesh Bais began by noting that "international law is blind to colonial wrongdoing". He then alluded to the transfer of Bengali people into what is now Rakhine State. Could the transfer of population be seen as a violation of international law? Geneva Convention IV from 1949 (Article 49(6)) forbids an occupying power from transferring part of its civilian population into the territory it occupies. Article 8(2)(b)(viii) of the ICC Statute prohibits the "transfer, directly or indirectly, by the Occupying Power of parts of its own civilian population into the territory it occupies".

This does not directly cover colonial wrongs in Burma. But we have an authorized investigation at the ICC in respect of Myanmar for these crimes *vis-à-vis* Rohingyas in modern times. So, do we have a double standard seen from the perspective of the Burmese? The same pattern can be seen with respect to India which was also colonized by the British. In this case, irresponsible border demarcations – the Radcliffe Line between India and Pakistan, and the McMahon Line between India and China – have led to gross human rights violations (via partition of Pakistan from India) as well as war (between India and Pakistan over Kashmir and between India and China over Tibet).

Ambassador Narinder Singh discussed access to international law, as elaborated in his fine foreword above. Former colonies face great chal-

---

[3] The audio-visual recording is available at https://www.cilrap.org/cilrap-film/191116-singh-bais/.

lenges in engaging with and availing themselves of international law. As colonies, they had no need to be dealing with or to gain experience in dealing with international law. He gave some poignant examples of the lack of capacity India has had, especially as relates to human resources. He also noted cases where post-colonial states had striven to exert agency in the international legal system, including the United Nations Convention for the Law of the Sea treaty negotiations, and suggested that this could serve as an example going forward.

Regarding these presentations on "The Parameters of the 'Colonial Wrongs' Problem", I have a couple of observations to make. First, colonial wrongs are not just about understanding the structures and dynamics of sectarian conflict, but also the colonial perpetrator group's behaviour in dealing with those structures and dynamics. For colonialism is not just about creating tensions among groups in its wake. It is also about modelling conduct that influences the groups after the colonizer departs. And this is true because, in a larger sense, colonization is itself an act of violence, a ripping of the social fabric, which perpetuates itself through post-colonial perpetration of violence between and among the groups that were its original victims.

Secondly, and similarly, colonial problems were not just structural or physical. Colonial powers often brought in bigotry, stereotyping, racism and inter-ethnic hatred via the European culture of racism and white superiority. As I mentioned during my comments on the Great Lakes panel at the conference, a prime example in this regard would be Rwanda.

There, first the German and then the Belgian colonizers injected into the colonized people the notion that Tutsis were superior to Hutus. The Tutsis, they informed the local populace, were supposedly a Nilotic people originating from Ethiopia. They were seen as taller, thinner, with aquiline noses, and a naturally more 'regal' bearing. In essence, according to this European mentality, the Tutsis seemed more 'Caucasian' and thus more capable, more intelligent, and more talented. They were made the administrators of Rwanda (and Burundi, for that matter). Hutus, on the other hand, were short, squat, with flat noses and thick heads. They were less like Caucasians and thus inferior, according to this twisted logic. This kind of attitude instilled tremendous resentment and hatred in the Hutus for the Tutsis and explains the virulence of the mass atrocity that followed decolonization.

Similarly, we learned in Jacques P. Leider's excellent presentation at the conference about the British colonial perception regarding the "Arakanese Mahomedans" as being indolent and inferior.

3.2. Patterns of Colonial Wrongs

3.2.1. The Great Lakes Region

Mutoy Mubiala began the case study portion of the conference programme with "Addressing Colonial Wrong-Doing in the Great Lakes Region of Africa".[4] The case studies appear in Part IV of this anthology. He focused on the colonial wrongs of Belgium in the Great Lakes Region. In particular, he looked at three objects of Belgian colonization: Rwanda, Burundi and the Democratic Republic of the Congo. His analysis helps instantiate two distinct types of patterns in terms of categories of colonial wrongs.

First, in Rwanda and Burundi, we have the example of the colonizer favouring one ethnic group over another and setting each group at odds against one another. In the aftermath of decolonization, there has been mass internecine violence between Hutus and Tutsis as a result of this reckless colonial policy. In the Democratic Republic of the Congo, we see another one of the colonial wrong patterns – transfer of civilians – in this case, ethnic Rwandans into eastern Congo. This has led to inter-ethnic violence between Banyamulenge and local Congolese in the Kivu provinces of the country.

3.2.2. Colonial Burma

The papers presented in this conference panel are available in Part III of this anthology. The panel started with Jacques P. Leider's presentation on "The Chittagonians in Colonial Arakan (Rakhine State): Seasonal Migrations, Settlements and the Socio-Political Impact".[5] Leider gave an outstanding account of an aspect of this civilian transfer practice during colonial Burma in respect of the settlement of Chittagonian agriculturalists moving into the region. This was a granular analysis of the situation, which shows some of the nuances of local identity and the role of the colonizers, local people, and those who moved into the area in question.

---

4   The audio-visual recording is available at https://www.cilrap.org/cilrap-film/191116-Mubiala/ and his written contribution appears as Chapter 15 below.

5   For the lecture, see https://www.cilrap.org/cilrap-film/191116-leider/. See Chapter 6 below.

Next Kyaw Yin Hlaing presented on "The Importance of Hearing Grievances Linked to Colonial Wrongs in Burma".[6] He explained why it can be useful to air colonial grievances in Myanmar. However, he also gave very helpful insights into how such discourse can be abused and even jeopardize efforts to deal with modern human rights violations. His Chapter 11 below elaborates on this risk in some detail.

3.2.3.   China and Japan

In this conference panel, LING Yan first presented "On the Relevance of Chinese Colonial Grievances to International Law".[7] She started with China's 'century of humiliation', which began with its defeat in the First Opium War in 1839, and lasting until it became the People's Republic of China in 1949. During this period, China endured being a semi-colonial and even a semi-feudal country at the hands of the British and the Japanese, among others.

LING proceeded to discuss China's attitude toward international law following this 'century of humiliation'. She focused, in particular, on respect for sovereignty and territorial integrity, non-interference with internal affairs, and treatment of the sovereign's citizens, peaceful settlement of international disputes, and Japan's war crimes. But she expressed frustration with Western powers treating international law as a tool to advance imperialistic aims, including a hypocritical human rights policy. This extends to treatment of Japanese war criminals after World War II, which has been weak as compared with investigation and prosecution of Nazi war criminals.

Claus Kreß looked at these two countries from the opposite perspective in "Inter-State Violence, Colonial Violence and ICL: Japan's Wars of Aggression and the Perception of Double Legal Standards".[8] He asked us to consider that, prior to World War II, Japan studied international law, starting from United States Commodore Matthew Perry's visit in 1853, and concluded that conquest was an acceptable norm. At the same time, it had been taking on board the examples and practices of European colonial powers with respect to their imperialist designs in Asia. In doing

---

[6]   His lecture is available at https://www.cilrap.org/cilrap-film/191116-hlaing/.

[7]   See Chapter 12 below, as well as the lecture at https://www.cilrap.org/cilrap-film/191117-ling/.

[8]   The audio-visual recording of the lecture can be seen at https://www.cilrap.org/cilrap-film/191117-kress/. His paper will be published by TOAEP as a stand-alone monograph.

so, the Land of the Rising Sun badly underestimated the legal revolution brought on by the Kellogg-Briand Pact, as featured in Oona Hathaway and Scott Shapiro's recent book *The Internationalists*.

The Japanese felt that the emerging norm against aggressive war was not airtight – there were exceptions (for example, the right of self-defence, the Chamberlain Doctrine, and the Monroe Doctrine). Thus, Western powers may have some responsibility for not disabusing Japan of its views regarding aggressive war. Immediately after the Tokyo Trial (or the International Military Tribunal for the Far East ('IMTFE')) – which put many Japanese leaders in the dock for war crimes and crimes against peace committed in and around the World War II – the Japanese witnessed how European colonizers maintained their colonies and even took up arms and employed blunt force in defence of their colonies in the region (for example, the Dutch in reference to their East Indies possessions, and the British in Burma). Technically, this did not violate any prohibition on the use of force. Thus, in this context, the Japanese leaders being found guilty of aggression at the IMTFE incurred Japanese ire and sparked a backlash.

In essence, Japan considered itself a victim of the double-standard problem in reference to colonial wrongs, which was perhaps best reflected in Judge Radhabinod Pal's voluminous dissent to the IMTFE judgement, which Professor Kreß referenced in opening his remarks. Indeed, per the *New York Times*, many of post-war Japan's nationalist leaders and thinkers have honoured Judge Pal as a hero, "seizing on — and often distorting — his dissenting opinion at the Tokyo trials to argue that Japan did not wage a war of aggression in Asia but one of self-defence and liberation". Plus, in the immediate post-war period, it would seem that the countries that sat in judgment of the Japanese did not embrace the principles upon which the Tokyo judgement was issued. In recent time, ironically, Japan has embraced the ICC's recent definition of, and jurisdiction over, the crime of aggression.

3.2.4. Indigenous Populations and Romani

Gunnar Ekeløve-Slydal's presentation was on "Past Wrongdoing Against Romani and Sami in Norway and the Prism of Modern International Criminal Law".[9] The Sami are an indigenous Finno-Ugric people inhabit-

---

[9] For the audio-visual recording of his lecture, see https://www.cilrap.org/cilrap-film/191117-ekelove-slydal/. See his comprehensive Chapter 17 below.

ing large swaths of the northern parts of Finland, Norway, Russia and Sweden. They are known as semi-nomadic reindeer herders (but also engage in agricultural practices, hunting and fishing, as well as the full range of professions not linked specifically to their traditional way of life). Norwegian policies, Ekeløve-Slydal explained to us, attempted to eradicate the Sami culture and way of life through assimilation techniques. The use of the Sami languages in schools and public life was not allowed, and the Sami were socially and economically ostracized in their own territories as the Norwegian government settled ethnic Norwegians in what was the traditional Sami homelands.

Similarly, the Romani, known colloquially as Roma or 'Gypsies', an Indo-Aryan ethnic group, traditionally itinerant, were the object of racist treatment by the Norwegian government. The Norwegians also sought to eradicate their culture, via enforced sterilization, removing children from Romani families and placing them in orphanages or with ethnic Norwegian families, and by enforced placement of Romani families in a labour colony.

This represents an infringement of core values protected by ICL and human rights (as reflected in the rays of these two being refracted and intersecting in a prism), including territorial and bodily integrity, equal access to the law, and protection of family, religion, language and culture. Although the Norwegians have attempted to atone for their sins via reparations programmes, support for Sami and Romani culture and languages, ceding some territorial control, and establishing truth commissions, many believe that they should be subjected to more serious justice mechanisms. This is especially true since they arguably committed genocide against the Romani.

In "Colonial Self-Exemption and Genocide in Canada", Asad Kiyani examined a similar phenomenon with respect to indigenous peoples in Canada, who were arguably the victims of genocide as well.[10] As much of this presentation revolved around an analysis of Third World Approaches to International Law ('TWAIL'), I will analyse the majority of it in the next Section of this chapter. I would note that Kiyani emphasized that TWAIL is about Third World people traditionally marginalized, not Third World *states*. Also, colonial exploitation is related to the notion of

---

[10]   See his Chapter 16 below. The audio-visual recording of his calmly-presented lecture is available in CILRAP Film at https://www.cilrap.org/cilrap-film/191117-kiyani/.

'sovereignty' as sovereignty was constructed, according to TWAIL, to permit colonial exploitation.

Based on these case studies, I have some thoughts on the analysis here regarding patterns. First, I think we can discern the following colonial wrongs or mismanagement templates:

1. bringing in other ethnic groups for labour or other economic exploitation (see colonial Burma with Bengali Indians transferred into Burma by the British and the Democratic Republic of the Congo with Banyarwanda being transferred into the Kivu region via the Belgians);

2. making one group supreme over another for purposes of proxy administration (see Rwanda and Burundi);

3. destroying indigenous structural institutions (for example, kingdoms, princedoms and fiefdoms) to create colonial structures that are incompatible with indigenous cultures and create chaos and inter-ethnic or group tensions (see Burma and Rwanda);

4. drawing borders based on imperialistic motives (for example, Sykes-Picot) leading to sectarian violence in places like Iraq between Sunnis and Shia or between Arabs and Kurds);

5. an entrenched or permanent colonial force seeking forced assimilation of indigenous peoples; and

6. outright destruction of a nation's culture, identity and sovereignty – that is, pure *debellatio* (and we ought to inquire as to whether this is a colonial wrong or mismanagement pattern in itself, or a condition preceding the imposition of other colonial wrongs or mismanagement patterns).

Second, in light of the elements laid out by Bergsmo in his introductory lecture regarding the core elements of the 'colonial wrongs' problem, I wonder whether other situations could or should be considered as part of this project. I would suggest that the inter-ethnic violence in Sri Lanka could be one of these. It involved the British colonial overlord favouring Tamils in what was then Ceylon, a post-colonization civil war, and contemporary efforts at transitional justice. Another case to consider is the Cambodian genocide in relation to French colonial conduct, as well as American actions in the region leading to the take-over of Cambodia by the Khmer Rouge, as Kevin Crow emphasized in his comments and has elaborated in his Chapter 13 below.

I believe it is good to include the situations regarding indigenous populations and related victims of colonialism. I also think United States slavery should be considered as the project grows over the coming years. Should African-Americans be entitled to some kind of justice mechanism in reference to these older crimes? For example, a truth commission? This is being vetted in the United States at the time of this writing, and would certainly also contemplate reparations. Similarly, comparable justice actions in relation to Native Americans in the United States, arguably the victims of genocide, seem long overdue.

3.3. General Theoretical and Policy Insights into the 'Colonial Wrongs' Problem

With respect to the *theoretical insights*, our first relevant conference presentation was Shannon E. Fyfe's "The Transfer of Civilians as a Collective Harm (and Wrong)".[11] In her paper – appearing as Chapter 10 below – she disaggregated 'wrongs' from 'harms'. She used transfer of civilians to do this. There are two aspects of this: transfer during colonial times and in post-colonial times. During colonial times, this was purportedly done for security or economic development. In Burma, there was a colonial social and political hierarchy with the British at the top, Chinese and Indians in the middle, and the Burmese at the bottom. *Colonial* transfer is currently seen as regrettable at worst, whereas *post-colonial* transfer is seen as problematic, illegal and punishable.

This creates two 'justice' problems. The first is a *distributive* justice problem (that is, who is actually tried for crimes?). This is when the objects of the justice process are limited by, for example, the timeframe of the ICC or the lack of a relevant crime (such as stoking ethnic tensions). Current domestic actors get held accountable but colonial actors do not. The second is a *substantive* justice problem: a defective protection of substantive rights (as opposed to focusing on the objects of justice). The modern legal framework does not allow for recognition of colonial wrongs.

Fyfe then distinguished 'wrongdoing' from 'harms'. To illustrate, she noted that a broken leg based on a hurricane is a harm with no wrong-

---

[11] The audio-visual recording of her lecture is available at https://www.cilrap.org/cilrap-film/191116-fyfe/.

doing. But if someone intentionally trips someone else, who falls into a third party's arms and falls in love, then there is wrongdoing but no harm.

Transfer of civilians into a population results in group harms. These should be acknowledged regardless of which actors or entities are responsible for them (that is, regardless of the nature of the wrongdoing). These harms accrue to the original occupants who are subjected to the migrants being forcibly introduced into their community. They also accrue to the persons forced to migrate later down the line. They may be subjected to persecution and ethnic cleansing, among other harms.

But this also entails wrongdoing. There are bad acts (for example, the way transfer is effected) and omissions (for example, displacing existing occupants of a territory or not providing housing for the migrants). These are morally indefensible and result in violations of the rights of others. Thus, this wrongdoing would apply to the British as colonizers, and perhaps to Burmese actors in carrying out what has been referred to as ethnic cleansing in recent times.

Fyfe concluded with two questions, in historical terms. First, what was the impact on the population locally as a result of the transfer of civilians? Second, what other mechanisms can be used?

We later heard from Ryan Mitchell in "Myanmar and the Hegemonic Discourse of International Criminal Law: Three Critiques".[12] He began by calling for ICL to engage in a "prophylactic" self-critique to avoid the risk of de-legitimisation based on its failure to grapple with colonial crimes. He referred to the *tu quoque* critique of ICL by Carl Schmitt as one potentially shared by any number of critics. From this, he noted that Schmitt's arguments were expressed via formalist objections intended to limit the scope of ICL, for example, the *nullum crimen sine lege* rule.

There are also available critiques of the recent efforts to exert jurisdiction over Myanmar, for example, the objections based on the *pacta tertiis* rule as applied to non-signatories of the Rome Statute. Using TWAIL conceptual tools (a critical account of how international law norms fail to address the realities of postcolonial states), a foray into rational-choice theory as a source for the logic of colonial practices, as well as conceptual history (looking at how international crimes are based on much longer

---

[12]   See his Chapter 9 below, as well as the audio-visual recording of his lecture in CILRAP Film at https://www.cilrap.org/cilrap-film/191116-mitchell/.

histories of discourse), Mitchell's critique was made on three levels: semantic, epistemic and genealogical.

Semantically, he noted that certain frictions between a state government and a 'people' can be based not on a denial of the latter's self-determination *per se*, but rather on the form in which self-determination claims are expressed. Here he cited Greek objections over the name of the state of Macedonia. This echoed comments over the semantic dimensions of the Rohingya issue and the question as to whether ICL, as a vocabulary, adequately reflects the nuances of post-colonial conflict situations. Subsequently, he addressed the epistemics of inter-ethnic conflict and distrust in post-colonial states, noting that, here too, ICL has no means of conceptualizing or referring to the strategies of 'divide and conquer' that often formed part of the basic logic of colonial rule. Third, in the mode of genealogical critique, he noted that newly-legislated crimes such as genocide are defined against much longer histories of (especially colonial) discourse and practice.

Formalist critiques of ICL frequently use the arbitrary character of its jurisdictional capacities to try to delegitimize the entire enterprise. In response, it might be preferable for international lawyers to more fully accept an anti-formalist position where 'legal gymnastics' are used not just to ensure accountability for states managing to squeeze through the jurisdictional bottlenecks of currently-existing mechanisms, but also to redefine those bottlenecks themselves in order to address older, colonial crimes.

Finally, in terms of theoretical presentations, we can return to the excellent analysis of Asad Kiyani in his presentations "Colonial Self-Exemption and Genocide in Canada", mentioned above. He relied on TWAIL principles to examine how Canada's self-exculpation from responsibility for the genocide of its indigenous citizens reflects the double standards inherent in international law as part of a project to exempt colonizers from the remit of the criminal process. He made the case for genocide against Canada in reference to its treatment of its indigenous population: killing, measures on birth (forced sterilization), forcible transfers (residential schools), and inflicting conditions on the group meant to bring about their destruction (malnourishment and bad housing). Paradoxically and hypocritically, Canada has fought against inclusion of 'cultural genocide' in reference to the 1948 Genocide Convention. Also, it has watered down the enforcement scope of its domestic statute criminalizing genocide. Further, it throws its financial, technical and human resources support to institutions that prosecute genocide *overseas*, including by winning favour with NGOs through generous funding. It even occasionally prosecutes foreign genocidaires on Canadian soil.

In the end, access to justice is denied to First Nations people in Canada not only by executive action in the international sphere and legislative action in the domestic sphere, but by an ontological deficit that presents itself in the judicial sphere. And it demonstrates the connection between traditional TWAIL treatment of international law to TWAIL's disaggregation of the state from its citizens, and to its problematization of continuing settler-colonial relationships outside the Global South.

As far as *policy insights*, certain speakers have focused on the risks of empowering modern perpetrators with the 'colonial wrongs' discourse. We heard warnings about this in the Burmese context from Kyaw Yin Hlaing. We heard similar warnings from Wolfgang Kaleck himself, who alluded to the risks of developing remedies for colonial grievances. He asked whether it could weaken international law or serve as a distraction from the need for reform or accountability in former colonial societies.

CHAN H.S. Icarus made this a point of emphasis in his presentation on "Use and Abuse of Colonial Grievances and Double Standards: China and the Five Principles of Peaceful Co-Existence".[13] He highlighted the 'Five Principles on Peaceful Co-existence' or the 'Panchsheel', namely: (1) mutual respect for territorial integrity and sovereignty; (2) mutual non-aggression; (3) mutual non-interference in internal affairs; (4) equality and co-operation for mutual benefit; and (5) peaceful co-existence. With reference to China (and, implicitly Hong Kong), he observed that formerly colonized States should not only be open about past colonial wrongs, but also come with clean hands without double standards, failing which, they only have themselves to blame for their condemnations falling on deaf ears.

3.4. Legal Issues Related to the 'Colonial Wrongs' Problem

In her lecture "Possible Impediments to Justice for Colonial Crimes: A Belgian Perspective", Crépine Uwashema focused on the case of the as-

---

[13] For the audio-visual recording, see https://www.cilrap.org/cilrap-film/191116-fyfe/.

sassination of Patrice Lumumba,[14] a criminal case filed by Lumumba's family before a Belgian domestic court. A threshold issue was whether the killing of Lumumba was a war crime. This, in turn, raised the issue of whether the killing was connected to a non-international armed conflict or an international armed conflict. If it could be charged as a crime, was it barred by the statute of limitations? Could Belgian courts be governed by the 1968 Convention on the Non-Applicability of Statutory Limitations to War Crimes and Crimes against Humanity? This is not clear but customary international law (as shown in jurisprudence of the Extraordinary Chambers in the Courts of Cambodia or 'ECCC') shows that it could be found that there was no statute of limitations bar.

Uwashema also addressed the establishment of parliamentary commissions of inquiry in Belgium. This could have negative consequences for criminal proceedings. For example, incriminatory statements can be made during the parliamentary inquiry stage without the due process protections of a criminal trial, but then the statement could be used during the criminal proceeding. She also examined Belgian state responsibility for the Lumumba assassination – there is no legal impediment here as the law has evolved to allow for criminal liability for the Belgian state. But this only results in an insufficient 'declaration of guilt'. There should also be reparations, restitution, and other relevant remedies.

We also heard from YANG Ken on "The Doctrine of *Debellatio* or Subjugation: Its Past and Contemporary Relevance".[15] As will be recalled, Bergsmo introduced the notion of *debellatio* in his introductory presentation. YANG Ken built on that and showed a gradual process of destroying Burmese institutions until they were eliminated. This resulted in taking Burmese sovereignty entirely, with the 1885 abolition of the Burmese Monarchy, at which point the British achieved *debellatio*. Although development of post-World War II *jus ad bellum*, as well as universalization of the principle of self-determination, seemed to have rendered the *debellatio* doctrine obsolete, the doctrine still had relevance in terms of Britain's 're-occupation' of Burma in 1945. More recently, it was germane with respect to the United States post-2003 occupation of Iraq. When fil-

---

[14] The lecture can be seen at https://www.cilrap.org/cilrap-film/191116-Uwashema/. Her Chapter 14 below is co-authored with her colleagues Christophe Deprez and Christophe Marchand.

[15] See his Chapter 4 below, as well as his lecture at https://www.cilrap.org/cilrap-film/191117-yang/.

tered through a TWAIL lens, we might conclude that the inalienability of sovereignty has remained a principle primarily for the Global North, whereas the Global South has been regarded as 'fair game' for the exercise of *debellatio*.

Matthias Neuner's conference presentation on "The Notion of Continuous or Continuing International Crime" considered the concept with regard to the emerging development of norms related to enforced disappearances, slavery, sexual slavery, conscription and enlistment of child soldiers, and unlawful deportation, among others.[16] From this survey, he concluded that the jurisprudence of international courts, the work of publicists, the International Law Commission and other (international) bodies, as well as international treaties and customary international law, allows credible application of the continuing/continuous crime customary doctrine to the forcible or unlawful transfer of populations in certain colonial and post-colonial contexts. But the exact details still need to be determined through the ICC's application and court decisions.

To these excellent ideas regarding legal concepts and tools that could be applied to dealing with the 'Colonial Wrongs' Problem, I would suggest we also consider the application, and/or deeper consideration of the doctrine of *uti possidetis juris* (Latin for 'as you possess under law'), a principle of international law that provides that newly-formed sovereign states should retain the internal borders formulated by their colonizers pre-independence.

I would also suggest studying the 'inter-temporal law', the principle that courts apply when a significant period of time has elapsed since the creation of an international norm. This takes into account subsequent changes in the relevant law. In the *Island of Palmas* case, the great arbitrator Max Huber invoked this principle as follows:

> As regards the question which of different legal systems prevailing at successive periods is to be applied in a particular case (the so-called intertemporal law), a distinction must be made between the creation of rights and the existence of rights. The same principle which subjects the act creative of a right to the law in force at the time the right arises, demands that the existence of the right, in other words its con-

---

[16] For his lecture, see https://www.cilrap.org/cilrap-film/191117-neuner/. His comprehensive written contribution appears as Chapter 5 below.

tinued manifestation, shall follow the conditions required by
the evolution of law.

This was alluded to by Wolfgang Kaleck in his presentation and
several times during the rich and frank consultations at the Yangon conference.

3.5. Mechanisms for Solving the 'Colonial Wrongs' Problem

In his conference presentation "Transitional Justice Policy Priorities: African versus European Agendas", Hugo van der Merwe examined transitional justice ('TJ') agendas that were at odds with one another.[17] His paper appears as Chapter 2 above, co-authored with Annah Moyo. The African Union adopted a "Transitional Justice Policy" in February 2019 that
makes reference to TJ potentially assisting societies "to come to terms
with the traumas of slavery, colonialism, apartheid, systematic repression
and civil wars". In contrast, the European Union's 2015 "Policy Framework on Support to Transitional Justice" contains no mention of the colonial era. Instead, it emphasizes States focus on narrower mandates (for
example, civil and political rights) and more recent periods of conflict
(despite suggesting that these processes should "aim to transform the society by identifying and dealing with root causes of conflict and violence"). With these contrasting approaches in mind, the analysis considered the evolution of international norms that have facilitated the focus on
colonial era abuses in TJ processes (including in truth commissions) and
how regional TJ frameworks either promote or marginalize these justice
demands.

Wolfgang Kaleck concluded the Yangon conference by exploring
this topic in "Double Standards in International (Criminal) Law Past and
Present: Thoughts on Ways Forward".[18] It appears as the opening Chapter
1 above. He raised several fundamental questions about the issues grap-
pled with at the conference: proper fora, parties, and time periods to cover.
He discussed the problems of horizontal selectivity and vertical selectivity
as being serious potential obstacles in terms of seeking justice. Double
standards are a reality. His presentation served as a capstone to the conference deliberations. He considered the many valuable double-standard
critiques of the unequal treatment of colonial wrongs versus current al-

---

[17] For the audio-visual recording of his lecture, see https://www.cilrap.org/cilrap-film/191117-merwe/.

[18] For the audio-visual recording, see https://www.cilrap.org/cilrap-film/191117-kaleck/.

leged contemporary crimes embedded in our modern system of international criminal justice. Kaleck mentioned the work of the European Center for Constitutional and Human Rights which, among other relevant projects, has sought justice for Herero and Nama communities for German colonial crimes committed in Namibia.

Kaleck gave an overview of potential mechanisms available to accommodate adjudication of colonial wrongs in situations of current mass atrocity, including the use of the courts, international and domestic, as well as alternative tools of addressing crimes of the past that can complement existing mechanisms. In fact, based on the conference presentations and deliberations, we can see a number of potential fora, parties, time periods, and conduct covered, and remedies for potentially dealing with colonial wrongdoing, as follows:

1. Potential fora:
    a. criminal justice mechanisms (international and domestic);
    b. human rights courts or bodies;
    c. alternative justice mechanisms (truth commissions or reparations bodies);
    d. national administrative commissions (such as the Rwandan National Commission for the Fight Against Genocide, which can serve as the basis to promote or advocate the accountability of former German and Belgian colonizers for their wrongdoing as a root cause of the mass atrocity committed in Rwanda in 1994, see Chapter 15 by Mubiala);
    e. national parliamentary commissions of inquiry (such as in Belgium for the Patrice Lumumba case, but note possible conflict or tensions with parallel criminal proceedings);
    f. joint claims tribunals (between the colonial victim countries and perpetrator countries, like the US-Iran Claims Tribunal);
    g. regional human rights organizations (for example, the African Union) setting up a claims chamber within that organisation;
    h. inter-State litigation before the ICJ (for example, the Democratic Republic of the Congo vs. Belgium in the Lumumba case; the Democratic Republic of the Congo vs. Rwanda/Uganda in reference to eastern Congo invasions/armed conflicts, new forms of colonialization) (ironically, The Gambia filed a case against My-

anmar, a fellow former British colony, before the ICJ for alleged genocide of Rohingya Muslims);

  i. domestic civil litigation (see Belgian July 2018 law lifting immunity for crimes committed by the State, but this can only result in a 'declaration of guilt'); and

  j. opinion tribunals (for example, for the Korean 'comfort women' in reference to Japan's war crimes during World War II).

2. Parties: colonizers vs. colonial subjects who represent the victims of colonialization (see Kaleck's Chapter 1 above). Corporations, arms traders.

3. Time period covered: how far back in time do we go? If there are layers of colonialism, which ones do we cover? For example, for the Democratic Republic of the Congo, do we go back to Leopold II in the 1800s, Lumumba in the early 1960s? If not, what is our cut-off point? This may depend on resource availability.

4. Conduct covered: should we concentrate only on the worst atrocities (for example, physical destruction, disappearance, or other types of physical persecution) or less serious ones (deprivation of economic and social rights)?

5. Remedies: these could include criminal punishment, reparations, and truth, among others. Which are most appropriate?

3.6. Colonial Wrongs, Memory and Speech Along the Atrocity Spectrum

The final substantive presentation at the Yangon conference was my own, on the topic "Colonial Wrongs, Memory and Speech Along the Atrocity Spectrum".[19] In the abstract, speech has incalculable intrinsic value. It can facilitate human interaction, organization, education, autonomy, self-actualization, tolerance and democratic governance. Certain speech in certain contexts, however, can be quite injurious – spurring division, ignorance, violence and anti-democratic governance. Within the crucible of atrocity, speech may be similarly Janus-faced. Its power to prevent mass violence cannot be disputed. But its capacity for enabling mass violence is similarly unquestionable. As mentioned in Kyaw Yin Hlaing's lecture, we have seen that in Myanmar with the hate speech of the extremist Buddhist

---

[19] You can see the audio-visual recording at https://www.cilrap.org/cilrap-film/191117-gordon/.

monk U Wirathu, a leadership figure in an anti-Muslim movement. At the time of writing, there is a Myanmar warrant of arrest against him related to his speech activities.

The issue arises: when and how may speech work for good or ill in relation to atrocity? In my scholarship, I have posited that the relationship between speech and atrocity should be analysed within a two-axis matrix. The first axis relates to chronology and divides into 'process' (referring to the cycle of atrocity) and 'pre-process' phases. The 'pre-process' phase indicates that a target group is successfully integrated into the social fabric and not subjected to untoward degrees of prejudice or discrimination. The 'process' (or atrocity cycle) phase consists of three critical junctures: (1) identification; (2) action; and (3) execution (with such criteria being derived from Gregory Stanton's 'Eight Stages of Genocide').

The second axis is qualitative and entails classifying speech as both 'salutary' and 'inimical'.

Returning to the chronology axis, during the pre-process phase, the focus must be on disseminating salutary speech. Such speech can go a long way towards preventing prejudice, discrimination and the formation of extremist groups. Dissemination can be achieved through various means, including fostering education with an emphasis on teaching pluralistic values, establishing pro-tolerance NGOs active in engaging with the citizenry, and safeguarding free access to channels of public communication. During the 'identification' stage when prejudice and discrimination are on the rise, promoting salutary speech may still play an important role in preventing atrocity. The question during this stage becomes whether salutary speech is still capable of negating inimical speech.

Let me suggest that this matrix has application in terms of the mechanisms for solving the 'Colonial Wrongs' Problem. Making reference to Bergsmo's suggestion in the Yangon conference programme that we consider creation of a new mechanism that can permit a space for airing colonial grievances in a potential mass atrocity or transitional justice context. In particular, he referred to possible creation of "a new tool that could be used to address such grievances, including ensuring the participation of relevant expertise in the listening to, analysing of, and otherwise engagement with the grievances through consultation or other processes". I am going to refer to this mechanism as the 'consultation process'. And I would like to suggest a kind of fusion between my atrocity spectrum framework and Bergsmo's consultation process.

More specifically, in the period before persecution reaches critical mass, when 'salutary' speech may help stem mass violence, we should consider that *discourse acknowledging colonial wrongs or mismanagement may constitute a type of salutary speech* within my framework that could ease the friction and thereby help prevent commission of core international crimes. This opportunity to rely on 'salutary speech', in the form of discourse acknowledging colonial wrongs or mismanagement, can be the object of Bergsmo's 'consultation process'. I am offering a conceptual temporal framework for when we can inject the 'consultation process' into a situation of potential atrocity and suggest how and to what extent it may be effective.

In conclusion, in the ICL field which tends to be extremely Western-centric, one of the strong points of CILRAP is that it has been quite inclusive of non-Western persons and perspectives. I think the diverse nature of participants at the Yangon conference and in this volume is evidence of that. But this is typical of CILRAP gatherings and its projects are always very inclusive of diverse viewpoints. What is amazing about the Yangon conference and the colonial wrongs project is the inclusion of a non-Western-centric perspective in a very substantial and substantive way. All participants in the Yangon conference made significant contributions in this regard. Reflecting on these contributions, as we have in this chapter, allows us to appreciate the project's scholarly insights in a very holistic way. This volume represents a remarkable body of scholarship and it has been gratifying to see how it has come together in its final form in this book. We should be grateful for these submissions and optimistic about their potential to generate further excellent scholarship as well as changes in the way ICL – and international law more widely – is perceived and dealt with.

PART II:
LEGAL NOTIONS

4

On Subjugation and the Case of Burma

YANG Ken[*]

4.1. Introduction

Like 'sovereignty', 'subjugation' is one of those 's-words' that today's international lawyers prefer not to talk about.[1] The reason is somewhat obvious: the United Nations ('UN') Charter – the written constitution of the international community since 1945 – seemed to have banished this inherently violent concept from the realms of international law. With Article 2(4) unequivocally safeguarding "territorial integrity" of states from belligerent force, seizing the entirety of the territory from the defeated state as a spoil of war – a phenomenon traditionally known as 'subjugation' – is no longer legally viable.

Subsequent development and practice have continued to reinforce this position. By 1967 – just as Hannah Arendt had noticed that "the very word 'expansion' has disappeared from our political vocabulary"[2] – the UN Security Council emphasized directly the "inadmissibility of the acquisition of territory by war" during the aftermath of the Six-Day War in the Middle East.[3] Therefore, when Schwebel attempted to justify Israeli occupation of Egyptian territory, he would have to go the extra mile and distinguish "defensive conquest" from "aggressive conquest", and went on to theorize Israeli occupation as being rooted in necessity and the prin-

---

[*] **YANG Ken** is a Researcher at the European University Institute in Florence. He holds degrees from Peking University Law School and Harvard Law School.

[1] This iconic disdain for the 's-word' was famously professed by Louis Henkin in 1999. See Louis Henkin, "That 'S' Word: Sovereignty, and Globalization, and Human Rights, Et Cetera", in *Fordham Law Review*, 1999, vol. 68, no. 1, p. 1.

[2] Hannah Arendt, *Imperialism: Part Two of the Origins of Totalitarianism*, Harcourt, Brace, Jovanovich, San Diego, CA, 1973, p. xix.

[3] United Nations Security Council ('UNSC') Resolution 242 (1967), UN Doc. S/RES/242, 22 November 1967 (https://www.legal-tools.org/doc/2e9040).

ciple of self-preservation – holding territory for the sake of fending off future aggressions – not territorial enlargement.[4]

Some argue that the world has, at least in principle, moved beyond wars of acquisitive character, and thus our laws no longer regulate the spoils to which victors have felt entitled for millennia.[5] While contemporary international lawyers are not unfamiliar with eruptions of armed conflict and allegations of illegal use of force, rarely do they confront situations where territorial aggrandizement had been the openly-professed goal.[6] Today, both victims of past colonization and current occupying powers would frame their experience as 'occupation',[7] a phenomenon parallel to 'conquest', meant to be temporary and constrained, short of seizing title. But even that may sound like an ugly word, for the peremptory norms of self-determination seemed to have left it little space.

Such modern antipathy against acquisitive wars explains why 'subjugation' has now been cast into oblivion: after all, what could appear greedier and more excessive than taking over an entire country and its population through military coercion? Even by classical standards, 'subjugation' was, by definition, extreme both with regards to its factual characteristics and legal consequence, and consequently occurred rarely compared to mere instances of 'conquest'. Referred by some earlier Anglophone publicists as 'complete conquest', 'subjugation' describes the dire situation where a defeated party in war has its entire armed force annihilated or neutralised, its full territory seized and controlled by the enemy, and its state institutions have been automatically dissolved or forcibly dismantled. From an international law standpoint, the materialization of the above facts meant that the state's sovereignty has been eliminated, the

---

[4] Stephen M. Schwebel, "What Weight to Conquest?", in *American Journal of International Law*, 1970, vol. 64, no. 2, p. 345.

[5] James Whitman, *The Verdict of Battle: The Law of Victory and the Making of Modern War*, Harvard University Press, Cambridge, MA, 2012, p. 255.

[6] For instance, most Russian and very few non-Russian scholars who had defended the incorporation of the Crimea into the Russian Federation characterized the event as a case of self-determination, rejecting the competing identification of the process as unilateral annexation. See Anthea Roberts, "Crimea and the South China Sea: Connections and Disconnects Among Chinese, Russian and Western International Lawyers", in Anthea Roberts *et al.* (eds.), *Comparative International Law*, Oxford University Press, 2018.

[7] During the author's visit to Yangon, Myanmar in November 2019, a sign was spotted in the colonial-era residence of former UN Secretary-General U Thant, which phrased British colonial presence in Burma as "occupiers".

victor was entitled to annex its territory, and the war was coming to an end. It is often associated with the Latin notion '*debellatio*', which could be literally translated as 'warring (the enemy) down', and is conventionally related to the brutal annihilation of Carthage by a vengeful Roman Republic.[8]

Perhaps due to their limited relevancy, the terms 'subjugation' and '*debellatio*' are sometimes treated in contemporary legal literature as synonymous. For early generations of lawyers, however, while the two notions substantively overlap, their exact meaning varies among authors.[9] In

---

[8] Italian historian Rocco Pezzimenti argued that actual Roman *debellatio* did not necessarily lead to "total destruction" of the enemy, but as "merely removing the instruments of *bellum*, of conflict, from the enemy". See Rocco Pezzimenti, "Roman Juridical Experience. The Reflections of Cicero", in Rocco Pezzimenti, *The Open Society and Its Friends: With letters from Isaiah Berlin and the late Karl R. Popper*, Millennium Romae, Rome, 1997, p. 16.

[9] Such division over the meaning of *debellatio* could be spotted in a speech by Oppenheim made in 1911, wherein he used the example of certain lawyers professing that *debellatio* "has no consequence in the point of law", as a dangerous example of international lawyers indulging in their "politico-jural convictions". Oppenheim, *The Future of International Law*, Clarendon, Oxford, 1921, p. 57. Oppenheim's statement suggests that certain jurists at the time had understood *debellatio* as not being able to generate any legal consequence by itself. It also should be noted that Oppenheim personally defined *debellatio* here as "annexation after effective conquest", which is extremely close to his definition of subjugation: "annexation turns conquest into subjugation", see Lassa Oppenheim, *International Law: A Treatise*, vol. 1, Longmans, London, 1905, p. 395, suggesting that the two notions can be equated from his understanding. In 1944, predicating the Allies' war-time slogan "unconditional surrender" would eventually materialize, Kelsen first invoked *debellatio* as the potential legal basis for the Allies' post-war treatment of Germany; see Hans Kelsen, "The International Legal Status of Germany to be Established Immediately Upon Termination of the War", in *American Journal of International Law*, 1944, vol. 38, no. 4; Hans Kelsen, "The Legal Status of Germany According to the Declaration of Berlin", in *American Journal of International Law*, 1945, vol. 39, no. 3; Hans Kelsen, "Is a Peace Treaty with Germany Legally Possible and Politically Desirable?", in *American Political Science Review*, 1947, vol. 41, no. 6. In 1950, Josef L. Kunz made an attempt to address the drastically different understandings over *debellatio* and subjugation. See Josef L. Kunz, "The Status of Occupied Germany under International Law: A Legal Dilemma", in *The Western Political Quarterly*, 1950, vol. 3, no. 4, p. 552. According to Kunz's summary, Continental publicists and their Anglo-American counterparts appropriate the notion *debellatio* differently. For Continental publicists, *debellatio* merely describe a factual situation where a state had been completely annihilated, yet it does not necessarily include the annexation of said country. Anglo-American lawyers believed that *debellatio* by definition consists of "the objective fact (conquest) [...] with the subjective animus of annexing the conquered enemy state", see Kunz, *op. cit.*, pp. 551-553. If Kunz was rights, the Continental–Anglosphere division over the use of *debellatio* is first and foremost a linguistic disagreement.

any event, with our reformed *jus ad bellum* framework banning any deliberate projection of lethal force onto the territory of another state (implied in the substitution of the more inclusive word "force" for "war" in Article 2(4)),[10] it seems only logical for lawyers to conclude that the doctrine of subjugation is "no longer operative".[11] In other words, if there is no 'right to conquer', there could be no 'right of conquest'. Subjugation, wrote Kunz in 1950, "is no longer of great actuality".[12]

This assessment, that the doctrine of subjugation is "no longer operative", might have been proven by recent history to be only partially true. One might argue that remnants of the doctrine of subjugation which prescribes the liquidation of sovereignty of a subdued political unit, has managed to retain its place within our modern legal landscape.[13] The most prominent example that substantiates such argument is the US occupation of Iraq following the Second Gulf War, which seemed to have ticked all of the boxes of for subjugation: the total defeat of enemy forces, exercising effective control over foreign territory, and, most importantly, the complete collapse of state institution.[14] Interestingly, US officials in charge of post-war state-building were not "shy about comparing the American role

---

[10] Tom Ruys, "The Meaning of 'Force' and the Boundaries of the *Jus ad Bellum*: Are 'Minimal' Uses of Force Excluded from UN Charter Article 2(4)", in *American Journal of International Law*, 2014, vol. 108, no. 2, pp. 159–210.

[11] James R. Crawford, "The Extinction of States", in James R. Crawford, *The Creation of States in International Law*, Oxford University Press, 2007, p.704, note 23; see also Eyal Benvenisti, *The International Law of Occupation*, Oxford University Press, 1993, pp. 94–96.

[12] Kunz, 1950, pp. 538–565, see above note 9.

[13] Therefore, it was only prudent of the editor for the entry *'debellatio'* in *Max Planck Encyclopedia of Public International Law* to note in the opening paragraph that "the continued existence of *debellatio* as a legal concept has been questioned", but not categorically ruled out. See Michael N. Schmitt, "Debellatio", in *Max Planck Encyclopedia of Public International Law*, Oxford University Press, 2009.

[14] Immediately after the occupation, the Coalition Provisional Authority issued Order Number 2 (23 May 2003) that directed the dissolution of Iraqi military, security and intelligence infrastructure. In recent years, there have been many inquiries into the consequences of this decision, especially how the disbanding contributed to the rise of extremism by both creating a vacuum and radicalizing former Sunni officers. See, for example, Mark Thompson, "How Disbanding the Iraqi Army Fuelled ISIS", *Time*, 28 May 2015; Patrick Wintour and Ewen MacAskill, "UK foreign secretary: US decision on Iraqi army led to rise of Isis", *The Guardian*, 7 July 2016.

---

in Iraq to that in post-World War II Germany and Japan",[15] with the former just happened to be the most prominent instances that some lawyers conceive as a modern-day exercise of subjugation.[16]

This eerie relevancy of subjugation could be explained by the fact that its substance falls outside of the familiar categories of *jus ad bellum* and *jus in bello* rules. Subjugation takes place under the framework of war: it presumes the occurrence of armed conflict and hostilities, as well as the legality of territorial aggrandizement. However, the doctrine of subjugation also prescribes the legal criteria for determining at what point sovereignty and juridical statehood should been seen as being unilaterally eliminated by the victorious party. American occupation of Iraq after the regime-changing war could thus be seen as a 'benign' version of subjugation parallel to the German experience, one that had eliminated Iraqi sovereignty but had spared Iraqi statehood. For some American lawyers who had then sought to justify the US transformation projects in Iraq, the doctrine of subjugation became the handy tool to clear potential legal hurdles and liabilities, especially constraints imposed by laws of belligerent occupation, which inhibits transformation of occupied territory per its original design. From his short piece published in the *American Journal of International Law*, former US diplomat David J. Scheffer went so far as to suggest that "occupation law should be returned to the box from which it came".[17]

The present chapter seeks to trace the doctrinal evolution of subjugation during the nineteenth and twentieth centuries, in the hope of shedding some light on how such a seemingly irrelevant notion has retained its place within the contemporary legal order. Section 4.2. reviews the sub-

---

[15] James Dobbins, Seth G. Jones, Benjamin Runkle and Siddharth Mohandas, *Occupying Iraq: A History of the Coalition Provisional Authority*, The Rand Corporation, Santa Monica, CA, 2009, p. 13. Similarly, Noah Feldman, a Harvard Law School constitutional law specialist who was part of post-war state-building effort, noticed in 2003 on his flight to the Middle East, that among his fellow colleagues who were still awake reading, "[w]ithout exception, they were reading new books on the American occupation and reconstruction of Germany and Japan". See Noah Feldman, *What We Owe Iraq: War and Ethics of Nation Building*, Princeton University Press, 2004, p. 1.

[16] It must be noted that the features of the US post-World War II occupation of Japan do not support the interpretation that *debellatio*/subjugation had been performed there; different from the case of Germany, Japanese capitulation (also in the form of "unconditional surrender") did not temper with government functions. See Schmitt, 2009, see above note 13.

[17] David J. Scheffer, "Beyond Occupation Law", in *American Journal of International Law*, 2003, vol. 97, no. 4, p. 860.

stance of 'subjugation' as manifested in international law treatises from mid-nineteenth century to early-twentieth century, a period defined by the European empires' turn to territorial expansion as well as their global rivalry for commercial success. The international law discipline at the time was moving from its classical phase to its positivist phase, constructing legal frameworks suitable to the realities of commercial empires. Due to the adversarial nature of war, international lawyers had in fact been hesitant to hand out explicit legal significance to conquests and annexations during their immediate pronouncement, as such legal determinations were likely to be haunted by the shifting tides of war. However, such concerns over contention was usually reserved for situations where European players were involved; a looser set of standards were applied to the colonial peripheries. Therefore, Section 4.3. below examines the subjugation of Burma as a case study, surveying how the doctrines involved were applied.

4.2. Subjugation as a Legal Notion in Positivist Treatises

It is important to register two facts before our examination of the notion of 'subjugation' begins. First, as Erich Kussbach has aptly pointed out, "notions of occupation, *debellatio*, subjugation and conquest, as used in legal literature, as a rule overlaps each other".[18] Therefore, one cannot offer a thorough articulation of 'subjugation' without simultaneously addressing the exact meanings of these neighbouring notions.

Second, throughout international law's positivist phase, publicists appeared to have encountered difficulties settling on a single terminology for addressing the phenomenon that we now associate with the notion 'subjugation'. Our current preference for 'subjugation' to describe the taking of territory in war after one belligerent party was entirely subdued and eliminated, can likely be attributed to Oppenheim and his landmark treatises, the original *International Law* (1905).[19] Interestingly, contemporary

---

[18] See Erich Kussbach, "Conquest", in Rudolf Bernhardt (ed.), *Encyclopedia of Public International Law*, vol. 1, North-Holland, Amsterdam, 1992, p. 120.

[19] Oppenheim, 1905, p. 287, see above note 9. The notion of 'subjugation' did appear in William Beach Lawrence (ed.), *Elements of International Law*, Little, Brown and Company, Boston, MA, 1855, when discussing the validity of treaties concluded against the backdrop of war ("for if they were not [held valid due to coercion], wars could only be terminated by the utter subjugation and ruin of the weaker party"), see *ibid.*, p. 240. This line was preserved in the eighth edition edited by Richard Henry Dana. While Dana discussed the phenomenon mainly under the headline "complete conquest", he also used the term subjugation in a non-technical fashion when discussing peace treaties ("But, if the war was begun

and preceding publicists had employed different expressions, ranging from "extinction by conquest" (Westlake, 1910),[20] "complete conquest" (Dana, 1866;[21] Halleck, 1861,[22] and 1866),[23] "absolute and unqualified conquest" (Wheaton, 1836),[24] to "(territorial acquisition completed through) entire submission and extinction of the state" (Vattel, 1773).[25] Intriguingly, by the time this subject was addressed in Crawford's *The Creation of States in International Law* (2006), he avoided 'subjugation' but used *debellatio* and occasionally equate the process to a now legally-dubious "annexation" which led to state extinction.[26] It is therefore important to note these differences, as well as continuities and discontinuities.

The fact that 'subjugation' had been conventionally articulated as some qualified form of 'conquest', suggests that our examination should first address this somewhat obsolete concept. We could begin with one understanding shared by positivist era publicists, namely that under the context of territorial acquisition,[27] conquest in its *ordinary* meaning re-

---

unjustly by the conqueror, and especially if for the purpose of subjugation, the moral aspect of the question would be altered"), see Richard Henry Dana (ed.), *Elements of International Law*, Little, Brown, and Company, Boston, MA, 1866, p. 722, footnotes supplemented by Dana.

[20] John Westlake, *International Law, Part I: Peace*, Cambridge University Press, 1910, p. 64.

[21] Dana (ed.), 1866, pp. 436, 449, 772, in footnotes supplemented by Dana, see above note 19.

[22] Henry Wager Halleck, *International Law; Or Rules Regulating the Intercourse of State in Peace and War*, H. H. Bancroft and Company, San Francisco, 1861, pp. 719, 775, 776, 810–841.

[23] Henry Wager Halleck, *Elements of International Law and Laws of War*, J.B. Lippincott Company, Philadelphia, 1866, p. 340.

[24] Henry Wheaton, *Elements of International Law, With a Sketch of the History of the Science*, Carey, Lea and Blanchard, Philadelphia, 1836, p. 252.

[25] Emer de Vattel, Joseph Chitty (eds.), *The Law of Nations; or Principles of the Law of Nature Applied to the Conduct and Affairs of Nations and Sovereigns*, T. and J. W. Johnson, Philadelphia, 1852, p. 386.

[26] Crawford, 2007, chapters 2 ("The Criteria for Statehood: Statehood as Effectiveness"), 16 ("Problems of Identity, Continuity and Reservation"), and 17 ("The Extinction of States"), see above note 11.

[27] Under a separate context that was the seizure of enemy property, 'conquest' had been used by Halleck to refer to "Towns, forts, lands, and all immovable property taken from an enemy", parallel to "captures made on the high seas, called maritime prizes". See Henry Wager Halleck, Sherston Baker (eds.), *Halleck's International Law: Or Rules Regulating the Intercourse of States in Peace and War*, vol. 2, C. Kegan Paul and Co., London, 1878, p. 115.

---

ferred merely to the *factual* situation where one state has taken possession of its adversary's territory as the result of military victory. A high threshold of effectiveness is incorporated into this definition in order to render it "actual conquest", as opposed to the scenario where "that force be overcome, and the original owner resumes his possession".[28] As framed by Oppenheim, such seizure "alone does not *ipso facto* make the conquering State the sovereign of the conquered territory".[29] This assertion followed a long pedigree that can be traced back to the time of Vattel,[30] where publicists maintained that conquest alone cannot immediately render legal rights over the fraction of territory it had seized during war, albeit such factual control constituted a necessary condition for future transfer of title. From this perspective, the common expression 'right of conquest' can be misleading, as it seems to rest title-acquisition on brute force alone, which was not accurate from a purely legal standpoint. Vattel, for instance, had written in a definitive tone about the need for "completing" the conquest for the purpose of generating title:

> Immovable possessions, lands, towns, provinces, become the property of the enemy who makes himself master of them: but it is only by the treaty of peace, or the entire submission and extinction of the states to which those towns and provinces belonged, that the acquisition is completed, and the property becomes *stable and perfect*.[31]

---

28 See Halleck, 1861, pp. 799–800, see above note 22; Oppenheim, 1905, pp. 287, 290, see above note 9.

29 Oppenheim, 1905, p. 287, see above note 9. Similarly, Halleck wrote in 1861 that "[b]y the term conquest, we understand the forcible acquisition of territory admitted to belong to the enemy. It expresses, not a *right*, but a *fact*, from which rights are derived". Halleck, 1861, p. 799, see above note 22.

30 O'Connell argued that Vattel's advocacy for territorial cession as foundation of territorial reconstruction constituted a critical break from prior feudal law traditions and had accommodated Europe's advancement into the Westphalia System. D.P. O'Connell, "Territorial Claims in the Grotian Period", in C.H. Alexandrowicz (ed.), *Studies in the History of the Law of Nations*, Springer, The Hague, 1970, p. 1.

31 Vattel, 1852, p. 386, see above note 25 (emphasis added). The same paragraph is supposed be included within the original 1758 edition of Vattel's *Law of Nation*. A later translation of the paragraph produced by Charles G. Fenwick reads: "real Property—lands, towns, provinces—become the property of the enemy who takes possession of them; but it is only by the treaty of peace, or by *the entire subjugation* and extinction of the State to which those towns and provinces belong, that the acquisition is completed and the ownership rendered permanent and absolute" (emphasis added), see Emmerich de Vattel, Charles G. Fenwick

This image of 'conquest' as an intermediate state short of permanently seizing sovereignty (title) may now appear counter-intuitive and alien, for its substance is actually a lot closer to what we today conceive as 'occupation'; in fact, positivist writers such as Halleck spoke of *"rights of conquest"* for addressing rights of the occupant,[32] while Oppenheim explicitly spelled out that military occupation *is* conquest.[33] Ironically, as conquest has "acquired the opprobrium which attaches to it in the twenty-first-century mind",[34] the two notions are often presented as dichotomic, with the latter presented as the lesser evil. Especially within contemporary literature on occupation law, both the phenomenon of 'military occupation' and its corresponding rules have been portrayed as a relatively progressive development, for they promise only temporary authority but not permanent foreign rule. This narrative on the sequential transition from conquest to occupation has been criticized as misleading, for it exaggerates the historical dominance of both norms and practices concerning conquest and its actual relationship to occupation. According to the French scholar Irénée Lameire, archival surveys showed that brute conquests during the sixteenth and seventeenth centuries had been mired in "precariousness" and uncertainty.[35] In Lameire's own words, the displacement of sovereignty was not always evident, and that "sovereignty is often fragmented, displaced in certain respects, not displaced in others: as a result there is a curious superimposition of sovereignty".[36]

From a historical perspective, both bodies of rules formulated around conquest and occupation could be conceived as legal regimes sustaining European territorial stability, sparing states from "the reign of *unregulated* force".[37] To clarify, 'stability' is not synonymous with "inalienability (of territorial sovereignty)", but rather aim to moderate the legal consequence of unilateral actions. According to German scholar August

---

(eds.), *The Law of Nations or the Principles of Natural Law*, Carnegie Institution, Washington, D.C., 1916.

[32] Halleck, 1861, p. 799, see above note 22.

[33] Oppenheim, 1905, p. 288, see above note 9.

[34] Peter M.R. Stirk, *A History of Military Occupation from 1792 to 1914*, Edinburgh University Press, 2016, p. 12.

[35] Peter M.R. Stirk, *The Politics of Military Occupation*, Edinburgh University Press, 2009, pp. 11–12.

[36] Stirk, 2016, p. 22, see above note 34.

[37] Sharon Korman, *The Right of Conquest: The Acquisition of Territory by Force in International Law and Practice*, Clarendon Press, Oxford, 1996, p. 95.

Heffter (1796-1880), the predominant principle of war among civilized nations was characterized not by tendencies for mutual annihilation (that is, 'complete conquest', 'subjugation', '*debellatio*'), but wars of limited duration and visions for re-establishing peace, with the abundance of peace treaties as testament.[38] This doctrinal insistence on peace treaty and formal cession was never meant to freeze territorial reconstruction through war, but to refrain practices of assigning *immediate* legal consequence to brute conquest or annexation when hostilities continued,[39] against which the sovereign's consent manifested in the form of peace treaties was conceived as the clear-cut cure. That being said, publicists also conceded that if time was indeed on the conqueror's side, then "mere lapse of time and the inability of the former sovereignty to recover its lost possessions" could still secure title over parts of another state, absent of complete conquest (subjugation) or cession.[40] Such scenario was later theorized as a separate mode of territorial acquisition known as 'prescription'.

It would also be useful to keep in mind the unique political structures under which these regimes had evolved. During the Middle Ages, forcible territorial seizure was constrained by the just war logic (which rejected unconditional 'right of conquest' with the exception of just war) and feudal law, including prevalent thoughts on knightly private warfare (which prioritized inflicting damage upon the adversary, instead of depriving "his inheritance, property or lands, which he held in lawful possession").[41] By the time Europe was engulfed in the Thirty Years' War (1618-1648), brute conquest was still considered by the French as an "inferior type of claim", and, in the eyes of the Spanish, "a threat to stability".[42] It was not until Europe gradually transitioned into a modern state system – one that had witnessed the ascendency of the principle of necessity as its guiding principle, driving political expansion in the name of self-

---

[38] Eyal Benvenisti, "The Origins of the Concept of Belligerent Occupation", in *Law and History Review*, 2008, vol. 26, no. 3, pp. 631–632.

[39] O'Connell, 1970, p. 1, see above note 30.

[40] Halleck, 1866, p. 340, see above note 22.

[41] Wilhelm G. Grewe, *The Epochs of International Law*, De Gruyter, Berlin, 2000, p. 122. Similarly, on the flipside, justifications on which wars of territorial acquisition had been fought also evolved. Infidelity during the Middle Ages when laws of Christendom prevailed, and nationalism after the French Revolution, were both conceived as legal justifications for territorial conquest in their respective historical eras.

[42] Stirk, 2009, p. 12, see above note 34.

preservation – that a new legal paradigm on territorial acquisition emerged to accommodate the era of *"voluntary* law of nations" (Vattel), and alongside it, new mechanisms of stabilization. Aside from requiring conquest to be complemented by sovereign volition, publicists also described other non-legal dynamics – most significantly the 'balance of power' – that serve as brakes against brute conquest. As Oppenheim had summarized in 1905:

> The conqueror has not in fact an unlimited possibility of annexation of the territory of the vanquished State. When the balance of power is endangered or when other vital interests are at stake, third Powers can and will intervene, and history records many instances of such interventions.[43]

Nevertheless, an exception was carved out, which addresses an extraordinary circumstance. Publicists who held that mere conquest cannot immediately displace sovereignty, also reserved the theoretical possibility that if brute conquest was so thorough in geographical scope and absolute in terms of military ferocity that the conqueror had not only established control over the entire realm of the enemy state, but had also annihilated its ruling institutions, then the sovereignty of the rival state itself should perish as a result. If a sovereign went so far as to extinguish another sovereign, then the issue of hostility and contention over territory would simply cease to exist. As a result, a 'complete conquest' (subjugation) was completed by none other than the conqueror himself.

It should be noted that at the time of those positivist treatises there obviously existed substantive confusion over the terminology of 'subjugation', prompting Halleck and Oppenheim to address the problem. Halleck distinguished the ordinary meaning of 'conquest' (which for him means 'occupation'), from its "more limited and technical meaning" which is when "the conqueror has acquired complete title" (that is, 'subjugation').[44] Oppenheim noted that people "speak of conquest as a title, and *everybody knows that subjugation after conquest is thereby meant"*.[45] One

---

[43] Oppenheim, 1905, p. 292, see above note 9. Westlake had noted that the logic of balance of power scrutinizes all sorts of territorial aggrandizement, and would treat the merger of crowns from marriage or inheritance the same way it treat subjugation. John Westlake, *Chapters on the Principles of International Law*, Cambridge University Press, 1894, pp. 120–122.

[44] Halleck, 1861, p. 775, see above note 22.

[45] Oppenheim, 1905, p. 287, see above note 9.

can presume Oppenheim's insistence on elevating 'subjugation' – rather than 'conquest' or 'annexation',[46] which he had used as *factual* conditions of a proper subjugation – as a distinct mode of territorial acquisition (parallel to that of occupation, accretion, prescription and cession), can be understood as part of the effort to disperse such perennial semantic confusion. Interestingly, following the swift 'death of conquest/subjugation' during the course of the twentieth century ('swift' when compared to the relative stability of the doctrines over 500 years, from the Great Discovery to the collapse of empires in the twentieth century), 'subjugation' has largely been absorbed by 'conquest' in legal discourse. Today, it is more often to find 'conquest' be placed next to 'discovery', 'cession' and 'occupation' as a mode of territorial acquisition.[47] Oppenheim's effort in untangling 'subjugation' from 'conquest' could be said to have lost its contemporary relevancy.

4.3. Subjugation Outside of Europe: The Annexation of Burma as an Example

As the previous section has indicated, the scholarly attention towards 'subjugation' as an original mode of acquisition should not be interpreted as highlighting its predominance in practice. Due to the high thresholds set by jurists in their doctrinal works, even some of the events they label as instances of subjugation could hardly pass their own tests.

The two examples cited by Oppenheim[48] – Prussia's subjugation of Hanover, Hessen-Kassel, Hessen-Nassau and Frankfurt am Main following the Austro-Prussian Seven Weeks' War (1866), and Britain's subjugation of the Orange Free State and the South African Republic amidst the Boer War (1900) – present much more complicated images of subjugation if examined closely. While historians agree that Prussia's annexation of the four German states in 1866 were indeed of unilateral nature and had

---

[46] It is quite interesting that 'annexation' was not even included in the index of the first edition of Oppenheim's *International Law*, 1905 (it was included in the third edition, 1920). It is mostly used to describe either subjugation or protectorates.

[47] For instance, the Max Planck Encyclopaedia of International Law has adopted the formulation of 'subjugation' designated as a sub-category within 'conquest' in its entry on "Territory, Acquisition". It is also interesting to note that nowadays, the notion 'title' has been preferred over the more classical expression 'modes of acquisition'. See Marcelo G. Kohen and Mamadou Hébié, "Territory, Acquisition", in *Max Planck Encyclopedia of Public International Law*, Oxford University Press, 2011.

[48] Oppenheim, 1905, p. 289, see above note 9.

---

eliminated them from the international scene,[49] it was implemented in a relatively gentle fashion, largely preserving local administrative structures.[50] Moreover, against the grand picture that was German unification, these episodes of conquest should not eclipse the contribution of the other peaceful methods.[51]

As for Britain's subjugation practice during the Boer War, it was in fact commonly cited by jurists as the textbook case for "premature annexation".[52] Boer forces had retained control of the said territories at the time the British commander announced proclamations of annexation (which would "henceforth form a part of His Majesty's dominions"), and an additional 36,000 British personnel were lost in the armed contention during the coming year.[53] Submission only came in May 1902, when the Peace of Vereeniging was signed. Jurists conceived it "not a treaty of peace proper", but terms of surrender, as subjugation had been completed and the Boer republic extinguished.[54]

Another often cited intra-Europe case of subjugation was that against the Papal States in 1870 initiated by the Kingdom of Italy, whose own unification relied in part on multiple cessions sought from Austria.[55] Interestingly, Italy maintained it had achieved *debellatio* against the Papal States when its forces occupied Rome, despite its forces had stopped at the boundaries of the Vatican City, leaving the supposed capital unoccupied. This fact had stemmed contentions over whether *debellatio* had been completed.[56]

---

[49] Randall Lesaffer (ed.), *Peace Treaties and International Law in European History: From the Late Middle Ages to World War One*, Cambridge University Press, 2004, p. 89.

[50] Hans A. Schmitt, "Prussia's Last Fling: The Annexation of Hanover, Hesse, Frankfurt, and Nassau, June 15–October 8, 1866", in *Central European History*, 1975, vol. 8, no. 4, pp. 332–333.

[51] Bodie A. Ashton, *The Kingdom of Württemberg and the Making of Germany, 1815-1871*, Bloomsbury, London, 2017, p. 156.

[52] O'Connell, 1970, p. 1, see above note 30.

[53] Coleman Phillipson, *Termination of War and Treaties of Peace*, E.P. Dutton and Company, New York, 1916, p. 23.

[54] *Ibid.*, p.17. Intriguingly, Oppenheim dated the subjugation of the Boer republics to year 1900.

[55] Erik Goldstein, *Wars and Peace Treaties: 1816 – 1991*, Routledge, London, 1992, pp. 13–18.

[56] Horace F. Cumbo, "The Holy See and International Law", in *The International Law Quarterly*, 1948, vol. 2, p. 612. Cumbo noted that the Italian government had subsequently ar-

Outside the European centre, a different set of rules of engagement had developed in parallel. The colonial encounter in the New World had given rise to the law of occupation, which replaced conquest as the primary language for legitimizing titles in the Americas.[57] By re-describing Native Americans as stuck in a primitive stage of economic and historical development, a new perception that the New World was relatively void of ownership was invented.[58] As Fitzmaurice noted, occupation as an original mode of territorial acquisition was essentially a unilateral doctrine of appropriation, as it gave no recognition to indigenous societies.[59] By the nineteenth century, as European powers raced for expansion in Africa – epitomized in Cecil Rhoades aspirational line "I would annex the planets if I could" – the continent was assumed to be a void of territorial sovereignty, thus theoretically opened to imposing sovereignty. In the case of nineteenth century Africa, such imposition was manifested in the creation of 'colonial protectorates' followed by formal 'annexation' – a legal notion that is also by its very definition unilateral.[60] While treaties of submission (capitulation) and protection were frequently drawn up as complements, they were theorized as ceding 'personal sovereignty' instead of territorial sovereignty due to the territories being only partly civilized

---

gued that "total and material occupation of a territory is not indispensable for 'debellatio'". Kunz argued that the Pope's temporal sovereignty and the Papal State had indeed come to an end by the conquest and subjugation of 1870. Yet, the international personality of the Holy See remained intact, supported by its continued interaction with other states. Josef L. Kunz, "The Status of the Holy See in International Law", in *American Journal of International Law*, 1952, vol. 46, no. 2, p. 311.

[57] One factor that had dampened the potency of conquest in legal arguments during the colonization of the Americas, was the prevalence of the 'Spanish Black Legend'. During the sixteenth and seventeenth centuries, Spain's rivals had utilized Spanish atrocities committed against Native Americans (conquest of the Aztecs and Incas) to demonize both the Spanish Empire and Catholicism. Such dynamic had prompted colonial powers to have their forcible seizure of native land "clothed in the more acceptable language of peaceful occupation". See Andrew Fitzmaurice, "Discovery, Conquest, and Occupation of Territory", in Bardo Fassbender and Anne Peters (eds.), *The Oxford Handbook of the History of International Law*, Oxford University Press, 2012.

[58] Andrew Fitzmaurice, *Sovereignty, Property and Empire, 1500–2000*, Cambridge University Press, 2014, p. 22.

[59] *Ibid.*, pp. 16–17.

[60] Rainer Hofmann, "Annexation", in *Max Planck Encyclopedia of Public International Law*, Oxford University Press, 2009.

(constituting merely *'territorium nullius'*).[61] Throughout the scramble for African territory, effective occupation usually came later than acquisition of the title.[62]

The gradual incorporation of Burma into British India through three Anglo-Burmese wars during the nineteenth century was, however, not a case of occupying savage lands. Britain did not depict itself as operating within a legal vacuum, nor did the British wish to. Historically speaking, European colonial enterprise in the East Indies had not always been characterized by overwhelming dominance, at least not in its early stages. Local authorities were given appreciation and respect, treated as potential allies rather than savages, in exchange for competitive edge *vis-à-vis* other European rivals.[63] Even until the end of the nineteenth century, Westlake cited "Asiatic empires" as the desirable model of non-Western populations successfully fulfilling the standards of civilization.[64]

However, as we can observe from the subjugation of Burma, such respect towards the Asiatic others also evolves in a way that reflects the latest power dynamics between colonial powers and local polity. Non-Western nations were subjected to the 'trial of strength' just to hold onto such quasi-equal status. Unfortunately, the great divergence between European powers and Asian societies – that is, the former's increasing economic and technological edge through the industrial revolution – had rendered such trials more difficult to endure.[65] There were a few lonely survivors. When Ethiopia successfully repelled Italian intrusion and denied its claim for protectorate in 1896,[66] this triumph had propelled it into the

---

[61] Fitzmaurice, 2014, p. 280, see above note 58. It must be mentioned that C.H. Alexandrowicz maintained opposite positions on both whether African political entities were indeed void of territorial sovereignty, as well as the characterization of the mode of acquisition. He maintained that the Partition was largely achieved through cessions in the form of bilateral treaties, see C.H. Alexandrowicz, "The Partition of Africa by Treaty (1974)", in C.H. Alexandrowicz, David Armitage and Jennifer Pitts (eds.), *The Law of Nations in Global History*, Oxford University Press, 2017, p. 257.

[62] Alexandrowicz, 2017, p. 257, see above note 61.

[63] Edward Keene, *Beyond Anarchical Society: Grotius, Colonialism and Order in World Politics*, Cambridge University Press, 2004, p. 79.

[64] Westlake, 1894, pp. 144–155, see above note 43.

[65] Jennifer Pitts, *A Turn to Empire: The Rise of Imperial Liberalism in Britain and France*, Princeton University Press, 2005, p. 15.

[66] C.H. Alexandrowicz, "The Role of Treaties in the European-African Confrontation in the Nineteenth Century (1975)", in Alexandrowicz, Armitage and Pitts (eds.), 2017, p. 292, see above note 61.

'Family of Nations'. Burma was not as fortunate, and was soon trapped in a vicious cycle triggered by its initial loss: foreign intrusions led to more domestic dysfunction; domestic failures in reform and modernization induced more external interference, until the state was completely extinguished; more impotence was always correlated to less significance in terms of international position, making it easier for Britain to exact legal rights unilaterally.

The cause of the initial clash between Britain and Burma – then under the reign of the Court of Ava, its last dynasty – was in fact Burma's expansion. Before its inglorious defeat at the hands of the British in 1826, the Burmese had secured a series of military victories, including rolling back three waves of Chinese intrusions between 1765 and 1769. Eventually, a series of unchecked conquests had created a common frontier between Bengal and Arakan.[67] Arakan was subjugated in 1785, completed with the deportation of Arakanese monarch King Thamada and all royal families, as well as the destruction of Arakan history chronicles.[68] Subsequent occupation was repressive, with Ava constantly demanding men and resources.[69] The ensued refugee exodus and on-and-off rebellions which had led to Burmese cross-border pursuits evolved into a security concern for the British. Frictions further intensified as Burma occupied Brahmaputra Valley, provoking the British to unilaterally declare protectorate over the Himalayan states of Cachar and Jaintia,[70] an unusual and legally dubious move so as to halt Burmese advance.[71] In any event, by the time the

---

[67] Thant Myint-U, *The Making of Modern Burma*, Cambridge University Press, 2001, p. 17.

[68] D.G.E. Hall, *Burma*, Hutchinson House, London, 1950, pp. 87, 94. On the destruction of Arakan history (the palm leaf chronicles), see Anthony Ware and Costas Laoutides, *Myanmar's 'Rohingya' Conflict*, Hurst Publisher, London, 2018, pp. 97–98, citing Arthur Phayre, *On the History of Arakan* (1844).

[69] Myint-U, 2001, pp. 17–18, see above note 67.

[70] *Ibid.*, p.18.

[71] The only prominent case where a power had *unilaterally* imposed protectorate status (through declaration) upon a protected state in the absence of a treaty was the case of Egypt, where Britain unilaterally proclaimed protectorate in 1914, ending Ottoman suzerainty during the outbreak of World War I. However, Britain had maintained occupation of Egypt since its conquest in 1882, which had rendered Ottoman authority largely nominal. In 1905, Japan also planned of unilaterally imposing protectorate over Korea in case a treaty was refused, but in the end was the treaty was indeed accepted. KIM Seung-young, *American Diplomacy and Strategy toward Korea and Northeast Asia, 1882–1950 and After: Perception of Polarity and US Commitment to a Periphery*, Palgrave Macmillan, New York, 2009, p. 58.

First Anglo-Burmese War (1824-1826) broke out, it had originated as "a clash between the two imperial powers".[72]

From the perspective territorial acquisition, the creation of British Burma was achieved through a curious hybrid of cession, unilateral annexation (prescription), and finally, complete subjugation. The legal consequence of the first war was most clear-cut. As the British Expeditionary Force continued to press on after two years of hard battle – the longest, most expensive expedition in British India's history and allegedly one of worst-managed in all British military history – Ava finally requested negotiation in 1826. Under the Treaty of Yandabo, the Court of Ava would end its westward expansion and interference in the Kingdom of Manipur as well as Assam, Jaintia and Cachar. It also agreed to cede the provinces of Manipur, Arakan and the Tenasserim, and pay an indemnity of one million pounds sterling.

By comparison, the Second Anglo-Burmese War (1852-1853) did not end with a peace treaty. The war began with the alleged mistreatment of two British citizens, interpreted by some British statesmen as another insult that the British could not afford to swallow, for "much importance was attached to ceremonies" in Ava, and that any more submission would be conceived as weakness "among Oriental nations". [73] Negotiation failed – some suspected to have been intentionally sabotaged – war ensued, and decisive British victory followed. Having successfully captured Pegu province, Indian Governor-General Lord Dalhousie who had entered the war without clear objectives,[74] wrote to the Court of Directors of the East India Company and stated his intention of annexing the newly occupied territory. He had observed that the Burmese had demonstrated no signs of submission, and as the monsoon rain would soon arrive, the latter was prone to wait out the war in Upper Burma. Since further advancement towards the Kingdom's capital would be infeasible both on military and economic grounds, permanently retaining Pegu should be pursued for keeping Burma in check and save Britain from future interventions. In his own words, occupying Pegu was about "compensation for the past, and

---

[72] Stephen L. Keck, *British Burma in the New Century, 1895–1918*, Palgrave Macmillan, London, 2015, p. 36.

[73] Charles Wood, "The Burmese War", in *Hansard*, vol. 124, 25 February 1853. According to the Earl of Derby, what was at stake was "the prestige of the British character in India", see the Earl of Derby, "The War With Ava", in *Hansard*, vol. 124, 24 February 1853.

[74] Myint-U, 2001, p. 104, see above note 67.

security for the future",[75] and to "hold the kernel of the Burmese Empire without encumbering ourselves with an armful of worthless rind".[76] Dalhousie was bent on this course of action, and planned to carry forward the annexation unilaterally even in the absence of formal cession, as forcing a capitulation could end up extracting unbearable tolls. In December 1852, the proclamation of annexation was sent to the King, along with a proposed peace treaty of only four articles: that there should be perpetual peace between the two States; that Pegu should be ceded to the British; that trade should be perfectly free and unrestricted; that there would be a fixed period for the treaty to be ratified. An additional letter threatened complete subjugation in case Burma attempted any intervention in Pegu.[77] The new King that had seized power through a timely revolt rejected the peace treaty but had also ended hostilities.

One British consul in China, Edward Harper Parker, later described this "transfer" as "by the novel process of a one-sided 'notification'".[78] It would take another three more years after the declaration to "pacify" the new territory,[79] although it was presented in February 1853 that "(Dalhousie) had established order sooner than it had been established in any province that had previously been annexed to the British Empire".[80] It was unclear whether the Court of Ava had sustained its protest against the occupation and annexation aside from its failed diplomatic effort in 1854. However, the carving away of Lower Burma as well as the imposed commercial treaty obligations (concluded in 1862) had all but restricted the Kingdom's capacity in adaptations, incapable of either carrying out needed reforms or contesting British encroachment in any realistic fashion.[81]

---

[75] James Hogg, "The Burmese War", in *Hansard*, vol. 124, 25 February 1853.

[76] Intelligence Branch, Army Headquarters, India, *Frontier and Overseas Expeditions from India, Vol. 5, Burma*, Mittal Publications, Delhi, 1983, pp. 90–91. In a Parliamentary speech made after the occupation and annexation of Pegu, the newly-captured territory was framed as "the most valuable provinces of the Burmese Empire", see *ibid.*

[77] Intelligence Branch, Army Headquarters, India, 1983, pp. 96–97, see above note 76.

[78] Edward Harper Parker, *Burma: With Special Reference to her Relations with China*, Rangoon Gazette Press, Rangoon, 1893, p. 100.

[79] Hall, 1950, pp. 113, 115, see above note 68.

[80] Hogg, 1853, see above note 75.

[81] Myint-U, 2001, p. 10, see above note 67.

Meanwhile, London remained mired in anxieties over the absence of a formal cession. Intriguingly enough, a memorandum produced by the prestigious Duke of Wellington back in 1829 for the Government of India, prepared for the occasion of "renewal of war with Ava", had surfaced in the House of Lords right after the annexation. The first paragraph provided:

> I concur with the Governor General in thinking that it will be absolutely necessary to retain possession of all that had fallen into the hands of the British troops [...] My opinion is, that it will be necessary to continue the preparations for carrying on the operations of the war till the Sovereign of Ava shall be convinced of the necessity of signing a treaty, by the provisions of which all these dominions will be *ceded* to the British Government, or *till the State of Ava shall be destroyed*. A mere military possession of these districts would be but an inglorious and little secure result of these successful operations.[82]

The relevancy of the Duke of Wellington's roadmap in 1853 following the creation of British Burma, reflected the British Empire's lasting anxieties over the legal, political and fiscal uncertainties generated by their latest expansion. British Burma's unstable foundation had rendered future failures in cultivating and maintaining a "friendly and subordinate government in Mandalay" much more unbearable,[83] due to its perceived significance for Indian security, and "radically" changing circumstances brought by "the French Intrigue (in Burma)".[84] Unfortunate for Burma, developments in the coming three decades would eventually propel an insecure British Empire to override its previous concerns over overextension. For one, the second half of the nineteenth century had witnessed the escalating competition between European powers for formal colonies,[85] as well as the rise of neo-mercantilism and protectionist policies. The two phenomena were indeed entangled, for what good could formal empire yield – maybe aside from the noble and selfless cause that was the 'civi-

---

[82]   The Earl of Derby, 1853, see above note 73.

[83]   Ernest C.T. Chew, "The Fall of the Burmese Kingdom in 1885: Review and Reconsideration", in *Journal of Southeast Asian Studies*, 1979, vol. 10, no. 2, p. 378.

[84]   D.K. Fieldhouse, *The Colonial Empires: A Comparative Survey from the Eighteenth Century*, The Macmillan Press, London, 1982, p. 173.

[85]   Of course, aside from formal colonies, commercial prerogatives were also pursued through other avenues such as mandates, concessions and spheres of influence.

lizing mission' – if the acquired sovereignty would not be used for constructing systems of tariff protection and imperial preferences, as well as guarding outbound investments?[86] Such new developments could be attributed to a series of factors, such as the newly unified and reinvigorated continental empires and their visions for imperialism, as well as new ideologies of national Darwinism.[87] Britain, then 'Workshop of the World', conceived this shift as an existential threat to her commercial predominance.

France's successful penetration into Indo-China from 1858 onwards provided that exact ground for precaution. In 1884, the French had finally established a protectorate over Annam and Tonkin through the Treaty of Hué. That same year, a commercial treaty was agreed by Paris and a Burmese mission, with the latter's calculation being that French recognition would "at least raise the diplomatic cost of Britain of any expansion at Mandalay's expanse".[88] Against this new development, Britain informed the French Foreign Minister that it had attached "special importance" to all related to Burma due to its "geographical position and its peculiar political relation with British India". Any special alliance or political understanding established between any other power and Burma would provoke serious objections from Britain. The French Minister later made a counter-inquiry, asking the British to point to any prior "special Treaty engagements [...] which precluded the Burmese from entering into independent political relations with other Powers". The result was the British being unable to identify any pre-existing arrangements of protection, one that would restrict the Burmese Kingdom's external sovereignty. The British Ambassador later went on to clarify that the British position on Burma was not based on specific formal arrangement or even general international law obligations; nor had it derived from a recognized "sphere of influence" that covered Upper Burma. Nevertheless, it was expected by the British that other powers would be "in friendly consideration" of established British interests, and that Britain should be able to rely on their ab-

[86] Bernard Semmel, *The Rise of Free Trade Imperialism: Classical Political Economy and Empire of Free Trade and Imperialism, 1750–1850*, Cambridge University Press, 1970, pp. 206, 226. See also John Gallagher and Ronald Robinson, "The Imperialism of Free Trade", in *The Economic History Review*, 1953, Second Series, vol. 6, no. 1, pp. 1–15.

[87] Andrew Fitzmaurice, "Liberalism and Empire in Nineteenth-Century International Law", in *The American Historical Review*, 2012, vol. 117, no. 1, p. 125.

[88] Thant Myint-U, *The River of Lost Footsteps: Histories of Burma*, Farra, Straus and Giroux, New York, 2008, p. 10.

stention.[89] At this point, British trust in the French had been fragile, and was further fractured by the claim by an Italian spy operating in Mandalay, that the then French Prime Minister Jules Ferry had promised French arms to Burma in secret, planned to be smuggled from Tonkin.[90] In the 1890s after Burma's subjugation, Britain would go on to stall French infiltration into Siam, so as to create a buffer state between British India and French Indo-China, so that a European War could be avoided.[91]

There were debates over which solution – annexation (subjugation) or protectorate – would be the more desirable political-legal option for settling 'the Burma problem'. By 1885, the word "annexation" had already developed a negative connotation in Britain. "I think it is the general feeling of this country – that our responsibilities are already heavy enough, that our Possessions [...] are sufficient to require the utmost care and vigilance, and that it is not desirable to increase either the one or the other", claimed the Colonial Secretary Edward Henry Stanley in the House of Lords in 1883.[92] In 1885, however, what had prevailed was the sense that "necessity has been forced upon us".[93] Even for the few who had advocated for the preservation of Burmese institutions (the monarchy and the Hluttaw, or council of state) out of practical concerns, also shared the concern that presence of past dynasty would drag the society with regards to needed transformation and progress:

> Burmese people are imbued with an almost superstitious veneration for the royal family. As long as the dynasty lasts, this veneration will continue [...] owing to the presence on the scene of a de facto sovereign of the reigning dynasty, and the impossibility of getting the people to bury their instincts, or sink their loyalty, so far as to suffer any authority to exist

[89] M.F. Lindley, *The Acquisition and Government of Backward Territory in International Law*, Longmans, Green and Co., London, 1926, p. 232.

[90] Myint-U, 2008, p.11, see above note 88; John L. Christian, "Anglo-French Rivalry in Southeast Asia: Its Historical Geography and Diplomatic Climate", in *Geographical Review*, 1941, vol. 31, no. 2, p. 279.

[91] Kees van Dijk, *Pacific Strife: The Great Powers and their Political and Economic Rivalries in Asia and the Western Pacific, 1870–1914*, Amsterdam University Press, 2015, p. 28.

[92] *Ibid.*, pp. 27–28 (italics added).

[93] The Earl of Kimberley, "Kingdom of Ava – Resolution", in *Hansard*, 22 February 1886.

on an equality with a prince of the royal blood. A protectorate, then, of the *ordinary kind* seems to be prohibited.[94]

A letter from then Secretary of State for India, Lord Randolph Churchill, to the Viceroy of India, Lord Dufferin, dated 18 November 1885 confirmed a similar thought process:

> It is French intrigue which has forced us to go to Burmah; but for that element we might have treated Theebaw with severe neglect. I do venture to hold very strongly that if you set up again Burmese monarchy, you do preserve *that germ of national independence which permits of foreign hostile intrigue*. Now the Indian government have a unique opportunity which may never recur for dealing very summarily with Burma.[95]

A formal proclamation of annexation – incorporating Upper Burma into British India – was announced on 1 January 1886, one month after King Thibaw was deported. Initial attempts were made to direct policies through the Hluttaw (council of state), but the results were perceived as unsatisfactory. By the time the Viceroy of India had arrived in Mandalay in February 1886, it was concluded that direct rule was the only option.[96] During this time, the capital had been unceremoniously looted, with many royal records destroyed:[97] "Some hundreds of Chinese carpenters hammered away night and day to metamorphise Theebaw's barbariously splendid palace into modern reception rooms for Lady Dufferin and suite".[98] The palace's principal throne rooms were transformed into the 'Upper Burma Club', which would later become the centre of expatriate social life.[99] All signs pointed to the fact that the indigenous officialdom was being displaced in totality.

From a legal standpoint, the subjugation of Burma was not accomplished by early 1886, since mere seizure of state capitals was not suffi-

---

[94] Edmond Charles Browne, *The Coming of the Great Queen: A Narrative of the Acquisition of Burma*, Harrison and Sons, London, 1888, pp. 228–229, citing Colonel Edward Sladen, former British Resident and political officer attached to the expedition (italics added).

[95] Ernest C.T. Chew, "The Fall of the Burmese Kingdom in 1885: Review and Reconsideration", in *Journal of Southeast Asian Studies*, 1979, vol. 10, no. 2, p. 379.

[96] Myint-U, 2001, p. 197, see above note 67.

[97] Keck, 2015, p. 73, see above note 72.

[98] Browne, 1888, p. 237, see above note 94.

[99] Andrew Selth, *Burma, Kipling and Western Music: The Riff from Mandalay*, Routledge, New York, NY, 2016, p. 119.

cient. Otherwise, Napoleon would have automatically been entitled to annex Prussia in 1806 and Austria in 1808 by occupying their capitals.[100]
Internal disorder and indigenous resistance triggered by the annexation
would require another seven years of "pacification" operations, to subdue
first the lowlands and then the upland areas.[101] To put an end to the resistance movement, the British military resorted to systematic destruction
of villages and replacement of local officers.[102] Active contention against
foreign occupation – both in form of military hostility and political-
diplomatic protest – had traditionally been understood as means of keeping sovereignty alive in the course of subjugation. As mentioned earlier,
ever since the unilateral annexation of Lower Burma, the Court of Ava
had lacked both the material power and the appropriate diplomatic apparatus to contest British claims, which the latter also conceived as unse-
cured. It was exactly such want that had driven Burma to initiate engagement with the French. By 1886, due to the swift demise of the central
government and abolition of the Monarchy, the British authority could
easily characterize its effort in pacification as "put[ting] down dacoity",
rather than acknowledging existence of powerful insurgencies and grass-
root resistance responding to conquest and annexation.[103] Nor had any
other powers had stakes high enough in Burma to contest British acquisition. Chinese reaction had at least occupied the minds of some British
statesmen,[104] but no reaction ensued. In the eyes of international law,
therefore, Burma was subjugated.

4.4. World War II and the 'Reconquest of Burma'

The political and military crisis preceding World War II as well as the war
itself played out as a stress-test for the updated territorial regimes that had
come into being during the interwar period, mainly due to the addition of

---

[100] Stirk, 2016, p. 271, note 104 (citing Arthur Lorriot, De la nature de l'occupation de guerre,
       Lavauzelle, Paris, 1903, p. 49), see above note 34.
[101] Myint-U, 2001, p. 199, see above note 67.
[102] Helga Turku, *Isolationist State in an Interdependent World*, Routledge, London, 2016, p.
       78.
[103] Keck, 2015, p. 176, see above note 72.
[104] Ughtred Kay-Shuttleworth, "Resolution", in *Hansard*, 22 February 1886. It was assured
       that there was "every reason to believe that that desire [to show a thoroughly friendly dis-
       position towards China] was heartily reciprocated by that country [China]".

Article 10 of the Covenant of the League of Nations,[105] and the Kellogg-Briand Pact of 1928. During this period, Japan, Italy, Germany and the Soviet Union all engaged in programmes of territorial expansion. Sometimes the power attempted to cloak the unilateral nature of the expansion with a veneer of self-determination, as was the case with the annexation of Austria under the Third Reich's threat of use of force. In other cases where aggressive military operations were front and centre, the powers rooted their territorial claims on the realization of *debellatio*, as was the case with Italy's annexation of Ethiopia in 1935 and the Soviet Union's occupation of Eastern Poland in 1939. Both powers asserted that the original state had ceased to exist following the belligerency. While Italy framed its annexation of Ethiopia as an old-fashioned conquest (and had subsequently managed to extract *de jure* recognition from many League members),[106] the Soviet Union had instead downplayed its own aggression in the dissolution of the Polish state, instead framing its intervention as redress against a situation of state disintegration that had already taken place. It was speculated that such legal strategy was devised so as to cir-

---

[105] The first sentence of Article 10 of the Covenant reads: "The Members of the League undertake to respect and preserve as against external aggression the territorial integrity and existing political independence of all Members of the League".

[106] While Italy was not at all subtle with its goals of annexing Ethiopia, it had in fact attempted to frame Ethiopia as the aggressor. On 3 October 1935, the day Italy launched its invasion, the Italian Government informed the League Council "that the warlike and aggressive spirit in Ethiopia had succeeded in imposing war against Italy". The Ethiopian Emperor left the country on 2 May 1936, and the capital Addis Ababa was captured three days later. The King of Italy signed a decree-law professing "the territories and peoples which belonged to the Empire of Ethiopia are placed under the full and entire sovereignty of the Kingdom of Italy" (Article 1). After the exiled Emperor challenged the Italian claim at the League Council on 10 May 10th, the Italian representative responded with the assertion that "Nothing resembling an organized Ethiopian State exists. The only sovereignty in Ethiopia is Italian sovereignty." See Robert Langer, *Seizure of Territory: The Stimson Doctrine and Related Principles in Legal Theory and Diplomatic Practice*, Princeton University Press, Princeton, 1947, pp. 132–133. While there had been concerns of premature annexation in 1936, Great Powers had acquiesced in the conquest during the immediate years, with the Britain's *de jure* recognition in 1938 considered as the landmark event that had settled all uncertainties. This reality was again confirmed in multiple memos produced by United Nations War Crimes Commission in 1946 and 1947, that due to the substantial number of recognitions garnered by the Italian Government after its conquest in 1936, it became apparent that "the 1935-36 War between Italy and Ethiopia was a war different from the Second World War". See United Nations War Crimes Commission, Committee I, Doc. No. 80, February 13, 1947, p. 3. United Nations War Crimes Commission, Committee III, Doc. No. 50, July 23, 1946, p. 2. On British recognition of Italy's annexation, also see CHEN Ti-Chiang, *The International Law of Recognition*, Stevens and Sons, London, 1951, p. 64.

---

cumvent pre-existing peace treaties concluded between Polish and Soviet governments; and by asserting that the Polish state ceased to exist, "the agreements between the Soviet Union and Poland have come to an end".[107]

Burma had also become a target of aggression during World War II. Japan's plan to establish the Greater East Asia Co-Prosperity Sphere did not initially involve seizure of Burma. However, as Japanese forces gradually locked into a stalemate with Chinese adversaries, the 'Burma Road', which ran from Rangoon to China and functioned as the crucial lifeline sustaining Chinese resistance, had emerged as a strategic imperative.[108] The assault began in December 1941, and within 1942 both British and Chinese forces were expelled from Burma. On 1 August 1943, Japan withdrew its military administration and granted Burma independence "within the Co-Prosperity Sphere"; the two governments immediately entered into an alliance, with Burma declaring war against the British Empire and the United States. It was not until 1944, following Japan's failed attempt to advance into British India, that the tides finally turned. The series of successful Allied offensive campaigns between late-1944 and mid-1945 was commonly referred to as the 'Reconquest of Burma'.

The non-legal expression 'Reconquest of Burma' did not indicate any sort of admission by Britain that sovereignty over Burma was at one point lost to Japan due to successful Japanese 'subjugation'. In fact, the term 'reconquest' was often appropriated to describe military campaigns aimed at retaking Allied colonial possessions across the Pacific that were considered to be only temporarily lost.[109] Nor had there been any serious attempt to validate Burma's release from British sovereignty. First, the conditions for a complete 'subjugation' were never really met: the Japanese forces did not control the frontier areas as British-Japanese hostilities

---

[107] Langer, p. 254, note 254. See also, George Ginsburgs, "A Case Study in the Soviet Use of International Law: Eastern Poland in 1939", *American Journal of International Law*, 1958, vol. 52, no. 1, pp. 70-72.

[108] Frank McLynn, *The Burma Campaign: Disaster into Triumph 1942-45*, Yale University Press, New Haven, 2010, p. 6.

[109] When searching the word 'reconquest' in *The New York Times* database, we notice that that the term mainly appears in war-time articles featuring military campaigns across the Pacific. See, for instance, "Road of Reconquest [of Hollandia (Dutch New Guinea)]", 25 April 1944; "Closing in on Guam", 12 July 1944; "Coming Attacks on Japan Must Cover Vast Distances", 17 September 1944; "Progress in the Palaus", 19 September 1944; and "Revival of the Philippines", 15 April 1945.

continued on the Bengal-Burmese frontier. Thus, Britain's claimed sovereignty over Burma endured World War II and was later reinstated when Japan was driven out.[110] As Morten Bergsmo points out in Chapter 7 below, the British strangely enough referred to their 'reoccupation' of Burma at the end of World War II, as if it was always an occupation. This reflects the British desire to establish rapid control by use of the military's civil administration, rather than the constitutional regime of the 1935 Burma Act.

Second, distinct from Italy's 'subjugation' of Ethiopia to which Great Powers had eventually acquiesced (partially due to the policy of appeasement), Japan's war-time conquest in Burma had never received any *de jure* recognition. Out of needs for war-time propaganda, the Allies had remained adamant in addressing the new administration another puppet-government controlled by Japan. Third, albeit the veneer of enabling 'co-prosperity' of Asian nations, Burma never regained its external sovereignty and important aspects of her internal sovereignty (on matters related to economy which were too important for Japanese war efforts not to be subjected to its control). Burma's nominal independence resembled the arrangement of a protectorate, which would require consent from the original sovereign.

But the war efforts against Japan ended up transforming Burmese nationalism. The Burma Act of 1935 had already separated Burma from British India as of 1937, granting Burma a form of semi-autonomy. Yet, the Burmese were largely excluded from the defence forces. World War II created an army comprised of Burmese and their military heroes, rekindling its proud military tradition, one that was terminated by the British

---

[110] J.J.G. Syatauw, *Some Newly Established Asian States and Development of International Law*, Martinus Nijhoff, The Hague, 1961, p. 78. The first contention appears to have been echoed by the International Military Tribunal at Nuremberg. In *In re Goering and Others*, the Tribunal stated: "In the view of the Tribunal it is unnecessary in this case to decide whether this doctrine of subjugation, dependent as it is upon military conquest, has any application where the subjugation is the result of the crime of aggressive war. *The doctrine was never considered to be applicable so long as there was an army in the field attempting to restore the occupied countries to their true owners, and in this case, therefore, the doctrine could not apply to the territories occupied after 1st September 1939*" (italics added). Yutaka Arai-Takahashi, *The Law of Occupation: Continuity and Change of International Humanitarian Law, and its Interaction with International Human Rights Law*, Martinus Nijhoff, Leiden, 2009, p. 37, citing the International Military Tribunal at Nuremberg, *In re Goering and Others*, Judgment, 1 October 1946, 13 AD 203, Case No. 92, para. 220.

subjugation.[111] Movement towards real independence for Burma had become irreversible at this point of history, although the British were late in
appreciating the full scope of the development.

4.5. Conclusions

In this chapter, I sought to examine the doctrine of 'subjugation' or '*debellatio*' presented in positivist treatises of the nineteenth and twentieth
centuries. The inquiry begins with an explanation of the unfamiliarity of
the concept itself as 'subjugation' presumed the admissibility of acquisitive wars, with territory and population as the ultimate spoils. Entering the
twentieth century, the prohibition of initially aggressive wars, later threat
or use of force, stripped away the prerequisite for 'subjugation' to possess
any legal significance. Technical differentiation between notions such as
'conquest' and 'subjugation' thus appeared obsolete and irrelevant. The
continuing process of outlawing war had also prompted changes in wording, with the violent, menacing 'conquest' replaced by the more opaque
and neutral notion of 'occupation'.

What then should be our takeaway from these distant histories
about 'conquest' and 'subjugation', and how do they relate to our current
legal order? First and foremost, as Section 4.2. indicates, it must be re-
membered that territorial regimes in international law did not solely serve
the purpose of legalising aggression and territorial expansion. The flipside
constituted rules and constraints for determining when something as valuable as territory is 'truly' taken. As part of the international legal discourse,
doctrines related to 'subjugation' also provide a discursive space in which
debates over the justice of aggression and domination may take place.

Second, national might – in the form of military power, domestic
political strength, and diplomatic mastery – is also a prerequisite for con-
tending against abrupt usurpation of territorial title. Those who contested
'subjugation' with the claim of 'premature annexation' were themselves
semi-peripheral states (in other words, already members to the family of
nations) and were able to survive the first blow of military intrusion (for
example, Orange Free State or Ethiopia). In the unfortunate case of Burma, as the Court of Ava failed to swiftly modernize itself, it lacked both

---

[111] Christopher Alan Bayly and Timothy Norman Harper, *Forgotten Wars: Freedom and
Revolution in Southeast Asia*, The Belkap Press of Harvard University Press, Cambridge,
2007, pp. 16–17.

the military-technical strength to stall British intrusion, as well as the diplomatic tools to contest British claims (Section 4.3.).

Third, and lastly, international lawyers should not deny the fundamental importance of force in international life and, thus, for the international legal order. The great disparity in terms of military technology and organization in the US–Iraq (Section 4.1.) and Britain–Burma wars (Section 4.3.) enabled the advantageous party to inflict violent and sudden death upon the weaker party. Such overwhelming defeats would have been unimaginable to Europe during the eighteenth and nineteenth centuries whence the classical rules on territorial acquisition and extinction of sovereignty derive. It seems likely that the world has moved past "the unipolar moment"[112] that lasted several decades, and that, for better or worse, the US is reluctant to engage in further "nation-building"[113] for the time being. International lawyers should nevertheless realise the extent of the discipline's entanglement with a violent past.

---

[112] Charles Krauthammer, "The Unipolar Moment", in *Foreign Affairs*, 1990–1991, vol. 70, no. 1.

[113] Philip Ewing, "'We Are Not Nation-Building Again', Trump Says While Unveiling Afghanistan Strategy", *National Public Radio*, 21 August 2017.

5

The Notion of Continuous or Continuing Crimes in International Criminal Law

Matthias Neuner[*]

5.1. Introduction

While most offences are committed in one single act, international criminal law also recognises a certain category of offences which have a continuing or continuous nature. For example, imprisonment[1] in violation of
fundamental rules of international law as defined in the Statute of the International Criminal Court ('ICC statute'), begins if a person is, without
justification, unlawfully deprived of his or her liberty and lasts until the
day on which the victim regains his liberty. The prohibited conduct is the
continuing unlawful detention of the victim. This main conduct is assisted
by a series of smaller acts (or omissions) which were necessary for the
detention, but which are absorbed by or consummated in the overall criminal conduct of deprivation of liberty: to arrest the victim, feed the person
in captivity, prevent attempts to flee, and to eventually release the victim.
To adequately capture the wrong and violation of the protected interest
(*Rechtsgut*), various domestic legal orders have specifically defined and
developed the notion of continuous or continuing crime. Can the same be
said about international criminal law?

This chapter discusses the notion of continuous or continuing crime,
its application to and current scope in international criminal law. The first
section below contains observations about the terminology, the definition,
and the notion itself. The second section analyses five offences and dis-

---

[*]   **Matthias Neuner** is Trial Counsel, Office of the Prosecutor ('OTP'), Special Tribunal for
Lebanon ('STL'). The views expressed in this chapter are those of the author and do not
necessarily reflect the views of the STL.
[1]   Rome Statute of the International Criminal Court, 17 July 1998, Article 7(1)(e) ('ICC Statute') (http://www.legaltools.org/doc/7b9af9/).

cusses whether and to what extend these qualify as continuous or continuing crime in international criminal law. Finally, a conclusion is offered.

5.2. Terminology, Definition and Notion

On the international level, there is currently no uniformly accepted terminology on continuous or continuing crime. This notion has neither been explicitly codified in international treaties, nor statutes of international criminal courts. The drafters of the ICC Statute decided to entrust the ICC judiciary with defining this notion, including its scope, and with applying it.[2] Instead of the drafters of the ICC Statute and the Elements of Crime ('EoC'), the judges' case law will decide. The ICC judges can rely on some case law of other international criminal tribunals where also judges had to decide for themselves, as the statutes and laws of these other tribunals were also silent.

5.2.1. Terminology

Judges or chambers from various international criminal tribunals seldomly referred to this notion. However, if the international judiciary made references, it uses no consistent terminology. Often a conflation between the adjectives 'continuous' and 'continuing' can be observed. Examples include continuous act,[3] continuous crime,[4] continuing offence,[5] continu-

---

[2] Mohamed M. El Zeidy, "The Ugandan Government Triggers the First Test of the Complementarity Principle: An Assessment of the First State's Party Referral to the ICC", in *International Criminal Law Review*, 2005, vol. 5, no. 1, p. 91.

[3] Blackstone's, Criminal Practice, Oxford University Press, 2018, para. A1.8 ('Blackstone's, Criminal Practice').

[4] Special Court for Sierra Leone ('SCSL'), *Prosecutor v. Charles Ghankay Taylor*, Trial Chamber II, Judgment, 18 May 2012, SCSL-03-01-T, paras. 118, 443, 1018, 1025, 1357, 1613 ('SCSL, TC judgment Taylor') (https://www.legal-tools.org/doc/8075e7/).

[5] UN General Assembly ('UN GA'), A/Res/47/133, 12 February 1993, containing the GA Resolution 47-133: Declaration on the Protection of all Persons from Enforced Disappearance, 18 December 1992, Article 17 ('GA Declaration Enforced Disappearance 1992') (https://www.legal-tools.org/doc/534c27/); International Criminal Tribunal for Rwanda ('ICTR'), *The Prosecutor v. Nahimana and Ngeze*, Appeals Chamber, Decision on Interlocutory Appeals, Joint separate opinion of Judge Chand Vohrah and Judge Rafael Nieto-Navia, 5 September 2000, ICTR 97-27-AR72 and ICTR 96-11-AR72, para. 7 ('ICTR, AC Interlocutory Decision Nahimana and Ngeze – separate opinion Vohrah and Nieto Navia') (https://www.legal-tools.org/doc/089520/); ICTR, *The Prosecutor v. Laurent Semanza*, Trial Chamber III, Judgment, separate and dissenting opinion of judge Pavel Dolenc, 15 May 2003, ICTR-97-20-T, para. 32 (https://www.legal-tools.org/doc/6e5e12/); Blackstone's, Criminal Practice, D11.32, see above note 3.

ing crime,[6] offence of a continuing nature[7] or continuous nature,[8] or permanent crime.[9] Trial Chamber II of the Special Court for Sierra Leone ('SCSL') referred to this notion as a prolonged offence of a continuous nature.[10]

These terminological differences indicate the early stage of transfer of this notion from the domestic to the international level and its application there. Conflation of terminology is indicative of the early stage of the process of defining and applying the notion which involves the efforts of various 'legislators', meaning chambers or individual judges in international criminal tribunals. They are assisted by scholars who analyse the case law and offer comments. Conflated use of terminology may also be a side-product of two elements: (1) absence of treaty law, and (2) the bench's composition.

Chambers in an international court are composed of judges of various legal and geographical backgrounds.[11] This requires that findings and efforts to transfer and develop a notion to the international level are subjected to 'compromise' among colleagues in the same chamber. Further, a *lacuna* regarding the details of the notion of continuous or continuing

---

[6] ICTR, *The Prosecutor v. Nsengiyumva*, Trial Chamber III, Decision on the Defence Motions Objecting to the Jurisdiction of the Trial Chamber on the Amended Indictment, 13 April 2000, ICTR-96-12-I, para. 28, p. 4 (https://www.legal-tools.org/doc/944793/); International Criminal Tribunal for the former Yugoslavia ('ICTY'), *Prosecutor v. Popović et al.*, Trial Chamber, Judgement vol. 1, 10 June 2010, IT-05-88-T, para. 876, p. 349 (https://www.legal-tools.org/doc/481867/).

[7] ICTR, *The Prosecutor v. Nahimana et al.*, Trial Chamber I, Judgement and Sentence, 3 December 2003, ICTR-99-52-T, para. 1044, p. 345 (https://www.legal-tools.org/doc/45b8b6/).

[8] ICC, *The Prosecutor v. Thomas Lubanga Dyilo*, Trial Chamber, Judgment pursuant to Article 74 of the Statute, 14 March 2012, ICC-01/04-01/06, para. 618, p. 282 (https://www.legal-tools.org/doc/677866/).

[9] ICC, *The Prosecutor v. Thomas Lubanga Dyilo*, Pre-Trial Chamber I, Decision on the Confirmation of Charges, 29 January 2007, ICC-01/04-01/06, para. 248, p. 85 ('ICC, PTC-Decision on Confirmation of Charges (Lubanga)') (https://www.legal-tools.org/doc/b7ac4f/).

[10] SCSL, *The Prosecutor v. Alex Tamba Brima et al.*, Trial Chamber II, Judgement, 20 June 2007, SCSL-04-16-T, paras. 39, 1280, 1820, pp. 31, 365, 502 ('SCSL, TC-judgment – AFRC') (https://www.legal-tools.org/doc/87ef08/); compare also International Convention for the Protection of all Persons from Enforced Disappearance, 20 December 2006, Article 8 (1)(b) ('2006 Convention on Enforced Disappearance') (https://www.legal-tools.org/doc/0d0674/).

[11] Compare ICC Statute, Article 36(8)(a), see above note 1.

crime exists due to absence of treaty law and written principles and rules of international law. To fill this *lacuna* poses a challenge for the judges who prefer to root their findings on firm ground. However, it was the decision of the negotiators in Rome to entrust to the judges the solving of this problem, which includes in effect the transfer of this notion, initially developed in domestic criminal law, to the level of international criminal law through case law.

The judges in international criminal tribunals could deliver a solid transfer by reverting to general principles of law derived from national laws of legal systems of the world.[12] The European Court of Human Rights ('ECtHR') chose this approach and distilled the relevant principle underlying the notion of continuous or continuing crime by comparing legislation of different European countries.[13]

A review of the current jurisprudence of international criminal tribunals reveals that none of these institutions has engaged in a comparable process on this notion yet. As a result, relevant findings of international criminal tribunals are usually brief and rather cryptic.

5.2.2. Definition

International criminal tribunals found in relation to certain offences that these constitute continuous or continuing crimes. However, they neither elaborated on the underlying notion of continuing crime nor on its scope in the context of individual crimes. Thus, until today, international criminal tribunals abstained from providing a definition of what this notion exactly entails. Therefore, guidance is sought from the work of the International Law Commission ('ILC'), case law of the ECtHR, scholars' writings and 'general principles of law derived from national laws of legal systems of the world'[14]. For laws of the United States of America, Black's Law Dictionary defines continuous crime as:

1. A crime that continues after an initial illegal act has been consummated; a crime that involves ongoing elements. [...]
2. A crime [...] that continues over an extended period.[15]

---

[12] *Ibid.*, Article 21(1)(b) and (1)(c).

[13] European Court of Human Rights ('ECtHR'), *Rohlena v. The Czech Republic*, Grand Chamber, Judgment, 27 January 2015, Application no. 59552/08, paras. 30–37, pp. 8–11 ('ECtHR, Judgment Rohlena v. Czech Republic') (https://www.legal-tools.org/doc/2bcff4/).

[14] Compare ICC Statute, Article 21(1)(c), see above note 1.

[15] Black's Law Dictionary, ninth edition, 2009, St. Paul, p. 427.

On the international level, there is neither in international nor in international criminal law, a widely accepted definition of what constitutes a continuous or continuing crime. The issue is further complicated as international law addresses various subjects, including States and individuals.

International criminal law addresses the individual by defining international crimes and assigning criminal responsibility to individuals. By contrast, the emerging law on state responsibility for internationally wrongful acts addresses States, not individuals. Keeping this distinction in mind, some limited guidance for what constitutes a continuous or continuing crime can be sought from the International Law Commission's ('ILC') draft code on the responsibility of States for internationally wrongful acts:[16]

> Article 14:
>
> Extension in time of the breach of an international obligation
>
> [...]
>
> (2) The breach of an international obligation by an act of a State having a continuing character extends over the entire period during which the act continues and remains not in conformity with the international obligation.

The ILC did not seek to define a continuous crime, but a continuous breach of international law. In the ILC's view three requirements need to be fulfilled: (1) the existence of an international obligation, (2) a conduct of a State which breaches this obligation, and (3) this breach continues.

Guided by the emerging international law on State responsibility, Joost Pauwelyn defines a continuous violation as a

> [b]reach of an international obligation by an act of a subject of international law extending in time and causing a duration or continuance in time of that breach.[17]

Pauwelyn's definition again contains the three aforementioned requirements, but his definition is broader than the ILC's in that it speaks about conduct committed by "subjects of international law". Thus, the

---

[16] UN, General Assembly resolution 56/83, A/RES/56/83, 12 December 2001, containing International Law Commission ('ILC'), Responsibility of States for Internationally Wrongful Acts, Yearbook of the International Law Commission, 2001, vol. II, Part Two, Article 14 ('ILC Draft Code State Responsibility') (https://www.legal-tools.org/doc/jj4mjf/).

[17] Joost Pauwelyn, "The Concept of a 'Continuing Violation' of an International Legal Obligation: Selected Problems", in *British Year Book of International Law*, 1995, vol. 66, p. 415 ('Pauwelyn, Continuing Violation').

author of the violation could be a State as well as an individual if the latter is a subject of international law. As international criminal law creates obligations such as 'do not enslave persons' or 'do not abduct civilians by illegal force and let them disappear', these prohibitions are addressed to human beings. However, there is an important difference between international law on responsibility of States and international criminal law. For international law it is generally sufficient that a conduct is prohibited, meaning defined by a norm of international law as wrongful. That in itself is insufficient for international criminal law. For a prohibition of international law to rise to the character of international criminal law, the norm must not only define the conduct as 'wrongful', but as criminal, meaning the norm defines the breach and provides for individual responsibility in form of a penal sanction.

The legal obligation has to arise out of a norm of international criminal law. Thus, for a continuous or continuing crime it is insufficient if a violation of (international) human rights law or of ordinary international law has occurred which then continues. Rather, an international legal norm is violated, and at this time the prohibition incurs individual criminal responsibility, meaning a penal sanction for an individual (and not responsibility for a State).[18] This understanding is in accordance with the principles of legality,[19] non-retroactivity,[20] and *nullum crimen sine lege*.[21] The ILC clarified:

---

[18] ICC Statute, Article 22(1), see above note 1; compare UN, ILC, Draft Statute for an ICC, 22 July 1994, Yearbook of the International Law Commission, 1994, vol. II, Part Two, Article 39 ('ILC Draft Statute for an ICC') (https://www.legal-tools.org/doc/9596bb/).

[19] ILC Draft Statute for an ICC, Article 39, see above note 18; UN, ILC, Draft Code of Crimes against the Peace and Security of Mankind ('CCaPSM'), Yearbook of the International Law Commission, 1996, vol. II, Part Two, Articles 2, 11 (https://www.legal-tools.org/doc/bb5adc/).

[20] Articles 11, 22 (1), ICC Statute, see above note 1; ILC draft CCaPSM, Article 13, see above note 19.

[21] UNGA, Universal Declaration of Human Rights, 10 December 1948, Resolution 217A III, UN Doc. A/810, Article 11(2) (https://www.legal-tools.org/doc/de5d83/); Third Geneva Convention relative to the Treatment of Prisoners of War, 12 August 1949, Article 49 (https://www.legal-tools.org/doc/365095/); UNGA, International Covenant on Civil and Political Rights, 16 December 1966, A/Res/2200(XXI)/A, Article 15 ('ICCPR') (https://www.legal-tools.org/doc/2838f3/); Additional Protocol II to the Geneva Conventions of 12 August 1949 and relating to the Protection of Victims of non-international armed Conflicts, 7 December 1978, Article 6(2)(c) (https://www.legal-tools.org/doc/fd14c4/); ICC Statute, Article 22, see above note 1.

> In the case of treaty crimes the principle [nullum crimen sine lege] has an additional and crucial role to play, since it is necessary that the treaty in question should have been applicable in respect of the conduct of the accused which is the subject of the charge. [...] In principle noncompliance with the *litera verba* of a treaty will not be sufficient to constitute a crime if the treaty did not apply to the accused, whether in accordance with its terms or—perhaps more importantly— because the treaty did not apply as law to the conduct of the accused.[22]

This refers to continuous or continuing crime as a (1) conduct which (2) violates an international criminal law obligation, and (3) this breach continues in time.

Regarding the third element, it is required that the breach of the obligation of international criminal law continues in time instead of being instantaneous only. 'Instantaneous' means that an act, for example, a shot with a revolver, resolves only on a specific moment in time or to a certain date. Thus, the conduct ceases to exist once the time-period necessary for the act's completion has expired.[23] For example, in an armed conflict, a State's air force shoots down a civilian airplane which lawfully flies through that State's airspace. This act constitutes murder[24] in the form of an instantaneous act as the shooting down of the airplane is a single act which was confined in time and killed all passengers on the plane. Only the effects of that singular act last, the taking of the passengers' lives, while the act itself, shooting a missile at the plane, has ended. Hence, this conduct is not an example of a continuous or continuing act.

By contrast, for a continuing crime it is required that the act continues and not merely its effects and consequences.[25]

---

[22] ILC Draft Statute for an ICC, Article 39, commentary para. 3, p. 55, see above note 18.

[23] Jean Salmon, "The Sources if International Responsibility, Ch. 27 Duration of the breach", in Crawford *et al.* (eds.), *The Law of International Responsibility*, p. 384 ('Salmon, Sources').

[24] ICC Statute, Article 7(1)(a), see above note 1.

[25] Pauwelyn, Continuing Violation, p. 419, see above note 17; compare ICTR, *The Prosecutor v. Nahimana et al.*, Appeals Chamber, Judgement, 28 November 2007, ICTR-99-52-A, para. 723 ('ICTR, AC judgment Nahimana (2007)') (https://www.legal-tools.org/doc/04e4f9/).

5.2.3. Notion

The notion emphasises that certain conduct constitutes an ongoing breach or a series of repeated breaches which continue in time, so considering the violation as ongoing characterizes and captures the entire wrong.

Regarding the continuing nature, domestic systems from the common and continental law traditions emphasize two different scenarios: they distinguish between continuing criminal offence ('infraction continue', 'Dauerdelikt', 'reato permanente' or 'trvající trestný čin') and a continuous offence ('infraction continuée', 'fortgesetzte Handlung', 'reato continuato' or 'pokračující trestný čin').[26]

5.2.3.1. Continuous Offence

Domestic legal systems and the ILC understand by 'continuous crime' an offence which consists of several discrete acts all of which contain the elements of the same (or similar) offence committed over a certain period of time.[27]

The ECtHR observed the following elements relating to objective (*actus reus*) or subjective (*mens rea*) criteria:[28]

1. criminal acts against the same legally protected interest ('Rechtsgut', 'bien juridique' or 'bene giuridico'); in addition, it is often required that the identities of the perpetrator and of the victim be the same on each occasion;

2. there is at least a similarity in the manner of execution of the individual acts (*modus operandi*), or there are other material circumstances connecting them which constitute a whole (*actus reus*);

3. there is a temporal connection between the different individual acts, which is to be assessed in the particular circumstances of each case;

4. there is the same, repeated criminal intent or purpose (*mens rea*) for all the individual acts, although they do not all have to be planned *ab initio*;

5. the individual acts comprise, either explicitly or implicitly, the constituent elements of the criminal offence(s).

---

[26] ECtHR, Judgment Rohlena v. Czech Republic, para. 28, p. 8, see above note 13.

[27] *Ibid.*, para. 28b.

[28] *Ibid.*, para. 33; compare also para. 72.

International Criminal Tribunal for Rwanda ('ICTR') judge Dolenc partially mirrored this approach in his separate opinion to the judgment in *Prosecutor v. Semanza:*[29]

> Each act in a series of separate but closely related acts fulfils all the elements of a certain criminalisation. In such circumstances, it is possible to regard the entire transaction, or series of repeated crimes as a single crime. For these acts to be joined together, certain linking elements should be taken into account, such as the repetition of the same kind of crimes, the uniformity of the perpetrator's intent, the proximity in time between the acts, the location, the victim or class of victims, the object or purpose and the opportunity.

This approach looks at each of several violations individually to check whether each, some or all of these acts are related to each other (or not) and thus can be assessed as continuing. If it is possible to consider the totality of the act as a series, then the conduct as a whole can be assessed as aggregating wrong.[30]

Regarding the responsibility of States, the ILC has adopted this approach of 'aggregating wrong' for composite acts:

> Article 15:
>
> Breach consisting of a composite act
>
> (1) The breach of an international obligation by a State through a *series of actions or omissions* defined in *aggregate* as wrongful occurs when the action or omission occurs which, taken with the other actions or omissions, is sufficient to constitute the wrongful act.
>
> (2) In such a case, the *breach extends* over the entire period starting with the first of the actions or omissions of the series and lasts for as long as these actions or omissions are repeated and remain not in conformity with the international obligation.[31]

---

[29] ICTR, *The Prosecutor v. Semanza*, Separate and Dissenting Opinion of Judge Pavel Dolenc to trial chamber judgment, 15 May 2003, ICTR-97-20-T, para. 32 (https://www.legal-tools.org/doc/6e5e12/).

[30] Kyle Graham, "The Continuing Violations Doctrine", in *Gonzaga Law Review*, 2008, vol. 43, no. 2, pp. 280, 283 ('Graham, Continuing violations').

[31] ILC Draft Code State Responsibility, Article 15 (emphasis added), see above note 16.

5.2.3.2.   Continuing Crime

Domestic legal systems and scholars understand by continuing crime a single act (or omission) which breaches an obligation of (international) criminal law and this violation lasts over a certain period of time.[32] Usually, the main act had caused an illegal situation and this status is prolonged through a series of essentially passive or partially active behaviour. For example, following the revolution in Iran in 1979, protesters entered the United States embassy and illegally detained the diplomatic and consular staff there for a prolonged period of time. The International Court of Justice ('ICJ') found that "the Iranian authorities (having withheld from the Chargé d'affaires and other staff the necessary protection and facilities to permit them to leave the Ministry in safety) have committed a continuing breach of their obligations".[33]

The ICTR omitted to define a continuing crime independently, but merely referred to Black's Law dictionary which relates to domestic United States law.[34]

Aysev identified five elements that make up a continuing crime:[35] (1) A precipitating act by the perpetrator(s) creates an unlawful state of affairs that is prolonged through the consummation period; (2) the *actus reus* of the crime continues to take place as long as the unlawful state of affairs is maintained by the subsequent conduct of the perpetrator(s); (3) the continuation of the unlawful state of affairs and the consequent harm is contingent upon the will of the perpetrator(s); (4) the legally protected interest of the victims continues to be infringed over the consummation period; and (5) the harm caused to the victim(s) accumulates over time.

---

[32] Compare ECtHR, Judgment Rohlena v. Czech Republic, para. 28(a), p. 8, see above note 13; compare for responsibility of states, Salmon, Sources, p. 386, see above note 23.

[33] Compare International Court of Justice ('ICJ'), *Case Concerning United States Diplomatic and Consular Staff in Tehran*, Judgment, 24 May 1980, ICJ Reports 1980, para. 78 (https://www.legal-tools.org/doc/4a9050/).

[34] ICTR, AC Judgment Nahimana (2007), para. 721, see also above note 25.

[35] Uzay Yasar Aysev, "Continuing of Settled? Prosecution of Israeli Settlements under Article 8(2)(b)(viii) of the Rome Statute", in *The Palestinian Yearbook of International Law*, 2019, pp. 50, 51 ('Aysev, Article 8(2)(b)(viii)').

The second approach does not aggregate wrongs, but divides the causes of conduct.[36] It dissects behaviour, instead of aggravating it (as the approach of continuous crime would).[37]

5.2.4. Effect of Continuous or Continuing Crime on Temporal Jurisdiction and Non-Retroactivity

If the notion of continuous or continuing crime is accepted on the international level, it may have an effect on the principle of non-retroactivity and temporal jurisdiction of an international criminal court.[38] If certain crimes continue and their commission has started before the temporal jurisdiction of an international tribunal, but continues to be committed into the period when the court's jurisdiction has started, then this notion is relevant for the principle of non-retroactivity and temporal jurisdiction of that court. International criminal tribunals have a defined temporal jurisdiction and the prosecution is entrusted with investigating and charging crimes which occurred within each tribunal's jurisdiction. Thus, the question poses itself what a prosecutor does with conduct of the accused person which preceded the time-period of temporary jurisdiction.

For example, the ICTR had temporal jurisdiction for crimes occurring after 1 January 1994.[39] What should a prosecutor do with an accused person who already committed crimes in 1993, meaning during the build-up phase for the genocide, but clearly outside the temporal jurisdiction of the ICTR?

5.2.4.1. ICC Negotiations

During the negotiations of the relevant articles in the ICC Statute, the issue of continuous or continuing crime was not openly but indirectly[40]

---

36   Graham, Continuing Violations, p. 283, see above note 30.

37   *Ibid.*, p. 281.

38   Compare ICC Statute, Articles 11, 24(1), see above note 1; Law on the Establishment of the Extraordinary Chambers, with inclusion of amendments as promulgated on 27 October 2004, NS/RKM/1004/006, Article 33 new (2) ('Law on ECCC') (https://www.legal-tools.org/doc/9b12f0/), in connection with ICCPR, Article 15, see above note 21.

39   Compare ICTR Statute, Article 1, as contained in UN Security Council resolution 955, UN Doc. S/RES/955, 8 November 1994 ('ICTR Statute') (https://www.legal-tools.org/doc/8732d6/).

40   Per Saland, "International Criminal Law Principles", in Roy S. Lee (ed.), *The ICC: The Making of the Rome Statute – Issues, Negotiations, Results*, Kluwer Law International, 1999, p. 196 ('Saland, Principles').

touched upon in relation to both the temporal jurisdiction of the ICC and the principle of non-retroactivity.

5.2.4.1.1.   Principle of Non-Retroactivity

At the Rome conference the discussions on non-retroactivity centred around whether to add a verb and, if so, which one. The inclusion of four verbs were discussed:

> No person shall be criminally responsible under this Statute for conduct [committed][occurred][commenced][completed] prior to the entry into force of the Statute.[41]

Each verb had a special nuance and different connotation when translated into the six official working languages which made agreement difficult so that the Coordinator of the Working group proposed to drop any verb in the sentence, a solution which was agreeable to the delegates.[42] The Drafting Committee added a footnote which provided that the "question has been raised as regards a conduct which started before the entry into force and which continues after the entry into force".[43] This footnote disappeared before the delegates were asked to adopt the final version in Rome.[44]

Following the adoption of Article 24 on non-retroactivity, the delegates negotiated a sister provision on temporal jurisdiction.

5.2.4.1.2.   Temporal Jurisdiction

A report by the Committee of the Whole during the Rome negotiations stated:

> 73. Article 8 ("Temporal jurisdiction"), as the representative of Lebanon had pointed out, did not cover acts that began before but *continued* after the entry into force of the Statute. Care should be taken not to bar prosecution for such acts,

---

[41] *Ibid.*

[42] *Ibid.*; William A. Schabas, *The International Criminal Court: A commentary on the Rome Statute*, Oxford University Press, 2010, p. 419.

[43] UN, Draft Report of the Drafting Committee to the Committee of the Whole, Part 3. General Principles of Criminal Law, UN Doc. A/CONF.183/C.1/L.65, 13 July 1998, p. 2 (https://www.legal-tools.org/doc/d78b35/).

[44] UN, Draft Statute for the International Criminal Court. Part 3, General principles of criminal law, UN Doc. A/CONF.183/C.1/L.76/Add.3, 16 July 1998, pp. 1–2 (https://www.legal-tools.org/doc/7595e9/).

> and the words "unless the crimes continue after that date" should be added at the end of paragraph 1.[45]

However, the proposed phrase which would have clarified the situation for continuous or continuing crimes was not adopted. Without such clarification, the ICC Statute now reads:

> Article 11 Jurisdiction *ratione temporis*
>
> 1. The Court has jurisdiction only with respect to crimes committed after the entry into force of this Statute.
> 2. If a State becomes a Party to this Statute after its entry into force, the Court may exercise its jurisdiction only with respect to crimes committed after the entry into force of this Statute for that State […].

Whether the non-inclusion of the clarifying phrase proposed by Lebanon means that the ICC is barred from adjudicating continuing crimes if their commission had begun before and continued after the ICC's jurisdiction began, needs to be decided by the judges.

5.2.4.1.3.   Inference of Negotiations on (Non-)Usage of the Notion of Continuous or Continuing Crime

What makes the question whether or not the notion of continuous or continuing crimes can be used confusing is that delegates agreed to using the verb "committed" in Article 11 ICC Statute, but could not agree on using any verb in Article 24(1) insofar the co-ordinator of the working group observed a "discrepancy that will not make it easy for the Court to resolve the issue of continuous crime".[46] Sadat argues that Article 24 is more restrictive than Article 11 and therefore excludes continuous crimes from the jurisdiction of the ICC.[47]

The only explanation the co-ordinator came up with regarding the discrepancy in usage of the verb "committed" in Article 11 was that a Turkish delegate made a very strong representation to that effect.[48] It follows that the omission or usage of a verb in Articles 11 and 24 appears to

---

[45]   UN Diplomatic Conference of Plenipotentiaries on the Establishment of an ICC, 9th meeting of the Committee of the Whole, UN Doc. A/CONF.183/C.1/SR.9, 22 June 1998, para. 73 (emphasis added) (https://www.legal-tools.org/doc/253396/).

[46]   Saland, Principles, p. 197, see above note 40.

[47]   Leila N. Sadat, *The International Criminal Court and the Transformation of International Law: Justice for the new Millennium*, Martinus Nijhoff, 2002, p. 186.

[48]   Saland, Principles, p. 197, see above note 40.

be a mere product of compromise in complex international negotiations, and not the result of negotiators deliberately omitting or including a verb in both provisions. Thus, the ICC may refrain from calling this discrepancy between both provisions a matter of substance.

5.2.4.2. Guidance in the Case Law of Other International Courts

Regarding the effect which the notion of continuous or continuing crime may have on the ICC's temporal jurisdiction, the judges may be guided by two other internationalised judicial institutions which decided this issue for their own jurisdictions and came to different conclusions: the Extraordinary Chambers in the Courts of Cambodia ('ECCC') confirmed its jurisdiction, while the ICTR denied it for conduct which had begun before the entry into force of its temporal jurisdictions.

5.2.4.2.1. ECCC

The Prosecution charged two senior accused persons, Nuon Chea and Khieu Samphan, not with carrying out the *actus reus* personally, but with having devised the common criminal purpose of a joint criminal enterprise and with having contributed in a relevant manner to its implementation. It was legally problematic that the acts of planning and devising the common criminal purpose related to conduct which had occurred before the beginning of the temporal jurisdiction of the ECCC on 17 April 1975.[49] The Trial Chamber convicted Nuon and Khieu including based on facts and conduct which had occurred before that date.[50] Both men appealed their conviction relying on the narrower temporal jurisdiction of the ECCC.[51]

---

[49] Law on ECCC, Articles 2 new, 5, see above note 38.

[50] ECCC, *The Prosecutor v. NUON Chea et al.*, Trial Chamber, Judgment, 7 August 2014, Case 002/01, 002/19-09-2007/ECCC/TC, paras. 878–891, 899, 900, 909, 918–931, 997–1003, 1014, 1015, 1039–1043, 1045, 1046 (https://www.legal-tools.org/doc/4888de/).

[51] ECCC, NUON Chea's Appeal against the Judgment in case 002/1, Supreme Court Chamber, 29 December 2014, 002/19-09-2007-ECCC-SC, paras. 627 635, 663 (https://www.legal-tools.org/doc/d36103/). Nuon argued: "In respect of the Phase I movement and Tuol Po Chrey, the Chamber relied almost entirely on *facts outside the temporal jurisdiction of this Tribunal*. Equally, the findings that Nuon Chea planned, instigated, and aided and abetted crimes committed during Phase II relied (in a more limited way) on facts *outside* the temporal jurisdiction", *ibid.*, para. 627 (emphasis added); ECCC, Mr. KHIEU Samphan's Defence Appeal Brief against the Judgment in Case 002/01, Supreme Court Chamber, 29 December 2014, 002/19-09-2007-ECCC-SC, paras. 9, 231 (https://www.legal-tools.org/doc/bf4c9f/).

The Supreme Court of the ECCC emphasized that the accused had engaged in a cluster of interrelated transactions together with the acts of those who personally carried out the *actus rei*, with all involved acting jointly with a criminal purpose as co-perpetrators.[52] The Supreme Court emphasized that

> it would be unnatural to break up such a protracted and complex transaction as it is only intelligible if all of its components are considered together.[53]

Highlighting the accused's participation in multi-actor criminal activity similar to joint criminal enterprise the chamber continued:

> [G]iven that the contributions of the Accused occurred *before* 17 April 1975 were part of a cluster of transactions of a joint criminal enterprise that *continued* over a period of time and brought to fruition the relevant *actus rei* committed within the jurisdictional period of the ECCC, the crime in question "was committed" *within* the temporal jurisdiction of the ECCC, [...] and the Accused remains responsible for them unless by 17 April 1975 he would have quit the joint criminal enterprise.[54]

5.2.4.2.2.   ICTR Appeals Chamber

Trial Chamber I convicted Ferdinand Nahimana for acts constituting incitement to genocide considering, *inter alia*, conduct which had occurred as early as in March 1992 and 1993,[55] prior to the ICTR's temporal jurisdiction which began 1 January 1994.[56] Particularly, the Trial Chamber held that

---

[52] Compare ECCC, *The Prosecutor v. Nuon and Khieu*, Supreme Court Chamber, Appeal Judgment, 23 November 2016, 002/19-09-2007-ECCC/SC, para. 215 ('ECCC, Appeal judgment Nuon *et al.*') (https://www.legal-tools.org/doc/e66bb3/).

[53] *Ibid.*, para. 215.

[54] *Ibid.*, para. 217 (emphasis added).

[55] ICTR, *The Prosecutor v. Nahimana et al.*, Trial Chamber I, Judgement and Sentence, 3 December 2003, ICTR-99-51-T, paras. 634, 667, 691 ('ICTR, TC judgment Nahimana') (https://www.legal-tools.org/doc/45b8b6/); namely para. 620: "The Chamber has considered the allegations regarding Nahimana's role as Director of ORINFOR in connection with the killings that took place in Bugesera in 1992. Although these events fall *outside the temporal jurisdiction* of the Tribunal, the Chamber considers the conduct of the Accused in this capacity with regard to these events *relevant to the charges against him*" (emphasis added).

[56] Compare ICTR Statute, Article 1, see above note 39.

---

the crime of direct and public incitement to commit genocide, like conspiracy, is an inchoate offence that *continues in time* until the completion of the acts contemplated. The Chamber accordingly considers that the publication of Kangura, from its first issue in May 1990 through its March 1994 issue, the alleged impact of which culminated in events that took place in 1994, falls within the temporal jurisdiction of the Tribunal to the extent that the publication is deemed to constitute direct and public incitement to genocide. Similarly, the Chamber considers that the entirety of RTLM broadcasting, from July 1993 through July 1994, the alleged impact of which culminated in events that took place in 1994, falls *within* the temporal jurisdiction of the Tribunal to the extent that the broadcasts are deemed to constitute direct and public incitement to genocide.[57]

On Appeal, Judge Pocar agreed with the Trial Chamber arguing:

Dans la mesure où des infractions sont répétées dans le temps et qu'elles sont liées entre elles par une intention ou un dessein commun, elles doivent être considérées comme une *infraction_continuée*, à savoir comme un crime unique. Il ne peut donc être question d'exclure une partie de cette infraction unique et de ne retenir que les actes commis après le 1er janvier 1994.[58]

'Infraction continuée' is to be translated as 'continuous crime'.[59] Indeed, before the judges was not one single act that continued, but a series of newspaper editions of Kagura which were published (same *modus operandi*) periodically (temporal connection) with the same intent (to incite genocidal acts).[60] However, the majority of the ICTR Appeals Chamber disagreed with the Trial Chamber and Judge Pocar:

---

[57] ICTR, TC judgment Nahimana, para. 1017, see above note 55 (emphasis added); compare also para. 1044, see above note 55.

[58] ICTR, *The Prosecutor v. Nahimana et al.*, Appeals Chamber, Judgment, partly dissenting judgment of Judge Fausto Pocar, 28 November 2007, ICTR-99-52-A, para. 2 (emphasis added) ('ICTR AC, dissenting opinion Judge Pocar, Nahimana') (https://www.legal-tools.org/doc/04e4f9/).

[59] ECtHR, judgment Rohlena v. Czech Republic, para. 28(b), p. 8, see above note 13. Contrary to this, the English translation of Judge Pocar's dissenting opinion erroneously used the term "continuing" crime.

[60] Compare elements (b), (c) and (d) of the test for continuous crimes as established by ECtHR, judgment Rohlena v. Czech Republic, para. 33, p. 10, see above note 13.

> [E]ven where *offences* may have commenced before 1994 and *continued* in 1994, the provisions of the Statute on the temporal jurisdiction of the Tribunal mean that a conviction may be based *only* on criminal conduct having occurred during 1994 […] the Appellants could be convicted only for acts of direct and public incitement to commit genocide carried out *in* 1994.[61]

This interpretation of the Appeals Chamber's majority is in line with an earlier reasoning of judges Nieto Navia and Vohrah who stated:

> in adopting the [ICTR] Statute, even crimes involving planning and preparation were specifically anticipated and debated among members of the Security Council. […] It extended the temporal jurisdiction of the Tribunal to January instead of April 1994 in order to capture crimes that may have involved planning and preparation. Extending it back further was rejected – thus only crimes committed after 1 January 1994 may be prosecuted before the International Tribunal.[62]

The majority of the Appeals Chamber advanced a strict interpretation of temporal jurisdiction requiring that it must be shown that (1) the crime with which the accused is charged was committed in 1994 (within the temporal jurisdiction of the ICTR), and (2) the acts or omissions of the accused establishing his responsibility occurred in 1994, and that, at the time of such acts or omissions, the accused had the requisite intent (*mens rea*) in order to be convicted pursuant to the mode of responsibility in question.[63]

The ICTR Appeals Chamber emphasized the principle that provisions conferring jurisdiction on an international tribunal or imposing criminal sanctions should be strictly interpreted, and accordingly the Trial Chamber was wrong to convict the accused of conduct that occurred prior to the temporary jurisdiction, meaning before 1 January 1994.[64]

---

[61] ICTR, AC judgment Nahimana (2007), para. 724 (emphasis added), see above note 25.

[62] ICTR, *The Prosecutor v. Nahimana et al.*, Decision on Interlocutory Appeals, Appeals Chamber, Joint Separate Opinion Vohrah and Nieto Navia, 5 September 2000, ICTR-96-11-AR72, para. 16 (https://www.legal-tools.org/doc/089520/); compare also para. 10, see above note 5.

[63] ICTR, AC judgment Nahimana (2007), para. 313, see above note 25.

[64] *Ibid.*, paras. 313, 314.

5.2.4.2.3.   Assessment

The approaches of the ECCC Supreme Court and the ICTR Appeals Chamber to temporal jurisdiction are different and incompatible. From a factual perspective, the ECCC's temporal jurisdiction commences on 17 April 1975, the day when the Cambodian capital Phnom Pen fell into the hands of the *Khmer Rouge*. Hence, the temporal jurisdiction appeared to exclude preparatory acts including planning. By contrast, the genocide in Rwanda unfolded in the second half of April 1994, but the ICTR Statute provides jurisdiction earlier, beginning already on 1 January of that year. The comparison of jurisdictional regimes reveals that the ICTR's temporal jurisdiction provided a three and a half months window during which a prosecutor can identify and charge acts of planning and preparation. By contrast, the Law on ECCC did not provide the same option.

Identifying the start of temporal jurisdiction of a court is a political decision that should be accepted by the judiciary. The majority of the ICTR Appeals Chamber accepted the will of the political decision-maker and advanced a strict interpretation of temporal jurisdiction. Judge Pocar, relying on the notion of continuous crime, found himself isolated.

In setting aside the will of the political decision-maker, the ECCC Supreme Court used an argumentation which is legally problematic, particularly regarding the allegation that the "cluster of transactions of joint criminal enterprise [...] continued" and it would be "unnatural to break up such a protracted and complex transaction".[65] A joint criminal enterprise ('JCE') is a mode of liability, not an offence as such. Hence 'continuous' contributions to a JCE cannot be regarded as a continuous crime, but at best as a continuous mode of liability. However, the notion of continuous or continuing crime does not apply to a continuous mode of liability.

Also, the Supreme Court's reasoning is problematic from the principle of legality point of view. The judges based their reasoning on one reference to domestic law in England and Wales.[66] It is doubtful that this approach from one jurisdiction is representative for the entire common law sphere. Furthermore, the accused were Cambodians and committed their crimes there, meaning in a country belonging to the civil law tradition. The approach by the Supreme Court is incompatible also with the

---

[65]   ECCC, Appeal judgment Nuon *et al.*, para. 215, see above note 52.
[66]   *Ibid.*, para. 216.

principle of strict interpretation[67] of temporal jurisdiction advanced by the ICTR and the SCSL. The latter approach is in line with jurisprudence of the Permanent Court of Justice and the ICJ.[68] Also, extending the temporal jurisdiction retroactively infringes the rights of the accused because, in case of doubt, the issue has to be decided in his or her favour.[69]

In conclusion, the Supreme Court should have vacated any conviction based on Nuon and Khieu's acts of planning and devising the criminal purpose of the joint criminal enterprise if such conduct had occurred prior to 17 April 1975. It should have been permitted for the Trial Chamber to factually rely on such acts of planning only as ingredients of elements for Nuon and Khieu's acts of contributing to the JCE within the temporal jurisdiction of the ECCC, meaning after 17 April 1975. The approach of the majority of the ICTR Appeals Chamber, on the other hand, is legally sound. The decision of the Supreme Court of the ECCC is not based on the notion of continuous or continuing crime, because the Supreme Court argued within the confines of a JCE, a mode of liability. As of today, judges at the ICC have refrained from referring to the continuous or continuing crime notion to extend the courts temporal jurisdiction.

5.3. Offences of a Continuous or Continuing Nature

This section discusses four international criminal law offences which are considered as continuous or continuing crimes, namely (1) enforced disappearance, (2) (sexual) slavery, (3) conscripting or enlisting children, and (4) transfer of population.

---

[67] Compare ICTR, AC Interlocutory Decision Nahimana and Ngeze, separate opinion Vohrah and Nieto Navia, para. 17, namely in footnote 22, see above note 5; ICTR, AC judgment Nahimana (2007), para. 313, see above note 25; compare SCSL, *The Prosecutor v. Sam Hinga Norman*, Appeals Chamber, Dissenting opinion of Justice Robertson, Decision on preliminary motion based on lack of jurisdiction (Child recruitment), 31 May 2004, SCSL-2004-14-AR72, para. 15, p. 12 ('SCSL Dissenting opinion Justice Robertson–Norman Appeal') (https://www.legal-tools.org/doc/098fbb/).

[68] The Permanent Court of Justice as well as the ICJ are hesitant and refused to entertain cases, deciding they lacked competence to do so (compare ICJ, Case of the Monetary Gold Removed from Rome in 1943 (Preliminary Question), Judgement of 15 June 1954, ICJ Reports (1954), p. 19 (https://www.legal-tools.org/doc/a23855/); ICJ, East Timor (Portugal v. Australia) Judgement, 30 June 1995, ICJ Reports (1995), p. 90 (https://www.legal-tools.org/doc/c7cf7e/); compare Status of Eastern Karelia, PCIJ, Series B, No. 5 and Interpretation of Peace Treaties, Advisory Opinion, ICJ Reports (1950), p. 65.

[69] Compare Law on ECCC, Article 33 new, see above note 38; ICC Statute, Article 24(2), see above note 1.

For each offence the analysis of the notion's basis follows the three requirements test: (1) an obligation of international criminal law, (2) is violated by conduct, and (3) the breach continues in time.

5.3.1. Enforced Disappearance

Enforced disappearance is a protracted offence.

5.3.1.1. Obligation of International Criminal Law

While enforced disappearance was prohibited internationally before 1992 already, it crystalized as an international crime based on customary international and treaty law through three acts: (1) a 1992 declaration of the United Nations ('UN') General Assembly, the offences' inclusion in (2) the Convention on enforced disappearance in 1994, and (3) the ICC Statute.

In 1978, the UN General Assembly expressed concern about enforced or involuntary disappearances.[70] In its first paragraph the resolution's preamble listed a number of human rights violations, but the General Assembly avoided the qualification of enforced disappearance as a(n) international) crime.

In 1992, the UN General Assembly declared that

> acts constituting enforced disappearance shall be considered a *continuing offence* as long as the perpetrators continue to conceal the fate and the whereabouts of persons who have disappeared and these facts remain unclarified.[71]

Adopting a proposal from the UN Commission on Human Rights[72] the UN General Assembly stated in 1993 that

> [a]cts constituting enforced disappearance shall be considered a *continuing offence* as long as the perpetrators continue

---

[70] UNGA, Disappeared persons, Resolution 33/173, 20 December 1978 (https://www.legal-tools.org/doc/splypg/).

[71] UNGA, Declaration on the Protection of all Persons from enforced disappearance, UN Doc. A/Res/47/133, 18 December 1992, published on 12 February 1993, Article 17 (https://www.legal-tools.org/doc/534c27/).

[72] Economic and Social Council, referring to the Commission on Human Rights document entitled "Report of the Working Group on the Declaration on the protection of all persons from enforced disappearance", E/CN.4/1992/19/Rev.1, 31 January 1992, Annex, Article 17(1) (https://www.legal-tools.org/doc/nju19t/).

> to conceal the fate and the whereabouts of persons who have
> disappeared and these facts remain unclarified.[73]

In 1994, the member States of the Organization of American States ('OAS') adopted a convention on forced disappearance of persons which stated: "This offense shall be deemed *continuous or permanent* as long as the fate or whereabouts of the victim has not been determined".[74]

The ICC Statute includes enforced disappearance of persons as a crime against humanity.[75]

5.3.1.2. Violating Conduct

The relevant conduct consists of two branches: (1) arrests, detention, or abductions, and (2) the refusal to acknowledge these acts, the deprivation of freedom or to provide information on the fate of the victims.[76] The negotiators of the ICC Elements of Crime agreed that to commit the offence of enforced disappearance it is sufficient that the perpetrator commits one of the two branches.[77] Still, situations exist in which a perpetrator is responsible for committing both prohibited branches.

5.3.1.3. Breach Continues in Time

During the negotiations for the ICC Elements of Crime of enforced disappearance of persons[78] the issue of continuous or continuing crime was indirectly touched upon.

5.3.1.3.1. Continuous or Continuing Nature?

Enforced disappearance begins when the victim disappears and lasts while authorities refuse to acknowledge that a deprivation of freedom had oc-

---

[73] GA Declaration Enforced Disappearance 1992, Article 17(1), see above note 5 (emphasis added).

[74] Organization of American States ('OAS'), Inter-American Convention on Forced Disappearance of Persons, 9 June 1994, Article 3(1) (emphasis added) ('OAS Convention on Forced Disappearance') (https://www.legal-tools.org/doc/7c67e0/).

[75] ICC Statute, Article 7 (1)(i), (2)(i), see above note 1.

[76] ICC, Elements of Crime, Article 7(1)(i), elements 1 and 2, p. 11 ('ICC EoC') (https://www.legal-tools.org/doc/3c0e2d/).

[77] Georg Witschel and Wiebke Rückert, "Article 7(1)(i) – Crime against Humanity of Enforced Disappearance of Persons", in Roy S. Lee (ed.), *The International Criminal Court: Elements of Crimes and Rules of Procedure and Evidence*, Transnational Publishers, Ardsley, NY, 2001, p. 100 ('Witschel/Rückert, Article 7(1)(i)').

[78] ICC Statute, Article 7(1)(i), see above note 1.

curred or to provide information about the fate and whereabouts of the victim. Thus, enforced disappearance occurs over a protracted period of time.[79] Specifically through the act of letting a victim 'disappear' an 'unlawful state'[80] is created which continues over a long period of time. This suggests that the offence has a continuing nature. Also, the legally protected interest, the liberty and eventually life, of the victim continues to be infringed throughout the period of disappearance; the continuation or the end of this unlawful state of affairs is contingent upon the will of the perpetrator and with the length of disappearance the harm caused for the disappeared person accumulates.[81] It would therefore be possible to consider this offence as a continuing crime.[82]

However, history has shown that criminal regimes may embark on series of enforced disappearances thereby targeting their enemies. To capture the systemic nature the qualification of such acts as continuous is helpful as this emphasises that the disappearances follow patterns (same *modus operandi*), they may be closely related in time (for example, to the takeover of power) and be driven by the same intent with each individual act constituting the same criminal offence.[83] Emphasizing the systemic nature of the crime, meaning that it often occurs as part of a 'series' of disappearances, one can argue that this offence has a continuous nature.

In 2006, the International Convention for the Protection of all Persons from enforced Disappearances explicitly mentioned the "continuous nature" of this offence.[84]

In 2010, the Working group on enforced or involuntary disappearances of the UN Office of the High Commissioner of Human Rights ('WG-Enforced Disappearances') commented:[85]

---

[79] Witschel/Rückert, Article 7(1)(i), p. 99, see above note 77.

[80] Aysev, Article 8(2)(b)(viii), p. 50, no.1, see above note 35.

[81] *Ibid.*, pp. 50, 51, no. 2–5.

[82] Inter-American Court of Human Rights ('IACtHR'), *Case of Blake v. Guatemala*, Judgment on Merits, 24 January 1998, separate opinion of Judge A.A. Cançado Trindade, para. 7 ('Separate opinion Cançado Trindade, Blake v. Guatemala') (https://www.legal-tools.org/doc/9096c1/).

[83] Compare elements (a) to (e) of the test for continuous crimes as established by ECtHR, judgment Rohlena v. Czech Republic, para. 33, p. 10, see above note 13.

[84] 2006 Convention on Enforced Disappearance, Article 8(1)(b), see above note 10.

Enforced disappearances are prototypical *continuous acts*. The act begins at the time of the abduction and extends for the whole period of time that the crime is not complete, [...] until the State acknowledges the detention or releases information pertaining to the fate or whereabouts of the individual.

5.3.1.3.2.   Principle of Retroactivity

Accepting the nature of this offence, the WG-Enforced Disappearances observed:

> This continuous nature of enforced disappearances has consequences with regards to the application of the principle of non retroactivity, both in treaty law and criminal law.[86]

This continuous nature caused concerns among delegations with regard to the temporal jurisdiction of the ICC. For example, if a victim was illegally detained before the ICC Statute entered into force in 2002 up until today, and the authorities deny that they were involved in this disappearance, would the ICC have jurisdiction? In March 2000 during the Preparatory Commission negotiations, a footnote was added to reflect the concerns, particularly of some Latin American states:

> Some delegations were of the view that the competence *ratione temporis* of the Court with respect to this crime should be clarified in the light of the relevant provisions of the Statute.[87]

This footnote was further modified to read in the final document in December 2000:

> This crime falls under the jurisdiction of the Court only if the attack referred to in elements 7 and 8 occurs after the entry into force of the Statute.[88]

---

[85] UNGA, adopting the Report of the Working Group on Enforced or Involuntary Disappearances, UN Doc. A/HRC/16/48, 26 January 2011, p. 11, section G, para. 39 ('Report, WG Enforced or Involuntary Disappearances') (https://www.legal-tools.org/doc/eb0ae2/).

[86] *Ibid.*

[87] UN Preparatory Commission for the ICC, Annex III, Elements of Crimes, Addendum, PCNICC/2000/L.1/Rev.1/Add.2, 7 April 2000, p. 14, footnote 30 (https://www.legal-tools.org/doc/5ca0b8/).

[88] ICC, Elements of Crime, Official Records of the Assembly of States Parties to the Rome Statute of the International Criminal Court, First session, New York, 3-10 September 2002, Part II.B, footnote 24 (https://www.legal-tools.org/doc/3c0e2d/).

This clarifies that the attack which led to the victim being abducted or detained, must have occurred after 1 July 2002, the point in time when the ICC Statute entered into force. By contrast, any enforced disappearances occurring before that date are not subject to the jurisdiction of the ICC.

5.3.1.3.3.   International Jurisprudence

In 1996, the Inter-American Court of Human Rights ('IACtHR') ruled in *Blake v. Guatemala*

> [I]n accordance with the aforementioned principles of international law which are also embodied in Guatemalan legislation, forced disappearance implies the violation of various human rights recognized in international human rights treaties, including the American Convention, and that the effects of such infringements – even though some may have been completed, as in the instant case – may be *prolonged continuously or permanently* until such time as the victim's fate or whereabouts are established.[89]

In 1998, Judge Cançado Trindade of the Inter-American Court of Human Rights referred to Article 3(1) of the OAS Convention on Forced Disappearance arguing that international norms typify forced disappearance as a "'continuing or permanent' crime while the fate or whereabouts of the victim is not established".[90]

In 2001, the ECtHR found in *Cyprus v. Turkey* regarding human rights violations occurring following the occupation of Northern Cyprus by Turkey that

> during the period under consideration, there has been a *continuing violation* of Article 5 of the Convention by virtue of the failure of the authorities of the respondent State to conduct an effective investigation into the whereabouts and fate of the missing Greek-Cypriot persons.[91]

At the time of writing, there is no decision of an ICC Trial Chamber on the continuous nature of the crime of enforced disappearance. However,

---

[89]   IACtHR, *Blake v. Guatemala*, Judgement on Preliminary Objections, 2 July 1996, para. 39 (emphasis added) (https://www.legal-tools.org/doc/a888e1/).

[90]   Separate opinion Cançado Trindade, Blake v. Guatemala, para. 7, see above note 82.

[91]   ECtHR, *Case of Cyprus v. Turkey*, Judgment, 10 May 2001, application no. 25781/94, para. 150 (emphasis added) (https://www.legal-tools.org/doc/bc22e8/).

former Judge Fernández de Gurmendi of the ICC expressed her view that enforced disappearance constitutes a continuous crime.[92]

5.3.2. (Sexual) Slavery

5.3.2.1. Obligation of International Criminal Law

Since at least 1904, several international treaties banned slavery[93] and sexual slavery,[94] though these instruments did not clarify explicitly that this offence is an international crime. However, since at least 1945 slavery has been consistently included as a crime in the charters of the International Military Tribunals Nuremberg ('IMT Nuremberg') and Tokyo, Control Council Law No. 10, as well as the Statutes of ICTY and ICTR.[95]

---

[92] ICC, *Situation in the Republic of Côte d'Ivoire*, Pre-Trial Chamber III, Corrigendum to judge Fernández de Gurmendi's separate and partially dissenting opinion to the Decision pursuant to Article 15 of the Rome Statute on the Authorisation of an Investigation into the Situation in the Republic of Côte d'Ivoire, 5 October 2011, ICC-02/11, para. 69 ('ICC, Fernández de Gurmendi's opinion on Côte d'Ivoire') (https://www.legal-tools.org/doc/eb8724/).

[93] Compare Convention to Suppress the Slave Trade and Slavery, 25 September 1926, Article 1 ('1926 Slavery Convention') (https://www.legal-tools.org/doc/12c9d8/); Supplementary Convention on the Abolition of Slavery, the Slave Trade, and Institutions and Practices Similar to Slavery, 7 September 1956, Articles 1, 3, 5–7 (https://www.legal-tools.org/doc/d038c8/); ICCPR, Article 8, see above note 21; Additional Protocol II to the Geneva Conventions of 12 August 1949, and relating to the protection of victims of non-international armed conflicts, 7 December 1978, Article 4(2)(f) (https://www.legal-tools.org/doc/fd14c4/).

[94] Compare International Agreement for the Suppression of the 'White Slave Traffic', 18 May 1904, 35 Stat. 1979, 1 L.N.T.S. 83 (https://www.legal-tools.org/doc/uf0h1u/); International Convention for the Suppression of the "White Slave Traffic", 4 May 1910, 211 Consol. T.S. 45, 1912 GR. Brit. T.S. No. 20, Article 1 and 2 (https://www.legal-tools.org/doc/9a9hlf/); League of Nations, International Convention for the Suppression of the Traffic in Women and Children, 30 September 1921 (https://www.legal-tools.org/doc/9d9c4q/); International Convention for the Suppression of traffic in women of full age, 11 October 1933, Article 1 (https://www.legal-tools.org/doc/sfu58r/); Protocol amending the International Convention for the Suppression of the "White Slave Traffic", 4 May 1949, Articles 1 and 2 (https://www.legal-tools.org/doc/wakv59/); UN, Convention for the Suppression of the Traffic in Persons and of the Exploitation of the Prostitution of Others, 2 December 1949, Articles 1 and 2 (https://www.legal-tools.org/doc/418154/).

[95] International Military Tribunal ('IMT Nuremberg'), Charter, London Agreement, 8 August 1945, Article 6(C) ('Statute IMT Nuremberg'); International Military Tribunal for the Far East ('IMT Far East'), Charter, 19 January 1946, Article 5(C); Control Council Law No. 10, Punishment of persons guilty of war crimes, crimes against peace and against humanity, 20 December 1945, Article II(1)(b) and (1)(c) (https://www.legal-tools.org/doc/ffda62/); ICTY Statute, Article 5(c) (https://www.legal-tools.org/doc/b4f63b/); ICTR Statute, Article 3 (c), see above note 39.

The IMT in Nuremberg convicted at least 13 defendants for slavery.[96] Based on Control Council Law No. 10, the US Military Tribunal issued convictions for enslavement against defendants in at least four cases.[97] The IMT Far East convicted at least two defendants for employing forced or slave labour.[98]

By contrast, sexual slavery was not included as an offence in the statutes of the IMT's, the ICTY and ICTR, but in the Statute of the ICC.[99]

5.3.2.2. Violating conduct

Based on the 1926 Slavery Convention, 'slavery' is defined as the exercise of any or all of the powers attaching to the right of ownership over a person.[100] The ICC Elements of Crime document lists various, illustrative

---

[96] IMT Nuremberg, Trial of Major War Criminals Before the International Military Tribunal, Nuremberg, Judgement Volume XXII, 1 October 1946, pp. 470, 477-478, 480-481, 486-491 ('IMT Nuremberg, judgement') (https://www.legal-tools.org/doc/d1427b/): for defendant Göring, see pp. 526-527; for defendant Keitel, see p. 536; for defendant Kaltenbrunner, see pp. 537-538; for defendant Rosenberg, see pp. 540-541; for defendant Frank, see pp. 542-544; for defendant Frick, see p. 546; for defendant Funk, see p. 552; for defendant von Schirach, see pp. 565-566; for defendant Sauckel, see pp. 566-568; for defendant Jodl, see pp. 570-571; for defendant Seyss-Inquart, see pp. 575-576; for defendant Speer, see pp. 577-579; for defendant Bormann see pp. 586-587.

[97] US Military Tribunal, *US v. Milch*, Judgement, 31 July 1948 (https://www.legal-tools.org/doc/9701a9/), reprinted in Trials of War Criminals Before the Nuremberg Military Tribunals under Control Council Law No. 10, Vol. II, 1997, pp. 790, 791, and Judge Fitzroy D. Phillips, concurring opinion, p. 866; US Military Tribunal, *US v. Pohl et al.*, Judgement, 3 November 1947 (https://www.legal-tools.org/doc/84ae05/), reprinted in Trials of War Criminals Before the Nuremberg Military Tribunals under Control Council Law No 10, Vol. V, (1997), p. 970; US Military Tribunal, *US v. Carl Krauch et al.* ('IG Farben'), Judgement, 30 July 1948 (https://www.legal-tools.org/doc/38b077/), summarised in Law Reports of Trials of War Criminals, The UN War Crimes Commission, Vol. X, 1997, p. 53; and US Military Tribunal, *US v. Friedrich Flick et al.*, Judgement, 22 December 1947 (https://www.legal-tools.org/doc/be375b/) reprinted in Trials of War Criminals Before the Nuremberg Military Tribunals under Control Council Law No 10, Vol. VI, 1997.

[98] IMT Far East, Judgment, 12 November 1948, reprinted in Röling and Rüter, *The Tokyo Judgment: The International Military Tribunal for the Far East*, 1977, Vol. I, pp. 388, 403 – 406, 413, 414, 416, 417; for defendant Kimura, see p. 452; for defendant Tojo, see pp. 462-463.

[99] ICC Statute, Articles 7(1)(g)-2, 8(2)(b)(xxii)-2, and Article 8(2)(e)(vi)-2, see above note 1; Eve La Haye, "Article 8(2)(b)(xxii)-2-Sexual Slavery", in Roy S. Lee, *The ICC: Elements of Crimes and Rules of Procedure and Evidence*, Transnational Publishers, 2001, p. 190.

[100] ICTY, Trial Chamber II, *Prosecutor v. Kunarac et al.*, Judgment, 22 February 2001, IT-96-23-T and IT-96-23/1-T, para. 540 ('ICTY TC judgment Kunarac') (https://www.legal-tools.org/doc/fd881d/); 1926 Slavery Convention, Article 1(1), see above note 93.

---

examples which are not exhaustive, such as "purchasing, selling, trafficking in persons, lending, bartering, or imposing a similar deprivation of liberty".[101]

In addition, sexual slavery requires that the perpetrator causes the victim to "engage in one or more acts of a sexual nature".[102]

5.3.2.3. Breach Continues in Time

International criminal tribunals differ as to whether the crimes of enslavement or sexual slavery are continuous or continuing crimes. The SCSL found that these crimes are continuous, but in relation to slavery the ICTY ruled cautiously, referring to the individual circumstances of each case.

5.3.2.3.1. ICTY

Trial Chamber II of the ICTY held in *Prosecutor v. Kunarac et al.*:

> The *duration* of the suspected exercise of powers attaching to the right of ownership is another *factor* that *may* be considered when determining whether someone was enslaved; however, its importance in any given case will depend on the existence of *other* indications of enslavement. Detaining or keeping someone in captivity, without more, would, depending on the circumstances of a case, usually not constitute enslavement.[103]

The ICTY Appeals Chamber concurred:

> The Appeals Chamber [...] observes that the *duration* of the enslavement is *not an element of the crime*. The question turns on the quality of the relationship between the accused and the victim.
>
> A number of factors determine that quality. One of them is the *duration* of the relationship. The Appeals Chamber

---

[101] ICC Statute, Article 7(2)(c), see above note 1.

[102] ICC EoC, Article 7(1)(g)-2, element 2, Article 8(2)(b)(xxii)-2, element 2, and Article 8(2)(e)(vi)-2, element 2, pp. 28, 37, see above note 76. The phrase "act of a sexual nature" is taken from a proposal by the United States (compare Preparatory Commission of the ICC, Proposal submitted by the USA, 4 February 1999, PCNICC/1999/DP-4/Add-2, Article 8(2)(b)(xxii)-2, element 2, and Article 8(2)(e)(vi)-2, pp. 16, 22 (https://www.legal-tools.org/doc/d6dfdc/).

[103] ICTY TC judgment Kunarac, para. 542, p. 194, see above note 100.

considers that the period of time, which is appropriate, will depend on the particular circumstances of each case.[104]

In relation to rapes occurring during the period of slavery the Appeals Chamber ruled:

> The Trial Chamber found that they had been repeatedly raped during the four-month period. Given the *continuous or repetitive nature* of the *offences* committed by the Appellant on the four women under his control [...].[105]

5.3.2.3.2.   SCSL

The SCSL without elaborating on its reasoning, confirmed in three cases that slavery is a continuous crime.[106] The same court also considered in two cases that sexual slavery constitutes a continuous crime.[107]

5.3.2.3.3.   Assessment

It remains to be seen how the ICC judges will rule. The cases in front of the SCSL related to victims who had to move with and serve the paramilitary troops in the war in Sierra Leone over months and years. The ICTY case related to victims who were more static, serving in soldiers' households or in facilities for up to seven months in Foča in Bosnia-Herzegovina.

However, while the ICC Statute and Elements of Crime envisage similar criminal conduct, other acts may be of a shorter duration, such as selling or bartering a person – both are acts that can occur within a short period of time. Similarly, certain acts relating to trafficking of a victim may be of a very short duration. For example, as part of human trafficking, a person is being received at a State's border, driven through the transit

---

[104] ICTY, Appeals Chamber, *Prosecutor v. Kunarac et al.*, Judgment, 12 June 2002, IT-96-23 and IT-96-23/1-A, para. 121, p. 37 (emphasis added) ('ICTY Appeals Chamber judgment Kunarac *et al.*') (https://www.legal-tools.org/doc/029a09/).

[105] ICTY Appeals Chamber judgment Kunarac *et al.*, para. 267, p. 82, see above note 104 (emphasis added).

[106] SCSL, TC judgment Taylor, paras. 118, 1613, pp. 53, 584, see above note 4; SCSL, Trial Chamber II, *Prosecutor v. Brima et al.*, Judgement, 20 June 2007, SCSL-04-16-T, paras. 39, 1820, 1826, pp. 31, 502, 503 ('SCSL, TC-judgment, AFRC') (https://www.legal-tools.org/doc/87ef08/); SCSL, *The Prosecutor v. Sesay et al.*, Trial Chamber I, Judgment, 2 March 2009, SCSL-04-15-T, paras. 2146, 2172, 2173, pp. 632, 639 ('SCSL, TC judgment Sesay') (https://www.legal-tools.org/doc/7f05b7/).

[107] SCSL, TC judgment Taylor, paras. 1018, 1025, 1474, pp. 393, 395, 441, see above note 4; SCSL, TC judgment Sesay, paras. 2172, 2173, pp. 639, see above note 106.

---

country to be released at the border of a third country or the victim is transported on a ship across the sea to a neighbouring country. The ICTY Appeals Chamber's view that the duration of the conduct is a "factor" but not an element, is flexible enough to allow the crime to be considered as continuous, continuing or instantaneous. Hence, the ICTY rightly pointed out that to qualify (sexual) slavery as a continuous crime depends on the circumstances of each individual case. Thus, the judges may check the test developed for continuous or continuing crimes, if the need arises.

5.3.3. Using, Conscripting, or Enlisting Children

The conduct of conscripting, enlisting or using children in hostilities was prohibited in the late 1970s. This prohibition later turned into an international crime, but it is contentious when this occurred.

5.3.3.1. Obligation of International Criminal Law

The 1977 Additional Protocol I to the Geneva Conventions from 1949 ('Additional Protocol I') prohibited the recruiting and use of child soldiers:

> The Parties to the conflict shall take all feasible measures in order that children who have not attained the age of fifteen years do not take a direct part in hostilities and, in particular, they shall refrain from recruiting them into their armed forces.[108]

While this provision prohibits such conduct, it stops short of penalising such acts because it is not listed as a grave breach in Article 85 or 11(4) of Additional Protocol I. Similarly, the second Additional Protocol to the Geneva Conventions from 1949 prohibits, but does not penalise, recruitment and use of children under 15 years of age in hostilities.[109]

Also, the Convention on the Rights of the Child adopted in 1989 prohibits, but does not penalise the recruitment and use of child soldiers

---

[108] Additional Protocol I to the Geneva Conventions of 12 August 1949 and relating to the Protection of Victims of International Armed Conflicts, dated 8 June 1977, Article 77(2) ('Additional Protocol I') (https://www.legal-tools.org/doc/d9328a/).

[109] Compare *ibid.*, Article 4(3)(c).

under the age of 15 years.[110] The same applies to Article 22(2) of the African Charter on the Rights and Welfare of the Child.[111]

In 1996, the Organisation of African Union exhorted African countries and its warring parties to "refrain from recruiting children under the age of 18 in armed conflict or violent activities".[112] Weeks later, the Security Council, addressing the situation in Liberia in West Africa, condemned "the practice of some factions of recruiting, training, and deploying children for combat".[113] However, during the debate in the Security Council, no delegate argued that recruiting or using children already constitute a crime in international law".[114]

In June 1997, the 'Cape Town Principles and Best Practices' were adopted which requested governments to adopt national legislation setting a minimum age of 18 years for recruitment, and that "persons responsible for illegally recruiting children should be brought to justice".[115]

In October 1997, the UN Committee on the Rights of the Child expressed concern about "abduction, killings and torture of children occurring in [the] area of armed conflict [in Northern Uganda] and the involvement of children as child soldiers".[116]

In June 1998, the President of the UN Security Council condemned recruitment and use of children in hostilities in violation of international

---

[110] UN, Convention on the Rights of the Child, 20 November 1989, A/RES/44/25, Article 38(2) and (3) (https://www.legal-tools.org/doc/f48f9e/).

[111] Organisation of the African Union, African Charter on the Rights and Welfare of the Child, 11 July 1990, OAU Doc. CAB/LEG/24.9/49 (https://www.legal-tools.org/doc/be2c54/).

[112] Organisation of African Union, Resolution 1659 on plight of African children in situation of armed conflict, 5 July 1996, para. 5 (https://www.legal-tools.org/doc/4feb6d/).

[113] UN Security Council Resolution 1071, 30 August 1996, S/RES/1071, para. 9 (https://www.legal-tools.org/doc/d4d772/).

[114] SCSL Dissenting opinion Justice Robertson–Norman Appeal, para. 42, p. 32, see above note 67.

[115] United Nations Children's Fund ('UNICEF'), Cape Town Principles and Best Practices' on the prevention of recruitment of children into the armed forces and on demobilization and social reintegration of child soldiers in Africa, 30 April 1997, p. 1 (https://www.legal-tools.org/doc/fce4d6/).

[116] UN, Committee on the Rights of the Child, 21 October 1997, CRC/C/15/Add.80, para. 19 (https://www.legal-tools.org/doc/s7mb7x/).

law. The Council stressed the "obligation of all States to prosecute those responsible for grave breaches of international humanitarian law".[117]

5.3.3.1.1. Negotiations for the ICC Statute

Already seven months earlier, in December 1997, the German delegation to the Preparatory Committee on the establishment of an ICC had submitted a reference paper to the Working Group on Definitions and Elements of Crime which contained for internal and international armed conflicts the following war crime: "forcing/recruiting children under the age of fifteen years to take direct part in hostilities".[118]

The negotiations in Rome included the war crime of using, conscripting or enlisting children in conflicts of an internal or international nature.[119] For an international armed conflict Article 8(2)(b)(xxvi) states: "Conscripting or enlisting children under the age of fifteen years into the national armed forces or using them to participate actively in hostilities". The sister provision for an internal armed conflict is almost identical, but refers instead of 'national armed forces' to "armed forces or groups".[120]

In May 2000, the Optional Protocol for the Convention of the Rights on the Child was adopted. It provides:

> States Parties shall take all feasible measures to prevent such recruitment and use, including the adoption of legal measures necessary to *prohibit and criminalize* such practices.[121]

5.3.3.1.2. Creating a crime for the SCSL Statute

In October 2000, more than two years after the adoption of the ICC Statute, the UN Secretary-General proposed to include into the Statute for the SCSL a child-related offence which was narrower in scope than the ICC Statute, namely:

---

[117] UN, Statement by the President of the Security Council, 29 June 1998, S/PRST/1998/18, p. 1 (https://www.legal-tools.org/doc/ahdype/).

[118] German delegation to the Preparatory Committee for the establishment of an ICC, 12 December 1997, Articles C(t) and D(f), pp. 4, 5 (https://www.legal-tools.org/doc/8oivv3/).

[119] ICC Statute, Article 8(2)(b)(xxvi) and 8(2)(e)(vii), see above note 1.

[120] *Ibid.*, Article 8(2)(e)(vii).

[121] UN, Optional Protocol to the Convention on the Rights of the Child on the involvement of children in armed conflict, 25 May 2000, A/RES/54/263, Article 4(2) (https://www.legal-tools.org/doc/669fb1/).

> Abduction and forced recruitment of children under the age
> of 15 years into armed forces or groups for the purpose of
> using them to participate actively in hostilities.[122]

This offence did not prohibit voluntary enlistment. It penalised enforced recruitment only, if this was preceded by an "abduction" of the child.

However, the President of the Security Council was critical of the proposed language, and suggested instead to use the language advanced in the ICC Statute on this offence "so as to conform [the proposed offence] to the statement of the law existing in 1996 and as currently accepted by the international community".[123] Article 4(3) of the SCSL Statute contains the wording proposed by the President of the Security Council: "Other serious violations of international humanitarian law [...] Conscripting or enlisting children under the age of 15 years into armed forces or groups or using them to participate actively in hostilities". This language is taken verbatim from Article 8(2)(e)(vii) in the ICC Statute.

5.3.3.1.3. When Did This Prohibition Become an International Crime?

Regarding the conflict in Sierra Leone, it became contentious in *The Prosecutor v. Norman* case which time the international prohibition against recruitment and use of child soldiers had crystalized to become an international crime. This issue was relevant insofar as the SCSL's Statute containing the child-related offence was adopted in 2002 and provided temporary jurisdiction retroactively, since 30 November 1996.[124]

In 2000, the UN Secretary-General had observed:

> the doubtful customary nature of the ICC Statutory crime
> which criminalizes the conscription or enlistment of children
> under the age of 15, whether forced or "voluntary", the crime

---

[122] UN Secretary General, Report of the Secretary-General on the establishment of a Special Court for Sierra Leone, 4 October 2000, S/2000/915, para. 15(c) and Enclosure: Article 4(c), pp. 4, 22 ('UNSG Report SCSL Establishment') (https://www.legal-tools.org/doc/4af5d2/).

[123] UN, Letter dated 22 December 2000 from the President of the Security Council addressed to the Secretary-General, S/2000/1234, para. 3 and Annex: Article 4(c), pp. 2, 5 (https://www.legal-tools.org/doc/1bi2bw/).

[124] SCSL, Statute, 16 January 2002, Articles 1(1), 4(c) ('SCSL Statute') (https://www.legal-tools.org/doc/aa0e20/).

which is included in article 4 (c) of the Statute of the Special Court is not the equivalent of the ICC provision.[125]

Justice Robertson agreed and, referring to the principles of strict interpretation and *nullum crimen sine lege*, argued that at the earliest by July 1998, with the adoption of the ICC Statute, could the enlistment of child soldiers be considered an international crime.[126]

However, the majority of the SCSL Appeals Chamber held that "[c]hild recruitment was criminalized before it was explicitly set out as a criminal prohibition in treaty law and certainly by November 1996".[127] Applying the *Tadić*-test, the SCSL concurred with the jurisprudence of the ICTY and ICTR, that authors of "egregious violations" of Additional Protocols I and II "must incur individual criminal responsibility for their deeds".[128] The reasoning of the SCSL is supported by the negotiations leading to the inclusion of the crime of recruitment or use of child soldiers. The United States had expressed its opinion that the prohibition of such conduct was more a human rights provision than a criminal law provision. The Coordinator of the Working Group observed that "the majority felt strongly that the inclusion [of this offence] was justified by the near-universal acceptance of the norm, the violation of which warranted the most fundamental disapprobation".[129] Also the ICRC regards the prohibi-

---

[125] UNSG Report SCSL Establishment, para. 18, see above note 122.

[126] SCSL Dissenting opinion Justice Robertson–Norman Appeal, paras. 15, 33, 41, 42, 45, 47, pp. 11, 12, 26, 30, 33, 34, 35, see above note 67.

[127] SCSL, *Prosecutor v. Sam Hinga Norman*, Appeals Chamber, Decision on preliminary motion based on lack of jurisdiction (Child recruitment), 31 May 2004, SCSL-2004-14-AR72(E), para. 53, p. 27 ('SCSL, Appeals Chamber Norman decision of the majority') (https://www.legal-tools.org/doc/42004d/).

[128] *Ibid.*, para. 30, referring to (1) ICTY, *Prosecutor v. Duško Tadić*, Appeals Chamber, Decision on the Defence Motion for Interlocutory Appeal on Jurisdiction, 2 October 1995, IT-94-1-AR72, paras. 94, 86–93 (https://www.legal-tools.org/doc/80x1an/), and (2) ICTR, *Prosecutor v. Akayesu*, Trial Chamber I, Judgment, 2 September 1998, ICTR-96-4-T, para. 616 (https://www.legal-tools.org/doc/b8d7bd/).

[129] Herman van Hebel and Darryl Robinson, "Crimes within the Jurisdiction of the Court", in Roy S. Lee (ed.), *The International Criminal Court: The Making of the Rome Statute – Issues, Negotiations, Results*, Kluwer Law International, 1999, p. 117 ('Van Hebel and Robinson, Crimes').

tion of recruitment and use of child soldiers as a war crime based on customary international law and treaty law.[130]

5.3.3.2. Violating conduct

Before the negotiations in Rome, the verbs 'forcing' or 'recruiting' had been included in the draft Statute.[131] As recruiting was understood to involve an active government policy, this verb was replaced with "conscripting" or "enlisting" which are more passive as they merely relate to the administrative act of recording a person's data in relation to the drafting process.[132] These acts refer to the moment the child joins the armed forces.[133] The act of conscripting includes the use of coercion or force,[134] such as an armed formation abducting a child to incorporate him or her into its units. By contrast, the act of enlisting refers to a voluntary decision made by a child.[135] Regarding the 'use' of the child to participate actively in hostilities, a long footnote had been added before the negotiations in Rome. Delegates conscious about the fact that the ICC judges would access the *travaux préparatoires* decided that no further clarifications would be made. The footnote read:[136]

> The words "using" and "participate" have been adopted in order to cover both direct participation in combat and also active participation in military activities linked to combat such as scouting, spying, sabotage and the use of children as decoys, couriers or at military checkpoints. It would not cover activities clearly unrelated to the hostilities such as food deliveries to an airbase or the use of domestic staff in an officer's married accommodation.

---

[130] Henckaerts and Doswald-Beck, *Customary International Humanitarian Law, Vol. I, Rules*, Cambridge University Press, 2005, pp. 584 (in section viii), 568–574 (discussing Rule 156: "Serious violations of international humanitarian law constitute war crimes").

[131] UN Report of the Preparatory Committee on the Establishment of an International Criminal Court, 14 April 1998, A/CONF.183/2/Add.1, p. 21, War crimes B (t) options 1 to 3 ('Preparatory Committee Draft Statute') (https://www.legal-tools.org/doc/816405/).

[132] Van Hebel and Robinson, Crimes, p. 118, see above note 129.

[133] Charles Garraway, "Article 8(2)(b)(xxvi) – Using, conscripting or Enlisting Children", in Roy S. Lee (ed.), *The International Criminal Court: Elements of Crimes and Rules of Procedure and Evidence*, Transnational Publishers, 2001, p. 205.

[134] ICC, PTC-Decision on Confirmation of Charges (Lubanga), para. 246, p. 85, see above note 9.

[135] *Ibid.*

[136] Preparatory Committee Draft Statute, p. 21, see above note 131.

However, use of children in a direct support function such as acting as bearers to take supplies to the front line, or activities at the front line itself, would be included within the wording.

5.3.3.3.   Breach Continues Over Time

ICC and SCSL jurisprudence consider each of the three variants of prohibited conduct (enlisting, conscripting or use of children under 15 years) as continuous crimes. Assuming that enlisting and conscripting refer to administrative acts then this would suggest that these acts are of an instantaneous nature. By contrast, the use of a child in activities relating to hostilities can, depending on the duration of the hostility, be of short, mid-term or even long duration.

ICC Pre-Trial Chamber I has observed:

> each individual instance of *enlistment* into the [*Force Patriotique pour la Libération du Congo*] FPLC, *conscription* into the FPLC or *use* to participate actively in hostilities of children under the age of fifteen gives rise to a crime within the jurisdiction of the Court. However, the Chamber considers it is advisable to treat (1) all instances of enlistment into the FPLC as a *continuous* war crime of enlistment of children under the age of fifteen into the FPLPC; (2) all instances of conscription into the FPLC as a *continuous* war crime of conscription of children under the age of fifteen into the FPLC; and (3) all instances of use to participate actively in hostilities of children under the age of fifteen by member of the [*Union des Patriotes Congolais*] UPC/FPLC as a *continuous* war crime of use to participate actively in hostilities of children under the age of fifteen.[137]

Pre-Trial Chamber I qualified each of the three variants of *actus rei* as constituting a continuous crime. Further, within these variants each act (of enlisting, conscripting and use of children) constitutes a discrete act that is completed[138] once one child is recruited or used in hostilities. The contextual similarities consist of several children being enlisted based on

---

[137] ICC, *The Prosecutor v. Thomas Lubanga Dyilo*, Pre-Trial Chamber I, Decision on the Prosecutor's Application for a warrant of arrest, Article 58, 10 February 2006, ICC-01/04-01/06, para. 91 (emphasis added), p. 44 (https://www.legal-tools.org/doc/af6679/); ICC, PTC-Decision on Confirmation of Charges (Lubanga), para. 248, p. 85, see above note 9.

[138] Compare element (e) of the test for continuous crimes as established by ECtHR, judgment Rohlena v. Czech Republic, para. 33, p. 10, see above note 13.

the same intention of the drafting officer or unit commander.[139] So all discrete acts of enlistment of one or several children are amalgamated into one continuous act as all acts of conscription protect the same legal interest:[140] the protection of children from bodily harm even if he or she has chosen to join an armed unit, as he or she will be exposed to danger. Similarly, all discrete acts of conscription are amalgamated into one continuous act, as they are all acts of use of children in hostilities.

ICC Trial Chamber I agreed with the qualification of enlisting and conscripting as continuous crimes.[141] Similarly, Trial Chamber II of the SCSL also qualified both variants as a continuous crime.[142] In addition this Chamber qualified the "use" of child soldiers in hostilities as a continuous crime: "the Trial Chamber has found that [...] children under the age of 15 were conscripted into the AFRC forces and/or *used* to participate in active hostilities [...]. Because of the *continuing* nature of *these crimes* [...]".[143]

The same Trial Chamber qualified in *Prosecutor v. Taylor* all three variants of enlisting, conscripting and using child soldiers in hostilities as a "continuous crime".[144]

By contrast, ICTR Trial Chamber I in *Prosecutor v. Sesay et al.* omitted to qualify the child soldier-related offences as continuous crime. Whether this was a mere omission is unclear. However, the judges determined that recruitment and training of child soldiers "began as early as 1991 and *continued* throughout the indictment period", meaning at least from November 1996 until September 2000.[145] The reference to this long period of time during which children were enlisted or conscripted is one indication of the continuous nature of this crime though the judges were not explicit on this point.

---

[139] Compare *ibid.* elements (b) and (d) of the test for continuous crimes as established by ECtHR.

[140] Compare *ibid.*element (a) of the test for continuous crimes as established by ECtHR.

[141] ICC, *The Prosecutor v. Thomas Lubanga Dyilo*, Trial Chamber I, Judgment pursuant to Article 74 of the Statute, 14 March 2012, ICC-01/04-01/06, paras. 618, 759, 1135, 1269, 1280, 1347, pp. 282, 337, 484, 547, 553, 585 (https://www.legal-tools.org/doc/677866/).

[142] SCSL TC-judgment, AFRC, paras. 39, 1820, pp. 31, 502, see above note 106.

[143] *Ibid.*, para. 1820, p. 502 (emphasis added).

[144] SCSL, TC judgment Taylor, para. 1357, p. 497, see above note 4.

[145] SCSL, TC judgment Sesay, paras. 1615, 2220, pp. 483, 651 (emphasis added), see above note 106.

5.3.4. Transfer of Own Population into Occupied Territory

The Prosecution and judges in Nuremberg attempted to address the problem of transfer of civilian population into occupied territories and, as such, their efforts constitute antecedents for subsequent codifications of the prohibition. The fourth Geneva Conventions from 1949 and its Additional Protocol I barred this conduct, and through the latter instrument this prohibition acquired the status of an international crime.[146] However, the exact scope of criminalised conduct is currently not clear. Scholars debate whether this uncertainty may have implications whether to qualify this offence as a continuous or continuing crime.

5.3.4.1. Obligation of International Criminal Law

The obligation in international armed conflicts not to transfer one's own population into occupied territory was in the Statute of the IMT Nuremberg. The indictment and the Judgment of the IMT in Nuremberg demonstrated a general awareness on the part of the prosecutors and judges of the problem of population transfers during occupations. Other international instruments such as the fourth Geneva Convention, Additional Protocol I and Article 8(2)(b)(vii) ICC Statute defined and further elaborated this obligation.

5.3.4.1.1. IMT Nuremberg

In 1942 representatives of nine countries occupied by the German Reich condemned war crimes including "mass expulsions" and "acts of violence thus perpetrated against civilian populations".[147] The Charter of the IMT in Nuremberg contained the war crime of "*deportation* [...] for any other purpose of *civilian population* of or *in* occupied territory".[148] The provision barred deportations, meaning forcible movement of persons over state borders. The object of these deportations was any "civilian population". Arguably, this could be the civilian population "of occupied territo-

---

[146] International Committee of the Red Cross ('ICRC'), Geneva Convention (IV) relative to the Protection of Civilian Persons in time of War, 12 August 1949, Article 49(6) ('ICRC, Geneva Convention IV') (https://www.legal-tools.org/doc/d5e260/); Additional Protocol I, Article 85(4), see above note 108; Van Hebel and Robinson, Crimes, p. 112, see above note 129.

[147] Resolution on German War Crimes signed by Representatives of nine occupied countries, 12 January 1942, London, Inter-Allied Review (https://www.legal-tools.org/doc/bb0570/).

[148] Charter of the IMT Nuremberg, Article 6(b), see above, note 95 (emphasis added).

ry" which had remained on the territory while the occupation occurred and the new authority deported it from there; or, this author submits, civilian populations (comprised of Germans or from other nations) which the new authority deported into the territory it occupied. The omission of the words 'forcible transfer' in the IMT Charter suggests that a forcible movement without crossing a state border or a movement *without* force, would not violate the obligation and thus not constitute a war crime under the IMT Charter (for example, if elements of the civilian population of the occupier chose to voluntarily move into the occupied territory).

However, count three (VIII)(J) of the indictment in the main trial at the IMT Nuremberg is ambiguously drafted on this point. Instead of mirroring the phrase 'deportation' of civilian population in occupied territory as it was used in Article 6(b) of the IMT's Charter, the count alleged that parts of the German population were "introduced" and "installed" in territory occupied by the German *Reich*:

Germanization of occupied territories

> In certain occupied territories purportedly annexed to Germany the defendants methodically and pursuant to plan endeavored to assimilate those territories politically, culturally, socially, and economically into the German Reich. The defendants endeavored to obliterate the former national character of these territories. In pursuance of these plans and endeavors, the defendants *forcibly deported inhabitants* who were predominantly non-German and *introduced* thousands of *German colonists*. [...]
>
> In the Department of Upper Rhine, Lower Rhine, and Moselle, the methods of Germanization were those of annexation followed by conscription.
>
> 1. From the month of August 1940, officials who refused to take the oath of allegiance to the Reich were expelled. On 21 September expulsions and deportation of populations began and on 22 November 1940, more than 70,000 *Lorrainers or Alsatians were driven into* the south zone of *France*. From 31 July 1941 onwards, more than *100,000 persons* were *deported* into the eastern regions of the Reich or *to Poland*. All the property of the deportees or expelled persons was confiscated. At the same time, 80,000 *Germans coming from the Saar or from Westphalia were installed* in Lorraine and 2,000

farms belonging to French people were transferred to Germans.[149]

The Prosecution at the IMT alleged that (1) the local French population from Alsace-Lorraine was deported to the South of France, and (2) Germans from Saar or Westphalia were then "installed". The use of this verb does not necessarily suggest the use of force, which deportation and Article 6(b) of the IMT's Statute require. Further, that parts of French civilian population from Alsace-Lorraine were forced to move to Southern France does, legally speaking, not constitute deportation as the population is *not* moved across a state border, but within the same occupied territory.

The IMT Judgment found:

> In Poland and the Soviet Union these crimes were part of a plan to get rid of whole native populations by expulsion and annihilation, in order that *their territory could be used for colonization by Germans.* [...]

> Hitler discussed with Rosenberg, Göring, Keitel and others his plan for the exploitation of the Soviet population and territory, which included among other things the evacuation of the inhabitants of the *Crimea and its settlement by Germans.* [...] In the West the population of Alsace were the victims of a German "expulsion action." Between July and December, 1940, 105,000 Alsatians were either deported from their homes or prevented from returning to them. A captured German report dated 7th August 1942, with regard to Alsace states that: "The problem of race will be given first consideration, and this in such a manner that *persons of racial value will be deported to Germany proper, and racially inferior persons to France*".[150]

Regarding the occupied Alsace-Lorraine, the judges found that the local population was deported into two directions: some towards Germany and others towards France, meaning away from Alsace-Lorraine. However, only the first movement, from Alsace-Lorraine to Germany constitutes deportation as this is movement over a state border. By contrast, the second movement, from Alsace-Lorraine to other parts of France, occurs

---

[149] IMT Nuremberg, Indictment, 19 November 1945, Count Three – War Crimes, VIII. Statement of the Offence" (emphasis added) (https://www.legal-tools.org/doc/23d531/).

[150] IMT Nuremberg, Judgement, pp. 456, 457, see above note 96 (emphasis added).

within the same occupied state and thus, this movement does legally speaking not constitute deportation. Further, the judges omitted to address the Prosecutor's allegations that 80,000 Germans from the Saar or Westphalia were "installed" in the occupied Alsace-Lorraine and, if so, whether this move could have amounted to deportation, meaning it occurred across a state border and involved force.

Regarding the Germans moving into the occupied Poland and the Soviet Union, particularly the Crimea peninsula the words "used" and "settlement" were again neutral, not suggesting that Germans moving into these regions were forced to do so. It can be concluded that with regard to the "Germanization of occupied territories" the judges assessed the main focus of the wrong as the forcible deportation of the local populations from the occupied territory across state borders. The IMT convicted Rosenberg and von Neurath for their contributions to the policies of Germanization.[151] Still, the Nuremberg Judgement remained vague regarding the movement of German civilians into occupied territory. It was particularly unclear whether the movement of German civilians to the occupied areas had involved force and thus constituted deportation in the sense of Article 6(b) of the IMT Charter.

5.3.4.1.2.   Geneva Convention IV

Article 49 of Geneva Convention IV provides the following in the event of an international armed conflict:

> (1) Individual or mass forcible transfers, as well as deportations of protected persons from occupied territory to the territory of the Occupying Power or to that of any other country, occupied or not, are prohibited, regardless of their motive.
>
> [...]
>
> (6) The Occupying Power shall not deport or transfer parts of its own civilian population into the territory it occupies.

Paragraph (1) deals with the original population which stayed or stays in the occupied territory. It is prohibited for the occupying authority to move this local population from the occupied territory to another country, whether to the one of the occupying power or a third country.

---

[151] *Ibid.*, pp. 238, 261, 295, 335.

The verb "shall" in paragraph (6) indicates that it is prohibited for the occupying power to deport or transfer its own population into the occupied territory.

Article 49(1) of Geneva Convention IV prohibits the illegal deportation of population from the occupied territory and subparagraph (6) the deportation of own population into occupied territory. However, subparagraph (6) is broader than the IMT Charter in that it also prohibits that own population is "transferred" to occupied territory. On the other hand, Article 49(6) requires that it is ones "own" population that moves into the occupied territory. Insofar it is narrower than the IMT Charter which prohibits the move of any civilian population into occupied territory.

The obligation contained in Article 49(6) of Geneva Convention IV, while constituting a prohibition, does not treat its violation as a grave breach,[152] meaning as a punishable crime. By contrast, Article 6(b) of the IMT's Charter constitutes a war crime.

5.3.4.1.3.   Additional Protocol I

In 1977, the Additional Protocol I determined that, for the purposes of international armed conflicts,

> the following acts shall be regarded as *grave breaches* of this Protocol, when committed wilfully, in violation of the relevant provisions of this Protocol, and causing death or serious injury to body or health:
>
> [...] the transfer by the Occupying Power of parts of its own civilian population into the territory it occupies, or the deportation or transfer of all or parts of the population of the occupied territory *within* or outside this territory, in violation of Article 49 of the Fourth Convention.[153]

The provision qualifies for the first time the wilful transfer of the occupying power's population into occupied territories as a grave breach.[154] In addition, the word "within" expands the prohibition by no

---

[152] Compare Henckaerts and Doswald-Beck, p. 462, see above note 130.

[153] Additional Protocol I, Article 85(4), see above note 108 (emphasis added).

[154] Van Hebel and Robinson, Crimes, p. 112, see above note 129; Herman van Hebel, "Article 8(2)(b)(viii) – The Transfer, Directly or Indirectly, by the Occupying Power of Parts of Its Own Population into the Territory it Occupies", in Roy S. Lee (ed.), *The ICC: Elements of Crimes and Rules of Procedure and Evidence*, Transnational Publishers, Ardsley, 2001, pp. 159, 160 ('Van Hebel, Article 8(2)(b)(viii) ICC Statute'); compare Henckaerts and Doswald-Beck, p. 462, see above note 130.

longer requiring that the occupied population which is being transferred has to cross a State boundary. Rather, the prohibition is violated already if the original population is transferred within the occupied territory.

5.3.4.1.4.   ICC Statute and Elements of Crime

Article 8(2)(b)(vii) of the ICC statute further extended the prohibition by adding the word "indirectly":

> The transfer, directly or indirectly, by the Occupying Power of parts of its own civilian population into the territory it occupies, or the deportation or transfer of all or parts of the population of the occupied territory within or outside this territory.

The additional phrase "directly or indirectly" stems from an Egyptian proposal which found support from the majority of States.[155] Under "indirectly" may fall a passive[156] stance by the Occupying Power which knowingly tolerates the transfer of its own population into occupied territory, or which fails to effectively prevent movement of its own population into occupied territory. However, a too expansive interpretation of the word "indirectly" was criticised by other delegations as it would overlap with other modes of liability covered by Articles 25 and 28 ICC Statute.[157]

5.3.4.1.5.   Conclusion on International Obligation

A two-fold international obligation exists for an occupying power: (1) not to deport or transfer the population staying in the occupied territory, and (2) not to transfer parts of its own population into the territory it occupies. With the adoption of Additional Protocol I to the Geneva Conventions and the ICC Statute, element (2) has been extended, as explained above. Since 1977, a wilful violation is considered as a grave breach which is to be pe-

---

[155] Van Hebel, Article 8(2)(b)(viii) ICC Statute, p. 159, see above note 154; Kearney, "On the Situation in Palestine and the War Crime of Transfer of Civilians into Occupied Territory", in *Criminal Law Forum*, 2016, p. 18, text preceding note 79 ('Kearney, Transfer of Civilians').

[156] Van Hebel and Robinson, Crimes, p. 113, see above note 129; UN, Commission on Human Rights, Preliminary Report prepared by Mr. A.S. Al-Khasawneh and Mr. R. Hatano, The human rights dimensions of population transfer, including the implantation of settlers, 6 July 1993, E/CN.4/Sub.2/1993/17, para. 15 ('UN Report on Population Transfers') (https://www.legal-tools.org/doc/bdqtn3/).

[157] Van Hebel, Article 8(2)(b)(viii) ICC Statute, p. 160, see above note 154.

nalised and can be subject to the adjudication of domestic and international criminal tribunals.

5.3.4.2.   Violating Conduct: Transfer

It is contentious precisely which conduct violates the prohibition. What does the word "transfer"[158] include? Currently there are no decisions of international criminal tribunals on this point and the academic literature is divided.

Some writers argue that only the arrival of one's own population in occupied territory is included in the word "transfer" ('position 1'). Others argue that the word "transfer" would include also the subsequent settlement including its duration ('position 2').[159] The disagreement is relevant insofar as it has consequences for whether the act of "transfer of own population" can be considered as being completed once the last group of one's own population has arrived, or rather whether the violation and thereby the criminal conduct continue during the settlement activities.

Zimmermann represents the first position, arguing that the transfer of population is complete with the arrival of one's own population in occupied territory, as a process of settlement would be not required.[160] This position would see the act of population transfer as either a series of instantaneous and discrete acts,[161] or as continuous acts[162] which stop once the last transfer of one's own population into occupied territory has occurred, or once the settlement starts, or once the occupying authority ends the occupation, hands over authority, and thus leaves the territory concerned.

According to the second position, the transfer includes subsequent settlement of one's own population in the occupied territory and thus is an ongoing process: individuals arrive to occupied territory and settle. As long as one's own population remains in the occupied territory and does

---

[158]   Article 49 (6), Geneva Convention IV, see above note 146; Article 85(4) of Additional Protocol I, see above note 108; Article 8(2)(b)(viii), ICC Statute, see above note 1.

[159]   Kearney, Transfer of Civilians, Section 5.2., see above note 155; Aysev, Article 8(2)(b)(viii), pp. 71–76, see above note 35.

[160]   Andreas Zimmerman, "Palestine and the International Criminal Court *Quo Vadis*: Reach and Limits of Declarations under Article 12(3)", in *Journal of International Criminal Justice*, 2013, p. 324 ('Zimmermann, Article 12(3)').

[161]   *Ibid.*

[162]   Aysev, Article 8(2)(b)(viii), p. 66, see above note 35.

not leave, this conduct would breach the international obligation. This view emphasizes the ongoing nature of the entire process (series of arrivals and settlement). Even if the occupying authority leaves one day, the violation may continue as the settlers may stay behind and continue their settlements.

To interpret what exactly the word "transfer" entails, the negotiators of the ICC Elements of Crime added footnote 44 which reads: "The term 'transfer' needs to be interpreted in accordance with the *relevant provisions of international humanitarian law* (IHL)".[163]

5.3.4.2.1.   Relevant Provisions of International Humanitarian Law

In 1979 and 1980, the UN Security Council emphasized that Israel's policy and practices of settling parts of its population and new immigrants in those territories constitute a violation of Geneva Convention IV.[164]

In 1981, the ICRC issued a resolution according to which "settlements in the occupied territories are incompatible with Articles 27 and 49 of the Fourth Geneva Convention".[165]

The 1997 draft of the 'Declaration on Population Transfer and the Implantation of Settlers' states:

> Article 3:
>
> Unlawful *population transfers* entail a practice or policy having the purpose or effect of *moving* persons *into or out of an area*, either within or across an international border, or within, into or out of an occupied territory, without the free and informed consent of the transferred population and any receiving population.
>
> Article 5:

---

[163] Report of the Preparatory Commission for the International Criminal Court, 2 November 2000, PCNICC/2000/1/Add.2, p. 28, footnote 44 (emphasis added) (https://www.legal-tools.org/doc/843931/); Van Hebel, Article 8(2)(b)(viii) ICC Statute, p. 161, see above note 154.

[164] UN Security Council Resolution 452, 20 July 1979, S/RES/452 (https://www.legal-tools.org/doc/946db2/); UN Security Council Resolution 465, 1 March 1980, S/RES/465, para. 5 (https://www.legal-tools.org/doc/d96c52/).

[165] ICRC, Resolution III: Application of the Fourth Geneva Convention of 12 August 1949, 14 November 1981, as issued during the 24th International Conference of the Red Cross in Manila, § 3.

> The *settlement, by transfer or inducement*, by the Occupying Power of parts of its own civilian population into the territory it occupies or by the Power exercising de facto control over a disputed territory is unlawful.[166]

Regarding "population transfer", the draft declaration distinguishes in separate articles between, the moving of persons into occupied territory, and their "settlement" there. At first sight, this distinction appears to suggest that transfer of population is only the movement,[167] while settlement is dealt in a different article; but this distinction is blurred because, according to Article 5, the settlement occurs (again) "by transfer". Thus, the declaration defines "transfer" of one's own population in a circular way, and treats it as satisfying both movement into occupied territory and establishment of settlements there.

The Declaration clarifies that the practices of population transfer and settlement "constitute international wrongful acts giving rise to [...] individual criminal responsibility".[168]

Furthermore, UN General Assembly resolutions have interpreted Article 49(6) of Geneva Convention IV in relation to settlements in Palestine:

> measures taken by Israel to change the [...] demographic composition [...] of the occupied territories [...] are null and void. [...] Israel's policy of *settling* parts of its population and new immigrants in the occupied territories constitute a flagrant *violation of the Geneva Convention* [...].[169]

In 1999, the same body again made reference to settlements, expressing "grave concern about the *continuation* by Israel of the *settlement*

---

[166] UN, Economic and Social Council, Commission on Human Rights, Sub-Commission on Prevention of Discrimination and Protection of Minorities, Draft Declaration on Population Transfer and the Implantation of Settlers, 27 June 1997, E/CN.4/Sub.2/1997/23, Annex II, Articles 3 and 5, p. 26 (emphasis added) ('UN Draft Declaration on Population Transfers') (https://www.legal-tools.org/doc/109f0j/).

[167] *Ibid.*, Article 3.

[168] *Ibid.*, Article 9.

[169] UN General Assembly, Report of the Special Committee to Investigate Israeli Practices Affecting the Human Rights of the Population of the Occupied Territories, UN Doc. A/RES/36/147C, 16 December 1981, para. 8 (https://www.legal-tools.org/doc/joncqh/); UN Doc. A/RES/37/88C, 10 December 1982, para. 8 (https://www.legal-tools.org/doc/f32c98/); UN Doc. A/RES/38/79D, 15 December 1983, para. 9 (https://www.legal-tools.org/doc/2yti78/); UN Doc. A/RES/40/161D, 16 December 1985, para. 11 (https://www.legal-tools.org/doc/g4i21u/).

activities, including the *ongoing construction* of the new settlement [...] *in violation of international humanitarian law, relevant UN resolutions*".[170]

In 1991, the ILC draft Code of Crimes against the Peace and Security of Mankind ('CCaPSM') also included the establishment of settlers in occupied territory as an exceptionally serious war crime.[171] The ILC stated in its commentary:

> it is a crime to *establish settlers* in an occupied territory and to change the demographic composition of an occupied territory. A number of reasons induced the Commission to include these acts in the draft article. Establishing settlers in an occupied territory constitutes a particularly serious misuse of power, especially since such an act could involve the disguised intent to annex the occupied territory. Changes to the demographic composition of an occupied territory seemed to the Commission to be such a serious act that it could echo the seriousness of genocide.[172]

In its 1994 draft statute for an international criminal court, the ILC again included the serious war crime of establishment of settlers in an occupied territory and changes to the demographic composition.[173] However, in the 1996 draft the reference to establishment of settlers was removed and replaced by language referring merely to transfer of population into occupied territory as in Article 85 of the Additional Protocol I to the Geneva Conventions.[174]

In conclusion, several resolutions adopted by the UN Security Council and General Assembly as well as the ILC in its draft CCaPSM from 1991 and in its ILC Draft Statute for an international criminal court from 1994 suggest that the prohibition of transfer of population into occupied territory includes settlement activities and that such conduct violates international humanitarian law, namely the Geneva Conventions. Howev-

---

[170] UN General Assembly, UN Doc. A/RES/54/78, 6 December 1999, preamble, p. 2 (https://www.legal-tools.org/doc/3x0085/).
[171] ILC, CCaPSM of 1991, Yearbook of the ILC 1991, vol. II, Part Two, A/46/10, Article 22(b), p. 104 (https://www.legal-tools.org/doc/251704/).
[172] *Ibid.*, Article 22(b), commentary para. 7, p. 105 (emphasis added).
[173] ILC, Draft Statute for an ICC, Article 22(2)(a), p. 15, see above note 18.
[174] ILC, CCaPSM of 1996, Yearbook of the ILC, 1996, vol. II, A/CN.4/L.532 [and Corr.1 and 3], Article 20(c)(i), commentary para. 11, pp. 38, 40, see above note 171.

er, while these resolutions express concern and condemn the practice of settlements, with the exception of the ILC's 1991 draft CCaPSM and its 1994 Draft Statute, they neither suggest that such violations amount to breaches or crimes nor that they would incur penal sanctions. Also, in its 1996 draft CCaPSM, the ILC no longer included the settlement activities in occupied territories as an international crime. This draft has not been adopted until today. Similarly, the 1997 UN Draft Declaration on Population Transfers, which qualified in Article 9 that population transfer and settlements give rise to individual criminal responsibility, is non-binding. Though this approach was known to the drafters of the ICC Statute in Rome, the chose not to include settlement activities.

5.3.4.2.2. Negotiations of the Statute of the International Criminal Court

The negotiators of the ICC Statute debated the issue whether the prohibition of transfer of population into occupied territory would also include settlements. The drafting of the war crime of transfer of population created heated debates and resulted at the Preparatory Committee in December 1997 in four options.[175] Option III(f)(i) prohibited "the *establishment of settlers* in an occupied territory and changes to the demographic composition of an occupied territory". This option was taken verbatim from the ILC's Draft Statute for an ICC from 1994.[176]

Also, the so called 'Zutphen draft' contained four options for this crime, and option 3(i) still contained the aforementioned prohibition of establishing settlements as proposed by the ILC in 1994:[177] Option 1: Transfer by occupying power of parts of its own civilian population into the territory it occupies; Option 2: transfer of own population into the territory it occupies, or deportation or transfer of all or parts of population of the occupied territory within or outside this territory; Option 3 i. the *establishment of settlers* in an occupied territory and changes to the demo-

---

[175] UN, Preparatory Committee on the Establishment of an ICC, 18 December 1997, A/AC.249/1997/L.9/Rev.1, section B(f), pp. 5, 6 (https://www.legal-tools.org/doc/787a4d/).

[176] ILC, Draft Statute for an ICC, Article 22 (2)(a), p. 15, see above note 18.

[177] UN General Assembly, Preparatory Committee on the Establishment of an ICC, Report of the Inter-Sessional Meeting from 19 to 30 January 1998 in Zutphen, The Netherlands, 4 February 1998, A/AC.249/1998/L.13, pp. 23, 24 (https://www.legal-tools.org/doc/7ba9a4/pdf/).

graphic composition; ii. (see option 2); and Option 4: exclusion of the provision.

In April 1998, the draft Statute for the ICC again contained four options including the aforementioned option 3i verbatim.[178]

However, during the ICC negotiations in Rome Option 3 i. which included an explicit reference to "establishment of settlers" was rejected, and a definition similar to Option 2 was adopted.

Subsequently, during the negotiations of the ICC Elements of Crime document, no proposal, whether from the Arab States, Switzerland, the United States or Turkey, sought to re-introduce or clarify that settlement activities could form part of the *actus reus* of this offence. Instead, delegations preferred to remain as close as possible to the narrower wording of the ICC Statute.[179] Thus, an historical interpretation of the word "transfer" indicates that the drafters of the ICC Statute and the ICC Elements of Crime, though cognisant of the UN Security Council and General Assembly resolutions, the ILC draft Statute from 1994, and the UN Draft Declaration on Population Transfers, did not agree to include settlements in the prohibition of transfer of population in the ICC Statute.

5.3.4.2.3.   Teleological Interpretation

Seeking a teleological interpretation of the word "transfer", some scholars suggest that the purpose of the prohibition is to preserve the legal interests of the indigenous population in the occupied territory, namely its right to self-determination, property rights, territorial integrity, and economic destitution of the land.[180] Scholars suggest that the perpetrator structurally pursues an end point, namely to transform the demographic composition or the political status of territory concerned by annexing and colonising it.[181] These scholars would include settlement activities in the prohibition.

---

[178] UN, Report of the Preparatory Committee on the Establishment of an ICC, 14 April 1998, A/CONF.183/2/Add.1, section War Crimes, B, f, option 3(i), p. 17 (https://www.legal-tools.org/doc/816405/).

[179] Van Hebel, Article 8(2)(b)(viii) ICC Statute, p. 160, see above note 154.

[180] Aysev, Article 8(2)(b)(viii), pp. 74, 79, see above note 35; Kearney, Transfer of Civilians, section VI, see above note 155.

[181] Christa Meindersma, "Legal Issues Surrounding Population Transfers in Conflict Situations", in *Netherlands International Law Review*, 1994, pp. 33, 34, 51; Kearney, Transfer of Civilians, p. 33, see above note 155.

5.3.4.2.4.   Assessment

At this point in time, the term "transfer" should be interpreted narrowly because the ICC negotiators were aware of these legal sources – whether the resolutions of the UN General Assembly or Security Council or the drafts of the ILC – but they made a conscious decision not to adopt the option which expressly mentioned settlements and thus chose a narrow interpretation. However, footnote 44 of the ICC Elements of Crime refers to an interpretation of "transfer" in "accordance with the relevant provisions of IHL". This is a dynamic reference, meaning it depends on future developments in international law, including the adoption of other treaties and declarations, whether "transfer" will be interpreted differently in the future.

Even the narrow interpretation – that transfer of population only includes the movement of one's own population to, but not its settlement in, occupied territory – will protect the legally protected interests or *Rechtsgüter*: preserve territorial integrity of the occupied State, the demographic composition of the original population under occupation, the physical harm of its members, and their property rights. The act of moving population precedes any settlement. The existence of settlements in occupied territory, while not fulfilling the *actus reus* of the crime as such, can still be used as evidence *post factum* when seeking to prove that earlier acts of movement of one's own population to occupied territory occurred.

Furthermore, the ICC negotiations added the phrase "directly or indirectly" in relation to acts of transfer in Article 8(2)(b)(viii) of the ICC Statute. The insertion of the word "indirectly" clarifies that "transfer" includes an occupying authority remaining passive.[182] Concerning such a passive attitude, the UN Special Rapporteur on population transfers observed:

> The term "transfer" implies purpose in the act of moving a population [...]. The State's role in population transfer may be *active or passive*, but nonetheless contributes to the systematic, coercive and deliberate nature of the movement of population into or out of an area. [...] The *State's role may involve financial subsidies, planning, public information,*

---

[182]   Van Hebel and Robinson, Crimes, p. 113, see above note 129.

> *military action, recruitment of settlers, legislation or other*
> *judicial action, and even the administration of justice.*[183]

In other words, population transfer interpreted as a mere movement could still be proven by circumstantial evidence on active or passive acts by the occupying authority.

A narrow interpretation is also in line with the principle of legality and *nullum crimen sine lege*, which is formulated as follows in the ICC Statute:

> The definition of a crime shall be strictly construed and shall not be extended by analogy. In case of ambiguity, the definition shall be interpreted in favour of the person being investigated, prosecuted or convicted.[184]

5.3.4.3. Breach Continues in Time

If one accepts a narrow interpretation of "conduct", then the transfer of the occupying power's own population occurs via multiple movements of individuals or groups who move into the occupied territory. These movements may occur at all times during which the occupation lasts.

The assessment whether these acts should be considered as continuous (or continuing) or instantaneous crimes depends on the facts of each case, including but not limited to the position of the perpetrator. The *de jure* and *de facto* position of each perpetrator has to be considered whether the perpetrator was in a high position in the occupying authority designing a policy of the occupying authority to permit movements into occupied territory; or a senior police commander who allowed movements into territory by advising staff manning check points to let settlers pass; or a businessman who earned his living organising the physical transfer to the occupied territories; or a mafia boss who benefitted from systematically trafficking persons into the occupied territory. This position will determine whether the perpetrator could engage in, facilitate, or at least acquiesce in a series of transfer acts into the occupied territory which violated the same protected interest, and whether each transfer followed a similar *modus operandi* and occurred in a temporal connection.[185] Furthermore,

---

[183] UN Report on Population Transfers, para. 15 (emphasis added), see above note 156.

[184] ICC Statute, Article 22(2), see above note 1.

[185] Compare ECtHR, judgment Rohlena v. Czech Republic, para. 33, elements (a) to (c), p. 10, see above note 13.

the same underlying intent of the perpetrator needs to be shown, and that each act met the elements of the offence of transfer of one's own population.[186]

It remains to be seen in each individual case whether the prosecution, apart from proving the elements of the offence itself, will manage to also demonstrate that the conduct constituted a continuous crime.

5.4. Conclusion

The notion of continuous or continuing crime is generally accepted in international criminal law. It was not expressly debated during the negotiations and neither included in the ICC Statute nor the ICC Elements of Crime document. Thus, the decision to what extent this notion may be applied by the ICC is left to its judges. With the exception of the Nuremberg and Tokyo Tribunals, other international criminal tribunals have already referred to this notion. But these references are brief and otherwise cryptic. Hence, the exact details and scope of this notion will have to be determined through future case law by the ICC. Only limited guidance comes from the jurisprudence of other international courts, such as the ECtHR, the ICJ, and the IACtHR, as well as from the ILC's draft code of state responsibility and general principles of law derived from national laws of legal systems of the world. Until today, no international criminal tribunal has engaged in an effort to distil a general principle to develop the notion of continuous or continuing crime.[187]

As a result, we face a conflated use of terminology when we approach this notion in international criminal law. Its exact elements are not clear. It needs to be seen whether the ICC will be willing to adopt the distinction between continuous or continuing crimes which the ECtHR acknowledges in its jurisprudence.[188]

---

[186] *Ibid.*, para. 33, elements (d), (e).

[187] Regarding some efforts to distil general principles, see ICTR AC, dissenting opinion judge Pocar, Nahimana, para. 2 in note, see above note 58; compare ECtHR, judgment Rohlena v. Czech Republic, paras. 31–33, pp. 9, 10, see above note 13; cf. Aysev, Article 8(2)(b)(viii), p. 42 in note 35, see above note 35.

[188] Compare ECtHR, judgment Rohlena v. Czech Republic, para. 28, p. 8, see above note 13. Note, however, that courts in Latin America tend to refer to the ECtHR's concepts of continuous or continuing crime in a reverse manner (cf. Aysev, Article 8(2)(b)(viii), p. 42 in note 34, see above note 35).

In the absence of such clarification by international criminal tribunals, this chapter has adopted a broad approach inspired by the ILC draft on state responsibility, modified to the requirements of international criminal law. According to this new approach, a continuous or continuing crime is (1) a conduct which (2) violates an international criminal law obligation, and (3) this breach continues over time.

Based on this approach, the chapter analysed whether five international crimes[189] can be considered as continuous or continuing crimes, or rather as instantaneous acts. The ICC Statute and international humanitarian law do, however, contain more offences than these five that have a continuous or continuing nature. The offences not analysed in this chapter are imprisonment, severe deprivation of liberty, enforced prostitution, apartheid and forced marriage.[190]

---

[189] They are (1) enforced disappearance, (2) slavery, (3) sexual slavery, (4) enlistment, conscription and use of child soldiers, and (5) transfer of population; see ICC Statute, Articles 7(1)(e), 7(1)(c), 7(1)(g)-2, 8(b)(xxvi), 8(e)(vii) 8(2)(b)(viii), see above note 1.

[190] ICC Statute, Articles 7(1)(e), 7(1)(g)-3, 7(1)(j), see above note 1. For forced marriage, see SCSL, TC-judgment, AFRC, paras. 703, 704, p. 217, see above note 106; SCSL, *Prosecutor v. Brima et al.*, Appeals Chamber, Judgement, 22 February 2008, SCSL-2004-16-A, paras. 181–195 (https://www.legal-tools.org/doc/4420ef/); SCSL, TC judgment Sesay, paras. 2306, 2307, 1298, 1474, see above note 106.

PART III:
COLONIAL BURMA

6

The Chittagonians in Colonial Arakan: Seasonal and Settlement Migrations

Jacques P. Leider[*]

6.1. Introduction

Muslim Chittagonians formed the dominant group of seasonal labourers and new settlers in north and central Arakan (now Rakhine State in Myanmar) during British colonial rule in Burma (1826–1948). The considerable growth of their settlements in the late nineteenth century was the defining factor which transformed Arakan's small pre-colonial Muslim community into the biggest Muslim group in Burma, concentrated in a densely populated border zone. The present chapter looks at these significant demographic and social changes, and responds to Morten Bergsmo's observation that the International Criminal Court Prosecution's legal approach in its request for a designated pre-trial chamber to authorize an investigation into alleged crimes in Rakhine State of 4 July 2019 "turns the spotlight on the demographic background of the conflict in northern Rakhine".[1]

The term 'Chittagonians' was commonly used in colonial sources as a catch-all name for a variety of people from Lower Bengal's Chittagong division, which bordered Arakan division (Burma). According to the geographical context in Burma itself, it could refer to Chittagonian seamen or shipwrights along the Irrawaddy (the 'lascars'), an array of Hindu and Buddhist traders, peddlers and cooks in Akyab and Rangoon, or mostly, as

---

[*] Dr. **Jacques P. Leider** is a Lecturer in the French School of Asian Studies (EFEO). He is the Scientific Co-ordinator of the EU-funded research project 'Competing Regional Integrations in Southeast Asia' (CRISEA). Research contributing to the present chapter has benefited from funding received from the European Union's Horizon 2020 research and innovation programme under grant agreement No. 770562.

[1] Morten Bergsmo, *Myanmar, Colonial Aftermath, and Access to International Law*, Torkel Opsahl Academic EPublisher, Brussels, 2019, p. 1 (https://www.toaep.org/ops-pdf/9-bergsmo).

was the case of Arakan, Muslim agriculturists and seasonal labourers. As Chittagonians were the biggest group of Bengalis in colonial Burma, they were presented as a distinct category of the migrant and residential Indian population in early twentieth century records. One may bear in mind that the name 'Chittagong' itself applied to a city, a port, a district, and, as mentioned, a Bengal division. 'Chittagonian' functioned as an inclusive ('being identified or identifying as Chittagonian') or exclusive generic ('Chittagonians as an Indian, non-indigenous race') in the colonial nomenclature before it became a site of contestation denoting unchecked immigration and cultural othering in the socio-political context of late colonial Arakan.

6.2. Chittagonians and Rohingyas

Seven decades after British rule has ended, discussion of the number and role of Chittagonian settlers in Rakhine history remains politically sensitive. The reason is that the Muslim Rohingyas, most of the Muslims in Rakhine State, consider references to the colonial-period 'Chittagonians' as attempts to deny their own sense of identity and legitimacy. In 1948, Muslim leaders from the Jamiat ul-Ulama of Maungdaw (in north Rakhine), who were calling for an autonomous Muslim region within the Union of Burma, stated in a petition submitted to state authorities that they were *not* Chittagonians, claiming indigeneity and a historical link to pre-colonial Arakan and its Muslim minority.[2] This refutation was reiterated many times. Rakhine Buddhists, adamantly rejecting post-World War II Rohingya claims, pointed to the colonial roots of most Muslims in north Arakan.

However, seventy years after the end of the colonial period, the overall majority, if not all Muslims in north Rakhine, identify as Rohingyas demonstrating an 'ethnifying' process of Muslim communities living mostly, but not exclusively, in the townships of Maungdaw, Buthidaung and Rathedaung townships.[3] The rise of the modern Rohingya movement

---

[2] Jamiat ul-Ulama Maungdaw, "Representation by the Muslims of North Arakan Claiming for an Autonomous State in the Buthidaung and Maungdaw Areas", in Home Department, Government of Burma, 24 February 1947.

[3] Territoriality matters in the context of identity formations. The successive exodus and ongoing flows of emigration from north Rakhine to East Pakistan/Bangladesh onwards to Pakistan and the creation of Rohingya diasporas in the Middle East, South and Southeast Asia have raised questions on existential conditions and the production of a deterritorialized Rohingya identity.

as the manifestation of a regional Muslim nationalism since the 1950s was instrumental in this development. The pattern of mutual exclusion has not been overcome but reinforced as waves of communal violence and acrimonious confrontations on social media in the twenty-first century show. The nexus of ethnic recognition and citizenship became most prominent with the debate about the implications and, as argued by many, unjust nature and arbitrary implementation of the 1982 citizenship law.[4] Until 1962, the north Arakan Muslim claims of ethnicity and indigeneity evolved in parallel in the domestic political arena with the struggle for an autonomous state.[5] However, the process of becoming and identifying themselves as Rohingya does not eradicate the colonial past of Chittagonian settlements which is no less a fact rooted in time and space. It is a chapter from which Rohingya writers have shied away, nearly leaving an historical blank, though sources suggest a diverse picture of a plurality of Muslims in Arakan both before and during the British colonial period.[6] Nonetheless, the term 'Chittagonian' is deeply resented because it was weaponized throughout decades of ethno-political contestation.

The challenges for historical research are not limited to the colonial legacy of Rakhine State. Current research faces a bewildering complexity

---

[4] For a detailed analysis, see Nick Cheesman, "How in Myanmar 'National Races' Came to Surpass Citizenship and Exclude Rohingya", in *Journal of Contemporary Asia*, 2017, vol. 47.

[5] The struggle of the Mujahid rebels (1947–61) with its looming threat of separatism dominated reporting on north Arakan in the 1950s. The conciliatory mood of Burmese politics under Prime Minister U Nu in 1960–62 hailed the promise of a political compromise for competing Buddhist and Muslim territorial claims. The creation of the short-lived Muslim-majority Mayu Frontier Administration in north Arakan is referred to by Rohingyas as a *de facto* recognition of their Rohingya identity.

[6] Maungdaw, 1947, see above note 2; "Address Presented by Jamiat Ul Ulema North Arakan on Behalf of the People of North Arakan to the Hon'ble Prime Minister of the Union of Burma on the Occasion of His Visit to Maungdaw on the 25th October 1948" (https://legal-tools.org/doc/wb3uz2). Mohammed Yunus writes: "It is totally misleading and ill-motivated to allege that bulk of the Muslims entered Arakan during British era. The fact is that many Muslim families, who had earlier been driven out by the Burmans, have returned to their homes in Arakan when peace prevailed there as explained by Phayre", see Mohammad Yunus, *A History of Arakan Past and Present*, Magenta Colour, Chittagong, 1994, p. 53; in his informative work, Abu Anin (alias U Kyaw Min) provides a detailed criticism of the British census records pointing out inconsistent classifications of Muslims. Abu Anin's presentation of "immigrants in Arakan" as being "mostly seasonal laborers" is representative of other Rohingya presentations, Abu Aaneen [alias Abu Anin or U Kyaw Min], "Towards Understanding Arakan History (Part II)", on *Kalaban Press Network*, 11 September 2007 (available on its web site).

of issues which have grown from unresolved ethno-political issues in the aftermath of World War II. While the situation was complex in 1948, it became increasingly violent and complicated over the following years and decades. Examples of these complications abound. When Burma became an independent state in January 1948, neither the Arakanese (Rakhine) Buddhists nor Muslims in north Arakan were constitutionally recognized as an ethnic group ('*lu myo*').[7] Arakanese were recognized as an indigenous ('*taing yin tha*') group but Sultan Ahmed, a leading political figure after the war, notes the controversies which arose at government level, both in late January 1947 and after Burma's independence a year later, regarding the right of "Muslims of Akyab district North" to vote linked to the underpinning issue of the recognition of their indigeneity.[8] Arakan became an ethnically denominated state only in 1974[9].

Rakhine's Buddhists see Rohingyas as the descendants of Bengali migrants of the colonial period, but have *also* seen them over time as people who, in shifting circumstances, crossed the border illegally after independence. These views were espoused by the Burmese/Myanmar authoritarian state after 1962. However, ethnic contestation was not the only cause of a festering communal dissent doubled by inequitable state policies that have not pacified but further torn apart the region. Security and border issues, poverty and underdevelopment joined the long list of factors to be considered. The triangular-shaped fronts of collision (including Buddhists, Muslims and the hegemonic state with its suspicion of centrifugal ethnic claims) saw occasional asymmetric political alignments as group and state interests were never in accordance but sometimes overlapping. State policies escalated the process of exclusion since the 1990s, but the Rakhine State and Rohingya issues remained on the margins of world attention. The internal displacement of tens of thousands of people in 2012 and the Rohingya mass flight to Bangladesh in 2016–17 brought to the fore the disenfranchisement, the *de facto* statelessness, and the transnational dimension of their refugee condition. Media attention also

---

[7]   'Arakanese' and 'Rakhine' are used without any difference of meaning to denote the Buddhist majority population of Arakan (Rakhine State). 'Arakan' and 'Arakanese' are terms found in most sources before 1989 and therefore used in line with references to such sources. 'Rakhine' is acknowledged as the official spelling today.

[8]   "Memorandum to the Government of the Union of Burma 18 June 1948" quoted in "Rohingya belong to Burma," *Arakan Monthly News and Analysis of the Arakan Rohingya National Organisation, Arakan (Burma)* 6 (2009), n° 1, p. 11.

[9]   Arakan State was officially renamed Rakhine State in 1989.

generated an exacerbation of hostility in the public discourse, nationally and internationally, and catalysed sectionalist interpretations.

In this context, the global acceptance of the right to identify and get recognition as 'Rohingyas' proceeded swiftly and in an uncontentious way. The sequential crises after 2012, including the narrative of earlier phases of violent conflict between Muslims and Buddhists, state-enforced marginalization, exclusion, disenfranchisement, and military-induced mass flights led to incriminations of ethnic cleansing and genocide, and established a harrowing account of Rohingya victimhood. With increasing visibility in the media, Rohingya history, an essential part of earlier campaigns to claim Rohingya legitimacy, shrank to a record of human rights violations. The importance of documenting Muslim victimhood is indisputable. However, it seems as if the paradigmatic shift from an obscurely communicated conflict to a widely publicized global issue implicitly made wider questions about the social, political and cultural history and its context in Rakhine State redundant. Yet, reading the modern history of north Rakhine Muslims backwards as a track record of state oppression is a narrow option. The region's past calls for a sensitive approach, but even radical solidarity with the oppressed must obviate determinism, a constricted focus on binary state-ethnic relations and pay sufficient attention to the *combinations* of injustice that have plagued the region and its people, including the majority Buddhist Rakhine population.

Moreover, complicated issues should not be made into taboos. 'Chittagonian' has surely become such a taboo. Political correctness cannot resolve the dilemma of using or skirting the term 'Chittagonian'. It becomes obvious when writing about World War II in Arakan. Rohingyas take credit for the participation of their ancestors in the anti-Japanese campaign of the British, while these men are invariably referred to as 'Chittagonians' in reports and memoirs. As the history of the 'now' in Rakhine State is changing rapidly and society and politics are in transition, investigating the roots of conflicts and the dynamics of change for the sake of transparency is demanding, but not superfluous. The history of Chittagonian settlers and the formation of local and regional Muslim identities, such as the emergence of the Rohingyas in north Rakhine, are interwoven and intimately connected. The colonial past is immanent in the present. A critical examination of the colonial archive should level the field for further debate and enlarge the space for co-producing knowledge that has been sorely lacking in the quest for justice for all groups and actors in the Rakhine State crises.

The present chapter investigates migrant Chittagonians who settled either temporarily or permanently in north Arakan, or were part of an annual, seasonal movement of agricultural laborers supplementing the workforce needed in Arakan's fluctuating rice economy from 1860s to 1930s. It draws on decennial census reports, gazetteers, annual reports and settlement reports of Lower Bengal and Burma. The chapter is divided into three parts. The first part starts with a brief note on borderlands, migrations and the colonial sources and their classification of Muslims. The second part explores the statistical evidence of the Bengal census and the textual evidence from Burma reports to illustrate and put into perspective the connection between Chittagonian migrations and the rice economy of Arakan. One important observation about the sources is that the colonial notes on seasonal migration, a highly visible phenomenon, are out of proportion with the record on the slow process of settlement migration. The third part presents the growth of Muslim communities in north Arakan, based on an exploration of numerical data from the census records. It also offers a critical view of evolving British classifications of the Muslim population. Moving from a general to a more specific, micro-level representation of data, the investigation of Chittagonian migrant communities at township level elucidates both temporal (migratory waves) and spatial (southward push) aspects of their growth.

This chapter concludes by arguing that the colonial state instrumentalized settlement migration for fiscal reasons, but failed to acknowledge the social and political impact of the Chittagonian settlement migration in the long run. Until before World War I, the wastelands in the borderlands were sufficient to absorb the inflow of newcomers, and communal tensions were a lesser risk. However, the threat of inter-ethnic strain was increasing in the subsequent decades. The seasonal migration, on the other hand, was a constant, recurrent phenomenon which functioned largely independently of social and political conditions in Arakan. The interdependence of Chittagonian coolie laborers and Arakanese rice growers created a symbiotic relationship which was significant and advantageous for both parties.

6.3. Borderlands, Migrations and Classifications

Borderlands are rightly considered to be complex areas because shared identities and inner frontiers overlap, while zones of friction and exclusion may arise from rivalling interests. British officers in Maungdaw in 1943 noted the contrast between the Buddhist villages north-west of the Naf River in what was Bengal (a majority-Muslim land) and the dense Muslim population on its south-eastern side, in Buddhist Burma's Akyab district, where they were stationed.[10] Coastal and hinterland migrations were a recurrent phenomenon in the frontier region of Arakan and Bengal (the north-east Bay of Bengal when viewed from the oceanside) throughout the last five centuries. They took place in opposite directions (alternating north to south/south to north movements) and various ways (individual and group migrations, invasions combined with deportations, forced resettlements for economic and military reasons, refugee movements, large exodus); they could be reverted (seeing the complete or partial return of refugee settlers) and could spill over into peripheral zones beyond the frontier region. They depended on or were impacted by changing economic and political conditions and included people of different religious and ethnic affiliation. Small Tibeto-Burman groups of the frontier region such as the Mro and Khumi, larger communities such as the Daingnet/Chakma, or the historically dominant populations such as Rakhine and Bengali speaking Muslims experienced voluntary or involuntary displacement within the Arakan-Bengal borderland.

Under British rule (1826–1948), the administrative border at the Naf River that separated Cox's Bazar sub-division (Chittagong district) and Akyab district (Arakan division) was not an impediment to human circulation via land or water. Transborder migration continued after the Government of Burma Act of 1935, which separated Burma and India. The Indo-Burman Immigration Agreement of 1941, an outcome of the enquiry on the 1938 anti-Indian riots and James Baxter's *Report on Indian Immigration*, did not impact the migratory flows between Arakan and Bengal before 1948. During the second half of the colonial rule when transborder migration was an important demographic factor, seasonal, temporary or settler migrants moving from Bengal to Arakan or inversely

---

[10] Robert Mole, *The Temple Bells are Calling A Personal Record of the Last Years of British Rule in Burma,* Pentland Books, Bishop Auckland, 2001, pp. 193-94.

were not counted or registered by the administration in Bengal or Burma. Only occasional estimations were established.

The language of the colonial archives reveals mindsets that are different from ours. Its vocabulary and syntax present late-nineteenth century and early-twentieth century views on the merits of immigration as a tool of civilizing progress; they demonstrate a colonial obsession with racial categorization underpinned by concepts of a moral economy which saw hard-working, land-conquering people (such as Bengali people from Chittagong) as agents of advancement, superior to other people often described as lazy, a term applied to various types of Southeast Asians in colonial settings, the Arakanese (Rakhine) being one such example. The colonial categorizing was not only a process of hierarchizing by racial and productivity criteria, but it also conditioned and formalized an interethnic 'othering' which impacted social and political relations.

However, the impression of a single homogenous colonial mind-set or a monolithic type of colonial knowledge would be mistaken. Views changed and seemingly moved by generational cohorts, interpretations of statistical data varied, and individual prejudice and opinions expressed in print could contradict or cut across state policies pursued in the name of progress. For that reason, colonial quotes no less than numerical figures, when cited as proofs or illustrations, need to be fleshed out with critical context.

The practice of decennial census reports started in British India in 1872. The two main criteria used to categorize the population in British Burma in the census reports of 1872, 1881, 1891, 1901 and 1911 was their religious affiliation and the language group they belonged to. This meant that independently of their origins, period of residence in Arakan, cultural roots, social integration, or their own sense of belonging, all the Muslims in Arakan found themselves grouped together under the heading of 'Muslims', while all those people (either Muslims or Hindus) who had ancient origins in Bengal and spoke dialectal forms of East Bengali were counted as Bengali speakers. On the other hand, since the early-nineteenth century, administrative and missionary descriptions pointed occasionally to a difference between local Muslims ('Arakan Mussulmans'/'Arakan Mahomedans') and 'Bengalis' or 'Indians' from Chittagong who were *new* immigrants. This difference between Muslim communities whose ancestors had lived in Arakan since the time of the Arakanese kings (that is, before 1785) and those who were post-1826 immigrant settlers was not relevant for their categorization in the census records.[11] In racialized terms, Chittagonians were classified as 'foreigners' because they were Indians who were not viewed as an indigenous population of Burma. While Muslims could be either indigenous or foreigners, the option for Muslims to choose expressly between the category 'Arakan Mahomedan' or 'Chittagonian' in survey operations was provided only in the census reports of 1921 and 1931.

British records (land tax settlements, census reports, annual administration reports, gazetteers) contain statistical information on different groups of people living in Arakan, their professional occupations, religious affiliation, seasonal migration, agricultural land expansion, and, in the early-twentieth century, increasingly detailed demographic data (population number, births, age, civil condition, gender ratio, infirmities, education). The individuality of migrant and acculturated Muslims is difficult to recover in the interstices of these matter-of-fact administrative documents. Their subjectivity is effaced because they appear as a mass, positively portrayed as diligent farmers and gardeners, but *anonymous*. They were faceless and voiceless in the sense that the motives of their migrations and the representations of their lives as trans-regional labourers or settlers did neither take shape in their own words nor in the descriptions of the colonial commentators. The same is obviously true for the mass of the resident Buddhist population, too, whose subjective experience of territorial, economic and demographic change remains hidden. The reconstruction of a portrait of the people hits severe limits as we encounter the constrictions of archival records.

6.4. Chittagonians and the Colonial Rice Economy in Arakan

Arakan had been a flourishing Buddhist kingdom between the fifteenth and seventeenth century, its majority population being the Arakanese (Rakhine), a group probably more internally differentiated by regional characteristics than in contemporary times. As the kingdom expanded along the coast and established hegemonic control over the coast from Lower Burma to Southeast Bengal, its population became more diverse including Muslims, Hindus and Christians coming from neighbouring India and Southeast Asia. The royal administration depended on the role of

---

[11] 1785 marks the beginning of Burmese rule in Arakan and 1826 the conclusion of the Yandabo treaty which put an end to the war between the court of Amarapura and the East India Company.

foreign elites as the kings defended their vast zone of coastal rule and opposed the Mughal expansion in Bengal. Muslim villagers were deported in great numbers to the centre of the kingdom to create buffer zones along the borders with Bengal. In hindsight, the history of the kingdom suggests the formation of a multi-layered presence of Muslims as a result of migrations and deportations.

After a period of decline and political breakup prompting calls for outside intervention, Arakan was annexed by Badon, the king of Myanmar, in late 1784.[12] The political, religious and cultural elites of Arakan were resettled in the neighbourhood of Amarapura, the royal capital, and the region entered a process of institutional and administrative integration. Unrelenting demand for manpower, however, and exorbitant taxation by the king led to a mass flight of tens of thousands of people from Arakan crossing the Naf River into the southern part of Chittagong, held by the British since 1761.[13] Yet, the Burmese court did not want to see its subjects run away at will, and political frictions with the East India Company ensued. Aggressions resulting from the cross-border movement of rebels and refugees poisoned the relations and were one of the causes of the First Anglo-Burmese War (1824-26).

The British military campaign had been horrifically expensive, and the British were keen to see the population of Arakan grow, agricultural production increase, and tax revenue cover the expenses of the administration and the garrisons. The economic history of Arakan during the colonial period was a history of the expansion of its agricultural lands and the growth of its rice production.[14] Exhausted by years of civil strife and fiscal mismanagement by its first British administrators, Arakan's population grew nonetheless rapidly after 1835. Many Arakanese Buddhist refugees who had fled to Bengal decades before returned; that movement lasted until the 1850s. The immigration of Bengalis, Burmese and Chinese

---

[12] On the history of the Mrauk U kingdom, see Jacques P. Leider, *Le Royaume d'Arakan, Birmanie, Son histoire politique entre le début du XVe et la fin du XVIIe siècle*, PEFEO, Paris, 2004; on the period of Burmese administration (1785–1824), see Jacques P. Leider, "Politics of Integration and Cultures of Resistance. A Study of Burma's Conquest and Administration of Arakan", in Geoffrey Wade (ed.), *Asian Expansions: The Historical Experiences of Polity Expansion in Asia*, Routledge, London, 2014, pp. 184–213.

[13] The Naf River was not, as occasionally stated, a border invented by the British.

[14] Tun Wai, *Economic Development of Burma from 1800 to 1940*, University of Rangoon, Rangoon, 1961.

was nominally encouraged. Rich alluvial soil and a stable taxation regime were vaunted as assets that could attract cultivators from Central Burma and East Bengal. Wages were higher in Arakan than in Bengal. However, flows of migrants varied according to local pull and push factors; immigrant settlers likely made choices based on a variety of opportunities and conditions. The border region, largely covered by jungle, was poorly populated and had been barely governed. Famines, over-population and cyclones in Bengal are rarely named in the sources as triggers of migration, but they must have played a role. Higher salaries, wastelands to be exploited, and a familiarity with social and geographical surroundings are factors traceable in the sources regarding Chittagonian migrants. Seasonal migration from neighbouring Chittagong to Arakan during the harvest period became a recurrent phenomenon after the Second Anglo-Burmese War (1852). Nonetheless, the region remained a backwater of Burma until the end of the colonial era, shut off towards the East by a mountain range, isolated by the lack of roads, and devoid of any major public or private investments in communications. The general growth of the agricultural population was a rare source of pride for administrators who had little else to report about progress. Industrial development and construction of basic infrastructure bypassed Arakan until the late twentieth century.

'British Burma' was formed in 1862 following the annexation of Lower Burma (1852), with a contiguous territory including Arakan and Tenasserim (both ruled since 1826) and Lower Burma.[15] Taxation of agriculturally exploited land in Arakan used to be settled *annually*. Starting in 1867, efforts were undertaken to make fiscal arrangements for longer periods (generally fixed for five or ten years). Such 'land revenue settlements' (1867–68, 1885–88, 1901–02, 1913–16) included information on the modes of cultivation and the cultivators; they are an important source to take stock of both seasonal and permanent migration of Chittagonians.[16]

---

[15] John Cady, *A History of Modern Burma*, Cornell University Press, Ithaca, NY, 1958, p. 93.

[16] Relatively few printed and nearly no manuscript documents relating to the fiscal and judicial administration of Arakan have survived for the period before the 1860s. A cyclone in late 1868 was invoked by the authors of the *Report on the progress of the Arakan division from 1826 to 1869* to explain the paucity of factual content in their compilation. Even a follow-up report dealing with the period up to 1875 was exceedingly thin. See *Report on the progress made in the Arakan division from 1826 to 1869*, Government Stationery, Rangoon, 1870; *Report on the progress made in the Arakan division from 1865/66 to 1874/75*, Government Stationery, Rangoon, 1876.

The administration of Arakan division was organized in three districts, from north to south, Akyab, Kyauk Phyu, and Sandoway. In 1865, the Arakan Hills Tract was separated from the Akyab district and became the Arakan Hills district mostly inhabited by Chin people. Demographic growth at district level can be investigated from annual reports. Akyab was the most populous district, stretching along the border with Bengal. It was divided into eight, later nine townships, with the population of a few towns and ports sometimes listed separately in the census reports. While the study of the population at *district* level is possible starting with the 1872 report, the study of settlement immigration at *township* level can only be undertaken from 1891 onwards, when the census reports included the so-called 'Provincial Tables'. Most townships saw an inflow of Chittagonian settlers, but it is only in the northern townships of Maungdaw and Buthidaung that Muslims came to form a majority. The peculiar conjuncture of trans-regional settlement migration remains for a large part elusive, because land migrations were not recorded. As stated above, the role of seasonal labourers was regularly confirmed in annual reports, census reports and gazetteers while the expanding settlements of Chittagonians in north Arakan were only marginally acknowledged even at the time when Chittagonians did already form a majority population along the border.

6.4.1. Settlement Migration and the Development of Arakan's Agriculture

During nearly forty years (1850–1890), British administrators in Arakan were eager to develop the transformation of waste lands into rice fields by settling migrants and providing fiscal advantages. East Bengal's Chittagonians became the biggest groups of migrants, first settling along the under-populated border with Bengal.[17] This was the township of Naaf, renamed Maungdaw in 1911, the name of its chief town. Seventy per cent of its population were Chittagonian migrants at the end of the 1880s.[18] The number of settlers then saw a steep increase in the 1890s as we will see below. The creation of Buthidaung township from a division of Rathedaung after 1901 resulted from a growing number of inland mi-

---

[17] English-language research on the development of agriculture in colonial Arakan does not seem to exist yet.

[18] *Report on the Settlement Operations in the Akyab District Season 1886–87*, Superintendent Government Printing, Rangoon, 1888, p. 3 ('Settlement Report in Akyab 1886–87').

grants crossing the Mayu Range to settle in the northern part of Buthidaung. However, the pool of available land was shrinking in the early years of the twentieth century reducing new settlements. Chittagonian migrants then probably started to move further south into other townships of Akyab district and the north of Kyauk Phyu district (Myebon) where their percentage in the 1930s still remained below 15.

In his *Report upon the Revenue Administration of the Province of Arracan for the year 1850–51*, Commissioner Arthur P. Phayre noted the "extensive demand for the rice of this district in foreign markets" and that "a larger export than ever before occurred". He concluded that "this large export, it may confidently be expected, will act as a stimulus for further cultivation". In Akyab, he reported, "wide tracts of country still remain waste".[19] At the same time, S.R. Tickell, Phayre's Assistant Commissioner, made a comment on the slowing increase of the capitation tax-paying population:

> it may be fairly inferred that the main source of our increase of population, which is Chittagong, is nearly exhausted; I believe I am correct in saying that the mass of the people who have immigrated from thence are the Arracanese, who fled the country on the incursions of the Burmese ... these have nearly all returned, and unless we can look to other quarters for an influx of population, we shall, I apprehend, have nothing to depend upon ere long, but the rising and future generations of the present inhabitants for an increase of population.[20]

Tickell was referring to the exodus to Bengal of tens of thousands of people from Arakan between 1795 and 1800, fleeing over-taxation and forced military recruitment, and their slow return during the 25 years of early British rule, a period sketched above. Tickell's pessimistic apprehension was unwarranted because Akyab's population kept on growing over the next decades, thanks to immigration from East Bengal, to a lesser

---

[19] "From Captain A.P. Phayre, Akyab, to the Secretary to the Board of Revenue, Calcutta, 22 October 1851", in *Reports on the Revenue Administration of Hazareebaugh, Arracan, Tenasserim Provinces, and Assam for 1850–51*, Bengal Military Orphan Press, Calcutta, 1853, pp. 16–17.

[20] *Ibid*, p. 27.

degree from Upper Burma (still an independent kingdom until 1886), and from Kyauk Phyu district (Ramree Island).[21]

Nonetheless, in the 1860s, immigration from Bengal stagnated, and while the percentage of people classified as indigenous 'Mahomedans of Burma' revolved around five per cent, the part of 'Indians' (that is, immigrants from Bengal) did not rise much beyond seven per cent.[22]

Efforts to facilitate the arrival of migrants were made. In the Rules for the settlement of land revenue in the Province of British Burma (1866), it was stipulated that

> bona fide cultivators may come into a circle under settlement, and cultivate unappropriated new land, and no question to be asked as to their right to do so. This stipulation includes any immigrant from foreign territory and any British subject.[23]

Lieutenant Colonel Stevenson, the Commissioner of Arakan, noted in his report of January 1869:

> Our want of population is well known; there is abundance of land to repay the toil of cultivators. [...]
>
> Under our revenue system every possible facility was offered to the cultivator to take up waste land, really available, however, only in districts where district officers took special care that *Thoogyees* (*that is*, village heads)

---

[21] "Burmese and Shans from Upper Burma come down in large numbers every year, and, though the majority return after a few months' stay, many no doubt remain and these, from their affinity with the natives, are the most useful class of colonists that come into the country; Of the Chinese immigrants, a good many settle in province; but the multitudes of Bengal and Madrasi labourers who arrive at the beginning of every dry season nearly all return to their homes as soon as the approach of the rainy weather brings their occupation to an end. Even of these, however, there must be an annually increasing residuum of permanent residents.", see *Report on the Administration of British Burma during 1876–77*, Government Press, Rangoon, 1878, p. 25.

[22] *Report on the Administration of the Province of British Burma for the year 1863–64*, Military Orphan Press, Calcutta, 1864; *Report on the Administration of the Province of British Burma for the year 1864–65*, Military Orphan Press, Calcutta, 1865; *Report on the Administration of the Province of British Burma for 1865–66*, Foreign Department Press, Calcutta, 1866; *Report on the Administration of the Province of British Burma for 1866–67*, Foreign Department Press, Calcutta, 1867.

[23] *Reports on the Revenue Settlement Operations of British Burma for the year 1867–68*, Office of Superintendent of Government Printing, Calcutta, 1869, vol. 1, p. 9 ('Revenue Settlement Operations Report 1867–68').

granted land within their powers as freely and with as little trouble to the applicants as the rules intended.[24]

Though Bengalis were already "the preponderating race [in] the Naâf township" in 1869, their immigration remained below British expectations until the late 1870s, because Chittagonians preferred to settle north of Naf River, in Bengal.[25]

> it is a pity immigration does not assume a more solid form, but there are many circumstances which tend to retard and hold it in check. The Chittagong district, which borders on the northern frontier, contains a very large expanse of country with a considerable area of waste land; vegetation is abundant, and but little labour is required to produce the necessaries of life. Being under British rule, with a comparatively light taxation, it would require attraction of a special nature to induce people from those parts to leave their homes and settle down in a strange land. [...] Natives from Chittagong know full well the condition of the country as regards the demand for labour [...].[26]

In 1874, a British initiative to bring Indians to Lower Burma generated mediocre results, and the project was abandoned a few years later when the government concluded that Indians, reluctant to relocate and pioneer the transformation of waste lands into rice fields, were more amenable to supply labour for industrial activities in cities. However, the situation in Arakan was different.

The flow of seasonal laborers, which we will discuss in the next section, was already a well-established part of the agricultural production cycle, but it did not respond to British ambitions to develop the land.

---

[24] *Ibid.*, vol. 1, pp. 29, 39.

[25] *Ibid.*, vol. 1, p. 82. Occasionally, later sources provide glimpses of the progress of settlement immigration during the period before 1890. R.B. Smart describing Payabyin, a village east of the Kalapanzin River in Buthidaung township, says that it was founded in 1864 "by settlers, Arakanese and Chittagonian, driven from the Maungdaw township by the pressure of immigration from Chittagong". The migrant pressure did not relent during the following years as Smart goes on saying that "It is interesting to note that after a further period of 50 years, many of these settlers have now migrated to the Yo *chaung* (*that is* creek) for the same reason". (R.B. Smart, *Burma Gazetteer Akyab District, vol. A*, Government Printing and Stationery, Rangoon, 1917, p. 240). Many of the Akyab District Gazetteer's village descriptions make also specific reference to the waste land grants.

[26] *Ibid.*, vol. 1, p. 30.

> The swarms of Indian coolies who flock to our parts every working season, and periodically return depriving the province of their permanent labour and of their accumulations, can scarcely be designated emigrants, as their visit was not an attempt at settlement, and their exodus has nothing in the nature of expatriation.[27]

Only in the late 1870s did settlement immigration take off with a modest, but regular flow of immigrants.

> The Bengalees come over from Chittagong into the Akyab district of Arakan, where there is an exceedingly scanty population and large tracts of culturable land, of which they can get grants on the most reasonable terms. The great drawback in their case is the want of capital to conduct agricultural operation on anything approaching a large scale; but, as it is, some 500 families now settle down annually in the district.[28]

A "Note on Waste Lands in Lower Burma for Cultivation" in Philip Nolan's 1888 *Report on the Emigration from Bengal to Burma and how to promote it* also stressed the need for more agricultural settlers in the Kaladan Valley (Arakan) and the minimal investments needed.

> District Officers might well devote attention to getting Bengali settlers here. There are large tracts of land which have passed out of production and large tracts that have never been cultivated that only require bunding to make them productive. The present inhabitants would no doubt object to grants on the ground of interference, prior claim, old possession etc. But any claims of this nature not entered in the settlement registers should be received with caution. Five years' exemption from revenue and second-class soil rates on new *pottahs* [29] would, I think, encourage Bengalis to settle.[30]

---

[27] *Report on the Administration of British Burma during 1875–76*, Government Press, Rangoon, 1877, p. 21 ('Burma Report 1876–76').

[28] *Report on the Administration of British Burma during 1877–78*, Government Press, Rangoon, 1879, p. 77.

[29] Pottah means "a deed of lease […] specifying the condition on which the lands are held and the value or proportion of the produce to be paid to the authority or person from whom the lands are held". See Horace Hayman Wilson, *A Glossary of Judicial and Revenue Terms and of Useful Words Occurring in Official Documents Relating to the Administration of the Government of British India*, W.H. Allen and Co., London, 1855.

Interestingly, the settlement officer quoted by Nolan compared the Kaladan township in central Arakan with the northern Naaf township, noting its optimal development. Up to 1888, Naaf township had already seen a considerable transformation of waste lands into rice fields and a steep growth of its immigrant population. The settlement officer reported that 70 per cent of the population were Bengalis, who occupied 79 per cent of the cultivated area, and accounted for 84 per cent of the tax-paying lands.[31] There was intense satisfaction and the Chief Commissioner declared himself ready "to consider any plan which the Commissioner [of Arakan] may propose for attracting Bengali immigrants if the privileges accorded by the Revenue Rules are not sufficient".[32]

> The Naaf tract presents some new features in the greater density of population, the preponderance of Bengalis, the greater value of land, the better condition of the cultivators, the higher rent of tenants' holdings, and the larger amount of land let out to tenants.[33]
>
> The density of the population of Bengal, coupled with ties of race and relationship, re-acts upon the agricultural condition of the Naaf which immediately adjoins Bengal. Pressure is met and overcome in view of compensating advantages [...].[34]

Immigration was promised to increase in the short run. In 1887, a settlement report for a land tract in the centre of Akyab district (Rathedaung and Ponnagyun townships) noted that Akyab's population had "considerably increased [...] and with it the demand for land":

> Bengalis from Chittagong, Burmans from Ramree and settlers from the hills are to be found in considerable numbers throughout the tract.[35]

---

[30] Philip Nolan, *Report on the Emigration from Bengal to Burma and how to promote it*, The Bengal Secretariat Press, Calcutta, 1888, p. 2.

[31] Settlement Report in Akyab 1886–87, see note 18.

[32] *Ibid.*, p. 2.

[33] *Ibid.*, p. 1.

[34] *Ibid.*, p. 3.

[35] *Report on the Settlement Operations in the Akyab District Season 1885–86*, Government Press, Rangoon, 1887, p. 2.

This growth took place even though taxation rates exerted an "unequal pressure". Taxation was comparatively higher than elsewhere in Burma and land was said to be poorer.[36]

The subsequent push of Chittagonians into Arakan (1891–1901) formed the last major episode of what was described ten years later for Burma in general as "an era of rapid expansion" when "fertile culturable land could be obtained for the simple cost of clearance".[37] On the one hand, this period connected evenly to the considerable rise of the population in the southern *'thanas'* of Cox's Bazar sub-division of Chittagong, on the Bengal side.[38] It went together with a move to colonize empty spots in south-east Bengal, and the migrant upsurge was therefore less an invasion of Arakan than an extension of the agricultural frontier of the sub-division of Cox's Bazar, as I will argue below. On the other hand, the increase of Muslim settlers in north Arakan led, according to British comments, to a displacement of Arakanese who moved out of the region. The rise of the Chittagonian community in north Arakan before World War I was, in conclusion, a process where a cluster of administrative, fiscal, territorial and ethnic factors jointly played into each other.

In the 1920s and 1930s, the consolidation of the percentage of Muslims in north Arakan and the fact that three quarters of the resident Muslims had been born in Burma shows that settlement immigration had lessened. New migrants, in smaller numbers, were moving further down south. Fertility, rather than immigration, would explain the rapid Muslim population growth in Maungdaw during the twenty years before World War II.[39]

The sober administrative language of the 1850s and 1860s had projected migration as an economic gain; the language of the 1870s and 1880s marked it as a positivist turn, emphasizing *progress* via land settlements and an improved condition of the people. The migrant wave in the

---

[36] *Ibid.*, pp. 2, 26.

[37] C. Morgan Webb, *Census of 1911* volume IX, Burma Report, vol. 1, Office of the Superintendent, Government Printing, Rangoon, 1912, p. 83.

[38] E.A. Gait, *Census of India 1901, volume VI B, The Provinces of Lower Bengal and their Feudatories, Provincial tables*, Bengal Secretariat Press, Calcutta, 1902, p. 10.

[39] The explanation of the 1931 census report that the 18 per cent increase of Maungdaw's population between 1921 and 1931 was essentially due to the immigration of 21,000 'Indians' is a bewildering statement. J.J. Bennison, *Census of India 1931 volume XI, Burma vol. 1, Report*, Office of the Superintendent, Government Printing and Stationery, Rangoon, 1933, p. 34.

last decade of the nineteenth century, however, led to more opinionated comments. Agricultural expansion was interpreted less in economic or demographic than racial terms. The migratory phenomenon was historicized as a matter of superior racial destiny.

Arakan Deputy Commissioner Smart's comment on the Chittagonian migrants is typical of the racialized representation of Indian migration to Burma in the early twentieth century:

> Since 1879 immigration has taken place on a much larger scale [...] Maungdaw township has been overrun by Chittagonian immigrants. Buthidaung is not far behind and new arrivals will be found in almost every part of the district. The later settlers, who have not been sapped of their vitality, not only do their own labour but it is not uncommon to find them hurrying on their own operations to enable such as can be spared to proceed elsewhere to add to their earnings by working as agricultural labourers, boatmen or mill coolies.[40]

British administrators were convinced that the rise of Burma's civilization at the end of the first millennium CE was due to their racial mixture with immigrant Indians (Brahmanism and Buddhism being essentialized by them as racial-cum-intellectual-and-cultural imports). In the case of Arakan which had had a different history of dynastic successions than Burma, they dismissed 'national' Arakanese legends that connected the Arakanese group, for religious and cultural reasons, to prestigious origins in north India (the land of the historical Buddha and his clan). Alternately, they turned to interpretations of the "character of the Arakanese people" as in the following comment of 1891:

> In some respects, they resemble the Burmans, but they do not have the same fascinating character [...] The Arakanese, it is said, approximate more closely to Hindu and Musalman customs in secluding their women. They are cleverer and more persevering than the Burmese generally. In the opinion of some, the Arakanese are a decaying race, but this opinion is strongly combated by others, who believe that the Arakan branch will outlive the Burman.[41]

A similar comment is found in the 1901 census report:

---

[40] Smart, 1917, p. 87; 241, see above note 25.
[41] H.L. Eales, *Census of 1891 Imperial Series, volume IX, Burma Report, Vol. 1*, Government Printing, Rangoon, 1892, p. 197.

> Save for a few Indian usages assimilated from his Chittago-
> nian neighbours and a trifle of Aryan ballast acquired from
> the same source, the Magh or Arakanese is, to all intents and
> purposes, a Burman, but a Burman, be it said, bereft of much
> of his charm.[42]

Statistical enquiries on language usage informed a parallel argument to the overall negative portrayal of the Arakanese. The seeming decline of the use of Arakanese as a language of communication, as stated in the 1901 census, bolstered a narrative on Arakanese degeneration, emphasizing the "phonetic disintegration" and the "decomposition" of the language. Arakanese was described as a "separate form of speech, dying hard", but "bound eventually to disappear", thus leading to the conclusion that "after another decennial census or two it will probably be possible to calculate fairly accurately the date by which it will have vanished off the face of Burma".[43]

Indian immigration was imagined as potentially re-invigorating. The penetration of Arakan by Chittagonians was going to follow the rules of a historical playbook according to which Indian migration and Indian influence had already determined the earlier course of Burmese history. The colonial beliefs in an Indian racial bonus flourished before World War I and applied both to Arakan and Burma. Nevertheless, colonial opinions disagreed on the outcome. On the one hand, there was a "prevailing tendency to assume that the Burmese as a race are doomed by the modern incursions of Indians into the province". Others opined that "just as in the past the Burmese tribes assimilated what was essential and what was advantageous from the immigrant Indian", so that there was "reason to believe that the present phase of Indian immigration is strengthening rather than weakening the hold of the Burmese on the province".[44]

A similar representation of deeply racialized, yet contrasting views is found in Major Enriquez' *Burmese Wonderland* (1922):

> In the north-east portion of Akyab, in the Buthidaung Sub-
> division, the population now consists chiefly of permanent

---

[42] C.C. Lowis, *Census of India 1901 Burma, volume XII, vol. 1*, Office of the Superintendent, Government Printing, Rangoon, 1902, p. 115.

[43] As the declared aim was to produce a "classification of the races", language was seen as the "most obvious and surest criterion of difference" to study the people of Burma scientifically. *Ibid.*, p. 112.

[44] Webb, 1912, p. 74, see above note 37.

Chittagonian settlers. [...] The Arakanese now tend to concentrate in the Sub-division of Kyauktaw. Some people think they must necessarily be submerged in time. Others believe that they will hold their own. Fortunately, they do not intermarry much with Chittagonians, and though rather an indolent race, have yet brains enough to be fairly prosperous, and in a few individual cases even rich.[45]

Not economic, ecological, territorial and cultural factors, but racial qualities were perceived as the determining factors of social change. An assumed pseudo-scientific nexus between a declining Arakanese majority and a zealous mass of Chittagonians was sufficient to rationalize the superficial observations made by the colonial elite. In this context, questions for the state to worry about social frictions and communal tensions would not arise. With the Victorian sentiment that law and order were the prerequisites of happiness, 'happiness' may have been tacitly assumed to prevail because the colonial state's subjects in Arakan did not cause trouble within its law and order regime.[46] This colonial mood of self-contentment was violently shaken by the 1938 Indian riots in Burma and radically put into question by the 1942 ethno-religious violence in Arakan. Nonetheless, in the case of Arakan, it did never lead to investigations into the complex regional context of mixed populations within the Bengal-Arakan borderlands.[47]

Chittagonians who settled in Arakan after the conclusion of the Treaty of Yandabo (1826) were welcome economic agents; they were industrious and reliably productive. Classified as cultural and ethnic 'foreigners' after having crossed an administrative border within British India, they did not become an object of study in themselves, nor was their demographic growth perceived as a factor of critical social impact in Burma.

At the outbreak of World War II, racial prejudice informed common knowledge on the border region propelled to become a major theatre of warfare. The *Report on Arakan (Akyab district and Arakan Hill Tracts)*,

---

[45] C.M. Enriquez, *A Burmese Wonderland A Tale of Travel in Lower and Upper Burma*, Thacker, Spink and Co., Calcutta, 1922, p. 59.

[46] I am paraphrasing from F.S.V. Donnison's preface to his book. F.S.V. Donnison, *Burma*, Ernest Benn Ltd., London, 1970, p. 11.

[47] Jacques P. Leider, "Territorial Dispossession and Persecution in North Arakan (Rakhine), 1942-43", Policy Brief Series No. 101 (2020), Torkel Opsahl Academic EPublisher, Brussels, 2020 (https://www.toaep.org/pbs-pdf/101-leider/).

produced by the General Staff at the British Army's headquarters in August 1942, stated under the heading "People" that "the Arakanese himself is lazy and careless", and had been "ousted [...] in agriculture and village trading" by "a large foreign element which has come in from India".[48] A year later, after the horrific ethnic vengeance campaign in the wake of the First Arakan Campaign, and with a view to rallying the Arakanese Buddhists to their cause, British ethnographic guidance for military behaviour towards civilians met along the front line in Arakan was updated.[49]

6.4.2. Seasonal Migration and Labour Dependency

Since the 1860s, British administrators in Arakan explained in their reports that the agriculture of Akyab district depended on hired labour.[50]

> During the reaping season, and indeed before, coolies from the Chittagong district come over in hundreds, and appear to do most of the real labour of the country in the northern parts as regards paddy cultivation.[51]

Many 'coolies' from Chittagong (and, to a lesser degree, from southern India and central Burma) came for the annual harvesting and transporting of paddy rice.[52] Temporary laborers were also employed during the ploughing season and for handling the paddy rice at the mills in

---

[48] General Staff of the British Army, *Report on Arakan (Akyab district and Arakan Hill Tracts)*, 1942 ('British Army General Staff Report'), National Archives of the UK, WO 230-1480.

[49] British Library IOR R-8-3, "Descriptions of the Inhabitants of the Arakan" produced by the General Staff, Eastern Army, "based on the Government of Burma's views on the names to be used in describing the different communities" set apart the "bulk of the population" being Buddhist Arakanese, recognized Arakanese Muslims ("long domiciled Mohammedan community"), Hill Tribes ("very simple and primitive") and Chittagonians (described as "domiciled Indians").

[50] An excellent description is Commissioner Lt. Col. Stevenson's paragraph on Chittagong coolies in Revenue Settlement Operations Report 1867–68, p. 81, see above note 23.

[51] *Ibid.*, p. 42.

[52] Chittagonian settlers were also involved in providing such labour: "The latter settlers who have not been sapped of their vitality, not only do their labour, but it is not uncommon to find them hurrying on their own operations to enable such as can be spared to proceed elsewhere to add to their earnings by working as agricultural labourers, boatmen or mill coolies". See Smart, 1917, p. 15, see above note 25.

Akyab port.[53] At the end of the season, laborers returned home. A description in the unmistakable colonial style reads as follows:

> large numbers of immigrants from Bengal and Chittagong reach the Akyab district penniless and on foot, but, at the close of the season, with full purses return by steamer to their homes.[54]

'Coolies' coming to Arakan came mostly by land, which was cheaper, but when crossing the Naf River at the border of Chittagong and Arakan divisions to step into Maungdaw township, their numbers were not recorded.[55] They returned more comfortably by direct steamers on the coastal sea road, boarding in Akyab where passenger numbers were reportedly recorded by port authorities.[56] The annual record of outbound passengers in Akyab port could tell us something about the yearly transport of people from Akyab to Chittagong, but it would still throw little light on migration as a whole. Migrants to Arakan may have been temporary migrants like Indians elsewhere in Burma, staying not just for a season, but for several years before returning home with their savings. In fact, numbers about emigration and immigration in the annual reports do

---

[53] Temporary labourers are understood to have spent several years in Arakan before returning home. "The greater part of the purely temporary sojourners arrive about the harvest season from Chittagong and Madras, and after rapidly amassing a sum, which for them is wealth, return to their homes, having spent from one to five years in the country working as labourers". See *Report on the Administration of British Burma during 1878–79*, Government Press, Rangoon, 1879, p. 14.

[54] *Report on the Census of British Burma taken on the 17th February 1881*, Government Press, Rangoon, 1883, p. 23 ('1881 census report'). See also *Report on the Administration of British Burma during 1874–75*, Government Press, Rangoon, 1876, p. 143; Burma Report 1875–76, 1877, p. 119, see above note 27.

[55] The 'land road' was a combined inland land and river road. Administrative reports do not contain any description of this road. World War II military descriptions of the "old Arakan road" vaguely indicate a footpath from Idgarh down south to Garjania (southern part of Bandarban) and onwards to Maungdaw. The "New Arakan road", most likely the colonial-period road of migrants, led from Cox' Bazar-Ramu south to Taungbro (also referred to as Tumbru) from where boats took passengers down the Naf River to Maungdaw. See British Army General Staff Report, see above note 48. A comprehensive note on the seasonal migration is found in Webb, 1912, p. 80, see above note 37.

[56] Data on immigration and emigration get scanty in the annual administration reports after World War I. Information on Akyab port's inbound and outbound passengers was only occasionally reported. Serial data from the port authorities in Akyab do not seem to have survived in the archives.

not tell us anything clear about either seasonal or settlement migrants. Take the *Report on the Administration of Burma for the year 1873–74*:

> The number of persons who left the Arakan Division in the year of report exceeded the number of immigrants according to the returns, viz., 6500, against 5035; but these figures can scarcely be correct, since many thousands of coolies travel between Chittagong and Akyab in steamers during the shipping season, and it is believed that many thousands more come into the division either by boat or overland.[57]

Nearly twenty years later, the 1891 Burma census confirmed this assessment, stating that the "immigration and emigration figures of Akyab are worthless".[58] Even for recording census figures, colonial administrators depended on the information provided by local '*thugyis*', formerly heads of groups of villages, who became tax collectors under the British and depended for their input on local village headmen. Nonetheless, the Arakan commissioners considered these figures as "tolerably correct", or noted that in rural districts, statistics were likely better than in towns, because "there is no reason why figures should not be accepted as fairly accurate".[59] Concluding comments sounded cautious:

> The figures of 1881 and 1891 would tend to prove that there is established in Burma a large and increasing colony of natives of India and their descendants.[60]

Even in the 1930s, when census records became more complex and detailed, administrators tersely noted that immigration by land was not put on record. State authorities did visibly not care much about the number of migrants from Bengal who entered north Arakan. The author of the annual report of 1933–34 made the following comment on the immigration and emigration figures:

> These figures relating as they do to passenger traffic by sea, take no account of the large numbers of agricultural labourers who enter Arakan by the overland route from Bengal and

---

[57] *Report on the Administration of Burma for the year 1873–74*, Government Press, Rangoon, 1875, p. 136.

[58] Eales, 1892, p. 176, see above note 41.

[59] *Report on the Administration of Burma for the year 1879–80*, Government Printing, Rangoon, 1881, p. 97.

[60] Eales, 1892, p. 176, see above note 41.

who cannot be counted. As many of these returned to Bengal by sea, the Arakan figures show a false balance.[61]

What was the annual number of seasonal migrants? Several tens of thousands each year on average, but the numbers seem to have fluctuated considerably. In the 1872 census report, the 'Collector of Chittagong' is quoted stating that "there are annually nearly 15,000 emigrants from Cox's Bazar alone to Arakan".[62] The *Report on the Administration of Burma for the year 1880–81* indicates 80,000, a considerable figure at a time when the general population of Arakan stood at around 590,000.[63] Yet three years later, the annual report even cited opinions putting it at "at 200,000; but this figure is probably much above the truth".[64] The *Akyab Gazetteer* of 1917, an important and fairly reliable source, put it at an average of 50,000.[65]

When the India-Burma Immigration Agreement of 22 July 1941 included a temporary stop to the migration of unskilled labour, "in Arakan, [...] an acute shortage of labor was immediately revealed and within a very short time after the signing of the Agreement, the Government of Burma had to ask the Government of India to allow the importation of 35,000 laborers into the Arakan Division".[66] The seasonal migration went on after World War II and still comprised up to 20,000 laborers.[67] It is unclear when it came to an end, given the regional insecurity after the war and the armed conflicts in Arakan in the period from 1947 to 1952 involv-

---

[61] *Report on the Administration of Burma for the year 1933–34*, Government Printing and Stationery, Rangoon, 1935, p. 110. In the census report of 1931, an explanation is provided on the recording of sea arrivals and departures. Port health officers counted arrivals themselves while asking companies for the number of departures. The records of shipping companies were estimations of tickets sold and children were not included. See Bennison, 1933, pp. 18–19, 34, see above note 39.

[62] *Report of the Census of British Burma taken in August 1872*, Government Press, Rangoon, 1875, p. 16, para. 79 ('Burma Census 1872 Report').

[63] *Report on the Administration of British Burma during 1880–81*, Government Press, Rangoon, 1881, p. 123.

[64] *Report on the Administration of British Burma during 1884–85*, Government Press, Rangoon, 1885, p. 64.

[65] Smart, 1917, p. 36, see above note 25.

[66] "Annual Report of the Agent to the Government of India in Burma for the Period January 1st to December 31st, 1941", British Library, IOR-B-M-3-1108.

[67] Commonwealth Relations Office, "Letter of Peter Murray, Foreign Office, to R.W.D. Fowler", 24 January 1949.

ing communist groups, Muslim rebels, paramilitary troops and regular army units in the countryside.

Against the background of these fluctuations, there are other factors that impacted the annual flow of seasonal workers. Quoting from a report on the land revenue administration for the year 1906–07, the census report of 1911 tells us:

> The Deputy Commissioner remarks that these Chittagonian coolies come to Akyab, only when crops fail in Chittagong and work is scarce, and that changes in contemplation in Chittagong may provide them in a few years with sufficient work at home.[68]

The same author concluded that these circumstances "foreshadowed" the "decline and even the extinction of this migration". This was not going to happen. The decrease of annual seasonal migrants from 1907 to 1911 was attributed to the taxation of the migrants, a new policy, as the migrants had not been targeted previously with a capitation tax.[69] There is no confirmation of any decline in subsequent years. The prospect of a decline of seasonal migration hailed, in the minds of British administrators, the prospect of seeing the Arakanese "come to their senses" and do the hard work once again themselves (rendered in the report as "productive of beneficial results").[70]

Throughout the colonial period, most British administrators took a negative view of Arakanese Buddhist farmers who hired Chittagonian coolies to do most of the hard work in the fields, calling it "excessive employment of hired labour".[71] However, even the indigenous Muslims in Kyauktaw depended on the imported labour:

> These men have often informed the Settlement Officer that they had got so out of the habit of doing hard manual labour that they were now absolutely dependent on the Chittagonian coolies who come yearly to help them over the most arduous of their agricultural operation, ploughing, reaping and earthwork.[72]

---

[68] Webb, 1911, p. 81, see above note 37.

[69] *Ibid.*

[70] *Ibid.*, p. 80.

[71] *Ibid.*

[72] Smart, 1917, p. 15, see above note 25.

The general picture of the Chittagonian seasonal migration remains diffuse. We do not know exactly when it started, and how it came to an end. We are left to imagine the lives and motivations of Bengali labourers in a seemingly unchanging flow back and forth between their homes and Arakanese rice fields. A satisfactory re-construction of the organization and conjuncture of the alternating movement throughout the eighty-year-period under review in this research is not supported by the sketchy sources. There are nonetheless two important takeaways.

The seasonal migration was simultaneously dependent on complex circumstances in Arakan and in Bengal. It had none of the simplicity hinted at in many of the short administrative descriptions. Arakan's Commissioner Stevenson noted in 1869 that "[n]atives from Chittagong know full well the condition of the country as regards the demand for labour and fix their own terms, being well aware that there is no competition in the market".[73] Other citations presented above, and not least the widely differing estimations of seasonal numbers, suggest a variety of reasons why the seasonal migration fluctuated. Besides famine due to poor harvests, the devastating cyclones of 1876, 1897 and 1919 destroying local livelihood in Bengal may have had an immediate impact.

The second insight is the symbiotic character of the co-operation of Buddhist and Muslim landowners in Arakan and seasonal labourers from Chittagong district. This Bengal-Arakan labour interdependence of agricultural production was a major aspect of the Arakanese rice-based economy promoted by the British. It seems as if it functioned smoothly, its dynamics unimpeded and independent of communal tensions that were soaring after World War I.

Seasonal migrations raise many more questions concerning the society, the economy and the lives of people in colonial Arakan. However, they constituted a marginal phenomenon in Burma, distinctively different from the mighty flow of Indian migrants to the port of Rangoon, which raised intense interest by contemporary decision-makers and later academic research alike.[74] Seasonal migration towards Arakan was definitely a minor issue within the context of Bengal's labour market, where the

---

[73] Revenue Settlement Operations Report 1867–68, p. 30, see above note 23.

[74] Usha Mahajani, *The Role of Indian Minorities in Burma and Malaya,* Vora and Co. Publishers, Bombay, 1960; Nalini Ranjan Chakravarty, *The Indian Minority in Burma –The Rise and Decline of an Immigrant Community,* Oxford University Press, London/New York/Bombay, 1971.

number of people recorded as migrants (because they crossed domestic, intra-Indian borders) counted in the hundreds of thousands.

6.4.3. Chittagonian Migrations: Insights from the Bengal Census

Chittagong district was one of Chittagong division's four districts, together with Tippera, Noakhali and the Chittagong Hill Tracts. Chittagong division itself was part of Eastern Bengal, which saw a rapid increase of its population after 1881. Bengal's census records do not provide explicit information about either seasonal, temporary or permanent migration to Burma or Arakan. Nonetheless, trends, figures, growth rates, and gender balance revealed by data from 1872 to 1931 (but more specifically 1891 to 1931, when provincial records were included in the census tables) provide a context which supports the descriptions made in Burma's administrative records of the seasonal and settlement migration of Chittagonians to Arakan.[75]

The corollary of the dominant Chittagonian male population recorded in the decennial records of Akyab District (Arakan) must be assumed to be a corresponding imbalance of a higher female population in the census records of Chittagong district. This is indeed what data at the district and *thana* level show.[76] Much colonial ink was spilled in comments about the higher percentage of the male population in the total pop-

---

[75] Sources used for the present section are the imperial and provincial tables of the Bengal census records from 1872 to 1931. See J.A. Bourdillon, *Report on the Census of Bengal 1881 volume II, Appendix B Statements I to XXI*, Bengal Secretariat Press, Bengal, 1883; J. A. Bourdillon, *Report on the Census of Bengal 1881 volume III*, Bengal Secretariat Press, Bengal, 1883, Appendix C, statements XXI to XXX; C. J. O'Donnell, *Census of India 1891, volume IV, The Lower Provinces of Bengal and their Feudatories*, Bengal Secretariat Press, Calcutta, 1892 (see the Administrative Tables); E.A. Gait, *Census of India 1901, volume VI B, The Provinces of Lower Bengal and their Feudatories*, Bengal Secretariat Press, Calcutta, 1902 (see the Provincial Tables); L.S.S. O'Malley, *Census of India 1911 Volume VI Bengal*, Bengal Secretariat Depot, Calcutta, 1913, Part II Tables; W.H. Thompson, *Census of India 1921 volume V Bengal*, Bengal Secretariat Book Depot, Calcutta, 1922, Part II Tables; A.E. Porter, *Census of India 1931 volume V Bengal and Sikkim*, Central Publications Branch, Calcutta, 1933, Part II Tables.

[76] The observation was first made by the author of the 1872 census report, explaining that in Akyab district, the balance was 53.56 per cent males to 46.44 per cent females, while in Chittagong, it stood at 47.5 per cent males to 52.5 per cent females. See Burma Census 1872 Report, p. 16, see above note 62.

---

ulation of India.[77] This was the norm in Bengal, too, with a single, barely varying exception, Chittagong district, which counted more women than men on average. In 1891, there were 8.67 per cent more women recorded than men; in 1931, the difference was still 5.55 per cent. This does not mean that the excess number of women in Chittagong's district population was a biological or an otherwise permanent phenomenon; the statistical difference denotes that when the census was taken (generally in February or March), there were more women recorded than men. The seasonal migration described by British administrators in Arakan is one very likely explanation for this observation. In absolute numbers, throughout the period under consideration, the excess varied between 43,000 to 52,000 for Muslim women and 1,500 to 13,000 for Hindu women. These numbers would admittedly request further study to unravel age cohorts and tease out the groups corresponding more immediately to the male-age cohorts recorded in the Akyab district tables of the Burma census.

The population of the Moishkhali-Kutubdia coastal *thana* (Cox's Bazar sub-division) in 1901 was recorded as *lower* by 7.3 per cent than in 1891. This loss was linked to the detrimental effect of the 1897 cyclone which did, as the census report tells us, almost as much damage as the one of 1876. During the 1881–1891 decade, the population recovered by 29.5 per cent while after a dip, it rose by 37.4 per cent from 1901 to 1911.[78] The huge gap of 25 per cent between the male and the female Muslim population in 1901 suggests that many men had left for seasonal work in Arakan. The total population must therefore have been higher during the 'none-harvesting-season' of the year. While the population of Moishkhali-Kutubdia increased considerably until 1911, the gender gap still remained at an impressive 16 per cent. If the gender gap (indicating a higher female population at the moment of the decennial census record) is, as I assume, a valid indicator for male Muslim seasonal migration to Arakan, the decreasing percentages in 1921 (12 per cent) and 1931 (9 per cent) may suggest that the number of seasonal workers from this region going to Arakan remained stable in absolute numbers.

Census figures do also provide strong contextual grounds for the flow of emigrants out of Chittagong district. Eastern Bengal saw a con-

---

[77] See, for example, Henry Beverley, "The Census of Bengal", in *Journal of the Statistical Society of London*, 1874, vol. 37, no. 1, pp. 69–113; Henry Beverley, "Census of Bengal, 1881", in *Journal of the Statistical Society of London*, 1883, vol. 46, no. 4, pp. 680–690.

[78] Thompson, 1922, p. 88, see above note 75.

siderable increase of its population from 1872 to 1931 in contrast with West Bengal. Census figures of Burdwan, Presidency and Rajshahi divisions show a moderate growth (13.7, 36.2 and 28.5 respectively) when compared with Dacca and Chittagong divisions (with 82 and 98.4 per cent respectively). However, within Chittagong division the population of the districts of Tippera and Noakhali more than doubled, while Chittagong district's population rose much less (59 per cent).[79] These general observations are only moderately helpful for our investigation, unless we focus our attention on the demographic growth in the individual 'thanas', the administrative units below the sub-divisional or district level.[80]

Chittagong district, which counted approximately 1.8 million people in 1931, was divided into the northern Sadar and the southern Cox's Bazar subdivisions. Cox's Bazar is the subdivision sharing a border with Arakan's Akyab district. The demographic growth of these two subdivisions from 1872 to 1931 was strikingly different. While the 'thanas' in Sadar subdivision had an average population growth of 28 per cent (excluding the fast growing urban agglomeration of Chittagong), the 'thanas' of Cox's Bazar subdivision had an average of 145 per cent.[81] This is not surprising because even in 1921, the southern part of Chittagong district was seen as "only partially developed" and attracted migrants.[82] Tek Naf, the 'thana' stretching along the Naf River opposite Burma, saw an unbroken population growth of 162 per cent in 60 years.[83] The settlement migration from Chittagong district in Bengal to Akyab district in Burma should therefore be seen, as I have argued above, in the perspective of a southward migratory push towards regions where new agricultural lands could be exploited in the late-nineteenth and early-twentieth century.

---

[79] The population increased strongly in the 1920s. The 1872–1921 increase was 43 per cent.

[80] Since 1982, a 'thana' is called 'upazila' in contemporary Bangladesh and defined as a sub-unit of a district. See "Upazila", on Wikipedia (available on its web site).

[81] For practical reasons, the figures of the census records have been aligned with the 'thanas' as they existed in 1872 when their number was still lower. 'Thanas' in Sadar division were Fatikchari, Hathazari, Raojan, Chittagong (Kotwali), Mirasarai, Sitakund, Patiya, Sitkania and Banshkali. 'Thanas' formed in 1921 include Rangunia, Double Moorings, Panchalais, Boalkhali and Anwara. English spellings of several of these terms vary.

[82] Thompson, 1922, p. 88, see above note 75.

[83] Cox's Bazar sub-division counted four 'thanas' in 1872: Cox's Bazar, Moishkhali (Maheshkhali), Teknaf and Chakaria. By sub-divisions, this number increased with the creation of new units: Ukhia (since 1911) and Ramoo and Kutubdia (since 1921). The percentage of 162 per cent for Tek Naf includes the data of the 'thana' of Ukhiya for the years 1911, 1921 and 1931.

Like Moishkhali-Kutubdia, the population of Teknaf-Ukhia area, opposite Maungdaw township (Arakan), was also lower in 1901 than in 1891, and it stagnated for another 20 years, rebounding only after World War I. In this case, however, there was no noteworthy gender gap to be observed in any of the five decennial census years, so that seasonal work (and a temporary absence of Muslim men) cannot explain the low level of the population. As the time period of this stagnation (the two and a half decades before World War I) matches quite exactly the growth phase of Chittagonian settlements in north Arakan, a likely hypothesis is the emigration of people from or coming through this area into Arakan. One may indeed suggest that people moved from elsewhere in Chittagong division, too, going further south-east and crossing the Naf River, but sources would not allow an assessment of their origins.[84]

Seasonal or temporary migrants also came from areas in Sadar subdivision further north. A gender gap indicating a higher female Muslim population fluctuating between 11 and 16 per cent in decennial records was a constant phenomenon in the '*thanas*' of Sitkania, Banshkhali and Anwara, bordering on Cox's Bazar subdivision. Patiya '*thana*' seems to have sent seasonal workers to Arakan until World War I, but less afterwards. On the other hand, in the late colonial period, seasonal workers seem to have come from much further away such as Hathazari, Mirsharai and Sitakund (all situated north of the city of Chittagong), a trend one can observe after 1901.

With few exceptions, the Bengal census data do not explicitly refer to or prove the migratory movements one observes in the record of Arakan, but both at macro and micro levels, they mirror and provide context to the rural demographic developments in Arakan.

6.5. Chittagonians and the Rise of a Self-Organized Muslim Society in North Arakan

The descriptive elements traced in colonial sources on the Chittagonian settlements in north Arakan suggest the genesis of a self-organizing collectivity forming besides Arakan's majority Buddhist society.

---

[84] Muslim men from the Cox' Bazar-Ramu area do not seem to have been involved in the annual seasonal migration, while the Chakaria area was less involved than neighbouring Moishkhali.

In the middle of the nineteenth century, north Arakan was under-populated; Chittagonian settlers joined a sparse Arakanese population, settlements grew with land grants, and waste lands became rice fields. British administrators outlined matter-of-fact differences between both population groups – their houses were built differently; the way of culti-vating was not the same – but their notes do not contain observations on cultural practices or social organization. The topic in which we are keenly interested in hindsight, such as village neighbourhoods, inter-ethnic rela-tions, and the power balance among the rural elites, are absent from de-scriptions.

Accounts reiterate the favourable British views of Chittagonian thrift, as explained above. Early on, the Bengali gardens had caught the eye of the administrators.

> This would show that the Bengalee holdings of paddy land are considerably smaller than those of the Mughs (*that is* Arakanese). In garden-land holdings [...] there is little difference in the area, but in the cultivation of miscellaneous produce, the Bengalees have certainly more land, and it is a class of cultivation in which they doubtless excel the Mughs.[85]

Early descriptions convey a picture of self-isolating communities.

> Natives of India are found chiefly in Maungdaw and on the waste land grants above Buthidaung, where they far out-number all other races. They live in their own villages and do not mix in any way with the Arakanese population. Whilst almost every Arakanese can talk Chittagonian, very few na-tives are acquainted with the language of their adopted coun-try and none can read it."[86]

However, it would be wrong to assume that Buddhist and Muslim societies did not interact and even influence each other in their social modes and habits. One may point to the transactional role of Muslim trad-ers, peddlers, fishermen and producers of dry fish.

Still, against the background of a very limited body of sources, there is surely a need to theorize Buddhist-Muslim relations to structure

---

[85] Revenue Settlement Operations Report 1867–68, p. 35, see above note 23.

[86] W.E. Lowry, *Report on the revision settlement operations in the Akyab district Season 1901–02*, British Burma Press, Rangoon, 1903, p. 5.

the rise and the presence of a concentrated Muslim community of largely migrant origins in north Arakan. While this challenge cannot be addressed in the present chapter, a few elements for such a discussion can be sketched. Any research on the 'Chittagonians', as outlined in the introduction of this chapter, is over-shadowed, not to say predicated, first, by the post-colonial rise of the Rohingyas as an ethnic expression of north Rakhine Muslims and as a localized movement in Burma's post-independence political landscape; second, by territorial claims formulated by North Rakhine Muslim leaders after the end of World War II; third, by the domestic contestation of Muslim claims for self-identification; and, fourth, by a process of legal exclusion, denial of rights and physical oppression led by the state. Our intention to understand regional history and connect the colonial past of the multiple populations of Arakan with the post-colonial conundrum of Rakhine State is therefore heavily impacted by the need to disentangle, in a long-term diachronic perspective, the conflicted histories of self-affirmation of both Buddhists and Muslims, the histories of intercommunal relations and victimization and the role of the state and the military in the late colonial and the post-colonial as well as the World War II period.

The issue of the so-called deep roots of the ethno-political conflict in Rakhine State is not a question about what went wrong at a particular moment in the past, but about the dynamics of an open-ended conflictual process, which emerged since the colonial period. Pace the intentions of those who want to rename pre-World War II Muslims of north Arakan 'Rohingyas' in the name of retro-projecting a sense of historical justice. Arguably, the selfhood of colonial Chittagonian migrants must also be recognized in its own right. Their existence should not be erased from the historical record, sacrificed to twenty-first century 'political correctness' or falsified. Many years before the Burmese state and its security forces became a dominating actor in Rakhine State, the Japanese invasion and the breakdown of the British administration (1942) opened a domestic political space filled by the ethnopolitical goals and territorial ambitions of both Buddhists and Muslims. Short- and long-terms interests were diverging, and both communities were turning to the state for recognition and validation. The issues of acculturated Arakanese Muslims or newly self-identifying Rohingya Muslims do not conflict with the evidence of migrant population growth. Acculturation and ethnification cannot, however, be discussed outside the rapidly changing social and political contexts hitting the Buddhist majority and the Muslim minorities in the Bengal-Arakan borderlands.

What comes to mind in the Myanmar context is the concept of the plural society seen by J.S. Furnivall as people who mix but do not combine, who meet in the marketplace but do not share culture. The concept of a 'parallel society', much discussed by German scholars in the early twenty-first century ('*Parallelgesellschaften*') points to ethnically distinctive communities in contemporary Western societies and the expression includes the notion of deliberate segregation which could be relevant to discuss the manifest process of alienation underpinning communal relations in Arakan/Rakhine State.

The way that ethno-religious communities competed for social, economic and political shares in the modernizing project of the colonial rulers further suggests the need for a bottom-up perspective. In a history from below, the ruthless prioritization of productivity undermined the traditional cultural hierarchy and turned upside down a territorial and social order where Buddhist Arakanese (with the exception of a tiny class of wealthy families) were receding while immigrants were expanding.

The sections below drawing on colonial census data present the growth of the Muslim community in Akyab district, particularly in Maungdaw and Buthidaung townships, demonstrate the impact of immigration as the major factor of Muslim population growth and provide an overview of migrant and indigenous Muslim communities in Akyab district. They provide important though unquestionably limited insights into Muslim communal formations and 'sedimentary' diversity. Yet these insights shed light on conditions right at the moment when communal riots broke out in 1942 pitting Muslims and Buddhists competing for the control of agricultural lands against each other.

6.5.1. The Growth of the Muslim Community in Arakan During the Colonial Period

The data contained in Burma census reports have been rightly criticized, first of all by British colonial administrators themselves looking back at the work of their predecessors. Criticisms extend to the quality of the numerical record, the reliability of the figures collected, the choice of categories to organize the data, and in more recent days, the racial and ethnicized classification, which essentialized the identities of people in ways that had little consideration for social change and inter-ethnic complexity.

Rohingya writers have criticized the British record of the Muslim population in Arakan arguing that there was no settlement immigration, because
Muslims included in the census records, taken early in the year, were actually seasonal migrants.[87] This is an important observation, but iit cannot
be answered in a fully satisfactory way, because, as mentioned above, we
do not know the volume of seasonal migrants in the census years more
than in any other year as it was not recorded. A difference of a few days
could indeed have a relevant impact on the total number to be recorded.[88]
The assumed over-estimation (mostly of Muslim men) must therefore
have declined, as the date of the census receded from mid-February to
mid-March from 1881 to 1921. Any over-estimation must also have had a
lesser impact, as the general population grew while there is no indication
that seasonal migration increased over time. There is one occurrence
where the difference must be taken into account, as it created a statistical
deviance. The 1872 census was taken in August, "during the rains after
the coolies had returned home", while the 1881 census was the earliest
census ever taken "in the height of the milling season".[89] Nonetheless, as
the present research shows, it is not the development of the total number
of Muslims in Akyab district which is the most relevant observation, but
the divergence in local community growth. It is the territorial aspect and
the social context that matter, much less than absolute numbers.

Despite many critical inputs on the deficiencies of the colonial
sources and the caveats to heed, the census figures are the only source
where we can find answers to questions on demographic change. As seen
above, the textual evidence on migration to north Arakan provides a continuous and therefore reliable indication about the flow of Chittagonian
immigration.

The 'imperial' and 'provincial' tables provide series of data to build
coherent arguments about the growth of the general population, the
growth of the Muslim communities, the proportions of different communities, and most importantly developments at a local level.

---

[87] The dates of the India and Burma census were 15 August 1872, 17 February 1881, 26 February 1891, 1 March 1901, 10 March 1911, 18 March 1921, and 24 February 1931.

[88] "A postponement of the record by ten days in the busiest portion of the emigration season
would cause a marked reduction in the number of immigrants to be entered". See Eales,
1892, p. 72, see above note 41.

[89] *Ibid.*

The present section argues that Chittagong immigration was social-ly and economically important, had a major impact on the demographic development of Arakan, and recreated the religious and social landscape of Akyab district.

Minor numerical differences between imperial and provincial tables for district and township totals are recurrent but statistically insignificant and remain un-noted. The small ethnic minority groups (such as Mro, Khami and Daingnak) are not taken into account in this research; the Kaman and Myedu communities are not included or discussed because they were numerically inconsequential, and were never distinguished offi-cially as separate groups before 1931. The districts under consideration are Akyab, Kyauk Phyu and Sandoway, leaving aside the Arakan Hill Tracts, which are irrelevant for the present investigation. The study of the Chittagonian immigration to Arakan is mostly a study of the Muslim mi-grant flow to the various townships of Akyab district. Myebon township, belonging to Kyauk Phyu district, is an exception; it was allegedly home of indigenous Muslims tracing their origins back to the seventeenth centu-ry, but became a destination for Chittagonian migrants after World War I.

To simplify comparisons, data of Kyauk Phyu and Sandoway, form-ing the south of Arakan, have been put together. Kyauk Phyu and Sando-way together formed 40 per cent of Arakan's population in 1872, but this percentage fell to 35 per cent until 1931. Akyab's rise was due to a num-ber of factors, three of the reasons are the extension of the land used for rice cultivation, Akyab port's rise as a trade hub, and the Chittagonian immigration. It is useful to recall that Chittagonians were not the only set-tlers coming to Arakan. Between the First and Second Anglo-Burmese Wars, Burmese from Lower Burma came to south Arakan, people from Upper Burma arrived after 1852, the arrival of Chinese, though marginal, was noted since the 1860s. Hindus were an economically relevant but numerically insignificant group during the entire colonial period, making up around 2.5 per cent of the population in Akyab district, but staying be-low 1 per cent anywhere else in Arakan. Nonetheless, Hindu Oriyas, non-Chittagonian Bengalis, and Muslim 'Madrassis' counted among the colo-nial immigrants, too. Domestic Buddhist migration from Ramree played an important role in the development of villages in the Rathedaung and Buthidaung areas and is frequently managed in gazetteers and census rec-ords.

From 1872 to 1931, the population of Akyab district grew by 130 per cent, the growth in Kyauk Phyu and Sandoway was 76 per cent (see Graph 1 below). Akyab district's population grew 42.6 per cent from 1870 to 1900 and only 24 per cent from 1900 to 1930. The author assumes that immigration declined as a factor of growth after World War I, as three quarters of the Muslim population were born in Arakan in 1931. Fertility became the essential growth factor.[90] Nonetheless immigration did not disappear and spilled over into the southern townships.[91]

Table 1 shows the growth of the population in Arakan division, Akyab district, and Kyauk Phyu-Sandoway districts. Akyab district's growth was driving the division's demographic growth. The surge between 1872 and 1881 has been explained above as a result of different dates for the census. The rise between 1891 and 1901 marks the most visible moment of growth due to immigration.

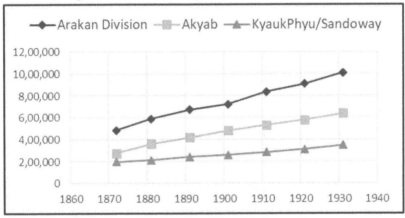

Graph 1: General population growth in Arakan division, Akyab district and Kyauk Phyu-Sandoway districts (1871-1931).

A comparative view of the growth of Muslim communities in Arakan division and Akyab district shows that Akyab district was driving Muslim population growth between 1872 and 1901 (Graph 2). In the early-twentieth century, the percentage of Akyab district Muslims in the total

---

[90] The British rule of thumb for the composition of a Buddhist household in Arakan was five and for a Muslim household six people.

[91] The 1921 and 1931 census differentiate between indigenous and immigrant Chittagonian and Bengali Muslims. The growth of the tiny Muslim communities in Kyauk Phyu and Sandoway was essentially due to migration.

Muslim population started to fall to some extent from its peak of 98 per cent. This may confirm, as I would assume, the increasing impact of immigration on the Muslim communities in the districts of Kyauk Phyu and Sandoway.

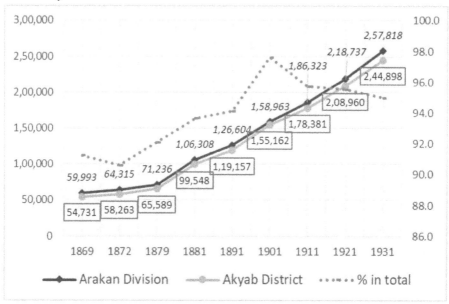

**Graph 2: A comparative view of Muslim population growth
in Arakan division and Akyab district.**

The share of Muslims in the total population of Arakan division grew under colonial rule. Muslims formed 12.24 per cent of the general population in 1869 and 25.56 per cent in 1931. In Akyab district, the percentage of the Muslim population went up from 20.67 per cent in 1869 to 38.41 per cent in 1931. These developments are represented in Graph 3. The surge appearing from 1879 to 1881 has already been explained as a statistical deviance due to the different dates of the census in 1872 and 1881. The increase during the 1891–1901 decade confirms the observations made by British administrators of a rise in Chittagonian settlers. The rise of the population in Naaf township then led to the creation of a new township to the east of Maungdaw, Buthidaung, which absorbed one-third of the former population of Rathedaung township and was included for the first time in the 1911 census.

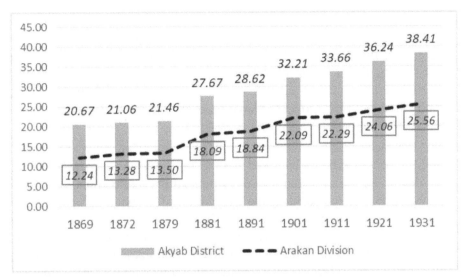

Graph 3: Percentage of Muslims in the total population of Arakan division and Akyab district

The graphs underscore the demographic importance of Akyab district and its population dynamics within Arakan division. A remarkable rise of the percentage of Muslims in the Akyab population took place from the late 1860s onwards with a decade of fast growth after 1891.

6.5.2. A Majority Muslim Society in North Arakan: The Case of Maungdaw and Buthidaung

To understand the territorial aspect and the social implications of the demographic increase of one group in comparison to the other, research needs to focus on the data at township level. Akyab's townships counted each between approximately 48,000 and 140,000 people in 1931. At the end of the colonial period, the percentage of Muslims in each of the nine townships of Akyab district varied between 4 per cent in Ponnagyun and 80 per cent in Maungdaw township. Buddhist-Muslim relations and communal cohabitation evolved in different shapes and contexts.

In Akyab township (the provincial capital including the port and surrounding villages), the Muslim percentage gyrated around 50 per cent between 1891 and 1931 with a population that did not substantially increase. Ponnagyun did not see any major percentual change of the Muslim share either. However, in Minbya and Pauktaw, there was a significant increase, from 7.2 per cent in 1891 to 14 per cent in 1931 for Minbya, and from 7.8 per cent to 12.8 per cent in Pauktaw. This may seem small, and absolute numbers are indeed small, but as the author has suggested elsewhere, it is this localized, but perceptible increase in combination with other factors, like a lesser availability of agricultural land and simultaneous Buddhist population growth in these townships of central Arakan, which could contribute to an explanation of the outbreak of the communal riots of 1942 in these townships.[92]

We lack a detailed record for Maungdaw township before 1891 when the census records included for the first time the provincial tables with details on the composition of its population. Chittagonian migrants formed already 70 per cent of the population of Maungdaw in 1891 and their uncontested domination was confirmed throughout the next forty years with a further steady increase. As mentioned above, prior to 1911, Maungdaw was called Naaf township, taking the name of the river separating Arakan from Bengal. Naaf/Maungdaw township was and remained by far the biggest township of Arakan division. It had nearly 100,000 people in 1891 and about 140,000 in 1931.

With the exception of Buthidaung (90,000 people in 1931), Maungdaw counted much more than the double of the population of any other township (having an average of 55,000). When land became scarce in Maungdaw, settlers moved over the Mayu Range into the Mayu and Kalapanzin River valleys where Buthidaung township was formed in 1908. Buthidaung had a majority Muslim population of nearly 60 per cent after World War I. Its territory had been cut off from Rathedaung township, as the Muslim-majority part of the latter. Rathedaung is situated further south on the eastern Mayu River side and any regional comparisons need to include this township. After the creation of Buthidaung township in 1911, Rathedaung's Muslim population fell back to a fifth of its total population, its level in 1891.

The following tables show the respective development of the Buddhist and Muslim populations in Maungdaw, Rathedaung and Buthidaung. When the 1890s saw an increase in migration, Maungdaw's population did *not* grow; it even receded. Buddhist Arakanese moved away under the migrant pressure, as the British administrators noted. But the Muslim population did not grow much either. However, in the Mayu Valley, the population of Rathedaung steeply increased, both the Buddhist (30 per

---

92   Leider, 2020, see above note 47.

cent) and the Muslim (255 per cent) communities grew, though at widely different speed.

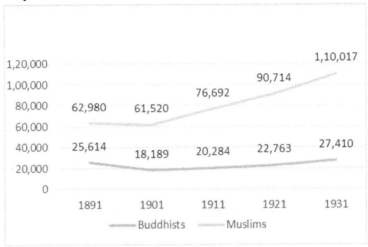

**Graph 4: Growth of the major population groups
in Maungdaw township (1891–1931).**

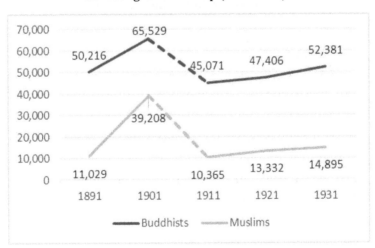

**Graph 5: Growth of the major population groups
in Rathedaung township (1891–1931).**

After 1901, Maungdaw's Muslims confirmed their regional predominance while the growth of its Buddhist population became disconnected from the rapid Muslim increase. Both in Rathedaung and Buthidaung, domestic migrants contributed to the growth of the Buddhist population after World War I. This growth was more marked in Buthidaung, an agricultural frontier zone, than in Rathedaung.

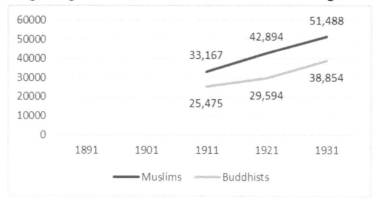

Graph 6: Growth of the major population groups of Buthidaung township (1911–1931).

Like Maungdaw, Buthidaung became the site of extreme communal violence in 1942 and 1943. Buddhists in Buthidaung first resisted Muslim aggressions that had been provoked by the explosion of anti-Muslim violence perpetrated in Minbya, Pauktaw and Myebon. But they were driven out of Buthidaung by campaigns in May 1942 and in the wake of the First Arakan campaign (December 1942–April 1943).[93] As an area where both Buddhist and Muslims competed for the ownership of land and the return on agricultural investment, the demographic balance (60:40) reflects a picture where no group would likely give in to pressure.

6.5.3. 'Arakan Mahomedans' and Chittagonians

The acculturated community of Arakan Muslims ('Arakan Mahomedans') was well described in the 1872 census and occasionally described by later colonial administrators.[94] Though it was a small group spread nearly all

---

[93] *Ibid.*

[94] The census of 1872 gives a valid description for the entire colonial period, contextualizing the group of local Muslims with regard to the immigrants:

The Mussulman population of Akyab, however, is not, as elsewhere in the province, alien, as they have for the most part been settled in the province for many generations, and, as the Commissioner of the division says, have little to distinguish them from the Arakanese, except their religion. These, and they are probably more than three-fourths of the Mussulmans of the district, have of course, their wives and families with them, and the examination of the distribution of the people according to age in the succeeding chapters shows that the disparity between the sexes is confined to the ages

over Arakan, its existence since pre-colonial times was never in doubt. They were the descendants of those Bengalis who had been deported by the Arakanese kings during war campaigns in Lower Bengal in the early seventeenth century and settled on royal lands in the Kaladan and Lemro Valleys, in the vicinity of Mrauk U (colonial 'Myohaung'), the former capital, and Kyauktaw.[95] However, being bundled together with other Muslims by the colonial administration and speaking an East Bengali dialect like the Chittagonians, they became nearly invisible statistically in the census from 1872 to 1921. The 1931 census introduced a racialized classification which drew a line between Chittagonian Muslims and Arakan Muslims; this enables a numerical differentiation of the two groups at township level. The present section will focus on the analysis of these data and the resulting profile of the indigenous Arakan Muslims.

With the formation of British Burma in 1862, bringing together Arakan, Tenasserim and Lower Burma, the administration of the colony was unified. The annual *Report on the Administration of the Province of British Burma* was first published for the year 1861–62 and the series ran until 1935–36, including occasionally brief ethnographic notes. As the British administrators had noted the presence of indigenous, acculturated Muslims in several ports along the coast, from Tenasserim to Arakan, they referred to these Muslim people as "Mahomedans of Burma". The annual reports of the 1860s classify around five per cent of the total population in Arakan as "Mahomedans of Burma"; the remaining seven per cent were categorized as "Indians", meaning recent immigrants.[96] In fact, this accul-

---

between 20 and 50 – that is to say, to the prime of life, – and is accounted for by thea able-bodied immigrants who bring no families.

See Burma Census 1872 Report, p. 16, see above note 62. Regarding their origins, the report noted:

There is one more race which has been so long in the country that it may be called indigenous, and that is the Arakanese Mussulman. These are descendants, partly of voluntary immigrants at different periods from the neighbouring province of Chittagong, and partly of captives carried off in the wars […].

Ibid., p. 30. See also Webb, 1912, p. 98, see above note 37.

[95] Stephan van Galen, "Arakan and Bengal The Rise and Decline of the Mrauk U kingdom (Burma) from the fifteenth to the seventeenth century AD" PhD, Leiden University, Leiden, 2008; Thibaut D'Hubert, *In the Shade of the Golden Palace Alaol and Middle Bengali Poetics in Arakan,* Oxford University Press, 2018.

[96] One may compare this total of 12 per cent with the 15 per cent indicated by Arthur P. Phayre 20 years earlier when he was the commissioner of the province; see Arthur P. Phayre, "Account of Arakan", in *Journal of the Asiatic Society of Bengal,* 1841, vol. 2, pp.

turated group was already identified much earlier among refugees and deportees from Arakan following the Myanmar conquest of 1784. Francis Buchanan identified such Muslims from Arakan in Burma's capital Amarapura (who used an East Bengali expression for Arakan, "Rooinga") during a visit in 1795, while the Reverend J.C. Fink, who missionized among the Arakanese refugees in Chittagong in the early-nineteenth century, called them "Mugh Mussulmans", "Mugh" being a common Bengali term for the Arakanese.[97] Besides, we may note that, not unlike British perceptions of the Arakanese, the colonial gaze first fixed the indigenous Arakan Muslims as "a hard working industrious race ... too well known to need any description", while later, their cultural assimilation with the Arakanese made them suspect as being "sapped of their vitality" to do hard labour.[98]

In 1921, the census categorized Muslims in Arakan with greater detail than before. People could identify, for the first time, as 'Arakan Mahomedans', or as belonging to any of these four categories: (1) Chittagonian Mahomedans born in Burma, (2) Chittagonian Mahomedans born outside of Burma, (3) Bengali Mahomedans born in Burma, and (4) Bengali Mahomedans born outside of Burma.[99] In the end, the number of 'Arakan Mahomedans' looked suspiciously low as it turned out to be the same as the estimation of their number in 1872. It confirmed to some extent the confusing indications found in earlier census. In 1911, for example, the estimation of their number was below 5,000. In 1931, on the other hand, Muslims identifying as 'Arakan Mahomedans' counted over

---

679–712. The 1872 census report contains inconsistent statements on the part of indigenous Muslims among the Muslim population as a whole. On page 3, we are told that between 24,000 and 25,000 "Arakanese Mahomedans" differ from the Buddhists "in little besides their religion". However, on page 16, it is suggested that three quarters of the total of Muslims in Arakan must be indigenous, and on p. 30, it is stated that there were 64,000 "Arakanese Mussulmans". This confusion can be amended with the help of the data of the 1860s, which make clear that 24–25,000 is the reliable figure. Some 64,000 was the total of Muslims in Arakan in 1872. The "three quarters" guess is an error, see Burma Census 1872 Report, see above note 62. I am grateful to Derek Tonkin for pointing out this issue.

[97] Robert Robinson, *Among the Mughs or Memorials of the Rev. J. C. Fink, Missionary in Arracan*, The Light Press, Calcutta, 1871, pp. 79–80; Francis Buchanan, "A comparative vocabulary of some of the languages spoken in the Burma Empire", in *Asiatick Researches*, 1798, vol. 5, pp. 219–240.

[98] Revenue Settlement Operations Report 1867–68, p. 83, see above note 23; Smart, 1917, p. 15, see above note 25.

[99] "Bengali" denoted people from Bengal who were not Chittagonians.

50,000. This last result was annotated with the comment that census officers on the ground had spent more time explaining the concept of 'Arakan Mahomedan' identity before recording the answer. In 1921, we are told, certain people who fit the profile of 'Arakanese Mahomedans' had in fact identified as 'Indians'.

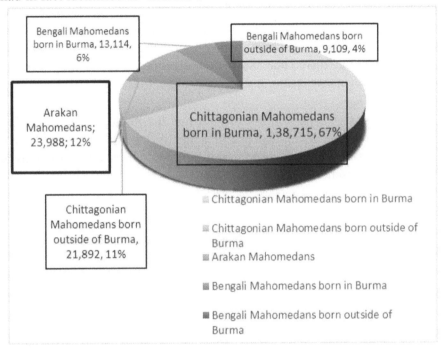

Graph 7: Muslim groups in Arakan according to the census of 1921.

While the colonial administration wanted to get closer to a definition of the supposed *racial* identity of its subjects, conditions and contexts of identity formation kept on changing.

The 1931 census further racialized the classification of people, and created novel categories. Immigrant Chittagonians and their descendants were "Indians" as belonging to the "Indian race", while local Arakan Muslims having mixed with the local population, belonged to the newly forged "Indo-Burman race" category. The fact that Indians were classified as foreigners, while mixed races were perceived as having historical roots in the country, produced a politically significant split.

The 1931 classification broke a line of continuity in numbering and grouping people so that the use of the 1931 census figures in comparison with earlier statistics needs some adjustments with inevitably imperfect results. The 1931 racial categories were as follows: (1) Burmese, (2) Other Indigenous, (3) Chinese, (4) Indian Hindu, (5) Indian Muslim, and (6) Indo-Burman races (referred to as "Others" in the provincial tables). In comparison with the religious groups of the previous census, Arakanese Buddhists and the hill tribes, formerly summed up separately as "animists", fell under the single "other indigenous" category in the imperial tables, while the Chinese emerged for the first time as a separate group. The racial difference between indigenous and foreign Muslims became a relevant criterion for classification which it had never been before.

As the 1931 census tables present the distribution of both Muslim groups at township level, we obtain a detailed picture to what extent Muslims identified as 'Arakan Mahomedans' and where they mostly lived. The result is presented in Graph 8.

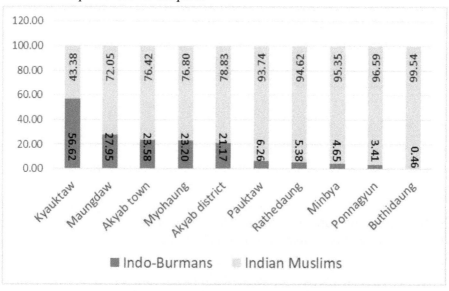

Graph 8: Percentage of 'Indian Muslims' and 'Indo-Burman Muslims' in the townships of Akyab district (Census of Burma, 1931).

The highest percentage of self-declared indigenous 'Arakan Mahomedans' was found in Kyauktaw, where Muslims formed 35 per cent of the total population. This reflects the ancient presence of Muslims near the royal capital Mrauk U (called Myohaung during the British period). Myohaung's substantial share of 23 per cent of Arakan Mahomedans calls for the same explanation. The lowest percentage (less than half per cent), on the other hand, is found in Buthidaung which had been created and evolved mainly as a township of new migrants, both Muslims and Buddhists. Nearly a quarter of Akyab's fishermen and traders claimed an indigenous identity as well which causes no surprise as the port at the mouth of the Kaladan River looked back on centuries of history. [100] In Pauktaw, Rathedaung, Minbya and Ponnagyun, four townships with smaller Muslim communities, the part of 'Arakan Muslims' was small, too.[101]

It is Maungdaw's 28 per cent of self-identifying Arakan Muslims which might at first come as a surprise. In the early-nineteenth century, Maungdaw was a tiny Buddhist village. A hundred years later, it was the centre of the most densely inhabited township of Arakan division. As shown above, both textual and numerical evidence underscore Maungdaw's rise as a settlement of immigrant Chittagonians. However, Maungdaw's society was, in comparison to Buthidaung and other townships, a society of first settlers and old residents and was not anymore, in the 1930s, the frontier region for agricultural entrepreneurs it used to be before 1900. One aspect of Maungdaw's Muslim society in the 1930s was its gender balance (male/female ratio) confirming its more

---

[100] Muslims accounted for 38 per cent of Akyab's population (Buddhists, 39 per cent, Hindus, 22 per cent). Akyab became the provincial capital in 1830, leading to the transformation of a village site into a rice-exporting port. The fact that nearly one quarter of the local Muslims identified as Arakanese Muslims – keeping a memory of ancient, pre-colonial roots in Arakan – underscores the historical presence of the Muslim fisher-village. Little is known in fact about Akyab's older history. Its religious composition barely changed during the late colonial period. In 1881, Muslims accounted for 40 per cent, Buddhists 38 per cent, and Hindus 19 per cent of the population (Christians and other religious communities counting for 3 per cent). See 1881 census report, p. 91, see above note 54.

[101] In Rathedaung township, 625 women identified as Arakan Muslims besides 176 men in the 1931 census. The male/female ratio is surprising. One possible explanation could be that these women were born as Buddhists, married Muslim men, converted to Islam and saw themselves as properly speaking Arakan Muslims. Inter-religious marriages are a subject that raises more questions in practice than can usually be answered with reference to the available sources. In general, the number of adult women was inferior to the number of male adults in both Buddhist and Muslim society in Arakan. So, it would seem unlikely that there were many interreligious marriages initiated by immigrant Muslim men. The legal situation of Buddhist women, who had converted to Islam, in family and inheritance disputes became a hot topic in colonial Burma's Buddhist society and remained so until today; it fed anti-Muslim polemics and was a matter of concern for the colonial rulers.

settled character; it did not have, like other townships, communities dominated by young Muslim males belonging to the 20–40-years cohort, typical for emerging and temporary migrant communities elsewhere.

This is a significant insight with regard to the interpretation of social and political trends which emerged under the onslaught of World War II and civil war conditions escalating in 1949. Kyauktaw and Myohaung Muslims could claim a distant Muslim heritage, but their numbers were few in comparison to Maungdaw's Muslims (see Graph 9). Calling oneself an 'Arakan Mahomedan' made clear that one did not want to be seen as a recent immigrant from across the border. The claim of belonging expressed by the adoption of 'Arakan Mahomedan' was due to expand.

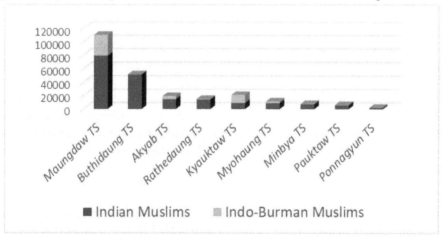

Graph 9: Quantitative levels of Muslims identifying as Chittagonians ('Indian Muslims') or Arakan Muslims ('Indo-Burman Muslims') (1931 Census of Burma).

Graph 9 illustrates the demographic ranking of Akyab's townships in terms of the total number of their Muslim population. It should be obvious that the two townships where Muslims formed a substantial majority were to play a dominant role among Akyab District's Muslims, due to their sheer demographic weight. Forty-five per cent of all Muslims in Akyab district lived in Maungdaw. The claims for the creation of an autonomous Muslim frontier zone were first raised in Maungdaw (in 1947) and Maungdaw's communal leaders (and, during the 1950s, its students at Rangoon University) played a pivotal role in the Rohingya movement. Neither Akyab's nor Kyauktaw's Muslims were critically involved in the rise of Arakan's Muslim sub-nationalism, which engulfed the region when the shackles of colonial rule loosened.

6.6. Conclusion

This chapter makes sense of the Chittagonian seasonal, temporal and permanent migration during the second half of the British colonial rule in Arakan (Rakhine State). It shows that the migratory flows from Bengal followed different dynamics. The settlement migration had a major social and economic impact, as it profoundly transformed the north of Arakan's Akyab district. Maungdaw and Buthidaung became densely cultivated and inhabited areas, which formed a stark contrast with the Buddhist majority areas further south.

The settlement immigration from Chittagong was not a chimera, and it cannot be confused with the seasonal migration and its symbiotic relationship with Akyab's rice production cycle. However, in the context of Bengal's colonial administration, seasonal and permanent migrations to Arakan formed, in quantitative terms, a minor phenomenon, and did not retain the attention of colonial administrators. Still, from an historical and economic perspective, the Chittagonian settlements in Arakan should not be isolated from their geographical origins. In the context of the Bengal-Arakan border region, the migratory flow matched the southward expansion of an agricultural frontier.

The investigation confirms that Muslim communities in Arakan were not a homogenous body, but formed a multi-layered and multi-sited religious group. The percentages and quantitative assessments derived from the 1931 census should not be essentialized or unduly extrapolated, because they offer just a snapshot of identities that were affected by changing circumstances. The erratic data of the pre-1931 census reports should not lead to the conclusion that 'Arakan Mahomedans' did not exist, came to exist lately, or appeared as a mere late trend to re-identify and shed off an immigrant profile. Our observations confirm the weakness and arbitrariness of colonial classifications. Yet, despite the indifference of the colonial apparatus to ethnic change, inconsistent and discontinuous classifications, and late colonial obsession with racial profiles, the records that were generated offer data which can be explored, re-examined, critically reviewed, and interpreted in respect of our own questions.

An attempt has been made to contextualize rather than interpret the data with regards to the later historical experience and the history of the 'now'. What this chapter contributes to research on the ethno-genesis of the Rohingyas, is the need for a greater awareness of complex and evolving Muslim identities during the colonial period. Studying the Chittagonian settlement migration is not in contradiction with the study of the Rohingyas and cannot be construed as conflicting with the sequential order of events. Understanding the rise of the modern Rohingyas means to understand another profound social and political transformation of the Muslims of north Arakan, inseparable from the colonial past. The socio-political process which conditioned post-colonial Muslim identities in Arakan was indebted to the radical breaks of World War II and the sequence of collective violence it ignited. This is an important chapter not included in this investigation. However, this process was rooted in the tension which was built up during the late colonial period and on which the administrative sources are mute. Nonetheless, the author suggests that demographic change was likely an important driver of these tensions which exploded with the communal riots of 1942. The question how Buddhists and Muslims were increasingly put into competition with each other for the control of land and resources calls for further analysis. How predictable was communal violence? How do colonial wrongs correlate with post-colonial injustice? It is against this background that the present investigation may function as an antidote to the 'confirmation bias' which has pervaded media dealing with the Rakhine State crisis since 2012, effectively preventing a transparent and balanced discussion of historical matters.

What the present research did not do is a comparative examination of the development of *both* population groups, Buddhists and Muslims. Identity formation among the Arakanese (Rakhine) Buddhists was similarly evolving as they did not exist as a homogenous group either, and were never categorized as uniformly such. The investigation also did not extract from the census data information on the composition of the population, age-cohorts and fertility, and did not pursue the question of male/female ratio. Such research would considerably flesh out the results presented here. It would notably show the influence that social habits of the majority population had on the minority group, and underscore the north-south divide in Arakan division which persists until today. Isolating the study of Buddhists and Muslims from each other is a methodological weakness, and while partial narratives feed victimhood narratives, they do not promote an understanding of the social and political gaps which came to divide the communities. The lack of demonstrating such underpinning complexity in this chapter is regretted. In view of broadening the social and political analysis, the role of Muslim and Buddhist rural and urban elites (political, administrative and educational) may be indicated finally as a relevant area for further research.

Myanmar, Colonial Aftermath, and Access to International Law

Morten Bergsmo[*]

7.1. Investigating in an Unusually Polarised Climate

On 4 July 2019, the Prosecutor of the International Criminal Court ('ICC') requested a designated pre-trial chamber to authorise an investigation into alleged crimes in Rakhine State in Myanmar since 9 October 2016.[1] The request was widely anticipated following a decision by ICC Pre-Trial Chamber I on 6 September 2018,[2] statements by the Prosecutor,[3] and var-

---

[*] **Morten Bergsmo** is Director, Centre for International Law Research and Policy (CIL-RAP). This chapter was first published on 15 August 2019 as Occasional Paper Series No. 9 (2019), Torkel Opsahl Academic EPublisher ('TOAEP'), Brussels, 2019 (https://www.toaep.org/ops-pdf/9-bergsmo). In the version that appears here the author has added some sources and updated where relevant. He thanks Antonio Angotti, CHAN Ho Shing Icarus, Wolfgang Kaleck, Claus Kress, Kyaw Yin Hlaing and SONG Tianying for their comments on the original version.

[1] ICC, Situation in the People's Republic of Bangladesh/Republic of the Union of Myanmar ('Situation in Bangladesh/Myanmar'), Office of the Prosecutor ('OTP'), Request for authorisation of an investigation pursuant to article 15, 4 July 2019, ICC-01/19-7 (146 pp.) ('ICC Prosecutor's Request') (http://www.legal-tools.org/doc/8a47a5/). The Prosecutor quotes a United Nations report which states that the objectives of the attacks by the Arakan Rohingya Salvation Army ('ARSA') in August 2017 "may not have been military, but aimed at eliciting a response by the [Myanmar Defense Services] (as in October 2016), with the broader goal of drawing renewed global attention to the Rohingya situation" (para. 64). She nevertheless holds that the alleged crimes committed by ARSA members "appear to fall outside the personal and territorial jurisdiction of the Court" (para. 65), seemingly excluding the possibility of forcible displacement.

[2] ICC, Situation in Bangladesh/Myanmar, Pre-Trial Chamber ('PTC') I, Decision on the "Prosecution's Request for a Ruling on Jurisdiction under Article 19(3) of the Statute", 6 September 2018, ICC-RoC46(3)-01/18-37 (http://www.legal-tools.org/doc/73aeb4/), in response to a request by the ICC Prosecutor on 9 April 2018 (ICC-RoC46(3)-01/18-1) (http://www.legal-tools.org/doc/4af756/). The Decision held that "acts of deportation initiated in a State not Party to the Statute (through expulsion or other coercive acts) and completed in a State Party to the Statute (by virtue of victims crossing the border to a State) fall within the parameters of article 12(2)(a) of the Statute" (para. 73), and if "at least an element of another crime within the jurisdiction of the Court or part of such a crime is com-

ious human rights reports.[4] It describes very serious allegations in tragic detail, centred around the crimes of deportation, persecution, and other inhumane acts. On 14 November 2019, Pre-Trial Chamber III authorised the commencement of an investigation into the Situation in Bangladesh/Myanmar,[5] and on 22 November 2019 the ICC Prosecutor confirmed that she will conduct such an investigation,[6] which is ongoing at the time of publication of this anthology. On 11 November 2019, The Gambia filed a case against Myanmar before the International Court of Justice ('ICJ') under the 1948 Genocide Convention.[7] In an Order dated 23 January 2020, the ICJ imposed three provisional measures confirming obligations Myanmar has as a State Party to the Genocide Convention and a bi-annual reporting obligation.[8] In a novel move, the Governments of Canada and the Netherlands stated their "joint intention to intervene in the matter of The Gambia v. Myanmar" on 2 September 2020.[9]

---

mitted on the territory of a State Party, the Court might assert jurisdiction pursuant to article 12(2)(a) of the Statute" (para. 74). The Prosecutor's Request follows this logic.

[3]   See, for example, ICC OTP, "Statement of ICC Prosecutor, Mrs Fatou Bensouda, on opening a Preliminary Examination concerning the alleged deportation of the Rohingya people from Myanmar to Bangladesh", 18 September 2018 (http://www.legal-tools.org/doc/32a147/).

[4]   Amnesty International's report, *"We Will Destroy Everything": Military Responsibility for Crimes Against Humanity in Rakhine State, Myanmar*, June 2018, ASA 16/8630/2018, stands out as being particularly thorough (http://www.legal-tools.org/doc/1358e2/).

[5]   ICC, Situation in Bangladesh/Myanmar, Pre-Trial Chamber III, Decision Pursuant to Article 15 of the Rome Statute on the Authorisation of an Investigation into the Situation in the People's Republic of Bangladesh/Republic of the Union of Myanmar, 14 November 2019, ICC-01/19-27 (https://www.legal-tools.org/doc/kbo3hy/).

[6]   ICC, Office of the Prosecutor, Statement of the Prosecutor of the International Criminal Court, Fatou Bensouda, following judicial authorisation to commence an investigation into the Situation in Bangladesh/Myanmar, 22 November 2019 (https://www.legal-tools.org/doc/paht1t/).

[7]   International Court of Justice, *Republic of The Gambia v. Republic of the Union of Myanmar*, Application Instituting Proceedings and Request for Provisional Measures, 11 November 2019 (https://www.legal-tools.org/doc/69p376/).

[8]   International Court of Justice, *Republic of The Gambia v. Republic of the Union of Myanmar*, Order of 23 January 2020, 23 January 2020 (https://www.legal-tools.org/doc/in5d55/). Myanmar filed its first, 195-page long report on 22 May 2020.

[9]   The Netherlands, Ministry of Foreign Affairs, Diplomatic statement, 2 September 2020 (https://www.legal-tools.org/doc/moqr0b/). The intention seems to be "to support these efforts which are of concern to all of humanity", and to "assist with the complex legal issues that are expected to arise and will pay special attention to crimes related to sexual and gender based violence, including rape" (*ibid.*).

International accountability for alleged crimes in Rakhine in 2017 has become a rallying cry of the international human rights movement. While recognising the gravity of the allegations that have been made, this chapter is not about these allegations or the ongoing processes of accountability, but about *how they may need to be supplemented*.

The former United Nations High Commissioner for Human Rights, Mr. Zeid Ra'ad al-Hussein, has played a leading role in condemning Myanmar for the alleged crimes in Rakhine and demanding international accountability. His rhetoric made headlines around the world after he publicly shamed Ambassador Kyaw Moe Tun, Myanmar's Permanent Representative to the United Nations in Geneva on 4 July 2018.[10] Mr. al-Hussein has continued his line on Myanmar after his term as High Commissioner ended, including by suggesting that genocide may have occurred in Rakhine.[11] Two of the Myanmar human rights mandates operating during his tenure adopted similar rhetoric.[12] Together, these actors

---

[10] See, for example, Nick Cumming-Bruce, "'Have You No Shame?' Myanmar Is Flogged for Violence Against Rohingya", *The New York Times*, 4 July 2018.

[11] See, for example, his audio-visual op. ed. "I Will Not Stay Silent. Our Leaders Are Failing Human Rights.", *The New York Times*, 6 May 2019. His co-authored op. ed. "The International Criminal Court Needs Fixing", *Atlantic Council*, 24 April 2019 (available on its web site) has also been seen as controversial. Observers have asked how Mr. al-Hussein could publicly attack the ICC in this manner when he served as the President of the Bureau of the Assembly of States Parties of the Court during the most critical period of its history. Indeed, no one contributed more to the election of the first ICC Prosecutor – widely considered the source of many of the problems that have plagued the Court since – than Mr. al-Hussein, as confirmed by the first Prosecutor in a recent publication, see Luis Moreno-Ocampo, "6. The International Criminal Court", in David M. Crane, Leila N. Sadat and Michael P. Scharf (eds.), *The Founders*, Cambridge University Press, 2018, pp. 95–125. Mr. al-Hussein also intervened in the start-up work of the ICC Office of the Prosecutor in ill-informed ways with significant negative consequences. It seems unavoidable that diplomatic failures around the ICC will be subjected to critical analysis, especially where it has unfairly complicated the work of the incumbent Prosecutor and Judges. See Morten Bergsmo, "Institutional History, Behaviour and Development", in Morten Bergsmo *et al.* (eds.), *Historical Origins of International Criminal Law: Volume 5*, TOAEP, Brussels, 2017, pp. 1–31 (http://www.legal-tools.org/doc/1c93aa/).

[12] The United Nations ('UN') independent international fact-finding mission on Myanmar, chaired by Mr. Marzuki Darusman, has suggested that "there is sufficient information to warrant the investigation and prosecution of senior officials in the Tatmadaw chain of command, so that a competent court can determine their liability for genocide in relation to the situation in Rakhine State", see Report of the independent international fact-finding mission on Myanmar, 12 September 2018, UN Doc. A/HRC/39/64, para. 87 (http://www.legal-tools.org/doc/61cb49/). It is difficult to understand how this respects the definition of the crime of genocide in the 1948 Genocide Convention as interpreted by the case

have contributed to the forging of a global moral narrative on Rakhine. This narrative is a part of the unusually blunt polarisation between the demand for international accountability by members of the international community, and the authorities of Myanmar.

This polarisation could become a problem for the ICC. For one, an exceptionally polarised environment can aggravate the challenge of group-think in refugee camps in Bangladesh,[13] cementing the risk of confirmation bias.[14] Potential witnesses may not adequately describe the con-

---

law of the ex-Yugoslavia and Rwanda Tribunals (– and I was responsible for legal submissions on genocide in the ex-Yugoslavia Tribunal's Office of the Prosecutor between 1994 and 2002). The ICC Prosecutor "has relied extensively" on the detailed report of the mission, see her Request, *supra* note 1, para. 29. UN Special Rapporteur for Myanmar, Ms. LEE Yanghee, also resorts to the genocide classification ("she is increasingly of the opinion that the events bear the hallmarks of genocide", see Report of the Special Rapporteur on the situation of human rights in Myanmar, 24 May 2018, UN Doc. A/HRC/37/70, para. 65 (http://www.legal-tools.org/doc/98d0a4/)). Moreover, by calling upon the authorities of Myanmar "to initiate a credible investigation into the killings in Kayah State by a body that is independent of the Tatmadaw" (*ibid.*, para. 39), she would seem to contradict Article 20(b) of the 2008 Constitution of Myanmar (http://www.legal-tools.org/doc/ea9567/).

As remarked in the online symposium 'On Myanmar' released by the Centre for International Law Research and Policy (CILRAP) (https://www.cilrap.org/myanmar/) on 14 August 2020, Dov Jacobs has pointed out that "nearly 500 (out of 775) footnotes" in the ICC Prosecutor's request to open an investigation "refer to various fact-finding or civil society reports. For the [Pre-Trial Chamber] decision [authorising the opening of the ongoing ICC investigation], nearly half of the footnotes refer to such reports". Jacobs has various methodological concerns and highlights "how it leads to the wholesale adoption of a one-sided narrative about the complex events that took place in Myanmar that underpins the rhetoric in fact-finding reports", see Dov Jacobs, "Limitations of Using Fact-Finding Reports in Criminal Proceedings: The Case of Myanmar", Policy Brief Series No. 118 (2020), TOAEP, Brussels, 2020 (http://www.toaep.org/pbs-pdf/118-jacobs/). Former United Kingdom Ambassador Derek Tonkin criticizes the UN Independent International Fact-Finding Mission on Myanmar on further grounds, see Derek Tonkin, "Mission Creep Untrammelled: The UN Fact-Finding Mission on Myanmar", Policy Brief Series No. 102 (2020), TOAEP, Brussels, 2020 (http://www.toaep.org/pbs-pdf/102-tonkin/).

It would seem that the anthology Morten Bergsmo and Carsten Stahn (eds.), *Quality Control in Fact-Finding* (TOAEP, Brussels, 2020, second edition (http://www.toaep.org/ps-pdf/19-bergsmo-stahn-second)) remains relevant for the UN Office of the High Commissioner for Human Rights.

13 See, for example, Hannah Beech, "The Rohingya Suffer Real Horrors. So Why Are Some of Their Stories Untrue?", *The New York Times*, 1 February 2018: "In any refugee camp, tragedy is commodified". See also SOMETAYA Ryuta, "Oppression Among the Oppressed: Inside Refugee Camps in Cox's Bazar", Policy Brief Series No. 105 (2020), TOAEP, Brussels, 2020 (http://www.toaep.org/pbs-pdf/105-sometaya/).

14 Moa Lidén, "7. Confirmation Bias in Investigations of Core International Crimes: Risk Factors and Quality Control Techniques", in Xabier Agirre, Morten Bergsmo, Simon De

---

text of international armed conflict or the crowd dimension of violations to life and the person in northern Rakhine communities from 25 August 2017.

An excessively polarised climate may also weaken recognition of the importance of turning every stone in making national investigations and prosecutions in Myanmar work. It would seem particularly important in the Myanmar context to avoid a general externalisation of accountability given the relative resourcefulness of its Office of the Judge Advocate General[15] as well as the security and constitutional realities of the country.[16]

Smet and Carsten Stahn (eds.), *Quality Control in Criminal Investigation*, TOAEP, Brussels, 2020; see also Moa Lidén, *Confirmation Bias in Criminal Cases*, Uppsala: Department of Law, Uppsala University, 2018, ISBN 978-91-506-2720-6 (doctoral thesis).

[15] SONG Tianying describes the domestic criminal justice accountability efforts, including by the Office of the Judge Advocate General, in her policy brief "Positive Complementarity and the Receiving End of Justice: The Case of Myanmar", Policy Brief Series No. 104 (2020), TOAEP, Brussels, 2020 (http://www.toaep.org/pbs-pdf/104-song/); see also CHAN H.S. Icarus, "'The People v. Myanmar': Of 'Compassion' in International Justice", Policy Brief Series No. 116 (2020), TOAEP, Brussels, 2020 (http://www.toaep.org/pbs-pdf/116-chan/). The Office has more than 90 staff members according to an e-mail message from the Office to the present author dated 10 July 2019 (including representatives based in regional commands). The military investigation into Rakhine allegations announced on 18 March 2019 (http://www.legal-tools.org/doc/03cf51/) falls under this Office. It has led to three convictions in the Gutarpyin case, the second court-martial concerning Rakhine 2017 crimes after the Inn Din case (where the ten convicted officers and soldiers were given an early pardon). On 15 September 2020, the Office announced that a third court-martial will start before the end of 2020, concerning allegations in Maung Nu and Chut Pyin, the most serious incidents in Rakhine in 2017 (see Press Statement by the Office of the Judge Advocate General, *Myawady in English*, 15 September 2020, p. 18 (https://www.legal-tools.org/doc/68qkxy/)). The Office also announced that it has started an investigation into "possible wider patterns of violations in the region of northern Rakhine in 2016-2017" (*ibid.*; see also Ministry of the Office of the State Counsellor, Statement by the Chairman of the Delegation of Republic of the Union of Myanmar at the General Debate of the 75th Session of the United Nations General Assembly, 29 September 2020, pp. 7–9 (https://www.legal-tools.org/doc/yd7ftx/). The ICC should welcome a possible prosecution by this Office of the Rakhine regional commander of the Myanmar Defence Services from 25 August 2017, who has already been discharged as an administrative sanction. The ICC Prosecutor's Request says that "the Prosecution will continue to review its assessment [of the military investigation] in light of new information as it becomes available", *supra* note 1, para. 246.

On the Independent Commission of Enquiry ('ICOE') – which submitted its final report of more than 450 pages on 21 January 2020 (see Executive Summary, 21 January 2020 (https://www.legal-tools.org/doc/h3k7jz/)) – the ICC Prosecutor's Request expresses that "it remains unclear if and how it is envisaged the ICOE's investigation will lead to

---

The Prosecution Request relies on the 6 September 2018 decision's[17] understanding of the crime of deportation and that a denial of the right to return may amount to the crime of other inhumane acts.[18] Both are welcomed as innovative by the international human rights community. This chapter does not engage with the jurisdictional assumptions underlying this understanding. It rather aims at highlighting that the Prosecutor's legal approach necessarily turns the spotlight on the demographic background of the conflict in northern Rakhine. That is a complex story, if not a minefield.

7.2. Transfers of Civilians into Burma

In navigating this terrain, persistent narrowing of the scope of analysis or sources entails risks.[19] A properly anchored understanding of Rakhine's demography needs to take into account relevant sources going back in time, not excluding the 1970s,[20] the 1950s,[21] and the late colonial period.[22]

---

criminal proceedings", but nevertheless makes assumptions about Myanmar law, *supra* note 1, paras. 251, 248. Under relevant laws of Myanmar, which are publicly available, the ICOE is a special investigations procedure, based on the Investigation Committees Act of 1 August 1949 (http://www.legal-tools.org/doc/039bfb/) whose earlier application and British colonial origin can be ascertained. The Court's characterisations of Myanmar law relevant to her ability to investigate and prosecute core international crimes require careful quality-control.

[16] In this context, the ICC Prosecutor's Request sweepingly claims that no "investigations or prosecutions are being, or have been undertaken by Myanmar authorities or in relevant third States, in relation to the potential case(s) identified in this Request and confidential *ex parte* Annexes 5 and 7, related to those who appear most responsible for the most serious crimes", *supra* note 1, para. 228. Quite apart from the accuracy of this description of the ongoing military investigation, does it encourage domestic investigation in Myanmar that the lists of potential cases and suspects are being withheld? Does this reflect a deeper understanding of the purpose of the principle of complementarity? We should avoid any perception of competition between international and national criminal justice.

[17] *Supra* note 2.

[18] ICC Prosecutor's Request, *supra* note 1, para. 75.

[19] Francis Wade's *Myanmar's Enemy Within: Buddhist Violence and the Making of a Muslim 'Other'*, Zed Books, London, 2017, is a popular reflection on identity, nationalism and history of Myanmar, so gripping that one almost does not realise that his analysis is virtually without footnotes. He barely touches on the British colonial period.

[20] To illustrate, this includes documents such as the 23 December 1975 minutes by the British Embassy in Rangoon of a meeting with the Bangladesh Ambassador K.K. Kaiser, during which the latter refers to "upward of ½ million Bangalee trespassers in Arakan whom the Burmese had some right to eject", quoted by former United Kingdom Ambassador Derek Tonkin, in "Exploring the Issue of Citizenship in Rakhine State", in Ashley South and Marie Lall (eds.), *Citizenship in Myanmar: Ways of Being in and from Burma*, Chiang Mai

---

University Press, 2018, p. 232. Ambassador Tonkin has pointed out to the author that this number may be described as higher than was stated due to confusion by the British Embassy at the time.

[21] Such as the United Kingdom Foreign Office, Research Department report "The Mujahid Revolt in Arakan", 31 December 1952 (http://www.legal-tools.org/doc/851b1e/). The report observes in paragraph 5 on pages 2-3:

> The great pressure of population in Bengal has led over the years to a steady movement southwards, with the result that the Chittagong district has become predominantly Indian-Muslim in character and has also become over-populated in relation to its resources; and there has naturally been an overspill into Northern Akyab [in Myanmar]. Particularly in the nineteenth century, when not only had the frontier been eliminated but also the extension of the Pax Britannica over India as a whole led to a rapid growth of population, this movement southwards developed and accelerated. In normal times, every year saw a large seasonal influx from Chittagong into Akyab district of coolies coming to work in the rice-fields: some went by sea direct to the port of Akyab, but many crossed the Naf river to Maungdaw and spread thence on foot. Naturally, some of them finally settled in the country, especially in the parts nearest their former homes, so that in 1917 the Settlement Officer reported that "Maungdaw township has been overrun by Chittagong immigrants. Buthidaung township is not far behind". [...] by 1931, the last year for which details of population are available, Indian Muslims, nearly all originating in Chittagong, formed 57 per cent of the population of the Maungdaw township and 56 per cent of the population of Buthidaung [...].

The ICC Prosecutor's Request notes that "according to statistics allegedly collected in 2016 by Myanmar's General Administration Department ("GAD"), Rohingya accounted for 93% of the population in Maungdaw Township in 2016, 84% of the population in Buthidaung Township", *supra* note 1, para. 38.

For Rakhine State as a whole, Frank S.V. Donnison wrote that the "population of Arakan in 1941 was slightly over a million, of whom some 600,000 were Arakanese and some 200,000 Chittagonian Indians, the rest being accounted for by various hill peoples and by minor communities in the plains. [...] The Chittagonian population had immigrated from Chittagong, some families many generations back, others recently. There was in addition, in peacetime, a seasonal and temporary immigration of agricultural labourers for the harvest. The Chittagonians were Muslim by religion and spoke the language of Chittagong", see his detailed study *British Military Administration in the Far East 1943-46*, Her Majesty's Stationary Office, London, 1956, p. 18 (part of the British government's multi-volume "History of the Second World War: United Kingdom Military Series", and as such described by the author as "contemporary history under official auspices", p. xiv).

See Chapter 6 above for a detailed analysis.

[22] Ambassador Tonkin remarks that 'Rohingya' is "an ethnic designation unknown to the former British administration", see *idem*, 2018, *supra* note 20, p. 222. He continues: "I have found not a single reference to the term "Rohingya" in any shape or form in any documents or correspondence, official or private, recording the 124 years of British rule in Arakan from 1824 to 1948" (p. 224); and adds: "The reason for this must surely be that the word means no more than "Arakaner" and is derived from the Bengali word for Arakan which is "Rohang" with a family taxonomic suffix – "gya"" (*ibid.*). There are obviously other views on this question. The argument of this chapter does not depend on any particular position or source on this or other historical details it touches upon. Azeem Ibrahim de-

It is not for this chapter to offer such a detailed chronicle, only to highlight relevant trends.

In his significant history of Myanmar, Dr. Thant Myint-U – grandson of the late U Thant, the third Secretary-General of the United Nations – soberly describes an important aspect of the current situation in Myanmar, including Rakhine State: "At the beginning of the [twentieth] century Indians were arriving in Burma at the rate of no less than a quarter million people a year. The numbers rose steadily until, in the peak year of 1927, immigration reached 480,000 people, with Rangoon exceeding New York City as the greatest immigration port in the world. This was out of a total population of only 13 million, the equivalent of the United Kingdom today taking 2 million people a year".[23] It may be appropriate to reflect on the sheer numbers for a moment. They only started to abate in the years after 1927. Aung San Suu Kyi referred in a 1991 publication to "a well-justified apprehension" among the Burmese late in the colonial period that "their very existence as a distinct people would be jeopardized if the course of colonial rule was allowed to run unchecked".[24]

The Burmese – who became a minority in their main city, Rangoon – had no say in this demographic transformation of their country. Britain fought three wars in order to occupy all of Burma and establish colonial rule by armed force.[25] To fuel her economic interests in rice pro-

---

bates Tonkin on the origins of 'Rohingya' identity, see his monograph *The Rohingyas: Inside Myanmar's Genocide*, Hurst & Company, London, 2018, pp. 30-31. But Ibrahim agrees with the specific trend discussed in this section, namely, large-scale migration "from British-ruled India to Burma before 1937" (p. 7). See Chapter 8 below for more detail on the colonial period.

[23] Thant Myint-U, *The River of Lost Footsteps: A Personal History of Burma*, Faber and Faber, London, 2007, pp. 185–86. Further research would probably provide more exact figures, taking into account immigration and emigration numbers, not limited to the port in Rangoon, but all major ports as well as land migration, to the extent such data is available. See Chapters 6 above and 8 below.

[24] Aung San Suu Kyi, *Freedom from Fear*, Penguin Books, London, 2010, pp. 103–04 (first published in 1991).

[25] In the words of Aung San Suu Kyi: "British annexation of Burma [...] was accomplished in three clear-cut phases spread out over little more than half a century. The first Anglo-Burmese War of 1824-6 ended with Arakan and Tenasserim passing under British rule; the second Anglo-Burmese War of 1852 added the province of Pegu to the British possessions; and, finally, the third Anglo-Burmese War of 1885 led to the subjugation of the whole country and brought an end to the Burmese monarchy", see *ibid.*, p. 84. The violence continued, starting with "a huge military deployment throughout the Irrawaddy Valley and continued with the large-scale and forced relocation of people. [...] Colonial magistrates

duction[26] and other sectors,[27] Britain allowed the transfer of millions of persons from her colonial India into Burma,[28] also leading to some conflicts between the Burmese and the immigrants.[29] In other words, Britain

---

were granted wide-ranging powers to move suspected rebel sympathizers, and dozens of villages were simply burned to the ground. Summary executions, sometimes by the half dozen or more, became routine, as did the public flogging of captured guerrillas", see Thant Myint-U, 2007, p. 29, *supra* note 23. To be sure, this refers to alleged conduct in 1886, not in Rakhine in 2017.

[26]   "Incomparably the most important [project for the re-occupation administration in Burma] was that for the revival of the rice trade" after the end of World War II, wrote Donnison, who explained that the concern at the time was that "no time whatever should be lost in reaching and developing the rice supplies of these exporting areas as soon as they were re-occupied", see *idem*, 1956, p. 263, *supra* note 21. Burma had become the largest exporter of rice in South-East Asia. Arakan was "a considerable rice-exporting area" (p. 264), since the "opening of the Suez Canal [in 1869] had favoured the production and the export of rice", see Jacques P. Leider, "Conflict and Mass Violence in Arakan (Rakhine State): The 1942 Events and Political Identity Formation", in South and Lall (eds.), 2018, p. 195, *supra* note 20.

[27]   Albeit facilitated by the British government, the basis of the British mass-transfers was commercial or military, not ideological. The South-East Asia Command "was concerned to import, for the period of [military administration at the end of World War II], a labour force of 150,000 to 200,000 men", as "labour required for the military forces", see Donnison, 1956, p. 316, *supra* note 21. For the situation where settlement could in part be based on ideological or religious conviction, see Morten Bergsmo, "Integrity as Safeguard Against the Vicissitudes of Common Justice Institutions", lecture presented in the Peace Palace, The Hague, 1 December 2018 (www.cilrap.org/cilrap-film/181201-bergsmo/).

[28]   Aung San Suu Kyi refers to this as an "unchecked influx of foreigners" which was "a major cause of the disintegration of traditional society", see *idem*, 2010, p. 101, *supra* note 24. She wrote in 1991 that "the increasing acreage of land brought under cultivation gave rise to a need for indentured labour which was supplied by India" (*ibid.*). Further: "Under British rule there was no control on the members of Indians and Chinese who came to seek their fortune in Burma" (*ibid.*, p. 66). Donnison refers to "unrestricted migration" from India, see *idem*, 1956, p. 315, *supra* note 21.

[29]   For example, "in 1938, on the pretext of an insult to the Buddhist religion, anti-muslim riots and massacres broke out, over most of the country, resulting in the death of some 200 Indians and the wounding of some 750 more", see *ibid.*, pp. 315–16. In May 1942, when the British forces withdrew from Rakhine as the Japanese advanced, "[c]ommunal strife and plundering [...] spread all over Arakan, Arakanese Buddhists massacring Chittagonians and Chittagonian Muslims massacring Arakanese each in the areas in which they predominated. [...] in the Muslim sphere all Buddhist pagodas and monasteries were razed to the ground, and the Burmese and Arakanese languages dropped out of use" (p. 21). Muslims had acted with "fanatical zeal to exterminate Arakanese Buddhists or to expel them from the areas of Muslim majority" (p. 22). Trying to analyse the impact of the 1942 events, Leider opines that in the "collective psyche of the Arakanese/Rakhine, the experience of 1942 toughened the perception of a demographic threat", see *idem*, 2018, p. 216, *supra* note 26. See also Jacques P. Leider, "Territorial Dispossession and Persecution in

---

transferred many more people into Burma than the overall number of Jewish settlers on the West Bank as of 1 January 2019, estimated at 449,508.[30] Why is this a relevant comparison?

The ICC Prosecutor has conducted a preliminary examination of alleged crimes in Palestine since 16 January 2015. Her annual reports on preliminary examination suggest that her main focus is "the settlement of civilians onto the territory of the West Bank" or so-called "settlement-related activities".[31] It is exactly this alleged transfer of civilians into the West Bank which human rights non-governmental organisations and some mainly-Muslim governments seek to have the ICC investigate and prosecute as a core international crime. Since the ICC Statute entered into force on 1 July 2002, its Article 8(2)(b)(viii) has prohibited the "transfer, directly or indirectly, by the Occupying Power of parts of its own civilian population into the territory it occupies". Israel – which, like Myanmar, is not

---

North Arakan (Rakhine), 1942-43", Policy Brief Series No. 101 (2020), TOAEP, Brussels, 2020 (http://www.toaep.org/pbs-pdf/101-leider/); and *idem*, "Mass Departures in the Rakhine-Bangladesh Borderlands", Policy Brief Series No. 111 (2020), TOAEP, Brussels, 2020 (http://www.toaep.org/pbs-pdf/111-leider/).

Despite this background, the British decided to recruit an irregular force in north Rakhine from September 1942 "to collect intelligence and to absorb the first pressure of any Japanese advance in the area" from "local Muslims who were ready to give their somewhat doubtful loyalty to the British as being the only allies in sight who might aid them to protect themselves against the Arakanese Buddhists" (see Donnison, 1956, pp. 21–22, *supra* note 21). This "V Force gained fame as an indispensable support for the British war effort in Arakan between late 1942 and 1945", and the Muslim "sacrifices for the British served as one of the main arguments to call for the creation of an autonomous Muslim zone in North Arakan" (see Leider, 2018, p. 202, *supra* note 26). Leider continues: "Informal suggestions and opinions to grant the Muslims such an autonomous territory had circulated among British military ranks during the war as they highly valued the contribution of V Force to the war effort" (*ibid.*). Some Muslim leaders were disappointed and blamed the United Kingdom: "The divide and rule policy of an Alien Govt. had created in the past a large measure of misunderstanding and distrust between our people and our Arakanese brethrens. This policy culminated in the massacre of 1942 of our people residing in various parts of Akyab District" (Jamiat ul-Ulama, cited in Leider, 2018, pp. 204–05, *supra* note 26). Interestingly, Churchill "regard[ed] Burma and contact with China as the most important feature in the whole [Eastern] theatre of war" (see Winston S. Churchill, *The Second World War. Volume IV: The Hinge of Fate*, London, 1951, Cassell & Co., Chapter 9 "The Invasion of Burma").

[30] Josef Federman, "West Bank settlers report surge in population growth", *The Times of Israel*, 6 February 2019 (available on its web site). This number excludes East Jerusalem.

[31] ICC, OTP, Report on Preliminary Examination Activities 2017, 4 December 2017, para. 59 (see paras. 51–78) (http://www.legal-tools.org/doc/e50459/).

an ICC State Party – does not consider its presence on the West Bank as occupation.[32]

Could Myanmar argue that the transfer of civilians into Burma prior to World War II – a process that has contributed significantly to the demographic makeup of, for example, Rakhine State – was a violation of international law? Such population transfers were only expressly prohibited by international law with the 1949 Geneva Convention IV Relative to the Protection of Civilian Persons in Time of War,[33] whose Article 49(6) provides that the "Occupying Power shall not deport or transfer parts of its own civilian population into the territory it occupies".[34] In other words, the transfers into Burma happened several years prior to the first express treaty prohibition of such conduct, and, as Matthias Neuner explains in Chapter 5 above, it is difficult to see this as a continuing crime.

Were that not the case, international lawyers would proceed to ask whether Burma was occupied[35] at the time of the transfers (a question of legal qualification on which the argument of this paper does not depend insofar as it concerns transfer of civilians into occupied *or similar territory*, including territory under forms of domination similar to occupation[36] – the value at stake is the same whether it was occupation or colonial rule). If the narrow answer is negative, what would be the effect of the British

---

[32] Theodor Meron's well-known dissenting advice when he served as the Legal Adviser of the Israel Ministry of Foreign Affairs is predicated on the assumption that there is a state of Israeli occupation, see his recent article "The West Bank and International Humanitarian Law on the Eve of the Fiftieth Anniversary of the Six-Day War", in *American Journal of International Law*, vol. 111, no. 2, pp. 357–75.

[33] See Convention (IV) Relative to the Protection of Civilian Persons in Time of War, 12 August 1949 (http://www.legal-tools.org/doc/d5e260/).

[34] Article 85(4)(a) of the 1977 Additional Protocol I made population transfer – "the transfer by the occupying Power of parts of its own civilian population into the territory it occupies" – a grave breach (http://www.legal-tools.org/doc/d9328a/).

[35] Eyal Benvenisti defines occupation as "the effective control of a power (be it one or more states or an international organization, such as the United Nations) over a territory to which that power has no sovereign title, without the volition of the sovereign of that territory" (see his monograph *The International Law of Occupation*, second edition, Oxford University Press, 2012, p. 3).

[36] Benvenisti observes that "foreign occupation has been likened by several UN General Assembly documents, including the Charter of Economic Rights and Duties of States, to colonialism" (making reference to UNGA resolutions 3281 (XXIX), 12 December 1974 (http://www.legal-tools.org/doc/3bf094/), and 3171 (XXVIII), 17 December 1973 (http://www.legal-tools.org/doc/438f4c/), *ibid.*, p. 17 (footnote omitted).

re-occupation of Burma at the end of World War II?[37] And further: was
Burma a sovereign nation at the time of the third Anglo-Burmese War?[38]

---

[37] After Britain had defeated Japan in Burma at the end of World War II, London invoked the
law of occupation as the legal basis for its authority in Burma, see Proclamation No. 1 of
1944: Military Administration issued by Louis Mountbatten as Supreme Allied Commander, South East Asia ("occupied by the Forces", see para. 1); see also Donnison, 1956, for
example, pp. 3, 33, 76, 113 and 263, *supra* note 21. Arakan had "a genuine and full military administration, the first in the Far East" (p. 15); cited by Benvenisti, 2012, p. 9, *supra*
note 35. A "power struggle developed" between the Civil Affairs Service (Burma) under
the South-East Asia Command and the Government of Burma in exile "under the direction
of the former and still titular Governor", see Philip Ziegler, *Mountbatten: The Official Bi-
ography*, Collins, London, 1985, pp. 317–23: "Damn it all, I'm *governing* Burma – not he,
whatever his title", wrote Mountbatten about the Governor (p. 318). The recognition that
the United Kingdom re-occupied Burma should affect our understanding of any earlier
British claims of *debellatio* or subjugation through the three Anglo-Burmese Wars. Why
would you re-occupy if your position is that the nation was subjugated decades earlier?
Benvenisti argues that "the law of occupation proved very useful to the reoccupants, who
invoked it in order to allow the military administrations wide discretionary powers unen-
cumbered by constitutional constraints" (*idem*, 2012, p. 9, fn. 42, *supra* note 35).

Benvenisti finds the doctrine of *debellatio* to be "a remnant of an archaic conception
that assimilated state into government", and it "has no place in contemporary international
law, which has come to recognize the principle that sovereignty lies in a people, not in a
political elite. The fall of a government has no effect whatsoever on sovereign title over the
occupied territory, which remains vested in the local population", see *ibid.*, p. 163. But it is
not so long ago that Georg Schwarzenberger condoned the doctrine, see his *International
Law as Applied by International Courts and Tribunals: Volume II, The Law of Armed Conflict*, Stevens & Sons, London, 1968, pp. 167, 296, 63, 139, 467. See the detailed discussion on 'subjugation' in YANG Ken, "On Subjugation and the Case of Burma", Chapter 4
above.

[38] See Anthony Anghie, *Imperialism, Sovereignty and the Making of International Law*,
Cambridge University Press, 2004, pp. 52–65 (the section "Defining and excluding the uncivilized"); M.F. Lindley, *The Acquisition and Government of Backward Territory in International Law: Being a Treatise on the Law and Practice Relating to Colonial Expansion*,
Longmans, Green and Co., 1926, pp. 24-47 ("Chapter IV. Inhabited Lands: State Practice"
and "Chapter V. International Law and Native Sovereignty").

As to whether Burma was a sovereign nation in 1885, see Thant Myint-U, 2007, chapters 6, 7 and 1 (in that order), *supra* note 23. John Sydenham Furnivall describes Burmese
King Mindon (1852-1878) as "probably the best sovereign of his line, and under his fostering care his people grew in numbers and prosperity", see J.S. Furnivall, *Colonial Policy
and Practice: A Comparative Study of Burma and the Netherlands India*, Cambridge University Press, 1948, p. 64 (on the subsequent pages he explains some of the king's policies
and results). He consistently refers to "the annexation of Upper Burma in 1886". See also
Frank S.V. Donnison, *Public Administration in Burma: A Study of Development During the
British Connexion*, Royal Institute of International Affairs, 1953, pp. 11–14.

Thant Myint-U's Chapter 1 details the British treatment of the last Burmese King Thibaw whose "archives [...] and almost all the other papers of the Court of Ava had gone up
in flames as drunken British soldiers set fire to the king's library soon after Thibaw's sur-

We ask these questions as international lawyers because we have a particular kind of meeting between norm and fact in mind, namely evidence of
alleged facts analysed in the light of the elements of the prohibition
against transfer of civilian population into occupied territory. But this is
not the only meeting between this norm and fact that is relevant in the
Myanmar context.

The prohibition in Article 49(6) of Geneva Convention IV was intended to "prevent a practice adopted during the Second World War by
certain Powers, which transferred portions of their own population to occupied territory for political and racial reasons or in order, as they claimed,
to colonize those territories. Such transfers worsened the economic situation of the native population and endangered their separate existence as a
race".[39] Burma was subjected to colonial practices, and the Burmese suffered economic consequences with the massive transfer of civilians from
British India. Does not her situation fall squarely within the generic legal
good or value protected by the prohibition against population transfer into
occupied territory? If the answer is in the affirmative, is this not important
to recognise if we want to understand the recent situation in Rakhine and
the excessive polarisation around accountability?

Not surprisingly, several delegates who spoke at the 1949 Diplomatic Conference were referring specifically to German and Japanese
practices during World War II.[40] In the indictment in the case against major war criminals before the International Military Tribunal at Nuremberg,
Count 3 – War Crimes, section '(J) Germanization of Occupied Territories' referred to how the defendants "introduced thousands of German
colonists", in order "to assimilate [certain] territories politically, culturally,

---

render. It was not until Lord Curzon visited as viceroy in 1901 that the wanton destruction
of the old buildings was ended and what was left of the Mandalay palace was preserved"
(p. 30). Two years later, Lord Curzon wrote that the greatest threat to British rule in India
(including Burma) was "the racial pride and the undisciplined passions of the inferior class
of Englishmen in this country", see Kenneth Rose, *Curzon: A Most Superior Person*,
Macmillan, 1985, p. 343. Benvenisti describes how some colonial powers did "not distinguish between conquest and occupation", enabling "the unilateral assumption of sovereignty over lands inhabited by what they deemed to be uncivilized peoples", *idem*, 2012, p.
32, *supra* note 35.

[39] Jean S. Pictet (ed.), *Commentary on IV Geneva Convention*, International Committee of
the Red Cross, Geneva, 1958, p. 283 (http://www.legal-tools.org/doc/7d971f/).

[40] See Final Record of the Diplomatic Conference of Geneva of 1949, vol. II-A, p. 664, cited
by Pictet (representatives of the Soviet Union, the Netherlands and Italy) (http://www.
legal-tools.org/doc/fb1a60/).

socially, and economically into the German Reich".[41] The Judgment quotes Adolf Hitler stating on 5 November 1937 that it is "not a case of conquering people but of conquering agriculturally useful space. [...] The history of all times – Roman Empire, British Empire – has proved that every space expansion can only be effected by breaking resistance and taking risks".[42] The Tribunal found that, "[i]n Poland and the Soviet Union these crimes were part of a plan to get rid of whole native populations by expulsion and annihilation, in order that their territory could be used for colonization by Germans".[43]

Indications are, however, that underlying the acceptance of the international law prohibition against the transfer of civilians into occupied territory was a general concern for the harm it causes, and not only a reaction against the practices of defeated Germany. Notably, the International Law Commission has commented that it is "an exceptionally serious war crime [...] to establish settlers in an occupied territory and to change the demographic composition of an occupied territory".[44] It expressed the

---

[41] International Military Tribunal, *The United States of America, the French Republic, the United Kingdom of Great Britain and Northern Ireland, and the Union of Soviet Socialist Republics v. Hermann Wilhelm Göring et al.*, Indictment, 6 October 1945, as amended 7 June 1946 (http://www.legal-tools.org/doc/23d531/). Three "aims and purposes of the [...] defendants" were identified in the indictment's Count 1 – The Common Plan or Conspiracy, section "IV. Particulars of the Nature and Development of the Common Plan or Conspiracy", "(B) Common Objectives and Methods of Conspiracy", the third of which was "to acquire still further territories in continental Europe and elsewhere claimed by the Nazi conspirators to be required by the 'racial Germans' as 'Lebensraum', or living space".

[42] Trial of the Major War Criminals before the International Criminal Tribunal Volume I – Judgment, p. 190 (http://www.legal-tools.org/doc/f21343/).

[43] *Ibid.*, p. 237. For findings on 'Germanisation', see pp. 238, 261, 295 and 335. See also Matthias Neuner, "The Notion of Continuous or Continuing Crimes in International Criminal Law", Chapter 5 above, who discusses how concerns related to population transfers during World War II were expressed through the Charter and Judgment of the International Military Tribunal in Nuremberg. The 1993 report on population transfer by Special Rapporteurs Mr. Awn Shawkat Al-Khasawneh and Mr. Ribot Hatano also discuss some documents on population transfer adopted during World War II, see UN Commission on Human Rights, Sub-Commission on Prevention of Discrimination and Protection of Minorities, "The human rights dimensions of population transfer, including the implantation of settlers", UN Doc. E/CN.4/Sub.2/1993/17, 6 July 1993, paras. 144–152 (https://www.legal-tools.org/doc/bdqtn3/).

[44] International Law Commission ('ILC'), Report of the Commission to the General Assembly on the work of its forty-third session, in *Yearbook of the International Law Commission*, 1991, vol. II, part 2, p. 105 (the offence appears as Article 22(2)(b) of the 1991 Draft Code) (http://www.legal-tools.org/doc/251704/). In the 1996 Draft Code (Article 20(c)(i)), the offence was formulated as the "transfer by the Occupying Power of parts of its own ci-

view that this "constitutes a particularly serious misuse of power, especially since such an act could involve the disguised intent to annex the occupied territory. Changes to the demographic composition of an occupied territory seemed to the Commission to be such a serious act that it could echo the seriousness of genocide".[45]

The 2005 customary law study of the International Committee of the Red Cross held that the prohibition against transferring civilian population into occupied territory is a norm of customary international law.[46] The study relied on a considerable number of legal sources, including resolutions of the UN Security Council,[47] the *Wall* Advisory Opinion of the International Court of Justice,[48] and the 2001 International Criminal Court Act of the United Kingdom.[49]

---

vilian population into the territory it occupies", see *idem*, Report of the Commission to the General Assembly on the work of its forty-eighth session, in *Yearbook of the International Law Commission*, 1996, vol. II, part 2, pp. 53–56 (http://www.legal-tools.org/doc/bb5adc/).

[45] ILC, 1991, *supra* note 44. This strong statement is hard to reconcile with the definition of the crime of transfer of civilians which does not require any violation of civilian life or physical integrity. Rather, the crime primarily harms an interest of the pre-occupation collective of the occupied territory, in its demographic state. Genocide, on the other hand, requires a specific intent to bring about the physical-biological destruction of a group in whole or in part.

[46] Jean-Marie Henckaerts and Louise Doswald-Beck, *Customary International Humanitarian Law, Volume 1: Rules*, Cambridge University Press, 2005, pp. 462–63, on what they designate as "Rule 130" (http://www.legal-tools.org/doc/78a250/). A detailed list of legal sources used in support of the position taken is found in *idem* (eds.), *Customary International Humanitarian Law, Volume II: Practice – Part 2*, Cambridge University Press, 2005, pp. 2956–70 (http://www.legal-tools.org/doc/d8df48/).

[47] See three resolutions adopted during the Jimmy Carter Presidency: Resolution 446 (1979), 22 March 1979 ("to desist from taking any action which would result in [...] materially affecting the demographic composition", and "not to transfer parts of its own civilian population into the occupied Arab territories" (para. 3) (http://www.legal-tools.org/doc/70334f/); Resolution 452 (1979), 20 July 1979 (http://www.legal-tools.org/doc/946db2/); and Resolution 476 (1980), 30 June 1980 (http://www.legal-tools.org/doc/130fa8/).

[48] International Court of Justice, *Legal Consequences of the Construction of a Wall in the Occupied Palestinian Territory*, Advisory Opinion, 9 July 2004 (with distinct individual opinions by, *inter alios*, Judges Thomas Buergenthal and Rosalyn Higgins): Article 49(6) of Geneva Convention IV "prohibits not only deportations or forced transfers of population such as those carried out during the Second World War, but also any measures taken by an occupying Power in order to organize or encourage transfers of parts of its own population into the occupied territory" (para. 120) (http://www.legal-tools.org/doc/e5231b/).

[49] Under the International Criminal Court Act (2001), ICC Statute Article 8(2)(b)(viii) is a domestic punishable offence (Sections 51(1) (England and Wales) and 58(1) (Northern Ireland), see Section 50(1) at the end, 50(6), and Schedule 8 (Article 8(2)(b)(viii)) (http://

The publicists Michael Cottier and Elisabeth Baumgartner explain that transfers of civilians into occupied territory have "severe humanitarian, economic, political and social long-term consequences, by changing the demographic composition of a territory, protracting conflicts and creating factual situations which are difficult to reverse".[50] They stress that the prohibition "aims at protecting the status [...] of occupied territory against the long-lasting effects of settlements by the Occupying Power and its population", continuing: "The transfer by an Occupying Power of its own civilian population into territory it occupies usually has substantial lasting consequences", involving change of the "demographic composition within the occupied territory".[51] The aim of the Occupying Power may be to "factually weaken the position of the resident population of the occupied territory and solidify its territorial and political claim over the territory".[52]

A more careful review of these and other sources suggests that German practices during World War II influenced the decision to include Article 49(6) in Geneva Convention IV, and allegations linked to Israeli settlements on the West Bank have had a significant impact on the subsequent criminalisation of the norm in international law.[53] There seems to be a distinct element of targeted reaction in both norm-evolutions: the prohibition was made with the Germans in mind; the crime, with the Israelis.

---

www.legal-tools.org/doc/e32fd7/). The United Kingdom's *Joint Service Manual of the Law of Armed Conflict*, Joint Service Publication 383, 2004, briefly states that "[m]embers of the occupying power's own civilian population may not be transferred to occupied territory", para. 11.55, p. 293 (http://www.legal-tools.org/doc/9dfeb2/).

[50] Michael Cottier and Elisabeth Baumgartner, "8. Paragraph 2(b)(viii): Prohibited deportations and transfers in occupied territories", in Otto Triffterer and Kai Ambos (eds.), *The Rome Statute of the International Criminal Court: A Commentary*, C.H. Beck, Munich, 2016, p. 405.

[51] *Ibid.* (all three quotations in the sentence).

[52] *Ibid.*

[53] "It is undoubtedly true that some of the Arab delegations insisting on inclusion of the provision were seeking to highlight activities by Israel in the occupied territories", see Robert Cryer, Håkan Friman, Darryl Robinson and Elizabeth Wilmshurst, *An Introduction to International Criminal Law and Procedure*, Cambridge University Press, 2007, p. 259. Judge Eli Nathan, head of the Israeli delegation to the Diplomatic Conference, in an explanation of vote on 17 July 1998, said that had the provision not been included, "he would have been able to vote in favour of adopting the Statute", see United Nations Diplomatic Conference of Plenipotentiaries on the Establishment of an International Criminal Court, Rome, 15 June–17 July 1998, Official Records, vol. II, p. 123 (http://www.legal-tools.org/doc/253396/).

This perception puts sincerity and consistency to the test. The International Law Commission arguably failed the test when it suggested that the conduct of transfer of civilians "could echo the seriousness of genocide", which is an exaggeration.[54] We face another test when Myanmar asks whether their concerns over the lingering harm caused by massive transfers of civilians into colonial Burma are not relevant to the international community.

7.3. In Search of a Response to the Sense of Double Standards

The ICC Prosecutor has opened an investigation into alleged crimes in Rakhine State in Myanmar at a time when, for a number of years, "[s]cepticism has [...] been mounting in the Global South where impunity for the massive human rights violations committed by Western colonial powers has been rife for more than half a century".[55] As the founder of the European Center for Constitutional and Human Rights, Wolfgang Kaleck, has pointed out: "Repeatedly, international criminal law has been portrayed as a tool of Western domination whose claim to universality is nothing more than an empty ideological superstructure".[56]

Myanmar has the potential to bring this sense of double standards to a head. Myanmar has suffered three colonial wars, systemic discrimination, demographic upheaval, and other violations for more than a century of colonial rule. By making deportation of Muslims from northern Rakhine State and the question of return the centrepiece of an ICC investigation – seemingly recognising a Rohingya identity as well-established[57] – the Prosecutor is inexorably turning the spotlight on the

---

[54] See *supra* note 45 with explanation.

[55] See Wolfgang Kaleck, *Double Standards: International Criminal Law and the West*, TOAEP, Brussels, 2015, p. i (http://www.toaep.org/ps-pdf/26-kaleck).

[56] *Ibid.*

[57] Ambassador Derek Tonkin notes that the "United Nations and Western governments are under pressure to accept the Rohingya identity. That is a political decision which only they can take. It is important though that their unqualified recognition of the Rohingya identity in Myanmar and overseas should not provide moral and political support to a highly questionable and pretentious narrative. Such an uncritical acceptance damages the prospects for reconciliation by further polarizing the Buddhist and Muslim communities": Tonkin, 2018, p. 239, see *supra* note 20. He refers to the encouragement "by a vociferous and well-coordinated international lobby" (p. 238), while recognising that "Rohingya might however also be seen to reflect an emerging, coalescing ethnic process among persons of Bengali racial origin designed as much as anything for self-protection in an increasingly hostile environment" (p. 230). Similarly, Jacques P. Leider refers to "a sense of shared destiny as

demographic reality and background of Rakhine State. If the massive transfer of civilians into Burma during the late colonial period is seen as irrelevant to international law and justice, this may feed criticisms that "threaten to undermine the legitimacy of international criminal law and [that] thereby adversely affect its potential to contribute positively to the collective coming to terms with international crimes".[58] Simply put, international law would be used against Burmese actors for current Rakhine violence, but it would be found to be silent on the past, colonial wrongs which make up part of the root causes of the violence. This can lead not only to estrangement from international law, but an anger which may negatively affect the necessary accountability processes.

U Thant – the third UN Secretary-General who showed us that Myanmar is no stranger to the idea of wider 'collective coming to terms'[59] – admired George Orwell and referred to his writings on colonialism to present the "strong resentment on the part of" the Burmese.[60] Orwell served with the Indian Imperial Police in Burma from 1922 to 1927, an experience which inspired his first novel *Burmese Days*: "In a job like that you see the dirty work of Empire at close quarters".[61] Are there relevant insights that can be extrapolated from this well-known novel on colonial practices? One of its main characters, Dr. Veraswami, an Indian who came to Burma during the British rule, strives to become a member of the local club, "the spiritual citadel, the real seat of the British power, the Nirvana

---

victims of state harassment" (Leider, 2018, p. 206, see *supra* note 26). These quotations – which point in different directions – show how controversial the identity question is. This chapter need not take a position on this question.

[58] Kaleck, 2015, p. i, *supra* note 55.

[59] Three years before Emmanuel Macron was born, he called for government leaders to take "fresh, new approaches on a planetary basis", informed by his "vision of a unified mankind", see U Thant, *View from the UN*, David & Charles, London, 1977, p. xviii. Note also the conclusion of his book: "I even believe that the mark of the truly educated and imaginative person facing the twenty-first century is that he feels himself to be a planetary citizen" (p. 454). Aung San Suu Kyi has remarked that a certain "meanness of spirit" was shown by the authorities over U Thant's funeral in Yangon, see her *Letters from Burma*, Penguin Books, London, 2010, p. 76 (first published in 1996). Whatever the circumstances at the time, this does not detract from the value of his book and legacy as Secretary-General.

[60] U Thant, 1977, p. 38, see *supra* note 59.

[61] George Orwell (né Eric Arthur Blair), *Shooting an Elephant and Other Essays*, Secker & Warburg, London, 1950, p. 79.

---

for which native officials and millionaires pine in vain".[62] Orwell describes how prejudice and self-righteousness among British colonisers fed discrimination and corrupted local communities.[63] The Burmese riot against the British community is crushed, but their anger succeeds in bringing down the Anglophile Dr. Veraswami. That non-British Anglophile representatives of the international community may trigger Burmese indignation just as much as British officials – the pen-holders of the Myanmar situation in the UN Security Council[64] – is one of the more obvious assumptions that can be distilled from Orwell's story. If such a representative happens to have worked intimately with the British Government during the negotiation and setting up of the ICC, Burmese sensitivity may be enhanced. But the anger could go further.

At first glance, it would primarily be a British problem if resentment for what Aung San Suu Kyi referred to as the "unchecked influx of foreigners"[65] grows as the ICC proceeds with its work and many Burmese come to feel that the language of international law has not been made for them, that there are in effect double standards. Europeans should not delight in the thought that this anger is not directed against Europe as such. Curiously, Orwell consistently refers to the "European Club", not the British or English club, although that is what it essentially was throughout British India.[66] As a strong supporter of the ICC, the European Union does indeed have an interest in avoiding extreme polarisation over the question of accountability for alleged core international crimes in Rakhine State.

---

[62] George Orwell, *Burmese Days*, Penguin Books, London, 2009, p. 14 (first published in 1934).

[63] Says Dr. Veraswami to his English friend: "'But, my dear friend, what lie are you living?' 'Why, of course, the lie that we're here to uplift our poor black brothers instead of to rob them. I suppose it's a natural enough lie. But it corrupts us, it corrupts us in ways you can't imagine. There's an everlasting sense of being a sneak and a liar that torments us and drives us to justify ourselves night and day. It's at the bottom of half our beastliness to the natives. We Anglo-Indians could be almost bearable if we'd only admit that we're thieves and go on thieving without any humbug.'", *ibid.*, p. 37.

[64] See, for example, "The UK Is 'Taking a Stand' to Bring Myanmar Leaders to Justice Over Rohingya Crisis", in *Global Citizen*, 5 September 2018 (http://www.legal-tools.org/doc/40cf22/).

[65] See *supra* note 28.

[66] See *supra* note 61.

There is even talk in Yangon of how the accountability issue has become a factor in wider geopolitical considerations.[67]

The purpose of this chapter, however, is neither to predict how far the polarisation over the issue of accountability for Rakhine allegations may go, nor to speculate on how the issue may affect great-power interests in the region. Rather, it seeks to trigger and bring more minds to bear on the question of what can realistically be done to meaningfully respond to the sense of double standards and to reduce excessive polarisation, while recognising the inherently confrontational nature of criminal justice at the level of suspects and prosecution and without in any way compromising interests of justice or peace.[68] This consultation needs to commence. This anthology will hopefully make a useful contribution. While international criminal lawyers may not be the obvious leaders of such an inquiry – indeed, some will ask what the problem is – they have a role to play. It is important that new measures designed will not impede requisite

---

[67] In his book *Where China Meets India: Burma and the New Crossroads of Asia*, Faber and Faber, London, 2011, Thant Myint-U discusses various aspects of Myanmar's relations with China, India and Western countries. Since his book was published, China has completed gas and oil pipelines from Yunnan Province across Myanmar to Ramree Island in Rakhine State, south of where the alleged crimes occurred in 2017. See SUN Yun, "On the Yunnan-Rakhine Corridor", Policy Brief Series No. 109 (2020), TOAEP, Brussels, 2020 (http://www.toaep.org/pbs-pdf/109-sun-yun/): "Western actors who have single-mindedly called for externalization of accountability for alleged crimes committed against Rohingyas in northern Rakhine have contributed significantly to the strengthening of ties between China and Myanmar, culminating with the signing of the key agreement on the Kyaukphyu deep-sea port [in Rakhine] in January 2020" (see also Thant Myint-U, *The Hidden History of Burma*, Atlantic Books, London, 2020, p. 247). For Indian and Bangladeshi geopolitical perspectives on Rakhine State, see Subir Bhaumik, "The India-Myanmar Kaladan Project: Vision and Reality", Policy Brief Series No. 106 (2020), TOAEP, Brussels, 2020 (http://www.toaep.org/pbs-pdf/106-bhaumik/), Devasheesh Bais, "Understanding Indian Responses to the Rohingya Crisis", Policy Brief Series No. 117 (2020), TOAEP, Brussels, 2020 (http://www.toaep.org/pbs-pdf/117-bais/), Shafqat Munir, "Geopolitics of Rakhine Region: A Bangladesh Perspective", Policy Brief Series No. 119 (2020), TOAEP, Brussels, 2020 (http://www.toaep.org/pbs-pdf/119-munir/), and Antonio Angotti, "Genocide and Constitutionalism in Bangladesh", Policy Brief Series No. 113 (2020), TOAEP, Brussels, 2020 (http://www.toaep.org/pbs-pdf/113-angotti/). See also NAKANISHI Yoshihiro and Antonio Angotti, "The Arakan Army: Violence in Rakhine State in Myanmar", Policy Brief Series No. 107 (2020), TOAEP, Brussels, 2020 (http://www.toaep.org/pbs-pdf/107-nakanishi-angotti/).

[68] This is done "in a context-sensitive manner" to avoid the "risk that such discussions will strengthen the position of nationalists and be used to promote discriminatory policies and agenda", see Kyaw Yin Hlaing, "The Importance of Hearing Colonial Wrongs in Myanmar", Chapter 11 below.

accountability mechanisms, but supplement them, an aspiration that was flagged earlier in this chapter.

There are recent examples of attempts to address historical wrong-doing also through the lens of current international law classifications. Initiatives in Canada (see Chapter 16 below),[69] Germany (Chapter 1 above),[70] and Norway (Chapter 17 below)[71] come to mind. It may be useful to consider such processes more closely, with a view to designing a *sui generis* approach for Myanmar.

The German track, which concerns violations that occurred in Namibia, a former German colony, is particularly promising, as it is largely driven by a desire to find ways to deal with the problem of double standards in the context of former colonies. It is a multi-pronged track with several projects. It does not to date amount to a hard-nosed application of so-called 'Third World Approaches to International Law' ('TWAIL') which would not necessarily help to resolve the challenge before us in Myanmar.[72] A focused approach may suit the area of international criminal law well, insofar as core international crimes seek to protect interests such as groups of persons against physical-biological destruction and innocent civilians against being killed or tortured, which are common global values in a different manner than, for example, development or economic growth.[73] A well-designed process for Myanmar, with TWAIL participa-

---

[69] Canada's National Inquiry into Missing and Murdered Indigenous Women and Girls produced various reports and activities between 1 September 2016 and 30 June 2019, including an advanced Internet presence (https://www.mmiwg-ffada.ca/).

[70] The European Center for Constitutional and Human Rights and partners have started a process to address the German genocide against the Ovaherero and Nama peoples in Namibia (1904-08), including a conference on "International Law in Postcolonial Contexts" (https://www.ecchr.eu/en/case/namibia-a-week-of-justice/) and an open letter to the German Government (http://www.legal-tools.org/doc/24a52c/).

[71] Norway has conducted a detailed public inquiry into the historical treatment of members of the Roma group in Norway, leading to the comprehensive report "Assimilering og motstand: Norsk politikk overfor taterne/romanifolket fra 1850 til i dag" ("Assimilation and resistance: Norwegian policy towards the Roma People from 1850 until today"), Norges offentlige utredninger 2015: 7 (http://www.legal-tools.org/doc/ca4c52/).

[72] Sergey Vasiliev, "The Crises and Critiques of International Criminal Justice", in *SSRN Electronic Journal*, January 2019, pp. 8–10, 13–15, gives an overview of TWAIL critiques of international criminal law: "TWAICL seeks to decolonise the conceptual and normative apparatus of international criminal law, by interrogating assumptions of geopolitical neutrality, universality and moral immaculacy of its standards, practices, and impacts" (p. 15).

[73] Sundhya Pahuja argues that international law generally "refuses to engage with its imperial history and well-documented intimacy with the powerful", see her monograph *Decolonis-*

tion, could perhaps offer the established discourse useful specificity and future-orientation.

Such a mechanism should not be limited by truth and reconciliation processes as we know them from other countries around the world. Thorough research on some of the historical events referred to in Section 7.2. above could, if properly undertaken, shed further light on several questions and begin to bridge the gap between competing and fragmented narratives.[74] It may also be useful to include analysis of the lead-up to the adoption of Article 49(6) of Geneva Convention IV in 1949 in the mandate of a mechanism.

7.4. Myanmar as an Opportunity to Address the Problem of Double Standards

The tragic killings and the disruption of the lives of hundreds of thousands in northern Rakhine have rightly given rise to the question of accountability. But at the same time, Myanmar offers us an opportunity to recognise the seriousness of the problem of double standards for former colonies, and to consider more systematically what can be done about it. As we have seen, what many Burmese perceive to be a root cause of the conflict and violence in Rakhine – the transfer of civilians into colonial Burma – has since become a crime under international law. But the past transfers into Burma are widely considered irrelevant under international law. The default view seems to be that the language of international law does not extend to this wrong and its long-lasting consequences – that this grievance has no access to international law. Reminding the Burmese of the important and obvious fact that demographic history cannot justify international crimes against Muslims in northern Rakhine – and Chapter 11 below reinforces the consideration – does not address this grievance.

---

ing International Law, Cambridge University Press, 2011, p. 1. The concepts of development and economic growth being her focus, she refers to "a pervasive rationality that successfully made a claim for the universality of a particular, or 'provincial' set of values originating in and congenial to the North" (p. 2, footnote omitted). Chapter 16 below by Asad Kiyani ("Avoidance Techniques: Accounting for Canada's Colonial Crimes") presents a nuanced correlation between TWAIL and international criminal law narratives.

74 Leider observes: "The interpretation that links the self-perception of the Arakanese/ Rakhine as victims of both Burmese oppression and Muslim immigration – a kind of grand historical narrative from 1785 down to the present – rather calls for a deeper investigation of social conditions and inter-ethnic relations in Arakan during the 1920s and 1930s", see *idem*, 2018, p. 217, *supra* note 26.

This chapter invites a consultation on the features of a process that could meaningfully respond to this sense of double standards and reduce excessive polarisation over the issue of accountability for allegations in Rakhine. Section 7.3. of the chapter sketches some desirable elements of such a process, without prejudicing the consultation which should take place with the participation of the Burmese and experts on double standards, colonialism and international law. Section 7.2. prepares the context of the discussion by analysing the factual background of the transfer of civilians into colonial Burma, and the evolution of the international law prohibition against, and criminalisation of, such transfers.

It will not be easy to make such a process successful. For one, this is not about the existing national and international accountability mechanisms for Rakhine allegations, or how the practice of transfer of civilians into colonial Burma should (not) affect these mechanisms, which are immediate points of orientation for international criminal lawyers. Neither is it narrowly about the technical definition or applicability of the crime of transfer of civilians into occupied territory.

For the process to succeed, emphasis needs to be placed on the *harm* which the prohibition against transferring civilians into occupied territory seeks to avoid – referred to by the International Law Commission as "[c]hanges to the demographic composition"[75] – that is, on the purpose of the norm. Such undogmatic, material recognition of past harm and its lingering consequences may start to foster better understanding and contribute towards reduced polarisation over the issue of accountability in Rakhine.

Despite these challenges, this chapter argues that it is worth trying to define and implement such a novel process. At least in situations where the transferred civilians remain a minority in the polity of the occupied territory, Myanmar shows that such transfers can cast shadows more than ten decades into the future. This risk of lingering long-term effect does not differ for the crime of deportation *out* of a territory, a fact which armed actors in Rakhine can ill afford to ignore.

---

[75] *Supra* note 44.

8

Migration from Bengal to Arakan During British Rule 1826–1948

Derek Tonkin[*]

> Migration from India to Burma is no new thing. It has been going on as far back as Burmese history can be traced through its chronicles and legendary lore.[1]

The record of Indian migration into Burma during British rule contrasts the purposeful influx of professional, skilled and unskilled workers into urban areas of Burma generally, notably to Rangoon City (Yangon), with the gradual, benign settlement of many tens of thousands of agricultural labourers from Bengal in Arakan (Rakhine State). Thanks to the porous nature of the border, these labourers came of their own volition, though generally encouraged to do so by the British administration. The migratory presence over the centuries of Muslim (and Hindu) communities in Arakan occurred so naturally that it was felt to be almost indigenous, so much so that any British responsibility for the post-war ferment in Arakan is questionable. In any event, the great majority of today's Rohingya can rightly feel that they belong in Myanmar. It seems unlikely that any principle of international law has been breached as a result of the Muslim presence in Arakan, but the former colonial power might well reassess its role critically.

---

[*] **Derek Tonkin** was Burma Desk Officer in the UK Foreign Office 1962–66. He was Ambassador to Vietnam 1980–82 and to Thailand and Laos 1986–89. This paper is a response to Morten Bergsmo, *Myanmar, Colonial Aftermath, and Access to International Law*, Occasional Paper Series No. 9 (2019), Torkel Opsahl Academic EPublisher, Brussels, 2019 (http://www.toaep.org/ops-pdf/9-bergsmo). The chapter was therefore first published as Occasional Paper Series No. 10 (2019) (https://www.toaep.org/ops-pdf/10-tonkin).

[1] James Baxter, *Report on Indian Immigration*, Superintendent, Government Printing and Stationery, Burma, Rangoon, 1941, foreword (https://legal-tools.org/doc/cc5cu2).

8.1. Introduction

At the 8133rd meeting of the UN Security Council on 12 December 2017, the representative of the Russian Federation, Vassily Nebenzia, observed during the course of the discussion on 'The Situation in Myanmar':

> In our view, what is needed most of all in order to agree on a settlement of the situation of mass movements of people across the Myanmar-Bangladesh border is goodwill on the part of both States. Unfortunately, it will be impossible to resolve matters if the two of them cannot come to a rapprochement on this age-old problem, whose foundation was laid in the previous century by a colonial administration, with its arbitrary drawing of borders and shifting of populations from one part of its colonial dominions to another. The role of the international community, including the United Nations, should be to assist bilateral efforts to surmount this crisis and its consequences.

8.2. Setting the Scene: The 1911, 1921 and 1931 Censuses of British Burma

British colonial records, notably annual and decennial censuses, trace in considerable detail the arrival of Indian migrant labour in Burma. These records highlight, however, the marked difference between what happened in Burma generally, and the special situation in Arakan (Rakhine) which has a long history of cross-border migration over the centuries, mainly from Bengal into Burma, but also in the opposite direction.

The British Burma Census report of 1911 noted that:

> With the exception of the agricultural immigrants from the district of Chittagong into Arakan, few Indians come to Burma with the intention of embarking in agriculture. The economic demand is not for agricultural but for urban labour, not for the raising of a crop but for its disposal [...].[2]

The report, however, also noted the presence in Arakan of "a huge indigenous agricultural Mahomedan population". Still, no attempt was made in the Census to assess the respective numbers of the indigenous

---

[2] See C. Morgan Webb, *Census of India, 1911*, vol. IX, Office of the Superintendent, Government Printing, Burma, Rangoon, 1912, part I, p. 76, para. 77 (https://legal-tools.org/doc/vcj9hs).

and migrant Muslim communities in Arakan, who were enumerated according to their 'tribes', and not according to their dates of arrival.

The Census Report of 1921 broke with previous practice and enumerated Muslims no longer according to tribe, but according to race, distinguishing two main historical Muslim groups in Arakan – indigenous pre-British rule ethnicities designated 'Indo-Burman' on the one hand, and British-era migrant ethnicities of Indian origin, notably Chittagonian, on the other. In this context, the Report noted:

> Akyab[3] is a special case because of its contiguity to India, the ease with which the boundary is crossed, and the special local conditions of a seasonal immigration which leads to the presence on the date of the census of a number of Indians who will return shortly after to India. Actually of the 201,000 Indians shown in Marginal Table 14 for Akyab 78,000 males and 76,000 females were born in the district; the phenomenon is as much an annexation of part of India by Burma as an invasion of Akyab by Indians.[4]

By the time of the Census Report of 1931, we read:

> In Akyab District itself 210,990 Indians were enumerated but only about one-tenth of them were enumerated in towns. In parts of Akyab District, Indians are so numerous that they should perhaps be regarded as indigenous.[5]

8.3. The Historical Background

In his report as Assistant Commissioner for Akyab on the Tax Settlement for the 1867–68 Season, Lieutenant G.A. Strover provided a brief description in October 1868 of the gangs of Chittagong coolies who crossed into Arakan every year for the reaping season. One of his concerns was how they might be encouraged to migrate permanently. This was not to happen until well after the opening of the Suez Canal in 1869 and the subsequent rapid expansion of international trade. It reads:

---

[3] Akyab District at the time included all of Northern Arakan except the Arakan Hill Tracts – today's Sittwe, Maungdaw and Mrauk-U Districts combined.

[4] See S.G. Grantham, *Census of India, 1921*, vol. X, Office of the Superintendent, Government Printing, Burma, Rangoon, 1923, part I, p. 220, para. 164 (https://legal-tools.org/doc/r84t1w).

[5] See J.J. Bennison, *Census of India, 1931*, vol. XI, Office of the Superintendent, Government Printing and Stationery, Burma, Rangoon, 1933, part I, p. 51, para. 25 (https://legal-tools.org/doc/7z9vl8).

52. During the reaping season, and indeed before, coolies from the Chittagong district come over in hundreds, and appear to do most of the real labour of the country in the northern parts, as regards paddy cultivation [...] The Arakanese in many parts do little or nothing themselves as regards manual labour, cheerfully paying the Chittagong coolies a fair rate of wages to gather in their crops rather than go to the trouble of doing it themselves, but even when paying for this work, they, as a rule, make very fair profits on the season's out-turn. As soon as the work is over, the coolies return to their homes, and re-cross our frontier, where they remain until the next season comes round. It is a pity immigration does not assume a more solid form, but there are many circumstances which tend to retard and hold it in check. The Chittagong district which borders the northern frontier contains a very large expanse of country with a considerable area of waste land, vegetation is abundant, and but labour is required to produce the necessaries of life. Being under British rule, with a comparatively light taxation, it would require attractions of a special nature to induce people from those parts to leave their homes and settled down in a strange land. Labour in this district is as scarce a commodity as in other parts of British Burma, and apparently more so. Natives from Chittagong know full well the condition of the country as regards the demand for labour, and fix their own terms, being well aware that there is no competition in the market: all circumstances combined there appears to be little chance of labour becoming more plentiful or cheaper than at present for years to come [...].[6]

As the Commissioner for Arakan, Lt. Col. J.F.J. Stevenson observed in his covering submission to the Chief Commissioner of Burma on 5 January 1869:

Our want of population is well known: there is an abundance of land to repay the toil of cultivators.

---

[6] G.A. Strover, "Letter from Lieutenant G.A. Strover, Assistant Commissioner, Revenue Settlement Department, Akyab, to the Deputy Commissioner, Akyab District", in *Reports on the Revenue Settlement Operations of British Burma, for the Year 1867-68*, vol. I, Office of Superintendent of Government Printing, Calcutta, 1869, p. 81, para. 52 (https://www.legal-tools.org/doc/0nw7me/).

The scholar Thibaut d'Hubert at the University of Chicago has referred to the nature of early migration into Burma from and through Bengal in his article "Pirates, Poets and Merchants: Bengali Language and Literature in Seventeenth-Century Mrauk-U". He writes:

> Muslims settled in Arakan in waves [...] Besides those 'willing' Muslim immigrants, we find slaves taken during the raids of Luso-Arakanese pirates in market-villages of the Delta area[7] [...] Besides the Bengali Muslims, other groups were present in Mrauk-U who were neither Bengali Turko-Afghans nor converted Bengalis [...].[8]

One cannot fail to notice the potential for diversity within Arakan's Muslim society itself. This diversity is confirmed by Alaol[9] who gave an extensive list of names referring to various kinds of Muslim individuals present in Mrauk-U under the reign of Satuidhammaraja (1645–52):

> Various individuals [coming from] various countries, informed about the delights of Rosang (i.e., Mrauk-U), came under the king's shadow: Arabs, Egyptians, Syrians, Turks, Abyssinians, Ottomans (Ruml), Khorasanis, Uzbeks, Lahoris, Multanis, Hindis, Kashmiris, Deccanis, Sindhis, Assamese (Kamarupi), and Bengalis (Bangadesi). Many sons of Shaykhs and Sayyids, Mughal and Pathan warriors.

One point is striking about this enumeration. Here Alaol does not encompass the whole Muslim community by saying that 'Musalmans' are present in Mrauk-U, but gives precise names related to particular places. He does not just name these places in a random order; he starts from the ones farthest afield (Arabia, Egypt, Syria, Central Asia, and Ethiopia), then he gives the nearer 'Hindustani' area (Lahore,

---

[7] The enslavement in the sixteenth and seventeenth Centuries of many tens of thousands of Muslims and Hindus brought by force to Mrauk-U was assuredly a violation of modern international law by the Arakanese Kingdom, but is not the subject of this dissertation.

[8] See Thomas de Bruijn and Allison Busch (eds.), *Culture and Circulation: Literature in Motion in Early Modern India*, Brill, Leiden/Boston, 2014, pp. 50–51 (https://legal-tools.org/doc/470u9m).

[9] Syed Alaol (1607–73), a prolific, renowned Bengali poet, captured in a remote area of Bengal by Portuguese pirates while on a boat with his father, and brought to Arakan.

Multan, Kashmir, Deccan, and Sindh) before finally introducing the regional area with Assam and Bengal.

Moving into the eighteenth century, a British writer, Major R.E.
Roberts of the East India Company, noted in his "Account of Arakan" in
1777 that:

> Almost three fourths of the inhabitants of Rekheng [Arakan]
> are said to be natives of Bengal, or descendants of such, who
> constantly pray that the English may send a force to deliver
> them from their slavery, and restore them to their country; in
> that case they have agreed amongst themselves to assist their
> deliverers to the utmost of their power.[10]

It is scarcely credible that 75 per cent of the inhabitants of Arakan
were at that time Bengalis, but it is I think beyond doubt that there was
already a substantial and settled Bengali community in Arakan, even if
many were killed or forced to leave when the Burmese invaded in 1785.
According to Rangoon University Professor Bertie Pearn, who in 1949
joined the UK Foreign Office as Head of South East Asia Research:

> By the year 1798, two-thirds of the inhabitants of Arakan
> were said to have deserted their native land. In one year,
> 1798, a body of no less than ten thousand entered Chittagong,
> followed soon after by many more; and while their compat-
> riots who had been longer settled there endeavoured to assist
> them, they were nevertheless reduced to a condition of the
> direct poverty, many having nothing to eat but reptiles and
> leaves.[11]

In the nineteenth century, after the British annexation of the territory in 1826, Sub-Commissioner Charles Paton published in 1828 a "Historical and Statistical Sketch of Aracan" – the main part of a Secret Report
dated 1826 in which he estimated (the same sentence in both reports) the
population of Arakan thus:

> The population of Aracan and its dependencies, Ramree,
> Cheduba and Sandoway, does not, at present, exceed a hun-
> dred thousand souls, and may be classed as follows: Mugs

---

[10] Cited in *Aséanie: Sciences humaines en Asie du Sud-Est*, 1999, vol. 3, p. 144 (https://legal-
tools.org/doc/luznxm). Major Roberts would not seem to have actually visited Arakan
himself.

[11] B.R. Pearn, "King-Bering", in *Journal of the Burma Research Society*, 1933, vol. 23, no. 2.

[Rakhine], six-tenths, Musselmans [Muslims], three-tenths, Burmese, one-tenth: Total 100,000 souls.[12]

8.4. The Paradox of the Indigenous Migrant

This 2:1 ratio of 'Mugs' to 'Musselmans' (or 7:3 ratio of Buddhists to Muslims) in 1826 – even on the assumption that the figures presented by Paton are little more than rough guesswork – is scarcely different from the ratio of Rakhine to Rohingya in the twenty-first century, and has led many to argue that there was no migration of substance into Arakan as British archives report, and that all that has happened is that many Muslims have simply returned to their 'ancestral lands' after their flight from Arakan, notably in 1785 when so many Arakan Muslims (and Buddhists) were deported to Ava after the Burmese invasion, or sought refuge in British-ruled Bengal until it was safe to return home. British records are indeed at times rubbished as unreliable, compiled only for colonialist purposes. The activist Maung Zarni in an article written in 2014 has observed:

> The fact that the British census and other official records did not include the category Rohingya says more about the short-comings of British pre-World War II social-science methodologies and political and economic power relations during the British colonial period than they do about the history of Rohingya identity.[13]

Even more pointedly, the Rohingya politician U Kyaw Min has flatly denied in an article critical of my own presentation that Bengalis and Chittagonians recorded in British censuses were permanently settled in Arakan:

> So called Bengali or Chittagonians in British census were mostly foreigners. Except business related persons and official staffs most of them were seasonal labourers, who did not bring their spouses. These foreigners were also included in British censuses. Professor Dr Than Tun named them as floating population. Once the working season is over, they

---

[12] See *Asiatic Researches; or, Transactions of the Society, Instituted in Bengal, for Inquiring into the History and Antiquities, the Arts, Sciences and Literature of Asia*, vol. XVI, Government Gazette Press by G.H. Huttmann, Calcutta, 1828, p. 372 (https://legal-tools.org/doc/eh58ce).

[13] See Maung Zarni and Alice Cowley, "The Slow-Burning Genocide of Myanmar's Rohingya", in *Pacific Rim Law and Policy Journal*, 2014, vol. 23, no. 3, p. 701 (https://legal-tools.org/doc/9xe3dk).

> returned to their native land. Rohingya has nothing to do with them [...] So called Chittagonian immigrants never took permanent settlement, only natives who formerly left Arakan came back and settled in their original places.[14]

U Kyaw Min would superficially seem to have the backing of British census records for his position. Thus the 1911 Census examines the seasonal migration between Chittagong and Akyab and notes:

> Every year, there is a periodic migration of coolies from Chittagong to assist in agricultural operations in Akyab. The amount of migration fluctuates greatly, falling to very small dimensions after a good season and rising considerably after a bad season in Chittagong. Only a comparatively small number remain permanently behind in Akyab, the majority returning to their homes in Chittagong after the reaping of the crops.[15]

My response to U Kyaw Min attempted, in a light-hearted vein, to correct the record.[16] The 1921 and 1931 censuses revealed a greater incidence of Chittagonian settlement in Akyab, additional to the admittedly small number of seasonal workers who stayed behind after the rice harvest. A later and more authoritative analysis is Chapter VII of the already mentioned Inquiry was completed in 1940 by the Financial Secretary, James Baxter, into Indian immigration to Burma and published shortly before the Japanese invasion.[17] The report is solely concerned with migrants who came after the British annexation of Arakan, not with indigenous Muslim communities. Chapter VII quotes the 1931 Census, which showed that in Akyab District, some 167,000 Indians (Muslim and Hindu) were born in Burma, against only 44,000 born outside. 'Born in Burma' can only mean resident in Burma, for the vast majority.

As a result of the Inquiry, the British Government of Burma negotiated with the British Government of India an agreement on immigration control which never came into effect, mainly because of the Japanese in-

---

[14] See "Why not Rohingya an antiquity? [Part 2]: An assessment on Rohingyas' genuineness", in *Rohingya Blogger*, 30 April 2014 (available on its web site).

[15] See Webb, 1912, p. 80, see above note 2.

[16] See Derek Tonkin, "The 'Rohingya' Identity: Arithmetic of the Absurd", in *Network Myanmar*, 9 May 2014 (available on its web site).

[17] See above note 1.

vasion. Nor was it ever likely to: it was widely opposed by political and commercial interests in India, as well as by Mahatma Gandhi:

> My study has led me to the conclusion that it is an unhappy agreement. It is panicky and penal. In the papers I find no reason to warrant any panic nor do I find any warrant for the severe punishment meted out to the Indians resident in Burma […][18]

Published on 22 July 1941, the text was reportedly only initialled, and never ratified. Even so, a provision about the suspension of all migration by unskilled labour came into immediate effect, causing outrage throughout India, and especially in Bengal whose Government declared that they had at no stage been consulted about or even made aware of the proposals in advance.[19]

In an address to visiting Prime Minister U Nu on 25 October 1948, the influential, quasi-political party Jamiat ul-Ulema of North Arakan (the Council of Scholars of North Arakan who included elected politicians like Sultan Ahmed and Abdul Gaffar) denied that there had ever been any substantive migration from the Chittagong region into Arakan at any time:

> We are dejected to mention that in this country we have been wrongly taken as part of the race generally known as Chittagonians and as foreigners. We humbly submit that we are not. We have a history of our own distinct from that of Chittagonians. We have a culture of our own. Historically we are a race by ourselves […] Our spoken dialect is an admixture of Arabic, Persian, Urdu, Arakanese and Beng[a]lis.[20]

This perspective has become the unshakeable, default mantra of Rohingya ideologues. It is now likely that the majority of Rohingyas hold

---

[18] See Mahatma Gandhi, "Statement to the Press", in *The Bombay Chronicle*, 25 August 1941; cited in *The Collected Works of Mahatma Gandhi (Electronic Book)*, vol. 81, Publications Division, Government of India, New Delhi, 1999, document 28 (https://legal-tools.org/doc/16g5wz).

[19] See *The Indo-Burma Immigration Agreement: A Nation in Revolt*, Indian Overseas Central Association by S. Satyamurti, New Delhi, 1941 for a detailed account of the opposition in India to the Agreement. It was effectively superseded by the Burma Immigration (Emergency Provisions) Act of 1947, which is still in force.

[20] See "Address presented by Jamiat ul-Ulema North Arakan: On Behalf of the People of North Arakan to the Hon'ble Prime Minister of the Union of Burma on the Occasion of His Visit to Maungdaw on the 25th October 1948", pp. 1–2 (https://legal-tools.org/doc/wb3uz2).

this perception of their indigeneity to be historically true, despite the sustained statistical evidence from British sources of migration over many decades. We should in the circumstances not be surprised at the current polarisation between the Rakhine Buddhist and Rohingya Muslim communities, the former claiming that the Rohingya are illegal migrants from Bengal, and the latter insisting on their historical indigeneity.

The British author Azeem Ibrahim would also seem to be in a state of denial about Chittagonian migration into Arakan during British rule. In his book *The Rohingyas: Inside Myanmar's Genocide*, he acknowledges that there was indeed substantial migration from British-rule India to most regions of Burma before 1937. But as regards Arakan he asserts:

> None of this significantly involved the Rohingyas, who mostly carried on working as farmers and fishermen on their own land rather than taking up work in the colonial administration.[21]

This denial of any migration of substance from Bengal to Arakan during British rule is compounded by his anachronistic use of the term 'Rohingya' which only emerged after Burma's independence in 1948. The designation was unknown to the British colonial administration. Indeed, the only historical source of reference to anything resembling 'Rohingya' prior to independence is to be found in an article in the 1799 Calcutta edition of Volume 5 of *Asiatic Researches* on the Languages of the Burma Empire by Francis Buchanan resulting from his visit to the Court of Ava as a member of a diplomatic mission in 1795.[22] The article has been the subject of intense speculation, but the absence of corroboration from any other independent source obliges us to take the reference only at its face value. We read:

> I shall now add three dialects, spoken in the *Burma* empire, but evidently derived from the language of the *Hindu* nation.

---

21 Azeem Ibrahim, *The Rohingyas: Inside Myanmar's Genocide*, C. Hurst & Co., London, 2018, p. 7.

22 See Michael Symes, *An Account of an Embassy to the Kingdom of Ava, Sent by the Governor-General of India, in the Year 1795*, W. Bulmer and Co. *et al.*, London, 1800 (https://legal-tools.org/doc/jeqk1p).

> The first is spoken by the *Mohammedans*, who have long been settled in *Arakan*, and who call themselves *Rooinga*, or natives of *Arakan*.[23]

Buchanan's article was widely cross-referenced by other scholars and encyclopaedists during the next 50 years or so, but all without exception gave Buchanan as their sole source. This did not however deter Ibrahim from proclaiming several of these supporting reference works to be independent sources for 'Rooinga' and its variants, despite the specific attribution to Buchanan in every case.[24]

Ibrahim's point of departure is the 1826 report by Arakan Sub-Commissioner Charles Paton quoted above which he interprets in his book as follows:

> Shortly after the British conquest, a survey carried out by Charles Paton indicated the population of the province was around 100,000. As with many British censuses of the colonial period, he focused as much on religion as ethnicity and identified that there were 30,000 Muslims split between three ethnic groups, a large community mainly in the north (the Rohingyas); the Kamans (a group descended from Afghan mercenaries who had served the previous dynasty); and 'a small but long established Muslim community around Moulmen [sic]'.[25]

It should however be noted that Paton does not refer anywhere in his Report to 'Rohingya', nor even to the Kaman, and the quotation at the end of the sentence is not from Paton but has been taken unattributably and inexplicably from the 1940 Baxter Report on Indian Immigration during British rule, written some 114 years later. For the Baxter Report, in a passing comment on quasi-indigenous Muslim communities in Arakan and Tennerassim we read:

---

[23] See *Asiatic Researches; or, Transactions of the Society, Instituted in Bengal, for Inquiring into the History and Antiquities, the Arts, Sciences and Literature of Asia*, vol. 5, printed verbatim from the Calcutta edition, J. Sewell *et al.*, London, 1799, p. 237 (https://legal-tools.org/doc/mhffl1) (indentation in the original).

[24] A detailed critique by me on this issue as well as highlighting numerous errors of historical fact: Derek Tonkin, "A Detailed Examination of Misinformation in Dr Azeem Ibrahim's Book *The Rohingyas: Inside Myanmar's Hidden Genocide*", in *Network Myanmar*, 1 March 2017 (available on its web site).

[25] Ibrahim, 2018, p. 6, see above note 21.

> There was an Arakanese Muslim community settled so long in Akyab District[26] that it had for all intents and purposes to be regarded as an indigenous race. There were also a few Mohamedan Kamans in Arakan and a small but long established Muslim community around Moulmein[27] which could not be regarded as Indian.[28]

Paton is again mentioned in Ibrahim's book. "Ostensibly working for the British Colonial Office, he was actually working for Britain's secret spy agencies".[29] It is true that Charles Paton, assisted by another more erudite and gifted Sub-Commissioner Thomas Robertson and Lieutenants Thomerson and Cammelin of the Royal Engineers, submitted a report graded 'Secret' to the Governor-General Lord Amherst, from which it is apparent that most of the work was completed not by Paton, but by Robertson, Thomerson and Cammelin, including all the interviews with village chiefs, both Muslim and Buddhist. At the time India was administered by the East India Company, not the Colonial Office, and the only reason for grading the report 'Secret' was that it was presented to the Governor-General through Chief Secretary George Swinton, who headed both the 'Secret' and 'Political' Departments. Paton was no more a spy than were Robertson, Thomerson and Cammelin. Paton's 1826 report was declassified only two years later and published as an article in *Asiatic Researches,* with the excision only of personality notes on village chiefs.[30]

8.5. The Repopulation after 1826 of 'Almost Depopulated' Arakan

The Indian Minority in Burma published in 1971 and authored by Dr. Nalini Ranjan Chakravarti is a mine of information about the Indian community in Burma and essential reading in this context, with a foreword by the renowned historian Professor Hugh Tinker who lauds Dr.

---

[26] Akyab District at the time was today's Sittwe, Mrauk-U and Maungdaw Districts combined.

[27] Moulmein, in its modern spelling of 'Mawlamyine', is not in Arakan in Western Burma, but in Tenerassim in Eastern Burma, in its modern versions Tanintharyi. As Sub-Commissioner for Arakan on the Western border, Charles Paton would not have presumed to make any comment about events in Tenerassim on the Eastern border.

[28] See Baxter, 1941, p. 4, see above note 1.

[29] Ibrahim, 2018, p. 29, see above note 21.

[30] An authoritative account of the Rohingya identity may be found in Jacques Leider, "Rohingya: The History of as Muslim Identity in Myanmar", in *Oxford Research Encyclopedia of Asian History*, Oxford University Press, May 2018.

Chakravarti's qualifications to write about this subject.[31] On Arakan's Muslims, Dr. Chakravarti has this to say:

> There is an overwhelming justification for separating the Moslems of Akyab District from other Indians. These Moslems are a permanently settled agricultural community of Arakan and are really Arakanese [...] Maungdaw Township with 90,000 Indians, Buthidaung Township with 45,000 Indians and Kyauktaw Township with 20,000 are at the border of Chittagong (Bengal, now East Pakistan) and more easily accessible from Chittagong than other parts of Akyab. They are indigenous people, living in those areas for generations and are Arakanese in dress and manner, though Muslim by faith.[32]

I have already shown that there were several waves of Muslim penetration into Arakan well before the British arrived. When the British invaded in 1824, they found the former Kingdom seriously depopulated. As Lieutenant General Albert Fytche, who became Chief Commissioner of British Burma, recalled:

> It is well known that when Arakan and Tenerassim first came into our possession, in 1826, they were almost depopulated, and were so unproductive, that it was seriously deliberated whether they should not be restored to Burma.[33]

It might even be argued that such was the depopulation of Arakan that, for all practical purposes, 1826 should be treated as 'year zero' when Arakan as a territory began to experience a virtual repopulation.

The First Anglo-Burmese War, unlike the Second and Third Wars, was no colonial war, but a clash of Empires. The East India Company had no wish to expand, but had to contend with aggressive imperial ambitions from the Burma King into Manipur and Assam, which the British were not prepared to tolerate. From 1826 to 1862, Arakan was administered as part of the Bengal Presidency. It became part of the Indian Province of British Burma after the Second Anglo-Burmese War. A further wave of

---

[31] See N.R. Chakravarti, *The Indian Minority in Burma: The Rise and Decline of an Immigrant Community*, Oxford University Press, New York, 1971.

[32] *Ibid.*, p. 17. This is in my view true of descendants of the pre-1824 settlers in the region of Kyauktaw and neighbouring Mrauk U, but not generally true of British-era Chittagonian migrants who settled in Maungdaw and Buthidaung.

[33] See Albert Fytche, *Burma: Past and Present*, vol. II, C. Kegan Paul & Co., London, 1878, p. 288.

Muslim migration started only later, as Arakan developed as a major rice exporter. The need for labour was paramount, and in the early years, some 10 per cent of the labouring population of the Chittagong region came across seasonally to harvest the rice and to work in the ports and elsewhere.

Eventually, many Chittagonians took the plunge. Some decided to stay on after the rice harvest, others just crossed the Naaf River into Arakan in search of a better life. They were encouraged to do so, both by the Governments of the Bengal Presidency and of British Burma who both sought stability among their respective work-forces during harvest time, not least in order to avoid premature harvesting in the northern parts of Arakan before the itinerant harvest gangs moved south.

I have already referred to the 1940 report on Indian immigration to Burma during British rule by the Financial Secretary, James Baxter.[34] He noted in Chapter VII, which is entirely devoted to immigration from the Indian Sub-Continent to Arakan during British rule, the preponderance of males over females in Arakan among Indian migrants and their descendants. The main ethnicities of the Indian population in Akyab District are given as follows:

	Male	Female	Total
Chittagonians	104,769	81,558	186,327
Bengalis[35]	10,998	4,588	15,586
Hindustanis	2,955	632	3,587
Oriyas	3,809	10	3,819

Table 1. Main Indian ethnicities in Akyab in 1940.

The Baxter Report noted that at the time some 86,000 male Indians were 'born in Burma' compared with 81,000 females, while 38,000 male Indians were born outside Burma against only 6,000 females. As Muslim families in Arakan were more prolific than Rakhine families, male immigrants were sooner or later generally able to find spouses among local Indian communities, though prospective wives were in short supply in both Muslim and Rakhine communities.

---

[34] See Baxter, 1941, see above note 1.

[35] Bengali origin outside the Chittagong region.

These figures are based on the 1931 Census, which distinguished between the majority 'Indian' British-era migrants or descendants on the one hand, and the minority quasi-indigenous 'Indo-Burman' descendants on the other, the latter listed mainly as Arakan Muslims (Yakhain-kala), Kaman and Myedu. Indo-Burmans numbered only 56,963 in the 1931 Census. Intermarriage with the local Rakhine community was historically far greater among Indo-Burman communities than among Indian communities.[36]

8.6. British Policy on Migration

British policy on immigration from Bengal to Burma was at the forefront of the 1888 report by Philip Nolan "Emigration from Bengal to Burma and How to Promote it". The report is primarily concerned with the promotion of the migration of agricultural labourers from impoverished Behar (Bihar) which was then in the Bengal Presidency and is today a State in India. There are however occasional references to Arakan (Araccan) and Chittagong. We read in the Report:

> To the Chittagong emigrants the differences between the wages current in their own district, which in this respect is the best in Bengal, and the Burma rates means an appreciable increase in comfort. To the Behari, it is often a matter of life or death […] In Burma any labourer can in a few years earn sufficient to establish himself as a cultivator, paying only the public revenue, assessed on all alike at a moderate rate, and absolutely free from all danger of disturbance. This a consideration which has great weight for the inhabitants of Chittagong who contribute a large proportion, perhaps a majority of Bengal immigrants […][37]

As an exercise in enlightened colonialism, it is difficult to fault the proposals in this Report. The intention was to develop unpopulated waste lands in various regions of Burma without disruption to or at the expense of indigenous communities.[38]

---

[36] "Rohingya" was not to make its first appearance until some 20 years later.

[37] See Philip Nolan, *Report on Emigration from Bengal to Burma, and How to Promote It*, Bengal Secretariat Press, Calcutta, 1888, paras. 9–10 (https://legal-tools.org/doc/cn7487).

[38] In the event, not all that many Biharis seem to have made the journey to and to have settled in Burma. The 1931 Decennial Census records only 508 male and 31 female Bihari speakers in the whole of Burma.

The Nolan Report notes that there is an area of some 296,000 acres of waste land in Akyab District fit for cultivation and which only requires clearing and "small bunding", work which can be carried out by the cultivators themselves.[39] The report quotes from the *Settlement Report for the 1886–87 Season in the Akyab District*:

> The great want in this tract[40] is population. The land if bunded is very productive, and if Bengalis could be induced to squat on it, I have no doubt that in a short time it would assume the same appearance as the Naaf[41] has now. I think that District Officers might well devote attention to getting Bengali settlers here. There are large tracts of land which have passed out of production and large tracts that have never been cultivated that only require bunding to make them productive. The present inhabitants would no doubt object to grants on the ground of interference with grazing, prior claim, old possession, [et]c. But any claims of this nature not entered in the settlement registers should be received with caution. Five years' exemption from revenue and second class soil rates on new pottas[42] would, I think, encourage Bengalis to settle.[43]

In his covering report, the Chief Secretary noted:

> The Chief Commissioner commends to the attention of the Commissioner of Arakan and the Deputy Commissioner of Akyab Mr Adamson's [the Settlement Officer] remarks on the want of communications and the want of population. He is prepared to consider any plan the Commissioner may propose for attracting Bengali immigrants if the privileges accorded by the Revenue Rules are not sufficient.

I have found no trace of any subsequent 'plan' to attract Bengali immigrants. Those who came paid their own travel expenses. In any case

---

[39] W.T. Hall, "Note on Waste Lands in Lower Burma Available for Cultivation", in Philip Nolan, *Report on Emigration from Bengal to Burma, and How to Promote It*, Bengal Secretariat Press, Calcutta, 1888, p. 2 (https://legal-tools.org/doc/cn7487).

[40] The tract concerned was the Kaladan Valley.

[41] The Naaf Valley tract included Maungdaw and Buthidaung.

[42] The meaning of 'potta' has not been found in any work of reference, but presumably means 'settled land'.

[43] See *Report on the Settlement Operations in the Akyab District: Season 1886-87*, Superintendent, Government Printing, Burma, Rangoon, 1888, p. 35 (https://legal-tools.org/doc/1o4bkb).

most immigrants from Bengal were illiterate and came from the rural areas of Chittagong district adjacent to Arakan. They were well aware from family connexions of the prospects for migration, which were primarily to settle on and acquire permanently tenancy of their own land. In Arakan there were hardly any British-owned estates or plantations requiring labour. The tax exemptions offered were the same for any new settlers, whether from Bengal, other districts of Burma or as far away as China. As Lt. Col. J.F.J. Stevenson, Commissioner for Arakan, noted as early as 1869 and so some 17 years before the rest of Burma came under British rule, in remarks typically prejudiced for the time:

> I may advert here to a measure which I took the liberty of advocating in my letter No. 36, dated 11 December last [1868], respecting the introduction of Chinese cultivators. This is not the place for discussing schemes. But I will say that if we could bring in cultivators of this race, we should be independent of Chittagonians, our only immigrants at present. The country would be improved as much by Chinamen as by any race of Bengalees, and the Burmese or Arakanese race would not deteriorate as it undoubtedly does by admixture with a low type Aryan type of people. And my remarks upon the Chinese race are equally applicable to the Shan people, who only require a little more encouragement to come in numbers from the Burman Shan States.[44]

8.7. Migration to Arakan During British Rule

In his article, Morten Bergsmo poses the intriguing question:

> Could Myanmar argue that the transfer of civilians into Burma prior to World War II – a process that has contributed significantly to the demographic makeup of, for example, Rakhine State - was a violation of international law?

I have some sympathy with this argument. It could be true of Burma as a whole. But as regards Arakan itself, the situation is less clear-cut. The British directly recruited few people in India for jobs in Arakan itself in the way that they organised or assisted the transfer of police (46 per cent), military (41 per cent), posts and telegraph (32 per cent), Western medical

---

[44] J.F.J. Stevenson, "Reports on the Revenue Settlement Operations of British Burma, for the Year 1867-68: Arakan Division", in *Reports on the Revenue Settlement Operations of British Burma, for the Year 1867-68*, vol. I, Office of Superintendent of Government Printing, Calcutta, 1869, p. 29, para. 71 (https://legal-tools.org/doc/0nw7me).

practitioners (58 per cent), subordinate public administration (about 30 per cent), railway workers (nearly 70 per cent), sea and river transport workers (about 51 per cent) for work in Burma generally.[45] Even the Chettiyar moneylenders who played such a dominant and controversial role in financing the rice industry in the Irrawaddy Delta played only second-fiddle to local financiers in Arakan. The agricultural labourers who settled in Arakan under British rule came primarily of their own volition. Yet encouragement to emigrate might in the circumstances which prevailed be held to be tantamount to irresistible inducement. Let us look at some migration statistics.

The first peace-time census in Arakan, for the capitation tax in 1829, assessed the population of Arakan at 121,288 by which time many of those, both Muslims and Buddhists, who had sought refuge in Bengal during Burman rule, had returned home. By 1832 the population had risen to 195,107 and by 1842 to 246,766. The Rev. G.S. Comstock (1847) recorded that the 1842 Annual Census estimated the population at the time at some 257,000:

> Of these about 167,000 were Mugs, 40,000 are Burmese, 20,000 are Mussulmans, 5,000 are Bengalese, 3,000 are Toungmroos, 2,000 are Kemees, 1,250 are Karens and the remainder are of various races, in smaller numbers and sundry other ethnic groups.

This would indicate, by 1842, an 8:1 ratio of Buddhists (Rakhine and Burmese) to Muslims in Arakan as a whole, not the 7:3 ratio of Charles Paton in 1826 noted above.

The population of Arakan trebled during the first 25 years of British rule from 100,000 or so to more than 350,000 (352,348 recorded in the 1852 Annual Census). I have already mentioned the reminiscences published in 1878 by the former Chief Commissioner of Burma, Lt. Gen. Albert Fytche. In *Burma: Past and Present*, he noted:

> This vast increase was due to immigration from provinces under Burmese government, and notably from Pegu […] The desertion of their own sovereign and country by these masses, and their voluntarily placing themselves under an alien rule, coupled with the vast increase of prosperity in every shape of the portion of Burma which has become British,

---

[45] Percentages of total Indian penetration in particular sectors are taken from Chakravarti, 1971, para. 13, see above note 31.

must, therefore, at least as far as British Burma is concerned, unequivocally convince the blindest admirer of native rule and institutions of the superiority of British over Native Rule; and that no portion of our great Eastern Empire is more important, with a great future before it, than our possessions in Burma.[46]

These migrants were Buddhist, not Muslim. Their arrival was voluntary. This process however was later reversed in Akyab District when the migration of Muslims from Bengal started in earnest after the opening of the Suez Canal in 1869, which saw the expansion of the rice trade throughout Burma and the development of Akyab Town (Sittwe) as a major international port. By the time of the first full census of 1872, the population of Arakan as a whole had reached 484,673. Buddhists at 364,023 (Rakhine and Burmese) still exceeded Muslims at 64,313 (Yakhain-kala pre-1824 settlers,[47] Chittagonians, Bengalis, Kaman, Myedu, Zerbaidis[48] etc.) by a ratio of nearly 6 to 1. However, in Akyab District 185,266 Buddhists were counted against 58,263 Muslims, a ratio of nearly 3 to 1. From then on, the ratio of Buddhists to Muslims in Akyab District showed a steady decline as migration from Bengal into the District gradually increased. By the time of the 1931 Census there were still more Buddhists (448,288) in Akyab District than Muslims (244,398). But the ratio had fallen to just under 2 to 1.[49]

British encouragement of Muslim settlement had certain repercussions. The pressures on the local Rakhine came however from two sources: Burmans ('Yanbyè' or Ramree islanders) already settled in Sandoway and Kyaukpyu moving into Akyab or arriving from adjacent Pegu Division,

---

[46] Albert Fytche, *Burma: Past and Present*, vol. I, C. Kegan Paul & Co., London, 1878, p. 256.

[47] Buchanan records that the Yakhain-kala or 'Rakhine strangers' called themselves 'Rooinga' or 'Natives of Arakan'. The word has survived until today as 'Rohingya', passing though many variations and being ascribed to a range of Arakan Muslim ethnicities over the years.

[48] For an explanation of this term, see C.C. Lowis, *Census of India, 1901*, vol. XII, Office of the Superintendent of Government Printing, Burma, Rangoon, 1902, pp. 110–11 (https://legal-tools.org/doc/umfjnv).

[49] Starting with the 1921 Census, the British administration enumerated Muslims in Arakan as either 'Indo-Burman' or 'Indian'. The two groups were subdivided into separate ethnic identities, none of them 'Rohingya'.

and Chittagonians migrating from Bengal into the north. As Robert Smart observed in his 1917 "Gazetteer on Akyab District":

> That the Arakanese are steadily being pushed out of Arakan by the steady wave of Chittagonian immigration from the west is only too well known. The reason why they cannot withstand this pressure is that they are extravagant and hire more labour than is necessary rather than do a fair share of the work themselves [...] the Arakanese not having been accustomed to hard manual labour for generations cannot and will not do it now. It has been brought home to him that if he will not do it himself he must give way to the thrifty and hard-working Chittagonian and his only reply is to move on. He has lived better and worked less than the despicable 'kula' and he does not mean to alter his ways now. The pressure from the Kyaukpyu and Sandoway districts must not be forgotten, and between the Chittagonian and the Yanbyè the Arakanese proper are not likely to survive[50] long.[51]

The Gazetteer, which in its final chapter presents demographic sketches of every township and sub-division of Akyab District, makes clear the extent of immigration from Bengal and the contrast between the old Indo-Burman and the new Indian settlers:

> Long residence in this enervating climate and the example set by the people among whom they have resided for generations have had the effect of rendering these people [pre-1824 Muslim settlers] almost as indolent and extravagant as the Arakanese themselves. They have so got out of the habit of doing hard manual labour that they are now absolutely dependent on the Chittagonian coolies to help them over the most arduous of their agricultural operations, ploughing, reaping and earthwork.

> Since 1879 immigration has taken place on a much larger scale and the descendants of the slaves are resident, for the most part, in the Kyauktaw and Myohaung [Mrauk U] townships. Maungdaw township has been overrun by Chittagonian immigrants. Buthidaung is not far behind and new arrivals will be found in almost every part of the district. The later

---

[50] But survive they did, and prosper.

[51] See R.B. Smart, *Burma Gazetteer: Akyab District*, vol. A, Superintendent, Government Printing, Burma, Rangoon, 1917, pp. 88–89 (https://legal-tools.org/doc/0odxg0).

settlers, who have not been sapped of their vitality, not only do their own labour but it is not uncommon to find them hurrying on their own operations to enable such as can be spared to proceed elsewhere to add to their earnings by working as agricultural labourers, boatmen or mill coolies.[52]

8.8. Muslim-Buddhist Communal Relations

What is perhaps remarkable is that these pressures on the Rakhine to move on did not lead to serious communal violence. There are reports of only isolated disputes among and between Chittagonians and Arakanese, mostly over land and rent, normal in almost any community. The Arakanese found that, for the prices Chittagonians were prepared to pay to buy land from them, they could purchase twice as much land further inland across the Arakan Yoma mountains among their own people.

Yet there is no doubt where British sympathies lay. Few colonial officials had a good word to say about the Rakhine. Bengali migrants were industrious; they paid their rent on time; they did not drink or gamble like the feckless and indolent Rakhine; they worked hard and prospered; their villages were generally better kept; they showed commercial enterprise. Such prejudices, impossible to conceal, may well have given rise to resentment among the Rakhine.

Yet in this context, the comments in 1957 of the Rakhine politician U Kyaw Min (not to be confused with the current Rohingya politician of the same name mentioned above) are worthy of note. U Kyaw Min was one of only eight British-educated Burmese, four of them Rakhine, formally recruited into the prestigious Indian Civil Service and authorized to use the initials 'I.C.S.' after their names. In a political tract on "The Arakan State", he noted:

> The problem of the Arakanese was the Chittagonian problem, not the Burmese. The Chittagonians, however, came to Arakan as servants and labourers and as such they were wanted in Arakan. They never were really a serious problem for they kept their place as servants and labourers and in the mofussil, where they came as peasants, there was enough room for them because of the lack of Arakanese farmers. The relations were always cordial. The first clash between them was with

---

[52] *Ibid.*, p. 90.

the advent of the Japanese in early 1942. But that is a story apart.[53]

This 'story apart' has been expertly analysed by Jacques Leider in "Conflict and Mass Violence in Arakan". He is rightly cautious in attributing responsibility. He notes:

> The terrible confrontation of 1942 had in fact tragic consequences for both communities. The inglorious events have never been a source of contentment or pride for any of the two parties. Actors on both sides of the social and religious divide have to share the responsibility for criminal behavior. Still, there is regrettably little reliable or detailed information on what triggered the violence in Minbya or Myebon, what happened thereafter and in which exact circumstances a wave of revenge killing occurred.[54]

There is a reference by both Jacques P. Leider and Morten Bergsmo to the 'divide and rule' policy of the British alleged by the Jamiat ul-Ulema in 1948 which had supposedly:

> created […] a large measure of misunderstanding and distrust between our people and our Arakanese brethren (a policy) […] [which] culminated in the massacre of 1942 of our people residing in various parts of Akyab District.[55]

I regard this 'divide and rule' shibboleth as little more than political opportunism designed to appeal to Prime Minister U Nu and to secure greater political representation in Parliament at the time. The allegation is not supported by any evidence and makes no reference to the dispossession and murder of Arakanese by Muslims in the northern part of the District, by way of retaliation. It is unlikely that U Nu was persuaded by this line of argument.

For most Buddhist Rakhine, the migration during British rule of many thousands of Bengali coolies and farmers was generally not unwel-

---

[53] See U Kyaw Min, *The Arakan State*, Pye Daw Tha Press, Kyaukmyaung, p. 2 (https://legal-tools.org/doc/oy113e).

[54] Jacques P. Leider, "Conflict and Mass Violence in Arakan (Rakine State): The 1942 Events and Political Identity Formation", in Ashley South and Marie Lall (eds.), *Citizenship in Myanmar: Ways of Being in and from Burma*, ISEAS Publishing, Singapore, 2017.

[55] "Address presented by Jamiat ul-Ulema North Arakan: On Behalf of the People of North Arakan to the Hon'ble Prime Minister of the Union of Burma on the Occasion of His Visit to Maungdaw on the 25th October 1948", p. 2, see above note 20.

come. The Rakhine were more than content to engage the labour of transient or permanent Bengali migrants during the rice harvest and as port workers at Akyab. I have already referred to the forced migration of Bengalis in the seventeenth and eighteenth centuries.[56] It is not unreasonable to suppose that, if Britain had not imposed its rule on Burma, the Rakhine themselves would have encouraged the Bengali influx into Arakan for precisely the same reasons as the British. Bengal was historically a source of labour and population for Arakan, forced or voluntary.

The nature of the Bengali presence in Arakan was well captured in the 1913–17 Revenue Settlement Report:

> The contrast between the native [Bengali] and Arakanese villages is very marked and can be seen even on the kwin map. The former are regularly laid out and every house has its fenced-in compound covering about half an acre and containing mango, jack and bamboos. Around the village are small plots of miscellaneous cultivation on which chillies and tobacco are grown as well as brinjals, maize and sometimes sugarcane. The compounds are kept free from weeds and are well swept. The houses are built in Indian style on a raised mud floor and are thatched with paddy straw in place of dhani. Though smaller on average than the houses of the Arakanese they are far from being mere hovels and their neat compounds give them an air of great comfort and prosperity. The people are well fed, well dressed and well housed, and there are nowhere any signs of any approach to poverty.
>
> The Arakanese villages on the other hand are irregular collections of mat and thatch cottages without compounds and frequently without shade. The villages are always untidy and towards the end of the hot weather dhani roofs in the last stages of disrepair give them a very poverty-stricken appearance. Wooden houses are rare, and a tin roof is almost unknown.[57]

The view that the present Rohingya crisis might be another colonial legacy has nonetheless come under scrutiny. Mohammad Shahabuddin,

---

[56] See above note 7 about the capture enslavement of many thousands of Bengali Muslims and Hindus during the Mrauk-U dynasty.

[57] Extract from para. 13 of the Report by R.B. Smart on the Revision Settlement Operations in the Akyab District Season 1913–17.

writing recently in the *Asian Journal of International Law*, observes guardedly:

> The continuation of colonial boundaries in the politico-legal imagination of post-colonial statehood is an established norm of international law. Although some international law-yers challenge this general application of the *uti possidetis* [literally "as you possess"] principle as a legally binding rule of international law, they nonetheless accept the pragmatic need for this principle, i.e. to maintain peace and stability. Ironically, as the example of the Rohingya crisis reveals, what seemed to be a solution at the time of decolonization turned out to be a recipe for humanitarian catastrophe [...] international law often fails to offer any adequate protection to vulnerable groups in society due to its normative reliance on individualism as well as weak enforcement mechanisms. The Rohingya crisis in Myanmar provides a perfect illustra-tion of these arguments, serving as a powerful reminder of the deep, enduring crisis of post-colonial statehood and its problematic engagement with international law.[58]

Writing in the Indian online magazine *The Wire*, Tathagata Dutta has argued that the Second World War and British wartime policies rup-tured Arakan's social fabric, though conceding that the troubles began when Arakanese Muslims "were massacred by rogue elements" within Aung San's Burma Independence Army and local Rakhine militants. He writes:

> The conduct of the British colonial administration, particu-larly in the closing days of the last Arakan Campaign in Au-gust 1944, continues to be a chequered one. Burmese inde-pendence in 1948 brought forth the deep divisions created in this period into the open. The Arakanese Muslims, for the first time facing direct Burmese rule once again, revolted and formed militant groups dubbed as 'mujahid bands'. They used arms and ammunition left behind by the British to take on the Burmese Army while the rest of Burma too flared up along ethnic lines. The British legacy today in Myanmar is

---

[58] See Mohammad Shahabuddin, "Post-colonial Boundaries, International Law, and the Mak-ing of the Rohingya Crisis in Myanmar", in *Asian Journal of International Law*, 2019, vol. 9, no. 2, p. 358.

perhaps the longest-running civil war in the world and a humanitarian crisis of gigantic proportions.[59]

Both Mohammad Shahabuddin and Tathagata Dutta describe Arakan Muslims historically as 'Rohingyas', though the use of this designation is surely an anachronism. The term[60] was, as I have already noted, unknown to the British who, like most Western countries, first used the designation in official correspondence only in 1991 to identify Arakan's Muslim population at the time of armed insurgency into Rakhine State by the Arakan Rohingya Islamic Front (ARIF) and the Rohingya Solidarity Organisation (RSO). These insurgent attacks led to the second large-scale exodus of Arakan Muslims into Bangladesh after the 1978 exodus in the wake of Operation Naga Min, designed to uncover illegal immigrants into Myanmar's border provinces.

I doubt though that today's Rohingya see Britain's wartime policies as responsible for their present plight. The British might perhaps have taken into greater account promises possibly made by British commanding officers in the heat of battle to Arakan Muslims to grant a measure of autonomy on independence, but there is nothing in British official archives to suggest that this possibility was at any time considered in London, either formally or informally. Far greater attention was given to the aspirations of the Karen who enjoyed a much strong political lobby in London, but they too failed to achieve their objective of achieving autonomy within or independence from the new Union of Burma.

It is also relevant that the Inquiry into the anti-Muslim riots which rocked Rangoon and several other cities in Burma in July 1938 reported only a very few minor incidents in the Sandoway (Thandwe) District of Arakan Division, and none at all in Akyab District itself.[61] The Final Report of the Riot Inquiry Committee noted:

---

[59] See Tathagata Dutta, "The Rohingya Crisis Is Another Colonial Legacy", in *The Wire*, 16 September 2019 (available on its web site).

[60] Francis Buchanan was surgeon and scientist to a diplomatic mission to the Court of Ava in 1795 where he met one or more persons deported from Arakan in 1785 who told him they were 'Rooinga' or 'Natives or Arakan'. Its etymology suggests that it means no more than 'Arakaner' and can be applied in Bangla-related languages to anyone resident in Arakan, whatever their ethnicity, on a par with 'New Zealander' or 'Londoner'.

[61] See *Final Report of the Riot Inquiry Committee*, Superintendent, Government Printing and Stationery, Burma, Rangoon, 1939 (https://legal-tools.org/doc/fg84bk).

> The scale of Indian immigration into Burma in the past and the comparative experience, ability, industry and thrift, and the relative success of the Indian financier and immigrant have, under present political influences, tended to obscure in the mind of the Burman the benefits his country has received, and will yet receive, from the Indians in the country and to create a real apprehension lest it may be continued so as to interfere with the prospects of the Burman himself in his own country. These apprehensions have been assisted to some extent by the complete breakdown in Burma, if not the complete abandonment, in the past of the policy of creating a self-supporting population of peasant proprietors of land, helped by legislation and free from the unsettling influences of artificial and fluctuating economic conditions.[62]

8.9. Concluding Observations

I must leave it to experts better qualified in international law to decide whether British policies and actions in encouraging migration into Arakan were a violation of this law on any count. I personally doubt this. Criticism has been made of the British failure to respect the traditional ruler in Burma as we did in practically every other territory colonized and how we thereby eliminated the Burmese sovereign's position as head of the Buddhist religion. There were also the less than diplomatic British decisions to govern Burma until 1937 as a province of India and not as a colony direct from London and to introduce opium as a revenue earner. Though these issues were not particularly relevant to Arakan, they would have had some proportionate effect. Chittagonians abstained from opium, but were happy to make a commercial profit selling it to their Rakhine neighbours.

Even so, and despite the indisputable historical record of the migration of their ancestors to Arakan mostly during British rule, today's Rohingyas, whom the British recorded in a kaleidoscope of ethno-linguistic designations other than Rohingya, can rightfully say that they were not brought to Arakan, but that they belong there.

To quote the Press Statement of former President U Thein Sein after talks with the present UN Secretary-General, António Guterres, on 11 July 2012, when the latter visited Myanmar as UN High Commissioner for Refugees:

---

[62] See *ibid.*, p. 289 (https://legal-tools.org/doc/53ecy0).

The President said that Bengalis came to Myanmar because the British colonialists invited them in prior to 1948, when Myanmar gained independence from Britain, to work in the agricultural sector. Some Bengalis settled here because it was convenient for them to do so, and according to Myanmar law, the third generation of those who arrived before 1948 can be granted Myanmar citizenship. He added that, if we look at the situation in Rakhine State, some people are the younger generation of Bengalis who arrived before 1948, but some are illegal immigrants claiming to be Rohingyas and this threatens the stability of the State. The Government has been looking seriously for a solution to this problem. The country will take responsibility for its native people, but it cannot accept illegal immigrant Rohingya in any way.[63]

U Thein Sein's reference to 'native people' might almost include Bengalis permanently settled in Rakhine State during British rule, but not post-1948 illegal entrants, whom the former President defined as 'Rohingya', adding yet another variant to the meaning of this designation, but possibly explaining why Daw Aung San Suu Kyi reportedly described Rohingya as 'Bangladeshi' (or more likely Bengali, as Bangladeshi is a nationality, not an ethnicity) when she met former Prime Minister David Cameron in the UK in 2013.[64]

By way of contrast, though, Senior General Min Aung Hlaing, the Commander-in-Chief of the Tatmadaw, told US Ambassador Scott Marciel in October 2017 that Britain was responsible for the presence of so many Bengalis in Rakhine State:

> The Bengalis were not taken into the country by Myanmar, but by the colonialists. They are not the natives [...] The native place of Bengalis is really Bengal.[65]

Though politically powerful in Myanmar, the Commander-in-Chief does not represent the Myanmar Government. State Counsellor Daw Aung

---

[63] See Unofficial Translation: Statement published on 12 July 2012 by the President's Office following a meeting on 11 July 2012 with the UN High Commissioner for Refugees António Guterres (https://legal-tools.org/doc/gejgk3).

[64] See Prasun Sonwalkar, "Rohingyas are Bangladeshis, Suu Kyi told David Cameron", in *Hindustan Times*, 19 September 2019 (available on its web site).

[65] See Robert Birsel and Wa Lone, "Myanmar Army Chief Says Rohingya Muslims 'Not Natives', Numbers Fleeing Exaggerated", in *Reuters*, 12 October 2017 (available on its web site).

San Suu Kyi, however, does, and she has been careful to avoid use of the term 'Bengali' or to allege that the Rohingya are 'illegal immigrants'.

The descendants of the many tens of thousands of Muslims and Hindus captured by Luso-Arakanese pirates and brought as slaves to Arakan in the sixteenth and seventeenth centuries might well ask what the British had to do with the compulsory resettlement of their ancestors. The Burman majority in Myanmar though might argue as well that it was not them, but the Arakanese who were responsible.

It is relevant in the context of citizenship to note what Deputy Head of Mission at the British Embassy in Rangoon, Roger Freeland, observed when reporting in a letter to the Foreign and Commonwealth Office in November 1982 on the promulgation of the 1982 Citizenship Law:[66]

> The new Law is blatantly discriminatory on racial grounds. If the new procedures that are being prepared turn out to be as rigorous as we suspect they will be, then the Law may in practice be even more discriminatory than its text pretends.
>
> On the other hand it would be possible to argue that the new Law is a generous and far-sighted instrument to resolve over a period of time an awkward legacy of the colonial era.[67]

This recognition of the British responsibility for the movement over the years of so many migrants from Bengal and beyond into Arakan is welcome, though as Ambassador Charles Booth commented in a letter to the Foreign and Commonwealth Office in May 1982 on the draft of the law when it appeared for public consultation in April 1982:[68]

> The new bill reflects little credit on the legislators and ultimately on the regime as a whole, and I see it as another move in Burma's policy of keeping itself "pure" of foreign involvement. Its immediate concern, I assume, is with illegal Bengali immigration into Arakan.[69]

---

[66] See Burma Citizenship Law, 15 October 1982, Pyithu Hluttaw Law No 4 of 1982 (https://legal-tools.org/doc/d3e586).

[67] See J.R. Leeland, "Burmese Citizenship Law", 25 November 1982, paras. 4–5 (https://legal-tools.org/doc/40czet).

[68] See "Suggestions Sought in Connection with the Burma Citizenship Draft Law", in *The Guardian Supplement*, 21 April 1982 (https://legal-tools.org/doc/y3eyxk).

[69] See C.L. Booth, "Burmese Citizenship Draft Law", 12 May 1982, para. 8 (https://legal-tools.org/doc/9o9mpo).

Mr. Nebenzia might wish to know that there was no need to transfer any agricultural labourers to Arakan; they were either there already, or simply walked across the border, or took a ferry across the Naaf River into Arakan, because their labour was needed; the border between Bengal and Arakan at the Naaf River was not created by the British, though they formally delineated it; it was established in 1666 for all practical purposes after the Mughal capture of Chittagong and the retreat of Arakan forces to the East Bank of the Naaf river and south of particular Arakan mountain ridges.

Union Minister U Kyaw Tint Swe observed on 28 September 2019 in his address to the UN General Assembly during the general debate at the 74th session:

> The British census of 1872 reported 58,255 Muslims in Akyab District (modern Sittwe). By 1911, the Muslim population had increased to 178,647. The waves of migration were primarily due to the requirement of cheap labour from British India to work in the paddy fields. Immigrants from Bengal, mainly from the Chittagong region, 'moved en masse into western townships of Arakan'.[70] As in other colonized territories across the world, our local population had no say whatsoever with regard to the seismic demographic transformation of their lands. Nevertheless, Myanmar accepts it as part of the chequered legacy for which we assumed responsibility when we won our independence in 1948. It was only in 1949, with the adoption of the fourth Geneva Convention, that international law expressly prohibited the transfer of civilians into occupied territories. But there was no recognition of the troublesome consequences of such operations.

Myanmar's view expressed above was confirmed in a letter dated 16 October 2019 to the UN Secretary-General as a document for the UN General Assembly. Ambassador U Hau Do Suan wrote:

---

[70] The quotation appears to have been taken from Thant Myint-U, *The River of Lost Footsteps: Histories of Burma*, Farrar, Straus and Giroux, New York, 2006, p. 185: "Muslim families from Chittagong, once the port of the Mrauk-U kings, moved en masse into the Western townships of Arakan, and in the rest of the province Bengalis, both Hindus and Muslims, arrived as doctors, clerks, schoolteachers and lawyers, forming an essential part of the new urban class". We might well ask what happened to these other Bengalis who settled down in other parts of the Province of British Burma. Most assuredly, they did not become 'Rohingyas', yet their descendants were of the same stock.

The issue of Rakhine State is one of the colonial legacies. Myanmar was a British colony for over one hundred years. During this period, the colonial power transferred hundreds of thousands of civilians mostly from British India (Chittagong region of present-day Bangladesh) to then Burma (Rakhine State) to propel the rapidly expanding rice production and export. In 1927 alone, there were more than 480,000 such transfers[71] into occupied colonial Burma. The British census of 1872 reported 58,255 Muslims in Akyab District (modern Sittwe).[72] By 1911, the Muslim population had increased to 178,647. The waves of migration were primarily due to the requirement of cheap labour from British India to work in the paddy fields in Rakhine State.[73] It was obvious that immigrants from Bengal, mainly from the Chittagong region had regularly moved en masse into western townships of Arakan during the British colonial period.[74]

For the record and in confirmation of the figures presented by the representatives of Myanmar in the United Nations, the following table is taken from R.B. Smart's Gazetteer of Akyab District 1917 based on the decennial censuses of 1872, 1901 and 1911:[75]

---

[71] This number very probably reflects the total of arrivals in Burma during 1927, the highest recorded year, but departures were also substantial. The Baxter Report 1940 notes 428,300 arrivals through ports in Burma, and 361,200 departures, a net inflow of 67,100 in 1927 through the ports. Few arrivals would have been visitors, but migrants would have been seasonal, short-term, longer-term and permanent. Departures would reflect many migrants returning home, often to be replaced by other family members, especially true of Chettiyars.

[72] See above note 3. Akyab District comprised present-day Sittwe, Mrauk-U and Maungdaw Districts combined.

[73] Though itinerant gangs of coolies were needed to harvest the rice crops, the main aim of the British-encouraged migration was to attract permanent settlers to reclaim and then farm waste and abandoned land.

[74] See Letter Dated 16 October 2019 from the Permanent Representative of Myanmar to the United Nations addressed to the Secretary-General, UN Doc. A/74/505, 18 October 2019 (https://legal-tools.org/doc/bl4y3d).

[75] At p. 86. I cannot reconcile the low figure for 'Burmese' (that is, Burmans) in 1872 with the estimates by Paton (1826) of 10,000 and by Comstock (1842) of 40,000 unless we suppose that after one or two generations Burmese Buddhist settlers became so integrated with the Arakanese that they regarded themselves as no longer Burmese. For the same reason, the recorded decline in the number of Arakanese from 1901 to 1911 possibly reflects the increasing use of the Burmese language over Arakanese. There are also minor discrepancies between Smart's figures and the census reports, for example, 'Mahomedans' at 58,255

Races	1872	1901	1911
Hindu	2,655	14,455	14,454
Mahomedan	58,255	154,887	178,647
Burmese	4,632	35,751	92,185
Arakanese	171,612	239,649	209,432
Shan	334	80	59
Hill Tribes[76]	38,577	35,489	34,020
Others	606	1,355	1,146
Total	**276,671**	**481,666**	**529,943**

Table 2: Racial composition reported by R.B. Smart.

It has already been noted that the paddy fields of Arakan were not British colonial estates, but were historically occupied mostly by the local Buddhist Rakhine population. Whether there was any deliberate 'transfer' of the Bengali population to settle permanently in Arakan or whether they came mainly of their own volition, whatever may have happened in the rest of the Province of British Burma, is the subject of this paper. My conclusion is that there is no persuasive evidence that the British colonial authorities actually arranged the transfer of Bengali migrants to Burma in any significant numbers; or, for that matter, of Burmese migrants from outside Arakan who would have been able to move so much more freely after the whole of Burma came under British control in 1886.

Even so, I would acknowledge that the British cannot deny the legacy of their historical presence in Arakan and Burma, and this should not be airbrushed out of the picture when the crisis in Rakhine is under discussion internationally. British responsibility did not disappear on Burma's independence on 4 January 1948.

---

appears as 58,263 in the 1872 Census: "Appendix I: Report on the General Census of 1872 Taken in the Arakan Division", in *Report on the Census of British Burma Taken in August 1872*, Government Press, Rangoon, 1875, para. 27 (https://legal-tools.org/doc/91gtbw).

[76]   Chin, Taungtha, Khami and Daignet.

9

Myanmar and the Hegemonic Discourse of International Criminal Law

Ryan Mitchell[*]

9.1. Introduction

The government of Myanmar is facing possible international legal liability for its policies in the Rakhine State. There are ongoing efforts at both the International Criminal Court ('ICC') and the International Court of Justice ('ICJ') to characterize actions of state officials as amounting to internationally wrongful acts, and to impose corresponding orders or penalties on this basis. In both cases, international crimes form the basis of the respective processes, though the specific crimes referred to, and the jurisdictional theories underlying the proceedings, are quite distinct.[1]

The question of Myanmar's and its officials' responsibility for alleged acts of violence by military personnel against civilians in Rakhine State puts into focus several dimensions of international legal liability in post-colonial situations. Indeed, for reasons that will be examined in this chapter, the case of Rakhine is a fitting point of departure to more generally reconsider certain key notions regarding state responsibility, wrongful acts, and the appropriate responses by international tribunals. The prosecutorial toolkit of a still broadly Eurocentric international criminal law, in particular, exhibits 'hegemonic' features that can lead to bitter divisions

[*] **Ryan Mitchell** is an Assistant Professor of Law at Chinese University of Hong Kong and holds a J.D. degree from Harvard Law School (2012) and Ph.D. degree from Yale University (2017).

[1] See International Criminal Court ('ICC'), *Situation in the People's Republic of Bangladesh/Republic of the Union of Myanmar*, Pre-Trial Chamber, Decision Pursuant to Article 15 of the Rome Statute on the Authorisation of an Investigation into the Situation in the People's Republic of Bangladesh/Republic of the Union of Myanmar, 14 November 2019, ICC-01/19-27 (https://www.legal-tools.org/doc/kbo3hy/); International Court of Justice ('ICJ'), *Republic of the Gambia v. Republic of the Union of Myanmar*, Application Instituting Proceedings and Request for Provisional Measures, 11 November 2019, 178-20191111-APP-01-00-EN (https://www.legal-tools.org/doc/69p376/).

over legitimacy when applied to territories still grappling with the legacies of colonialism.[2]

The use of international criminal law processes today to address centuries of conflict and enmity in Rakhine raises concerns that:

> [t]o focus on individual guilt instead of, say, economic, political or military structures, is to leave invisible, and thus to underwrite, the story those structures have produced by pointing at a scapegoat. Criminal law is a weak and vulnerable strategy to cope with large crises: the more we insist on its technical character, the more we look away from its role in strengthening one narrative over others, and the more the trial will ratify the hegemony of that power on whose shoulders justice sits.[3]

In line with these concerns, the present chapter identifies and elucidates three dimensions of critique that may be usefully directed towards the legal frameworks currently being applied to the Rakhine situation. It aims not to provide arguments for any 'exculpation' of Myanmar state actors, or to justify *tu quoque* objections to the enforcement of international norms,[4] but rather to interrogate the modes by which international law allocates culpability and pose the question as to whether these might be improved.

The chapter will first address critiques based on the *ontology* of international law, as applied to Myanmar and its internal conflicts. It will ask whether the transplantation of the (historically European) conceptual

---

[2] See, for example, Martti Koskenniemi, *The Politics of International Law*, Bloomsbury Publishing, 2011, p. 234: "one should note the hegemonic trends within the spectacular rise of international criminal law". On hegemony and "hegemonic techniques" in international law more generally, see *ibid.*, pp. 219–240. On the hegemonic dynamics of international law as a continuation of the "civilizing mission" of colonial powers, see, for example, the discussion in Frédéric Mégret, "Where Does the Critique of International Human Rights Stand? An Exploration in 18 Vignettes", in Fred Varela, Justo Corti and John Haskell (eds.), *New Approaches to International Law: The European and the American Experiences*, Springer Science and Business Media, 2012, noting, *inter alia*, that the "colonial moment will not go away that easily because it helped forge some of the very basic concepts of international law and human rights". *Ibid.*, p. 9.

[3] Koskenniemi, p. 235, see above note 2.

[4] See Wolfgang Kaleck, *Double Standards: International Criminal Law and the West*, Torkel Opsahl Academic EPublisher, Brussels, 2015, p. 14 (https://www.toaep.org/ps-pdf/26-kaleck): discussing *tu quoque* ['you too'] objections by which defendants aimed at "undermining the political legitimacy of the court in general" by pointing out biases in its allocation of liability.

---

vocabulary of states, territories, and 'peoples' has contributed to, or directly caused, the very crimes it is now used to define. That this is the case is suggested by the contrasting manifestations of the doctrines of *uti possidetis* and of national self-determination in Myanmar's international legal history.

Second, the chapter undertakes a critique on the basis of the *epistemic* features of international criminal law, specifically in relation to the deep causes of civil disorder and inter-ethnic conflict. In particular, postcolonial violence takes on a very different character when viewed as part of a much longer chain of interactions. The current tribunal processes have not yet taken into account the unique economies of (dis)trust, based on the logic of division-and-conquest, that formed an essential element of colonial rule beginning with the East India Company's acquisition of Arakan. Where such policies have significantly contributed to subsequent outbreaks of violence, it may be proper to address this context when theorizing legal responsibility.

Third, this chapter will inquire as to the genealogical development of specific legal doctrines that form the basis of the Myanmar proceedings at the ICC and the ICJ. It will evaluate the claim that these doctrines have been structured in such a way as to create forms of liability for newly-independent former colonies that are not applied to their former colonizers, a problem raised by Morten Bergsmo in Chapter 7 above. The use of flexible interpretations of jurisdictional standards, at times rising to the level of legal fictions, is part of the normal repertoire of international tribunals. This may at times be defensible in order to bring justice to bear on situations of conflict or atrocity. However, there is no clear reason why courts should adopt this attitude of jurisdictional maximalism only or primarily in respect to former colonies. If spatial jurisdictional barriers can be relativized in order to bring the once-colonized before international tribunals, then temporal barriers to jurisdiction protecting erstwhile colonizers from liability should be as well.

Finally, on the basis of these three critical perspectives, the chapter will conclude by asking whether there is any prospect for addressing colonial era wrongs in the context of the current proceedings involving Myanmar. It will present the suggestion that some applications of judicial creativity and flexibility – of the sort frequently used *vis-à-vis* formerly colonized states – can appropriately impose liability upon Myanmar's former colonizer as well. While the individualized, prosecutorial dynamics of the ICC seem to preclude any expansive inquiry into such forms of liability, the Myanmar proceedings at the ICJ may offer a point of departure from which they could be addressed.

9.2. Ontological Critique

9.2.1. Rakhine Before the Nation-State

Two battles in 1757 helped to determine the future of the region of Arakan, which is now known as Rakhine State of western Myanmar. The Kingdom of Arakan was at this time still ruled by the dynasty based at Mrauk-U. For centuries its majority-Buddhist population remained independent both from successive Burmese dynasties and the Hindu and Muslim polities to the west, despite periods of nominal Mughal suzerainty, and exhibited an extensive cultural hybridization between these and other influences.[5] This autonomy would soon be lost, however, and the later inter-ethnic and inter-religious tensions that would take root in the region – and which continue today – would be shaped in important ways by this process.[6]

Both of the fateful battles of 1757 concerned not Arakan itself, but rather its neighbours. To the east, the new Konbaung Dynasty of the Bamar people overcame the final opposition of the Mon Hanthawaddy Kingdom at the Battle of Pegu. This victory followed the momentous Battle of Syriam of the previous year, in which the Konbaung founder Alaungpaya – the known as 'Maitreya' or 'The Buddha of the Future' – had also defeated the Mon and the French forces supporting them. Following this decisive victory, the Konbaung rulers would turn their attention to other wars, including expansion into Siam, repelling successive invasions by China's Qing Dynasty, and, by the 1780s, the conquest and "Buddhist restoration" of Arakan.[7]

---

[5] Like other frontier zones, Arakan constituted a "middle ground"; that is, a place "of fluid cultural and economic exchange where acculturation and the creation of hybrid political institutions were contingent on local conditions". Such zones generally tended to exhibit very contested processes of nation-state incorporation. Charles Patterson Giersch, *Asian Borderlands: The Transformation of Qing China's Yunnan Frontier*, Harvard University Press, 2006.

[6] See Jacques P. Leider, "Politics of Integration and Cultures of Resistance: A Study of Burma's Conquest and Administration of Arakan (1785–1825)", in Geoff Wade (ed.), *Asian Expansions*, Routledge, 2014, pp. 196–225.

[7] *Ibid.*; see also Aye Chan, "The Development of a Muslim Enclave in Arakan (Rakhine) State of Burma (Myanmar)", in *SOAS Bulletin of Burma Research*, 2005, vol. 3, no. 2, pp. 396–420; Mohammad Shahabuddin, "Post-colonial Boundaries, International Law, and the

The other battle in 1757 that helped to create some of today's dynamics in Rakhine State was the Battle of Plassey, in which the East India Company defeated the resistance of the Nawab of Bengal and obtained *de facto* control over this region to the immediate west of Arakan. From this point, the Company would consolidate its control over not only this region, but all of India. Before the period of Company rule gave way to that of the British Raj, Arakan and some other Konbaung-controlled regions would be annexed to colonial India via the First Anglo-Burmese War of 1824-1826.[8]

If the later geopolitical conquests of Arakan were in significant part spurred by these military events unfolding on either side, the juridical transformations of the region were in part decided by another event of 1757: the Swiss jurist Emer de Vattel's completion of his manuscript on the *Droit des Gens*, which he first published at Neuchâtel at the end of that year.[9] In Vattel's work, which is sometimes considered the "first distinctively modern international law treatise",[10] he opens with a discussion of "what is meant by a nation or state", that is, those entities whose "society" is the basis of the law he is describing. According to Vattel, nations are "bodies politic, societies of men united together for the purpose of promoting their mutual safety and advantage by the joint efforts of their combined strength".[11] The members of the nation, meanwhile, "deliberate […] and take […] resolutions in common; thus becoming a moral person, who possesses an understanding and a will peculiar to herself, and is susceptible of obligations and rights".[12]

None of these ideas, of course, originated with Vattel. Yet his clear compilation of them, along with the many other concepts and norms dis-

---

Making of the Rohingya Crisis in Myanmar", in *Asian Journal of International Law*, 2019, vol. 9, no. 2, pp. 334–358.

[8] Nick Robins, "The Corporation that Changed the World: How the East India Company Shaped the Modern Multinational", in *Asian Affairs*, 2012, vol. 43, no.1, pp. 12–26.

[9] Ben Holland, "The Moral Person of the State: Emer de Vattel and the Foundations of International Legal Order", in *History of European Ideas*, 2011, vol. 37, no. 4, pp. 438–445.

[10] Frederick G. Whelan, "Vattel's Doctrine of the State", in *History of Political Thought*, 1988, vol. 9, no. 1, pp. 59–90.

[11] Emer de Vattel, *The Law of Nations, Or, Principles of the Law of Nature, Applied to the Conduct and Affairs of Nations and Sovereigns, with Three Early Essays on the Origin and Nature of Natural Law and on Luxury*, in Béla Kapossy and Richard Whatmore (eds.), Indianapolis, Liberty Fund, 2008.

[12] *Ibid.*, p. 67.

cussed in his *Droit des Gens*, would soon become a dominant reference point for discussions of the law of nations in both legal and diplomatic contexts until well into the nineteenth century. The juristic premise of a state as a "moral person" with a "will", as the sole possessor of international obligations and rights, meant that states, and only states, could have the characteristics of "liberty and independence". Only a state so recognized by international legal society could be "mistress of her own actions, when they do not affect the perfect rights of others".[13] The natural corollary of this status, of course, was that "a people that has passed under the dominion of another is no longer a state, and can no longer avail itself directly of the law of nations". The law of nations, after all, was "the law of sovereigns".[14]

These concepts did not fit well to the realities on the ground in Arakan, or indeed in the conflicts that were reshaping its larger region. The Konbaung ruler who would conquer Arakan in 1785 did so in the name of an agenda aiming to "restore" its Buddhist faith, to "purify […] the *sasana* [Buddhist monastic orders]", and also to confer additional legitimacy on his own rule as a '*dhammaraja*' or righteous king.[15] Symbolic of this aim was the seizure of the eschatologically important Mahamuni Buddha Image, symbolic of divinely-sanctioned rulership, and its transport to Mandalay.[16] Rather than as a separate "moral person" with its own "will" *or* as a "people […] under the dominion of another", the Konbaung construed Arakan as an integral, if recently estranged element of a primordial, theologically-defined polity.

The Arakanese and their culture were to be "absorbed" on this basis of a posited supra-state identity encompassing both them and their new Burmese rulers.[17] While this involved at times negotiating with or seeking to avoid the alienation of the new Konbaung subjects, it also involved major new policies of reorganization and administrative homogenization with other territories. Both spatial divisions and such signifiers as seals and coinage were to be changed to match the new situation of rule.[18] More

---

[13] *Ibid.*, p. lv–lxiii.

[14] *Ibid.*, p. 85.

[15] Leider, 2014, p. 188, see above note 6.

[16] *Ibid.*

[17] *Ibid.*, p. 194.

[18] Than Tun (ed.), *The Royal Orders of Burma, A.D. 1598-1885, Part Four: A.D. 1782-1787*, Center for Southeast Asian Studies, Kyoto University, 1987, p. 182.

seriously, much of the preëxisting leadership and elites were exiled post-conquest, such that "the whole supporting infrastructure of Arakanese kingship disappeared".[19]

Meanwhile, the great power taking effective control of Bengal after the 1750s was also not a sovereign state after the Vattelian mould, but rather the East India Company, exerting various forms of formal and informal influence over local political actors and pursuing policies aimed at maximal commercial expansion. One of the great turning points in this process, and indeed what is often regarded as the moment that effectively inaugurated Company rule, was the handing over of the rights of *Diwani* tax and revenue administration in Bengal via the Treaty of Allahabad in 1765.[20] Over the next years, English commercial control took ever firmer root throughout the region, and increasingly permeated neighbouring Arakan as the nearest gateway to the Burmese market.[21]

The forces shaping Arakan's fate from the mid-1750s onwards thus consisted in large part of, on the one hand, expansive Burmese claims to rulership based on permutations of traditional Buddhist political cosmogony, and, on the other, the changing colonial dynamics of an informal British economic empire gradually taking on characteristics of formal political administration. In no sense did Arakan or its people(s) during this period come to take on the status of a recognized 'moral person' accorded identifiable agency. Only following the annexation of the territory from the Burmese to Company-controlled Bengal by 1826 would the qualities of Vattelian sovereignty come to be ascribed to the Arakanese, in retrospect, as a set of rights already lost.

9.2.2. New Rights of Possession

The Anglo-Burmese War of 1824-1826 unfolded amidst decades of cross-border movements of peoples – initially, especially of Arakanese fleeing Burmese policies of conscription and taxation in support of wars elsewhere.[22] Not only did this lead to a depletion of the local population, but also formed the basis for insurgencies and raids into Burmese-controlled Arakan from Company-ruled Bengal. By the 1810s, there was an aware-

---

[19] Leider, 2014, p. 189, see above note 6.
[20] Robins, 2012, p. 18, see above note 8.
[21] Chan, 2005, pp. 399-401, see above note 7.
[22] Leider, 2014, pp. 195-200, see above note 6.

ness among colonial officials of the desire of some Arakanese rebels to instigate conflict between the English and the Burmese.[23] Refusal to turn over rebels in English-controlled territory to Burmese authorities, and the latter's claims to 'inheriting' ancient Arakanese rights to land then in Company hands added to conflicts resulting in the first of the major nineteenth century Burmese defeats.

Arakan was first construed as a unit for the assignation of territorial sovereignty via the Treaty of Yandabo (1826), which also imposed the huge indemnity of one million pounds sterling upon the defeated Burmese. Signed between "the Honorable East India Company [...] and his majesty the King of Ava", this treaty provided in Article 13 that:

> To prevent all future disputes respecting the boundary line between the two great Nations, the British Government will retain the conquered Provinces of Arracan (sic) [...] and His Majesty the King of Ava cedes all right thereto. The [...] Arakan Mountains [...] will henceforth form the boundary between the two great Nations on that side. Any doubts regarding the said line of demarcation will be settled by Commissioners appointed by the respective governments [...] of suitable and corresponding rank.[24]

From this point on, the territorial boundaries of Arakan and its neighbouring region would be defined by European-style surveying methods. Meanwhile, just as the region's borders would now be legally fixed for the first time, the land itself would be recharacterized in Western legal terms. Along with the *imperium*, or political sovereignty over the new territory, there were conferred the legal rights of public *dominium*, or ultimate property ownership, that could also be expropriated by the sovereign by the corresponding right of *dominium eminens* (that is, eminent domain).[25] Such rights would pass between sovereigns after war via the international law doctrine of *uti possidetis*, which accorded recognition of

---

[23] *Ibid.*, p. 200.

[24] Treaty of Yandabo, 24 February 1826, Article 13.

[25] See Vattel, p. 659, see above note 11. Cf. Richard Lesaffer, "A Master Abolishing Homework? Vattel on Peacemaking and Peace Treaties", in V. Chetail and P. Haggenmacher (eds.), *Vattel's International Law from a XXIst Century Perspective*, Brill, 2011: "The necessity [...] which allowed the prince to cede a part of his State also allowed him to dispose of the private property or even the persons of his subjects. *The dominium eminens* of the sovereign granted him the right to dispose of the assets of all people subject to his sovereignty for the common good".

rights over currently-possessed territories at the agreement of peace. As Vattel put it:

> Since each of the belligerents claims to have justice on his side, and since there is no one to decide between them [...] the condition in which affairs stand at the time of the treaty must be regarded as their lawful status, and if the parties wish to make a change in it the treaty must contain an express stipulation to that effect. Consequently, all matters not mentioned in the treaty are to continue as they happen to be at the time the treaty is concluded.[26]

Three features of *uti possidetis* as it was then construed are significant. First, the 'freedom' with which rights were alienated was often fictional, instead being, as in Burma, the outcome of military conquest or coercion. Second, sovereign rights depended in no way upon opinions of those living in the territories over which title was conferred – indeed this had been quite explicit in international legal doctrine already in the time of Grotius.[27] Third, the general *dominium* over a territory also entailed the rights to determine ownership of lands in the sense of private law, such as, for example, to collect rents.

It is important to keep in mind the extent to which the Company's acquisition of territories functioned not only as a proxy for extending British imperial sovereignty, nor just the forceful prying open of new commercial markets, but also often as the 'land-grabbing' of a landlord or rentier *par excellence*.[28] The acquisition of Arakan came at a time when the Company was facing severe financial difficulties (indeed, it would for this

---

[26] Lesaffer, 2011, p. 373, see above note 25.

[27] Hugo Grotius and Richard Tuck (eds.), *The Rights of War and Peace*, I.III.VIII, Indianapolis, Liberty Fund, 2005: "Neither is that true which is supposed, that all Kings are constituted by the People. The contrary sufficiently appears from the Examples I have already alleged, of a Master of a Family that receives Strangers into his Lands, upon Condition of Subjection; and of Nations reduced under one's Dominion by the Right of War".

[28] It would be instructive to compare the Company's transformation of land tenure in colonial Arakan with the processes of enclosure used throughout the British colonial world and, indeed, earlier in the British Isles themselves beginning in the seventeenth century. See Umut Özsu, "Grabbing Land Legally: A Marxist Analysis", in *Leiden Journal of International Law*, 2019, vol. 32, no. 2, pp. 215–233 (describing how "social relations in an environment that is only just beginning to undergo integration into the capitalist mode of production are characterized by a significant measure of what Marx terms 'extra-economic' coercion – the use of direct, unconcealed violence to compel dispossession and subjugate labour-power".).

---

reason soon lose its commercial role via its restructuring by Charter Act of 1833),[29] and it made use of the newly-acquired territories in seeking to balance its books.

Some preëxisting features of the distribution of property in Arakan, as well as in colonial Burma in general, would contribute to shaping the political economy of Company rule. As Gunnar Myrdal wrote in 1968, "hardly a single big absentee landlord of the feudal type existed in precolonial Burma", and, rather than confronting the sorts of population pressures that would lead to land concentration, there had instead been endemic manpower shortages.[30] Not only did this result in a lack of large-scale agricultural operations, it also meant that "[w]hen the British occupied the territory [...] [they] described it as an area where scarcely a rich man was to be found".[31] The colonial power moved into this "land [...] tilled by peasant cultivators", and began to develop commercial agriculture at scale.

As an American missionary noted in the 1840s: "All the land in Arakan belongs to the East India Company", while "cultivators [...] retain the land which they have once leased, as long as they cultivate it, and regularly pay the stipulated rent to Government".[32] Government revenues, meanwhile, benefited from this situation of proprietorship while also gearing local agricultural production towards export as far as Europe.[33] The maintenance of these economic policies required new manpower, and this was in large part provided for by "a flood of immigration from Bengal [that] drove the natives into the more distant villages".[34] Colonial policies to encourage this immigration contributed to forming the community that is now generally referred to internationally as the 'Rohingya', and helped

---

[29] See Huw Vaughan Bowen, *The Business of Empire: The East India Company and Imperial Britain, 1756–1833*, Cambridge University Press, 2005, p. 258.

[30] Gunnar Myrdal, *Asian Drama: An Inquiry into the Poverty of Nations, Vol. II*, Pantheon, 1968, p. 1042.

[31] *Ibid.*

[32] G.S. Comstock, "Notes on Arakan: By the Late Rev. G. S. Comstock, American Baptist Missionary in That Country from 1834 to 1844", in *Journal of American Oriental Society*, 1849, vol. 1, no. 3, pp. 221–58, 231.

[33] J.S. Furnivall, *Colonial Policy and Practice: A Comparative Study of Burma and Netherlands India*, Cambridge University Press, 1948, p. 114.

[34] *Ibid.*, p. 102.

set the course for key aspects of the regional inter-ethnic conflicts that continue to this day.[35]

Even the very general overview of early colonial administrative policies provided here should suffice to establish one basic initial conclusion. The process of bringing 'Burma' into the framework of international law via colonization based on the doctrines of sovereign statehood, *uti possidetis*, and *dominium*, among others, has played a significant role in later events. It not only generated a conceptual vocabulary of state sovereignty as a plenary 'right' to be (re)acquired by a unitary, homogenous 'national' community, but also set in place new political and economic hierarchies in which certain groups, among them the Arakanese and, later, the Bamar, were relegated to an inferior status *vis-à-vis* both the colonizers and their favoured subjects.

These dynamics continued through the period of colonial rule, including after full annexation of Burma in 1885 and the elimination of the Konbaung Dynasty following the Third Anglo-Burmese War. The next section provides an overview of relevant policies during the subsequent colonial period and their consequences for the formation of a functioning unitary state. The lack of a pre-existing ontology of state identity encompassing Burmese, Buddhist Arakanese, and Muslims in Arakan that could be 'revived' in later eras was not ameliorated by colonial era policies, but rather greatly exacerbated by the systematic foreclosing of any opportunity for subjects to form co-operative inter-group relations. The importation of Western legal and economic structures furthered this process.

9.3. Epistemic Critique

9.3.1. Colonialism and Distrust

Not only Myanmar, but many post-colonial states face profound, and at times insurmountable, difficulties in crafting a unitary 'national' identity after independence. In part, this reflects the conglomeration of different peoples into a shared territory based on the principle of *uti possidetis* as it was applied in the context of mid-twentieth century decolonizations to

---

[35] Census data supports the view that the great majority of the Rohingya community can trace their background to these periods of immigration. See Jacques P. Leider's Chapter 6 above, as well as his "Competing identities and the hybridized history of the Rohingyas", in *Metamorphosis: Studies in social and political change in Myanmar*, 2015, pp. 151-78. See also Derek Tonkin's Chapter 8 above.

mean the maintaining of existing legally-recognized borders.[36] As Matthew Craven has written, the application of this model to the handing over of territorial sovereignty was in inherent tension with the supposed guiding principle of 'national self-determination'. Indeed, the latter concept largely "lost its decisive import by reason of the impossibility of self-determination meaning anything but independence within inherited borders".[37]

As the previous section indicated, the importation of this Vattelian framework of legal subjects and rights itself helped set the stage for conflict. However, it was also the case that specific, long-term policies pursued by the colonial authorities worked to make unitary identity unlikely or impossible. Indeed, the deliberate prevention of subjects' establishing any such identity outside of the colonial state is arguably inherent to the logic of colonial rule. Administration of Arakan, and Burma in general, exhibited the features of a 'divide and conquer' strategy commonly employed in colonial regimes.[38] At root, this strategy calls for the creation of conditions of impossibility for the solidarity of opposing groups, including via techniques such as limiting their mutual communications, providing them incompatible incentives, or actively punishing manifestations of such solidarity.[39]

It is important to recognize that this has very often been a *conscious* and *effective* means for the rule over large territories and populations by minority groups (such as colonizers). There is thus a contrast between mere *tertius gaudens* (literally: 'the third rejoices'), which refers to situations in which a third party passively benefits from the infighting of two groups, and intentional projects of *divide et impera*, as it was termed by the Romans.[40] The latter, as emulated by later colonizers, calls for active interventions.

From the perspective of the colonizer, groups that would jointly benefit from collaborating together to oppose the outsider must be

---

[36] Matthew Craven, *The Decolonization of International Law: State Succession and the Law of Treaties*, Oxford University Press, Oxford, 2007; cf. Shahabuddin, 2019, p. 346, see above note 7.

[37] Craven, 2007, p. 205, see above note 36.

[38] Eric A. Posner, Kathryn E. Spier, and Adrian Vermeule, "Divide and Conquer", in *Journal of Legal Analysis*, 2010, vol. 2, no. 2, pp. 417, 450–451.

[39] *Ibid.*, p. 418.

[40] *Ibid.*

stopped from doing so. This calls for altering the perceived costs and benefits of their working together. One way of doing so is by actually changing those costs and benefits: The colonial strategy of 'bribing' members of minority groups by giving them more prestige and ability to participate in the colonial system, as the British generally did in Myanmar with Indian subjects, is an example.[41]

Whether or not initially deliberate, the dynamics of migration and political-economic administration of the colonial authorities, from the very beginning of Company rule in Arakan, were ideally suited to these ends. As has already been noted, colonial economic imperatives in the newly conquered space led to a dynamic in which "the growth of population led to a minute subdivision of the land into tiny parcels".[42] That population growth was in substantial part from Chittagong (Chattogram) and other parts of Bengal.

During the subsequent period of colonial rule, many towns in Arakan and elsewhere became largely Indian in population, as did important offices of colonial administration. This process is described in detail in Chapter 6 above. Differential treatment helped to ensure that Indian and Arakanese or Bamar subjects had no basis for mutual solidarity or trust. Indeed, the basic architecture of the state, such as the law courts, also became "the prerogative of Indians […] as there were few Burmans with a general education sufficiently advanced to study western law, [and] there were still no law classes" well into the colonial period.[43]

Over the course of colonial period, additional trends or policies of political economy helped to promote these dynamics. Particularly significant was "the introduction of land sales and the opening of the countryside to moneylenders", of whom the latter were, again, often Indian colonial subjects pursuing new opportunities to the east.[44] If acquisition of Burmese territories had originated in a direct 'land-grab' by the Company, policies by the early twentieth century were such that 'land-grabbing' could become a general feature of private economic relations in Arakan

---

[41] Robert H. Taylor, "Party, Class and Power in British Burma", in *Journal of Commonwealth and Comparative Politics*, 1981, vol. 19, no. 1, pp. 44–62.

[42] Furnivall, 1948, p. 102, see above note 33.

[43] *Ibid.*, p. 136.

[44] Myrdal, 1968, p. 1042, see above note 30.

and the Irrawaddy Delta.[45] While moneylenders might have "found it more profitable [...] to avoid land ownership" and instead charge high interest rates to peasant cultivators, the unsustainable financial situation of these borrowers led to much loss of title.[46]

This existing trend was greatly exacerbated by the post-World War I era. The colonial Land and Agriculture Committee estimated that, between 1930 and 1937 alone, the amount of land in Lower Burma's important rice-growing regions held by "non-agriculturists" (that is, landlords based in cities) rose from 19 per cent to 50 per cent. Of these, roughly half were Chettiar moneylenders.[47] The displaced Arakanese and Burmese peasants lacked the means to buy back ownership stakes in such land. Notably contributing to this dispossessed status were colonial changes to the structure of financial credit: traditional rules for borrowing against land held that the borrower could always recover alienated real property upon full repayment "even after generations",[48] but "British courts came to treat such conditional sales [that is, land forfeited as collateral] as final". Interest debts could also accrue far beyond previous limits, and such customs as "labourers' [...] prior claim upon the produce" of agricultural work, that is, "security of payment" as a legal right, were annulled.[49]

Colonial era policies, or indeed the very structure of colonial rule in many of its dominant aspects, thus promoted distrust. This was true in the *collective* sense of fostering distrust between 'native' ethnic Bamar and Arakanese *vis-à-vis* immigrants from British India accorded higher status as members of the mercantile and administrative class. Yet, it was also true in the *individual* sense of newly-imposed credit relationships, and underlying legal doctrines, according members of the majority peasant population the status of financially and politically distrusted subjects, prone to dispossession of their property at once upon failure to meet colonial authorities' standards for productivity, and not invited into positions

---

[45] Chan, 2019, p. 400, see above note 7.

[46] Andrus J. Russell, *Burmese Economic Life*, Stanford University Press, 1947, p. 67; see also Furnivall, 1948, p. 118, see above note 33: "A large number of natives of India are permanently settled in the seaports and large villages, and they have driven the more apathetic Burman out of the more profitable fields of employment".

[47] *Ibid.*, pp. 69–70.

[48] Myrdal, 1968, p. 1043, see above note 30.

[49] Furnivall, 1948, pp. 134–135, see above note 33.

of state authority or influence. The imposed English common law legal frame joined with the colonial political frame, and the economic frame of new, alienating debt and commercial structures, all disempowering Arakanese and Bamar subjects. What they had left were memories of an increasingly mythical Buddhist-monarchical golden age.

9.3.2. Knowing the Independent Polity

Another common technique for preventing solidarity, applied in colonial contexts, calls for the closing down of channels of communication. In game theoretic terms, colonizers aim to ensure that neither of the two (or more) parties that might co-operate to the colonizers detriment, but to their own benefit, know that their counterparts are also prepared to pursue this 'Pareto equilibrium' (situation of optimal co-operation).[50] Shutting down of 'insurrectionist' media, preventing the formation of independence-oriented associations, and punishment of any acts of organization or advocacy to these ends are frequently adopted to break down such forms of unsanctioned communication. Such policies were indeed applied in colonial Burma.[51]

Importantly, where resistance to British rule *did* arise, it was generally organized not upon the basis of nationalism or anti-colonialism *per se*, but rather framed in religious terms. As noted above, pre-colonial political legitimacy in Arakan and among the Burmese had been construed primarily in terms of Buddhist cosmogony. That this was the primary or only vector for a communal sense of solidarity in resistance meant that the mass immigration of non-Buddhist subjects was well-suited to reduce risks to colonial rule.

Mass migration from Bengal into Rakhine, among other related measures, thus greatly helped to create circumstances in which no stable and unified opposition could articulate shared interests in resistance. Migration of Muslim settlers into Arakan was encouraged and even at times lauded by the colonial officials in racialized, social Darwinian terms. This dynamic of competition was greatly exacerbated during the conflicts of World War II, during which Muslims and Buddhists in Arakan fought, and

---

[50] Posner, Spier and Vermeule, 2010, p. 423, see above note 38.
[51] See, for example, Jordan Carlyle Winfield, "Buddhism and Insurrection in Burma, 1886–1890", in *Journal of the Royal Asiatic Society*, 2010, vol. 20, no. 3, pp. 345–367.

committed atrocities against each other's civilian populations, as proxies for British and Japanese colonial administrations.[52]

Following independence in January 1948, many Muslims in Rakhine articulated the 'Rohingya' identity and called back to an affiliation with Arakan predating the Burmese conquest of 1785. Like other ethnic minority groups in Myanmar's border regions, they sought political autonomy. This was viewed as anathema by the Bamar-dominated post-independence administration, which sought, above all, to maintain a unified, 'Burmanized' nation-state inheriting the full political and economic powers relinquished by Britain.[53] These conflicts, of course, became an 'internal' matter for the new state, as the doctrine of *uti possidetis* was applied and the notion of national self-determination was relegated to its subordinate, even decorative role.[54]

Both domestic and international legal doctrines continued to reinforce the notion of the unitary sovereign state as the transcendent prize to be captured by successful revolutions. The new state constitution of Myanmar adopted requirements of *jus sanguinis* in defining citizenship, dual nationality, and restricted immigration.[55] Meanwhile, courts applied full protections of sovereign immunity, even in cases of claims against British colonial authorities or over goods expropriated during wartime occupation.[56]

Inter-ethnic tensions and struggles over autonomy continued to reflect the colonial-era legacy of distrust. This was given regular expression during the process of forming the new state. At a meeting of the Burma Constituent Assembly in September 1947, for example, the soon-to-be first prime minister of independent Burma, U Nu, expressed the point that the:

---

[52] See Chapter 6 above by Jacques P. Leider. See also his "Conflict and Mass Violence in Arakan (Rakhine State): The 1942 Events and Political Identity Formation", in Ashley South and Marie Lall (eds.), *Citizenship in Myanmar: Ways of Being in and from Burma*, 2018.

[53] Frank H. Golay *et al.*, *Underdevelopment and Economic Nationalism in Southeast Asia*, Cornell University Press, 1969, pp. 211–212.

[54] See Craven, 2007, see above note 36.

[55] Golay, 1969, p. 215, see above note 53.

[56] *U Kyaw Din v. The British Government*, 14 July 1948, International Law Reports, 1956, p. 214; *U Zenya v. Secretary of State for War*, 2 February 1949, International Law Reports, 1956, p. 402.

---

wealth of Burma has been enjoyed firstly by the big British capitalists, next the Indian capitalists, and next the Chinese capitalists. Burmans are at the bottom, in poverty, and have to be content with the left-over and chew-over bones and scraps from the table of foreign capitalists […] The moment we have the power, we will have to do away with this unfair, one-sided economic system.[57]

From the very beginning, the new state was plagued by both inter-ethnic conflicts, insurgencies, and internal political struggle culminating in the *coup d'état* of 1962. Post-independence economic policies led first to largely unsuccessful efforts to attract foreign investment, and then to wide-ranging nationalizations of most major industries. 'Burmanization' of industries went hand-in-hand with attempts to submit them to state oversight in an uncertain (if not hostile) international economic environment.[58]

The formal transfer of sovereignty from the British Empire to the newly independent administration was not matched by a concomitant transfer of state capacity. Neither did the preceding century of colonial rule establish clear and uncontested rights of legitimate rule that could be effectively transferred to new local rulers, as presumed by the doctrine of *uti possidetis*. Rather, there has ensued another near century of ongoing 'internal' conflict in which successive regimes have sought to achieve full Vattelian *imperium* and *dominium* over a homogenous territory, while other groups, the Rohingya included, have pursued their own claims to a valid, independent political status. That there is no shared frame in which such claims can be reconciled is a lack directly attributable to Myanmar's colonial history, and indeed could be considered a form of epistemic violence.[59] The only way for any of the country's groups to know itself as possessing the international legal rights of a 'moral person' was to exercise the full powers of the former colonizer.

As the following section will discuss, when international criminal law and doctrines of state responsibility are brought to bear on Myanmar today, formal legal statehood creates the relevant architecture of liability and jurisdiction. However, aspects of this jurisdictional paradigm clash

---

[57] U Nu, *Towards Peace and Democracy*, Ministry of Information, Rangoon, 1949, pp. 2-4.

[58] Golay, 1969, pp. 234-240, see above note 53.

[59] See Kenneth MacDonald, "Epistemic Violence: The Body, Globalization, and the Dilemma of Rights", in *Transnational Law and Contemporary Problems*, 2002, vol. 12, no. 1, p. 65.

intensely with substantive legal or political issues as perceived by many actors in post-colonial contexts; in particular, the positing of state identity as something 'already achieved'. By contrast, members of post-colonial polities may view themselves as still striving to (re)construct a state identity not yet established. The claim that these considerations should influence current international law responses to conflict in Myanmar (and elsewhere) will now be evaluated.

9.4. Genealogical Critique

9.4.1. Addressing Jurisdictional Hegemony

That international tribunals, particularly international criminal tribunals, might operate in a hegemonic fashion is a longstanding claim in some corners of international law scholarship.[60] In general, one can identify the critiques that, *inter alia*, exercises of international jurisdiction often replicate colonial power relationships, with former colonies in practice bearing the vast majority of liability;[61] that human rights concerns "are potentially so broad that they can be used to justify interference on any range of issues";[62] and that the very paradigm of criminal law-style "enforcement" and "compliance" serves to "displace discussions about the justice or even

---

[60] See, for example, Koskenniemi, 2011, see above note 2; Mégret, 2012, see above note 2; see also, for example, Joel Colón-Ríos, "Constituent Power, the Rights of Nature, and Universal Jurisdiction", in *McGill Law Journal/Revue de droit de McGill*, 2014, vol. 60, no. 1, pp. 127–172. These concerns have been shared by states. See, for example, the UN General Assembly, Sixth Committee, Summary record of the 12th meeting on 12 October 2011, UN Doc A/C.6/66/SR.12, 16 November 2011 (https://www.legal-tools.org/doc/b1zbul/) at which the representative from Argentina described universal jurisdiction as potentially "be[ing] perceived as a tool for interference in the internal affairs of other States or as a hegemonic jurisdiction exercised by developed countries against nationals of developing countries". At this same meeting, concerns over the implications of universal jurisdiction upon state sovereignty or the principle of non-interference were also expressed by delegates of Iran, Sudan, Swaziland, Zambia, Venezuela, Malaysia and Senegal.

[61] See, for example, Suzan M. Pritchett, "Entrenched Hegemony, Efficient Procedure, or Selected Justice: An Inquiry into Charges for Gender-Based Violence at the International Criminal Court", in *Transnational Law and Contemporary Problems*, 2008, vol. 17, p. 265; Christopher R. Rossi, "Hauntings, Hegemony, and the Threatened African Exodus from the International Criminal Court", in *Human Rights Quarterly*, 2018, vol. 40, no. 2, pp. 369-405.

[62] Mégret, 2012, p. 23, see above note 2.

---

the conceivability of interference",[63] by which former colonies have sought ontological security.

Criticisms of phenomena such as the ICC's overwhelming focus on African cases and defendants by the time of writing, or on its reluctance to open investigations into alleged crimes by powerful developed states (only very recently somewhat mitigated)[64] have been paired with more general claims that the institution, or international criminal law as a whole, represents the twenty-first century continuation of the 'civilizing mission' of former colonial empires.[65] Even more than in the standard imaginary of international human rights law, international criminal processes can naturally take on the characteristics of a drama in which the main roles are those of savage, victim, or saviour,[66] with the Hague-based institution in the third role, the former colony in the first.

It is certainly the case that former colonies themselves did not initiate the 'project' of international human rights law. Rather, they for the most part engaged in international fora and processes aimed at reinforcing the hard-won status of sovereigns entitled to rights against foreign interference. Independent Burma was not only typical in this respect, but a leader. Mid-twentieth century attempts to foster solidarity between formerly-colonized peoples, including the Bandung Conference of 1955 in which Burma played a significant role, explicitly centred upon mutual respect for Vattel-style state sovereignty.[67]

This was also the case with respect to the new human rights treaties that emerged following the World War II. The Universal Declaration of Human Rights ('UDHR') and the Genocide Convention,[68] both of 1948, were adopted at a time when the Netherlands was at war to hold on to its

---

[63] *Ibid.*

[64] ICC, *Situation in the Islamic Republic of Afghanistan*, Appeals Chamber, Judgment on the appeal against the decision on the authorisation of an investigation into the situation in the Islamic Republic of Afghanistan, 5 March, 2020, ICC-02/17OA4 (https://www.legal-tools.org/doc/x7kl12/).

[65] Claire Nielsen, "From Nuremberg to The Hague: The Civilizing Mission of International Criminal Law", in *Auckland University Law Review*, 2008, vol. 14, p. 81.

[66] Makau Mutua, "Savages, Victims, and Saviors: The Metaphor of Human Rights", in *Harvard International Law* Journal, 2001, vol. 42, no. 1, p. 201.

[67] See Final Communiqué of the Asian-African Conference of Bandung, 24 April 1955.

[68] Convention on the Prevention and Punishment of the Crime of Genocide, adopted 9 December 1948, entered into force 12 January 1951 ('Genocide Convention') (https://www.legal-tools.org/doc/498c38/).

colonial control of Indonesia; France was doing the same in Vietnam; and the British Empire was similarly engaged in a struggle to keep hold of many of its colonies. 'National self-determination' was not incorporated into either of these sources of international law in a robust sense. Indeed, a more robust role for self-determination would have obstructed both colonizers seeking to hold their possessions and newly-independent regimes seeking to assert full control of the territories they had inherited via *uti possidetis*.[69]

There was thus from the beginning of the post-war system no agreed-upon norm of self-determination reaching beyond the veil of statehood to confer a particular *form* of autonomy to sub-state groups. This was left up to internal settlement by newly liberated peoples, some of them in situations of deep mutual distrust and enmity, lacking any shared ontological or epistemic basis for a unified state identity. That this was the case in Rakhine, in particular, has been suggested by the first two sections of this chapter.

Meanwhile, the governments of these fragile new polities were also concerned over possible new forms of intervention. For example, when Burma signed the Genocide Convention in 1949, it included reservations as to Article VIII, which provides that parties "may call upon the competent organs of the United Nations to take such action under the Charter of the United Nations as they consider appropriate for the prevention and suppression of acts of genocide", though it was the only state to do so.[70]

In the context of 1949, it was relatively clear what "actions" Article VIII could refer to: either direct military intervention by the UN ('United Nations') Security Council (as was soon to occur in a different context on the Korean Peninsula) or, alternatively, international criminal tribunals of the sort that had recently concluded their work at Nuremberg and Tokyo. The fact that newly-independent Burma did *not* issue a reservation over Article IX (as several others did), which provides for inter-state disputes settled at the ICJ, suggests that it viewed Article VIII as entailing more intrusive measures.

Today, as Myanmar faces potential liabilities both via potential prosecution of state officials at the ICC *and* via inter-state proceedings at the ICJ under the Genocide Convention, questions of hegemony are clear-

---

[69] See Craven, 2007, p. 183, see above note 36.
[70] Genocide Convention, see above note 68.

ly implicated. They play out quite differently in respect to the two cases, however. The following sections will examine in turn issues involved in the former and the latter proceedings and conclude with suggestions as to how their hegemonic dimensions might be mitigated or equalized.

9.4.2. Tactical Legal Fictions

International criminal law jurisprudence has long featured the use of 'creative' workarounds to overcome jurisdictional objections based on the Vattelian model of coequal state sovereignty.[71] This was already the case with regards to the first successful international criminal tribunals at Nuremberg and Tokyo, at which claims regarding the universal moral prohibition of aggressive war were the main basis for retroactive application of this new crime, though the 1928 Kellogg-Briand Pact also played a subordinate role.[72] Yet, already in the aftermath of World War I, more than two decades earlier, there had already been tentative efforts to prosecute officials of the defeated Central Powers, albeit largely unsuccessful ones.[73]

Though Kaiser Wilhelm was never prosecuted and lived out his days in exile, this precedent has recently been cited at the ICC as marking the beginning of the project of international criminal liability for heads of state. Specifically, it was discussed in detail in the context of the 2019 Appellate Chamber ruling on the duties of Jordan, and other Rome Statute Parties, to arrest the indicted former Sudanese President Omar al Bashir.[74] In a concurring opinion signed by four of the five judges of the majority opinion, the attempted prosecutions after World War I were cited to justify the notion that international custom had long since dispensed with head of

---

[71] William Schabas, "Customary Law or Judge-Made Law: Judicial Creativity at the UN Criminal Tribunals", in *The Legal Regime of the International Criminal Court*, Brill Nijhoff, 2009, pp. 75-101; Shane Darcy and Joseph Powderly (eds.), *Judicial Creativity at the International Criminal Tribunals*, Oxford University Press, 2010.

[72] Micaela Frulli, "The Contribution of International Criminal Tribunals to the Development of International Law: The Prominence of *Opinio Juris* and the Moralization of Customary Law", in *The Law and Practice of International Courts and Tribunals*, 2015, vol. 14, no. 1, pp. 80–93.

[73] See, for example, overview in William A. Schabas, *The Trial of the Kaiser*, Oxford University Press, 2018.

[74] ICC, *The Prosecutor v. Omar Hassan Ahmad Al Bashir*, Judgment in the Jordan Referral re Al-Bashir Appeal, Appeals Chamber, 6 May 2019, ICC-02/05-01/09-397 (https://www.legal-tools.org/doc/0c5307/).

state immunity *vis-à-vis* international tribunals.[75] Although this example did not play as conspicuous a role in the judgment, the two were highly compatible. In both cases, the notion of a 'vertical' obligation to the ICC that supersedes 'horizontal' obligations between states was the dominant principle at work.

Most states in the world today (certainly in formerly-colonized Africa, the Middle East, and Southeast Asia) continue to insist upon sovereign and head of state immunity in their dealings with each other, albeit with gradually increasing (mostly non-criminal) exceptions, for example, for commercial conduct.[76] The custom of these arguably specially-affected states was not, however, considered in relation to the Appellate Chamber's finding that customary head of state immunity does not exist with respect to international tribunals.[77] The tactical legal fiction was deployed that the 'relevant' form of custom was that *vis-à-vis* international courts (only in existence since 1920), and that this displaced ancient custom on general head of state immunity. By asserting a newfound Hohenzollern genealogy, the ICC 'discovered' its jurisdiction.

Such legal fictions are not infrequently used to overcome obstacles to jurisdiction based on state sovereignty. This was fully on display on 14 November 2019, when Pre-Trial Chamber ('PTC') III of the ICC authorized the Prosecutor to launch an investigation into the "Situation in the People's Republic of Bangladesh/Republic of the Union of Myanmar".[78] Echoing an earlier response to the Prosecutor, the PTC found that this in-

---

75 ICC, *The Prosecutor v. Omar Hassan Ahmad Al Bashir*, Appeals Chamber, Joint Concurring Opinion of Judges Eboe-Osuji, Morrison, Hofmański and Bossa, 6 May 2019, ICC-02/05-01/09-397-Anx2 (https://www.legal-tools.org/doc/5dfc08/).

76 Pierre-Hugues Verdier and Erik Voeten, "How Does Customary International Law Change? The Case of State Immunity", in *International Studies Quarterly*, 2015, vol. 59, no. 2, pp. 209–222.

77 On "specially-affected" status and the head of state immunity issue, see Kevin Jon Heller, "Specially-Affected States and the Formation of Custom", in *American Journal of International Law*, 2018, vol. 112, no. 2, pp. 191–243.

78 ICC, Pre-Trial Chamber, Decision Pursuant to Article 15 of the Rome Statute on the Authorisation of an Investigation into the Situation in the People's Republic of Bangladesh/Republic of the Union of Myanmar, 14 November 2019, ICC-01/19-27 (https://www.legal-tools.org/doc/kbo3hy/).

vestigation is warranted, despite Myanmar not being a party to the ICC's Rome Statute.[79]

The ruling on jurisdiction consisted primarily of an interpretation of Article 12(2)(a) of the Rome Statute, which requires that "at least one legal element of a crime within the jurisdiction of the Court or part of such a crime is committed on the territory of a State Party".[80] The specific crime in question, deportation, is defined in Article 7(2)(d) of the Rome Statute in general terms that consist of a forced expulsion of a targeted civilian population from "the area in which they were lawfully present without grounds permitted under international law".[81]

Thus, per this theory of jurisdiction, the ICC could pursue prosecutions of Myanmar officials, regardless of the state's consent, if an element of the crime of deportation was committed "on the territory" of ICC State Party Bangladesh. The novelty and creativity of this argument was widely noted.[82] Here, as in the *Al Bashir* matter, was the deployment of a tactical legal fiction to overcome a barrier to jurisdiction.

The exertion of this novel theory of jurisdiction, however, ran counter to the traditional general principle of international law *pacta tertiis nec nocent nec prosunt*, often referred to by shorthand as *pacta tertiis*. This rule holds that "agreements create neither obligations nor rights for third party states".[83] As a third-party state to the Rome Statute, this would presumably apply to Myanmar. The ICC's PTC did briefly examine this

---

[79] ICC, Pre-Trial Chamber, Decision on the Prosecution's Request for a Ruling on Jurisdiction under Article 19(3) of the Statute, 6 September 2018, ICC-RoC46(3)-01/18-37 ('Decision on the Prosecution's Request for a Ruling on Jurisdiction') (https://www.legal-tools.org/doc/73aeb4/).

[80] *Ibid.*, p. 36.

[81] Rome Statute of the ICC, 17 July 1998, Art. 7(2)(d) (http://www.legal-tools.org/doc/7b9af9/).

[82] See, for example, Mark Kersten, "Justice for the Rohingya? An Amicus Brief and the Road(s) to Accountability", *Justice in Conflict*, 26 June 2018 (available on its web site): "the option currently seems to be rather clear: have the ICC investigate deportation or do nothing at all […] it is this creative and novel use of the Rome Statute that acts as a reminder of the promise of the ICC – laying the groundwork for justice when no one else is willing to do so".

[83] See, for example, Robert Y. Jennings, "The Progressive Development of International Law and its Codification", in *British Year Book of International Law*, 1947, vol. 24, p. 301; United Nations, Vienna Convention on the Law of Treaties, 23 May 1969, Article 34 (https://www.legal-tools.org/doc/6bfcd4/) ('Vienna Convention'): "A treaty does not create either obligations or rights for a third State without its consent".

problem in its judgment of 6 September 2018. Yet it quickly disposed of this objection, first by pointing to Article 34 of the Vienna Convention on the Law of Treaties, which provides for the ability of customary international law to supersede the presumption against a lack of validity for a rule *vis-à-vis* third-party states.[84] Moreover, as the PTC noted, *jus cogens* norms of international law can also be the basis for such exceptions. The exact relation of the *jus cogens* doctrine to the case was, however, left unspecified.[85]

As with head of state immunity, these claims that preëxisting jurisdictional protections for sovereign states have been superseded by new customary norms worked to exert jurisdiction over former colonies, not their colonizers. It is true that with the UDHR Article 13 norm on the freedom of movement and the subsequent 1951 Convention Relating to the Status of Refugees, forced deportation became clearly identified as a wrongful act in positive international law texts. However, at no point then or since was a clear jurisdictional norm developed via identifiable state practice that criminal prosecutions as to this wrong should ignore the principle of state consent.[86]

The history of forced populations transfers by Western states themselves, of course, is centuries long. The annexation of Burma as an administrative subdivision of India and its subsequent experience of colonial rule, as detailed in the opening sections of this chapter, reflect this history. Indeed, when ancestors of many of today's Rohingya were moved into Arakan by colonial authorities, pursuing political and economic interests and "[driving] the natives into the more distant villages",[87] this might well have violated some of the same norms or values against forced migration at issue in Rakhine today.

---

[84] Vienna Convention, Article 38, see above note 83 ("Nothing in articles 34 to 37 precludes a rule set forth in a treaty from becoming binding upon a third State as a customary rule of international law, recognized as such".), cited in Decision on the Prosecution's Request for a Ruling on Jurisdiction, p. 18, see above note 79.

[85] Decision on the Prosecution's Request for a Ruling on Jurisdiction, see above note 79.

[86] It can also be noted that forced population transfers survived well into the inter-war period as a key facet of League of Nations governance involved in both 'minority protection' and Mandate activities. They were also a major facet of post-World War II efforts to redraw the map of Europe. Matthew Frank, "Reconstructing the Nation-State: Population Transfer in Central and Eastern Europe, 1944–8", in *The Disentanglement of Populations*, Palgrave Macmillan, London, 2011, pp. 27-47.

[87] Furnivall, 1948, p. 102, see above note 33.

Should this be recognized as part of the same chain of activity that has caused Myanmar state officials to face potential criminal liability? What, if any, responses could be taken to do justice to this still quite living history? Given that the ICC exercises only criminal jurisdiction, and prosecutes only individuals charged with intentional violations of legal norms, there are likely insurmountable barriers to any liability for nineteenth and early-twentieth century colonial era wrongs to be adjudicated in this forum. The ICJ, however, may be a more promising venue for bringing some form of justice to bear on colonial wrongs.

9.4.3. Redistributing Liabilities

As has been noted above, newly-independent Burma signed onto the Genocide Convention with a reservation as to Article VIII, which arguably applied to non-consent-based international criminal law proceedings or to humanitarian interventions, but had no reservation as to Article IX. The latter provides as follows:

> Disputes between the Contracting Parties relating to the interpretation, application or fulfilment of the present Convention, including those relating to the responsibility of a State for genocide [...] shall be submitted to the International Court of Justice at the request of any of the parties to the dispute.[88]

It is upon this basis that The Republic of the Gambia filed a complaint to the International Court of Justice on 11 November 2019.[89] The Application Instituting Proceedings ('Application') argued that Myanmar was in violation of its obligations under the Genocide Convention with relation to state policies targeting the Rohingya community in Rakhine.

As is clear from this jurisdiction-conferring article, the Application concerns a state-to-state dispute. This quality of the proceedings is further reinforced by Article 36(1) of the ICJ Statute, which empowers the Court to hear "all cases which the parties refer to it and all matters specially

---

[88] Genocide Convention, Article IX, see above note 68.
[89] ICJ, *The Gambia v. Myanmar*, Application Instituting Proceedings and Request for Provisional Measures, 11 November 2019, 178-20191111-APP-01-00-EN ('Application') (https://www.legal-tools.org/doc/69p376/).

provided for [...] in treaties and conventions in force";[90] such "treaties and conventions" are, of course, those among states.

The assumption that Myanmar is a Vattelian state entity exercising full *imperium* and *dominium* within its territories – rather than a weak and still-forming polity, in which formally-governing civilian state actors have only limited control over military activities – forms the basis for the ICJ proceedings. It is also at work in the ICJ ruling on preliminary measures of late January 2020. There, the Court stated that the "context invoked by Myanmar does not stand in the way of the Court's assessment of the existence of a real and imminent risk of irreparable prejudice to the rights [of Rohingya] protected under the Convention".[91] On the basis of this risk, it ordered Myanmar to "take all measures within its power" to prevent new acts of violence against the Rohingya.[92]

This order is likely justified, given the generally-established incidents of violence committed by Myanmar military personnel against Rohingya civilians in Rakhine, some of which have already been acknowledged by the country's own Independent Commission of Enquiry,[93] and given that the judges could not be seen to be passive during the proceedings in the face of the serious allegations made by The Gambia. As to the ultimate merits of the case, these will likely turn on whether the ICJ finds it can assign a 'genocidal intent' to the State.[94] This is a less certain matter, and it is one that involves construing the nuances of official acts and policies, many of which may have only a formal imprimatur of approval from the civilian government but, in substance, be the result of decisions by military actors.[95]

---

[90] Statute of the ICJ, 26 June 1945, Article 36(1) ('ICJ Statute') (https://www.legal-tools.org/doc/fdd2d2/).

[91] ICJ, *The Gambia v. Myanmar*, Application of the Convention on the Prevention and Punishment of the Crime of Genocide, Order, 23 January 2020 (https://www.legal-tools.org/doc/in5d55/).

[92] *Ibid.*, p. 3.

[93] "Executive Summary of the Independent Commission of Enquiry's Final Report", 21 January 2020 (https://www.legal-tools.org/doc/h3k7jz/).

[94] See Application, p. 13, see above note 89.

[95] For an argument to this effect, see Pon Souvannaseng, "Rohingya genocide case: why it will be hard for Myanmar to comply with ICJ's orders", *The Conversation*, 1 February 2020 (available on its web site).

In documents like The Gambia's Application, facts such as the refusal of Myanmar civilian officials to accept the use of the 'Rohingya' designation for Muslims in northern Rakhine are used as evidence to link particular alleged atrocities to a collective state intent to violate "the rights of the Rohingya group to exist as a group".[96] This conflict over naming, however, does not necessarily indicate a threat against "the very existence of [a] certain human group [...]".[97] Groups sharing borders, let alone those within the same polity, inevitably not merely 'coexist' but also define themselves in relative terms. A certain form of identity-claim can create profound anxieties in another group due to the manner in which it is expressed. One might point to relatively mundane scenarios such as the naming conflict between Greece and what is now 'North' Macedonia. There, a specific *way* of defining the latter's existence produced a sense of existential anxiety in its southern neighbour.[98] Similarly, the term 'Rohingya' invokes an understanding of Arakan that is in tension with narratives rooted in Konbaung-era politics. For civilian leaders to insist upon naming issues certainly reflects disputes over political ontology, but may not be "incitement to commit genocide".

Certainly, the conflict in Rakhine has been a much more violent scenario than the conflicts over Macedonian identity. Yet it is possible that attribution of genocidal intent to "the state of Myanmar", and specifically to its civilian officials, might indeed mischaracterize what is "a protracted problem of ill-treatment of ethnic minorities in Myanmar rather than of genocide".[99] Ultimately, of course, this will be a matter for the parties to argue and the Court to determine. In doing so, it might aid in securing an accurate outcome, and one viewed as legitimate by all parties (to the extent possible), if the Court would acknowledge and, perhaps, directly respond to the underlying historical context of colonial wrongs in Rakhine, which several chapters in this anthology invite.

---

[96] *Ibid.*, p. 43.

[97] Reservations to the Convention on the Prevention and Punishment of the Crime of Genocide, Advisory Opinion of 28 May 1951, I.C.J. Reports 1951, p. 23 (https://www.legal-tools.org/doc/52868f/).

[98] Thimios Tzallas, "Macedonia name dispute: Problem solved?", *LSE European Politics and Policy (EUROPP) Blog*, 20 June 2018.

[99] ICJ, *The Gambia v. Myanmar*, Application of the Convention on the Prevention and Punishment of the Crime of Genocide, Separate Opinion of Judge Xue Hanqin, 23 January 2020 (https://www.legal-tools.org/doc/4l6if9/).

Simply to 'keep in mind' the context of colonial history when adjudicating this dispute, and to clearly refer in the Court's statements of the facts of the case to various colonial wrongs that contributed to recent conflicts, would doubtless be a good way to begin. However, by itself this would not result in acts of the former colonial state bearing any material form of liability. The appearance of a hegemonic imbalance of liabilities would remain for those local actors sensitive to this context.

Instead, one way for such liability actually to be imposed might be via joinder of a claim by Myanmar against the United Kingdom for policies during or after the colonial era that may have constituted violations of customary international law. Given the many direct causal factors linking colonial policies with later conflicts, this might aid the Court in finding an adequate resolution of the dispute. There are several possible jurisdictional theories by which such a claim might be joined to the proceedings, but they vary with respect to their basis in precedent or likely treatment by the Court.

First, the United Kingdom itself could intervene as a third party to the litigation, having an interest in addressing its own historical liability for exacerbating inter-ethnic conflict and (potentially) facilitating genocide. This would be quite improbable, however.[100] Readers are referred to Derek Tonkin's Chapter 8 above for the perspectives of a former British Ambassador. It is also unlikely that Myanmar could directly involve the United Kingdom in the present case via a 'cross-claim'. Article 80(1) of the ICJ Rules of Court allows *counter*-claims that are "directly connected with the subject-matter of the application and must come within the jurisdiction of the Court".[101] Such claims have so far been restricted to those by the respondent against the applicant state.[102]

---

[100] ICJ Statute, Article 63(1), see above note 90 provides: "Should a state consider that it has an interest of a legal nature which may be affected by the decision in the case, it may submit a request to the Court to be permitted to intervene". Surely addressing one's own legal responsibility for historical wrongs would constitute an "interest of a legal nature".

[101] ICJ, Rules of Court, 24 March 1922, Article 80(1) (https://www.legal-tools.org/doc/e12a04/).

[102] The counter-claims involved in *Bosnia and Herzegovina v. Serbia and Montenegro*, however, did implicate conduct or rights of third states (that is, Croatia). ICJ, *Bosnia and Herzegovina v. Yugoslavia*, Application of the Convention on the Prevention and Punishment of the Crime of Genocide, 17 December, 1997 (https://www.legal-tools.org/doc/8769f0/).

In principle, however, one might doubt whether the United Kingdom is indeed properly considered a "third party" to the dispute. This is, however, again a question of political ontology that is tightly bound together with colonial history. The Gambia was occupied by the British Empire from 1758, and from 1825-1948 both it and Arakan were British colonial possessions. Litigation over any policies enacted during that period could be viewed as having occurred within a single polity. Even after the United Kingdom acceded to the Genocide Convention on 30 January 1970, the British monarch Elizabeth II was still "Queen of the Gambia", and head of state of the latter. A Governor-General served as her constitutional delegate until 24 April of the same year, when The Gambia abolished the monarchy to become a "republic within the Commonwealth".[103] A claim against the United Kingdom for conduct during those three months of 1970, for example, its failure to offer any action to mitigate its previous policies exacerbating inter-ethnic conflicts or to provide economic assistance to reduce the risk of future genocides, could involve the obligations of all three parties.

It may be doubtful, however, that the Court would be willing to read Article 80(1) against the grain in order to allow a *cross*-claim against the United Kingdom (such jurisdictional gymnastics tend to flow in the direction of imposing liability Southward, not Northward). A more likely jurisdictional approach would be for Myanmar to file a separate claim against the United Kingdom for acts of genocide or conspiracy, incitement, attempt, or complicity during the colonial period itself. Myanmar could then request the joinder of this related claim to the present litigation with The Gambia.[104]

Though the Genocide Convention had not yet been drafted or put into effect during the British colonial rule of Arakan and Burma, there could surely be a strong argument that this Convention only codified existing customary norms prohibiting "[d]eliberately inflicting on the group conditions of life calculated to bring about its physical destruction in whole or in part", with "intent to destroy" that group, again, "in whole or

---

[103] "African Affairs at Westminster", in *African Affairs*, 1965, vol. 64, no. 255, pp. 107–115.

[104] Joinder of cases brought by different parties over closely-related subject matter has previously been used by the ICJ in the *South West Africa cases* (Liberia and Ethiopia v. South Africa) and the *North Sea Continental Shelf cases* (Federal Republic of Germany/Denmark; Federal Republic of Germany/Netherlands).

in part".[105] If this customary norm did already exist before 1948, then should Myanmar and the United Kingdom's respective ratifications of Article IX of the Convention perhaps simply be understood as mutual acceptance of ICJ jurisdiction over claims as to the existing wrong of genocide, *whenever* they occurred?

Jurisdictional flexibility is on constant display with respect to former colonies in international law, especially wherever international crimes are at issue. Whether or not states have signed particular instruments can matter little, and many *spatial* barriers to jurisdiction can be overcome by deploying creative readings of customary international law or of various tribunals' jurisdictional rules. Yet *temporal* barriers to claims against former colonial empires tend to be treated as sacrosanct.[106] Is this incongruity justified?

A joined claim against the United Kingdom for colonial-era policies would not impede any findings of the Court regarding current obligations of Myanmar or necessary measures for the latter to take *vis-à-vis* the Rohingya. However, it could perhaps lead to the former colonial power bearing some obligations to either support or even fully bear the costs of, for example, reparations of injuries stemming in large part from colonial policies. Appropriate measures could properly be informed by the 2001 Draft Articles on Responsibility of States for Internationally Wrongful Acts of the International Law Commission, which provide for, for example, resti-

---

[105] Genocide Convention, Article II, see above note 68; for an argument that the customary international law norm against genocide predates the Convention, see John Quigley, in *The Genocide Convention: An International Law Analysis*, Routledge, 2016, vol. 63. For further discussion of genocide's pre-1948 history, see, for example, Jens Meierhenrich, *Genocide: A Reader*, Oxford University Press, 2014; Jeremy Sarkin, *Colonial Genocide and Reparations Claims in the 21st Century: The Socio-Legal Context of Claims under International Law by the Herero against Germany for Genocide in Namibia, 1904-1908*, ABC-CLIO, 2008; Alexander Laban Hinton, Andrew Woolford and Jeff Benvenuto (eds.), *Colonial Genocide in Indigenous North America*, Duke University Press, 2014.

[106] Allan D. Cooper, "Reparations for the Herero Genocide: Defining the Limits of International Litigation", in *African Affairs*, vol. 106, no. 422; Regina Menachery Paulose and Ronald Gordon Rogo, "Addressing Colonial Crimes Through Reparations: The Mau Mau, Herero and Nama", in *State Crime Journal*, 2018, vol. 7, no. 2, pp. 369–388. On retroactivity, see Sarkin, 2018, pp. 110–113, see above note 105: "In 1946, genocide was already accepted as a crime [...] The 1948 Convention did not 'create' the crime, but merely codified and clarified this type of criminal conduct [...] it could be argued that [...] the Convention has a valid retrospective effect [...] it can [thus] be applied to events predating its coming into force".

tution (Article 35), compensation (Article 36), and satisfaction (Article 37).

The symbolic costs imposed by Article 37 in terms of measures such as formal apologies and acknowledgments of breach can be as significant as the economic costs of the former two articles.[107] Indeed, measures of this sort can be paired with recommended steps such as truth commissions, commissions of inquiry, or other transitional justice mechanisms. Especially as compared with ICC prosecutions, such measures might better fulfil aims of reducing enmity and "reconstruct[ing] moral and social systems devastated by violence".[108] Any measures ordered on the basis of British liability might also go far towards changing the perspectives of at least some in Myanmar sceptical of the Court's legitimacy or the fairness of its procedure. It would help reconcile the post-colonial condition with the project of accountability, making the latter seem more like a common project.

9.5. Conclusion

This chapter has reviewed three general critiques of the application of the international criminal law paradigm to inter-ethnic conflict in Myanmar's Rakhine State. It has noted that the process of imposing the legal ontology of the nation-state on colonized peoples has created situations of uncertainty and conflict over how, and by whom, sovereign status can be claimed. Rather than merely proving an awkward fit with different political traditions, the transmission of international legal personality to polities inheriting colonial borders via *uti possidetis* has led to intractable conflicts over state identity. The multivalent readings of Arakan's history now serve as the basis for incompatible claims to the rights and privileges of Vattelian statehood.

Second, this chapter presented an analysis of the ways in which specific colonial policies served to create or exacerbate relationships of distrust, especially by disempowering and marginalizing the majority community of Buddhist "peasant cultivators" in Arakan. The transfer of population from Bengal and the transformation of economic and social life in the region, including especially the imposed precarity of agricultur-

---

[107] International Law Commission, Draft Articles on Responsibility of States for Internationally Wrongful Acts, 2001 (https://www.legal-tools.org/doc/10e324/).

[108] Martha Minow, *Between Vengeance and Forgiveness: Facing History after Genocide and Mass Violence*, Beacon Press, 1998, p. 88.

al labour and the adoption of preferential policies towards non-local colonial subjects, created profound barriers to the later development of any unitary political community. Mutual recognition and co-operation, which require epistemic resources establishing the trustworthy or good faith motivations of one's interlocutors, were systematically impeded by colonial era administration.

Third, the chapter related these factors to the genealogy of international criminal law norms and institutions, noting in particular the unidirectional, arguably 'hegemonic' character of interpretation often used to ensure liability before tribunals for formerly-colonized states. It noted examples of this flexibility with regards to the ICC investigation of the situation in Rakhine and the potential scope of prosecutions, which could end up putting excessive liabilities on civilian officials. It then argued that, in the ICJ proceedings brought by The Gambia under the Genocide Convention, there may be an opening for jurisdictional flexibility in the opposite direction, to allow claims over colonial-era wrongs that shaped ongoing conflicts.

10

The Transfer of Civilians as a
Collective Harm (and Wrong)

Shannon Fyfe[*]

10.1. Introduction

The great promise of international institutions was that they would bring all peoples under the rule of law, where rights would be protected regardless of where one came from. Yet colonialism and its lingering effects continue to present a challenge for international institutions aimed at achieving this ideal. The International Criminal Court ('ICC'), for instance, has been criticized on two fronts for its failures to acknowledge or address the impacts of colonialism on the Global South.

First, critics have argued that there is a *distributive justice* problem in international criminal law, since the ICC has no jurisdiction over the bad acts of colonial powers in the nineteenth and early-twentieth centuries. While there is no accountability for these bad actors, accountability is sought for current bad actors within communities which suffered at the hands of colonial powers. That one is rightly held legally accountable for one's actions, while another is not, does not change the fact that one has been rightly held legally accountable for one's actions. But the imbalance in the distribution of accountability is a problem for both the actual and perceived legitimacy of the ICC.

Second, critics have argued that there is also a *substantive justice* problem in international criminal law, as the legal framework seeking accountability for current bad actors cannot adequately consider the lingering impacts of past colonial wrongs. As many Third World Approaches to International Law ('TWAIL') scholars have noted, it might be the case that the international community's insistence on ensuring that individual

---

[*] **Shannon Fyfe** is an Assistant Professor of philosophy at George Mason University, where she is also a fellow at the Institute for Philosophy and Public Policy, and an Adjunct Professor at the Antonin Scalia Law School.

leaders are subject to international criminal justice is unfair, given that "the causes of violence are rooted in histories of colonial subject formation, contested governance and resource ownership".[1]

International crimes related to the movement of people, including deportation and transfer of civilians into occupied territory, offer a clear example of how the two distinct phases of bad acts challenge our goals of achieving substantive and distributive justice. In this chapter, I analyse the collective harm which the prohibitions against transferring civilians seek to avoid, as well as the corresponding wrongdoing. Throughout, I use the illustrative case of the transfer of civilians into and out of Myanmar to motivate and develop my account, though it is of wider applicability.

In distinguishing the harm from the wrongdoing, I proceed in two steps. First, I analyse the specific sort of collective harms caused by deportation and the transfer of civilians into occupied territory, using an objective list account of well-being and harm. An objective list of well-being interests should contain those things without which it will be impossible for a group, and its individual members, to fulfil "more ultimate aspiration",[2] including continuing to exist as a community and maintaining its demographic composition. One notable aspect of this first step is to explain these harms without propping up racist or xenophobic claims that a community is entitled to be homogenous, and thus permitted to exclude 'outsiders' on the basis of their race or country of origin. I then consider the wrongfulness of the acts separately, in order to assess responsibility in light of the harm caused by the discrete acts, but while also taking into account larger questions of responsibility and oppression.

Disaggregating questions of harm and wrongdoing, I argue, is a critical step in understanding how we should go about preventing, interrupting, and holding individuals responsible for crimes related to the transfer of civilians, in part because the articulation of the harms does not rely on the ability of an international criminal justice institution to identify an individual who is responsible for the harm. While international law should endeavour to develop in ways that reduce both the distributive and substantive justice problems, it cannot and should not attempt to erase the impact of the subjugating and oppressive effects of colonial international

---

[1] Kamari Clarke, "Rethinking Africa through Its Exclusions: The Politics of Naming Criminal Responsibility", in *Anthropological Quarterly*, 2010, vol. 83, no. 3, pp. 625–651, 628.

[2] Joel Feinberg, *Harm to Others*, Oxford University Press, 1984, p. 37.

law, as well as colonial actors. Accordingly, we ought to identify and articulate harms, past and present, before we identify (and hold accountable, either through the law or through public acknowledgment) the individuals, collectives, and historical forces responsible for the harms.

10.2. The Transfer of Civilians: A Justice Problem

In this section, I consider two distinct ways that the transfer of civilians has been viewed: transfer of civilians during colonial power, and transfer of civilians by post-colonial societies.

10.2.1. Transfer of Civilians Under Colonialism

It was considered one of the most important tasks of colonial powers in the nineteenth century to stay in control of the demographics of their colonies.[3] This required censuses to be held on a regular basis within their colonies, and to enact policies in light of their findings. Colonial administrators enacted "special laws and policies relating to distinct nonmajority groups" in the name of security and continued governance.[4] There is evidence that minority populations were able to gain the favoured status of European colonial powers by embracing Christianity or through other methods of demonstrating their loyalty.[5] These colonial policies continue to impact "understandings of ethnicity and patterns of ethnic relations in postcolonial states".[6] Throughout the parts of the world controlled by colonial powers, these sorts of practices contributed to immediate and ongoing ethnic conflicts.

In colonial Burma (now Myanmar), for instance, the British gained power over the territory through the use of armed force in the nineteenth century, and proceeded to enact policies to serve its own economic interests.[7] This included allowing the transfer of millions of individuals from

---

[3] Azeem Ibrahim, *The Rohingyas: Inside Myanmar's Hidden Genocide*, Hurst & Company, London, 2016, p. 44.

[4] Benedict Kingsbury, "'Indigenous Peoples' in International Law: A Constructivist Approach to the Asian Controversy", in *American Journal of International Law*, 1998, vol. 92, p. 427.

[5] *Ibid.*

[6] *Ibid.* For a detailed survey, see Donald L. Horowitz, *Ethnic Groups in Conflict*, University of California Press, 1985.

[7] Jacques P. Leider, "Conflict and Mass Violence in Arakan (Rakhine State): The 1942 Events and Political Identity Formation", in South and Lall (eds.), *Citizenship in Myanmar: Ways of Being in and from Burma*, ISEAS – Yusof Ishak Institute and Chiang Mai Univer-

its neighbouring colony of India, which resulted in two-layered colonial economic exploitation: "the British occupied the top of the colonial hierarchy, socially, economically, and politically; the Indians (and to a lesser extent Chinese) dominated the middle layer; and finally the Burmese, especially tradition-bound Buddhists, were at the bottom".[8] As Morten Bergsmo notes in the concept note for this project, the beginning of the twentieth century was marked by Indians "arriving in Burma at the rate of no less than a quarter million people a year. The numbers rose steadily until, in the peak year of 1927, immigration reached 480,000 people, with Rangoon exceeding New York City as the greatest immigration port in the world".[9] The Burmese, "who became a minority in their main city, Rangoon [–] had no say in this demographic transformation of their country".[10]

10.2.2. Transfer of Civilians Under Post-Colonialism

Following World War II, former colonies began to gradually gain independence, but they were left with conflicts either fostered or created by colonial powers, particularly on the basis of ethnicity or religion. The consequence of the colonial administrations was that "many states have complex mixes of ethnic groups, and there are many regions with ethnic groups splintered across multiple states".[11] While most states have found their way forward, in some post-colonial societies, these conflicts have resulted in mass violence against or between different sects, including genocides and ethnic cleansings aimed at changing the demographic makeup of a community.

---

sity Press, Singapore and Chiang Mai, 2018, p. 195; Jacques P. Leider, "Territorial Dispossession and Persecution in North Arakan (Rakhine), 1942-43, Policy Brief Series No. 101 (2020), Torkel Opsahl Academic EPublisher, 2020 (https://www.toaep.org/pbs-pdf/101-leider/), p. 2.

[8] Maung Zarni and Alice Cowley, "The Slow-Burning Genocide of Myanmar's Rohingya", in *Pacific Rim Law and Policy Association*, 2014, vol. 23, p. 698; see also John S. Furnivall, *Colonial Policy and Practice: A Comparative Study of Burma and the Netherlands India*, Cambridge University Press, 1948.

[9] Morten Bergsmo, "Myanmar, Colonial Aftermath, and Access to International Law", Occasional Paper Series No. 9 (2019), Torkel Opsahl Academic EPublisher, 2019 (http://www.toaep.org/ops-pdf/9-bergsmo), quoting Thant Myint-U, *The River of Lost Footsteps: A Personal History of Burma*, Faber and Faber, London, 2007, pp. 185–86. See also Chapter 7 above.

[10] *Ibid.*, p. 6.

[11] Ibrahim, 2016, p. 49, see above note 3.

The situation in Myanmar appears to have followed the latter pattern. While there have been various attempts by the majority Buddhist Burmese population to address the demographic changes that occurred during colonial rule, the most serious has been the persecution of the Rohingya Muslims in northern Rakhine State in western Myanmar. The Rohingya have been subjected to killing, violence, and forced displacement through cycles of inter-communal violence since the 1940s. The "dominant narrative of many Burmese about the Rohingyas is one of illegitimate 'invasion' by a threatening 'outsider'".[12] This is in spite of the historical fact that while the Rohingyas may not have been Burmese hundreds of years ago, today the Rohingyas are Burmese, both politically and under international law.[13]

Continuing to look at Myanmar as an example, there have been several attempts to use international law as a tool of accountability for the perpetrators of violence against the Rohingya. In 2017, the United Nations ('UN') Human Rights Council established a Fact-Finding Mission to gather the facts and circumstances of alleged human rights violations and abuses in Myanmar.[14] The Independent International Fact-Finding Mission on Myanmar, in its final report from September 2019, details that the Rohingya people are "the target of a Government attack aimed at erasing the identity and removing them from Myanmar, and [...] this has caused them great suffering".[15] The final report notes that the Rohingya face violence, structural discrimination under the law, movement restrictions, forced labour, and forced displacement into Bangladesh.[16]

Based on the findings of the UN Fact-Finding Mission,[17] The Gambia accused Myanmar of committing genocide against the Rohingya Mus-

---

[12] *Ibid.*

[13] See *ibid.*, Chapter 1.

[14] United Nations General Assembly ('UNGA'), Situation of Human Rights in Myanmar, UNHRC, thirty-fourth session, UN Doc. A/HRC/Res/34/22, 24 March 2017 (https://www.legal-tools.org/doc/842442/).

[15] UNGA, Detailed findings of the Independent International Fact-Finding Mission on Myanmar, UNHRC, forty-second session, UN Doc. A/HRC/42/CRP.5, 16 September 2019 (https://www.legal-tools.org/doc/fdy4p1/).

[16] *Ibid.*

[17] For criticism of the recommendations made by the Fact-Finding Mission, see Derek Tonkin, "Mission Creep Untrammelled: The UN Fact-Finding Mission on Myanmar", Policy Brief Series No. 102 (2020), Torkel Opsahl Academic EPublisher, 2020 (http://www.toaep.org/pbs-pdf/102-tonkin). Tonkin argues that the Fact-Finding Mission

lims before the International Court of Justice ('ICJ') in November 2019.[18] The filing requests provisional measures to protect the Rohingya people.[19] In January 2020, the ICJ ruled that Myanmar was required to implement emergency measures to protect Rohingya Muslims, and preserve any evidence of possible genocide.[20] Additionally, in July 2019, the ICC Prosecutor requested authorization from Pre-Trial Chamber III to open an investigation into the situation in the People's Republic of Bangladesh and the Republic of the Union of Myanmar.[21] In November 2019, Pre-Trial Chamber III authorized the Prosecutor to investigate alleged crimes related to the persecution of the Rohingya.[22] While many would argue that the response to the plight of the Rohingya has been slow and inadequate, there are international bodies pursuing resolutions under international law.

10.2.3. A Justice Problem

The two realms of civilian transfer have not been considered within the same framework. The colonial transfer of civilians is seen as regrettable at most, and not something for which particular groups or individuals can be or will be held responsible. The post-colonial transfer of civilians, on the other hand, is seen as something for which groups and individuals should be held morally and legally responsible, in part because we now have the international justice mechanisms that allow for such attributions of re-

---

overstepped its mandate in issuing specific recommendations for action to the Government of Myanmar and the international community, especially the UN Security Council. Tonkin also claims that the Fact-Finding Mission's final report is based on historical bias and misinformation.

[18] International Court of Justice ('ICJ'), *The Gambia v. Myanmar*, Application of the Convention on the Prevention and Punishment of the Crime of Genocide, Application instituting proceedings and Request for the indication of provisional measures, 11 November 2019 (https://www.legal-tools.org/doc/69p376/).

[19] *Ibid.*

[20] ICJ, *The Gambia v. Myanmar*, Application of the Convention on the Prevention and Punishment of the Crime of Genocide, Order on provisional measures, 23 January 2020 (https://www.legal-tools.org/doc/in5d55/).

[21] ICC, *Situation in the People's Republic of Bangladesh/Republic of the Union of Myanmar*, Pre-Trial Chamber, Decision Pursuant to Article 15 of the Rome Statute on the Authorisation of an Investigation into the Situation in the People's Republic of Bangladesh/Republic of the Union of Myanmar, 14 November 2019, ICC-01/19-27 (https://www.legal-tools.org/doc/kbo3hy/).

[22] *Ibid.*

---

sponsibility. This disparity reflects two different but related types of injustice, which I outline below.

10.2.3.1. Distributive Injustice

Some critics have argued that since there is no accountability for colonial bad actors, it is not fair for current bad actors to be held responsible for similar acts. Because its mandate only concerns events that have taken place since 2002, the ICC, for instance, does not have jurisdiction over colonialists, nor does it have jurisdiction over certain crimes, such as creating ethnic tensions, that are outside the scope of its mandate. The passage of time has likely reduced any world-wide demand for moral accountability as well. This distributive injustice is plausible as a reason why a post-colonial state like Myanmar might not want to participate in international criminal justice institutions designed largely by Western states. Western complicity in colonial and post-colonial violence does not absolve the individuals who are committing atrocities from individual responsibility for their actions, and it should not prevent the individuals from being held accountable for their crimes. As stated above, that an individual is rightly held legally accountable for one's actions, while another is not, does not change the fact that an individual has been rightly held legally accountable for one's actions. The ICC can prosecute individuals who have overseen mass killing in their own nations, and because that is what the ICC can rightly do, that is what it should do. But as I will argue below, this does not mean that we should not use other methods to properly recognize the bad acts of the West.

10.2.3.2. Substantive Injustice

Another justice concern relates to the fact that the modern legal framework does not allow for adequate consideration of the lingering impacts of past colonial wrongs. Antony Anghie and B.S. Chimni claim that the history of colonialism makes "Third World peoples acutely sensitive to power relations among states and to the ways in which any proposed international rule or institution will actually affect the distribution of power between states and peoples".[23] While Anghie does not think it is possible for the Global South to dispense with international law altogether, he does

---

[23] Antony Anghie and B.S. Chimni, "Third World Approaches to International Law and Individual Responsibility in Internal Conflicts", in *Chinese Journal of International Law*, 2003, vol. 2, no. 1, pp. 77–103, 78.

argue that international law must develop a better understanding of the ongoing impacts of colonialism.[24]

Ifeonu Eberechi claims that it "is almost impossible to come across an armed conflict in Africa without a colonial component, as most wars have highlighted the ethnic composition of the African societies – a socio-political mess that white colonialism created".[25] This applies to many post-colonial societies, including in Southeast Asia. He argues that responsibility for grave crimes in post-colonial societies should also fall on the shoulders of the international actors who contributed to the conditions of conflict, and notes that the ICC's model of individual responsibility fails to apportion responsibility in this way.[26] As many TWAIL scholars have noted, it might be the case that that the international community's insistence on ensuring that individual leaders are subject to international criminal justice is unfair, given that "the causes of violence are rooted in histories of colonial subject formation, contested governance and resource ownership".[27]

It might be the case that international law is necessarily unjust, especially in terms of substance and distribution, and thus post-colonial states should be wary of participating in the international law enterprise at all. But as with the claims about distributive injustice, concerns about substantive injustice should at least push us to identify an alternative method of acknowledgment and responsibility attribution for colonial powers.

10.3. The Harm of Civilian Transfer

In this section, I offer an account of harm, first distinguishing between harm and wrongdoing, which is the subject of the next section, before surveying the most compelling theories of harm. In a *legal* sense, we can think of the concept of 'harm' as defining what a legislative body might be permitted to legitimately outlaw. If we begin with the assumption that individuals may act as they choose, then a legislature is only justified in

---

[24] Antony Anghie, "The Evolution of International Law: Colonial and Postcolonial Realities", in *Third World Quarterly*, 2006, vol. 27, no. 5, pp. 739–753, 752.

[25] Ifeonu Eberechi, "Armed Conflicts in Africa and Western Complicity: A Disincentive for African Union's Cooperation with the ICC", in *African Journal of Legal Studies*, 2009, vol. 3, no. 1, pp. 53–76, 56–57.

[26] *Ibid.*, p. 76.

[27] Clarke, 2010, p. 628, see above note 1.

interfering with this liberty in order to prevent or reduce harm. But questions related to harm are broader than the legal questions of permissible legislative coercion, and if we think that the criminal law relies on its moral legitimacy, then we must begin with the *moral* concept of 'harm'. Accordingly, in what follows, I break down these moral questions before I turn to the legal implications. I endorse a well-being theory of harm and a preference theory of well-being for individuals. I consider the difference between individual and group-based harms, and I endorse an objective list theory of well-being for groups. Finally, I apply this theory to harm that can result from transferring civilians.

10.3.1. Harm and Wrongdoing

Before we can analyse the concept of 'harm', we must be able to distinguish it from the concept of 'wrong' or 'wrongdoing'. We could actually distinguish between wrongs, harms, and wrongful harms, since there are harms that do not result from wrongful conduct, and there are wrongs that do not result in harm.[28] Joel Feinberg offers one compelling account of harm and wrongdoing, in which he identifies two relevant senses of 'harm'. The first involves a setback to interests, and the second involves one person wronging another person.[29] A setback to interests need not have been caused by intentional human action, and could instead be the result of weather or an accident. We would say that a painful, broken leg caused by weather or an accident was a harm, but we would not attribute it to another person's wrongdoing.

The second sense of 'harm' involves wrongdoing. A painful, broken leg that results from intentional tripping would be a setback to interests that involves wrongdoing. Notice that harm does not have to result from wrongdoing, such as where I intentionally trip someone, and instead of breaking her leg she bumps into a stranger and they fall in love. But since our aim is to answer questions about harms where we can identify an entity that is at least partially culpable with respect to the harm, or acts that society could legitimately criminalize,[30] and where some kind of setback

---

[28] See Derek Parfit, *Reasons and Persons*, Clarendon Press, Oxford, 1984, Chapter 15. Parfit argues that it is possible for one to act wrongfully without negatively impacting the interests of an identifiable person.

[29] Feinberg, 1984, pp. 31–36, see above note 2.

[30] J.S. Mill notably argues for the Harm Principle, which claims that "the only purpose for which power can be rightfully exercised over any member of a civilized community,

to interest occurs, I will use Feinberg's definition of harm because it captures both the result and the wrongful action.

In accordance with the harm principle, Feinberg sets up the following as the conditions under which Person A ('A') *harms* Person B ('B'):

1. A acts (perhaps in a sense of "act" broad enough to include acts of omission [...])

2. in a manner which is defective or faulty with respect to the risks it creates to B, that is, with the intention of producing the consequences for B that follow, or similarly adverse ones, or with negligence or recklessness in respect to those consequences,

3. A's acting in that manner is morally indefensible, that is, neither excusable nor justifiable; and

4. A's action is the cause of a setback to B's interests, which is also

5. a violation of B's right.[31]

The harm aspect of this definition is found in condition 4.[32] Thus, a harm is (1) a wrongful act that (2) sets back or invades the interest of another person.[33] These interests can be either (1) well-being interests or (2) rights-based interests,[34] as I consider in the next sub-section, in which I depart from Feinberg by taking up well-being interests rather than rights-based interests as the best way to understand harm.

Wrongdoing, or the wrongfulness aspect of harm, is captured by conditions 1, 2, 3, and 5 of Feinberg's definition. It is based on one's moral or legal culpability for an action. A person can be said to wrong another person "when he treats him unjustly",[35] where the injustice consists of the morally indefensible actions taken under conditions 2 and 5 above. I return to the concept of wrongfulness in Section 10.4.

---

against his will, is to prevent harm to others". John Stuart Mill, *On Liberty*, 1859, David Bromwich and George Kateb (eds.), Yale University Press, New Haven, 2003, p. 80. See also Feinberg, 1984, p. 3, see above note 2.

[31] Feinberg, 1984, pp. 105-06, see above note 2.

[32] *Ibid.*, p. 106.

[33] Parfit, 1984, chapter 15, see above note 28.

[34] Feinberg, 1984, pp. 34-35, see above note 2.

[35] *Ibid.*, p. 107.

10.3.2. Harm and Interests

According to Feinberg's definition, harm is understood in terms of set-backs to interests, so the first step in analysing harm will be to explore the different kinds of interests that could be harmed. I consider rights-based interests and well-being interests in turn.

10.3.2.1. Rights-Based Interests

A rights-based account of harm explains harm by identifying the rights one possesses, either naturally or via convention, and establishing that a harm has occurred when one of those rights has been violated. For instance, a proponent of the rights-based account would claim that if B has a right not to be displaced from her home without her consent, then A's non-consensual removal of B from her home sets back B's rights-based interest in her home, even though he does not harm B in any other way, that is, her well-being is not affected.[36] Appeals to human rights are based on this sort of argument. Thus, if one has a right to own and inhabit property under a natural law theory of human rights, or under international human rights law, one who has had their property taken unjustly has experienced a harm via rights-violation.

However, it seems that rights-based interests cannot actually be identified without appealing to well-being. The reason why we might be justified in experiencing harm (or even acting in self-defence to prevent that harm) is not simply based on the narrow view that we have inviolable rights, but rather that what we see as impermissible actions are grounded in our preferences related to our well-being. So, whether or not there is a plausible rights-based account that identifies rights in terms of their likely impact on well-being, we must look at well-being interests to develop a robust account of harm.

10.3.2.2. Well-Being Interests

An alternative account of harm looks at harm to well-being interests. Welfare interests include interests in "the continuance for a foreseeable interval of one's life",[37] "the integrity and normal functioning of one's body", [38] "the absence of groundless anxieties and resentments, the capacity to

---

[36] This example is modified from Alan Wertheimer, *Consent to Sexual Relations*, Cambridge University Press, 2003, p. 93; see also Feinberg, 1984, p. 107, see above note 2.

[37] Feinberg, 1984, p. 37, see above note 2.

[38] *Ibid.*

engage normally in social intercourse and to enjoy and maintain friend-ships, at least minimal income and financial security, a tolerable social and physical environment, and a certain amount of freedom from interfer-ence and coercion".[39] These interests are "those general all-purpose inter-ests" that must be satisfied for an individual to pursue her "particular goals and aims".[40] Thus the concept of well-being interests can be seen as universal, whether or not we subscribe to an objective understanding of which interests count as well-being interests. It is clear, however, that harm to welfare interests will have an impact on "the whole network of [an individual's] interests", since they are prior to the fulfilment of "more ultimate aspirations".[41]

If we look at the above case of being removed from one's home from the perspective of well-being interests, the list of interests we care about could either be subjective or objective. On a subjective list account of well-being interests, if B does not identify or experience a harm that has occurred as a result of the removal, we would say that B's subjective interests have not been harmed. However, on an objective list account of well-being, B's interest in bodily integrity, financial security, and capacity to engage in social interactions have all been negatively affected, and therefore her well-being has been negatively affected as well. I look more closely at these theories of well-being in the following sub-section.

10.3.3. Harm and Well-Being

There are three main theories about assessing the quality of a person's life: mental state views, preference-based views, and objective list views.[42] Mental state theories "hold that the quality of a life for the person who lives it is determined completely by [...] its experiential quality",[43] and since experience is largely subjective, these theories broadly focus on

---

[39] *Ibid.*

[40] *Ibid.*

[41] *Ibid.*

[42] Judith Jarvis Thomson, *The Realm of Rights*, Harvard University Press, Cambridge, MA, 1990, p. 205; Wertheimer, 2003, pp. 94-95, see above note 36; Thomas Scanlon, "The Status of Well-Being", in Grethe B. Peterson (ed.), *Tanner Lectures on Human Values*, University of Utah Press, Salt Lake City, 1998, p. 99; Derek Parfit, "What Makes Someone's Life Go Best?", in Russ Shafer-Landau (ed.), *Ethical Theory: An Anthology*, John Wiley and Sons, Oxford, 2013; Thomas Scanlon, *What We Owe to Each Other*, Harvard University Press, Cambridge, MA, 1998.

[43] Scanlon, 1998, p. 113, see above note 42.

self-evaluation of how a life is going. Only something that has an effect on the "quality of one's experience" counts as a contributor to well-being.[44] This branch of theories often focuses on the mental states of pleasure or happiness,[45] where harm to well-being consists in the introduction of pain or unhappiness, but mental states other than happiness can be captured by these sorts of theories, such as life satisfaction or a more general emotional well-being.[46] Yet happiness-based theories, or hedonism, boasts several attractive features. It is a straightforward way of looking at what it means for a life to go well, since pleasure and the absence of suffering is a simple way of answering this question. As Daniel Haybron illustrates, when we think of what makes intense nausea bad, we are focused on what it *feels* like, as the "badness appears to be brutely phenomenological, residing in the quality of the experience itself".[47] Self-evaluation of one's emotional state or life satisfaction will be similarly focused on how one feels.

But what makes these views straightforward is arguably what makes them weak: they are too simplistic. As demonstrated by Nozick's experience machine thought-experiment,[48] most people think about their own welfare as having "more than just positive states of mind".[49] It fails to capture everything we might think it wrong with certain obvious harms, such as death, but also the precarity of home or community. It can account for any suffering that might occur prior to death, the fact that one no longer experiences 'any' mental states after death (as far as I know). But mental state theories cannot account for other aspects of harm. One does not "experience" death, but one may experience whatever leads up to death. And would we want to say that someone who has been impacted by the transfer of civilians has not been harmed if she was not specifically aware of the migration statistics? Some might, but I would disagree with a view that cannot account for a way in which an individual who does not 'experience' the feeling of being displaced or had the demographic fabric of her

---

[44] *Ibid.*

[45] Parfit, 1984, p. 493, see above note 28.

[46] Daniel M. Haybron, "Mental State Approaches to Well-Being", in Matthew D. Adler and Marc Fleurbaey (eds.), *The Oxford Handbook of Well-Being and Public Policy*, Oxford University Press, 2016, p. 347.

[47] *Ibid.*, p. 354.

[48] Robert Nozick, *Anarchy, State, and Utopia*, Basic Books, New York, 1974, p. 42.

[49] Haybron, 2016, p. 355, see above note 46.

community altered could still have been harmed. It might be true that some harms are so minor that we would not necessarily call them harms if they are not experienced as such by a victim. But those are not the sorts of harms we are considering here, and thus I will not go any further into this possibility.

Preference-based theories hold that the quality of a person's life is a matter of the extent to which that person's preferences or desires are satisfied".[50] These views claim that the "quality of a person's life depends (in part) on whether one's actual subjective desires are fulfilled, but it does not require that one actually *experience* the fulfillment of the desire".[51] Preference-based theories differ from experiential theories in that they appeal to more than just the "present features of our lives that are introspectively discernible".[52] Rather, they appeal to all preferences one might have about her life, and are tied to the correspondence between these preferences and actual states of affairs.[53] There are several different versions of preference-based theories, with different requirements for what constitute suitable desires. Some views look straightforwardly at the satisfaction of current desires, while others look at the overall satisfaction of desires over a lifetime. Still others require that desires be informed in some way, so as to avoid the criticism that some people lack the information necessary to 'properly' formulate desires. On any of these views, "[y]our well-being has to do with what is in your self-interest",[54] and this is hard to argue with on its face. These views appear to be necessarily tied to reality in a way that mental state views are not, yet they still account for the subjective preferences of an individual in analysing her well-being. The harm of displacement to someone who prefers to continue to inhabit their land, or to exert some (perhaps only indirect) control over her state's migration policies is easily captured by these views.

Yet the difference between the distinctive preference-based views reveals a challenge. Either we want to give full deference to someone's expressed desires, or we want to couch these desires in some way. If we

---

[50] Scanlon, 1998, p. 113, see above note 42.

[51] Wertheimer, 2003, pp. 94-95, see above note 36 (emphasis added).

[52] Parfit, 2013, p. 294, see above note 42.

[53] *Ibid.*

[54] Krister Bykvist, "Preference-Based Views of Well-Being", in Matthew D. Adler and Marc Fleurbaey (eds.), *The Oxford Handbook of Well-Being and Public Policy*, Oxford University Press, 2016, p. 330.

opt for the first view, we may accept certain preferences that have been somehow limited due to the particular circumstances of one's upbringing, especially involving limited access to information. If we take the other route, and require that desires must be 'informed', we seem to be veering into objective territory in which someone's true preferences might not meet the standard for counting as preferences, based on what the preferences are, or what went into their formation. An individual's desire to associate mostly with people who share her religion, for instance, should not necessarily be discounted simply because we might think there is something inherently valuable about heterogeneous communities.

Objective theories assert that "certain things are good or bad for people, whether or not these people would want to have the good things, or to avoid the bad things".[55] On these accounts, there are "standards for assessing the quality of a life that are not entirely dependent on the desires of the person whose life it is".[56] Rather, for example, "knowledge, achievement, and moral virtue can be good in your life and their absence bad even if you're not in fact attracted to them",[57] and thus they count toward your well-being. Harm consists of denial of these objective goods, whether or not an individual experiences the denial as harm or has a preference for these particular goods. This has the benefit of permitting external assessment of well-being, and can allow for the institutional provision of resources in order to achieve well-being.

It might be the case that most would agree on at least some objective features of well-being, such as those listed above, or such as those that are regularly found in international human rights documents. But that claim seems to be tied to our preferences – if we tried to come up with a list of objective goods, we would only want to include those things for which we have a preference. Otherwise we would have a hard time accepting that the good is objectively 'good'. And this arguably causes objective list theories to collapse into preference-based theories. Deportation or economic hardship would likely be captured as harms under nearly any objective list we could imagine, but the story we tell about why has to do with our *preferences* for liberty and economic security.

---

[55] Parfit, 2013, p. 296, see above note 42.

[56] Scanlon, 1998, p. 113, see above note 42.

[57] Thomas Hurka, "Objective Goods", in Matthew D. Adler and Marc Fleurbaey (eds.), *The Oxford Handbook of Well-Being and Public Policy*, Oxford University Press, 2016, p. 380.

At the level of the individual, the harm caused by the transfer of civilians will not look good no matter which conception of well-being we adopt. Whether you are losing your community's identity due to the decisions of a colonial power, or you are being forcibly removed from your community, your home, and your land, all of these accounts seem to be capable of capturing these harms. But the most compelling of these three accounts, when assessing harm to the individual, is the preference-based set of views. The experiential view is too limiting, in that someone's life can go well as long as they are oblivious to certain pains or wrongdoings. The objective list views are also too limiting, in that they determine what will contribute to the well-being of individuals without taking into account their own view of what will make their lives go best, and what will not detract from it. Individuals should be able to identify their own preferences, and be understood to be doing well, or to be harmed, based on the satisfaction of these preferences.

The preference-based views might look like a problem for application of the harm principle. If goods are whatever individuals (or groups) desire, and harms are what they desire to avoid, then it may be hard to identify a wrongful action as a harm. If condition 4 is purely subjective, and "B's interests" can be based on anything B desires (or does not desire), then it may be difficult to assess the other conditions based on what B sees as her interests. This would make it challenging to justify the criminalization of behaviour, if everyone had idiosyncratic desires. Yet this assumes that there is no way to generalize about individuals' preferences. While we would not want to claim that an particular individual has necessarily experienced a particular harm, or preferred to avoid that harm, we can make generalizations about the sorts of harms that individuals prefer to avoid when we identify what sorts of harms should be criminalized by a society, and in the next sub-section I argue that we should.

10.3.4. Group-Based Harms

The preceding account is persuasive if we think about harms to individual persons. But reliance on the subjective preferences in order to determine well-being is less plausible if we try to think about harming a group, such as the groups who have been harmed by colonial and post-colonial actors. We need to be able to capture both the collective and individual aspects of a group, and acknowledge the shared and differing experiences.

Raimo Tuomela distinguishes between the 'I-mode' and the 'we-mode' in terms of ways we can think about individuals who are part of groups, particularly in terms of how they act (although I expand on this view elsewhere to include harms as well). The 'we-mode' approach is based on the idea that "the primary acting agent in central group contexts is the group viewed as an intentional agent, while the individual members of the group are the primary ontological agents acting as representatives for the group".[58] In short, the 'we-mode' allows us to acknowledge that individuals in a group are socially constructed by the group.[59] The 'I-mode', on the other hand, involves individuals acting for their own private reasons, even if we still acknowledge that the individual is part of a group. This way of thinking also allows us to capture the fact that individuals experience harms differently, even while harms are directed at an entire group.

The preference-based views align with the 'I-mode', acknowledging the individual preferences one might have with respect to oneself as an individual and as a group member. But the 'we-mode' demands something beyond the aggregation of individual preferences, and the identification of a set of collective preferences seems much more challenging than the identification of a collective intention. Thus, the objective list views will be more appropriate for assessing whether or not a group has been harmed (as a group) through a setback to their collective interests. Since individuals will have a variety of preferences as to how they see their lives going best, adopting and utilizing an objective list of goods that capture fundamental aspects of humanity is a better way to assess collective harm. While I do not want to suggest that there is an extensive list of goods that are objectively better (such as reading poetry or drinking expensive wine), I would adopt an objective list that coheres with the fundamental aspects of humanity as what constitute well-being interests. That is, an objective list of well-being interests should contain those things without which it will be impossible for the group, and its individual members, to fulfil "more ultimate aspirations".[60] These include such interests

---

[58] *Ibid.*, p. 2. Frank Hindriks challenges this view on the basis that groups cannot have intrinsic intentionality. See Frank Hindriks, review of *Social Ontology: Collective Intentionality and Group Agents*, Raimo Tuomela, in *Economics and Philosophy*, 2015, vol. 31, no. 2.

[59] Raimo Tuomela, *Social Ontology: Collective Intentionality and Group Agents*, Oxford University Press, 2013, p. 2.

[60] Feinberg, 1984, p. 37, see above note 2.

as bodily integrity, some minimum amount of financial security (or at least a guarantee that existing security cannot be arbitrarily taken away by a state power), and the ability to live in a social community with others. At a bare minimum, widespread and arbitrary deprivation of these interests would constitute harm to a group.[61]

Now that we have an account of what (minimally) counts as a setback to the interests of a group, I turn to the particular harms of civilian transfer as it impacts individuals and groups, and analyse how we should understand these as harms.

10.3.5. The Harm of Civilian Transfer

Broadly, both the colonial and post-colonial movements of people meet the definition of 'domicide', which is the deliberate destruction of home against the will of the home dweller.[62] The setback to one's interests in the form of having a home destroyed could certainly be caused by a natural disaster or other force other than the intent of humans. But since we are only focused on the loss of home at the hands of intentional actors, the term 'domicide' best describes our cases. I argue that we should understand home to constitute something much more substantial than mere shelter or housing. Rather, we should understand home to involve our families and our political community, united in the pursuit of the common good, which we get from Aristotle.[63] On a more modern view, we can dis-

---

[61] Larry May defends an "international harm principle" which identifies the following principle of group-based harm: "To determine if harm to humanity has occurred, there will have to be one of two (and ideally both) of the following conditions met: either the individual is harmed because of that person's group membership or other non-individualized characteristic, or the harm occurs due to the involvement of a group such as the State". Larry May, *Crimes against Humanity: A Normative Account*, Cambridge University Press, 2005, p. 83.

[62] See J. Douglas Porteous and Sandra E. Smith, *Domicide: The Global Destruction of Home*, McGill-Queen's University Press, Montreal, 2001. The concept is not a legal concept, yet there are parallels found in property, tort, contract, and criminal law, as well as international human rights law and international humanitarian law, all of which recognize the right to own private property or real property, and place limits on behaviour related to using, taking, or destroying property. For example, the US Constitution provides that "private property [shall not] be taken for public use, without just compensation", US Constitution amendment V. The US Supreme Court has ruled on what constitutes a "public use" and "just compensation", providing federal parameters on how states may (and may not) take property away from their residents. See, for example, Supreme Court of the United States, *Kelo v. City of New London*, 545 U.S. 469 (2005); *Monongahela Navigation Co. v. United States*, 148 U.S. 312 (1893); *United States v. Miller*, 317 U.S. 369 (1943).

[63] See Aristotle, *Politics*, translated by C.D.C. Reeve, Hackett Publishing, Indianapolis, 1998.

---

tinguish 'home' from 'dwelling' or 'house' as the latter notions are physical structures used by people for living, while the concept of home involves a special kind of relationship with place and those who are a part of that place. Access to a 'home' is the sort of preference that must be fulfilled in order to succeed in fulfilling most other desires.

10.3.5.1. Transfer of Civilians as an Individual Harm

The first sort of harm related to the loss of home corresponds to the actions of post-colonial citizens in deporting or otherwise displacing individuals from particular communities (ethnic or religious groups in particular). There are many physical, economic, social, and psychological harms that result from the loss of home, including bodily and economic insecurity, as well as the experience of being isolated from a group of other like-minded individuals. As Claudia Card explains, "[s]ocial vitality exists through relationships, contemporary and inter-generational, that create an identity that gives meaning to a life. Major loss of social vitality is a loss of identity and consequently a serious loss of meaning for one's existence".[64]

The second sort of harm corresponds with the actions of colonial powers in transferring or permitting the transfer of large numbers of individuals from other colonial territories to a community. The influx of non-local people to a community could disrupt the political community, the sense of pursuit of the common good, and the relationship one might have with a place. This harms individuals insofar as they may be discriminated against by migrants who arguably lack the same kind of political rights to inhabit their community, and there may be direct economic harms from policies that favour migrants for jobs. Over time, the impact of these policies can multiply as the chasm between the colonial administration and the poor colonial citizens grows, resulting in a disempowered and bitter populace.

One danger in relying on the preference-based theory of harm is that it could permit individuals to justify racist or xenophobic views, and seek to exclude migrants on the basis that they are 'harmed' by the influx of people of different racial or national backgrounds. The idea that an individual is entitled to build a community with only people who look and talk and pray like her is not, by my lights, a permissible preference insofar

---

[64] Claudia Card, "Genocide and Social Death", in *Hypatia*, 2003, vol. 18, no. 1, p. 63.

as the non-fulfilment of that preference constitutes a harm. Accordingly, we must disambiguate two different effects of migration. First, we can consider the harms an individual might suffer from the transfer of civilians from another community, where the transferring power intends to negatively impact the individual and her community and make it impossible for the individual to achieve her aspirations. These harms might occur in the face of occupation or another form of domination, rather than self-determined migration. This is not the same as the second sort of harms, those that result from the ordinary, self-determined movement of migrants into a community, including the corresponding change to the demographic makeup that occurs within the community.

10.3.5.2. Transfer of Civilians as a Collective Harm

When it comes to group harm, it becomes even more clear why we do not want to rely on victims' subjective experience, regardless of the particular experience of some (or even nearly all) of the individual members of the group. The 'we-mode' requires us to establish a collective interest, and this involves establishing certain objective goods, the denial of which results in harm to the group and its individual members. When a victim group has been determined by the actions of a perpetrator group, the perpetrators are concerned with harming through the denial of objective goods. They are not focused on denying any particular victim the satisfaction of her preferences, or the experience of happiness, except insofar as these denials contribute to the harming of the victim group as a collective. The focus is on the group, and thus the analysis of the harm must be tied to collective, objective interests.

The harm resulting from the transfer of civilians into a population includes the aggregative effect of the individual harms (which may vary by person), but also some harms that arguably cannot be captured solely by the experience of individuals, such as the demographic changes. A community may have a collective preference in maintaining the stability of their own community, especially in a particular geographic area, and ensuring that they have the ability succeed on economic, social, and political terms. Again, since these seem like they are nearly universal preferences, it is also reasonable to capture these as objective goods. The influx of migrants certainly does not necessarily threaten these objective goods (see below). But if the migrants are arriving without any choices having been made by the original community, and the migrants are receiving preferential treatment, this could result in two harms. First, it might result in the economic, political, and social discrimination of the original inhabitants. And second, the preferential treatment can feed into resentment and conflict between the original inhabitants and migrants, and as we have seen, these conflicts can last long after the colonial powers have ceded their administrative authority.

As noted above, relying on a preference-based view of harm could justify racism or xenophobia, and this becomes even starker when we look at group-based preferences and harms. Even if we adopt an objective list view, as I argue we should, these racist or xenophobic preferences could be incorporated into a disingenuous argument for protecting one's own 'community', that is, one's own race or ethnicity. The desire to build a community in which the members feel supported, able to fully develop their identities, and able to fulfil their aspirations is compelling. But when this desire is used to justify a homogenous community, and used to justify racist or xenophobic policies of exclusion and hatred, the end is no longer permissible. Further, the inability to protect the community from migrants does not constitute a harm. So again, we must disambiguate the legitimate harms to a community, where the community and its members are prevented from living full lives, from situations involving ordinary migration.

The harm resulting from being displaced or deported also includes the aggregative effect of the individual harms. The 'I-mode' captures the suffering of individuals who have watched their children murdered or their homes burned to the ground, the phenomenological experiences of loss. But there is also something over and above this aggregation that occurs when something like deportation, or ethnic cleansing, or genocide occurs. When a group faces killing or forced displacement due to another group's desire that they be removed completely, either from the planet or the state or the community, the psychological, social, economic, and physical impacts are severe. Nearly all groups have a preference that their group continue to exist in the future (although individuals could be part of the group and not share this desire), so this is again a preference, but would also be found on any objective list.

For both types of collective harm, a group is focused on perpetrating objective harms, or denying objective goods, to the victim group. Thus, the interests that are fundamental to the ability of the victim group to fulfil its ultimate aspirations, collectively and individually, are the best way to think about collective harm. The existence of their home, and other collective aspirations of a group are threatened by the transfer of civilians into or out of a territory. All of the collective aspirations of a group might be threatened by the transfer of civilians into or out of a territory. Accordingly, these transfers result in a clear setback to interests, and thus an individual and group harm. In the next section, we can turn to the other aspect of harm under the harm principle: the wrongful nature of the act, and what follows from wrongfulness of civilian population transfers.

10.4. The Wrong of Civilian Transfer

I used Feinberg's definition of harm in Section 10.3.2., in which he distinguishes between the wrongfulness of an act and the harmfulness of an act. I have analysed the aspect of harm that corresponds with the setback to the victim's interests, and I will now turn to the conditions that correspond to wrongfulness. Because I have already established the harmfulness of civilian transfers, I go directly to the act of transfer as a way to draw out its wrongfulness.

Wrongdoing, or the wrongfulness aspect of harm, consists of four conditions. First, it is an act, or possibly an omission. Second, it is performed "in a manner which is defective or faulty with respect to the risks it creates" to another person, that is, with intent to produce certain adverse consequences, or "with negligence or recklessness in respect to those consequences".[65] Third, the action is morally indefensible, that is, not saved by an excuse or justification. Fourth, it violates the rights of another person. I consider each condition in turn, with respect to the transfer of civilians.

10.4.1. Action

Transferring civilians involves an initial action, either transferring/permitting the transfer of migrants into an existing community, or displacing communities from their existing community. Particular instances of transfer may include other acts that cause setbacks to the individuals or communities, as well as omissions like a failure to provide alternate housing options or the ability to communicate with friends or family members. These actions are aimed at destroying home or community.

---

[65] Feinberg, 1984, pp. 105-06, see above note 2.

10.4.2. Manner

The manner in which the acts or omissions of one who transfers civilians are 'defective' or 'reckless' is straightforwardly established. Whether we only acknowledge the minimal objective list interests, or take into account the most pressing desires of an individual on a desire satisfaction view of interests, the denial of interests like freedom of movement, freedom of association, and a place to sleep clearly constitute adverse consequences. Moreover, a perpetrator would be hard-pressed to deny that these adverse consequences are reasonably foreseeable, if not guaranteed, by his actions. Thus, a perpetrator who engages in the transfer of civilians likely has the intent to produce the adverse consequences, and accordingly their actions could constitute domicide.

We could, however, imagine a British administrator who does not possess this intent, yet still engages in the practice of transferring civilians into an occupied territory and thus contributes to the adverse consequences. He might be less responsible than his compatriots, although he likely could not avoid responsibility altogether. This might be one of the only distinctions between post-colonial and colonial transfers of civilians: we can conceive of this (perhaps negligent) British administrator, whereas we cannot conceive of a Burmese individual 'negligently' burning down the homes of Rohingyas. Yet when we turn to moral responsibility, the distinction may disappear, as the Burmese individual's responsibility may be mitigated by the impact of those British policies on her community. In effect, the responsibility appears similar.

10.4.3. Moral Indefensibility

Feinberg uses the concept of moral indefensibility to refer to "actions and omissions that have no adequate justification or excuse".[66] A justification changes the status of an act itself, so that an act that was otherwise impermissible or wrong (like deporting) becomes a permissible act. An excuse, however, does not change the status of the act. The act is still wrong, but the person acting is considered 'not blameworthy' for the act. I consider several potential justifications here and one potential excuse.

---

[66] *Ibid.*, p. 108.

10.4.3.1. Colonial Transfer of Civilians

One justification that might be offered draws on the problem I noted earlier with respect to migrants and homogenous communities. The British could claim that the Burmese people only stood to benefit from the introduction of new, diverse civilians into their communities. They could claim it should always be permissible for individuals to migrate when it is done in accordance with the law. By these lights, any discomfort on the part of the Burmese could be blamed on racism or xenophobia. However, this justification ignores the role the British government played in transferring civilians, and the role that they played in structuring the Burmese society so that the Burmese people suffered direct harm as a result of the influx of civilians.

A more likely defence that could be offered by the British (or other colonial powers) is that the British only did what was necessary to maintain control over and provide security for the Burmese people. This sort of consequentialist justification could be used to dismiss any harms that came from their actions, as long as the British were successful in maintaining security for the Burmese people. Taking this defence a bit further, they might even claim that they would be justified in their actions as long as they *intended* to provide security for the Burmese people, regardless of whether or not they were successful. Such a flat-footed consequentialist justification is not persuasive either, given that the argument could permit mass violence against a portion of the Burmese people in service of providing security for the rest of the Burmese people.

10.4.3.2. Post-Colonial Deportation of Rohingya

Turning now to a justification that might be offered by some Burmese today who claim that Rohingyas are not Burmese, and therefore they have no right to live in Rakhine State. Ibrahim is of the view that members of "the military, ethnic extremists, Buddhist fundamentalists and the NLD" [the political party National League for Democracy] think that "the Rohingyas have no right to be in the country. Time and again it is written that they are 'Bengalis' and should live in their own country – Bangladesh".[67] Chapter 11 below analyses this in further detail than this chapter warrants. Here we simply note that Ibrahim claims that this narrative developed in the years following the end of colonial rule, as the military gradually

---

[67] Ibrahim, pp. 16-17, see above note 3.

"created a new logic whereby only Burman Buddhists could really be loyal citizens".[68] Government officials repeat the narrative that the Rohingyas are really Bengali migrants, and the national laws do not recognize most Rohingyas as full citizens,[69] but Muslims have lived in today's Rakhine State for centuries. Chapters 6 and 8 above discuss the migration from today's Bangladesh into Rakhine during the British colonial period. This chapter need not address these factual issues, except to note that under international law the Rohingyas born in Rakhine should be granted citizenship by the Burmese government, and in any event there is no defence for their forced removal from their homes and villages.

Burmese who participate in forced deportations of Rohingyas might offer one excuse, and it is related to the distributive and substantive justice problems I noted at the beginning of this chapter. They might claim that since they (or their families or their communities) were harmed by the British and their colonial practice of transferring civilians into Burma, and the British were not held responsible, they should not be held responsible for the parallel harms they are causing to the Rohingyas. Such an excuse should not be successful, but as I noted earlier, the claim should not be ignored. There must be a mechanism for acknowledging wrongdoing on the part of colonial powers, in order to validate and acknowledge the harms suffered by the Burmese people. But the fact that this mechanism does not exist yet does not provide a defence to those who perpetrate harms against the Rohingyas. It does not justify their actions, nor does it provide a reason to withhold blame from the participants.

10.4.4. Rights Violation

The final criterion of a wrongful act of harm requires that the harm constitute a rights violation. Feinberg defines a right as a "valid claim which an individual can make in either or both of two directions".[70] The first involves claims that could be made against specific individuals to meet their obligations, or as demands for non-interference.[71] The second involves claims against the state to meet their obligations, or as demands for non-

---

[68] *Ibid.*, p. 17.

[69] Socialist Republic of the Union of Burma, Burma Citizenship Law, 15 October 1982 (https://www.legal-tools.org/doc/d3e586/).

[70] Feinberg, 1984, p. 109, see above note 2.

[71] *Ibid.*

interference, or "claims to the legal enforcement of the valid claims he has against other private citizens".[72]

Some claims will be both moral claims against an individual, and legal claims against the state. Criminal acts, for instance, will usually involve both moral and legal claims. The forced transfer of persons is a crime in most jurisdictions in the world, so there is almost certainly a legal right not to be subjected to these sorts of violations (or the results thereof). However, even if the transfer of civilians does not constitute a legal rights violation, it is a moral rights violation. A moral right, according to Feinberg, is "a claim backed by valid reasons and addressed to the conscience of the claimee or to public opinion".[73] Based on the well-being interests account of the harm of the transfer of civilians, it seems that there are valid reasons to think that individuals have a moral claim right to be free from these harms, whether we consider natural rights or rights that we have from being part of a particular community or having a particular sort of home. The right to move freely (within reason) and maintain control over one's own body (within reason) and to maintain the ability to associate with particular individuals (again, within reason) are seriously violated by the transfer of civilians. Accordingly, based on the foregoing analysis, perpetrators of these wrongs, such as the British as a colonial power, the Burmese state that is sanctioning the displacement of Rohingyas, and the corresponding individual members of these groups, engage in wrongful acts of harm.

10.5. Conclusion: Post-Colonial Alternative Justice Mechanisms?

I have established that the transfer of civilians, during both colonial and post-colonial periods, constitutes a serious harm to individuals and collectives. I have also established that the current system of international criminal law cannot account for at least one of these sorts of harms, and possibly both. The next step, which I cannot fully explore here, is to consider what alternative mechanisms could be created to properly acknowledge these harms and attribute responsibility.

Given the length of time that has passed since the end of the colonial era, most individuals will not be available to participate in truth commissions, in Myanmar or in other post-colonial communities. Accordingly,

---

[72] *Ibid.*

[73] *Ibid.*, p. 110.

any truth-telling that occurs will not necessarily be first-person accounts. Instead, we might imagine a form of truth-telling that provides for the public exhibition of historical records and accounts of population transfers from the colonial period. Such an exhibition would not focus on punishment like an international criminal trial, nor would it focus on reconciliation. Instead, the focus would be on acknowledgement, and perhaps on collective accountability and apology, should representatives of colonial powers be willing to participate. But it seems that the acknowledgement is the crucial aspect of the process, and the aspect over which the post-colonial community has the most control.

These processes should occur simultaneously with justice mechanisms aimed at establishing harm and wrongdoing for current situations relating to population transfer, whether those mechanisms are criminal, truth-focused, or a combination of the two. Justice demands that all of these harms and wrongs, regardless of when they occurred, must be brought into daylight.

11

The Importance of Hearing
Colonial Wrongs in Myanmar

Kyaw Yin Hlaing[*]

11.1. Introduction

The three Anglo-Burmese wars between 1824 and 1885 resulted in most of modern-day Myanmar being added to the British Empire. 'Ministerial Burma' (which included the central lowlands, and the coastal areas of Rakhine and Tanintharyi) was administered directly, while the so-called 'frontier areas' (the Chin, Kachin, and Shan areas) were ruled indirectly through existing local authorities. Except for a brief period during World War II when it was occupied by the Japanese, Myanmar remained under British control until independence on 4 January 1948. During this period, the colonial authorities committed specific acts and instituted policies which have been felt as 'wrongs' and given rise to grievances in the post-colonial period.

This chapter focuses on current perceptions of colonial wrongs. It is less concerned with the factual detail of what happened during the colonial period than with how perceived colonial wrongs have shaped national discourse since independence. In taking this approach, it aims to highlight both the importance of understanding colonial wrongs as an influence on policy and attitudes in Myanmar, and the danger of focusing on these historical issues as grievances to be redressed. It stresses the active role that

---

[*] Dr. **Kyaw Yin Hlaing** is the Executive Director of the Center for Diversity and National Harmony in Yangon, Myanmar (since 2015). He has previously served as an Assistant Professor at the National University of Singapore (2001-2007) and the City University of Hong Kong (2007-2013), where he was also the Coordinator of the Development Studies Program (2008-2013) and Associate Director of the Southeast Asian Research Center (2012-2013). He was the Director of the Political Dialogue Program of the Myanmar Peace Center and an Adviser to the President of the Union of Myanmar (2013-2015). He holds a B.A. (Hons.) from Mandalay University, and M.A. (Government) and Ph.D. degrees from Cornell University. He received the 2020 M.C. Bassiouni Justice Award.

political actors and community leaders in Myanmar have played in shaping the memory of colonial grievances, inevitably resulting in an intertwining of these issues with domestic political agendas. In particular, it notes the extent to which nationalists invoke colonial grievances as a justification for restrictive policies and racist attitudes. Any discussion of colonial grievances in Myanmar needs to be aware of this context and approach the issue carefully in order to avoid exacerbating existing problems and tensions.

The first part of the chapter focuses on four specific grievances (immigration of foreigners, exploitation of farmers, exploitation of local women, and 'divide and rule' policies), noting their prevalence in current discussions. The second part turns to the ways in which colonial grievances have been used by influential actors and have shaped domestic laws and policies. The third section considers the situation in Rakhine State as a case study of the ways in which colonial grievance narratives can exacerbate inter-communal tensions. The fourth part follows on from the discussion of the situation in Rakhine State to consider how attitudes towards the international community have been influenced by the memory of colonization, particularly but not exclusively in the context of Rakhine State. The final section considers what these facts mean for a discussion of colonial wrongs in Myanmar and the risks and benefits of such an approach.

11.2. Perceived Colonial Grievances

The experience of colonization was marked by a loss of control – politically, economically and socially. Within these broad themes popular understandings of colonial wrongs have focused on a number of specific policies and developments. Among the most commonly invoked 'wrongs' are: the bringing of Indian and other migrants to Myanmar; the exploitation of local farmers by foreigners; the exploitation of local women by foreigners; and 'divide and rule' policies. What these issues share is a sense that current problems or (perceived) injustices are the result of acts or policies by the colonial authorities.

One issue Burmese nationalists and politicians regularly refer to as a major colonial wrong is the influx of foreigners into what is today Myanmar, brought by the colonial administration. During the colonial period people from different parts of the British Empire were able to enter colonial Burma freely. By the time of independence this had resulted in the presence of a number of immigrant populations. One that received particular negative attention both during and after the colonial period were immigrants from the Indian sub-continent. Immigrant communities lived in their own enclaves and their interactions with indigenous people were limited to market places.[1] The association of these immigrants with the colonial regime, and the fact that Indians were preferred over locals for positions in the administration, civil service, and police, added to tensions relating to access to land and economic opportunities. Popular narratives have continued to frame these groups as 'outsiders' rather than seeing them as part of the social and demographic makeup of Myanmar. This has encouraged racial intolerance and discrimination, which are linked to fears that these 'immigrant' populations will (try to) take control, through force, by becoming the demographic majority, or by economic means.

To illustrate with situations in colonial Rangoon, a large Indian community lived in the same neighbourhood in downtown Rangoon and had very little interaction with the local people. Moreover, a prominent Myanmar political writer described:

> Betel nut sellers, donut sellers, cloth merchants, store owners and wholesalers, all are Indians. Indians are everywhere: shoe makers to factory owners, policemen to high court judges, medical orderlies to physicians, prison guards to prison wardens, all positions are monopolized by Indians.[2]

A nationalist leader also recalled that the Bamar and other indigenous people felt like foreigners in their own land. The same nationalist leader stated:

> In those days, if you want to get things done, you must be able to speak Indian. Otherwise, you would be looked down upon. Of course, we loathed Indians and the colonial administration because of that. To tell you the truth, such negative and hostile sentiments by indigenous people against Indians served as the underlying reasons for the anti-Indian and anti-Muslim riots in colonial Burma.[3]

The negative attitude Bamar Buddhists developed against Muslims underlay all anti-Muslim riots throughout the post-colonial period. The

---

[1]   John Furnivalle, *Colonial Policy and Practice*, New York University Press, 1956, pp. 303-312.
[2]   Maung Thein Pe, "Indo-Burma Conflict", *Socialism and Our Burma*, Saok Phyant Cheeyay, Rangoon, 1954, p. 174.
[3]   Interview with a nationalist leader, 23 March 1998.

Buddhist organizations that led the anti-Indian and anti-Muslim riots in colonial Burma continued to exist, and to disseminate anti-Muslim narratives, in the post-colonial period. Some religious leaders went so far as to say that keeping Muslims in check was a way of saving the country from the negative impacts of colonial wrongs.[4]

The questions of economic exploitation and the exploitation of women are also linked to these fears of domination by 'immigrant' populations. Like most colonies, colonial Burma suffered considerable economic exploitation. The economy during the colonial period was largely controlled by British companies, while immigrants from other parts of the British Empire were employed as labourers. In addition to these general trends, popular memory singles out the role of the '*Chettyars*'. These Indian money-lenders provided loans to Burmese farmers. The local farmers lack of financial knowledge, combined with the economic depression in the 1930s, saw many become unable to repay the loans and then forced to forfeit their lands to these '*Chettyars*'. A Karen farmer noted in 1928:

> Tersely and pointedly speaking, Chettyar banks are fiery dragons that parch every land that has the misfortune of coming under their wicked creeping. They are a hardhearted lot that will wring out every drop of blood from their victims without compunction, for the sake of their own interest. One proof of this: 30 or 40 years ago, nine of 10 villagers in the country owned land; now it is the reverse, and the one that has anything, has the same tied up in the hand of the Chettyar rightly [is indebted to the Chettyar] [...] Suffice it to say that the swindling, cheating, deception and oppression by the Chettyars in the country, particularly towards the ignorant folks, are well-known and are to a large extent responsible for the present impoverishment of the land.[5]

Recalling how local people suffered at the hands of '*Chettyars*', a prominent nationalist leader and politician, Thakin Chit Maung, made a similar assessment of the lives of farmers in the 1930s:

> All residents of my village including my family were farmers. We did not understand the modern capitalist economy. Chettyars took advantage of us. We lost our land, money and houses. That's why many young people from our village

---

4   Interview with a monk activist, 3 May 2004.
5   Report of the Burma Provincial Banking Enquiry Committee, 1929/30, vol. I, p. 31.

joined the Saya San Peasant Rebellion. I got a chance to see him (Saya San). He was trying to right the wrong inflicted on our people. That's why we all viewed him as our national hero and leader.[6]

One of the main focuses for concerns about the social and societal impact of colonization and of immigration has been the question of religion. Although the majority of the population are Buddhists, concern is often expressed about Christianity and Islam taking over and wiping out Buddhism in the country. The two main perceived risks in this respect are that members of these religions will have more children than Buddhists, and that they will marry and convert Buddhist women. In both cases, the received wisdom is that this will eventually lead to Buddhists becoming a minority population. The association of these risks with colonialism is due to the perception that the presence of considerable populations of Christians and Muslims dates to the colonial period. In general, Christianity was actively promoted by missionaries who came to Myanmar during the colonial period. Islam was mostly brought less formally, via the immigration of Muslims. Although, it should be noted that there were already Muslim populations in Myanmar before colonization. These differences – notably the fact that members of the current Christian population are seen as the descendants of locals who were converted, while Muslims are the descendants of immigrating Muslims – may help to explain why the Muslims have been subject to particular negative perceptions. Moreover, religion has become another marker of difference for the already ethnically different population who are identified as immigrants.

The current concern with the idea of Muslims marrying Buddhist women engages the concern about loss of social identity to conversion and to the risk of immigrant groups pushing out locals. At the same time, they reflect traditional attitudes towards women, who are assumed to need protection rather than seen as possessing agency. They also encode the idea that women who marry outside their community will lose their social identity and take on that of their husband, in this instance particularly religious identity.

The continuing relevancy of perceived grievances relating to the descendants of people who entered Myanmar during the colonial period highlights the failure of integration. This failure is itself blamed on colo-

---

[6] Interview with a nationalist leader, 12 September 2002.

nization, which is seen as having created a plural (rather than integrated) society in Myanmar. In addition to being blamed for the endurance of tensions between the original population and the descendants of those who immigrated during the colonial period, colonial policies are blamed for the fragmentation of society and tensions between groups within Myanmar. To this day colonial 'divide and rule' policies are cited as a cause of inter-communal tensions. It is particularly common to hear such complaints in the context of the peace process where they are invoked by governmental actors as an explanation for the origins of ethnic armed conflict. Representatives of the ethnic armed organizations also frequently mention colonial legacies as both a cause of conflict with the Burmese authorities, and as a complicating factor in attempts to promote co-operation among ethnic armed organizations and, more generally, the ethnic groups which they represent. It is notable that since independence many Burmese politicians and administrators viewed the so-called 'divide and rule' policy of the colonial administration as the main source of ethnic armed conflicts in Myanmar. The post-colonial school textbooks and government propaganda argued that some ethnic minority members engaged in armed struggles mainly because colonial administrators had placed a wedge between the Bamar and ethnic minority political leaders. Until 1988, many citizens appeared to have shared this 'blame colonialism' view, such that whenever they did not like the sentiments expressed by someone, they would refer to him or her as having a 'colonial mentality'. It was only after the nationwide protest that toppled the military-dominated socialist regime, that people started attributing more blame to the incompetent and corrupt authoritarian government than to the colonial administration. Nevertheless, officials from successive military governments between 1962 and 2010, as well as analysts close to these autocratic governments, continued to suggest that Myanmar is still being affected by the colonial administration's 'divide and rule' policy.[7]

Discussion of this issue often implies that the ethnic divisions were deliberately created by the colonial administration and therefore frames the legacy of these policies as a 'colonial wrong'. To an extent this may be true. The colonial administration and British observers were largely responsible for the codification of ethnic identities and ascribed particular

---

[7] The author personally witnessed, at talks and seminars, analysts and former officials from the military regime blaming colonial rule for most socio-political and economic problems in Myanmar.

characteristics to different ethnic groups. They were also probably aware of the advantages, in terms of maintaining supremacy, of ensuring divisions among the colonized peoples. On the other hand, the intent of such policies should not be overstated. The codification of ethnic groups represented a particular worldview as much as deliberate policies of 'divide and rule'. Moreover, the differences in administration between different parts of colonial Myanmar were, to a great extent, dictated by pragmatic considerations of the ease and benefits of direct versus indirect control. Such divisions were largely driven by economic rather than political considerations. Nonetheless, the belief that the British played off different groups against each other and the fear that on the one hand the Bamar (particularly the political elite and the Defence Services) and on the other the international community are engaged in similar policies to weaken inter-communal unity are very present.

11.3. The Use and Abuse of Colonial Grievance Narratives in National Debate

The previous section highlighted a number of issues that are perceived as colonial wrongs and which have an ongoing relevance. Since independence in 1948, a range of laws and policies have aimed to (or claimed to aim to) rectify these wrongs. The perceived problems left by the colonial period have also been taken up by various influential leaders of the post-colonial era and used to bolster their position, to rally support, or to explain current problems. A particular problem has been the use of colonial grievances and the related fears of being taken over and exploited by foreigners, to bolster nationalist (and ethno-nationalist) agendas. This has exacerbated the problems noted above with colonial grievances being used to entrench divisions based on ethnicity and religion. Righting colonial wrongs has become a way to justify discrimination and racial hatred.

Soon after independence, the government enacted the 1954 Buddhist Women's Special Marriage and Succession Act, which aimed at protecting the rights of Buddhist women married to non-Buddhist men. Needless to say, this law was introduced to protect the Buddhist Burmese who were married to 'foreigners' or men of different faith groups.

In 1962, the military took control of the country and established the military-dominated 'Socialist Government'. The Socialist Government introduced a number of policies and measures, with claim that they would bring 'genuine independence' to the people. In the name of 'liberating' the country's economy from foreign companies and compradors, the Socialist Government nationalized the economy and demonetized the largest currency note. The Socialist Government also passed a new Tenancy Law in 1963, which was designed to protect local farmers. Although the Socialist Government was toppled by mass protests in 1988, its anti-colonial economic policies were initially welcomed by a large majority of poor people. A farmer who wholeheartedly supported the Socialist Government recalled:

> My family lost everything we had during the depression in 1930. We never recovered. We genuinely thought that the Socialist policies would bring the country's economy back into the hands of the majority people. We welcomed the nationalization plan. Most people would not admit this, as the socialist policies led Myanmar to become a 'Least Developed Country (LDC)'.[8]

Beyond economics, the Socialist Government also tried to liberate the country from the influence of Western culture, for example, by stopping the teaching of university courses in English and the wearing of western dress at social and official functions. The leader of the Socialist Party, Ne Win, infamously disrupted a Christmas party with a Western music band without knowing that the party had been organized by his own children. Throughout the 1980s, popular magazines in Myanmar were not allowed to print any photographs with people in Western dress.

The Socialist Government tried to right the problem with immigrants by enacting a new citizenship law. The 1982 Citizenship Law is a good example of both the ways that rectifying perceived colonial wrongs have been included in laws and the problems with the way these issues have been approached. The Citizenship Law sets out an extremely restrictive view of who belongs in Myanmar. It creates three categories of citizenship, which provide a formal structure for defining some citizens as belonging less and having fewer rights than others. These distinctions are based on ethnicity and the duration (in terms of both time and number of generations) of residence in Myanmar. The law provides 'taing-yin-tha' – defined as members of ethnic groups which were settled in Myanmar before 1823 (that is before the start of colonization) – with a particular privileged status. These factors suggest a link between the Citizenship Law

---

[8] Interview with a former leader of the Peasant Asyayone, 22 November 1998.

and the perceived immigration of foreigners during and after the colonial period. This link and the association with fears of being ruled by foreigners were made explicit in the speech given by Ne Win on the adoption of the law:

> During the period between 1824 and the time we regained independence in January 1948, foreigners, or aliens, entered our country unhindered under various pretexts. [...] We, the natives or Burmese nationals, were unable to shape our own destiny. We were subjected to the manipulations of others from 1824 to 4 January 1948.[9]

Later in the same speech, he explains that the law allows persons who entered the country during the colonial period to be citizens as they were no longer able to return to their places of origin:

> Such being their predicament, we accept them as citizens, say. But leniency on humanitarian ground cannot be such as to endanger ourselves. We can leniently give them the right to live in this country and to carry on a livelihood in the legitimate way. But we will have to leave them out in matters involving the affairs of the country and the destiny of the State. This is not because we hate them. If we were to allow them to get into positions where they can decide the destiny of the State and if they were to betray us we would be in trouble.[10]

These statements highlight the fear that the local population will lose control and links this to the colonial period, both directly and through the emphasis on these people as individuals who immigrated during the colonial era. The speech also makes clear that the intention of the 1982 Citizenship Law was to resolve a problem that was a legacy of the colonial period; namely, the presence in the country of various people of different ethnicities and origins, who had themselves or whose ancestors had arrived in Myanmar during the colonial period and whose citizenship status was (at least partially as a result of this migration) unclear or contested. It is significant for the framing of colonial wrongs in Myanmar that these people are seen as a problem and as a threat. The majority of those concerned were not British or formal representatives of the colonial power, but members of other colonized peoples. However, there is no expression

---

[9] U Ne Win's Speech on the Citizenship Law, *Working People's Daily*, 9 October, 1982.
[10] *Ibid.*

of solidarity on this basis and no sense that these people might also be considered victims of colonization. Instead, the presence of these people is itself considered a problem and they are progressively framed as perpetrators of that wrong.

As a means of addressing the perceived problem of populations who immigrated during the colonial period and the danger of these groups taking control, the law is problematic. It gestures towards the idea of integration, that is, of bringing these groups into the social and political structures of the majority population, by allowing third generation 'associate' and 'naturalized' citizens to become full citizens. However, at the same time it entrenches a distinction between 'taing-yin-tha' and other citizens and formalizes the idea that some citizens may be discriminated against based on ethnicity and duration of residence. In doing so, it perpetuates the visible presence of a distinct population identified as a threat and as a residue of colonialism. The restriction of the rights of 'associate' and 'naturalized' citizens, for example, with regard to the right to form political parties and stand for election, reinforce these attitudes.

The adoption of laws and Ne Win's speech demonstrate the attitudes towards people who immigrated during the colonial period that was being put forward by the government. However, it is important to remember that the 1982 Citizenship Law was adopted following popular consultations (although it is unclear how much impact these had on the final text of the law). Despite the criticisms of external actors it remains widely accepted and popular with the local people. This suggests that the attitudes it puts forward, and the concerns to which it sought to respond, have an ongoing resonance with the population as a whole.

This popular endorsement may reflect the extent to which colonial wrongs and particularly the fear of loss of sovereignty have been internalized by the population. When the military had once again taken control of the country under the name of the State Law and Order Restoration Council ('SLORC') after the Socialist Government, it reinterpreted the 1982 Citizenship Law and distinguished ethnic nationality ('taing-yin-tha') and non-ethnic nationality citizens by formally issuing a list of 135 indigenous races in Myanmar. The Socialist Government had considered all full citizens as 'taing-yin-tha', allowed the third generation of 'associate' or 'naturalized' citizens to become full citizens, and at least theoretically, all full citizens had equal rights. Under the SLORC, those who do not belong to one of the officially recognized 'national races' can never be 'taing-yin-

tha'. Under the 2008 Constitution written by the military government, only '*taing-yin-tha*' citizens can run for the presidency and the vice-presidency. When new citizenship identification cards were issued to the public, Muslims were not allowed to claim their ethnicity as Bamar; they could only choose to be recognized as Bengali, Pakistani, or Indian. Although the military government was terribly unpopular and its Constitution was rejected by the pro-democracy movement, its reinterpretation of the citizenship law was rarely questioned by a large majority of '*taing-yin-tha*' citizens.

The Socialist Government and the subsequent military governments also 'abused' colonial grievances to destroy the reputations of their opponents. Both regimes referred to their critics as 'informants of the (neo-colonialist) Central Intelligence Agency'. The military government also repeatedly tried to denigrate Daw Aung San Suu Kyi by highlighting her marriage to an Englishman – "citizen of the country that enslaved Myanmar and masterminded the murder of the national hero, her father, General Aung San".[11] In addition, there is evidence that the military government actively promoted negative attitudes towards Muslims. One activist monk revealed that he had published some anti-Muslim pamphlets in the early 2000s, with the help of some officers from the military government. Some government officials later admitted that anti-Muslim narratives and discourses were disseminated whenever the pubic was unhappy with the government. A retired government official explained:

> The anti-Muslim sentiment among the Myanmar people has been so strong since the colonial days. It is easy to divert public attention by spreading rumors about how Muslims have abused Buddhists – especially Buddhists. In the early 1990s, the Mandalay Regional Commander tried to find a ruby that disappeared when the British took over Mandalay Palace. There was a rumor at the time that the ruby had been hidden on the body of the Mahamuni Buddha statue. People have been putting gold leaves on the body of the statue for several decades and those who tried to find the ruby had to break the gold on the body apart. Many monks and Buddhist laypeople were very upset with what the regional commander had done, and planned to organize a protest. However, the

---

[11] Kyaw Yin Hlaing, "Daw Aung San Suu Kyi: A Burmese Dissident Democrat," in Lowell Dittmer, ed., *Burma or Myanmar? The Struggle for National Identity,* World Scientific, 2010, p. 135.

planned protest turned into an anti-Muslim riot when someone came into the meeting and said that his niece had been
raped by her Muslim employer. This is one of several examples of how the military government abused long-held public
grievances to serve their interests.[12]

Additionally under the military government, government newspapers regularly mentioned the massacres by the British during the colonial
period as a colonial grievance.

It should be noted that the public did not hold the same level of interest or concern across all colonial grievance narratives disseminated by
the military government. The government's anti-colonial propaganda was
made more effective when reinforced by other influential societal actors,
who spread similar narratives. For example, many influential religious
leaders shared anti-Muslim narratives in their daily interactions and
through their sermons. A study conducted by the author in 2004 and 2005
indicated that the public believed in the anti-Muslim rumours spread by
the government mainly because other popular religious leaders had endorsed these rumours. This may also explain why agents from the military
government worked with some religious leaders in promoting anti-
Muslim sentiments. In contrast, popular opinion was resolutely un-
swayed by official narratives about the then-opposition leader, Daw Aung
San Suu Kyi. A popular writer went so far as to say: "In fact, the military
government helped her [Daw Aung San Suu Kyi] out. The more anti-
Aung San Suu Kyi propaganda the government disseminated, the more
people loved her".[13]

The Thein Sein Administration, which had come into power after
the 2010 elections held by the military government, stopped using anti-
Muslim narratives to divert public attention. However, because the Thein
Sein Government did not take effective actions to contain the activities of
anti-Muslim nationalist groups, many anti-Muslim riots broke out in various parts of the country. In order to win the support of Buddhist nationalists, the government passed four 'race and religion laws' in 2015. These
laws make inter-religious marriages and the conversion of women, on
marriage to a non-Buddhist spouse, more difficult. In both cases the specific concern with Buddhist women helps make clear the interest of the

---

[12] Interview with a retired government official, 1 November 2004.
[13] Interview with a writer, 4 November 2004.

laws. They are less concerned with women's rights so much as with the perceived danger of women marrying out of their community. This is seen as potentially exploitative of the women, hence the need to protect them from such marriages. Buddhist nationalists framed the 2015 Race and Religion Protection Laws as necessary to protect Myanmar as a Buddhist nation and to prevent the country being overrun by Muslims.[14]

It is not, however, inevitable that anti-colonial measures will be popular or will always continue to be popular. As evidenced by the 1963 Tenancy Law mentioned above, although the measures were popular at the time and people had believed they would bring benefits to local farmers, labourers, and businesses which had failed to flourish even after independence, with the benefit of hindsight it is clear that these measures in fact had a negative impact on the economy and are therefore now criticized by locals.

11.4. Colonial Grievances Narratives in Rakhine State

The inter-communal tensions in Rakhine State and the narratives constructed by different communities around the outbreaks of violence provide a demonstration of the ways in which colonial grievances are invoked and can have a toxic legacy.

Throughout the colonial period, Rakhine State, like other parts of Myanmar, saw an influx of foreign workers, including a large number from the Indian sub-continent. Many of these immigrants were Muslims, which added to the tensions with the primarily Buddhist population. The latent tensions erupted into violence in 1942. The context within which this fighting occurred was the retreat of the British in the face of Japanese attacks. The Muslims largely aligned with and were armed by the British, while the ethnic Rakhine aligned with other ethnic groups who seized this opportunity to fight for liberation from Britain with the support of the Japanese. Despite these larger alliances the fighting in Rakhine State was almost entirely between local communities, and although the broader conflict may have been a factor it cannot be entirely blamed for the brutality of the violence.

The 1942 violence continues to be invoked today as background to inter-communal tensions and is felt as an unresolved issue by members of both Rakhine and Rohingya communities. Although the context of World

---

[14] Interview with a religious leader, 9 December 2018.

War II and the extent to which this was inter-communal violence, rather than violence by the colonial power against the colonized population(s), means that it does not fall neatly into the category of what might be considered 'colonial wrongs', in Rakhine State it is perceived as a colonial grievance and highlights the pre-Independence tensions around the Muslim population. The Muslim population was already seen as having come to Myanmar under the aegis of the colonial power, and with their support; they were therefore associated with the colonial power. The Muslims fighting for the British rather than with those calling for independence reflects this perceived alignment with the colonial power rather than the native population.

In the post-colonial period, the fears associated with this population have focused around the idea that they would try to take control of Rakhine State and will become the majority population by procreating faster, marrying local women, and converting Buddhists. More than 60 percent of the participants of a survey with 1,200 Rakhine community members believed that Muslims would take over Rakhine State if they had the opportunity, and almost all survey participants believed that the Muslim population has grown at an alarming rate and should be controlled.[15] Some Rakhine nationalists openly stated that Muslims are merely guests in Rakhine State and that they should not act like they are owners of the state.[16] For current purposes the question of how realistic these fears are is less significant than the extent to which they reflect the (perceived) colonial grievances of the Rakhine (and more broadly the Burmese): the presence of immigrants, and the loss of economic, social, and political control of their country. These factors have contributed to subsequent outbreaks of inter-communal violence and the increasing tension between communities. Moreover, the colonial legacy of segregated rather than cohesive communities has contributed to the split between the communities and the difficulties in promoting reconciliation.

Rakhine nationalists and extremist community leaders have used these fears to strengthen their positions. The positioning of the Muslim population as a residue of colonialism and a source of ongoing injustice helps to frame them as a problem to be resolved or a wrong to be re-

---

[15] The survey was conducted by a group of young researchers under the supervision of the author.
[16] Interviews with five Rakhine community leaders, December 2012.

dressed. The colonial grievances narrative also helps to understand why the fear that the Muslims mean to take control of Rakhine State by becoming a majority and/or driving out the Rakhine is so pervasive. It is this fear that drives popular support for repressive measures targeting the Muslim population and enables Rakhine to see themselves as the victims of the problems in Rakhine State. Not surprisingly, although they disliked the military government, a large majority of Rakhine people supported the government's tough policies against Muslims in Rakhine State. Many Rakhine community members believed they needed to discriminate Muslims and to contain their expansion, in order for Rakhine State not to become a Muslim state.[17]

It should be noted that negative narratives were not spread only by the Rakhine. Muslims have also developed anti-Rakhine discourses on the basis of their own grievances. The clashing narratives of the Rakhine and the Muslims have fuelled inter-communal tension. They promote backward-looking policies – ones that aim to resolve problems from the past – rather than forward-looking policies such as efforts to promote development and inter-communal harmony, which would help all communities in Rakhine State. In this way, colonial grievance narratives have contributed to the negative nature of the discourse and the tendency to treat policies on key issues such as citizenship as a zero-sum game, benefiting either the Rakhine or the Muslims but never both.

Within the Rakhine community, the framing of the presence of the Muslims as a 'colonial wrong' to be redressed has contributed to the dominance of nationalists and the limited space for divergent views. The communal violence that took place in 2012 and afterwards provided further fuel for nationalists to come up with more anti-Muslim narratives and a revisionist, anti-Muslim history of Rakhine State. Moderate Rakhine leaders may feel unable to promote greater interaction with Muslims or reconciliation measures because these would be so unpopular with the population as a whole. To take such a position therefore risks both loss of influence (as the leaders' views are no longer aligned with those of their community) and even attack from extremist elements.

---

[17] Ten Focus Group Discussions with Rakhine community leaders from 2016 to 2018.

11.5. Understanding Attitudes to the International Community in the Context of Colonial Grievances

The colonial history and residual fears of loss of control as well as the belief that external actors may use 'divide and rule' tactics to try and weaken local actors and undermine cohesion help to explain local attitudes towards the international community. In this context it should be noted that many people in Myanmar have little understanding of the international community and particularly of the variety of actors involved; they do not understand the different roles of bodies such as embassies, non-governmental organizations ('NGOs'), UN agencies, and the International Criminal Court or International Court of Justice.

The situation in Rakhine State provides an illustration of the problem. The Rakhine and other groups see the international community as biased in favour of the 'Rohingya' and as oblivious to or uncaring about the former's suffering. In serious conversations with more than a thousand Rakhine community members between 2012 and 2020, all of them wondered why the international community did not wish to take into account the sufferings of the Rakhine people. Many of them noted that there were bad people in both communities and that all communities in Rakhine State suffered in the communal violence. Many Rakhine therefore wondered why, even then, the international community and media only sympathized with the Muslim community and why members of the international community and media were not prepared to say that there were perpetrators in all communities. One Rakhine woman activist once asked the author:

> The UN and other international communities always talk about conflict sensitivity. What we do must be conflict-sensitive. Why do they not act as they preach? What they have done on the ground has divided the communities further. Some Rakhine nationalist leaders have gone so far as to say that what the international community is doing can split Rakhine State. Please tell the international organizations and media that they should be more conflict-sensitive.[18]

By and large, the Rakhine and nationalists in Myanmar see the actions of the international community as interfering with national sovereignty. Rather than being taken as an attempt to assist, the involvement of the international community in situations such as Rakhine carries over-

---

[18] Personal conversation with a Rakhine woman activist, 8 August 2017.

tones of colonization that feed into fears of loss of power, control of land, and economic opportunities. This fear of loss of sovereignty contributes to the rejection of mechanisms such as the UN's Fact-Finding Mission or international criminal justice approaches. To accept such a mechanism would be to allow the international community to assert control over the highest powers in Myanmar and to dismiss Myanmar's justice system as inadequate; an assertion of power and of superiority that recall colonial attitudes.

The question of double standards also arises in this context. It is rarely explicitly invoked as such, except in so far as other groups complain that their sufferings are ignored or dismissed by actors focusing on 'the Rohingya'. However, this concern can be seen as underlying some of the resistance to the international community. Myanmar and its people are aware of their comparative lack of power and that no similar condemnation has focused on the wrongs done to them or others during the colonial period. This may be framed as a question of the international community bullying weaker states rather than as a matter of double standards, but the complaint of injustice underlies both. Although currently UN agencies and international organizations operating in Rakhine State have tried to improve their relationship with the Rakhine community, and Rakhine community members have started saying less negative things about the UN and other international NGOs in Rakhine State, there is still a view that comments made at international symposiums and meetings organized by the UN and other international organizations are very one-sided. In addition, locals consider the position of one UN agency to be reflective of the stance of the entire UN system.

11.6. Conclusion: Benefits and Risks of using Colonial Grievances as a Framework for Discussing Problems in Myanmar

Like many other countries, modern Myanmar was shaped by the experience of colonization. The legacies of colonization can be seen in the demographics of the country, in its laws, and in the outlook of the population. Moreover, a shared understanding of colonial grievances – of the wrongs done by the colonial administration and never remedied – have become internalized as part of the history of Myanmar as understood by its inhabitants. However, this understanding of colonial grievances and the responses to it in law, policy, and perception are not value-neutral. This chapter has attempted to show how these grievances have been shaped and exploited by political actors, particularly nationalists, to support a specific agenda. In this way, the understanding of colonial grievances has contributed to the development of discriminatory policies, inter-communal tensions, and misogynistic policies. It has fuelled the spread of Buddhist nationalism and has been used to justify internal repression.

These observations are not intended as a rejection of the thesis that colonial wrongs should be examined through the lens of international law, nor of the arguments in favour of some form of reparation for colonial wrongs. Nor is there any intention to minimize the damage done by colonization, in Myanmar or elsewhere. They are however a warning about approaching the subject without careful consideration of the specific context of each country and its relations to its colonial past. Understanding the colonial history of Burma is helpful to understanding modern Myanmar, but taking at face value evaluations of colonial wrongs and implementing solutions put forward by actors interested in exploiting this history for political gain may be problematic. An approach to current issues which draws on the perceived colonial wrongs may help identify the fears, concerns, and priorities of the population or provide a basis for discussions on ways to heal divisions and promote inter-communal harmony. This is how I understand this anthology and the project of which it forms part. However, unless approached in a context-sensitive manner there is a risk that such discussions will strengthen the position of nationalists and be used to promote discriminatory policies and agenda. Moreover, if such a discussion is initiated or driven by international actors it is likely to be treated with suspicion by locals as external actors attempting to impose their own priorities and values on Myanmar.

It is important to ask what is the purpose of any discussion of colonial wrongs or of proposed reparation measures. The question of how such discussions will impact all populations in former colonies and the political discourse of these States must be considered; what is helpful in one context may be actively harmful in another. The focus of efforts to address colonial wrongs and the double standards of international law must be on measures which will help all peoples and promote sustainable peace. Promoting accountability and the legitimacy of international law are valid considerations, but are less important than the lives and well-being of the populations (of all kinds) living in former colonies. Myanmar, like many other countries, suffered grievous wrongs as a result of colonization. Wrongs which continue to have an impact today. Acknowledging the impact of colonization is a valuable step, and measures which take both the history and the perceived grievances into account have the potential to help heal these enduring grievances. However, such measures must be carefully designed and implemented so that they do not exacerbate discriminatory attitudes and policies or fuel dangerous political agenda.

PART IV:
OTHER FORMER COLONIAL TERRITORIES

12

On the Relevancy of
Chinese Colonial Grievances to International Law

LING Yan[*]

> *It is crucial that we understand the past*
> *if we are to address today's challenges.*
>
> LIU Daqun

Colonial grievances of one hundred years have been recorded in modern Chinese history. The grievances have a long-lasting impact on many aspects of China's positions on international law and diplomatic policies. The first part of this chapter recalls the Chinese history of the 'century of humiliation' when China was a semi-colonial and semi-feudal country. The second part of the chapter discusses the impact of the colonial grievances on China's attitude towards international law. It focuses on the issues concerning respect for sovereignty and territory integrity, non-interference in internal affairs and human rights, peaceful settlement of international disputes, and Japanese war crimes.

12.1. Past Colonial Wrongs

12.1.1. Colonial Wrongs Done to China by Colonial Powers

China has a history of some 5,000 years. Dynasties have been changed many times since the Qin Dynasty which united the whole land under its control for the first time, to the establishment of the present government in 1949. Mostly, the Han people ruled China, except in the Yuan Dynasty when Mongolians ruled China for about 100 years, and the Qing Dynasty when Manchu ruled China for about 300 years. However, China does not

---

[*] **LING Yan** is a Professor at China University of Political Science and Law (CUPL). She is Co-Director of CILRAP's LI Haopei Lecture Series.

consider itself as a colony in those days; instead, she identifies herself as a multi-ethnic country.

Colonial grievances of one hundred years have been recorded in the modern Chinese history since the late Qing Dynasty. The Western colonial powers wanted to do more business with China, while the Chinese feudal rulers adopted a policy of seclusion. The policy and measures taken by the Qing government to ban opium smoking and opium trade became a blasting fuse for the first Opium War in 1840. Great Britain opened the door of China by opium and forces. China was forced to sign the Treaty of Nanking, the first of several unequal treaties, on 29 August 1842 after China lost the war. The Qing government of China accepted all the proposals and clauses put forward by Britain, meeting most of their requirements.

According to the Treaty,[1] China lost parts of territory by ceding Hong Kong Island to the United Kingdom, severely damaging China's sovereignty and territory integrity. China opened up several cities as trading ports, allowing British businessmen to trade freely without being subjected to 'official licensing guild'. China also allowed British people to pay import-export taxes and custom duties in China based on a tax rate that China and Britain had jointly agreed. These articles of the Treaty undermined China's autonomy on trade and tariff matters. Furthermore, China paid a compensation of 21 million Yuan to the United Kingdom.

The next year, the British government forced the Qing government to conclude the Treaty of Humen as an appendix to the Treaty of Nanking, which redefined the most-favoured-nation treatment and consular jurisdiction enjoyed by Britain. In 1844 and 1845, following in British footsteps, the United States, France, Belgium, Sweden and other countries also coerced the Qing government to sign similar treaties, obtaining consular jurisdiction and missionary power in China in ways that further undermined China's sovereignty.

China's failure in the first Opium War and the conclusion of a series of unequal treaties have brought about fundamental changes in Chinese society. China gradually became a semi-colonial and semi-feudal country.

During a period of about one hundred years – the so-called 'century of humiliation' – China experienced many foreign invasions and wars,

---

[1]　WANG Tieya (ed.), *Zhongwai jiu yuezhang huibian* [a compilation of old treaties and agreements between China and foreign countries], SDX Joint Publishing Company, Beijing, 1957, vol. 1, p. 31.

including the following: the above-mentioned first Opium War with Britain in 1840–1842, then the second Opium War with Britain and France in 1856–1860, the Sino-French War in 1883–1885, the Sino-Japanese War in 1894–1895, the invasion of Germany troops to Jiaozhou Bay in 1897, the Siege of the International Legations in 1900, the Russo-Japanese War in 1904–1905 (a war in north-eastern China between Russia and Japan over the control of the Korean Peninsula and the Chinese Liaodong Peninsula), and the Japanese war of aggression against China in 1931–1945.

During these wars, the foreign troops massacred Chinese people on a large scale. For example, in 1900, the allied forces of eight powers burned, killed and plundered Tanggu Town, turning the town of more than 50,000 people into the ruins of nobody, and leaving only 100,000 people alive in Tianjin, which prior to the attack had one million inhabitants.[2] In short, these wars and invasions not only grossly violated China's sovereignty and territory integrity, but they also caused heavy casualties among the Chinese and destroyed the property of many Chinese families.

As a result of China's failure during these wars, the colonial powers forced China to sign 300 to 400 unequal treaties,[3] such as the Treaties of Tianjin with Britain, France, the United States and Russia in 1858, the Treaty of Aigun with Russia in 1858, the Treaties of Peking with Britain, France and Russia in 1860, the Treaty of Tianjin with France in 1885, the Treaty of Shimonoseki with Japan in 1895, the Kiautschou leasehold Treaty with Germany in 1898, and Boxer Protocol with 11 Western colonial powers in 1901.

Through such unequal treaties, China ceded her territory Hong Kong Island and Kowloon to Britain; Taiwan, the Pescadores and the Liaotung peninsula to Japan; and more than 1.5 million square kilometres of territory to Russia. In addition, 10 foreign states (Britain, Japan, France, Russia, Germany, the United States, Portugal, Belgium, Italy and Austria-Hungary) got 35 concessions (leased territories) from China, such as Dalian, Kuantung, Zhanjiang, Guangzhouwan, Weihai, Tianjin and almost all of the city of Shanghai.[4] These concessions were occupied and governed

---

[2] State Council of the People's Republic of China, Human Rights in China, November 1991 ('First White Paper on Human Rights in China').

[3] ZHANG Zhenpeng, "On Unequal Treaties", in *Modern Chinese History Studies*, 1993, no. 2, p. 19.

[4] See WANG Tieya, 1957, pp. 35–36, 54, see above note 1.

by foreign powers enjoying extraterritoriality. Each concession allowed its own citizens to inhabit, trade, travel and convert others to their own religion. Concessions had their own police force to enforce the consular law of that concession. Originally, Chinese were forbidden to live in most of the concessions. But eventually by the 1860's, most concessions permitted Chinese to live there to provide services. However, the Chinese were treated like second-class citizens. In 1885, some foreigners even put up a sign at the gate of the Park in the French Concession of Shanghai saying that "Chinese and dogs are not allowed to enter", to insult the Chinese people's dignity. In addition, the colonial powers plundered China's wealth on a large scale.[5]

It is against this background that the term 'century of humiliation' was developed, referring to the period of foreign invasion and colonialism of parts of China.

12.1.2. War Crimes Committed in China by Japanese Imperialists

Up until the present time, the Chinese government and people have been keenly remembering the heinous crimes committed by Japan in China during World War II. Japan occupied three north-eastern provinces of China after the 18 September 1931 Incident, turning them into a Japanese colony. The Japanese military waged ruthless and inhumane aggressive war against China between 1937 and 1945. They burned houses, killed soldiers and civilians, and looted wherever they went, causing immeasurable losses. Some have estimated that as many as 3 million soldiers and 18 million civilians died, and that as many as 100 million people were left homeless.[6]

The report submitted by the Chinese government to the Far East Commission on the losses during China's Anti-Japanese War recorded tremendous losses. A total area of more than 1.5 million square kilometres, in more than 1,500 counties and cities in 26 provinces, had been occupied by Japanese troops, accounting for more than 70 per cent of the total area that Japan occupied in Asia. More than 10 million people were killed or

---

[5] First White Paper on Human Rights in China, see above note 2.

[6] Ezra F. Vogel, *China and Japan Facing History*, The Belknap Press of Harvard University Press, 2019, p. 282.

injured directly as a result of the war, and at least more than 20 million people were harmed by the war.[7]

The 'First White Paper: Human Rights in China' published by the State Council of the People's Republic of China in November 1991 pointed out that during the eight years of war of aggression, more than 930 cities in China were occupied by Japan, with direct economic losses of USD 62 billion and indirect economic losses of more than USD 500 billion. Japan's infringement of China's sovereignty and plundering of social wealth deprived the Chinese people of the minimum living conditions.[8]

12.2. Impact of Colonial Grievances on China's Attitude Towards International Law

The modern history of China since the Opium War is also a history of the Chinese people's bravery and indomitable struggle with the colonial powers to maintain national unity. After nearly 110 years of fighting, the Chinese people finally drove the colonial powers out of Mainland China. Although the establishment of the current regime in China in 1949 ends the 'century of humiliation', the Chinese government often distrusts the Western powers and have a suspicion that they will never stop their conspiracy to split China and oppose China's reunification. The grievances linked to the 'century of humiliation' have had a long-lasting impact on China's attitude towards international law and diplomatic policies.

International law originated in Europe, largely in the seventeenth century, at a time when China's Qing government (1644–1840) adopted the policy of arrogance and seclusion. Qing officials were completely unfamiliar with the Western world,[9] let alone international law. They even treated the foreign envoys according to a tributary system. The Opium Wars opened the door of China to the Western powers. That led to the introduction of international law to China. It was an American missionary, M.A.P. Martin, who translated into Chinese for the first time in 1864 *Ele-*

---

[7]   CHI Jingde, *Zhongguo dui Ri kangzhan sunshi diaocha shishu* [A History of China's Investigation of the Loss of the War of Resistance Against Japan], published by the National History Museum of Taiwan, 1987, p. 210.

[8]   First White Paper on Human Rights in China, see above note 2.

[9]   ZENG Fanyan, "Deep Enlightenment from the Painful Lesson", in *Journal of Guizhou Normal University*, 1990, no. 3, p. 38.

ments of International Law written by the American diplomat Wheaton.[10] Only then did China start to know international law.

12.2.1. The Principle of Respect for State Sovereignty and Territory Integrity

As mentioned above, China suffered greatly from the foreign invasion and aggression. When the Chinese stood up – as the revolutionary leader Chairman Mao announced in 1949 – China wanted to prevent foreign invasion and aggression from ever happening again. Since then, China has persistently urged that States should put aside their differences in social systems and ideologies, and co-exist peacefully. In the 1950s, China, India and Myanmar jointly initiated the 'Five Principles of Peaceful Coexistence':

- mutual respect for sovereignty and territory integrity;
- mutual non-aggression;
- non-interference in each other's internal affairs;
- equality and mutual benefit; and
- peaceful coëxistence.

The five principles have been written into China's Constitution and included in more than 160 communiqués on the establishment of diplomatic relations between China and others.[11] In China's view, the Five Principles of Peaceful Coexistence reflect the political opinions, interests and demands of developing countries for the construction of a new international order. It enriches and develops the essential principles of international law enshrined in the Charter of the United Nations ('UN'), and makes an important contribution to the cause of peace and development of mankind.[12]

The first and most important of the five principles is mutual respect for sovereignty and territory integrity. Sovereignty is always an essential interest of Sates and the basis of international law. Theoretically, the Chinese government acknowledges that the connotation and scope of sover-

---

[10] Rune Svarverud, *International Law as World Order in Late Imperial China*, Brill, Leiden, 2007, p. 88.

[11] LIU Zhengmin, "Following the Five Principles of Peaceful Coexistence and Jointly Building a Community of Common Destiny", in *Chinese Yearbook of International Law*, Law Press, China, 2014, p. 3.

[12] LI Shishi, "Enriching the Connotation of the Five Principles of Peaceful Coexistence in the New Era", in *Chinese Yearbook of International Law*, Law Press, China, 2014, p. 7.

eignty has been developing since World War II, but the core of sovereignty remains the same. State sovereignty not only means territorial integrity, political independence, state equality, and non-interference in internal affairs, but also the duties of States to respect each other's fundamental rights of sovereignty and to fulfil international obligations.[13]

China tends to consistently show sympathy towards developing countries when dealing with international crises. She seeks to resolve problems under the principle of respect for State sovereignty. Sovereignty and territorial integrity amount to a sensitive issue for China. When it comes to any threat to carve up Chinese territory or when any separatist movement appears, the Chinese government and people will feel a strong sense of shame and anger because of the history of foreign invasion and occupation. The former Communist Party leader DENG Xiaoping had the foresight to counsel that China should hide her capacities and bide her time. He instructed to wait for a proper time to settle territorial problems with neighbouring countries by preserving China's position on sovereignty over the disputed territory, but temporarily leaving aside the issue and instead enjoy mutual benefit from joint exploration of resources.

But nowadays, Chinese leaders' attitude towards territorial issues has become stronger and stronger. Take the Diaoyu Islands and islands in the South China Sea as an example. After the Japanese Government's 'nationalization' of the Diaoyu Islands in 2011, the then Chinese Prime Minister WEN Jiabao responded that the Diaoyu Islands are China's inherent territory. On the issues of sovereignty and territory, the Chinese government and people will never budge an inch.[14] Talking about the islands in the South China Sea, President XI Jinping pointed out that they have been China's territory since ancient times. The islands were the legacy left by ancestors. The Chinese people will not allow anyone to infringe upon China's sovereignty and related rights and interests.[15] Regarding the freedom movement in Hong Kong at the time of writing in 2019, President XI

---

[13] MA Xinmin, "Protected Interests and Values Underlying the Five Principles of Peaceful Coexistence: The Balance between National Interests and Common Interests of the International Community", in *Chinese Yearbook of International Law*, Law Press, China, 2014, p. 18.

[14] "Premier Wen Jiabao: Never Budge an Inch on Sovereignty and Territorial Issues", *CCTV* 11 September 2012 (available on its web site).

[15] "Xi Jinping: The South China Sea Islands the Legacy of the Ancestors Should Not Be Violated", *China*, 19 October 2015 (available on its web site).

warned: "Separatist activities in any place in China will be smashed into pieces, and external forces' support for separatists in China will be considered as delusional by Chinese people".[16]

It is not the topic of this chapter to discuss territorial and sovereignty issues in depth. Basic familiarity with China's history and the 'century of humiliation' may help readers to understand why Chinese patriotism and national unity surge each time issues concerning China's sovereignty and territorial integrity come up, and why the Chinese government provides a strong response against any threat of infringement of her territory or sign of separatism.

12.2.2. Non-Interference and Human Rights

Due to the Western origins of international law, for a long time, Chinese scholars confined their study of the theory of international law to its class character and ideology.[17] Before China opened the door to the world in the 1970s, the *People's Daily* newspaper once put forward a 'five never policy':

- never allow foreign investment;
- never ally with foreign countries;
- never accept foreign loans;
- never participate in capitalist international government organizations; and
- never generate foreign debt.[18]

These principles demonstrated China's negative views on international organizations and Western countries at the time.

Similarly, the modern conception of human rights is mostly Western in origin.[19] In the view of the Chinese government, for historical reasons, the first thing to do for Chinese human rights is to secure the right to sub-

---

[16] "Xi Jinping: Any Attempt to Split China is an Idle Dream", *China*, 13 October 2019 (available on its web site).

[17] For example, ZHOU Ziya, "On the Nature of Modern International Law: Class Character, Uniqueness, Mandatory and Continuation", in *Academic Monthly*, 1957, no. 7, pp. 67–72.

[18] LYU Yiwei, "The Timely Adjustment of China's View of Sovereignty and Human Rights in the Early Stage of Reform and Opening Up", in *Journal of South-Central University for Nationalities (Humanities and Social Sciences)*, July 2017, vol. 37, no. 4, p. 123.

[19] Colleen Good, "Human Rights and Relativism", in *Macalester Journal of Philosophy*, 2010, vol. 19, no. 1, p. 28.

sistence. Without national independence, there would be no guarantee for the people's lives.[20] The former Deputy Foreign Minister LIU Huaqiu explained: "As a people that used to suffer tremendously from aggression by big powers but now enjoys independence, the Chinese have come to realize fully that state sovereignty is the basis of the realization of human rights".[21]

Accordingly, China strictly adheres to 'sovereign independence' and 'non-interference in internal affairs'. Sovereign independence entails, on the one hand, that each State enjoys the fundamental rights of sovereign independence, by which the state has full competences in domestic and foreign affairs; on the other hand, no foreign interference is allowed in internal affairs of a sovereign State.[22] China also has an impression that the United States and some other Western countries, for the purpose of promoting their social systems and ideologies and curbing the peaceful development of developing countries, have not fully evaluated human rights in their own and other countries according to recognized standards. They have pursued double standards of human rights.[23] It is a consistent practice of Western countries to accuse one country of violating human rights and protect the others in regional affairs, and accuse one party to a conflict in internal affairs of violating human rights and protect the other.[24]

With the continuous development of globalization, many Western scholars have commonly formed the view that national sovereignty has lost its omniscient authority. With the interaction and interdependence of the whole world, human rights have crossed national boundaries and become a global issue. There is no national boundary for human rights protection. Human rights rank above national sovereignty. So, up to the 1990s, a main issue debated among Chinese scholars of international law was the relationship between sovereignty and human rights, that is, whether state sovereignty ranks above human rights or on the contrary.

---

[20] First White Paper on Human Rights in China, see above note 2.

[21] Stephen C. Angle, *Human Rights and Chinese Thought: A Cross-Cultural Inquiry*, Cambridge University Press, 2002, p. 242.

[22] ZHOU Gengsheng, *International Law*, Vol. 1, The Commercial Press, 1976, p. 188.

[23] FANG Guangshun and SONG Zongbao, "The Double Standards of Human Rights in the Practice of Western Countries", in *Leading Journal of Ideological and Theoretical Education*, 2012, no. 11, p. 54.

[24] *Ibid.*, p. 55.

The view that human rights are subsumed under the rights of national sovereignty and interests of the collective, has prevailed in the Chinese circle of international law. The government has argued: "Owing to tremendous differences in historical background, social system, cultural tradition and economic development, countries differ in their understanding and practice of human rights"; and: "the issue of human rights falls by and large within the sovereignty of each country".[25] It means the protection of human rights cannot be used as a pretext to interfere in a State's internal affairs. Therefore, it is not surprising to hear comments like this: "Other people don't know better than the Chinese people about the human rights condition in China and it is the Chinese people who are in the best situation to have a say about China's human rights situation".[26] This statement reflects the government's attitude towards human rights and non-interference in China's internal affairs. However, a commentator has pointed out that this position "effectively works to shield a state's domestic human rights abuses from international criticism".[27]

Nevertheless, there have been some changes in China's attitude towards human rights issues. China has actively participated in international human rights fora. China has acceded to several international conventions on human rights, and publicly supported the Universal Declaration of Human Rights. After entering the second decade of the twenty-first century, China's emphasis on the principle of sovereignty is no longer simply to adhere to the lines of 'absolute sovereignty' and 'human rights are purely internal affairs'. This is due to China's recognition of the mainstream consciousness of the international community that, in some circumstances, human rights no longer belong to internal affairs of a state. But China still affirmed the value of culture relativism. She has tied cultural relativism and the sovereignty principle together and uses the relativist view of human rights as a defence of non-interference in a State's internal affairs.[28] On several occasions, China has asked Western countries to take full ac-

---

[25] First White Paper on Human Rights in China, see above note 2.

[26] CNN, "China's Foreign Minister berates Canadian reporter over human rights", 2 June 2016 (available on its web site).

[27] Uyen P. Le, "A Culture of Human Rights in East Asia: Deconstructing 'Asian Values' Claims" in *U.C. Davis Journal of International Law and Policy*, 2012, vol. 18, no. 469, p. 11.

[28] LYU Yiwei, "The Development and Maturity of China's Sovereignty and Human Rights View After 1990s", in *Journal of Yantai University (Philosophy and Social Science Edition)*, 2017, vol. 30, no. 6, p. 44.

count of the huge developmental differences, cultural traditions, and so-cial conditions of States, rather than imposing their value on others. China believes that the concept of human rights has historical and cultural rela-tivity. She stresses the focus of human rights protection should be on the situations of racial discrimination, colonialism, and foreign aggression; and that the principles of sovereign independence and non-interference in the internal affairs of States should be respected. Although China has changed her original view of absolute sovereignty over human rights, the historical root-cause can still be found from her current position on sover-eignty, human rights and non-interference of internal affairs.

12.2.3. Peaceful Settlement of Disputes by Negotiation

China has grown up from being a semi-colonial and semi-feudal society, to a developing country. Because of the humiliating diplomacy of the past, China cherishes her independence. China has therefore consistently advo-cated for peaceful settlement of international disputes, and peaceful han-dling of relations and historical problems with other countries. China's government holds the view that, firstly, the peaceful settlement of interna-tional disputes must abide by the purposes and principles contained in the United Nations Charter and the basic norms of international law. Special emphasis should be placed on principles such as respect for the sovereign-ty and territorial integrity of States, non-use of force or threat of force, and non-recognition of the legality of the results of the threat or use of force.

Secondly, the Chinese government believes dialogue is an effective means to settle international disputes peacefully. Because it will not only help to enhance mutual understanding, clarify facts, and resolve conflicts between the countries concerned, but also to avoid deepening a dispute that could bring disaster to the people of both parties. The former Minister of Foreign Affairs WU Xueqian stated in the United Nations General As-sembly in 1986 that peaceful settlement of international disputes through dialogue is a correct means. As a matter of fact, only through negotiation and equal consultation, can States overcome the contradiction and differ-ence of interests between them, prevent international conflicts, and main-tain world peace.[29]

---

[29] WANG Houli's statement on peaceful settlement of international disputes at the Sixth Committee of the 41st session of the UN General Assembly, in *Chinese Yearbook of Inter-national Law*, Law Press, 1987, p. 829.

There are many means to settle international disputes peacefully. Negotiation, enquiry, mediation, conciliation, arbitration, judicial settlement, and resort to regional agencies or arrangements are listed in the means of pacific settlement of disputes in Article 33 of the United Nations Charter. China has always advocated the settlement of disputes between regions or countries through negotiation or consultation. Through negotiation, China has solved the problems of dual nationality with Southeast-Asian countries, demarcation with neighbouring countries, and, most significantly, the return of Hong Kong and Macao from the United Kingdom and Portugal.

China has always been very cautious in the settlement of international disputes through judicial means. In the early 1970s, after China had recovered her United Nations seat, the Chinese government refused to recognize the statement of the Kuomintang government accepting the compulsory jurisdiction of the International Court of Justice ('ICJ'). China has never entered into a special agreement with any other country to submit disputes to the ICJ. China has made reservations on the settlement of international disputes through the ICJ when signing, ratifying or acceding to international conventions that contain dispute-settlement clauses.

In the international treaties concluded between China and foreign countries, almost no arbitration clause is included or accepted except for some economic and trade agreements. In practice, China always refuses to settle disputes by international arbitration. For instance, after the armed conflict between China and India occurred in the border area in 1962, the Indian government proposed to settle the dispute by international arbitration. The Chinese government rejected India's proposal, saying that the border dispute between China and India is a major issue concerning the sovereignty of the two countries, involving more than 100,000 square kilometres of territory. Therefore, direct negotiation between the two parties is the only means to settle the dispute. It is not possible to find a solution through any forms of international arbitration.[30]

In recent years, the Philippines sued China by establishing an arbitration tribunal, according to Annex VII of the United Nations Convention on the Law of the Sea ('UNCLOS'), to resolve the disputes in the South

---

[30] ZHAO Jinsong, "Primary Exploration of China's Peaceful Settlement of International Disputes", in *Science of Law (Journal of Northwest University of Political Science and Law)*, 2006, no. 1, p. 100.

China Sea between China and the Philippines. The Chinese government firmly upholds its sovereignty over the Spratly Islands, and insists that China and the Philippines have reached their consensus on settling the South China Sea issue through bilateral negotiation and consultation in a number of bilateral documents.[31] China made its position clear: no acceptance, no participation, no recognition, and no implementation of the international arbitration on this matter.[32]

Why does China refuse to settle international disputes by judicial means? There are several reasons. As mentioned before, compared with Western countries, China is a late-comer in the international community, and did not to the same extent participate in the rule-building process. Therefore, in the eyes of the Chinese people, the ICJ is a tool for Western powers to carry out international political struggles. Furthermore, in the official or academic circles of China, most people still adhere to the concept of absolute sovereignty and believe that they cannot give part of her sovereignty to international institutions. The cultural difference between China and Western countries also plays a role. The Chinese traditional culture takes Confucianism as its core. It prefers harmony among people rather than frequent resort to lawsuits to resolve disputes.

The most relevant reason may be found in China's semi-colonial history. As we all know, after the Opium War in 1840, China gradually became a semi-colonial and semi-feudal country and was bullied by colonial and imperialist powers. The past experience taught people in China that Western powers had not treated China fairly, and international law was only a tool for the so-called civilized countries to invade China.[33] The unequal treaties imposed upon China humiliated the country and the people, and caused them significant suffering over several decades.

For example, China participated in the Paris Peace Conference of 1919 as a victor of World War I, but China's sovereignty was not respected, and her fundamental rights and interests were not guaranteed by the

[31] The State Council Information Office of the People's Republic of China, a white paper titled "China Adheres to the Position of Settling Through Negotiation the Relevant Disputes Between China and the Philippines in the South China Sea", in *Chinese Journal of International Law*, 2016, vol. 15, no. 4, pp. 909–933.

[32] Some scholars have different view. See for example, WANG Sheng and ZHANG Xue, "Judicial Approach to International Dispute Settlement and China's Response", in *Contemporary International Relations*, 1996, no. 10, pp. 32–38.

[33] ZHAO Jinsong, 2006, p. 100, see above note 30.

Western colonial powers. The Western colonial powers ignored the reasonable requirements of China to take back all the rights and interests in Shandong from Germany. Instead, they decided to transfer all the rights and interests of Germany in Shandong to Japan, which led to the outbreak of the May Fourth Movement against imperialism and feudalism.

Furthermore, Japan occupied three provinces in Northeast China by force in 1931. The League of Nations sent an investigation team to these provinces for field investigation, as China requested. Although, based on the investigation mission's report, the General Assembly of the League of Nations confirmed Japan's aggression against China, it did not take any action to stop Japan's occupation.

This gave the Chinese people an impression that international organizations and their judicial organs are not reliable to safeguard rights and interests of China. The Chinese government does not trust international judicial organs to apply international law impartially and make a fair and just determination. The arbitration award of the international arbitration tribunal on the dispute in South China Sea between China and Philippines has been criticized for applying double standards.[34] China would rather have the matter under her own control by resolving international disputes or problems without third party involvement.

12.2.4. Japanese War Crimes

12.2.4.1. Investigation and Prosecution of Japanese War Crimes

It is often mentioned that, up until now, the Japanese government has not fully admitted its guilt for waging war of aggression in the manner that the German government has. The right-wing of Japan has even attempted to completely deny it. One of the crucial reasons is that the international community, Japan and China have not endeavoured to investigate and prosecute the Japanese war crimes committed in China thoroughly.

It is well known that after World War II, the Allied States established International Military Tribunals to prosecute the German Nazi war criminals and Japanese perpetrators. In addition to the International Mili-

---

[34] LUO Guoqiang, "Analysis on the Preliminary Award of the South China Sea Arbitration Case", in *Foreign Affairs Review*, 2016, no. 2, pp. 13, 16; LEI Xiaolu and YU Minyou, "Criticism in Light of International Law on the Adjudication of the Historical Rights Involved in the South China Sea Arbitration Case", in *International Studies*, 2017, no. 2, pp. 11, 18, 19. The different views by scholars on the South China Sea arbitration are difficult to found in public media due to strict censorship.

tary Tribunal's prosecution of the major Nazi war criminals in Nuremberg, the Allies continued to prosecute German war criminals in their occupied German areas. Israel and European countries have never given up the efforts to hunt down and arrest Nazi criminals. In 1960, Israel brought Adolf Eichmann, a notorious war criminal, from Argentina for trial in Israel. Franz Radmacher, another war criminal, was then arrested in the Middle East. The international community realized that quite a number of heinous war criminals remained in various parts of the world, and they could not be allowed to get away with their crimes. With the efforts of many countries and international organizations, the United Nations General Assembly adopted the Convention on the Non-Applicability of Statutory Limitations to War Crimes and Crimes Against Humanity on 26 November 1968, which gave renewed impetus to the world-wide pursuit of Nazi war criminals. Since then, whenever Israel and European countries found a clue to war criminals, they would track them down. It was reported that Sandor Kepiro, a 97-year-old former Hungarian officer and Nazi war criminal was on trial in Hungary in 2011.[35] Nazi war criminals were also prosecuted in German domestic courts. Germany began to investigate Nazi crimes in the late 1950s and has tried thousands Nazi war criminals. As a consequence, Nazi war criminals have had almost nowhere to hide in post-war Germany and the world, whereas up until now Japan itself has never prosecuted war criminals within Japan.[36]

In comparison, the International Military Tribunal for the Far East ('IMTFE') only prosecuted 28 Class A Japanese war criminals after World War II. More than 100 major war criminals were arrested by the international prosecutor's office. The initial plan was to have trials of a second, third and even fourth case of Japanese major war criminals. However, the trials did not continue after the first trial of 28 accused. As a result, many major war criminals escaped punishment. In addition, in order to quickly end the Tokyo trial, no comprehensive investigation and prosecution was conducted for crimes such as forced labour of civilian workers, sexual

---

[35] "97 years old World War II major Nazi suspect on trial in Hungary", *CCTV*, 6 May 2011 (available on its web site).
[36] FUJITA Hisakazu, "The Tokyo Trial: Humanity's Justice V Victors' Justice", in YUKI Tanaka *et al.* (eds.), *Beyond Victor's Justice? The Tokyo War Crimes Trial Revisited*, Nijhoff, 2011, p. 16.

slavery, and testing and use of biological and chemical weapons.[37] In November 1950, the United States released KISHI Nobusuke, an infamous Class A war criminal. In 1950s, a number of Japanese war criminals, who had not been prosecuted, returned to Japan's government circles. KISHI Nobusuke even became the Minister of Foreign Affairs in 1954, and Prime Minister in 1957.

In China, the Kuomintang government established a commission for war crimes and promulgated several regulations for the investigation and prosecution of war crimes[38] after Japan's surrender. Ten military tribunals were set up in Beiping, Shenyang, Nanjing, Guangzhou, Jinan, Hankou, Taiyuan, Shanghai, Xuzhou and Taipei to try war criminals. It was reported that by the end of January 1949, these national military tribunals had sentenced more than 140 accused to death, and more than 400 to fixed-term imprisonment or life imprisonment. The laws and regulations on which these trials were based were much more detailed than the law promulgated by the new government in 1956.[39] Many trials of Japanese war criminals conducted by the national military tribunals were, in my view, fair and just. But there were also defects and mistakes. In the late stage of the trial, due to the domestic situation at the time, the government ordered the shutdown of some military tribunals. Trials were either speeded up or hastily concluded. Some defendants were transferred to the Nanking Military Tribunal. Finally, these military tribunals had hurried to try and convict 445 out of 2,200 war crime detainees by the end of the trials

---

[37] TSUNEISHI Kei-ichi, "Reasons for the Failure to Prosecute Unit 731 and Its Significance"; JIA Bing Bing, "The Legacy of the Tokyo Trial in China"; Ustinia Dolgopol, "Knowledge and Responsibility: The Ongoing Consequences of Failure to Give Sufficient Attention to the Crimes Against the Comfort Women in the Tokyo Trial", in YUKI Tanaka *et al.* (eds.), *Beyond Victor's Justice? The Tokyo War Crimes Trial Revisited*, Nijhoff, 2011, pp. 177–206, 213, 243–262.

[38] These regulations are "Measures for the Investigation of Enemy Crimes (revised) in September 1945"; "Measures for the Disposition of War Criminals" in January 1946 (15 articles); "Measures for the Trial of War Criminals" (10 articles), which was revised and renamed as "Regulations for the Trial of War Criminals" (35 articles, which refine the concept of war criminals, the conduct of war crimes, the period of prosecution, the matters that cannot be exempted from criminal responsibility, the responsibility of commanders and the sentencing standards); and "Rules for Implementation of the Measures for the Trial of War Criminals" in 1946 (which made detailed provisions for the prosecution, arrest and trial of war criminals).

[39] In 1956, the Standing Committee of the National People's Congress passed a decision on handling the Japanese war criminals in custody during the war of aggression against China. There are only six articles in total.

---

in April 1949,[40] and the rest were repatriated to Japan without charges. OKAMURA Ningji, who resisted surrendering to the Communist Party when Japan was defeated, was pronounced not guilty and released. His trial was criticized to be a miscarriage of justice.

After the founding of the new government in 1949, more than 1,000 Japanese war criminals were arrested or transferred to the government of the People's Republic of China in early 1950s. The government, on the one hand, showed sympathy to the sentiment of the people who had suffered significantly from the Japanese brutal aggression, and realized that the indignation of the Chinese people would not be pacified without trial of the Japanese war criminals. As the then Premier ZHOU Enlai said, the Japanese war criminals must be investigated, prosecuted and punished, which the government had owed to people.[41] On the other hand, the government adopted a 'policy of leniency', namely, only a few accused of serious war crimes should stand trial with no death penalty and no life imprisonment.[42]

As a result, of more than one thousand Japanese war crime-detainees, only 45 were selected to stand trial because of the gravity of the crimes they had committed. The others were re-educated and rehabilitated. The trial and re-education of Japanese war criminals were successful in the sense that all accused persons pleaded guilty and the others who were exempted from prosecution were also determined to be reformed and unlikely to re-engage in war of aggression. But the shortcomings were also obvious. Like the Tokyo Tribunal, war crimes such as compelling Chinese civilians to forced labour in Japan during the war, testing and use of bacterial and chemical weapons in China, and forcing comfort women to provide sexual services for Japanese military personnel were not prosecuted. From 1956 to 1964, all Japanese prisoners of war including the convicted persons were released and repatriated to Japan.

In short, the criminal responsibility for Japan's war of aggression has not been completely settled.

---

[40] Ta Kung Pao [大公报], 27 January 1949 (Shanghai edition) in XU Jiajun, "Tilanqiao Prison and the Imprisonment, Trial and Enforcement of Japanese War Criminals", *Shanghai Local Records*, 2005, no. 4.

[41] LIU Wusheng and DU Hongqi (eds.), *The Military Activities of Zhou Enlai (II)*, Central Documentary Publisher, Beijing, 2000, p. 392.

[42] SHU Gong, "China's Trial of Japanese War Criminals in 1956", in *Across Time and Space*, 2006, no. 6, p. 20.

Actually, the government's position on the war criminals was profoundly affected by political considerations. After the San Francisco Peace Conference in 1951, from which China was precluded, Japan followed the United States line towards the newly established Chinese government and signed a bilateral peace treaty with the Taiwanese authorities in 1952, which created a serious obstacle to the normalization of Sino-Japanese diplomatic relations. In view of this, the Chinese government saw the normalization of diplomatic relations between China and Japan as a priority in its policy toward Japan.[43] The government explained that the reason for adopting the policy of leniency was that a decade had elapsed since the end of World War II, and the status of the two countries in international affairs had changed significantly, so adopting a policy of leniency would be helpful to promote the normalization of Sino–Japanese diplomatic relations as well as to ease and stabilize the international situation.[44] Barak Kushner has commented that the "CPC was very clearly using the trials as a means of bending Japanese public opinion toward a more favorable viewpoint of China, putting the war in the rear view while moving forward toward normalization".[45] After the Chinese government made the decision to treat the Japanese prisoners of war leniently, the then Japanese Foreign Minister SHIGEMITSU Mamoru issued a statement, expressing his pleasure at China's release of prisoners of war and his willingness to expand trade with China as much as possible.[46]

When the international community continued the criminal justice pursuit of Nazi criminals, China was busy with domestic class struggles in the first 30 years of the new government. At one stage, it denied the trial the Kuomintang government conducted because of the *OKAMURA Ningji* case. The trial documents of the Tokyo Military Tribunal went missing while the domestic trial documents of Japanese war crimes were not ac-

---

[43] LI Ying, *Details of the History of the Republic*, People's Publishing House, 2010.

[44] WANG Zhanping (ed.), *Trial Justice: Prosecution of Japanese War Criminals Before the Special Military Tribunal of the Supreme Court*, People's Court Publisher, Beijing, 1990, p. 2.

[45] Adam Cathcart, "Resurrecting Defeat: International Propaganda and the Shenyang Trials of 1956", in Kerstin von Lingen (ed.), *War Crimes Trials in the Wake of Decolonization and Cold War in Asia, 1945-1956: Justice in Time of Turmoil*, Palgrave Macmillan, 2016, p. 268.

[46] LUO Pinghan, On China's policy towards Japan in the mid-1950s and its relations with Japan, *The History of the People's Republic of China*, 27 September 2009 (available on its web site).

cessible to scholars and people. The historical materials of the trials, including the indictment, trial records, evidence and some of the judgments were lost or not made public for a long time. Reports and research on war crimes trials had disappeared from sight. Some lawyers who worked for the Tokyo trial – such as Mr. MEI Ru'ao, the Judge of the Tokyo Tribunal, Mr. ER Sen, the prosecution advisor, and Mr. GAO Wenbin, the secretary to the prosecution and translator – had been labelled and persecuted as rightist or anti-revolutionary. The others were removed from law-related jobs by reassigning them either to foreign language teaching positions or as librarians.[47]

12.2.4.2. Reparation and Apology

The Potsdam Proclamation of 1945 issued by China, the United States and the United Kingdom made the principle of Japan's war reparation clear. Japan may keep the industrial equipment and objects necessary for its economic operation, and the rest can be used for reparations.[48] Reparations were not only an important way to recover the economy of the war-torn allies, but also an important means to punish Japan's aggression and prevent the revival of militarism. Since China was the country that suffered the most, the former Chinese government claimed that China should receive at least 40 per cent of the war reparations.[49] However, after the surrender of Japan, the former Chinese government only received a symbolic compensation of about USD 22.5 million, a small part of the 15 per cent of the compensation promised to China.[50] This is perceived as extremely unfair by the Chinese people.

The right of China to claim compensation was further waved by the Chinese government as part of the policy of leniency and as a gesture of good-will to Japan. In ZHOU Enlai's view, the cost of compensation would eventually be inflicted on the Japanese people rather than the Japa-

---

[47] XIANG Zhejun, the Chinese Prosecutor at the International Military Tribunal for the Far East, worked at the Shanghai Institute of Finance and Economics (1960-1965); NI Zheng-yu, advisor to Prosecution, worked as a Director of Library and Russian teacher at Tongji University (1954–1956); WU Xueyi, advisor to Prosecution, worked as a librarian at China Medical Institute; QIU Shaoheng, secretary and assistant to the Chinese Prosecutor, worked at Shanghai Foreign Language Institute.

[48] *Collection of International Treaties (1945-1947)*, World Affairs Publishing House, 1959, p. 78.

[49] *Selected Materials of Modern Chinese History (1945-1949)*, vol. 3, pp. 75–76.

[50] Foreign Relations of the United States, vol. 6, pp. 376–377.

nese government.[51] Several years later, CHEN Yi, the former Vice Premier and Foreign Minister, made it clear that the

> Chinese government and the Chinese people have always looked forward, not backward, to the relation between China and Japan. At present, what the Chinese and Japanese governments need to work together is, first of all, to promote the normalization of relations between the two countries.[52]

The Chinese government formally waved to Japan her claim of war reparations in 1972 when the two states established diplomatic relations. Nevertheless, it is the government's view that the Chinese people have never given up their compensation claims to Japan. During the Japanese war of aggression against China, Japanese troops systematically carried out the policy of 'burning all, killing all, looting all' in China, massacred numerous innocent civilians, and caused thousands of major tragedies in the occupied areas. Of the millions of casualties in China, 30 million were civilians. More than 10 million of them were forcibly captured by the Japanese army as labourers and enslaved. Nearly 200,000 Chinese women were cruelly forced to be 'comfort women'. In addition, a large number of properties were destroyed and plundered. Chinese civilians make up the largest civilian victim group of World War II. Some Chinese victims have been filing lawsuits in the Japanese courts since the 1990s, but so far, they have not received any of their deserved compensation.

In comparison, Germany's attitude towards the victims of its war crimes committed during World War II is much better than that of Japan. In the early 1950s, Germany began to implement war compensation. In 1956, the parliament of the Federal Republic of Germany passed a law for compensation to the Nazi victims. It has paid compensation to victimized countries and Jewish people.[53] The German government has been making profound introspection and sincere atonement for its historical wrongdoings. On 7 December 1970, Willy Brandt, the then Chancellor of the Federal Republic of Germany, knelt in profound apology in front of the monument to the Warsaw Ghetto Uprising. The Chinese ambassador to Ireland

---

[51] GAO Fanfu, "The Friendly Element of the China's Waiver of the Compensation Claim to Japan", in *Journal of Studies of China's Resistance War Against Japan*, 2008, no. 2, p. 204.

[52] LI Ying, *Details of the History of the Republic*, People's Publishing House, 2010.

[53] YANG Deli, "Über Die Fragen in den Reparationen Deutschlands", in *Deutschland-Studien*, 1996, vol. 11, no. 1, pp. 30–33.

commented that Brandt's kneeling down in penitence helped to guide Germany out of the defendant's seat.[54]

On the contrary, in 1982, 1986 and 2003, the history textbook for primary and secondary schools designated by the Japanese Ministry of Culture was revised, distorting history and glorifying the action of aggression. Besides, each Japanese prime minister has paid homage to the Yasukuni Shrine in Tokyo, which also honours 14 Class A war criminals who were responsible for the aggression against China. These facts have grasped the attention and provoked the anger of the Chinese government and people. The Memorial Hall of the Victims in the Nanjing Massacre by Japanese Invaders has been established and opened to the public in 1985. The Chinese government pointed out that whether Japan can correctly understand the history of Japanese aggression in the past is an important matter of principle.[55] Japanese war crimes became a hot topic in 2005 when the Japanese Ministry of Culture approved a history textbook that downplayed Japan's role in World War II, and Prime Minister KOIZUMI paid the fifth homage to the Yasukuni Shrine. The Chinese people's anti-Japanese sentiment surged and Sino-Japanese relations deteriorated to a low point in a year which marked the 60th anniversary of the end of World War II. Tens of thousands of people in more than 20 cities in China demonstrated against Japan. The Japanese embassy, consulates, companies and enterprises became the targets of angry protesters. The behaviour of the Japanese politicians reflects that Japan has adopted an erroneous attitude towards its history of aggression. It is not difficult to understand why this has provoked fury in China.

As Japan's leaders are still refusing to admit the guilt of war crimes and the Japanese government has never made a formal apology to the Chinese people with regard to the war,[56] the Chinese government began to take more actions to refresh the memory of Japan's aggression and atrocities. The official documentation in the Central Archives has been opened to researchers since 2005. Some of them were published in printed version in 2009. The State Archives Administration released in 2014 a daily online publication of scanned, hand-written confessions of 45 war crimi-

---

[54] LUO Linquan, "Japan's leaders are still stubbornly refusing to admit their war crimes", *Phoenix Television*, 24 January 2014 (available on its web site).

[55] "China reserves the right to further respond to Japan's revision of textbooks", *CCTV*, 11 April 2002 (available on its web site).

[56] JIA Bing Bing, 2011, p. 209, see above note 37.

nals prosecuted in Shenyang and Taiyuan in 1956.[57] China made a film about the Tokyo Trial in 2006, though, later than the Japanese films about the Tokyo Trial made in 1983 and 1998 respectively. In 2014, the Seventh Session of the Standing Committee of the 12th National People's Congress adopted a decision to establish National Memorial Day on 13 December for the Nanking Massacre and to mourn the victims of the massacre. A Centre for Tokyo Trial Studies was also created in 2011. The transcripts of the trial proceedings of the IMTFE in both English (60 volumes) and Chinese (12 volumes) have been published in 2013 and 2018 respectively.

12.3. Conclusion

As Judge LIU Daqun has stated: "It is crucial that we understand the past if we are to address today's challenges".[58] From China's past experience, it is easy to understand China's attitude towards international law, especially why China emphasizes respect for sovereignty and territorial integrity, non-interference of internal affairs, and peaceful settlement of international disputes by negotiation and dialogue. As a victimized country of colonial wrongs and war crimes, China supports the prosecution of core international crimes. China has nominated judge candidates every time to the International Criminal Tribunal for the former Yugoslavia.

China has actively participated in the preparatory work for the establishment of the International Criminal Court ('ICC'), and has been closely observing the function and performance of the Court. The Chinese observer to the Assembly of ICC Member States stated that when the judicial work of an international judicial institution is criticized by many Member States for the existence of selective justice; when its actions may endanger the stability, social harmony and national reconciliation of a country; and when it is challenged by many countries and people, it should rethink whether its work is consistent with the purposes and principles of the establishment of the institution.[59]

---

[57] "Xinhua Insight: Japanese war criminal confessions renew Chinese anger", *Xinhua English*, 15 July 2014 (available on its web site).

[58] LIU Daqun, Foreword, in Suzannah Linton (ed.), *Hong Kong's War Crimes Trials*, Oxford University Press 2013, p. viii.

[59] The Chinese representative and Deputy Director of the Department of Treaties and Law, MA Xinmin, addressed the Thirteenth Session of the Assembly of States Parties to the

Currently, the Western countries remain the dominant law-making power in many fields of international law. The Chinese government stands for placing attention on the interests of all mankind as guidance for the development of international law.

Regarding the atrocities committed by Japanese war criminals, it is difficult to remove overnight the grievances accumulating over the years. It requires efforts by both Japan and China. On the side of Japan, to wash away memories of the sins and crimes committed by Japanese militarists, the Japanese government should acknowledge the history without bias or distortion. It should engage in profound introspection, and make 'solemn and sincere apologies' to China for the atrocities committed, including massacres, torture, rapes, and live human experiments of biological warfare. Furthermore, Japan should do what it can in penitence and atonement to unequivocally and irreversibly renounce militarism, and to prevent militarism and fascism from coming back. In addition, Japan should take concrete action to promote reconciliation and peaceful development between the two countries and their peoples.[60] What Canada, Germany and Norway are currently doing may be a useful approach for Japan's consideration.[61]

On the side of China, she can proceed to the investigation and prosecution of the Japanese war crimes that have not been investigated and prosecuted,[62] because statutory limitations do not apply to war crimes and crimes against humanity. It is said that the Allies set up several international military tribunals in Yokohama, Japan, to prosecute Japanese class B and C war criminals after the Tokyo trial. China's personnel also participated in the trials. However, almost no trial documents or research have been published as China was in intense civil war at the time.

Rome Statute, December 2014, see the text in the *Chinese Yearbook of International Law*, 2014, pp. 814–815.

[60] LUO Linquan, "Japan's leaders are still stubbornly refusing to admit their war crimes", *Phoenix Television*, 24 January 2014 (available on its web site).

[61] Morten Bergsmo, *Myanmar, Colonial Aftermath, and Access to International Law*, Torkel Opsahl Academic EPublisher, Brussels, Occasional Paper Series No. 9 (2019), p. 18 (http://www.toaep.org/ops-pdf/9-bergsmo).

[62] It is reported that 15 victims of the 'Chongqing bombing' or their families filed a civil lawsuit with the Chongqing High People's Court on 10 October 2012, formally asking the Japanese government to publicly apologize to the victims and provide compensation.

Ignoring the trial of Japanese war criminals conducted by the Kuomintang government is not helpful for exposure of the Japanese war crimes committed in China. More trial documents should be collected and opened to the public, to expose the atrocities of Japanese war criminals. Having a people's tribunal[63] like the one held for comfort women in 2000[64] can be an alternative, to stir the Japanese government to face up to responsibility for Japanese war crimes.

The purpose of awakening people's memory of past colonial grievances is not to take revenge for humiliation, but to prevent repetition of past tragedies and disasters. It should not be used as a political tool to incite national hatred. In dealing with past grievances, a balance should be found between national interests and people's interests.

---

[63] See Andrew Byrnes and Gabrielle Simm (eds.), *International Peoples' Tribunals: Their Nature, Practice and Significance*, Cambridge University Press, 2018.

[64] Women's International Tribunal on Japanese Military Sexual Slavery, *The Prosecutors and the Peoples of the Asia-Pacific Region v. Hirohito Emperor Showa and others*, PT-2000-1-T, Judgement, 4 December 2001, cited in Wolfgang Kaleck, *Double Standards: International Criminal Law and the West*, Torkel Opsahl Academic EPublisher, Brussels, 2015, p. 41 (https://www.toaep.org/ps-pdf/26-kaleck).

13

Winds of Justice:
Post-Colonial Opportunism and
the Rise of the Khmer Rouge

Kevin Crow[*]

13.1. Introduction: Justice and Temporal Jurisdiction

On the slightly cloudy Thursday morning of 7 August 2014, at the Extraordinary Chambers in the Courts of Cambodia ('ECCC'), the Trial Chamber read its finding that former leaders of the Khmer Rouge were guilty of crimes against humanity in Case 002/01. Shortly thereafter, one Cambodian man and two American men gathered on a podium outside the Court's curved façade to address a crowd of reporters.[1] After the Deputy Prime Minister of Cambodia, Sok An, thanked the United Nations ('UN') Secretary General and UN Special Expert on UN Assistance for "continuing to raise the money that made the voluntarily funded court possible",[2] David Scheffer addressed the media with the following words: "Today, the winds of international justice swept through the fields, forests, and towns of Cambodia where millions perished".[3]

Scheffer's words are reminiscent of what Alex Hinton referred to as 'San's Dream' in his book *The Justice Façade*. San's Dream is a notion taken from a pamphlet that portrays an idyllic NGO-funded vision of a Cambodia where conviction by trial for past wrongs frees the present from 'bad dreams' of the past.[4] The dream promoted via cartoon is meant

---

Kevin Crow is Assistant Professor of International Law and Ethics at Asia School of Business and International Faculty Fellow at MIT Sloan School of Management.

[1] These three were Deputy Prime Minister of Cambodia Sok An, UN Special Expert David Scheffer, and United States ('US') Ambassador-at-Large for War Crimes Stephen Rapp.

[2] See Eben Saling, "Press Conferences Detail Triumphs, Defeats, and Plans in the Aftermath of Case 002/01", *Cambodia Tribunal Monitor*, 7 August 2014 (available on its web site).

[3] *Ibid.*

[4] See Alexander Hinton, *The Justice Façade: Trials of Transition in Cambodia*, Oxford University Press, 2018.

Publication Series No. 40 (2020) – page 391

to explain to everyday working folks in Cambodia why the ECCC is so necessary, why justice must be served. According to the cartoon, once former Khmer Rouge leaders are convicted, 'justice' will come in the form of new dreams of a bright future, and the shirtless sandal-clad Uncle San will be free from the bad dreams that haunt him presently, finally ready to sleep peacefully in his hammock which hangs amidst the "fields [and] forests [...] of Cambodia".[5] While this vision of justice will seem suspect to anyone who has spent time at the ECCC, I want to suggest that Scheffer was right in a sense that 'international justice' is like the wind: you can see that it is there because it ruffles some leaves, but once it blows through, its substance is revealed as fleeting; it has changed little in its wake.

This chapter sets aside those well-known criticisms of the Court: the allegations of judicial corruption, *ex parte* communications, and systematic exclusion of local co-lawyers especially during the tenure of Co-Prosecutor Andrew Cayley;[6] the opportunities for governmental tampering built into the procedure of the Court;[7] and the widespread impression in the legal community that the Trial Chamber's analysis case 002/01 left something to be desired (for example, competence).[8] Instead, this chapter focuses on the roles of the US and China building up to the 4.5-year reign of the Khmer Rouge in an effort to highlight the absurdity of the ECCC's 4.5-year temporal jurisdiction (1974–1979). This is not because of the specific time-frame, but because the very concept of 'international justice' at the Court does not gel with local conceptions of justice, which in turn do not gel with time-frames. The roles of the US and China illustrate how

---

[5] See *ibid*. See also Saling, 2014, see above note 2. The quote is from David Scheffer's statement to the press, cited above.

[6] Colin Meyn, "International Prosecutor Resigns From KR Tribunal", *The Cambodia Daily*, 10 September 2013; Zach Zagger, "ECCC judges order prosecutor to retract public request for further investigations", *Jurist*, 18 May 2011 (available on its web site); Michael Karnavas, *Judicial Ethics in the International Tribunals*, Lecture, ADC-ICTY Twelfth Defence Symposium, 24 January 2014; Documentation Center of Cambodia, "Chronology of the Khmer Rouge Tribunal" (available on its web site).

[7] For a detailed discussion on these procedural flaws, see my forthcoming commentary on the S-21 case: Kevin Crow, *Commentary on Prosecutor v. Duch (ECCC)*, André Klip and Steven Freeland (eds.), *Annotated Leading Cases of International Criminal Law*, vol. LX, Intersentia, 2020.

[8] David Cohen, Melanie Hyde and Penelope Van Tuyl, *A Well-Reasoned Opinion? A Critical Analysis of the First Case Against the Alleged Senior Leaders of the Khmer Rouge (Case 002/01)*, East-West Center, 2015.

even imaginaries of 'international justice' fail to consider how lingering legacies of colonial wrongs enabled non-colonial powers to exploit Cambodia – how, by design, holistic views of 'causation' and therefore 'justice' were procedurally excluded from the realm of possibility at the ECCC. The form a 'legitimate' legal argument could take was predefined temporally, thereby rendering arguments that accounted for a broader range of culpability than 4.5 years to be legally 'illegitimate'.

To put this argument in context – and without ever attempting to recount 'entire' histories of French Indochina, the Kingdom of Kampuchea, China, the Khmer Rouge, the Vietnam War, the UN, or the US – this chapter begins with a brief background on Cambodia's transition from a French colonial control around 1954 (13.2.). Drawing from prevailing accounts on the history of the period as well as Khmer Rouge documents,[9] which are very briefly summarized, it argues the Khmer Rouge would not have come to power *but for* the intervention of the US in supporting Lon Nol and would not have sustained itself *but for* the support of Mao's China (13.3.).

During the immediate post-Khmer Rouge era, not only did the UN continue to recognize the Khmer Rouge as the 'legitimate' government of Vietnam-controlled Cambodia,[10] the US and UN also limited aid to Cambodia for 13 years during a period when its infrastructure was utterly destroyed: Cambodia had no currency, no education system, indeed, no economy.[11] During these 13 years, Khmer Rouge archival records were neglected and in many cases destroyed,[12] and Vietnamese leadership along with later-Prime Minister Hun Sen manifested (through the post-

---

[9] All found in David Chandler, Ben Kiernan and Chanthou Boua (eds.), *Pol Pot Plans the Future: Confidential Leadership Documents from Democratic Kampuchea, 1976-1977*, Yale University Press, 1988.

[10] Michael Vickery, *Cambodia, 1975-1982*, Silkworm, 1984; David Chandler, *A History of Cambodia*, fourth edition, Perseus, 2008; Ben Kiernan, *The Pol Pot Regime: Race, Power, and Genocide in Cambodia Under the Khmer Rouge, 1975-1979*, Yale University Press, 1998; Philip Short, *Pol Pot: Anatomy of a Nightmare*, Owl, 2004; *Kampuchea: Decade of the Genocide, Finnish Inquiry Commission*, 1982 ('Kampuchea'); Ben Kiernan, *How Pol Pot Came to Power*, Verso, 1985; Julia Lovell, *Maoism: A Global History*, Penguin, 2019.

[11] See, for example, David Chandler, "Cambodia Deals with its Past: Collective Memory, Demonization and Induced Amnesia", in *Totalitarian Movements and Political Religions*, 2008, vol. 9, no. 2, p. 355.

[12] See, for example, Viviane Frings-Hessami, "Khmer Rouge Archives: Appropriation, Reconstruction, Neo-Colonial Exploitation and Their Implications for the Reuse of the Records", in *Archival Science*, 2019, vol. 19, no. 2.

CPK government) interests in burying the history of Cambodia whilst la-belling the Khmer Rouge 'genocidal'. Let me be clear on this point: I am not suggesting the crimes of the Khmer Rouge were not horrific. I am merely pointing out that 'legally-speaking' none of the Khmer Rouge leaders have been convicted for the form of genocide presented at many of the Phnom Penh museums established under Vietnamese and United Nations Transitional Authority in Cambodia ('UNTAC') rule. The trial Chamber's conviction for genocide of a minority Muslim population only held against Nuon Chea, and was on appeal at the time of his death in 2019.[13] After Nuon Chea's death, the ECCC Supreme Court Chamber terminated proceedings that would have brought about a final judgment whilst simultaneously declining to vacate the verdict of the trial Cham-ber.[14] The former action was mandated by domestic law, but the sole au-thority cited in drawing the latter interpretation regarding the presumption of innocence was a 1988 European Court of Human Rights Case of highly questionable relevance.[15] Setting aside those legal questions, the point here is to draw attention to an aesthetic of justice that exists in narrative outside of the law, yet influences both the public perception of the Court's legitimacy and the legal arguments presented as legitimate within the Court.

What factors drove this narrative? Definitive answers to such ques-tions are often elusive, but it is clear that Hun Sen's government pushed to encapsulate 'guilt' around the nucleus of the Pol Pot clique. Indeed, dur-ing the years when the Khmer Rouge still held sway in northern Cambo-dia, both Hun Sen and Vietnamese leadership sought through museums and archives to ensure that the Khmer Rouge could not reverse the dwin-dling of its influence.[16] I suggest here that by the ECCC's genesis in 2006, this collection of circumstances had produced a situation in which fair trial was impossible, not only because of the intervening decades of

---

[13] For the Nuon Chea situation, see ECCC, Interoffice Memorandum, 15 August 2019, F46/5.1 (https://www.legal-tools.org/doc/f9icy1/).

[14] ECCC, Case No. 002/19-09-2007-ECCC/SC, Supreme Court Chamber, Decision on Ur-gent Request Concerning the Impact on Appeal Proceedings of Nuon Chea's Death Prior to the Appeal Judgment, 22 November 2019, F46/2/4/2 (https://www.legal-tools.org/doc/3lboek/).

[15] European Court of Human Rights, *Barberà, Messegué and Jabardo v. Spain*, Judgment, Application No. 10590/83, 6 December 1988. The ECCC cites para. 77, but see also para. 68, 78 (https://www.legal-tools.org/doc/a84e3a/).

[16] *Ibid.*

memory manipulation, but also because of the lack of any clear and reliable evidence of direct 'orders' or 'commands', as required by the ECCC
Statute and customary international law.[17] Thus, just like a strong wind,
the ECCC brushes along the surface of Cambodia only for a (long) moment; while it might cool the heat, it passes without substantively impacting the State. Its vision of 'justice' is as temporal as its jurisdiction (13.4.).
With these points aired, I offer some concluding remarks on adversarialism and evidence (13.5.).

13.2. (Hi)Stories of (In)Justice: Colonial Wrongs

During World War II, France's grip on its colonies in Indochina weakened
considerably. In March 1945, after years of deference to French bureau-
cracy, Japanese forces interned the French administration (which had been
allowed to run relatively undisturbed during Nazi occupation) and offered
independence to the three Indochina States.[18] Then-King Sihanouk took
up the offer: he abrogated all French treaties and established a new Basic
Law.

But in September 1945, British and French troops arrived to disarm
Japanese troops and restore French authority.[19] France then introduced a
number of democratic reforms in the years that followed that were more
threatening to the elites of Cambodia than the occupation of the Japanese
or the re-establishment of the French protectorate.[20] In this way – and in
broad strokes – the intellectual city-leftists associated with Sihanouk came
to be associated with French colonial suppression in the eyes of the rural
populations.[21] Those elites sought to keep rural Cambodians, who comprised the vast majority of the population, from exercising the authority

---

[17] Law on the Establishment of the Extraordinary Chambers, with inclusion of amendments
as promulgated on 27 October 2004, NS/RKM/1004/006, Article 1, 29 (https://www.legal-
tools.org/doc/e66d31/). In reference to customary international law, the ECCC Law relies
upon the Cambodian Criminal Code in place in 1956, the Geneva Conventions of 1948,
the Genocide Convention of 1949, and for procedural matters, Cambodia's accession to the
ICCPR in 1966. See, generally, *ibid*. For a discussion on crimes against humanity as customary international law, see Kevin Crow, "International Law and Corporate Participation
in Times of Armed Conflict", in *Berkeley Journal of International Law*, 2019, vol. 37, no.
64.

[18] Vickery, 1984, see above note 10; Chandler, 2008, see above note 10.

[19] *Ibid.*

[20] *Ibid.*

[21] Chandler, 2008, see above note 10.

their numbers would glean from democratic reforms. Thus, the earliest resistance groups began in the 1940s, at first seeking only freedom from various forms of encroachment (under the Issarak) and only later sorting out ideological positions in the later 1940s and early 1950s.[22] By the time Sihanouk was able to consolidate power after 'peacefully negotiating' for independence in 1954, and by abdicating his 'King' title so he could take on political responsibilities as 'Prince', the Khmer Rouge was still a relatively unorganized and unthreatening political movement emanating from the villages.

Part of what drove the animosity toward Sihanouk was the perception amongst the "little people" (as he called the roughly 85 per cent of the population who lived on the countryside)[23] that – after all of his dramatic opposition to French occupation[24] – there was too much deference to American interests at the Geneva Agreement of 1954 and too little post-independence involvement of the peasantry with politics.[25] The countryside was still paying taxes to an unresponsive central authority, only now it was a Cambodian one rather than a French one. There was also the fact that the Geneva Agreement represented a defeat for virtually all progressive currents of Cambodian politics. Unlike the French agreements with Vietnam and Laos, Cambodia had to disarm its revolutionary forces, they were allowed no re-grouping zone, and they were left with little choice but to reintegrate into a Cambodia they did not desire – one under the rule of Sihanouk and (in the eyes of the Khmer Rouge[26]) his neo-colonialist conservative supporters.[27]

There were many factors that weakened Sihanouk's grip in the decade after the Geneva Agreement, but the beginning of the end was economic deterioration. Although Sihanouk's flirtation with intellectual leftists such as Ieng Sary and Khieu Samphan ended with attempted and actualized purges, their socialist ideals gained enough sway in Sihanouk's party by the early 1960s to inspire a number of reforms. In 1963, relations were broken with the Capitalist South Vietnam, import-and-export trade

---

[22]   *Ibid.*

[23]   Lovell, 2019, see above note 10.

[24]   Sihanouk publicly offered his life in exchange for Cambodian independence. See Vickery, 1984, see above note 10.

[25]   *Ibid.*

[26]   Chandler, 2008, see above note 10.

[27]   Vickery, 1984, see above note 10.

---

and banks were nationalized, and, by early 1964, American aid programmes were terminated. Khieu Samphan had recommended all of these actions, years earlier. Finally, in May 1965, all diplomatic relations with the US were cut off.

After 1963, economic conditions steadily deteriorated. Sihanouk's reforms were in practice (though not by necessity) means to disguise further concentration of Cambodia's economic wealth in the hands of Sihanouk's favourite players, who were often given control over 'nationalized' institutions and allowed to run them for private profit. While Sihanouk retained a certain level of 'good king' or 'God King' awe from even radical left peasants, his party subordinates did not. In-party tensions grew as well, as many Phnom Penh business-minded politicians found Sihanouk's policies erratic and short-sighted; they preferred a closer alliance with American interests. By the time Sihanouk swung towards American interests again in late 1969, it was too late.

13.3. (Hi)Stories of (In)Justice: Opportunism

Both the United States and China sought to overthrow the government of Sihanouk for different reasons. While the United States saw Sihanouk's policy of neutrality as a barrier to its war in Vietnam – especially to its aim of cutting off transportation of personnel and supplies between North and South Vietnam through the north of Cambodia – and while it supported the Khmer Serei and Lon Nol due to their friendliness of free market ideals, China saw early on in the Khmer Rouge's ideology an opportunity to enact Mao's cultural revolutionist ideals of radical class abolition, currency abolition, and agricultural self-sufficiency as a means to achieve a 'pure' Communist State. Both the United States and China succeeded in manipulating the political landscape in Cambodia and both contributed greatly to the rise and tragic outcomes of the Khmer Rouge. This subsection turns first to the series of actions surrounding the United States and Lon Nol (13.3.1.), and then to China's involvement with the Khmer Rouge (13.3.2.).

13.3.1. The United States and Lon Nol

The United States (hi)story building up to 1975 primarily revolved around its interests in Vietnam. In 1955, after Sihanouk abdicated his 'King' title to his father in order to retain his position as the head of State, he founded a national party, the Sankum, which came to dominate the legislature. It was a one party State; opposition efforts were undermined or suppressed. When Sihanouk declined to join Southeast Asia Treaty Organization (SEATO) – one of many Cold War alliance efforts curated by the US – stressing adherence to Cambodia's commitment to neutrality, the United States began to covertly support opposition forces (Khmer Serei) that it felt might be necessary to gain a firmer grip against Communist spread in an era when the now-infamous 'domino theory' still fell on receptive and powerful ears.[28] Eventually, when relations with Thai and Southern Vietnamese neighbors supported by the United States cooled, Cambodia ended its United States military aid programme and, as mentioned above, broke off diplomatic relations with Washington in 1965.

At the same time, Sihanouk was fuelling Khmer Rouge-esque perceptions that his regime was nothing more than a puppet for neo-colonial powers by conducting purges of far left voices in Phnom Penh and elsewhere.[29] As already noted, anti-Sihanouk narratives had bubbled since the late 1940s, but most of the animosity was directed against his allies due to his 'good king' image. But beginning with the French reoccupation of Cambodia after World War II, an anti-feudal narrative had burgeoned and gained steam amongst the Issarak, the Khmer People's Revolutionary Party (KPRP), and eventually the Khmer Rouge. During the first half of the 1960s, narratives that once viewed Sihanouk as a Cambodian extension of French bourgeoisie control, shifted to ones that viewed him as a puppet for American interests. Indeed, Pol Pot repeatedly referred to the Prince as "an agent of the United States". After 1965, these narratives too lost sway. By 1969, Pol Pot had dropped his anti-Sihanouk rhetoric, and after Lon Nol seized power in 1970 with the support of United States forces, Sihanouk (exiled in Beijing) aligned himself with the Khmer Rouge, calling on his supporters to join the resistance. Most records indicate that Beijing, and in particular Premier ZHOU Enlai, played a vital role in curating this transition.[30]

---

[28] This was the popular idea among United States diplomats during the Cold War that if one domino (State) 'fell' (to Communism), the rest would quickly topple. See, for example, Peter Leeson and Andrea Dean, "The Democratic Domino Theory: An Empirical Investigation", in *American Journal of Political Science*, 2009, vol. 53, no. 3, p. 533.

[29] Vickery, 1984, see above note 10; Chandler, 2008, see above note 10; Kiernan, 1998, see above note 10; Short, 2004, see above note 10; Kampuchea, 1982, see above note 10; Kiernan, 1985, see above note 10; Lovell, 2019, see above note 10.

[30] Lovell, 2019, see above note 29.

There were two primary interwoven factors that spurred United States intervention in Cambodia. The first was rice and the second was the escalation of US intervention in Vietnam. Cambodia's economy depended on taxing rice exports which, in 1964, had reached record highs, but with more US and Northern Vietnamese troops needing sustenance in 1965, and with more Vietnamese crops being destroyed, large amounts of rice were smuggled from Cambodia to Vietnam. Indeed, US intelligence from the period indicated that Sihanouk anticipated a 1965 drop in revenue and planned to sell rice secretly to the Vietnamese.

Moreover, Vietnamese troops increasingly used northern Cambodia as a safe passage to escape US fire. For some time already, the US had been secretly planting landmines in northern Cambodia targeting Vietnamese trails, but during the years from 1969 to 1973, this offensive escalated dramatically. Without notifying the US Congress, the Nixon Administration dropped over 500,000 bombs on Cambodia and deployed US troops over its border. By the time these interventions subsided in 1974, an estimated 700,000 Cambodians had been killed, thousands of homes destroyed, and economic devastation engulfed the region. Thousands of refugees then fled to urban areas where they were treated as second class citizens; much of the population was entirely dependent upon US food aid. Indeed, production of rice had fallen to less than 20 per cent of the quantity required to feed the country, and with Lon Nol's regime more concerned with power retention than infrastructure, there was little opportunity to boost production. This collection of conditions has led Ben Kiernan, one of the leading voices on the history of the period, to conclude that "Pol Pot's revolution would not have won power without US economic and military destabilization of Cambodia".[31] These conditions also likely bolstered the Khmer Rouge's later obsession with boosting agricultural production per hectare to levels that were later revealed to be impossible.[32]

As noted above, the Khmer Rouge was a relatively small movement before the US intervention. But it won broader support by espousing guerilla war against both the Americans and the Lon Nol government in Phnom Penh installed by the Central Intelligence Agency ('CIA'). The Khmer Rouge used the US bombings to mobilize fighters against Lon Nol;

---

[31] Kiernan, 1998, see above note 10.
[32] See ECCC, Case 002/01, Trial Chamber, 2013.

when they seized the city of Battambang in 1975, they tore apart two B-52 bombers with their bare hands; when they seized Phnom Penh later that year, they evacuated residents partially under the pretence that American B-52s were about to bomb the city. The abrupt withdrawal of US forces in 1975 during the final weeks of the Vietnam War led to the collapse of the Lon Nol regime and opened the way for Pol Pot to come to power. Some have suggested that the abrupt ending of US food aid was as much a factor in the starvation that spread across Cambodia after Lon Nol as the policies of the Khmer Rouge.

Some sources argue that covert American operations began 1965 under the Johnson administration just after Sihanouk severed diplomatic ties. They suggest that there were 2,565 sorties into Cambodia from 1965 to 1968, with 214 tons of bombs.[33] When the Khmer Rouge seized power in 1975, the US and UN were quick to recognize the Democratic Party of Kampuchea (DPK) as the 'legitimate' State authority, and refused to change that designation long after the Vietnamese liberation in 1979. This has led some commentators to question the sincerity of UN involvement with Khmer Rouge trials at the ECCC. As one commentator put it:

> The UN has declared its involvement is necessary to guarantee "accountability," [but] its real concern is to prevent the proceedings from probing what happened in the years before and after the Khmer Rouge held power. Any genuine investigation would be obliged to begin in 1969, when the US, as part of its war against Vietnam, indiscriminately and illegally bombed Cambodia to prevent it being used as a supply line and safe-haven by Vietnamese liberation fighters.[34]

In sum, there were at least two political reasons why the US bombed Cambodia in the early 1970s: rooting out the North Vietnamese troops on Cambodian soil, and protecting the Lon Nol regime from Cambodian communist forces.[35] Not only did this contribute to economic slowdown, corruption in government, and political upheaval, it also legitimated the Khmer Rouge narrative that Cambodia was under siege, that the Capitalists would stop at nothing to destroy them. This, combined

---

[33] Taylor Owen and Ben Kiernan, "Bombs Over Cambodia: New Light on the US Air War", in *The Asia-Pacific Journal*, 2007, vol. 5, p. 5.

[34] James Conachy, "Cambodia: Khmer Rouge Trial Expected by End of Year", *Word Socialist Web Site*, 11 September 2001 (available on its web site).

[35] Owen and Kiernan, 2007, see above note 33.

with the withdrawal of the US forces and the abrupt cut in US support for the CIA-installed Lon Nol government, paved the way for the Khmer Rouge to easily seize Phnom Penh in 1975.

13.3.2. China and the Khmer Rouge

Chinese and Soviet policy toward Cambodia through the 1950s and 1960s was identical to that toward the Vietnamese – that is, to maintain Cambodia's neutrality even if it meant holding back local revolutionary forces.[36] In 1958, Sihanouk attempted to strengthen diplomatic and economic ties with China and signed a trade agreement with the Democratic Republic of Vietnam.[37] While several sources suggest that both Vietnam and the United States were willing to maintain Sihanouk against the Cambodian revolutionary Communists,[38] most emphasize that Sihanouk's neutral, non-Communist Cambodia was valuable to the Vietnamese war effort as a safe haven for troops and agricultural production.[39] But China was also one of Sihanouk's main foreign supporters, providing economic aid important for the country's material progress and for strengthening Sihanouk's post-monarchy regime.[40]

The official line pushed by the People's Republic of Kampuchea – Cambodia's present political authority – is that the course of the Khmer Rouge under Pol Pot was determined by China's desire for hegemony over Southeast Asia, and that there was a Chinese hand behind the policies adopted by the Pol Pot clique. This (hi)story finds its anchor in the 1954 Geneva Agreements, where Cambodian revolutionaries were essentially left politically powerless to manifest ideological change.[41] But both Chinese and Russian negotiators pressed this outcome, and some have commented that it was the fear of United States military intervention – including the threat of nuclear weapons – that drove this position, rather than active Chinese expansionism. The most recent accounts of the build

---

[36] Chandler, 2008, see above note 10.

[37] Vickery, 1984, see above note 10.

[38] Vickery, 1984, see above note 10; Chandler, 2008, see above note 10; Kiernan, 1998, see above note 10; Short, 2004, see above note 10; Kampuchea,1982, see above note 10; Kiernan, 1985, see above note 10; Lovell, 2019, see above note 10.

[39] Kiernan, 1998, see above note 10; Short, 2004, see above note 10.

[40] On the factories given to Cambodia as part of the Chinese aid program, see *Far Eastern Economic Review* (9 May 1963), pp. 319–22. See also Kiernan, 1985, see above note 10.

[41] See Geneva Agreements, 21 July 1954.

up to Lon Nol's coup in 1970 indicate that the narratives of Chinese expansionism, while actually motivating foreign policy from the United States side, were not a reality in China.[42] The United States vastly overestimated China's interest in Southeast Asia and its ability to support the interests it did have in the region. It was the perception of impending Chinese hegemony more than the reality that determined United States foreign policy.

That said, long before the Khmer Rouge came to power – indeed, even before Lon Nol's military coup – Chinese authorities were courting both Sihanouk and Khmer Rouge leadership. And even as Sihanouk's reign was falling apart, Mao stood on a balcony with a near-exiled Sihanouk, fully aware of the fact, yet declaring, "Long live Cambodia! Long live Prince Sihanouk!" before crowds on Tiananmen Square.[43]

In his more realistic moments, Sihanouk realized that there was a strong current of political manipulation: he wrote in his own diaries that the Cambodian People's Party ('CPP') would "spit me out like a cherry pit".[44] Yet he seemed at once naïve and self-interested in his consistent readiness to work with Mao and ZHOU, and to accept their push toward Khmer Rouge support, in the years immediately after Lon Nol took power. No one can know exactly what motivated him – various records indicate a craving to return to things as they were before Lon Nol,[45] a willingness to acquiesce to Chinese interests so long as his lifestyle remained a few notches above the "little people" he once ruled,[46] or in the most charitable estimations emanating from Cambodian sources, a susceptibility to deception and manipulation despite his best intentions[47] – but we can know that, when it served the CPP most, Sihanouk called on the subjects still loyal to him to join with formerly despised Khmer Rouge forces against Lon Nol, and that it is unlikely that the Khmer Rouge would have ever attained the forces it gained but for Sihanouk's call to arms.[48]

---

[42] Lovell, 2019, see above note 10.
[43] *Ibid.*
[44] *Ibid.*
[45] See *ibid.*
[46] *Ibid.*
[47] For example, Dith Pran, *Survival in the Killing Fields*, Roger, 1987.
[48] Lovell, 2019, see above note 10.

Even if China lacked hegemonic authority, it nevertheless had a strong influence upon the Khmer Rouge leadership. This influence came in at least two forms. The first was through the ideological influence of Maoism and the second was through aid and trade funding. Diplomatic records from both China and the Khmer Rouge during this period are notoriously difficult to come by. Nevertheless, with respect to the former of these, a leaked conversation between the first meeting between Mao and Pol Pot would suggest a fan-like relationship:

> Pol Pot (exceptionally excited): We are extremely happy to be able to meet the great leader Chairman Mao today!

> Mao: We approve of you! Many of your experiences are better than ours. China does not have the right to criticize you […] You are fundamentally correct […] Right now [in China], we have […] a capitalist country without capitalists […].

> Pol Pot: […] In future, we will be sure to act according to your words. Since I was young, I have studied many of Chairman Mao's works, in particular those concerning people's war. The works of Chairman Mao have led our entire party.[49]

Other records indicate that Ieng Sary often travelled with copies of Mao's books, the French translations, thoroughly marked with copious notes.[50]

The latter of China's two forms of influence was motivated through its rivalry with Vietnam. While China supported Sihanouk in the years prior to Lon Nol, it also welcomed the idea of a Southeast Asian Communist movement that distanced itself from Hanoi. This offered Pol Pot greater flexibility in the years before 1970, and when the United States evacuated Phnom Penh in 1975, China almost immediately provided aid and enormous shipments of supplies. In the years following, China gave copious amounts of military aid as well as hundreds of training personnel, and Cambodia provided China with thousands of tons of rice, harvested through forced labour in its burgeoning work camps.

But even as early as 1976, Chinese economic aid began to wane. Some have suggested that this was because Cambodia's demands were

---

[49] Dan Tong, '1960–70 niandai de Xihanuke, boerbute yu Zhongguo' [Sihanouk, Pol Pot and China in the 1960s–70s], excerpt from Lovell, 2019, see above note 10.

[50] *Ibid.*

too great; others have suggested that ZHOU Enlai's death that year jeopardized the relationship, either because Cambodian leadership became suspicious of China or because ZHOU's (disputed)[51] plan to return Sihanouk to power no longer had a champion.[52]

Nevertheless, it is clear that by 1975 China had replaced the United States as the primary benefactor nation and therefore as the actor with the most power to make Cambodia its 'satellite', but that by late 1977 it had little interest in doing so, at least not in collaboration with Khmer Rouge leadership. It rather appeared to pull back, either still hoping that the smoke would soon clear and that it would be able to support Sihanouk's re-ascension to leadership,[53] or unable to cope with Cambodia as its own domestic problems grew in severity.[54] At any rate, Beijing continued to recognize the legitimacy of the Khmer Rouge government, as did the UN, long after 1979 when the ECCC's temporal jurisdiction cuts off.

Some commentators have suggested that Beijing's two-track foreign policy fomented suspicion and postponed peace in Cambodia.[55] That is, Beijing both backed the Khmer Rouge as a strongly-supported insurgence capable of removing Lon Nol, and recognized Prince Sihanouk as the official leader of Cambodia.[56] Like Washington, Beijing continued to support the Khmer Rouge even after it was completely conquered by the Vietnamese troops in early 1979. In 1984, then-Vice Premier DENG Xiaoping said of the Khmer Rouge: "I do not understand why some people want to remove Pol Pot [...] it is true that he made some mistakes in the past but now he is leading the fight against the Vietnamese aggressors".[57]

At the very least, such impressions illustrate the contingency of the act of creating a 'justice'-producing legal mechanism upon the political, cultural and temporal vantage points of those who seek it.

---

[51] *Ibid.*

[52] Vickery, 1984, see above note 10; Chandler, 2008, see above note 10.

[53] Vickery, 1984, see above note 10.

[54] Lovell, 2019, see above note 10.

[55] Sopheada Phy, Peace and Conflict Monitor, "Getting Away With Murder: The Khmer Rouge Tribunal", *Global Policy Forum*, 11 November 2008 (available in its web site).

[56] David Ablin and M. Hood, *Revival: The Cambodian Agony*, Routledge, 1990.

[57] Nayan Chanda, Ben Kiernan and William Shawcross, "An Exchange on Cambodia", *The New York Review of Books*, 27 September 1984.

13.4. After the Khmer Rouge: Justice as Temporal as the Wind

The sections above stress the point that justice is not a universal concept. Not infrequently, there are divergences between local and 'international' understandings of how justice should unfold and where it should take place. Some cultures seek forms of justice through investigatory and judicial means. Other cultures seek it through situating an event within temporalities that reach across multiple lifespans and generations. Even institutions that engage in investigation and adjudication take different form in different places and emphasize different procedures or facts as legally significant.

One poignant example of this, and of the mismatch between 'international justice' and local understandings of justice, can be found in Hinton's work.[58] On the basis of over 300 interviews with victims of the Khmer Rouge, Hinton emphasizes that in Cambodian society, adversarialism (the Court) creates a barrier between victims and perpetrators who seek reconciliation as the ultimate form of justice.[59] An adversarial court is not the place to find justice; in fact, adversarial constructs such as 'verdicts', 'sentences', and attributions of definite fault, undermine through their very procedure a justice that is reflective of Cambodian culture. In Cambodian understandings of Karma (a central element of Cambodian society), anger and antagonism are pointless, even if present, since the people responsible for bad acts (even crimes against humanity) carry the consequences for those acts with them through their present life and into the next. Thus, rather than seeking justice through conviction, many of the victims that participate in ECCC proceedings do so in order to locate the places where their loved ones were buried, because only then can monks administer proper burial rights, which will grant rebirth to the deceased, and in this way (rather than through conviction), achieve justice.[60]

The UN's hybrid justice in Cambodia also rings hollow because of the lack of any meaningful recognition of past wrongs on the part of the organization itself. For example, one Oxfam Report published in 1988 noted that Cambodia was "the only third world country [...] denied Unit-

---

[58] Alexander Hinton, *The Justice Façade: Trials of Transition in Cambodia*, Oxford University Press, 2018.

[59] *Ibid.*

[60] *Ibid.*

ed Nations development aid".[61] While exact records describing (lack of) humanitarian aid are difficult to find,[62] the absence of international cash in Cambodia during the pre-UNTAC period is well known. As Chanthou Boua put it:

> For thirteen years, from 1979 to 1992, Cambodia did not receive UN development aid. The reason is that the government of the State of Cambodia was not recognized by the UN or Western countries, the donors of UN funds, despite the fact that it was this government which ended the suffering and genocide perpetrated by the Khmer Rouge regime [...] 8.5 million Cambodians living under the Hun Sen regime continued to be punished by the world community.[63]

Following the overthrow of the Khmer Rouge in 1979, the United States, China and European States continued to recognize the Khmer Rouge as the legitimate government of Kampuchea (as Cambodia was renamed from 1975 to 1991). Indeed, the UN blocked all international assistance to the new, Vietnamese-backed regime and opposed all calls for the arrest and trial of Khmer Rouge leaders. This persisted even until 2000 when Kofi Annan halted negotiations on the establishment of the tribunal (the negotiations began after the United States started calling for the tribunal in 1997).[64]

Reverberations of this support continued amongst the international community into the 1990s, and in fact, the shift from Khmer Rouge support begot visions of justice more harmonized with the local culture. One UN ambition when it took over Cambodia in 1991 was 'reconciliation' – it discussed something akin to truth and reconciliation commissions – meaning in that context that no official attempt to investigate and adjudicate the past would be made. Thus, for the two years that UN troops occupied the country in the early 1990s, no steps were even taken against Khmer Rouge leaders.

---

[61] Eva Mysliwiec, *Punishing the Poor: The International Isolation of Kampuchea*, Oxfam, 1988.

[62] Kampuchea, 1982, see above note 10 (claiming that the international humanitarian aid documents for Cambodia are not all available).

[63] Chanthou Boua in Ben Kiernan (ed.), *Genocide and Democracy in Cambodia: The Khmer Rouge, the United Nations and the International Community*, Yale University Southeast Asia Studies, 1993.

[64] Allan Yang, "No Redemption – The Failing Khmer Rouge Tribunal", in *Harvard International Review*, 2008, vol. 29, no. 4.

Prior to the UNTAC years, throughout the 1980s, the Khmer Rouge received international support. In addition to the large supply of weapons, China continued to support the Khmer Rouge with a yearly USD 100 million long after 1979.[65] From 1979 to 1986, the United States gave USD 85 million to the Khmer Rouge.[66] And from 1979 to 1991, European governments provided substantial military equipment.[67] Indeed, United States military support for the Khmer Rouge remained unchanged despite the Vietnamese withdrawal from Cambodia in 1989.[68] Meanwhile, Australia actively called for an amnesty to be given to the Khmer Rouge on the condition that it lay down its arms, and the UN agencies went along with Great Power policies and suggestions.

So when David Scheffer declared that "the winds of international justice swept through the fields, forests, and towns of Cambodia where millions perished", his words described a particular conception of justice that assumes its own universality. Yet, as we have seen, this conception is geographically and temporally bound, rooted in Western and not Cambodian conceptions of justice, and is therefore in some sense a normative aspiration rather than substantive declaration. Indeed, the ECCC's primary function does not appear to be to attain some estimation of 'justice' that reflects Cambodian culture, but to maintain a certain narrative of 'just' global power relations.

Of course, when atrocities occur as complex as those that took place in Cambodia, actors will seek to create narratives of the past to serve purposes in the present, whether those purposes are deterrent or political or otherwise motivated. In some sense, actors are always 'using' the past because there is no 'God's-eye view': we do not and cannot have a singular 'truth' of the past – stories of societies do not move along single narratives – there are always multiple winners and losers. In my view, the broader lesson here is that a binary view of 'justice' – one that understands actors as only discretely occupying categories such as 'convicted' or 'acquitted' or 'perpetrator' or 'victim' or even 'accused' – is a procedural function inherent to adversarial judgment. As such, adversarial

---

[65] Kiernan, 1993, see above note 63.

[66] *Ibid.*

[67] Raoul Marc Jennar, "Cambodia: Khmer Rouge in Court", *Le Monde diplomatique*, October 2006 (available on its web site).

[68] George Chigas, "The Politics of Defining Justice After the Cambodian Genocide", in *Journal of Genocide Research*, 2000, vol. 2, no. 2, p. 245.

judgment in some contexts should be resisted at the same time as evidentiary and thereby narrative accuracy should be pursued. Adversarial judgment by its nature pits narratives against each other and chooses winners – a 'correct' (hi)story. By contrast, accurate evidence can be interpreted in a variety of ways over time and across space.

13.5. Conclusion

The sections above have argued that, because Lon Nol would not have come to power but for US intervention; because the Khmer Rouge would not have gained Sihanouk's (and Beijing's) support but for Lon Nol's seizure of power; and because the US's abrupt severance of support for Lon Nol created a power vacuum in the immediate post-Vietnam War moment, the Khmer Rouge would not have come to power *but for* US intervention. Moreover, because at the dawn of the Khmer Rouge's reign, Kampuchea depended upon economic aid from and sales of rice to China; and because many of the cadres that bolstered the Khmer Rouge's initial seizure and sustenance of power from 1974 to roughly 1976 did so after Sihanouk blessed the Khmer Rouge at Beijing's behest, the Khmer Rouge would not have sustained itself *but for* Chinese intervention.

The sections above have also argued that, by the ECCC's genesis in 2006, intervening decades of memory manipulation, and evidentiary damage both political and collateral, have produced a situation in which, for example, evidence of past archival manipulation or present corruption at the Court is clearer and more reliable than the evidence of direct 'orders' or 'commands' found in the archives to convict 'those most responsible' for the deaths of around two million Cambodian nationals between 1975 and 1979.

Reliable evidence itself is not necessarily the guiding light on the path to justice. Indeed, as Hinton's interviews of the families of Khmer Rouge victims forcefully demonstrated, 'international justice' is not necessarily international. And if justice itself is a concept in constant flux across space and time, perhaps the ECCC's greatest flaw is the assumption that adversarialism can reflect 'justice' and 'accuracy' at the same time as procedure and circumstance necessitate that evidentiary accuracy is unobtainable, especially within a myopically defined temporal jurisdiction.

To provide a final example, the archive of the Tuol Sleng (S-21) – the largest in Cambodia – is actually composed of records found in several places and brought together by an insurgent government (the Vietnam-ese).[69] When the Khmer Rouge lost power in 1979, many records disap-peared, were stolen, misappropriated or destroyed.[70] During the 1980s, the remaining records were kept in poor conditions and remained uncata-logued. Some records known to have been in the archive in 1979 later dis-appeared, and some records were later added to the archive. Thus, the re-liance by the ECCC on the Tuol Sleng archive, curated by the same gov-ernment that destroyed many of the records, is in effect partial reliance on a Vietnamese narrative of Khmer Rouge records. Open discussions along these lines would, in my view, better serve the interests of 'justice'.

The interests of 'justice' would also be served by discussions on whether evidence should be collected with the aim of processing it through procedural systems that seek and are geared toward conviction and punishment for actions that took place in a limited temporal space, rather than collecting and verifying evidence through non-prosecutorial means with the aim of meeting community definitions of justice.

---

[69] See, for example, Hessami, 2019, p. 255, see above note 12.
[70] *Ibid.*

14

Possible Impediments to Justice for Colonial Crimes: A Belgian Perspective

Christophe Marchand, Crépine Uwashema and Christophe Deprez[*]

14.1. Introduction

Justice for colonial wrongs is a difficult matter. Collective or individual responsibilities have rarely been established in history.[1] This may be described as an 'accountability gap'.[2] While this gap may partly be due to circumstantial and factual reasons, it is also the result, specifically, of legal impediments that are faced by victims in their quest for justice. Such impediments exist on the plane of international(ized) justice, at the level of former colonies, as well as in the domestic legal order of former colonial States.

This chapter takes the latter perspective as a starting point. Drawing from our experience in assisting victims of colonial crimes and their families in Belgium, we will seek to examine the 'accountability gap' from

---

[*] **Christophe Marchand**, **Crépine Uwashema** and **Christophe Deprez** are all attorneys at JUS COGENS, a Brussels-based, small-size law firm specialising in human rights and international criminal issues. Deprez is Associate Lecturer at the University of Liège and a Visiting Professor at the University of Lille and at Aix-Marseille University. He holds a Ph.D. from the University of Liège. Marchand qualified as an attorney in 1996 and is a partner at and founder of JUS COGENS. He has extensive experience in international criminal cases and in human rights litigation, including before the European Court of Human Rights and United Nations monitoring bodies. Uwashema is a partner at JUS COGENS. She holds master's degrees in law from the Vrije Universiteit Brussel and Université libre de Bruxelles.

[1] See Wolfgang Kaleck, *Double Standards: International Criminal Law and the West*, Torkel Opsahl Academic EPublisher, Brussels, 2015, p. i. See also, pointing at a few recent, domestic attempts to address this issue, Morten Bergsmo, "Myanmar, Colonial Aftermath, and Access to International Law", in Occasional Paper Series No. 9 (2019), Torkel Opsahl Academic EPublisher, Brussels, 2019, pp. 17–18.

[2] See also Chapter 15 below by Mutoy Mubiala ("Addressing Colonial Wrong-Doing in the Great Lakes Region of Africa").

the perspective of the criminal law and practice of a former colony. We will do so by presenting a selected series of concrete legal impediments that victims may face in litigating at the Belgian level, as well as potential solutions to tackle them.

The analysis will be structured in four sections, each addressing one specific, possible legal impediment. Firstly, the characterization of colonial wrongs as war crimes will be examined, with a discussion on legal nature of colonial conflicts under international humanitarian law ('IHL') and possible implications in terms of criminal prosecutions in Belgium (Section 14.2.). Secondly, the chapter will address the non-application of statutory limitations for international crimes and its contours in the Belgian experience (Section 14.3.). Thirdly, we will turn to the Belgian experience in establishing parliamentary commissions of inquiry on colonial wrongs, and the impact that such process may have in the context of criminal proceedings (Section 14.4.). Fourthly and finally, in light of recent legislative developments, the chapter will leave the domain of individual responsibility and turn to novel perspectives on the criminal liability of Belgium as a State (Section 14.5.).

14.2. Prosecution for War Crimes and the Classification of Armed Conflicts

From a legal perspective, the characterization of colonial wrongs as international crimes is of key importance to the efforts to bring those responsible to justice. This is because in many legal systems, the catalogue of international crimes – whether war crimes, crimes against humanity or genocide – triggers the application of a series of derogatory tools (either procedural or substantive in nature) that are specific to this category of offences. This includes the application of specific modes of liability,[3] the ban on immunities,[4] or, as will be further examined below,[5] the application of specific norms pertaining to statutory limitations.

---

[3] See, for example, in the Belgian context, Article 136*septies* of the Criminal Code (for a commentary, see Damien Vandermeersch, "Les violations du droit international humanitaire", *in Les infractions – Volume 5: les infractions contre l'ordre public*, Brussels, Larcier, 2013, pp. 140–145).

[4] See, for example, in the context of the Rome Statute of the International Criminal Court ('ICC'), 17 July 1998, Article 27 ('ICC Statute') (http://www.legaltools.org/doc/7b9af9/).

[5] At Section 14.3.

Among international crimes, war crimes are the ones that have probably been most commonly associated with colonial, decolonization or post-colonial contexts. As Kaleck observes: "War crimes were a common feature of colonial wars",[6] also in the context of struggles of independence against Belgium.[7] This includes Congo (then Zaïre) in the early 1960's.

On 17 January 1961, soon after the 30 June 1960 independence, Congo's first Prime Minister, Patrice Lumumba, was assassinated in Katanga (which had recently seceded from the newly independent Congo), in the presence of both Belgian and Katangese officials.[8] His corpse was dissolved in acid.[9] Patrice Lumumba was known to have attracted strong opposition from Belgian officials due to his highly critical position towards the former colonial State and its remaining interests in Congo.

In 2001, a commission of inquiry[10] was established within the Belgian Parliament to elucidate the circumstances of this crime. In its final report, the commission came to the conclusion that "some members of the government of Belgium and other Belgian actors bear a moral responsibility in the circumstances that led to the death of Lumumba".[11]

Unsatisfied with this timid finding, in June 2011 the family of Patrice Lumumba lodged a criminal complaint with a Brussels-based investigative judge, on grounds of the (Belgian) nationality[12] of ten suspected participants to this crime.[13] This complaint soon came to raise a debate on the precise characterization of the crime that had been committed against Patrice Lumumba. Could his assassination indeed qualify as a war crime –

---

[6] Kaleck, p. 28, see above note 1.

[7] *Ibid.*, p. 27.

[8] Enquête parlementaire visant à déterminer les circonstances exactes de l'assassinat de Patrice Lumumba et l'implication éventuelle des responsables politiques belges dans celui-ci, Rapport, *Doc. Parl.*, 2001-2002, no. 50-0312/007, pp. 838–839 in particular.

[9] *Ibid.*, p. 824.

[10] On such mechanism in the Belgian context, see below at Section 14.4.

[11] Enquête parlementaire visant à déterminer les circonstances exactes de l'assassinat de Patrice Lumumba et l'implication éventuelle des responsables politiques belges dans celui-ci, Rapport, *Doc. Parl.*, 2001-2002, no. 50-0312/007, p. 839. Our own translation of "certains membres du gouvernement belge et d'autres acteurs belges ont une responsabilité morale dans les circonstances qui ont conduit à la mort de Lumumba".

[12] Jurisdiction to prosecute international crimes in Belgium based on active nationality is consolidated in Article 6, 1 *bis* of the Preliminary Title to the Belgian Code of Criminal Procedure (Titre préliminaire du Code de procédure pénale).

[13] At the time of writing, only two of them were still alive.

especially in the specific forms of murder, torture or inhuman treatment, serious injury to body or health, other outrage upon personal dignity, deprivation of the rights of fair and regular trial, and/or unlawful deportation or transfer? And, in the affirmative, should it be considered a war crime committed in an international or in a non-international armed conflict?

While the classification between international and non-international armed conflicts has, on the face of it, limited significance in the Belgian criminal system (this is because the catalogue of war crimes enshrined since 1993[14] in Article 136*quater* of the Belgian Criminal Code consists of a list that is common to both international and non-international conflicts),[15] the nature of the armed conflict that was ongoing at the time may still be relevant in connection with the requirements of legality and non-retroactivity in criminal proceedings. This is because, under the latter principles, "a person may only be held criminally liable and punished if, at the moment when he performed a certain act, the act was regarded as a criminal offence by the relevant legal order".[16]

In the *Lumumba* case, the firm position of the family of Patrice Lumumba was and still is that, in light of relevant IHL principles,[17] the situation in Congo in January 1961 qualified as an international armed conflict ('IAC'). In short, this is because Belgian troops were still present in Congo in January 1961, because Belgium was actively contributing to the secessionist movements in both Katanga and Kasaï provinces, and because United Nations ('UN') and Union of Soviet Socialist Republics ('USSR')

---

[14] Loi du 16 juin 1993 relative à la répression des violations graves du droit international humanitaire, Belgian Official Journal (Moniteur belge), 5 August 1993.

[15] See, for example, Éric David, *Éléments de droit pénal international et européen*, second edition, Brussels, Bruylant, 2018, vol. 2, p. 1229. This certainly contrasts with what usually applies in other legal systems (see, for example, the duality of ICC Statute, Article 8, see above note 4).

[16] Antonio Cassese, "Nullum Crimen Sine Lege", in Antonio Cassese (ed.), *The Oxford Companion to International Criminal Justice*, Oxford University Press, 2009, p. 438.

[17] See Article 2 common to the four 1949 Geneva Conventions as interpreted, for example, by International Criminal Tribunal for the former Yugoslavia ('ICTY'), *Prosecutor v. Tadić*, Appeals chamber, Judgment, 15 July 1999, IT-94-1-A, para. 84 (https://www.legal-tools.org/doc/8efc3a/); ICC, *Prosecutor v. Lubanga*, Trial Chamber I, Judgment pursuant to Article 74 of the Statute, 18 March 2012, ICC-01/04-01/06-2842, para. 541 (https://www.legal-tools.org/doc/677866/). For a general commentary, see, for example, Andrew Clapham, "The Concept of International Armed Conflict", in Andrew Clapham, Paola Gaeta and Marco Sassòli (eds.), *The 1949 Geneva Convention: A Commentary*, Oxford University Press, 2015, pp. 3–26.

troops were also involved on the ground at that time.[18] As it is not seriously disputable that war crimes committed during international armed conflicts were already reflected in customary international law at that time,[19] and because the legality principle under international law does not oppose the prosecution of international crimes based on their customary nature,[20] Patrice Lumumba's complaint was, in our view, fully admissible.

When this question was raised before the investigative section of the Brussels Court of Appeal ('chambre des mises en accusation'), the perspective of the office of the federal prosecutor ('parquet fédéral') was slightly different. While agreeing that the murder of Patrice Lumumba could be characterized as a war crime and could lawfully lead to a criminal trial, the prosecutor considered that the situation in Congo, back in January 1961, did not consist of an international but of a non-international armed conflict ('NIAC'). In turn, this alternative position raised the question whether the criminalization of war crimes was already customary, back in 1961, also in time of non-international armed conflicts – which, according to the prosecutor, it was.[21]

---

[18] See Georges Abi-Saab, *The United Nations Operation in the Congo, 1960-1964*, Oxford University Press, 1978, especially pp. 7–47.

[19] See, already in 1949, Geneva Convention (I) for the Amelioration of the Condition of the Wounded and Sick in Armed Forces in the Field, 12 August 1949, Article 49 (https://www.legal-tools.org/doc/baf8e7/); Geneva Convention (II) for the Amelioration of the Condition of Wounded, Sick and Shipwrecked Members of Armed Forces at Sea, 12 August 1949, Article 50 (https://www.legal-tools.org/doc/0d0216/); Geneva Convention (III) Relative to the Treatment of Prisoners of War, 12 August 1949, Article 129 (https://www.legal-tools.org/doc/365095/); Geneva Convention (IV) relative to the protection of civilian persons in time of war, 12 August 1949, Article 146 (https://www.legal-tools.org/doc/d5e260/).

[20] See, for example, ICTY, *Prosecutor v. Tadić*, Appeals chamber, Decision on the Defence Motion for Interlocutory Appeal on Jurisdiction, 2 October 1995, IT-94-1-A, paras. 128–129 ('Tadic Decision on the defence motion for interlocutory appeal on jurisdiction') (https://www.legal-tools.org/doc/80x1an/); ICTY, *Prosecutor v. Hadžihasanović, Alagić and Kubura*, Appeals chamber, Decision on Interlocutory Appeal Challenging Jurisdiction in Relation to Command Responsibility, 16 July 2003, IT-01-47-AR72, paras. 35, 44–46 and 55 (https://www.legal-tools.org/doc/608f09/).

[21] Brussels Court of Appeal ('chambre des mises en accusation') ('BCA'), *Prosecutor and Lumumba v. Huyghe et al.*, FD.30.99.10/11, Federal prosecutor's submissions to the Brussels Court of Appeal, 7 June 2012.

In its 12 December 2012 decision,[22] the Brussels Court of Appeal, while not directly addressing the nature of the armed conflict at that time and place, concurred that, *prima facie*, the complaint and proceedings were admissible and had to carry on.

This decision has been criticized – including in the media[23] – by one commentator.[24] According to the latter (who argued that the conflict in Congo was non-international at that time), "[i]t is only from the beginning of the 1990's that the concept of war crime has been extended to grave breaches of international humanitarian law committed in (…) non-international armed conflicts".[25]

Surely, this statement must be nuanced.[26] When, in the *Tadić* case, the International Criminal Tribunal for the former Yugoslavia ('ICTY') was called upon to decide that during the 1990's ex-Yugoslavia war NIAC-based violations of IHL were already recognized as war crimes, the Tribunal also built on many pre-1990's (and indeed pre-1960's) declarations, military handbooks and other materials suggesting ancient customary status, for example, in relation to the 1936-1939 Spanish civil war or to the 1947 civil war in China.[27]

---

[22] BCA, *Prosecutor and Lumumba v. Huyghe et al.*, FD.30.99.10/11, Interlocutory judgment n°. 4358, 12 December 2012.

[23] Pierre d'Huart, "Affaire Lumumba: "il n'y a pas eu crime de guerre"", *La Libre Belgique*, 12 December 2012.

[24] Pierre d'Huart, "Affaire Lumumba: vers un non-lieu?", in *Journal des Tribunaux*, no. 6517, 2013, pp. 282–285.

[25] *Ibid.*, p. 282 (our own translation of "[c]e n'est qu'à partir du début des années 1990 que la notion de crime de guerre s'est étendue aux violations graves du droit humanitaire commises dans (…) les conflits armés non internationaux").

[26] See, also of this view, Jacques B. Mbokani, "Le lien de connexité entre le crime et le conflit armé dans la définition des crimes de guerre", in Diane Bernard and Damien Scalia (eds.), *Vingt ans de justice internationale pénale*, Les dossiers de la Revue de droit pénal et de criminologie, no. 21, La Charte, 2014, p. 44 (noting: "[t]he least we can say is that this statement comes as a surprise. Even more surprising is that [the author] cites Eric David and Antonio Cassese, although this is not what these eminent professors meant to say in the excerpts that the author refers to"; our own translation of "[l]e moins qu'on puisse dire, est que cette affirmation étonne. Plus étonnant encore, c'est qu'il cite à son appui Eric David et Antonio Cassese, alors que ce n'est pas ce que ces éminents professeurs ont voulu dire dans les passages auxquels l'auteur se réfère").

[27] Tadic Decision on the defence motion for interlocutory appeal on jurisdiction, paras. 100–102 in particular, see above note 20.

In fact, it very much seems that no international or internationalized criminal body has ever had the chance to question whether, in the early 1960's, grave breaches of IHL committed in time of NIAC could already qualify as war crimes under customary international law. In the context of the *prima facie* assessment that it was called upon to conduct on 12 December 2012, the Brussels Court of Appeal suggested that they could. In the view of Patrice Lumumba's family, this is an important step in filling the accountability gap for colonial wrongs.

14.3. The Non-Applicability of Statutory Limitations for International Crimes

The existence of statutory limitations is a recurring question in efforts to tackle impunity for international crimes. This is certainly true of colonial crimes, which tend to be brought to justice several decades after they were committed – if ever indeed. This is yet another challenge in the *Lumumba* case that deserves some attention.

It is not disputed that, in the Belgian (written) legislative framework, both the existence of war crimes and the suppression of statutes of limitation for their prosecution are the result of a 1993 piece of legislation that entered into force on 15 August 1993.[28] As a result of this legislation, and despite its subsequent, profound amendment (especially in 2003),[29] Article 21 of the Preliminary Title to the Belgian Code of Criminal Procedure[30] provides that the prosecution of war crimes, crimes against humanity and genocide in Belgium cannot become time-barred. The possible challenge with respect to this provision, as we shall see below, pertains to its *ratione temporis* scope.

It should first be recalled that Belgium is far from being isolated on the exclusion of statutory limitations for international crimes. On the international level, important steps have been taken in this direction, especially with a view to preventing impunity for World War II crimes.[31] On 26 November 1968, the Convention on the non-applicability of statutory

---

[28] Loi du 16 juin 1993 relative à la répression des violations graves du droit international humanitaire, Belgian Official Journal (Moniteur belge), 5 August 1993.

[29] Loi du 5 août 2003 relative aux violations graves du droit international humanitaire, Belgian Official Journal (Moniteur belge), 7 August 2003.

[30] Titre préliminaire du Code de procédure pénale ("Preliminary Title").

[31] See Florence Bellivier, Marine Eudes and Isabelle Fouchard, *Droit des crimes internationaux*, Paris, Presses Universitaires de France, 2018, p. 351.

limitations to war crimes and crimes against humanity was adopted under the auspices of the UN.[32] A similar initiative was replicated a few years after that within the Council of Europe, with the adoption in 1974 of the Convention on the non-applicability of statutory limitation to crimes against humanity and war crimes.[33] Although it is true that neither of these instruments gained much support (Belgium still became a party to the 1974 Council of Europe Convention in 2003), many legislators decided to go along and to adopt 'imprescriptibility' clauses for international crimes. This is how Article 21 of the Preliminary Title to the Belgian Code of Criminal Procedure came into existence – along with, for example, Article 213-5 of the French criminal code[34] and Article 29 of the Statute of the International Criminal Court.[35]

The *ratione temporis* scope of this provision, which entered into force on 15 August 1993, must then be questioned. Does it apply to all crimes, whenever committed and whether or not they would have normally become time-barred before 15 August 1993? Does it apply to past crimes, but only insofar as they had not reached statutory limitation by 15 August 1993? Or does it apply to crimes committed after 15 August 1993 only? In other words, can Article 21 of the Preliminary Title be applied in relation to the assassination of Patrice Lumumba – a crime for which, if it were not for Article 21, the statutory limitation would have normally expired after 10 years under Belgian law as it applied at that time?[36]

The international and comparative experience reveals important differences in approach on this issue. To only mention one obvious contrast

---

[32] United Nations, Convention on the Non-Applicability of Statutory Limitations to War Crimes and Crimes against Humanity, 11 November 1970, *Treaty Series*, vol. 754, p. 73 (https://www.legal-tools.org/doc/4bd593/).

[33] Council of Europe, European Convention on the Non-Applicability of Statutory Limitation to Crimes against Humanity and War Crimes, 27 June 2003, ETS No. 082 (https://www.legal-tools.org/doc/302b1c/).

[34] This provision, which was introduced pursuant to a law no. 64-1326 of 26 December 1964, provides for the non-applicability of statutory limitation to crimes against humanity and genocide. War crimes, on the other hand, may still become time-barred after 30 years under Article 462-10 of the French Criminal Code (https://www.legal-tools.org/doc/418004/).

[35] "The crimes within the jurisdiction of the Court shall not be subject to any statute of limitations".

[36] Loi du 17 avril 1878 contenant le titre préliminaire du Code de procédure pénale, telle que modifiée par la loi du 30 mai 1961, Belgian Official Journal (Moniteur belge), 10 June 1961, Article 21.

at treaty level: while the 1968 UN Convention applies to all crimes "irrespective of the date of their commission" (Article 1), the 1974 European Convention is limited to crimes "committed after its entry into force" or "committed before such entry into force in those cases where the statutory limitation period had not expired at that time" (Article 2). The question, in short, is thus whether Article 21 of the Preliminary Title should be interpreted in accordance with the UN or European conventional model.

Under common principles of Belgian judicial law and practice, when norms of a procedural character are newly adopted, they normally apply immediately to all new situations, but also to all continuing effects of situations that arose prior to the legislative amendment in question.[37] Theoretically, this would seem to suggest that, insofar as it entered the Belgian legislative framework on 15 August 1993, the ban on statutory limitations for international crimes should normally apply to crimes committed after 1993, to older crimes for which the statutory limitation had not been reached by 15 August 1993, but – *prima facie* – not to crimes which had already become time-barred by that date. As far as ordinary crimes are concerned, this position has been confirmed in Belgium both by the Cour de cassation and by the Cour constitutionnelle.[38]

This general position, however, may not be in line with international and comparative practice as far as *international crimes* are specifically concerned. As other precedents indicate, and although human rights practice seems to generally echo the general solution described above,[39] sev-

---

[37] Article 2 and 3 of the Belgian Code of Civil Procedure, as interpreted by consistent case law (see, for example, Cour de cassation, 24 April 2008, *Pasicrisie*, 2008, p. 993; for many further references, see Franklin Kuty, *Principes généraux du droit pénal belge – Tome 1: la loi pénale*, third edition, Brussels, Larcier, 2018, p. 294).

[38] Cour de cassation, 12 November 1996, no. P.95.1171.N (available at www.juridat.be); Cour constitutionnelle, 4 April 2019, no. 54/2019, *Revue de droit pénal et de criminologie*, 2019, no. 6, pp. 824–828.

[39] Though the European Court of Human Rights ('ECtHR') clearly accepts the extension of a limitation period before its expiry (ECtHR, *Coëme and others v. Belgium*, Judgment, 22 June 2000, no. 32492/96, 32547/96, 32548/96, 33209/96 and 33210/96, para. 149 ('ECtHR Coëme v. Belgium') (https://www.legal-tools.org/doc/0f1fd3/)), the Court seems more careful and less consistent when it comes to "restoring the possibility of punishing offenders for acts which were no longer punishable because they had already become subject to limitation". Compare ECtHR, *Kononov v. Latvia*, Judgment, 24 July 2008, application no. 36376/04, para. 144 (https://www.legal-tools.org/doc/56dc40/); ECtHR, *Kononov v. Latvia*, Grand Chamber, Judgment, 17 May 2010, application no. 36376/04, paras. 228–233 (https://www.legal-tools.org/doc/ed0506/); ECtHR *Coëme v. Belgium*, para. 149.

eral arguments have been successfully put forward in judicial history to support the assertion that this general model does not apply, as such, to prosecution for international crimes.[40]

When faced with similar challenges, the Extraordinary Chambers in the Courts of Cambodia ('ECCC'), for instance, have decided that the principles of legality and non-retroactivity do not apply at all to limitation periods and to other procedural matters, but only to purely substantive issues.[41] Another chamber within the ECCC further suggested that, in any case, limitation periods do not run for the time during which the State's prosecutorial and investigative machinery has not been functioning properly.[42]

In our view, however, the most convincing argument rests with general international law – especially in the form of custom.[43] This has been the French Court de cassation's approach in the *Barbie* case, when it decided that the non-applicability of statutory limitation for crimes against humanity was not only the result of Article 213-5 of the French Criminal Code (mentioned above), but that it also stemmed from a pre-existing norm of international law – as such, there was thus no retroactivity and the principle merely confirmed by Article 213-5 could rightfully apply to the crimes committed by Claus Barbie during World War II.[44]

In the *Lumumba* case, neither the office of the federal prosecutor nor the Brussels Court of Appeal raised the *ratione temporis* scope of Article 21 of the Preliminary Title to the Belgian Code of Criminal Proce-

---

[40] On the non-applicability of statutory limitations in light of the specific nature of international crimes, see Yasmin Q. Naqvi, *Impediments to Exercising Jurisdiction over International Crimes*, The Hague, T.M.C. Asser Press, 2010, pp. 211–214.

[41] Extraordinary Chambers in the Courts of Cambodia ('ECCC'), *Prosecutor v. NUON Chea et al.*, Pre-Trial Chamber, 15 February 2011, no. 002/19-09-2007-ECCC/OCIJ (PTC 145 and 146) D427/2/15, para. 183 (https://www.legal-tools.org/doc/592afb/). Also of this view, see Claus Kreß, "*Nullum poena nullum crimen sine lege*", in Rudiger Wolfrum (ed.), *The Max Planck Encyclopedia of Public International Law*, Oxford University Press, 2010, para. 20 (https://www.legal-tools.org/doc/f9b453/).

[42] ECCC, *Prosecutor v. Kaing Guek Eav (Duch)*, Trial Chamber, Decision on the defence preliminary objection concerning the statute of limitations of domestic crimes, 26 July 2010, no. 001/18-07-2007-ECCC/TC (E187), para. 14 (https://www.legal-tools.org/doc/2466c7/).

[43] For a detailed analysis on the notion that customary international law precludes the use of statutes of limitation over international crimes, see Naqvi, 2010, pp. 192–209, see above note 40.

[44] French Cour de cassation (crim.), 26 January 1984, no. 83-94.425.

---

dure as a possible impediment to the admissibility of the criminal prosecution initiated by Patrice Lumumba's family. The prosecutor observed
that "under Article 21, para. 1, of the Preliminary Title to the Belgian
Code of Criminal Procedure, criminal prosecution for [international
crimes] cannot become time-barred",[45] and the court concurred that "the
Belgian [trial] judge might indeed be competent over these facts [which]
cannot become time-barred under Article 21, paragraph 1, of the law of 17
April 1878 containing the Preliminary Title to the Belgian Code of Criminal Procedure".[46]

This is, to the best of our knowledge, the first and only court decision in Belgian judicial history in relation to this issue. In 1999, however,
a Belgian investigating judge called upon to investigate crimes committed
by Augusto Pinochet had already decided as follows: "it must be concluded that there exists a customary norm of international law establishing the
non-applicability of statutory limitations for crimes against humanity and
that this norm is applicable in the domestic legal order".[47] The 12 December 2012 Court of Appeal decision in the *Lumumba* case strongly suggests – as does the latter investigating judge's order and as other domestic
courts have also done before – that the ban on statutory limitations for
serious colonial crimes also applies to any past offence, as this principle
not only results from the relevant legislative framework in Belgium, but
also, has some superior roots in the international legal order.

14.4. The Establishment of Parliamentary Commissions of Inquiry and Possible Implications on Criminal Proceedings

On 9 December 1999, a proposition to establish a Parliamentary Commission of inquiry in charge of determining the exact circumstances of the

---

[45] *Prosecutor and Lumumba v. Huyghe et al.*, FD.30.99.10/11, Federal prosecutor's submissions to the Brussels Court of Appeal, 7 June 2012 (our own translation of "conformément
à l'article 21 § 1ier du titre préliminaire du code d'instruction criminelle, l'action publique
relative à des [crimes internationaux] ne peut être prescrite").

[46] *Prosecutor and Lumumba v. Huyghe et al.*, FD.30.99.10/11, Brussels Court of Appeal
(chambre des mises en accusation), Interlocutory judgment no. 4358, 12 December 2012
(our own translation of "le juge belge pourrait en effet (…) être compétent pour connaître
de ces faits [qui] sont imprescriptibles en application de l'article 21, paragraphe 1er, de la
loi du 17 avril 1878 contenant le titre préliminaire du Code d'instruction criminelle").

[47] Brussels Investigating Judge, 6 November 1998, *Revue de droit pénal et de criminologie*,
1999, p. 289 (our own translation of "il y a lieu de conclure à l'existence d'une règle cou-
tumière de droit international consacrant l'imprescriptibilité des crimes contre l'humanité
et que cette règle est applicable en droit interne").

assassination of Patrice Lumumba and the possible involvement of Belgian politicians was submitted to the Belgian Chamber of Representatives. On 2 February 2000, the establishment of the said commission was approved and eventually, on 16 November 2001, a report of almost one thousand pages regarding the parliamentary inquiry was published.[48] As mentioned above,[49] this commission came to the timid conclusion that "some members of the government of Belgium and other Belgian actors bear a moral responsibility in the circumstances that led to the death of Lumumba". The implications of this parliamentary commission of enquiry on the ongoing criminal proceedings regarding the assassination of Lumumba in Belgium have not yet come to light. However, some procedural concerns may already be raised based on the Belgium *Transnuklear* case (see below).

By virtue of Article 56 of the Belgian Constitution and the law of 3 May 1880 on parliamentary inquiries ('the law of 3 May 1880'), the Chamber of Representatives and the Senate[50] may establish commissions of inquiry. A member of Parliament can request that an inquiry be held. This request is handled in the same manner as a bill. After a debate in committee, the request goes to the plenary meeting for discussion and voting. If the request is approved, the branch of Parliament in which the request was made must appoint the commission of inquiry, upon which the investigation can proceed. According to the law of 3 May 1880, the inquiry may be held by the Chamber or the Senate in plenary or by a special commission. In practice, a special commission always conducts inquiries. The commission of inquiry and its chairperson hold the same powers as an investigating judge. This means that they can, amongst other things, call on and hear witnesses and experts. For some investigative measures such as a restriction of the freedom of movement, a seizure of material goods, a house search, perception and recording of private communication and telecommunication, a judge has to be appointed under the law of 3 May 1880.[51] Upon completion of the inquiry, the rapporteur designated by the commission gives an account of the results of the inquiry to the plena-

---

[48] Enquête parlementaire visant à déterminer les circonstances exactes de l'assassinat de Patrice Lumumba et l'implication éventuelle des responsables politiques belges dans celui-ci, Rapport, *Doc. Parl.*, 2001-2002, no. 50-0312/006 and no. 50-0312/007.

[49] See above at Section 14.2.

[50] These are the two branches of the Belgian Parliament.

[51] Article 4, para. 4, of the law of 3 May 1880.

ry session. The plenary examines the report and makes a statement about the possible conclusions, recommendations or resolutions of the commission of inquiry.[52]

An inquiry initiated by the Chamber of Representatives or the Senate does not replace possible investigations by the judiciary. The law of 3 May 1880 provides that in case a parliamentary inquiry coexists with a judicial investigation, the parliamentary inquiry must not hinder the course of the judicial investigation.[53]

Belgium has an ancient practice of establishing parliamentary commissions of inquiry in relation to sensitive issues such as colonial matters.[54] In the past, the power of inquiry was used primarily for legislative initiatives that should allow a more efficient functioning of the legislative bodies and lead to legislative initiatives. Over the years, parliamentary commissions of inquiry have been used in response to certain heavily, emotionally charged files, such as the *Parliamentary commission of inquiry into the events in Rwanda*,[55] the *Parliamentary commission investigating the legal and illegal exploitation and trade of natural resources in the Great Lakes region in view of the current conflict situation and Belgium's involvement*,[56] the parliamentary commission of inquiry to investigate the murder of Patrice Lumumba and possible Belgian responsibilities, and, more recently, the more comprehensive and newly-established parliamentary commission on Belgium's colonial past.[57]

---

[52] The mechanism of parliamentary commissions of enquiry as explained by the Belgian Senate. Belgian Senate, "Parliamentary committees of inquiry" (available on its web site).

[53] Article 1 of the law of 3 May 1880.

[54] See, for example, Chambre des Représentants de Belgique, Commission parlementaire, chargée de faire une enquête sur les événements qui se sont produits à Léopoldville en janvier 1959, 27 March 1959, 1958-1959, no. 3.

[55] Sénat de Belgique, Commission d'enquête parlementaire concernant les événements du Rwanda, 6 December 1997, 1997–1998, no. 1-611/7.

[56] Sénat de Belgique, Commission d'enquête parlementaire chargée d'enquêter sur l'exploitation et le commerce légaux et illégaux de richesses naturelles dans la région des Grands Lacs au vu de la situation conflictuelle actuelle et de l'implication de la Belgique, 20 February 2003, 2002-2003, no. 2-942/1.

[57] Chambre des représentants de Belgique, Commission spéciale chargée d'examiner l'état indépendánt du Congo (1885-1908) et le passé colonial de la Belgique au Congo (1908-1960), au Rwanda et au Burundi (1919-1962), ses conséquences et les suites qu'il convient d'y réserver, 17 juillet 2020, 2019–2020, no. 55-1462/001.

The Belgian practice of establishing parliamentary inquires raises some concerns which may hinder effective and fair criminal proceedings, and which might contribute to fostering an accountability gap.

Procedural issues and tension between a parliamentary inquiry and a judicial investigation – when both are investigating the same matter at the same time – were illustrated in the Belgian *Transnuklear* case. This case concerned two industrialists who were suspected of having made profit out of scams with hazardous nuclear waste. The two industrialists were eventually acquitted by the Antwerp Court of Appeal in May 1993 because of a serious violation of their right to a fair trial, which led according to the Court of Appeal to the inadmissibility of the criminal proceedings. This decision was based on the fact that the two industrialists had in fact been obliged to make confessions under oath before a parliamentary commission of inquiry and that, afterwards, an investigating judge had built on those statements made under oath to further interrogate the two industrialists. The Court considered that questioning under oath persons who are subject to a criminal investigation on facts that are the object of the criminal investigation is a clear violation of defence rights, if the statements made before the commission of inquiry are then used to incriminate the concerned persons in the context of the criminal investigation.[58]

The question must therefore be raised whether the practice of parliamentary commissions of inquiry may lead to an accountability gap in the sense that the defence can rely on this case law to evade criminal responsibility in case information from parliamentary commissions of inquiry are subsequently used in criminal proceedings.

After this judicial precedent, the law of 3 May 1880 has been modified by a law of 30 June 1996 amending the law of 3 May 1880 on parliamentary inquiries and Article 458 of the Criminal Code.[59] Article 8 of the law of 3 May 1880 now provides that "he who is summoned to be heard as a witness is obliged to appear and to comply with the summons, under penalty of imprisonment of eight days to six months and a fine of five hundred francs to ten thousand francs", but that the professional secrecy referred to in Article 458 of the Belgian Criminal Code can be in-

---

[58] See also Cour de cassation, 6 May 1993, *Pasicrisie*, 1993, I, no. 225.

[59] Loi du 30 juin 1996 modifiant la loi du 3 mai 1880 sur les enquêtes parlementaires et l'article 458 du Code pénal, Belgian Official Journal (Moniteur belge), 16 July 1996.

voked, and that any witness may invoke the fact that, by making a truthful statement, he could expose himself to criminal prosecution and therefore will refuse to testify.[60] However, a refusal to answer during a parliamentary inquiry based on the fact that the concerned person could expose him- or herself to criminal prosecution, could raise a negative suspicion and could still lead to the public prosecutor pressing an investigation. It has been advocated[61] that the possibility of having parallel parliamentary inquiries and criminal investigation on the same facts, should be made impossible in Belgian law.

The legislative amendment after the *Transnuklear* case does not, in our opinion, address all the possible procedural impediments that could be thought of regarding the correlation between Belgian parliamentary inquiries and criminal investigations.

It is not clearly established by current Belgian legislation, for instance, whether information considered as confidential during a parliamentary commission of inquiry[62] may be used in a criminal proceeding if

---

[60] Under the French, original version of Article 8 of the law of 3 May 1880:

Toute personne autre qu'un membre de la Chambre qui, à un titre quelconque, assiste ou participe aux réunions non publiques de la commission, est tenue, préalablement, de prêter le serment de respecter le secret des travaux. Toute violation de ce secret sera punie conformément aux dispositions de l'article 458 du Code pénal.

Les témoins, les interprètes et les experts sont soumis devant la Chambre, la commission ou le magistrat commis, aux mêmes obligations que devant le juge d'instruction.

Tout un chacun peut être appelé comme témoin. La convocation se fait par écrit et, au besoin, par citation. [...]

Les témoins et les experts prêtent ensuite le serment de dire toute la vérité et rien que la vérité. [...]

Toute personne citée pour être entendue en témoignage sera tenue de comparaître et de satisfaire à la citation sous peine d'un emprisonnement de huit jours à six mois et d'une amende de cinq cents francs à dix mille francs. Les dispositions du livre I du Code pénal, sans exception du chapitre VII et de l'article 85, sont applicables.

Sans préjudice de l'invocation du secret professionnel visé à l'article 458 du Code pénal, tout témoin qui, en faisant une déclaration conforme à la vérité, pourrait s'exposer à des poursuites pénales, peut refuser de témoigner.

[61] For example, by Jacques Velu, Attorney General at the Cour de cassation, during the solemn opening session of the Court on 1 September 1993.

[62] Article 3, para. 4, of the law of 3 May 1880 provides that:

Les membres de la Chambre sont tenus au secret en ce qui concerne les informations recueillies à l'occasion des réunions non publiques de la commission. Toute violation de ce secret sera sanctionnée conformément au règlement de la Chambre [...].

necessary for the establishment of the truth, whether declarations made under oath during a parliamentary commission of inquiry can be subjected in some situations to an adversarial debate in order to protect the equality of arms during the criminal proceedings, whether the outcome of such commissions might lead to situations where the *ne bis in idem* principle would or could be raised by the defendant, etc.

Other questionable consequences of parliamentary inquiries on criminal proceedings could include possible leaks of information from the parliamentary inquiry[63] that would be detrimental to the (necessary) secrecy of criminal investigations, and the obligation of undergoing questioning under oath during a parliamentary inquiry which is not always compatible with the right to remain silent.

On the other hand, the law of 3 May 1880 does not provide specific guarantees pertaining to effective legal assistance during the parliamentary inquiry, regarding questions such as access to the case file and equality of arms. Not only do parliamentary commissions raise concerns regarding the rights of the concerned persons during the inquiry, but also regarding the consequences of the parliamentary inquiry on any parallel judicial investigations.

As the *Transnuklear* case has shown, establishing parliamentary commissions of inquiry may arguably, paradoxically, reinforce the accountability gap. In case a parliamentary inquiry and a judicial investigation are ongoing at the same time or relate to the same facts, the practice of parliamentary inquiry commissions in Belgium may result in judicial investigations not having any effect or might raise some risks as to the (in)admissibility of criminal proceedings,[64] as a result of remaining gaps in Belgian legislation regarding procedural rights during parliamentary inquiry and criminal proceedings.

14.5. The Criminal Liability of Belgium as a State

On 30 July 2018, the law of 11 July 2018 amending the Criminal Code and the Preliminary Title of the Code of Criminal Procedure as regards

---

La commission peut lever l'obligation de secret sauf si elle s'est expressément engagée à le préserver.

[63] Despite the above-mentioned provision of Article 3 of the law of 3 May 1880.

[64] Like it was the case in the *Transnuklear* case.

---

the criminal liability of legal persons entered into force in Belgium.[65] The most significant changes implemented by this legislation concern the alignment of the criminal regime for legal and individual persons, making both liable for any criminal offense to which they contributed, and the abrogation of the criminal immunity of legal entities governed by public law.

Since July 2018, legal entities governed by public law can thus be held criminally responsible for offenses committed in their name or on their behalf. With respect to this specific category of legal persons, however, only a simple declaration of guilt can be pronounced, in accordance with the amendment of Article 7*bis* of the Belgian Criminal Code.[66]

Prior to this legislative reform, Article 5 of the Belgian Criminal Code excluded certain legal entities governed by public law from its scope, namely: the Belgian federal State, the regions, the communities, the provinces, rescue zones, pre-zones, agglomeration of Brussels, municipalities, multiple municipality zones, intra-municipal territorial bodies, the French Community Commission, the Flemish Community Commission, the Common Community Commission, the public social welfare centres, associations without legal form and non-profit organizations in the course of incorporation. Some of these legal entities of public law had been until then qualified as political, given that they have an organ directly elected according to democratic rules. They therefore enjoyed criminal immunity.

The new law of July 2018 can be considered a small but important step towards covering certain existing accountability gaps regarding the criminal responsibility of the Belgian State – including, possibly, for colonial wrongs –, in two ways in particular.

---

[65] Loi du 11 juillet 2018 modifiant le Code pénal et le titre préliminaire du Code de procédure pénale en ce qui concerne la responsabilité pénale des personnes morales, Belgian Official Journal (Moniteur belge), 20 July 2018.

[66] Article 7*bis*, last paragraph, of the Belgian Criminal Code provides that: "En ce qui concerne l'Etat fédéral, les Régions, les Communautés, les provinces, les zones de secours, les prézones, l'Agglomération bruxelloise, les communes, les zones pluricommunales, les organes territoriaux intracommunaux, la Commission communautaire française, la Commission communautaire flamande, la Commission communautaire commune et les centres publics d'aide sociale seule la simple déclaration de culpabilité peut être prononcée, à l'exclusion de toute autre peine".

Firstly, the new legal regime provides for the possible coexistence of criminal liability for both natural and legal persons. Prior to the legislative amendment, Article 5 of the Belgian Criminal Code did not provide systematically that a natural person and a legal person could be convicted at the same time. When the legal person's liability was incurred due to the intervention of a natural person exclusively, only the one person (either the natural or the legal person) who had committed the most serious offence could be held criminally responsible. Article 5 of the Belgian Criminal Code thus previously provided for an exoneration of responsibility for the person who had committed the least serious fault (this was unless the offence was committed "knowingly and intentionally"; in such a case, coexistence of criminal liability remained possible). Since 30 July 2018, this principle of non-concurring liability has been abolished. Article 5 of the Belgian Criminal Code now stipulates that "the criminal liability of legal persons does not exclude that of natural persons who have committed or participated in the same acts". The general rules on liability and participation in criminal offences as provided in Article 66 *et seq.* of the Belgian Criminal Code now apply in those situations.[67]

Secondly, the law of 11 July 2018 introduced a form of criminal liability for legal persons governed by public law. The Belgian State and its many decentralized entities – such as the regions, the communities, the provinces, and the Brussels agglomeration – are now considered as legal persons who may be criminally liable. This means that the law now allows victims to file a criminal complaint in Belgium, against the Belgian State, including for colonial wrongs.

Despite these two amendments, we have to note that with respect to legal entities governed by public law, such as the Belgian State, only a penalty consisting of a "mere declaration of guilt" may be imposed pursuant to Article 7*bis*, paragraph 3, of the Belgian Criminal Code. Other penalties existing for natural persons as well as other legal persons (such as fines, confiscation, dissolution, and prohibition from practicing) are explicitly excluded by the Belgian Criminal Code for legal entities governed by public law. In the context of colonial wrongs, this may be problematic for achieving an effective reparation for victims before a criminal court. Measures which plaintiffs may expect to be taken by a State who is con-

---

[67] "La responsabilité pénale des personnes morales n'exclut pas celle des personnes physiques auteurs des mêmes faits ou y ayant participé."

sidered criminally responsible for a colonial wrong usually do not only consist in a *mere declaration of guilt*, but may also consist in taking steps to prevent a recurrence of the colonial wrongdoing, the payment of compensation for the caused loss, the restitution of colonial objects, etc. Victims could, however, consider trying to obtain some of these measures through civil proceedings subsequent to a criminal *declaration of guilt*. Furthermore, it is questionable whether a 'mere declaration of guilt' can be considered as an effective criminal sentence given that it is neither privative nor restrictive of freedom, of private property or of any other right.

At last, pursuant to Article 2 of the Belgian Criminal Code, no crimes can be punished with penalties that were not prescribed by law at the time when the crime was committed. In addition, if the penalty determined at the time of the judgment differs from that determined at the time of the crime, the least severe penalty will be applied.[68] Article 2 of the Belgian Criminal Code prohibits the retroactive application of criminal law when it is to an accused's disadvantage. The principle of non-retroactivity of criminal law[69] applies both to the provisions defining the offence and to those setting the penalties incurred. Bearing these principles in mind, the law of 11 July 2018, which entered into force on 30 July 2018, will only apply to crimes committed after that date. Criminal liability of the Belgian State can thus only exist for criminal offences committed after the date of the entry into force of the new law. This means that an accountability gap in relation to the criminal liability of the Belgian State still exists for any colonial wrongs committed before 30 July 2018 (which certainly applies to a big part of colonial wrongdoing) given that the old rules continue to govern this period. The Belgian State thus continues to enjoy criminal immunity for any colonial or post-colonial wrongs committed prior to 30 July 2018. The future will tell if arguments can be raised successfully before courts with a view to countering this accountability gap, as has been the case in relation to the non-applicability of statutory limitations for international crimes.[70]

---

[68] See also above at Section 14.1.

[69] Also embodied in Council of Europe, European Convention on Human Rights, 4 November 1950, Article 7 (https://www.legal-tools.org/doc/8267cb/), and UN, International Covenant on Civil and Political Rights, 23 March 1976, Article 15 (https://www.legal-tools.org/doc/2838f3/).

[70] See also above at Section 14.3.

14.6. Conclusion

There is still a long way to effective justice for colonial crimes within the Belgian legal system. As exposed above, different impediments might still be faced by victims in their quest for accountability. Also important are the procedural questions regarding the correlation between Belgian parliamentary inquiries and criminal investigations discussed above.

A potential recommendation to tackle impediments mentioned earlier in the chapter, with a view to countering existing accountability gaps, would relate to the difficulties concerning the *ratione temporis* scope of different mechanisms in the context of colonial wrongs. Given the fact that most of the cases concerning colonial crimes tend to be brought to justice several decades after they were committed, it could be envisaged by the Belgian legislator to provide specific regulations with a view to duly addressing the temporal impediments and to better taking into account the particular historical and practical reasons which often place victims of colonial wrongs in an uneasy position to seek justice after several years or decades have lapsed.

15

Addressing Colonial Wrongs
in the Great Lakes Region of Africa

Mutoy Mubiala[*]

15.1. Introduction

Since decades, the Great Lakes Region of Africa has been facing serious human rights and international human rights violations, including genocide, war crimes, and crimes against humanity. According to various fact-finding undertaken, these atrocity crimes are among the lingering consequences of colonial wrong-doing in the region, which includes the ethnic-based 'divide and rule' policy developed by former colonial powers (Germany and Belgium) in Burundi and Rwanda, as well as forced transfers of Banyarwanda populations into eastern Democratic Republic of the Congo ('DRC'). These two colonial wrongs have grounded ethnic conflicts and related atrocities in these three countries.

International law's response to the atrocity crimes has been characterized by the polarization on post-colonial actors and the exclusion of the colonial wrong-doing from the accountability processes, despite its identification as main root cause of post-colonial conflicts and atrocities in the region. In concrete terms, while post-colonial perpetrators have faced justice and were held accountable for their crimes, including by both criminal and non-criminal transitional justice mechanisms on national and international levels, no accountability processes were engaged or initiated to address colonial wrong-doing. There is, therefore, an 'accountability gap' contributing to unequal access to international law. In certain instances, this 'accountability gap' has contributed to the criticism of double stand-

---

* **Mutoy Mubiala** is an Associate Professor of International Human Rights Law at the University of Kinshasa, Democratic Republic of the Congo. He worked as a Human Rights Officer at the Office of the United Nations High Commissioner for Human Rights ('OHCHR') from 1994 until his retirement in 2019. He holds a Ph.D. in International Relations (specializing in International Law) from the Graduate Institute for International and Development Studies (University of Geneva).

ards in international law, in general, and, in particular, international criminal law and justice. This situation contrasts with the emerging initiatives, including in Canada, Norway and Germany, illustrating "the attempt to address historical wrong-doing [...] through the lens of current international law classifications".[1]

International law emerged from the European context, since as early as the sixteenth century. This period coincided with the European colonial expansion to other continents, including Africa, the Americas and Asia. The European-based international law provided legitimacy to colonialism, thus ignoring to address its wrong-doing. When achieving independence, Third World countries, mostly grouped in the Non-Aligned Movement, contested the Western-based international law and contributed, in some instances, to its reform through the United Nations ('UN') General Assembly and other relevant fora (diplomatic conferences), as referred to by Ambassador Narinder Singh in his Foreword above. In addition to these official channels, scholars from the Third World, led by the Indian School of International Law, have contributed to the development of Third World Approaches to International Law ('TWAIL'). One of the main themes of their scholarly efforts has been, so far, the critical review and analysis of the legal implications of colonial policies, including those in Africa.[2]

Within this framework, this chapter aims to examine the legacy of colonial wrong-doing in the Great Lakes Region ('GLR') and to think of how to address its lingering negative consequences in the post-colonial era. The ultimate goal of this chapter is to contribute to the doctrinal efforts aimed at developing a new tool for inclusive access to international law. The chapter is divided into three main parts: (1) fact-work on the legacy of the colonial wrong-doing to post-colonial mass atrocity crimes in the GLR; (2) responses provided so far to these atrocities, their scope and limits; and (3) formulation of action-oriented proposals on transitional justice mechanisms to address the existing 'accountability gap' between colonial and post-colonial actors. Before examining these substantive

---

[1] See Morten Bergsmo, *Myanmar, Colonial Aftermath, and Access to International Law*, Occasional Paper Series No. 9 (2019), Torkel Opsahl Academic EPublisher, Brussels, 2019, pp. 17–18 (https://www.legal-tools.org/doc/64a8fc/). That concept paper appears as Chapter 7 above.

[2] See, for example, James Gathi, Obiora Okafor and Antony Anghie, "Africa and TWAIL", in *African Yearbook of International Law*, 2010, vol. 18, pp. 9–13.

points, it is important to provide a brief historical background of the German and Belgian colonial wrong-doing in the GLR.

15.2. Colonial Wrong-Doing and Its Lingering Negative Consequences in the Great Lakes Region

The German colonial ruling was ethnic-oriented and -based, including in Burundi and Rwanda. Belgium, which inherited these two colonies from Germany under the Mandate and Trusteeship regimes established by the League of Nations and the United Nations respectively, consolidated this system. In addition, by proceeding to successive forced transfers of Rwandan populations into eastern part of its colonial territory of Congo, in particular in the province of North-Kivu, Belgium effectively engaged in a 'divide and rule' policy in this context. The colonial ethnic-based rule was subsequently exacerbated by the dictatorial post-colonial regimes in the three countries, thus leading to ethnic-based violence and the related recurrent perpetrations of mass atrocity crimes, including genocide, war crimes, and crimes against humanity. Examining the German approach to the colonization, Mohammad Shahabuddin outlined the following:

> Conceiving the ethnic 'other' as backward and primitive by the dominant cultural group of each epoch is a norm of international relations that dates back to antiquity [...]. Thus, irrespective of the origin of international law, it is evident that the body of rules governing international relations had been informed by notions of superior 'self' and inferior ethnic 'other'. Among different regional systems of international law in antiquity and the Middle Ages, which were limited in their application, modern European international law having its root in the sixteenth-century jurisprudence emerged as a universal norm of interstate relations through the nineteenth-century colonial expansions. Since then, it has become the dominant language of European civilisation; it is the European 'self' that defines and deals with the non-European 'other' through international law, among other means.

> Yet, within this dichotomy of the European 'self' and the non-European 'other', we can observe how the nineteenth-century European discourse on national self-images, within the framework of the liberal and conservative traditions, are reflected in the conception of the non-European 'other', and hence in corresponding policies dealing with the latter. This

is best substantiated by the nineteenth-century colonial projects. On the one hand, the justifications for colonial missions were expressed in light of the concept of the 'nation' in
the metropolis along the lines of liberal or conservative traditions. On the other hand, the same traditions explained the
science of race -social Darwinism – in the parallel monogen-
ic-assimilationist or polygenic-exclusionist streams to inform
the hierarchical relationship between the Europeans and the
natives in the colonies. During this period of empire building,
as well as we shall soon see, the nineteenth-century jurists of
both traditions, not only justified the colonial project, but also the atrocities associated with it.[3]

In Africa, Germany implemented its colonial policy through several
means, including the extermination of local populations (the Herero and
Nama peoples from South West Africa) and the application of the 'divide
and rule policy' in the GLR along the lines of ethnic-belonging to the Tutsi and Hutu communities (Burundi and Rwanda). Belgium, which succeeded to Germany as the League of Nations Mandate power and then the
United Nations Trusteeship power, consolidated the German approach.

One main consequence of the ethnic-based colonization of Germany and Belgium in the GLR has been ethnic conflicts leading to mass
atrocity crimes, including genocide, war crimes and crimes against humanity, in Burundi, the DRC and Rwanda. Placed in the contemporary
context, these wrongs constitute core international crimes, according to
the contemporary international humanitarian law ('IHL'), international
human rights law ('IHRL'), and international criminal law ('ICL'), which
prohibit both ethnic and racial discrimination and forced transfers of population by an occupying power.

15.2.1. Ethnic and Racial Discrimination

Ethnic and racial discrimination are prohibited in IHRL (the 1965 International Convention on the Elimination of All Forms of Racial Discrimination) and included among crimes against humanity provided in the Rome
Statute of the International Criminal Court (Article 7). If implemented in
the current period, the 'divide and rule' policy of Germany and Belgium
in Rwanda and Burundi would be addressed through the application of the

---

[3] Mohammed Shahabuddin, "The Colonial 'Other' in the Nineteenth Century German Colonization of Africa, and International Law", in *African Yearbook of International Law*, 2010,
vol. 18, no. 1, pp. 15–17.

relevant provisions of international law. The inability to do so, for temporal jurisdiction reasons, leads to an 'accountability gap' between the colonial and post-colonial perpetrators of these crimes in the two countries.

15.2.1.1. Rwanda

Among the fact-finding mechanisms engaged in the inquiry on the genocide and other mass atrocity crimes perpetrated in Rwanda in 1994 which dealt with the identification of root causes of the crimes, one can mention the Special Rapporteur of the UN Human Rights Commission on the human rights situation in Rwanda and the International Panel of Eminent Personalities established by the Organization of African Unity.

15.2.1.1.1. The UN Human Rights Commission's Special Rapporteur on Rwanda

On 25 May 1994, the UN Human Rights Commission adopted a resolution establishing the mandate of the Special Rapporteur on the situation of human rights in Rwanda. In accordance with the resolution, the Special Rapporteur was tasked with the following mandate:

> (a) To report to the Commission on Human Rights on the situation of human rights in Rwanda, including the root causes and responsibilities [...].
>
> (b) To make available to the Secretary-General systematically compiled information on violations of human rights and of international humanitarian law.[4]

The Special Rapporteur, accompanied by the author of this chapter (then his assistant), carried out several field missions and submitted his reports to the Commission and the United Nations General Assembly. In his first report, submitted while the armed conflict and massacres were still on-going in the country, the Special Rapporteur recommended, *inter alia*, the following short-term and medium-term measures:

> 72. The United Nations, in cooperation with OAU, should take appropriate steps to:

---

[4]   UN Economic and Social Council, Report of the Situation of Human Rights in Rwanda submitted by Mr. R. Degni-Ségui, Special Rapporteur of the Commission on Human Rights, under paragraph 20 of Commission Resolution E/CN. 4/S-3/1 of 25 May 1994, UN Doc. E/CN.4/1995/7, 28 June 1994, p. 3 (emphasis added) (https://www.legal-tools.org/doc/q8r4kb/).

Induce the parties to the conflict to negotiate, in good faith and with due regard to the Arusha Agreement of 4 August 1993, the terms for peace, democratic transition and national reconciliation and unity; and

Call on the parties to implement in good faith the agreements thus reached. The agreements must not in any way provide, as part of a political settlement, for the impunity of those responsible for acts of genocide and other crimes against humanity. On the contrary, they must establish mechanisms for the effective punishment of those responsible. That is one of the prerequisites for national reconciliation and unity. [...]

74. The United Nations should, within the framework of the peace negotiations:

Stress the need for national reconciliation and unity. In this regard, the new constitution should contain provisions for the prohibition and severe punishment of acts of incitement to ethnic hatred and violence. No official document, national identity card, driving licence, family registration book or the like should contain any reference to membership of an ethnic group. Any ethnically based party or association should be prohibited; [...].

75. Pending the establishment of a permanent international criminal court, the United Nations should establish an ad hoc international tribunal to hear the evidence and judge the quality parties or, alternatively, should extend the jurisdiction of the international tribunal on war crimes committed in the former Yugoslavia.[5]

This last recommendation was rapidly implemented by the UN Security Council which, by its Resolution 935 (1994) of 1 July 1994, established the International Commission of Experts to

examine and analyse information submitted pursuant to the present resolution, together with such information as the Commission of Experts might obtain, through its own investigations or the efforts of other persons or bodies, including the information made available by the Special Rapporteur on Rwanda, with a view to providing the Secretary-General with its conclusions on the evidence of grave violations of

---

[5]   *Ibid.*, pp. 18–19.

international humanitarian law committed in the territory of Rwanda, including the evidence of possible acts of genocide.[6]

As a result of the preliminary report of the Commission of Experts on Rwanda, the Security Council established the International Criminal Tribunal for Rwanda ('ICTR') by its Resolution 955 (1994) of 14 November 1994.[7] According to the author of this chapter, writing elsewhere,

> [t]he Commission of Experts on Rwanda, based on the experience of the Commission of Experts on the former Yugoslavia, recommended in its preliminary report the expansion of the jurisdiction of the ICTY to the crimes committed in Rwanda. For practical reasons, while establishing a second ad hoc tribunal for Rwanda (based in Arusha, Tanzania), the Security Council provided both the ICTY and the International Criminal for Rwanda ('ICTR') with a common prosecutor and chamber of appeals based in The Hague.[8]

For his part, and in accordance with his mandate, the Special Rapporteur on Rwanda also examined the root causes of the Rwandan conflict and their contribution to the related atrocities. In his third report to the UN Human Rights Commission, he outlined:

> General situation: the causes of the genocide
>
> 12. Two years after it occurred, the genocide as a phenomenon in the etymological sense, continues to generate numerous works and studies and much research supplementing the reports of human rights observers. All in all, these investigations tend to confirm the original hypothesis contained in the preliminary report (E/CN.4/1995/7), particularly regarding the underlying causes of human rights violations, which represent the main focus of this report.
>
> 13. These causes are many, varied and complex. For the sake of simplicity, they are divided here, without any scientific

---

[6]   United Nations ('UN'), Security Council Resolution 935 (1994), UN Doc. S/RES/935 (1994), 1 July 1994 (https://www.legal-tools.org/doc/1594bd/).

[7]   *Ibid.*

[8]   Mutoy Mubiala, "The Historical Contribution of International Fact-Finding Commissions", in Morten Bergsmo *et al.* (eds.), *Historical Origins of International Criminal Law: Volume 4*, Torkel Opsahl Academic EPublisher, Brussels, 2015, pp. 518–519 (https://www.toaep.org/ps-pdf/23-bergsmo-cheah-song-yi); Lyal S. Sunga, "The Commission of Experts on Rwanda and the Creation of the International Criminal Tribunal for Rwanda: A Note", in *Human Rights Law Journal*, 1996, vol. 16, no. 3, pp. 121–124.

pretensions, into three main categories: politico-historical, economic and socio-cultural.

(a) The politico-historical causes

14. Although it is not possible to establish any genuine order of precedence among the various causes, the politico-historical dimension seems to be the most important because of its conditioning and determining effect on the others. It is both political and historical in that the basis of the conflict between the two groups, Hutu and Tutsi is political – i.e. power – and is rooted in the history of this people. Responsibility lies less with the ancestors of past centuries than with the authorities of more recent periods, firstly colonization and then the African regimes.

15. Although pre-colonial Rwanda was inhabited by the same peoples as are found there today, namely, the Hutus (of Bantu origin), the Tutsis (of Hamitic descent) and the Twas (pymoid type), these peoples, organized in more or less autonomous kingdoms, did not constitute opposing dominant and dominated 'ethnic groups'. These kingdoms were bound to the Mwami (king) within a feudal monarchic system by a contract of patronage known as "ubuhake". Moreover, the division of labour whereby Hutus were farmers and Tutsis herders, which placed economic power in the hands of the latter, did not become established as a fixed and close system like the caste system. It was possible to move from one category to the other [...].

16. *It was the colonizers, first the Germans then the Belgians, who as part of their policy of divide and rule, depended on the Tutsi group to govern the conquered territory under a system of indirect rule, thus upsetting the existing social equilibrium. The resulting imbalance gradually became more marked, marginalizing the Hutus. Moreover, in order to give an ideological flavour to their concoction and thus consolidate it, they created the myth of the superiority of the Tutsis over the two other ethnic groups, thus institutionalizing the ethnic division. This ideology of discrimination was not only reflected in the indication of ethnic group on identity cards, but also reinforced in the schools. The Belgian colonialists supported the Hutu social revolution only because they felt betrayed by Tutsi allies' demands for independence.*

17. With independence, the political dimension became more closely linked with the ethnic dimension, so that the conflict became essentially one of opposition between Hutus/republicans and Tutsis/feudal-monarchists. The new regime, presided over successively by Grégoire Kayibanda and Juvénal Habyarimana, regardless of the official line on national unity, completed the work of the colonialists by exacerbating ethnic rivalries and using them as a basis for its own survival [...].[9]

This led to the 1994 conflict and its related mass atrocity crimes. The report of the Special Rapporteur also addressed the regional implications of this conflict, with its massive refugee influxes in the neighbouring countries, in particular DRC. Therefore, in addition to the recommendations relating to the prosecution of the presumed authors of the genocide and crimes against humanity committed in Rwanda and the provision of international support for the strengthening of the national judicial system, the Special Rapporteur made an important recommendation to the UN to provide support for a comprehensive settlement of the crisis in the GLR, as follows:

195. The United Nations should:

(a) Urgently convene, in agreement with the Organization of African Unity, an international conference on the Great Lakes with a view to solving the problems of the region as a whole and, if necessary, arrange for a special session of the Commission on Human Rights to consider the specific dimension of the protection and promotion of human rights; (b) Adopt a comprehensive strategy based on an integrated approach to the problems of the Great Lakes subregion aimed at (i) achieving a peaceful and lasting settlement of the Great Lakes conflict; and (ii) preventing the outbreak of a general conflict threatening the stability of the region as a whole.[10]

---

[9] UN Economic and Social Council, Report on the Situation on Human Rights in Rwanda submitted by Mr. René Degni-Ségui, Special Rapporteur of the Commission on Human Rights, under paragraph 20 of resolution S-3/1 of 25 May 1994, UN Doc. E/CN.4/1997/61, 20 January 1997, pp. 5–6 (emphasis added) ('Rwanda HRC Report 1997') (https://www.legal-tools.org/doc/uyth7j/).

[10] *Ibid.*, p. 45 (para. 195).

The International Conference on the Great Lakes Region ('ICGLR'), convened from 2003 to 2006. It was backed by the UN and AU to address the aftermath of the Rwandan genocide and its regional consequences. The negotiation process, in which this author was involved as the Office of the United Nations High Commissioner for Human Rights' ('OHCHR) focal point, made an important effort towards developing regional human rights protocols[11] to help prevent future mass atrocity crimes. These instruments include, among others, the Protocol on Judicial Cooperation and the Protocol for the Prevention and the Punishment of the Crime of Genocide, War Crimes, and Crimes Against Humanity and All Forms of Discrimination. The latter was influenced by the ICTR's judgements on hate-based related crimes (the so-called 'Media case').

Unfortunately, even though the ICGLR discussed the root causes of the conflicts in the GLR, it did not address colonial wrong-doing and its lingering negative consequences in the region. In the perspective of the North-South relationship, ICGLR, as well as other relevant fora,[12] only discussed the funding of the reconstruction of the affected countries by the former colonial powers, mostly with the European Union.

15.2.1.1.2. International Panel of Eminent Personalities on the Rwandan Genocide

Traumatized by the Rwandan genocide perpetrated in 1994, Member States of the Organization of African Unity ('OAU') initiated a process of an account of this tragedy. In 1997, at the initiative of the then-Ethiopian Prime Minister, Meles Zenawi, the Central Organ of the OAU Mechanism for Conflict Prevention, Management and Resolution established the International Panel of Eminent Personalities (the 'Rwanda Panel') to investigate the Rwandan genocide and the surroundings events.[13] As reflected in the report of the OAU Secretary-General on the establishment of an

---

[11] See Mutoy Mubiala, "Les droits de l'homme dans le processus de la Conférence internationale sur la région des Grands Lacs", in Chile Eboe-Osuji (ed.), *Protecting Humanity: Essays in International Law and Policy in Honor of Navi Pillay*, Martinus Nijhoff, Leiden, 2010, pp. 81–91.

[12] See, for example, Centre Nord-Sud, "Forum de Lisbonne. La région des Grands Lacs: vers un nouveau dialogue Nord-Sud (Lisbonne, 15-16 mai 1997)", 16 May 1997.

[13] The Panel composed of Sir Qett Ketumile Masire (former President of Botswana, Chair); General Ahmadou Toumani Touré (former Head of State of Mali); Ms. Lisbet Palme (Sweden); Ms. Elle Johnson-Sirleaf (Liberia); Justice P.N. Bhagwati (India); Senator Hocine Djoudi (Algeria); and Ambassador Stephen Lewis (Canada).

international panel of eminent personalities to investigate the genocide in Rwanda and the surrounding events, the mandate of the Panel was as follows:

> The Panel is expected to investigate the 1994 genocide in Rwanda and the surrounding events, starting from the Arusha Peace Accord to the fall of Kinshasa as part of efforts aimed at averting and preventing further wide-scale conflicts in the Great Lakes Region. It is, therefore, expected to establish the facts about how such a grievous crime was conceived, planned and executed, investigate and determine culpability for the failure to enforce the Genocide Convention in Rwanda and in the Great Lakes Region, and to recommend measures aimed at redressing the consequences of the genocide of the genocide and at preventing any possible recurrence of such a crime.[14]

Going beyond the limited temporal scope of its mandate, the Rwanda Panel addressed the issue of the root causes, the role of the colonial wrong-doing in this context, and its lingering negative consequences in post-colonial Rwanda. The Rwanda Panel, *inter alia*, has stated as follows:

> 2.3. […] Let us look briefly at the historical background. The first thing an outsider must understand is that there exists today two conflicting versions of Rwandan history, one favoured essentially buy Hutu, the other reflecting the present government's stated commitment to national unity. The fundamental historical debate revolves around whether ethnic differences between Rwanda's Hutu and Tutsi existed before the colonial era. The two groups themselves disagree profoundly on this issue, and each can find certain authorities to support their position. Certainly, there were Hutu and Tutsi for many centuries. The former had developed as an agricultural people, while the Tutsi were predominantly cattle herders. Yet the two groups had none of the usual differentiating characteristics that are said to separate ethnic groups. They spoke the same language, shared the same religious beliefs, and lived side-by-side; intermarriage was not uncommon. Relations between them were not particularly confrontational; the historical record makes it clear that hostilities were much

---

[14] International Panel of Eminent Personalities to Investigate the 1994 Genocide in Rwanda and the Surrounding Events, "The Roots of the Crisis to 1959", *Rwanda: The Preventable Genocide – Report of International Panel of Eminent Personalities*, July 2000, p. 9.

more frequent among competing dynasties of the same ethnic category than between the Hutu and the Tutsi themselves.

[...]

2.8. Having said that, we now come to two of the great culprits in this tragic saga. From 1895 to 1916, Rwanda was a German colony. In 1916, in the midst of the First World War, Germany was forced to retreat from its east African territories and was replaced in Rwanda and Burundi by Belgium. For the next 45 years, the Belgians controlled the destinies of Rwanda, Burundi, and the Congo. Virtually all authorities (including both Hutu and Tutsi) agree that first Germany, but above all Belgium, organized the colony very much along the lines that Mwami Rwabugiri had drawn, though the colonizers made those lines far more rigid, inflexible, and self-serving. But the point to be noted is that they did not have to do so. The interpretation that the European powers were merely maintaining the status quo as they had found it ignores their power to impose on their new African acquisitions more or less whatever form of governance they chose.

[...]

2.10. Colonizer and the local elite also shared an interest in endorsing the pernicious, racist notions about the Tutsi and the Hutu that had been concocted by missionaries, explorers, and early anthropologists in that period. The theory was based both on the appearance of many Tutsi – generally taller and thinner than were most Hutu – and European incredulity over the fact that Africans could, by themselves, create the sophisticated kingdom that the first white men to arrive in Rwanda found there. From the thinnest of air, an original racial fantasy known as the Hamitic hypothesis was spun by the first British intruders. It posited that the Tutsi had sprung from a superior Caucasoid race from the Nile Valley, and probably even had Christian origins. On the evolutionary scale then all the rage in Europe, the Tutsis could be seen as approaching, very painstakingly, to be sure, the exalted level of white people. They were considered more intelligent, more reliable, harder working, and more like whites than the "Bantu" Hutu majority.

2.11. The Belgians appreciated this natural order of things so greatly that, in a series of administrative measures between 1926 and 1932, they institutionalized the cleavage between the two races (race being the explicit concept used at the time before the milder notion of ethnicity was introduced later on), culminating in identity cards that were issued to every Rwandan, declaring each to be either Hutu or Tutsi. This card system was maintained for over 60 years and, in a tragic irony, eventually became key to enabling Hutu killers to identify during the genocide the Tutsi who were its original beneficiaries.

[…]

2.13. The ramifications of the Belgian system could hardly have been clearer. Between 1932 and 1957, for example, more than three-quarters of the students in the only secondary school in the small city of Butare were Tutsi. Ninety-five per cent of the country's civil service came to be Tutsi. Forty-three out of 45 chiefs and all but 10 of 559 sub-chiefs were Tutsi.[15]

The Belgian colonial system negatively impacted the post-colonial governance in Rwanda, during which the division between Hutu and Tutsi was exacerbated. According to the Rwanda Panel:

3.2. […] One view of Rwandan history insists that the movement for independence was largely engineered by the Belgians and the Catholic hierarchy in order to replace their erstwhile Tutsi collaborators with a more co-operative Hutu administration. This interpretation makes the Rwandans nothing but pawns in a European game. In fact, the so-called Rwandan Revolution of 1959 to 1962 was assisted by these outsiders, but it was imposed by them.

[…]

3.6 There was to be no Rwandan revolution. It is technically true that within a mere three years a Tutsi-dominated monarchy under colonial rule gave way to a Hutu-led independent republic. But in practice, the changes mostly affected the top rungs of Rwandan society. A small band of Hutu, mainly from the south-centre and, therefore, not representative of even of the entire new Hutu elite, replaced the tiny Tutsi elite. They were back with enthusiasm by the Catholic church and their former Belgian colonial masters. Accepting the racist premises of their former oppressors, the Hutu now treated all

---

[15] *Ibid.*, pp. 9–11.

Tutsi as untrustworthy foreign invaders who had no rights and deserved no consideration. The well-being of the peasant farmers, who comprised the vast majority of the population, was not a prominent consideration of the new leadership. In the remarkably though and prescient words of a 1961 UN Trusteeship Council report, "[t]he developments of these last 18 months have brought about the racial dictatorship of one party…An oppressive system has been replaced by another one…It is quite possible that some day we will witness violent reactions on the part of the Tutsi."

[…]

3.10. The first violence occurred in late 1959. Already the political climate was tense, with the death of the King in mid-year in suspicious circumstances. Under the leadership pf Grégoire Kayibanda, a graduate of the Catholic seminary and co-signatory of the manifesto, a predominant Hutu party had emerged – Mouvement Démocratique rwandais/Parti du mouvement de l'émancipation Hutu, or Parmehutu. When Tutsi youth beat up a Parmehutu activist, Hutu rushed to exploit the moment. They retaliated, and civil war broke out. The Belgians and church leaders were both blatantly partial to their new Hutu friends. The White Fathers gave strategic advice to some of the Hutu leaders and, in general, blessed their cause. At the same time, the senior Belgian military officer on the spot directed events on behalf of the Hutu, while his troops, when they were not passively standing by, were actually encouraging Hutu attacks against Tutsi.

[…]

3.12. Huge numbers of Tutsi fled the areas of the most fierce fighting, some 10,000 taking refuge in neighbouring states […].[16]

Based on its findings on the role of the colonial 'divide and rule' policy in post-colonial deadly conflicts in Rwanda and, while commending the establishment and operation of the ICTR, as well as the efforts made to revitalize the Rwandan justice system, the Rwanda Panel demonstrated the challenges for them to ensure justice and reconciliation, in particular in view of the perception of double standards in the prosecution and trial of the offenders and perpetrators. It then raised the issue of post-

---

[16] *Ibid.*, pp. 15–17.

conflict reconciliation by non-judicial means and referred to some foreign and African experiences (including South Africa).[17]

In its recommendations to the international community, the Rwanda Panel, *inter alia*, urged

> all those parties that have apologized for their role in the genocide, and those who have yet to apologize, to support strongly our call for the [UN] Secretary-General to appoint a commission to determine reparations owed by the international community to Rwanda.[18]

This recommendation could be an entry point for addressing the responsibility of the two former colonial powers (Germany and Belgium) for their respective wrong-doing and its lingering negative consequences in Rwanda and Burundi.

15.2.1.2. Burundi

As noted by the Rwanda Panel:

> 3.22. Under German colonialism, Rwanda and Burundi had been merged into a single colony called Rwanda-Urundi for administrative purposes. Later they became, first, League of Nations Mandate Territories and then United Nations Trust Territories under Belgian administration, and were separated once again. Both countries gained independence from Belgium in 1962. In each, the ethnic mix is about 85 per cent Hutu and 15 per cent Tutsi. Neither country experienced open conflict between the two groups before their movements for independence.
>
> 3.23. The interconnectedness of the two nations has been clear since independence, when events in Rwanda offered what an authority calls "a powerful demonstration effect on both Hutu and Tutsi in Burundi, causing enormous mutual distrust between them" [...].[19]

Recurrent ethnic clashes occurred between the Hutu and Tutsi in Burundi, including in 1962, 1966, 1973, 1988 and 1993. The latter resulted from the assassination of the first Hutu democratically elected president, Melchior Ndadaye, and led to a bloody civil war from 1993 to 2000,

---

[17] *Ibid.*, pp. 183–185.

[18] *Ibid.*, p. 263.

[19] *Ibid.*, p. 19.

ended by the signature of the Arusha Peace Agreement in August the same year. Several fact-finding mechanisms were deployed to investigate the alleged international crimes committed in the context of this conflict. According to its Resolution 1012 (1995) of 28 August 1995, the UN Security Council requested the Secretary-General to establish an international commission of inquiry, which was mandated:

> (a) to establish the facts relating to the assassination of the President of Burundi on 21 October 1993, the massacres and other related serious acts of violence which followed;
>
> (b) to recommend measures of a legal, political and administrative nature, as appropriate, after consultation with the Government of Burundi, and measures with regard to the bringing to justice of persons responsible for those acts, to prevent any repetition of deeds similar to those investigated by the commission and, in general, to eradicate impunity and promote national reconciliation.[20]

The Commission addressed the root causes of the conflict in Burundi. In its final report, it noted that:

> 78. Burundi was a unified, independent kingdom, occupying the central highlands, at the time of the German conquest in 1893. The royal caste, the Baganwa, was placed above both the Hutus and Tutsis and claimed to have a mixed ancestry. Under the King and other Baganwa, both Hutu and Tutsi exercised positions of power and prestige. There is no record of ethnic massacres from the pre-colonial period. Judicial authority was exercised by the King himself, by the local chiefs appointed by him, and by wise men designated by consensus on each hill, the Bashingantaye.
>
> 79. During German colonial dominance, which ended in 1916, and during the Belgian mandate that followed, the country was governed formally through the King (indirect rule). In the last years of the mandate the King had become a mere figurehead. Colonial administration generally favored the Tutsis at the expense of the Hutus, accentuating the social and economic differences between them. The Belgians

---

[20] UN Security Council Resolution 1012 (1995), UN Doc. S/RES/1012 (1995), 28 August 1995 (https://www.legal-tools.org/doc/80c1a0/). The Commission composed of Edilbert Razafindralambo (Madagascar), Chairman; Abdelali El Moumni (Morocco); Mehmet Gtney (Turkey); Luis Herrera Marcano (Venezuela); and Michel Maurice (Canada).

administered Burundi together with Rwanda from Bujumbura. Burundians and Rwandese were a minority of the population of Bujumbura until independence.

[…]

81. To understand the post-independence political process in Burundi, it is necessary to be aware of the parallel process in its twin country, Rwanda. Both countries have the same culture, virtually the same language, and the same "ethnic mix". They are roughly equivalent in size, in population and in geographical characteristics. In Rwanda, however, the royal family and the nobility were Tutsi. Tutsis had exercised for centuries the monopoly of power. Rwanda had been a unified, independent monarchy even longer than Burundi at the time of German conquest.

82. To counter Tutsi pressure for independence on their terms, the Belgians favored a Hutu uprising in Rwanda in 1959, which led to a state of emergency and the effective end of Tutsi supremacy. Independence was granted in 1962 under an elected Hutu Government led by Grégoire Kayibanda. Tutsis lost all effective political power. In December of the following year, there was a massacre of some 20,000 Tutsis by Hutus, the first in recorded history, and great numbers went into exile. Persecution and exile of Tutsis continued during the years that followed. Most of these exiles went to Uganda, but a great number settled in Burundi and other countries.

83. In Burundi, the political struggle became increasingly ethnic […].[21]

The Commission found that genocidal acts were committed by the Hutu against Tutsi, but recommended thorough investigations to refine its findings. It also recommended the reform of the judicial system to have an impartial administration of justice to address impunity.[22]

In 2015, a post-electoral crisis occurred in Burundi, after the contested presidential elections of May 2015. The country faced serious and widespread human rights violations. On 30 September 2016, the UN Hu-

---

[21] Letter Dated 25 July 1996 from the Secretary-General Addressed to the President of the Security Council, UN Doc. S/1996/682, 22 August 1996, pp. 19–20 (https://www.legal-tools.org/doc/3070be/).

[22] *Ibid.*, pp. 55–57.

man Rights Council established a commission of inquiry on Burundi "to conduct a thorough investigation into human rights violations and abuses committed in Burundi since April 2015, to determine whether any of them may constitute international crimes and to identify their alleged perpetrators".[23] In its first report to the Council, the Commission concluded that:

> 81. In the light of its investigations, the Commission finds that extrajudicial executions, arbitrary arrests and detentions, enforced disappearances, acts of torture and cruel, inhuman or degrading treatment and sexual violence have persisted in Burundi from April 2015 to the time when the present report was drafted.

> 82. The Commission has reasonable grounds to believe that several of these violations, committed mostly by members of the National Intelligence Service, the police, the army and the Imbonerakure, constitute crimes against humanity.[24]

Based on these findings, the Commission made, *inter alia*, the following recommendation regarding the accountability mechanisms:

> 80. In view of the lake of independence of the Burundian judiciary and the impunity enjoyed in respect of the gross violations committed by agents of the State and members of the ruling party, including the Imbonerakure, the Commission believes that the Burundian State is neither willing nor able genuinely to investigate or prosecute those violations. It therefore falls to the International Criminal Court to investigate those violations and establish criminal responsibility in respect thereof.[25]

The International Criminal Court ('ICC') already opened an investigation into the situation in Burundi in 2017 (see Section 15.2.3.2.3. of this chapter).

15.2.2. Forced Transfers of Population, with Special Reference to Eastern Democratic Republic of the Congo

International humanitarian law prohibits forced transfers of population, as discussed in Chapters 5, 7 and 10 above. What happens in the time of war

---

[23] UN General Assembly, Report of the Commission of Inquiry on Burundi, UN Doc. A/HRC/36/54, 11 August 2017, p. 1 (https://www.legal-tools.org/doc/a787e6/).

[24] *Ibid.*, p. 17.

[25] *Ibid.*, p. 16.

also often occurred in the context of the colonization, including in the GLR. This was the case with the forced transfers by the Belgians of waves of Banyarwanda into eastern DRC. These led to a significant change in the demographic composition of the Kivu provinces, causing, in the colonial aftermath, complex ethnic conflicts including land competition and nationality issues. Local conflicts have evolved in a regional war on the territory of the DRC, and its occupation by certain neighbouring countries. So far, apart from fact-finding, international, regional and national justice mechanisms involved have not addressed the issue of colonial wrongdoing and its legacy of mass atrocity crimes perpetrated there.

Prior to the Belgian administration of Rwanda, the North Kivu province in the DRC comprised of a balanced proportion of indigenous communities, including the Hunde, Nyanga and Nande ethnic groups. As an author outlined:

> Ethnic balance started to de-equilibrate with the 'implantation' of large numbers of Rwandan Hutu peasants in North Kivu, organized by the colonial administration. Facing a need for labor force on their plantations as well as demographic pressure and famine in Rwanda, the colonizers simply transferred workers and their families from Rwanda to North Kivu, obviously underestimating the impact of this imposed exodus on existing local ethnic and socio-political structures. This migration was institutionalized by the Mission d'Immigration des Banyarwanda (MIB) in 1937. The Belgians brought 85,000 Rwandan Hutus to Masisi between 1937 and 1955 (Mathieu/Mafikiri Tsongo 1998). The latter were settled in the Hunde-dominated heartland of Masisi in the autonomous enclave of Gishari.
>
> [...]
>
> The change in demographics as well as the additional property-oriented way of securing access to land gave rise to intensified political and land competition. This competition has predominantly occurred across ethnic lines and, therefore, resulting dynamics and tensions have been ethnically translated. Fuelled by the fear of losing their land to 'the others', people and communities from all sides hence have got mobi-

lized and radicalized with respect to identity, nationality and ethnicity.[26]

Fact-finding has demonstrated the role of forced transfers of Banyarwanda population into eastern DRC and their legacy of post-colonial mass atrocity crimes committed there. Forced transfers of Banyarwanda into eastern DRC as a main historical cause of the ethnic violence occurring in this area was outlined by Roberto Garreton, former Special Rapporteur on the Situation of Human Rights in Zaire (now DRC), in his first report to the UN Commission on Human Rights in 1995:

> A. Ethnic conflicts in Northern Kivu
>
> 85. The Northern Kivu region that borders on Rwanda and Uganda has some three million inhabitants, of whom approximately one-half are indigenous to the area, the rest belonging to the category of the Banyarwanda or persons of the Hutu, Tutsi or Twa ethnic groups of Rwandese origin. The Banyarwanda account for 80 per cent of the population of the Masisi area or the Bwito community, yet most public and government posts have almost always been filled by indigenous inhabitants.
>
> 86. The tribal problems in this region of Zaire are due to the frontiers of the country established by the Act of Berlin of 1885 and the Brussels Convention of 11 August 1910, under which many persons of the neighbouring State of Rwanda were annexed to Congo. Between 1939 and 1954 some 80,000 Rwandese were recruited by Belgian colonists to work on plantations. Following the removal of King Mwami Kigeri V in 1959, Tutsi political refugees arrived in the region, and this influx was followed by the clandestine emigration of persons endeavouring to join their families on the other side of the Rwandese frontier. Since July 1994, approximately 1.2 million Hutus from Rwanda have become refugees in Zaire, particularly in the vicinity of the town of Goma. Others have moved towards the Masisi, Rutschuru and Walikale areas in order to join the Banyarwanda Hutus already settled there.

---

[26] Johannes Beck, "Contested Land in the Eastern Democratic Republic of the Congo. Anatomy or the Land-Related Intervention", in *IFHV Working Paper*, 2012, vol. 2, no. 2, Institute for International Law of Peace and Armed Conflict ('IFHV') at the Ruhr University Bochum, pp. 10–11.

87. The tension between the Hunde, Nyanga and Nande ethnic groups (also called Bahunde, Banyanga and Banande or
indigenous inhabitants of the area) and the Banyarwanda,
which was due above all to land distribution problems, has
been exacerbated by political factors connected with electoral procedures and laws governing nationality.

88. From a legal standpoint, legislation on nationality is one
of the main causes of the ethnic conflict. Decree Law No.
71-020 of 26 March 1971 granted nationality on a collective
basis to the Banyarwanda who, thereby acquired certain
rights, such as the right to vote and to stand for election.
However, Law No. 81-002 of 29 June 1981 amended previous legislation granting Zairian nationality solely to those
who could prove that their ancestors had lived in Zaire since
1885. The application of this Law, because of its retroactive
nature, would revoke the rights acquired by the Banyarwanda.[27]

While contested land and nationality of the Banyarwanda population in the Kivus have been the immediate cause of these conflicts and the
related atrocities, forced transfers of the Banyarwanda by the former colonial power (Belgium) into eastern DRC grounded these post-colonial
developments. As in the cases of Rwanda and Burundi, the Belgian colonial wrong-doing in eastern DRC raises the question of the responsibility
of former colonial powers in this regard.

This issue is not specific to Africa and the GLR. As rightly observed
by Morten Bergsmo about colonial forced transfers in Myanmar:

[…] Britain fought three wars in order to occupy all of Burma and establish colonial rule by armed force. To fuel her
economic interests in rice production and other sectors, Britain allowed the transfer of millions of persons from her colonial India into Burma, also leading to some conflicts between the Burmese and the immigrants. In other words, Britain transferred many more people into Burma than the overall number of Jewish settlers on the West Bank as of 1 January 2019, estimated at 449,508. Why is this a relevant comparison?

---

[27] Report on the situation of human rights in Zaire, prepared by the Special Rapporteur, Mr.
Roberto Garreton, in accordance with Commission resolution 1994/87, UN Doc.
E/CN.4/1995/67, 23 December 1994, pp. 17–18 (original footnotes omitted)
(https://www.legal-tools.org/doc/2hyzhf/).

The ICC Prosecutor has conducted a preliminary examination of alleged crimes in Palestine since 16 January 2015. Her annual reports on preliminary examination suggest that her main focus is "the settlement of civilians onto the territory of the West Bank" or so-called "settlement-related activities". It is exactly this alleged transfer of civilians into the West Bank which human rights non-governmental organizations and some mainly-Muslim governments seek to have the ICC investigate and prosecute as a core international crime. Since the ICC Statute entered into force on 1 July 2002, its Article 8(2)(b)(viii) has prohibited the "transfer, directly or indirectly, by the Occupying Power of parts of its own civilian population into the territory it occupies". Israel – which, like Myanmar, is not an ICC State Party – does not consider its presence on the West Bank as occupation.

Could Myanmar argue that the transfer of civilians into Burma prior to World War II – a process that has contributed significantly to the demographic makeup of, for example, Rakhine State – was a violation of international law? Such population transfers were only expressly prohibited by international law with the 1949 Geneva Convention IV Relative to the Protection of Civilian Persons in Time of War, whose Article 49(6) provides that "Occupying Power shall not deport or transfer parts of its own civilian population into the territory it occupies". In other words, the transfers into Burma happened several years prior to the first express treaty prohibition of such conduct.

Were that not the case, international lawyers would proceed to ask whether Burma was occupied at the time of the transfers (a question of legal qualification on which the argument of this paper does not depend insofar as it concerns transfer of civilians into occupied *or similar territory*, including territory under forms of domination similar territory – the value at stake is the same whether it was occupation or colonial rule). If the narrow answer is negative, what would be the effect of the British re-occupation of Burma at the end of World War II? And further: was Burma a sovereign nation at the time of the third Anglo-Burmese War? We ask these questions as international lawyers because we have a particular kind of meeting between norm and fact in mind, namely evidence of alleged facts analysed in the light of the

elements of the prohibition against transfer of civilian population into occupied territory.[28]

Bergsmo's observations can apply, *mutatis mutandis*, to the situation in eastern DRC. If the Belgian forced transfers of Banyarwanda
population into eastern DRC occurred under modern international law,
they would be considered wrongful. However, at that time, this colonial
practice was not prohibited by international law. As seen above, those
forced transfers of Banyarwanda population into eastern DRC contributed
to the post-colonial conflict environment in the GLR, leading to the perpetration of widespread human rights violations and international crimes.
Several transitional justice processes aimed at addressing serious violations of IHL, IHRL and ICL have been implemented in this context, in the
three countries under review by this chapter.

15.2.3. Transitional Justice Processes and Consultations in the Post-Colonial Great Lakes Region

15.2.3.1. Rwanda

In response to the perpetration of mass atrocity crimes, the government of
Rwanda took the initiative to request the establishment of an *ad hoc* international criminal tribunal for Rwanda by the UN Security Council, as
well as to set up special chambers within the Rwandan judicial system to
prosecute the presumed authors of genocide and other international crimes
committed in the context of the Rwandan conflict. The government also
organized a conference on 'Genocide, Impunity and Accountability', in
Kigali, from 1 to 5 November 1995, which adopted a number of recommendations:

> 1. The Conference denounces the basic role played by the
> ethnistic ideology and calls upon the Rwandese Authorities
> to resolutely undertake the struggle against this ideology
> through all possible ways, especially through education pro-
> grammes, adult education, the media and political and dip-
> lomatic speeches.
>
> 2. The Conference requests rigorous enforcement of existing
> Rwandese laws which suppress racism and ethnic considera-
> tions and recommends, just like in the case of French and
> Belgian laws banning the negation of the Jewish genocide,

---

[28] Bergsmo, 2019, pp. 6–10, see above note 1 (the numerous and unusually enriching footnotes have been omitted here). See also Chapter 7 above.

the adoption of a law prohibiting any Rwandese citizen or foreigner residing in Rwanda from denying or relativizing the 1994 genocide; with due respect to internal regulations connected with the freedom of expression. This law will also apply to organizations and associations established in Rwanda; violations of this law may lead to sanctions or expulsion from the Rwandese territory.

3. The Conference calls on the political class to avoid succumbing to temptations to ethnic fundamentalism, not to aggravate any particularism whatsoever and not to allow ethnic displays.

4. The Conference requests the Christian Churches to really ponder on the close correspondence between the evangelic message and fetishization of the ethnic group as it emerges from speeches and actions of a number of their pastors and their congregations, in such a way as to contribute to the pacification of hearts and minds […].

5. The Conference requests communication professionals to avoid falling prey to the ethnicism trap in their remarks and to contribute to the development of a critical mind towards any racist manipulation.

6. The Conference calls upon intellectuals to devote themselves to the task of finally writing the country's history in a critical and documented manner in accordance with methods befitting this discipline, so as to come out of mythological and ideological reconstructions.

7. The Conference solemnly invites the authorities to urgently gather all documentations on the 1994 genocide and crimes against humanity in order to fight the negationism.[29]

15.2.3.1.1. Criminal Accountability Mechanisms

In addition to the ICTR and ICTY, criminal accountability mechanisms for genocide and other international crimes committed in Rwanda in 1994 have included special chambers in the Rwandan justice system. The cooperation between the two international and national judiciaries progressively increased as we approached the completion of the ICTR's operation.

---

[29] Office of the President, Republic of Rwanda, "Recommendations of the Conference held in Kigali from November 1st to 5th, 1995, on: 'Genocide, Impunity and Accountability: Dialogue for a National and International Response'", The Office, Kigali, December 1995, pp. 10–11.

15.2.3.1.1.1. The ICTR and ICTY

The ICTR was tasked by the UN Security Council to prosecute and try the presumed authors of the alleged genocide and crimes against humanity committed in Rwanda and neighbouring countries from 1 January to 31 December 1994. It operated from early 1995 to the end of 2015. During the 20-year period of its activities, the ICTR indicted a total of 93 persons and completed the trials of 80, mostly among the organizers and planners of the above-mentioned crimes. The ICTR handed-over 5 cases to national jurisdictions (Rwandan and French), and transmitted 3 others to the Mechanism for the ICTR and ICTY established by the UN in 2012.[30] Evaluating the outcome of the ICTR, Human Rights Watch observed:

> The ICTR was only ever expected to try a small number of suspects: primarily those who played a leading role in the genocide. To some extent, it has performed this task, and has tried and convicted several prominent figures, including former Prime Minister Jean Kambanda, former army Chief of Staff Augustin Bizimungu and former Ministry of Defence Chief of Staff Colonel Théoneste Bagosora. The ICTR also set precedents in the development of international criminal law, such as the first-ever prosecution of rape as genocide in the case of a former *bourgmestre* (mayor), Jean-Paul Akayesu.[31]

In addition, in the Media case, the ICTR clarified the role of hate speech in incitement to perpetrate genocide. According to Judge Byron:

> 2. Freedom of expression and hate speech-based crimes
>
> [...] In the Media Trial, the Trial Chamber recalled the important protection of international law on the right to freedom of expression. However, it also recalled that both the International Covenant on Civil and Political Rights and the Convention for Elimination of all Form of Racial Discrimi-

---

[30] International Criminal Tribunal for Rwanda ('ICTR'), "Key Figures of ICTR Cases", October 2019 (available on its web site).

[31] Human Rights Watch, "Rwanda: Justice after Genocide 20 Years On", 28 March 2014, p. 5 (available on its website); Larissa J. van den Herik, *The Contribution of the Rwanda Tribunal to the Development of International Law*, Martinus Nijhoff, Leiden, 2005; George W. Mugwanya, "The Contribution of the International Criminal Tribunal for Rwanda to the Development of International Criminal Law", in Chacha Murungu and Japhet Biegon (eds.), *Prosecuting International Crimes in Africa*, Pretoria University Law Press, Pretoria, 2011, pp. 69–96.

nation not only allowed, but required the prohibition of advocacy of racial hatred. The Trial Chamber also extensively dealt with the related jurisprudence of the European Court of Human Rights.

However, the Chamber felt that the developed international human rights standards had to be adapted to the context: It argued that at issue was 'not a challenged restriction of expression but the expression itself. Moreover, the expression charged as incitement to violence was situated, in fact and at the time by its speakers, not as a threat to national security but rather in defense of national security, aligning it with state power rather than in opposition to it'.

The Chamber analyzed particular articles published in Kangura and specific broadcasts. It noted that some of the communications cited by the Prosecution were protected by the freedom of expression. The Trial Chamber underlined the importance of distinguishing, for example, between the discussion of ethnic consciousness and the promotion of ethnic hatred. Similarly, public discussion of the merits of the Arusha Accords, which had aimed at ensuring peace in Rwanda before the genocide, however critical, constituted a protected exercise of free speech. [32]

The main criticism of the ICTR's outcome has been the one-side justice resulting from the prosecution of the Hutu leaders, while no single member of the Tutsi-led government was indicted, prosecuted and tried.

15.2.3.1.1.2. Special Chambers in the Rwandan Justice System

The above-mentioned 1995 Kigali Conference's report served as the basis for the development of national accountability, including the adoption by the parliament of the necessary legislative reform for the prosecution and trial of the presumed authors of genocide, as well as the development of alternative ways to address the consequences of the latter, with a view to promoting national reconciliation. Accordingly, the parliament of Rwanda adopted a law establishing special chambers within the Rwandan judiciary (thereafter 'special chambers') on 30 August 1996 (Act No. 8/96). It es-

---

[32] See Dennis C.M. Byron, "Hate Speech and the Rwanda Genocide: ICTR Jurisprudence and Its Implications", in Chile Eboe-Osuji (ed.), *Protecting Humanity: Essays in International Law and Policy in Honour of Navanethem Pillay*, Martinus Nijhoff, Leiden, 2010, pp. 53–66.

tablished specialized chambers within the courts of first instance tasked with the exclusive competence to prosecute all alleged perpetrators of international crimes and offences committed between 1 October 1990 and 31 December 1994. These crimes and offences included the following:

> (a) Crimes of genocide or crimes against humanity as defined in the 1948 Convention on the Prevention and Punishment of the Crime of Genocide, the Geneva Convention relating to the Protection of Civilian Persons in Time of War, of 12 August 1949, and its Additional Protocols, and the Convention on the Non-Applicability of Statutory Limitations to War Crimes and Crimes against Humanity of 26 November 1968, all three of which have been ratified by Rwanda; and (b) Offences covered in the Penal Code, which the Public Prosecutor's Office alleges, or the defendant admits, were committed in connection with the events surrounding the genocide and crimes against humanity.[33]

While complementary, the special chambers and the ICTR differed on several elements. On *ratione materiae*, the special chambers had jurisdiction over genocide and crimes against humanity. The special chambers were allowed to sentence the accused to death, while the maximum penalty decided by the ICTR was life. This explains why the ICTR did not authorize the transfer of cases to the special chambers before the death penalty was abolished in Rwanda. In addition, the special chambers were to apply the Rwandan Penal Code.

On *ratione temporis*, the jurisdiction of the special chambers covered the period from 1 January 1990 to 31 December 1994, wider than the temporal scope of the ICTR's mandate. The obvious goal of this extension was to cover the events that occurred since the commencement of the civil war in 1990.

Finally, on *ratione personae*, while the ICTR was focusing on the planners and organizers of the genocide and other mass atrocity crimes, the special chambers dealt with four categories of the presumed authors of the crimes: (1) the organizers and planners; (2) the persons who have committed or encouraged to commit the genocide and the related crimes in their official capacities (local authorities, militia and religious authorities); (3) the persons who have systematically committed criminal acts;

---

[33] Rwanda HRC Report 1997, p. 18, see above note 9.

and (4) the accomplices of intentional homicides or serious assaults having caused the death of victims.[34]

Evaluating the outcome of the special chambers after two decades, Human Rights Watch wrote:

> In 1996, Rwanda adopted a new law governing the prosecution of genocide-related crimes. Genocide trials began in December the same year in a charged environment. The legal framework for these prosecutions was established, but the day-to-day demands on the newly reformed justice system were unmanageable. Numerous defendants were convicted without legal assistance as defence lawyers were scarce and often too afraid to defend genocide suspects. The international non-governmental organization Lawyers without Borders (*Avocats sans frontières*) provided important assistance through a pool of national and foreign lawyers, but the needs far outweighed their capacity [...]. By 1998, the total prison population had reached 130,000, but only 1,291 people had been tried. It became apparent that it would take decades to prosecute those suspected for involvement in the genocide [...]. To overcome this challenge, the Rwandan government devised a novel system for trying genocide cases: gacaca.[35]

International and national criminal justice (including the ICTR, ICTY and the special chambers) have dealt with individual criminal responsibility to address impunity, thus implementing the retributive approach to justice. However, it has been unable to ensure the expected reconciliation. As far as the ICTR is concerned, one author has observed:

> The quest of extending the role of tribunals beyond its traditional mission of justice to embrace the difficult need of reconciliation after mass atrocities has revealed itself to be challenging. This difficulty is most clearly illustrated in the case of the ICTR, whose mission is to bring about Rwandan reconciliation through justice. The implementation of this mission that was doubted by some members of the Security Council, including Rwanda itself, at the time of setting up the ICTR is becoming a difficult experiment, with positive results but also with some negative outcomes capable even of undermining the aimed objective of national reconcilia-

---

[34] *Ibid.*, pp. 18–19.
[35] Human Rights Watch, 2014, pp. 3–4, see above note 31.

tion. The problem of co-operation between the Tribunal and Rwanda, the difficulties of circumscribing individual responsibility without condemning the whole community, the problem of singling out and punishing some criminals and leaving the rest unpunished, the abuse of pardon and clemency, and finally the absence of the victim in a criminal process pretending to restore his situation are some of the difficult problems hampering the proclaimed mission of reconciliation assigned to the ICTR […].

If retributive justice has to be considered as a tool for reconciliation should it not reach the big and the small criminal? […].

The search for collective rather than individual responsibility has even been identified, in some cases, as likely to lead to more national reconciliation. Retributive justice that emphasizes individualization of the crime and punishment is opposed restorative justice that looks for a collective responsibility by focusing 'on restoring victims, restoring offenders, and restoring the communities'. In the specific case of African societies it as even argued that in order to reach reconciliation the 'whole community must take responsibility for the traumas' […].

The problem of recourse to collective responsibility remains the potential for abuse. If Germans as a people should not be equated with Nazi, and Hutu as a group to 'genocidaire', 'Interahamwe' or 'Impuzamugambi' as a group should be condemned, banned, and declared liable before the courts.[36]

15.2.3.1.1.3. Co-operation Between the ICTR and the Rwandan Judiciary

The relationship between Rwanda and the ICTR has been globally difficult, in particular at the inception and the operation of the ICTR. One should remember that Rwanda, as a non-permanent Member of the UN Security Council, voted against the adoption of Resolution 955 (1994) establishing the ICTR, even though this resolution was adopted at its request. The main reason for its opposition to the resolution was the non-

---

[36] Jean Marie Kamatali, "The Challenge of Linking International Criminal Justice and National Reconciliation: The Case of the ICTR", in *Leiden Journal of International Law*, 2003, vol. 16, pp. 115 and 125–126.

inclusion of the death penalty in the Statute of the Tribunal. This remains a contentious issue until Rwanda abolished the death penalty in its legislation, thus paving the way to the improvement of its co-operation with the ICTR. According to ICTR:

> Various aspects of the work undertaken by the Tribunal depend significantly on the cooperation of States [...] To interview witnesses and conduct investigations, locate fugitives and arrest them, protect or relocate witnesses, or to require their appearance at trial, the Tribunal must obtain full cooperation from States [...]. On 27 October 2002, when Rwanda had de facto suspended its cooperation with Arusha, President Navanethem Pillay addressed the United Nations General Assembly, calling its attention to the fact that: 'Many States have assisted the ICTR in arranging contact with and facilitating the travel of witnesses. Some witnesses had no travel documents and special travel documents were easily arranged. However some months in 2002, the ICTR experienced difficulties over the flow of witnesses from Rwanda. The non-appearance of witnesses from Rwanda has disrupted the careful planning of the judicial calendar and is a severe setback to the judicial work [...]. Of the 122 defense witnesses that came to the ICTR this year, 8 came from Rwanda. The issue of travel of witnesses from Rwanda must be resolved, for trials hearing prosecution testimony to resume on time. I have invited the Minister of Justice and Institutional Relations in Rwanda, Honourable Minister Jean de Dieu Mucyo, the President of the Supreme Court of Rwanda, Judge Simeon Rwagasore and Prosecutor General of Rwanda, Mr. Gerald Gahima, to observe firsthand the judicial proceedings at the ICTR. It is my hope that my invitation would be accepted'.
>
> Starting in the Fall 2003, when the Prosecution anticipated a number of cases to Rwandan judicial authorities as part of a strategy outlined by the new Prosecutor Hassan Bubacar Jallow, the Tribunal noted in its annual report, that 'there is a more frequent or constant presence of the Prosecutor in Rwanda, the location of the crime and of the Investigations Division of the Office. This has enabled the Prosecutor to exchange ideas with the Rwandan Government on a regular basis and to attend to problems as they emerge. There has also been, as a result of the constant of frequent presence of

the Prosecutor in Rwanda, a more in-depth discussion on the transfer of cases to Rwanda [...].

As part of its completion strategy the Tribunal amended its Rules of Procedure and Evidence by introducing Article 11 bis, which allows the court to transfer cases to national jurisdictions while the Prosecutor assisted Rwandan authorities in drafting and adopting legislation to permit Kigali to receive cases from the ICTR.[37]

The ICTR's support for the revision of the Rwandese legislation provides a good example of positive complementarity. However, the latter was absent with regard to restorative transitional justice mechanisms established in Rwanda.

15.2.3.1.2. Restorative Transitional Justice Mechanisms

The recommendations of the Kigali Conference paved the way to the adoption of national accountability mechanisms, including the revived traditional Gacaca courts and the National Commission for the Fight Against Genocide.

15.2.3.1.2.1. Gacaca Courts

On 26 January 2001, the Rwandan parliament adopted the Organic Law No. 40/2001 establishing the Gacaca courts, tasked with prosecuting the genocide and crimes against humanity committed between 1 October 1990 and 31 December 1994.[38] Inspired by the traditional Gacaca, the revived Gacaca courts' main objective was to try the presumed authors of the mentioned crimes while promoting reconciliation at the community-level. They were initially tasked to address minor crimes or offences, including the destruction of properties. Due to the shortcomings of the special chambers, they have inherited cases from the latter. After a pilot starting in 2002, these courts became fully operational in 2005 and were closed in 2012. In terms of their outcome, a United Nations document provides this assessment:

---

[37] ICTR, "International Criminal Tribunal for Rwanda, Model or Counter Model for International Criminal Justice? The Perspective of the Stakeholders", International Symposium, Geneva, 9–11 July 2009, pp. 50–51.

[38] Rwanda, Journal Officiel de la République du Rwanda No. 14, 13 July 2001. This Law was amended on 19 June 2004 and 18 June 2008.

In the Gacaca system, communities at the local level elected judges to hear the trials of genocide suspects accused of all crimes except planning of genocide. The courts gave lower sentences if the person was repentant and sought reconciliation with the community. Often, confessing prisoners returned home without further penalty or received community service orders. More than 12,000 community-based courts tried more than 1.2 million cases throughout the country.

The Gacaca trials also served to promote reconciliation by providing a means for victims to learn the truth about the death of their family members and relatives. They also gave perpetrators the opportunity to confess their crimes, show remorse and ask for forgiveness in front of their community. The Gacaca courts officially closed on 4 May 2012.[39]

For its part, the AU Panel of the Wise wrote:

[...] it is important to note that the *gacaca* was a compromise that recognized the inability of the country's judicial system to deal with trials after mass atrocities. The *gacaca* tribunals should, therefore, be seen as a locally appropriate and pragmatic mechanism to address impunity and contribute to reconciliation. The *gacaca* experience illustrates the possibilities of using a nuanced approach to combine customary African values with international criminal law and human rights practices to overcome intractable conflict.[40]

In its above-mentioned and cited report, Human Rights Watch is more critical about of the operation of the Gacaca courts:

The expectation that gacaca could deliver national-level reconciliation in a matter of few years, especially so soon after genocide, was unrealistic from the outset. But gacaca's potential for contributing to reconciliation was hindered by difficulties in revealing the truth, as some participants lied or remained silent due to intimidation, corruption, personal ties, or fear of repercussions. In addition, gacaca did not deliver on its promises of reparations for genocide survivors: survivors received no compensation from the state, and little resti-

---

[39] UN Department of Public Information, "The Justice and Reconciliation Process in Rwanda", March 2014, p. 2 (available on its web site).

[40] African Union Panel of the Wise, *Peace, Justice, and Reconciliation in Africa: Opportunities and Challenges in the Fight Against Impunity*, International Peace Institute, New York, 2013, p. 35.

---

tution and often overly formulaic apologies from confessed
or convicted perpetrators – casting doubt on the sincerity of
the some of these confessions. While gacaca may have
served as a first step to help some Rwandans on the long
path to reconciliation, it did manage to dispel distrust between many perpetrators and survivors of the genocide.[41]

The literature is divided on the Gacaca courts. Some authors, with a
focus on the novel approach to the prosecution of international crimes,
have positive account on them.[42] Others are of the view that the Gacaca
courts failed to meet human rights standards in their functioning.[43]

15.2.3.1.2.2.   National Commission for the Fight Against Genocide

On 16 February 2007, the Rwandan parliament adopted a law on the attributions, organization and functioning of the National Commission for
the Fight against Genocide ('National Commission on Genocide'). Article
4 of this law provides the Commission's mandate:

> 1° to put in place a permanent framework for the exchange
> of ideas on genocide, its consequences and the strategies for
> its prevention and eradication;
>
> 2° to initiate the creation of a national research and docu-
> mentation centre on genocide;
>
> 3° to advocate for the cause of genocide survivors both with-
> in the country or abroad;
>
> 4° to plan and coordinate all activities aimed at commemo-
> rating the 1994 genocide;
>
> 5° to elaborate and put in place strategies that are meant for
> fighting genocide and its ideology;

---

[41]   Human Rights Watch, 2014, p. 5, see above note 31.

[42]   See among others, Bert Ingelaere, "The Gacaca Courts in Rwanda", in Luc Huyse and
Mark Salter (eds.), *Traditional Justice and Reconciliation after Violent Conflict: Learning
from African Experiences*, IDEA, Stockholm, 2008, pp. 25–59; Shannon E. Powers,
"Rwanda's Gacaca Courts: Implications for International Criminal Law and Transitional
Justice", in *Insights*, 2011, vol. 15, pp. 1–7; Anne-Marie de Brouwer and Etienne Ruveba-
na, "The Legacy of the Gacaca Courts in Rwanda: Survivors' Views", in *International
Criminal Law Review*, 2013, vol. 13, pp. 937–976.

[43]   Danielle L. Tully, "Human Rights Compliance and the Gacaca Jurisdictions in Rwanda",
in *Boston College International and Comparative Law Review*, 2003, vol. 26, pp. 401–413;
Christian Garuka, "Genocide as Prosecuted by the International Criminal Tribunal for
Rwanda and Gacaca Courts in Rwanda", in Chacha Murungu and Japhet Biegon (eds.),
2011, pp. 221–231, see above note 31.

6° to seek for assistance for genocide survivors and pursue advocacy as to the issue of compensation;

7° to elaborate and put in place strategies meant for fighting revisionism, negationism and trivialization;

8° to elaborate and put in place strategies meant to solve genocide consequences such as a trauma and other diseases which resulted from genocide;

9° to cooperate with other national or international organs with similar mission.[44]

This provision includes some elements which can serve as the basis to promote or advocate the accountability of former German and Belgian colonizers for their wrong-doing as a root cause of the mass atrocity crimes committed in Rwanda in 1994, including genocide. Pending this, the National Commission has played a catalyst role in achieving the memorial aspects of the 1994 genocide. In particular, it had been involved in the celebration of the international day devoted to the latter and its annual celebration on 7 April in Kigali, which has received worldwide attention and participation. In addition, the Rwandan Commission played a role model for the establishment of national committees for the prevention of genocide and other atrocity crimes in the framework of the ICGLR's Regional Committee for the Prevention of the Crime of Genocide, War Crimes, Crimes against Humanity and all Forms of Discrimination.[45]

15.2.3.2. Burundi

The 2000 Arusha Peace Agreement provided a power-sharing scheme along the lines of the ethnic belonging, including in the government and armed forces. It also provided for the establishment of mechanisms to address the culture of impunity in Burundi. In this framework, the institution of Bashingatahe, wise persons similar to Inyangamugaho (members of traditional Gacaca in Rwanda) received large support, while the government finally opted for the establishment of a truth and reconciliation

---

[44] Rwanda, Law no. 09/2007 of 16/02/2007 on the attributions, organisation and functioning of the national commission for the fight against genocide, 16 February 2007, Article 4 (https://www.legal-tools.org/doc/a416eb/).

[45] See Mutoy Mubiala, "Le Comité régional pour la prévention du génocide de la Conférence internationale sur la région des Grands Lacs", in Emmanuel Decaux et Sébastien Touzé (ed.), *La prévention des violations des droits de l'homme. Actes du colloque des 13 et 14 juin 2013*, Pedone, Paris, 2015, pp. 115–123.

commission ('TRC'). However, the ICC has intervened to address the serious violations of human rights and international crimes occurring in the country in the context of the electoral crisis since 2015.

15.2.3.2.1. Bashingantahe

Traditional Bashingantahe were originally elected as the judges at the local level. They played an important peace-making role in their respective communities. During the colonial and post-colonial rules, their role has evolved after their appointment as civil servants. Despite this evolution, they are still well-appreciated. During the 1993 crisis, it was reported that several of them provided protection to people at risk of killings. Their role was populated during the Arusha Peace Talks. Some participants proposed the revival of the institution as a restorative transitional justice mechanism, while others advocated for their integration in the membership of the proposed TRC. The challenge was to select reliable Bashingantahe among the 34,000 identified throughout the country in 2000, with the support of the United Nations Development Programme ('UNDP'), due to the perception of the progressive transformation of the institution during the colonial and post-colonial rule.[46] This favoured the option for the proposed TRC as a transitional justice mechanism.

15.2.3.2.2. The TRC

The UN was requested to support the implementation of the Arusha Peace Agreement on the design and operation of transitional justice mechanisms. The UN support was provided in accordance with the recommendation made by the 1995 International Commission of Inquiry for Burundi. In this regard, the UN deployed several missions to assist in the design of accountability mechanisms. All these missions faced a serious challenge in the refusal by the government of Burundi of an *ad hoc* or mixed court. It expressed its preference for the creation of a truth and reconciliation commission. Even for the implementation of this option, the discussions were long and laborious.

---

[46] See, *inter alia*, Philippe Ntahombaye and Zénon Manirakiza, *Le rôle des techniques et mécanismes traditionnels dans la résolution pacifique des conflits au Burundi*, UNESCO, Bujumbura, 1997; Zénon Manirakiza, "L'institution des Bashingantahe. Entre tradition et modernité", in *Au Cœur de l'Afrique*, 1999, vol. 65, pp. 209–238; Tracy Dexter, "L'institution des Bashingantahe au Burundi et son rôle dans la situation post-conflit", in *Justice en période de post-conflits. Actes du Colloque international (Bujumbura, Source du Nil, 20-22 septembre 2005)*, UNESCO, Bujumbura, 2005, pp. 185–193.

The author of this chapter had the opportunity to participate in an OHCHR's technical support mission to Bujumbura, in June 2011, to assist the government and stakeholders in the drafting of the terms of reference of the proposed TRC. One of the conflicting points was the determination of the temporal scope of its jurisdiction. Some participants, in particular the officials, were defending the year of the independence of the country (1962) as the starting point of the temporal jurisdiction of the proposed TRC. Others, including civil society organizations, backed by the donor community, advocated the inclusion of the colonial period. Even Belgian diplomats and missionaries consulted were favouring the second option, stating that Belgium would participate in the process if this option was retained. The latter would enable to address the colonial wrong-doing in the country. Finally, the Law enacting the TRC, adopted by the parliament on 15 May 2014, limited its temporal jurisdiction to the period from 1 July 1962 (the Independence Day) to 4 December 2008 (the date of end of the armed conflict).

According to Article 6 of the enacting law, the TRC is tasked with the following mandate:

> Les missions de la Commission sont les suivantes:
>
> 1. Enquêter et établir la vérité sur les violations graves des droits de l'homme et du droit international humanitaire commises durant la période allant de la date de l'indépendance le 1er juillet 1962 au 4 décembre 2008, date de la fin de la belligérance. La Commission prend en compte la gravité et le caractère systématique et collectif des violations.
>
> Les enquêtes visent notamment à:
>
> élucider les violations des droits politiques, civils, économiques et sociaux majeurs;
>
> a) établir les responsabilités individuelles et celles des institutions étatiques, des personnes morales et des groupes privés;
>
> b) déterminer la nature, les causes et l'étendue des violations précitées, y compris les antécédents, circonstances, facteurs, contexte, motifs et perspectives qui ont conduit à ces violations;
>
> c) identifier et cartographier les fosses communes et tout autre endroit d'enterrement non reconnu par la

loi, prendre les mesures nécessaires à leur protection, procéder à l'exhumation éventuelle des corps aux fins d'un enterrement digne.

2. Qualifier toutes les violations indiquées au point 1 du présent article.

3. Publier:

a) la liste des personnes disparues, assassinées et celles des victimes et des témoins qui renoncent à l'anonymat;

b) la liste des personnes, autant burundaises qu'étrangères, qui se sont distinguées dans la protection des vies humaines pendant les différentes crises;

c) la liste des victimes qui ont accordé le pardon ainsi que celle des auteurs ayant bénéficié du pardon.

4. Proposer:

a) un programme de réparations comportant à la fois des mesures individuelles et collectives, tant matérielles que morales et symboliques;

b) la mise en place d'un programme d'actions visant à promouvoir le pardon et la réconciliation;

c) une date de la Journée nationale de commémoration des victimes des violations des droits de la personne humaine;

d) l'érection, sur des sites identifiés, de monuments de la réconciliation et de la mémoire aux niveaux national, provincial et local;

e) la conception et la réalisation d'autres ouvrages et œuvres symboliques;

f) les réformes des institutions pour garantir la non répétition des événements du passé, afin de bâtir une société burundaise et démocratique;

g) la réécriture d'une histoire la plus partagée par tous.

5. Contribuer, notamment par une recherche documentaire, à la réécriture de l'histoire du Burundi pendant la période

> couverte par le mandat, afin de permettre aux Burundais une version largement partagée et acceptée des événements.[47]

It goes without saying that Article 6(1)(c) of the above-mentioned enacted law provides a window for addressing the colonial wrong-doing as a root cause of ethnic conflicts and the related atrocities committed in Burundi. However, the ongoing post-electoral crisis, which commenced in 2015, has not enabled the TRC to efficiently operate, thus anticipating its failure to address impunity and to achieve reconciliation. As a consequence of international crimes perpetrated, the ICC has opened an investigation into the situation in the country.

15.2.3.2.3. The ICC and Burundi

As far as Burundi is concerned, the ICC Prosecutor Fatou Bensouda opened a preliminary examination of the situation in Burundi on 25 April 2016.[48] She subsequently submitted her report on the preliminary examination, in which she concluded that she has reasonable basis to believe that crimes against humanity were committed in Burundi during the period under review, and requested ICC Pre-Trial Chamber III to authorise an investigation regarding these crimes. On 9 November 2017, the Pre-Trial Chamber adopted its decision authorising the ICC Prosecutor to open an investigation regarding crimes within the jurisdiction of the Court allegedly committed in Burundi or by nationals of Burundi outside Burundi since 26 April 2015 until 26 October 2017.[49] The ICC has continued its investigations even if Burundi withdrew from the Rome Statute. The ICC's press release on the decision to authorise an investigation provides as follows:

> Pre-Trial Chamber III, considered that the supporting materials presented by the ICC Prosecutor, including victims' communications submitted to the Prosecutor, offer a reasonable basis to proceed with an investigation in relation to crimes against humanity, including: a) murder and attempted murder; b) imprisonment or severe deprivation of liberty; c) torture; d) rape; e) enforced disappearance and f) persecution, allegedly committed in Burundi, and in certain instances out-

---

[47] Burundi, Loi N° 18 du 15 mai 2014 portant création, mandat, composition, organisation et fonctionnement de la Commission Vérité et Réconciliation, Bujumbura, 2014.

[48] ICC, Office of the Prosecutor, Report on Preliminary Examination Activities 2017, 4 December 2017, p. 62 (https://www.legal-tools.org/doc/e50459/).

[49] ICC, "ICC judges authorise opening of investigation regarding Burundi situation", Press Release, 9 November 2017 (available on its web site).

side of the country by nationals of Burundi, since at least 26 April 2015. The Chamber noted that, according to estimates, at least 1,200 persons were allegedly killed, thousands illegally detained, thousands reportedly tortured, and hundreds disappeared. The alleged acts of violence have reportedly resulted in the displacement of 413,490 persons between April 2015 and May 2017.

The crimes were allegedly committed by State agents and other groups implementing State policies, including the Burundian National Police, national intelligence service, and units of The Burundian army, operating largely through parallel chains of command, together with members of the youth wing of the ruling party, known as the "Imbonerakure".

The ICC Prosecutor is not restricted to the incidents and crimes described in the decision but may, on the basis of the evidence, extend her investigation to other crimes against humanity or other crimes within the jurisdiction of the Court (i.e. genocide or war crimes), as long as she remains within the parameters of the authorised investigation.[50]

The above-mentioned communiqué announcing the ICC's authorization to the Prosecutor to open investigation on Burundi raised the implications of Burundi's withdrawal from the ICC Rome Statute, as well as the issue of co-operation with the ICC:

The Pre-Trial Chamber found that the Court has jurisdiction over crimes allegedly committed while Burundi was a State party to the ICC Rome Statute. Burundi was a State Party from the moment the Rome Statute entered into effect for Burundi (1 December 2004) until the end of the one-year interval since the notification of Burundi's withdrawal (26 October 2017). The withdrawal became effective for Burundi on 27 October 2017. Accordingly, the Court retains jurisdiction over any crime within its jurisdiction up to and including 26 October 2017, regardless of Burundi's withdrawal. As a consequence, the Court may exercise its jurisdiction even after the withdrawal became effective for Burundi as long as the investigation or prosecution relate to the crimes allegedly committed during the time Burundi was a State Party to the Rome Statute. Moreover, Burundi has a duty to cooperate with the Court for the purpose of this investigation since the

---

[50] *Ibid.*

investigation was authorised on 25 October 2017, prior to the date on which the withdrawal became effective for Burundi. This obligation to cooperate remains in effect for as long as the investigation lasts and encompasses any proceedings resulting from the investigation. Burundi accepted those obligations when ratifying the Rome Statute. [...]

Lastly, the Chamber noted that, according to available information, the Burundian authorities have remained inactive in relation to potential cases arising out of the situation in Burundi. Despite the establishment of three commissions of inquiry and certain proceedings before domestic courts, the Chamber found that these steps were either deficient or did not concern the same persons or the same crimes that are likely to be the focus of an ICC investigation. Accordingly, there is no conflict of jurisdiction between the Court and Burundi.[51]

It should be noted that, so far, Burundi has refused to co-operate with the ICC, thus undermining the possibility for the latter to contribute to addressing impunity in the country, including through positive complementarity. The Burundian position differs significantly from the co-operative attitude of its neighbouring DRC.

15.2.3.3. Democratic Republic of the Congo

According to Angèle Makombo, former UN senior political affairs officer:

The political and economic rivalries between the Banyarwanda and the indigenous Congolese, which were contained during the colonial period, escalated after independence in 1960 [...]. In 1962, 1964 and 1965, clashes broke out between these two different communities resulting in hundreds of casualties [...]. In 1993, Banyarwanda peasants and indigenous Congolese ethnic groups began to attack each other with machete and spears, resulting in the death of some 3,000 persons and displacing another 300,000. The violence continued unabated in the Masisi and Walikale regions without any person responsible for the situation being brought to justice [...]. In September 1996, South Kivu former deputy governor stated in a radio broadcast that if the Banyamulenge did not leave Zaïre within a week, they would be interned in camps and exterminated. The Banyamulenge's re-

---

[51] *Ibid.*

sponse was to join forces with the support of neighbouring countries to launch the rebellion which put an end to Mobutu's regime.[52]

The war engaged in this context resulted in widespread atrocities. To address the latter, the government of the DRC referred the situation to the ICC in 2004. So far, this has led to several cases before the Court. In addition, the government also adopted transitional justice measures to address mass atrocity crimes, including the establishment of a TRC the same year. The failure of the latter and further fact-finding by the OHCHR Mapping Team led to recommendations in 2010 for the establishment of new transitional justice mechanisms.

15.2.3.3.1. The ICC and the Situation in the Democratic Republic of the Congo

According to the International Coalition for the ICC, the

> conflict in the Democratic Republic of Congo (DRC) is one of the world's deadliest since World War II. Since 1998, some 5.4 million are reported to have died from war related causes. Civilians in the regions of Ituri and North and South Kivu have borne the brunt of fighting between government forces and local militias, often backed by regional powers, over control for territory and rich mineral resources. Political and ethnic tensions have resulted in years of grave international crimes including mass murder, the use of child soldiers, pillage, sexual and gender based crimes, among others. For many years, victims and civil society have demanded accountability at the national and international levels.

> The ICC investigation opened in 2004 – its first-ever – has focused on the leaders of several armed militia and rebel groups suspected of war crimes and crimes against humanity. The DRC ratified the Rome Statute in April 2002. A law incorporating ICC crimes into domestic law and facilitating cooperation with the Court was adopted in 2015, after many years of civil society advocacy. There have also been several prosecutions of grave crimes in special domestic courts in eastern DRC.

---

[52] Angèle Makombo, "Civil Conflict in the Great Lakes Region: The Issue of Nationality of the Banyarwanda in the Democratic Republic of the Congo", in *African Yearbook of International Law*, 1997, vol. 5, pp. 51–54.

Thomas Lubanga who was commander-in-chief of the FPCL as well as resident of its political arm known as the Union of Congolese Patriots (UPC), became the first person to be tried and convicted by the ICC. He serves 14 years in prison for war crimes of enlisting and conscripting children under the age of 15 years and using them to participate actively in hostilities (child soldiers). On 8 July 2019, ICC Trial Chamber VI found Bosco Ntaganda guilty, of 18 counts of war crimes and crimes against humanity committed in Ituri, DRC, in 2002-2003, including sexual violence.

On 19 December 2015, Mr. Lubanga was transferred to a prison facility in the DRC to serve his sentence of imprisonment. In 2017, Trial Chamber II set the amount of Mr. Lubanga's liability for collective reparations at USD 10,000,000, which was approved by the Appeal Chamber in 2019. Apart from Lubanga, the ICC also convicted German Katanga and Bosco Ntaganda of charges of war crimes and crimes against humanity. Katanga was sentenced to a total of 12 years' imprisonment. Bosco Ntaganda's conviction is the third conviction in the situation of the DRC. He was the co-accused in the case against Thomas Lubanga and served as his military chief as the Deputy Chief of the FPCL/UPC. He eluded justice until his surrender to the ICC in 2013. On 8 June 2019, he was convicted of 18 crimes of war crimes and crimes against humanity, including rape and sexual slavery by Trial Chamber VI. The verdict could be the ICC's first final conviction for charges of sexual and conflict-related violence. Currently, Mr. Ntaganda is appealing the decision.[53]

It follows from this account that all closed and pending cases relating to the situation in the DRC before the ICC have concerned, so far, leaders of armed groups in the eastern region of the country. In its decisions on some of these cases, the ICC has made valuable contributions to international law, including on the criminalization of conscription and use of child soldiers and sexual violence as a means of war. The main criticism of the ICC's work on the DRC has been its inability to develop positive complementarity with the national justice system. As the Open Society outlined in a report:

---

[53] International Coalition for the ICC, "Democratic Republic of Congo" (available on its web site).

In creating the International Criminal Court (ICC), the drafters of the Rome Statute assigned primary responsibility for dealing with its specified crimes to national authorities. The ICC may exercise jurisdiction only where a state is not willing and able to carry out 'genuine' investigations and prosecutions of war crimes, crimes against humanity, and genocide. This principle of complementarity not only sets forth a key test for admissibility of cases in The Hague; it also places a heavy burden on individual states to help achieve the Rome Statute's overarching goal: ending impunity for grave atrocities.

While the ICC plays a critical role as a court of last resort, it will never have the capacity to deal with more than a handful of cases at one time. By supporting the development of political will and legal and functional capacity at the state level, complementarity gives more victims a chance at justice for horrendous crimes, makes proceedings more accessible to affected communities, contributes to deterrence through the promotion of accountability at the national level, and enables national authorities to invest in the creation of functional criminal justice systems capable, ultimately, of ending cycles of mass atrocities. The realization of complementarity in post-conflict states is an important component of conflict resolution and prevention. [...]

The international community has undertaken numerous efforts to help meet both general and more specific challenges to the credible prosecution of international crimes in DRC. MONUSCO has provided security, logistical support, and expertise in support of proceedings in the military justice system. Donors have backed various trainings in investigation, prosecution, and judging of international crimes, as well as the building, rehabilitation, and equipping of judicial infrastructure.

Yet a lack of government respect for the independence of the judiciary, the chronic underfunding of the justice sector, an unwillingness to pursue sensitive cases, and a mixed record of cooperation with the ICC all raise questions about the DRC government's commitment to genuine justice for Rome Statute crimes. The country's limited capacity to plan and coordinate policy in the justice sector, including complementarity policy, is compounded by poor coordination among donors active in justice-sector support and a largely dysfunctional mechanism for coordination between relevant government agencies and donors. But perhaps the greatest challenge to realizing complementarity in the DRC is the lack of strategy for complementarity programming. Agreement on a specific complementarity mechanism, perhaps a model court, may be the best way to focus resources in a manner that can build domestic capacity, tap into existing rule-of-law programming, and deliver justice for atrocities in the near term.[54]

An appropriate complementarity strategy in the DRC should include both criminal justice and non-judicial transitional justice tracks.

15.2.3.3.2. From Failed Truth and Reconciliation Mechanism to Proposed Transitional Justice Mechanisms

In the DRC, a TRC was established in 2004 by an organic law adopted in accordance with the 2002 Global and Inclusive Agreement signed at the Inter-Congolese Dialogue in Sun City (South Africa). For political and governance reasons, the Congolese TRC did not achieve its mission, as planned. However, during the two years of its operation, it was involved in the mediation of several local conflicts, in particular in the troubled eastern DRC.[55] However, the failed TRC did not take action to address colonial wrong-doing at the origins of the situation in this area, in particular forced transfers of the Banyarwanda into the North-Kivu. It would be the appropriate forum to address this issue.

In 2008, the UN Secretary-General requested the OHCHR to take the lead in mapping the international crimes, in co-operation with the UN Department of Peacekeeping Operation ('DPKO') and the UNDP. The OHCHR's Mapping Team was mandated to:

> [c]onduct a mapping exercise of the most serious violations of human rights and international humanitarian law committed within the territory of the Democratic Republic of the Congo between March 1993 and June 2003.

---

[54] Eric A. Witte, *Putting Complementarity into Practice: Domestic Justice for International Crimes in the DRC, Uganda, and Kenya*, The Open Society Foundations, New York, NY, 2011, pp. 5–6.

[55] Mutoy Mubiala, "Les commissions de vérité et de réconciliation et la justice en Afrique", in *Congo-Afrique*, 2015, vol. 55, p. 104.

Assess the existing capacities within the national justice system to deal appropriately with such human rights violations that may be uncovered.

Formulate a series of options aimed at assisting the Government of the Democratic Republic of the Congo in identifying appropriate transitional justice mechanisms to deal with the legacy of these violations, in terms of truth, justice, reparation and reform, taking into account ongoing efforts by the Congolese authorities, as well as the support of the international community.[56]

An OHCHR press release published the day of the presentation of the Mapping Report to the UN Human Rights Council, on 1 October 2010, provided:

In her foreword to the report, UN High Commissioner for Human Rights Navi Pillay states that "no report can adequately describe the horrors experienced by the civilian population" in the DRC (formerly Zaire), "where almost every single individual has an experience to narrate of suffering and loss."

"While it neither aims to establish individual responsibility, nor lay blame, the report – in full candour – reproduces the often shocking accounts by victims and witnesses of the tragedies they experienced", she says.

"The report is intended as a first step towards the sometimes painful but nonetheless essential process of truth-telling after violent conflict [...] it looks to the future by identifying a number of paths that could be pursued by Congolese society to come to terms with its past, to fight impunity, and to face its contemporary challenges in a manner that prevents the re-occurrence of such atrocities."

While the report's gruesome inventory of serious violations dramatically underscores the need for justice, the DRC's ability and willingness to address the issue remains limited, the reports says, noting that poorly functioning judicial institutions "have left millions of victims with nowhere to turn and no opportunity to have their voices heard."

---

[56] OHCHR, *Commissions of Inquiry and Fact-Finding Missions on International Human Rights Law and International Humanitarian Law: Guidance and Practice*, United Nations, New York, 2015, p. 127.

> The very limited number of prosecutions of those alleg-
> edly responsible for serious violations of human rights and
> of international humanitarian law committed in in the DRC
> "has only encouraged further serious violations, which con-
> tinue to this day", the report says. "[...] Because of the mul-
> tiple dimensions of seeking justice for the possible crimes
> committed in the DRC, it is crucial that a holistic policy of
> transitional justice be implemented, which will involve the
> creation of diverse and complementary mechanisms, both
> judicial and non-judicial."
>
> Those mechanisms could include a variety of options
> examined in the report, including creation of a mixed juris-
> diction, possibly involving "hybrid courts" with both nation-
> al and international staff, creation of a new Truth and Recon-
> ciliation Commission; reparation programs; and reforms of
> both the legal sector and the security forces. Inclusive na-
> tional consultations should be held to give the overall pro-
> cess credibility and legitimacy.[57]

The OHCHR Mapping Report recommended options on transitional justice mechanisms and processes in the DRC, including the establishment of special chambers in the Congolese judicial system, hybrid courts and a new TRC.[58] The Congolese Senate has refused to establish hybrid courts including foreign magistrates. For its part, the proposed TRC is yet to be established.

To conclude on the GLR transitional justice experiences, the author of this chapter refers to a thought he made elsewhere regarding the legacy of African traditional justice systems for the restorative dimension of transitional justice in Africa:

> In inspiring African TRCs and revived traditional justice sys-
> tems, African ancestral conciliatory procedures contributed
> to the enhancement of restorative transitional justice, contra-
> ry to retributive mechanisms prevailing in Latin and Central
> America and (the UN ad hoc international criminal tribunals,
> hybrid tribunals, ICC). A more balanced and integrated ap-

---

[57] "UN Releases D.R. Congo Report Listing 10 Years of Atrocities, Identifying Justice Options", United Nations Organization Stabilization Mission in the DR Congo, 1 October 2010 (available on its web site).

[58] OHCHR, "Rapport du Projet Mapping concernant les violations les plus graves des droits de l'homme et du droit international humanitaire commises entre mars 1993 et juin 2003 sur le territoire de la République démocratique du Congo", August 2010, pp. 458–522.

proach between retributive and restorative transitional justice would help 'humanize' the evolution of international criminal justice and the rule of law, while contributing to the fight against impunity.[59]

15.2.3.4. Retributive v. Restorative Transitional Justice in Africa

The restorative focus of African transitional justice is reflected in the AU Transitional Justice Policy, which provides several tools for developing restorative transitional justice processes and consultations, including reconciliation and social cohesion, reparations, redistributive (socio-economic) justice, memorialization, and diversity management, and detailed benchmarks for their implementation, as follows:

Reconciliation and Social Cohesion

60. Reconciliation is both a goal and a process premised on building the trust necessary for a degree of cooperation between individuals and communities. Full redress and reparation are essential to building reconciliation. Reconciliation involves addressing legacies of past violence and oppression, reconstructing broken relationships and finding ways for individuals and communities to live together.

61. Reconciliation may be strengthened by further efforts to achieve forgiveness between victim(s) and perpetrator(s), including expressions of remorse and willingness to make reparations.

62. Social cohesion requires healing, which includes regard for each other's suffering; coming to terms with the totality of what happened; promoting shared truth; constructing a common narrative about the past, justice and the need to restore and experience a sense of security; and overcoming a sense of victimization.

---

[59] Mutoy Mubiala, "The Contribution of African Traditions and Norms to United Nations Human Rights Law", in *Human Rights and International Legal Discourse*, 2010, vol. 4, pp. 233–234; see also Hlengiwe Mkhize, "Truth Commissions: Actors in the Reconciliation Process", Paper presented at the twenty ninth Round Table on "Justice and Reconciliation: An Integrated Approach", International Institute of Humanitarian Law, International Committee of Red Cross, San Remo, 7–9 September 2006; Idris A. Abuelgasim, "The Debate on Restorative Justice", Paper presented at the twenty ninth Round Table on "Justice and Reconciliation: An Integrated Approach", International Institute of Humanitarian Law, International Committee of Red Cross, San Remo, 7–9 September 2006.

63. Benchmarks and standards for effective reconciliation and social cohesion may include:

i. Programmes that promote social cohesion, coexistence and reconciliation at all levels of society;

ii. Programmes that address structural inequalities, and promote inclusive development, equitable management of diversity and social cohesion;

iii. Measures securing human rights for all and promoting truth recovery through truth commissions and public trials to satisfy appeals for justice;

iv. Education programmes which reinforce equality, dignity and common humanity;

v. Institutions, programmes and platforms that bring members of different groups together;

vi. Offers of forgiveness and provision of facilities for platforms for mediation and psychosocial support.

Reparations

64. Reparative justice consists of effective and adequate financial as well as non-financial redress or restitution for violations or losses suffered.

65. The forms that reparation takes are:

i. Material reparation, which may include the restitution of access and/or title to property taken or lost, rebuilding of property destroyed by violence, and provision of a job, a pension and monetary compensation;

ii. Healing complements and completes truth and reconciliation and constitutes one of the objectives of truth and reconciliation. It is the process by which affected individuals and communities mend the physical and psychological wounds that they have suffered and recover from the emotional and moral effects of violence;

iii. Rehabilitation, which is the provision of basic services, including victim-specific support such as medical and psychosocial services, as well as services specific to women and children;

iv. Collective reparation, which may include the restitution of communal lands; rebuilding health, education, security, judicial and other public service infrastructure as well as the livelihood systems of affected communities, with due regard to the interests of children and youth; and compensation in the form of money or services to the community;

v. Moral reparation, which involves non-material forms including disclosure of facts about the actors and circumstances of a victim's mistreatment or death, public acknowledgement and apology, the identification and exhumation of the bodies of loved ones and provision of support for burial ceremonies and memorialization.

66. Benchmarks and standards for successful reparative justice may include:

i. Member States should develop comprehensive and holistic policy frameworks that not only provide for public reparation programmes, but also encourage nongovernmental reparation initiatives along with transparent and administratively fair procedures to access reparation, and institutions to administer them effectively;

ii. Reparation programmes should be transformative and promote equality, non-discrimination and participation of victims and other stakeholders. They should build solidarity across victim communities, restore dignity, be fair and just and tailored in their form to the needs of different categories of victims, particularly children and youth;

iii. Member States should adopt holistic approaches to reparations for harm inflicted by sexual and gender-based violence which address the societal structures and conditions that permit such violations;

iv. Reparation should be prompt, adequate and effective in addressing the harm suffered by the victim;

v. The reparation programme should have a clear strategy for resource mobilization – this could include a reparation fund;

vi. Where it is expected that there will be a significant time lapse before a full reparation programme is implemented, there should be provision for interim reparations;

vii. Guidelines for coordination between the different actors involved in reparations programmes must be developed to ensure that the approach is comprehensive and the widest range of groups affected by the conflict are reached;

viii. There should be proper oversight of reparation programmes, which may include submission of regular reports to the appropriate designated body regulated by national law.

Redistributive (Socio-Economic) Justice

67. Redistributive (socio-economic) justice entails the socio-economic and development measures designed to rectify structural inequalities, marginalization and exclusion for achieving social justice and equitable and inclusive development.

68. Along with the reparative measures, forward-looking redistributive measures that address underlying socio-economic marginalization and exclusion and contribute to preventing relapse to violence should be adopted.

69. The benchmarks and standards for redistributive justice may include:

i. Land reform and protection of property rights, including traditional ownership, access and use of land and resources on land, having regard to the need to guarantee the inheritance and property rights of women in accordance with national laws;

ii. Affirmative action development packages for historically marginalized groups/regions and those affected by violence, having regard to inequalities within communities, particularly those affecting women, including displaced and refugee women;

iii. Adoption of all-inclusive and equitable fiscal and development strategies as well as wealth/resource-sharing and power-sharing arrangements.

70. The implementation of policies that offer educational and employment opportunities for youth, including through prioritizing and mobilizing investment in social services such as technical and vocational training, infrastructural development and rural agricultural and pastoralist development schemes.

Memorialization

71. Memorialization entails the measures beyond the immediate transitional period that are necessary for truth, reconciliation and healing, involving public acknowledgement of

victims and institutionalizing both societal dialogue across generations and non-impunity in national discourse.

72. Acknowledging that respect for the dead is a fundamental human obligation and a prerequisite for peace and reconciliation among the living, the AUC has set an international precedent by establishing a continental human rights memorial, the African Union Human Rights Memorial (AUHRM). Based on the ethics and practices of memory and education, the AUHRM project helps to remind warring parties and peacemakers of the value of memorialization as an expression of respect for the dead and survivors of violence and for confronting atrocities.

73. Memorialization could include commemorative activities, erection of monuments and symbols, renaming of public spaces or buildings, review of artistic or cultural expressions as well as national symbols and holy days and/or revision of history texts and educational curricula. As a long-term inclusive process, it requires a policy foundation ensuring the sustained engagement of a range of actors, targeting the youth in particular.

74. Benchmarks and standards for successful memorialization may include:

i. Participation: Memory initiatives should promote inclusion of multiple voices across political, class, ethnocultural and generational lines, paying particular attention to women and other marginalized groups, including at local and community levels;

ii. Complementarity: Memory initiatives should foster transformative justice and build on and take forward the works of complementary mechanisms of truth, justice, reparation and non-impunity;

iii. Process: Memorialization should foster intergenerational dialogue and involve educational activities targeting children and youth, including through commemorative programmes and annual ceremonies;

iv. Multiple narratives: Memorialization should allow for the expression of multiple narratives, recognizing the inevitability of multiple discourses and different understandings of the past as well as varying experiences of different groups, including women, children, youth and vulnerable groups such as persons with disabilities;

v. Intergenerational focus: Memorialization processes should prioritize and promote the active inclusion of younger generations as agents for change and as a guarantee of non-recurrence of violence.

Diversity Management

75. The diversity management element of the AUTJP addresses the group dimension of conflicts and violations where violence was organized and perpetrated on the bases of race, ethnicity, colour, sex, language, religion, political or any other opinion, national and social origin, fortune, birth or other status. This is particularly important in societies where ethnocultural and religious polarization and animosity feature as prominent parts of conflicts or where violence targets particular ethnic, religious or regional groups.

76. Benchmarks and standards for constructive diversity management may include:

i. Recording and acknowledging the identity dimension of violence in the criminal and truth and reconciliation dimension of TJ, having regard to the gendered dimension of such violence;

ii. Instituting educational programmes that target stereotypes and social prejudice and promote respect for ethnocultural diversity and the dignity of fellow human beings, irrespective of their origin, through school curricula, religious and cultural teachings, radio and television shows;

iii. Establishing policies and institutions that promote national cohesion and tolerance and accommodation between members of different communities;

iv. Regulatory measures for combating hate speech on the basis of religion, ethnicity and language and similar acts that incite violence and fuel communal divisions and tension;

v. Periodic dialogue between and celebration of diversity involving religious, community and political leaders as well as representatives of affected communities, targeting in particular the youth and youth groups;

vi. Institutional measures that ensure equitable representation of members of various communities in national and
local decision-making structures, with particular regard to
representation of members of the most marginalized
communities or regions.[60]

So far, the above-mentioned restorative justice tools have been unable to address colonial wrong-doing, thus contributing to the criticisms of
'double standards' of international law. This explains the need to examine
how the latter can contribute to addressing colonial wrongs and crimes.

15.2.4. Relevancy of International Law to Address Colonial Wrongs

International criminal law as experienced in the operation of the ICC and
other transitional justice mechanisms in the GLR has been unable to address the 'pre-accountability' of former colonial powers for their wrong-
doing under the Western-centric international law. Moreover, the implementation of criminal responsibility is irrelevant for States, and individual
criminal responsibility has terminated for most colonial perpetrators, who
already died, as illustrated by the Lumumba case before the Belgian
courts, as described in Chapter 14 above.

However, the author of this chapter is of the view that international
law relating to State responsibility could be used to address colonial
wrong-doing. The United Nations International Law Commission ('ILC')
has contributed to the codification and progressive development of State
responsibility over four decades, in two subjects: (i) the responsibility of
States for internationally wrongful acts, and (2) the liability of States for
the injurious consequences of acts not prohibited by international law
(causal liability). Rules developed in the two fields can be used to address
colonial wrong-doing.

15.2.4.1. State Responsibility for Internationally Wrongful Acts

According to international law, States are responsible for internationally
wrongful acts attributable to them.[61] As far as the GLR is concerned, the

---

[60] African Union ('AU'), "Transitional Justice Policy", AU, Addis Ababa, 2019, pp. 12–15;
see also, African Commission on Human and Peoples' Rights ('ACHPR'), "Study on Transitional Justice and Human and Peoples' Rights in Africa", ACHPR, Banjul, 2019, pp. 15–
16.

[61] See Pierre-Marie Dupuy, "Quarante ans de codification du droit de la responsabilité internationale des Etats. Un bilan", in *Revue générale de droit international public*, 2003, vol.
107, pp. 305–348.

litigation relating to the territorial occupation of the DRC by neighbouring countries before the African Commission on Human and Peoples' Rights (ACHPR) and the International Court of Justice ('ICJ') provides good examples of the implementation of State responsibility for internationally wrongful acts, including serious violations of IHL, IHRL and ICL. Before examining this jurisprudence, it is important to provide a brief account on the relevant facts.

15.2.4.1.1. Background to the Territorial Occupation

As is well-known and recorded, Mobutu's collapse was followed, in 1998, by a deadly regional conflict, called 'Africa's First World War', involving the armed forces of several GLR-countries on the territory of the DRC, including Burundi, Rwanda and Uganda. These three neighbouring countries of the DRC intervened militarily in eastern DRC, officially to back the Tutsi population at risk of genocide and to fight against the Hutu armed groups revived from the former Rwandese Armed Forces (ex-FAR) in exile in the Kivus. Widespread atrocity crimes were committed in this context and have continued to be perpetrated by the armed groups operating in eastern DRC, several of which being rebel groups from the neighbouring countries.[62] Leaders of these armed groups claimed that they were creation for self-defence or the protection of their respective ethnic communities, some of which are interconnected with Tutsi and Hutu in Burundi, Rwanda and Uganda. In addition to backing several of these armed groups and militia, the latter countries have made direct military interventions on the territory of the DRC, occupying a portion of its eastern region during a certain period.

To address the occupation of its territory by Burundi, Rwanda and Uganda, the government of the DRC moved before several bodies, including the African Commission on Human and Peoples' Rights ('African Commission') and the ICJ.

15.2.4.1.2. Case before the African Commission on Human and Peoples' Rights

As the monitoring body of the African Charter on Human and Peoples' Rights ('African Charter'), the African Commission is tasked with receiving and reviewing inter-state and other communications (Article 55 of the

---

[62] See, among others, Joan Casòliva and Joan Carrero, *The African Great Lakes. Ten Years of Suffering, Destruction and Death*, Cristianisme i Justicia, Barcelona, 2000.

Charter), including individual communications. In the context of the former, on 8 March 1999, the DRC submitted a communication against Burundi, Rwanda and Uganda, summarized as follows:

> The case concerned a Communication made by the Democratic Republic of the Congo (DRC) to the African Commission alleging violations of the African Charter on Human and Peoples' Rights (African Charter) and international law including the Geneva Conventions 1949 and Additional Protocols, the UN Charter and UN Declaration on Friendly Relations. It was also the first interstate communication filed before the African Commission on Human and Peoples' Rights (the Commission).
>
> The DRC alleged that armed forces from Burundi, Uganda and Rwanda had been occupying its border provinces in the eastern part of the country and committing mass violations of human rights and international law. Such alleged violations included the mass killing of civilians and the siege of a hydroelectric dam (civilian run) resulting in the cut off of electricity to homes, schools and hospitals – which led to the deaths of patients dependent on life support systems. The DRC further alleges, in particular against the Ugandan soldiers, the deliberate spread of HIV/AIDS amongst the local population by the perpetration of rape. Further allegations were the mass looting of civilian property and the natural mineral wealth in the region, as well as the forced movement of populations from the region into 'concentration camps' in Rwanda in order to establish a 'Tutsi land'.[63]

At its session of May 2003, the African Commission adopted a report on this case, according to which it:

> considered that there was an effective occupation of parts of the Complainant States' territory which constituted a violation of the Charter which requires the Commission, by virtue of Article 23, to uphold international law including the UN Declaration of Friendly Relations and the UN Charter.
>
> The alleged human rights violations stemmed from this illegal occupation and were in direct violation of the Charter and international law. Articles 60 and 61 of the African Char-

---

[63] ACHPR, *DRC v. Burundi, Rwanda and Uganda*, Communication, 29 May 2003, Communication 227/99, p. 1 (https://www.legal-tools.org/doc/1d1ea8/).

ter require the Commission to draw inspiration from international law on human and peoples' rights which includes the Geneva Conventions of 1949 and the Additional Protocols. The acts of violence alleged – killings, rapes and mutilations – while still in effective occupation of the eastern provinces of the DRC were considered by the Commission to be inconsistent with the Geneva Convention relative to the Protection of Civilian Persons in Time of War 1949 and Additional Protocol 1.

Furthermore, the Commission held that there was a violation of Article 2 of the African Charter concerning non-discrimination in the enjoyment of rights, as the violations were directed at victims based on their national origin.

Further violations of specific rights in the African Charter were found including violation of the protection assured to the family as the fundamental unit of society and the violation of the freedom to leave and return to one's country, which were compromised by the forced displacement of the population out of the region.

The Commission declared that violations of international law, such as the Additional Protocol 1 to the Geneva Conventions, had taken place by the siege of the hydroelectric dam in lower Congo which resulted in the cutting off of electricity to schools, homes and hospitals. This additionally compromised Articles 16 and 17 of the African Charter – the rights to the best attainable physical and mental health and the right to education.

The Commission urged all states to abide by international law and urged Rwanda, Uganda and Burundi to withdraw from DRC territory. The Commission also recommended that adequate reparations be made on behalf of the victims of human rights violations committed by the armed forces of the respondent states whilst in effective occupation of DRC territory.[64]

---

[64] *Ibid.*

The jurisprudence of the African Commission in this case was complemented by the judgment of the ICJ in the *Case Concerning Armed Activities on the Territory of the Congo.*[65]

15.2.4.1.3. Cases before the International Court of Justice

For the same facts as stated above, the DRC brought a case against Uganda and Rwanda before the ICJ on 23 June 1999. For reasons of jurisdiction, the ICJ decided that the case concerning the latter was not admissible.[66] However, it received the case regarding Uganda and issued a ruling on 19 December 2005. In this case, the ICJ addressed several issues, including the use of force, belligerent occupation, violations of IHRL and IHL, and illegal exploitation of natural resources. The DRC requested reparation for the injury caused by Uganda's wrongful acts. According to its judgment, the Court:

> *Finds* that the Republic of Uganda, by engaging in military activities against the Democratic Republic of the Congo on the latter's territory, by occupying Ituri and by actively extending military, logistic, economic and financial support to irregular forces having operated on the territory of the DRC, violated the principle of non-use of force in international relations and the principle of non-intervention;
>
> [...]
>
> *Finds* that the Republic of Uganda, by the conduct of its armed forces, which committed acts of killing, torture and other forms of inhumane treatment of the Congolese civilian population, destroyed villages and civilian buildings, failed to distinguish between civilian and military targets and to protect the civilian population in fighting with other combatants, trained child soldiers, incited ethnic conflict and failed to take measures to put an end to such conflict; as well as by its failure, as an occupying Power, to take measures to respect and ensure respect for human rights and international humanitarian law in Ituri district, violated its obligations un-

---

[65] International Court of Justice, *Armed Activities on the Territory of the Congo (Democratic Republic of the Congo v. Uganda)*, Judgment, 19 December 2005, p. 168 ('Armed Activities Uganda Judgment') (https://www.legal-tools.org/doc/8f7fa3/).

[66] International Court of Justice, *Armed Activities on the Territory of the Congo (New Application: 2002) (Democratic Republic of the Congo v. Rwanda)*, Judgment, Jurisdiction and Admissibility, 3 February 2006, p. 6 (https://www.legal-tools.org/doc/1d7775/).

der international human rights law and international humanitarian law;

[…]

Finds that the Republic of Uganda, by acts of looting, plundering and exploitation of Congolese natural resources committed by members of the Ugandan armed forces in the territory of the Democratic Republic of the Congo and by its failure to comply with its obligations as an occupying Power in Ituri District to prevent acts of looting, plundering and exploitation of Congolese natural resources, violated obligations owed to the Democratic Republic of the Congo under international law;

[…]

(5) Unanimously,

Finds that the Republic of Uganda is under obligation to make reparation to the Democratic Republic of the Congo for the injury caused;

(6) Unanimously,

Decides that, failing agreement between the Parties, the question of reparation due to the Democratic Republic of the Congo shall be settled by the Court, and reserves for this purpose the subsequent procedure in the case.[67]

The issue of reparation by Uganda has not yet been settled. According to the media, the Congolese government has requested Uganda to pay USD 100 billion and the latter has not agreed with this amount. The continuing contentious discussions between the two countries have led to the re-submission of the case to the ICJ (the review of which was suspended again in November 2019, at the request of the two countries).

15.2.4.2. State Liability for Injuries Caused by Acts Not Prohibited by (Colonial) International Law

Contrary to international responsibility, causal liability proceeds from the injuries caused as a consequence of lawful acts or acts not prohibited by international law (for example, activities relating to hazardous products such as nuclear tests). As mentioned above, colonization was not consid-

---

[67] Armed Activities Uganda Judgment, pp. 116–117, see above note 65; see Auguste K. Mampuya, "Responsabilité et réparation dans le conflit des Grands-Lacs au Congo-Zaïre", in *Revue générale de droit international public*, 2004, vol. 108, pp. 679–707.

ered as unlawful act under the Western-centric international law applicable during the colonial period and even today. This provided colonial powers with the opportunity to engage in their wrong-doing. However, as demonstrated by fact-finding, the latter caused lingering negative consequences illustrated by the perpetration of mass atrocity crimes in the GLR. While not criminalized under the colonial period, these atrocities led up to international crimes under post-colonial international law. Colonial wrong-doing, which consists of acts currently criminalized, remains unaddressed through international criminal responsibility, non-applicable to States.[68] However, the accountability of former colonial powers can be addressed through liability for acts not prohibited by (colonial) international law. Causal liability differs from the responsibility for internationally wrongful acts in their consequences. As an author outlines as follows:

> The following are the consequences of a wrongful act, according to article 42, paragraph 1, of the draft articles on State responsibility (Part Two), which are deemed to codify in this respect customary law: (a) *restitutio naturalis*, (b) compensation by equivalent, (c) satisfaction and (d) guarantees for non-repetition.

> In cases of lawful acts, not all of these consequences would apply; satisfaction and guarantees of non-repetition certainly would not apply.

> Compensation by equivalent may be applicable whether the antecedent act is wrongful or not, although the regime regarding the burden of proof may be subject to different rules, depending on whether it corresponds to a wrongful act (responsibility) or to a lawful one (liability). In the field of liability, maximum limits (ceilings) may be imposed upon compensation, whereas in that of responsibility, the *Chorzow* rule imposes *in integrum restitutio*.[69]

In the case study under review, former colonial powers (namely Germany and Belgium) should compensate the affected countries and communities for their past wrong-doing, because of the lingering negative consequences (mass atrocity crimes) of the latter (causal liability). This

---

[68] See Robert Rosenstock, "An International Criminal Responsibility of States?", in *International Law on the Eve of the Twenty-First Century. Views from the International Law Commission*, United Nations, New York, 1997, pp. 265–285.

[69] Julio Barboza, "*Sine Delicto* (Causal) Liability and Responsibility for Wrongful Acts in International Law", in *ibid.*, p. 324.

leads to a novel and emerging principle of 'pre-criminal accountability' for colonial wrong-doing. This could be explained by the fact that, even though colonial wrongs were not criminalized under the Western-centric (colonial) international law, they have caused injuries to their former colonies and their communities. In addition, similar acts are criminalized, now, by post-colonial law, in particular the Rome Statute of the ICC. The latter explicitly criminalizes "Apartheid" (Article 7(1)(j)), which developed as a colonial crime in South Africa. According to Article 7(2)(h) of the Statute:

> "The crime of apartheid" means inhumane acts of a character similar to those referred to in paragraph 1, committed in the context of an institutionalized regime of systematic oppression and domination by one racial group over racial group or groups and committed with the intention of maintaining that regime.

Under the Rome Statute, forced transfers of population are considered, either, as crimes against humanity (Article 7(1)(d)) or as war crimes (Article 8(2)(a)(vii)). Under contemporary international law, forced transfers of populations – an expanded practice under colonial rule in Africa, Asia and elsewhere – would amount to crimes against humanity (for example, transfer of Banyarwanda into eastern DRC) or war crimes (the case of Burma during the wars against the British colonizer).

The 1968 Convention on the Non-Applicability of Statutory Limitations to War Crimes and Crimes Against Humanity, entered into force on 11 November 1970, provides that the

> States Parties to the present Convention,
>
> Recalling resolutions of the General Assembly of the United Nations 3 (I) of 13 February 1946 and 170 (II) of 31 October 1947 on the extradition and punishment of war criminals, resolution 95 (I) of 11 December 1946 affirming the principles of international law recognized by the Charter of the International Military Tribunal, Nürnberg, and the judgement of the Tribunal, and resolutions 2184 (XXI) of 12 December 1966 and 2202 (XXI) of 16 December 1966 which expressly condemned as crimes against humanity the violation of the economic and political rights of the indigenous population on the one hand and the policies of apartheid on the other,
>
> Recalling resolutions of the Economic and Social Council of the United Nations 1074 D (XXXIX) of 28 July 1965 and

1158 (XLI) of 5 August 1966 on the punishment of war criminals and of persons who have committed crimes against humanity,

Noting that none of the solemn declarations, instruments or conventions relating to the prosecution and punishment of war crimes and crimes against humanity made provision for a period of limitation,

Considering that war crimes and crimes against humanity are among the gravest crimes in international law,

Convinced that the effective punishment of war crimes and crimes against humanity is an important element in the prevention of such crimes, the protection of human rights and fundamental freedoms, the encouragement of confidence, the furtherance of co-operation among peoples and the promotion of international peace and security,

Noting that the application to war crimes and crimes against humanity of the rules of municipal law relating to the period of limitation for ordinary crimes is a matter of serious concern to world public opinion, since it prevents the prosecution and punishment of persons responsible for those crimes,

Recognizing that it is necessary and timely to affirm in international law, through this Convention, the principle that there is no period of limitation for war crimes and crimes against humanity, and to secure its universal application,

Have agreed as follows:

Article I

No statutory limitation shall apply to the following crimes, irrespective of the date of their commission:

(a) War crimes as they are defined in the Charter of the International Military Tribunal, Nürnberg, of 8 August 1945 and confirmed by resolutions 3 (I) of 13 February 1946 and 95 (I) of 11 December 1946 of the General Assembly of the United Nations, particularly the "grave breaches" enumerated in the Geneva Conventions of 12 August 1949 for the protection of war victims;

(b) Crimes against humanity whether committed in time of war or in time of peace as they are defined in the Charter of the International Military Tribunal, Nürnberg, of 8 August 1945 and confirmed by resolutions 3 (I) of 13 February 1946 and 95 (I) of 11 December 1946 of the General Assembly of the United Nations, eviction by armed attack or occupation and inhuman acts resulting from the policy of apartheid, and the crime of genocide as defined in the 1948 Convention on the Prevention and Punishment of the Crime of Genocide, even if such acts do not constitute a violation of the domestic law of the country in which they were committed.

Article II

If any of the crimes mentioned in article I is committed, the provisions of this Convention shall apply to representatives of the State authority and private individuals who, as principals or accomplices, participate in or who directly incite others to the commission of any of those crimes, or who conspire to commit them, irrespective of the degree of completion, and to representatives of the State authority who tolerate their commission.

Article III

The States Parties to the present Convention undertake to adopt all necessary domestic measures, legislative or otherwise, with a view to making possible the extradition, in accordance with international law, of the persons referred to in article II of this Convention.

Article IV

The States Parties to the present Convention undertake to adopt, in accordance with their respective constitutional processes, any legislative or other measures necessary to ensure that statutory or other limitations shall not apply to the prosecution and punishment of the crimes referred to in articles I and II of this Convention and that, where they exist, such limitations shall be abolished.[70]

There has been some useful State practice under these principles, including the French and Belgian national legislation, concretizing this international normative development. This has made possible the prosecution and trial of Nazi criminals, including Klaus Barbie, by the French courts (Lyon, 1987). It has also facilitated the admissibility of complaints, such as that submitted to the Belgian courts by the family of the first elected Congolese Prime Minister, Patrice Lumumba, with the support of the Jus Cogens Team, as described in Chapter 14 above. One can also

---

[70] Convention on the Non-Applicability of Statutory Limitations to War Crimes and Crimes Against Humanity, 11 November 1970 (https://www.legal-tools.org/doc/4bd593/).

mention the Belgian initiative to establish parliamentarian commissions of inquiry of situations involving colonial wrongs, including the assassination of Lumumba.[71]

That said, there is a need to go beyond individual cases to adopt a holistic or global approach. From a victim-centred perspective, there is a need for justice – to fight against impunity for colonial wrongs and crimes. In particular, the new international law provides a window of opportunity for pending justice, by lifting or dropping the temporal limitation to the prosecution of the presumed authors of war crimes and crimes against humanity. In this regard, this chapter is proposing the establishment of *ad hoc* joint claims tribunals that can appropriately address collective colonial wrongs.

15.2.4.2.1. Proposal for the Creation of Joint Claims Tribunals to Address Accountability for Colonial Wrongs

International law provides several examples of joint litigation bodies established along the lines of arbitral tribunals, for example, the Iran-United States Claims Tribunal. It is suggested to establish joint claims tribunals inspired by this model, including representatives of both the concerned former colonial power and the country affected. Representatives of the UN and relevant regional organizations (the EU, AU or ICGLR) could supplement the composition of such bodies. The names of these bodies would include those of the involved countries (for examples, Germany-Namibia Claims Tribunal or Belgium-DRC Claims Tribunal).

Such tribunals should review different contentious aspects of serious colonial wrong-doing based on the claims submitted by the affected countries or communities. The tribunals should enable civil society organizations, academics and representatives of local communities to participate in their processes. Their outcome could include issuance of apologies or public acknowledgment of the harm caused to the affected countries or collective compensation measures (education, health and development programmes) by former colonial powers.

Regarding the applicable law of such tribunals, they should apply the normative framework of 'transitional justice law', including the 1997 Set of Principles for the Protection and Promotion of Human Rights

---

[71] See Chapter 14 above by Christophe Marchand, Crépine Uwashema and Christophe Deprez.

through Action to Combat Impunity (the Joinet Principles),[72] the 2005 UN Basic Principles and Guidelines on the Right to a Remedy and Reparation for Victims of Gross Violations of International Human Rights Law and Serious Violations of International Humanitarian Law (the van Boven Principles),[73] as well as the 2005 Updated Set of Principles for the Protection and Promotion of Human Rights through Action to Combat Impunity. The latter provides for the following general obligations of States to take effective action to combat impunity:

> Impunity arises from a failure by States to meet their obligations to investigate violations; to take appropriate measures in respect of the perpetrators, particularly in the area of justice, by ensuring that those suspected of criminal responsibility are prosecuted, tried and duly punished; to provide victims with effective remedies and to ensure that they receive reparation for the injuries suffered; to ensure the inalienable right to know the truth about the violations; and to take other necessary steps to prevent a recurrence of violations.[74]

The above proposal of joint claims tribunals benefits from the project initiated by the European Center for Constitutional and Human Rights and its partners to address the genocide of the Ovaherero and Nama peoples from Namibia by the German colonizer.[75] The German track aims to go beyond the ongoing bilateral negotiations between the governments of Germany and Namibia about this issue, in order to include academics,

---

[72] UN Economic and Social Council, Question of the impunity of perpetrators of human rights violations (civil and political), Revised final report prepared by Mr. Joinet pursuant to Sub-Commission decision 1996/119, UN Doc. E/CN.4/Sub.2/1997/20/Rev.1, 2 October 1997, Annex II (https://www.legal-tools.org/doc/ykahvz/).

[73] The right to a remedy and reparation for victims of violations of international human rights and humanitarian law, Note by the High Commissioner for Human Rights, UN Doc. E/CN.4/2005/59, 21 December 2004, Annex I (https://www.legal-tools.org/doc/dd5602/). This text was endorsed by the UN General Assembly by its Resolution 60/147 on 16 December 2005, UN Doc. A/RES/60/147, 21 March 2006 (https://www.legal-tools.org/doc/bcf508/).

[74] Impunity, Report of the Independent Expert to Update the Set of Principles to Combat Impunity, Diane Orentlicher, Addendum: Updated Set of Principles for the Protection and Promotion of Human Rights through Action to Combat Impunity, UN Doc. E/CN.4/2005/102/Add.1, 8 February 2005, pp. 7–8, 12–13 and 16–17 (https://www.legal-tools.org/doc/639fa9/).

[75] Bergsmo, 2019, p. 18, see above note 1.

civil society organizations and other relevant stakeholders from the two countries.[76] As Bergsmo outlined, regarding its relevancy for Myanmar:

> The German track, which concerns violations that occurred in Namibia, a former German colony, is particularly promising, as it is largely driven by a desire to find ways to deal with the problem of double standards in the context of former colonies. It is a multi-pronged track with several projects. It does not to date amount to a hard-nosed application of so-called 'Third World Approaches to International Law' ('TWAIL') which would not necessarily help to resolve the challenge before us in Myanmar. A focused approach may suit the area of international criminal law well, insofar as core international crimes seek to protect interests such as groups of persons against physical-biological destruction and innocent civilians against being killed or tortured, which are common global values in a different manner than, for example, development or economic growth. A well-designed process for Myanmar, with TWAIL participation, could perhaps offer the established discourse useful specificity and future-orientation.[77]

This thinking is also applicable to the three countries of the GLR (Burundi, DRC and Rwanda) examined in this chapter. So far, beyond political and academic rhetoric – mostly limited to the slave trade, colonial exploitation of natural resources, robbery of cultural property as well as the related call for reparation or restitution – no concrete project on transitional justice processes and consultations has been developed to address the colonial wrong-doing and its legacy for subsequent mass atrocity crimes committed in the GLR. The German track relating to Namibia provides, therefore, a momentum and a window of opportunity for developing and implementing such a project for the GLR. This could fill a gap in past transitional justice processes in the GLR which have only responded to post-colonial human rights abuses, failing to address colonial wrong-doing.

---

[76] Wolfgang Kaleck (ed), *Colonial Repercussions: Namibia*, European Center for Constitutional and Human Rights ('ECCHR'), Berlin, 2019.

[77] Bergsmo, 2019, p. 18, see above note 1 (footnotes omitted). See Chapter 7 above.

15.2.5. Conclusion

The Great Lakes Region of Africa has been facing protracted conflicts characterized by mass atrocity crimes, including genocide and crimes against humanity. To investigate these crimes, the international community, in particular the United Nations and the African Union, deployed many fact-finding mechanisms in the affected countries, including Burundi, the Democratic Republic of the Congo, and Rwanda. These fact-finding and inquiry mechanisms were mandated, among others, to identify the root causes of serious violations IHRL, IHL and ICL. Such fact-finding has documented widespread serious violations while identifying colonial wrong-doing among the root causes of those violations.

It results from the analysis of the practice of past and ongoing non-judicial transitional justice processes in the three countries under review that no initiative was yet taken, so far, to address colonial wrong-doing. It is surprising and disappointing to exclude the external dimension of past human rights abuses and to deal only with internal or local accountability for the lingering negative consequences of colonial wrong-doing. As tasked by their mandating bodies, international criminal accountability mechanisms, including the ICTR, ICTY and the ICC (which has been dealing with the situations in the DRC and Burundi), have limited (as anticipated) their operation to the prosecution and trial of the perpetrators (mostly the planners and organizers) of international crimes committed in the post-colonial era. This has excluded, not only minor offenders (causing an impunity gap), but also former colonial actors (leading to an 'accountability gap'). This illustrates the fact that individual criminal responsibility is not sufficient, *per se*, to address impunity and accountability for serious human rights violations and international crimes. If the impunity gap between main perpetrators and minor offenders could be addressed by national or hybrid courts, criminal justice, at both national and international levels, is unable to address the root causes of those crimes.

Meanwhile, international law provides other possible frameworks to address the lingering negative consequences of colonial wrong-doing, including State liability, as codified by the UN International Law Commission. This chapter has identified the causal liability of former colonial powers for injuries caused by acts not prohibited by past Western-centric international law as a possible legal foundation of former colonial powers' accountability for their wrong-doing in Africa, in general, and in the GLR, in particular.

This chapter, therefore, suggests the establishment of 'joint claims tribunals' on the model of the US-Iran Claims Tribunal, involving the concerned former colonial powers (Germany and Belgium) and the affected countries and communities in the GLR (Burundi, DRC and Rwanda). These tribunals should also engage with civil society organizations, academics, and other relevant stakeholders from both sides. This recommendation is made with reference to the project of the European Center for Constitutional and Human Rights aimed at addressing Germany's accountability in the extermination of local peoples in South West Africa (now Namibia), during German colonial rule. The chapter argues that the proposed transitional justice mechanism – by giving effect to State liability for the former colonial powers for their wrong-doing and to subsequent compensation for the affected countries or communities – would contribute to responding to the criticisms of 'double standards' of international law. The ICC should support such proposed mechanisms. The latter could complement international criminal justice, while ensuring equal access to international law in Africa and worldwide.

PART V:
INDIGENOUS PEOPLES

16

Avoidance Techniques: Accounting for Canada's Colonial Crimes

Asad G. Kiyani[*]

16.1. Introduction

Canada's reputation in contemporary international criminal law is quite positive. Since the 1990s, Canadian diplomats and lawyers have been deeply involved in developing and staffing international criminal tribunals, and internationally supporting the push for international criminal justice. Canada provided diplomatic and logistical support for the *ad hoc* tribunals for the former Yugoslavia and Rwanda, as well as other tribunals in Sierra Leone, Lebanon and Cambodia. More famously, the Canadian delegation played a pivotal role in consensus-building during the Rome Conference negotiations for the future International Criminal Court ('ICC'), was the first state to pass laws implementing the Court's Rome Statute, and embarked on an international campaign to encourage other states to ratify and implement the Statute.

This paper explores the contrast between the Canadian enthusiasm for justice internationally, and the reluctance to permit or pursue accountability at the domestic level. While Canada has – with some notable exceptions – prosecuted or supported the prosecution of all manner of international crimes committed overseas, it has noticeably avoided the question of accountability mechanisms for crimes committed by the Canadian state against indigenous peoples in Canada.

The next section examines the history of Canadian support of overseas international criminal justice, and its avoidance of domestic justice for

---

[*]   **Asad G. Kiyani** is Assistant Professor at University of Victoria Faculty of Law, and holds a LL.B. degree from Osgoode Hall Law School, LL.M. degree from Cambridge University, and Ph.D. degree from the University of British Columbia. This research is funded in part by the 2017 Antonio Cassese Prize for International Criminal Law Studies, and the Hessel Yntema Prize for Comparative Law.

international crimes. It outlines Canada's role in the development of international criminal institutions, and the basis for its positive reputation. It also outlines the countervailing arguments, pointing at both the specific field of international criminal law, as well as state inaction in respect of overseas human rights violations. Thus, Canada is both inattentive and sometimes opposed to remedies of international crimes, as well as an exporter of human rights violations through its inadequate regulation of business interests. Similar arguments of inattentiveness and opposition to remedies can be raised in respect of these interests.

The next section describes Canada's parallel lack of action in the domestic sphere. It outlines the basic premises of the argument that the Canadian state has committed (and continues to perpetrate) numerous human rights violations and international crimes against Indigenous peoples living in Canada. While not all of these violations can be defined as international crimes, many can. What connects the human rights and international criminal violations is the state's historical and continuing indifference towards its Indigenous peoples, which is reflected in its indifference towards overseas human rights violations. Thus, Canada's reputation as a human rights leader and as a proponent of international criminal law is undermined by its activities (and inactivity) overseas, as well as its domestic actions.

Having established these dual sets of failings, the next section explains the legal mechanisms through which Canada has created obstacles to domestic accountability. Both international and domestic law were operationalized in ways that made it exceedingly difficult to recognize the repression of Indigenous peoples as crimes. This, in turn, diminished demands for justice by shifting them from the legal to the political sphere. The emphasis in this section is on the intentional limiting of the definition of genocide in both international and domestic law.

The chapter concludes by drawing out some themes that connect the notion of colonial crimes to contemporary moves for international criminal justice. As with many other states, Canada's support of international criminal justice has always been measured and calculated, often with a view towards distinguishing its treatment of its own colonial crimes from those of other states.

This analysis of Canadian involvement in international human rights violations and international criminal justice is rooted in Third World Approaches to International Law ('TWAIL'). While TWAIL was informally a guiding force for some international legal scholars for an extended period of time – as seen in the works of Bedjaoui,[1] Abi-Saab[2] and Sornarajah[3] – it arose as a formal discipline in the 1990s.[4] Arguably, the earliest example of TWAIL in the realm of international criminal law is that of Radhabinod Pal's famous dissent at the Tokyo Tribunal,[5] which remains relevant to this day.[6]

The first self-identifed TWAIL scholarship on international criminal law comes from Antony Anghie and Bhupinder Chimni, who outline two important points.[7] First, as in other areas of international law, TWAIL in international criminal law remains concerned with the fate and interests of the 'ordinary peoples' of the Third World. The key question is always how international law and practice recognize and serve these 'ordinary peoples'. What this means is that TWAIL is *not* reflexively about affirming state sovereignty. Rather, in the same way that modern international criminal law focuses on individual criminal responsibility, TWAIL puts people and not the state at the forefront. This means, as Anghie and Chimni say, that the TWAIL scholar will sometimes find herself aligned with the state, and sometimes opposed to that same state.[8]

This insight is fundamental to understanding the relevance of TWAIL beyond limited and questionable notions of the 'Third World'. The central tension that TWAIL identifies is that between the sovereign state and its

---

[1] Mohamed Bedjaoui, *Towards a New International Economic Order*, Holmes & Meier, New York–London, 1979.

[2] See, for example, George Abi-Saab, "The Development of International Law by the United Nations" in Frederick Snyder and Surakiart Sathirathai (eds.), *Third World Attitudes toward International Law: An Introduction*, Martinus Nijhoff, Leiden, 1987, pp. 221–230.

[3] Muthucumaraswamy Sornarajah, *The International Law on Foreign Investment*, 4th ed., Cambridge University Press, 2018 (first published in 1994).

[4] See James Thuro Gathii, "TWAIL: A Brief History of Its Origins, Its Decentralized Network, and a Tentative Bibliography", in *Trade Law and Development*, 2011, vol. 3, no. 1 pp. 26–64.

[5] Radhabinod Pal and Akira Nakamura, *Dissentient Judgment of Justice Pal: International Military Tribunal for the Far East*, Kokusho-Kankokai, Tokyo, 1999. The dissenting judgment of Justice Pal is available in the ICC Legal Tools Database (https://www.legal-tools.org/doc/38eba7/).

[6] Latha Varadarajan, "The trials of imperialism: Radhabinod Pal's dissent at the Tokyo tribunal", in *European Journal of International Relations*, 2015, vol. 21, no. 4, pp. 793–815.

[7] Antony Anghie and B.S. Chimni, "Third World Approaches to International Law and Individual Responsibility in Internal Conflicts", in *Chinese Journal of International Law*, 2003, vol. 2, no. 1, pp. 77–103.

[8] *Ibid.*, p. 83.

subjects. While the idea of international law is naturally tethered to interactions *between* sovereign states, and sometimes the effects of one sovereign state's acts on the subjects of another sovereign state, TWAIL focuses on the form of the state as a product of international interactions and the central configurator of both international and domestic interactions.References to the 'Third World' aspect of TWAIL risk being overly literal and excessively functional to the extent they suggest either that TWAIL is only relevant to the geographic territory of the 'Third World', or that 'Third World' is an unhelpful, unidentifiable analytic category. TWAIL scholars identify the salience of the concept of 'Third World' not in categorical terms, but rather in shared experiences of colonialism and, now, post-colonialism; it is a sensibility born of a particular set of interactions that both interprets and predicts other future interactions.

The relevance of TWAIL to the Canadian development of international criminal law and the domestic treatment of Indigenous peoples turns on this understanding of TWAIL as centred on the state, its form, and its role. As I have argued elsewhere, TWAIL can meaningfully inform understandings of the development of international criminal law, particularly definitions of international crimes,[9] and the selectivity of the field – including the use (or non use) of international criminal law domestically.[10] In turning this lens on the Canadian involvement in international criminal law, new connections and disjuncts become apparent.

Three benefits accrue from applying TWAIL to the Canadian context. First, it helps demonstrate the instability of the notion of a 'domestic' context, as distinct from an international one, through the application of international law theory and methods. Canada is a federal state, but many of its Indigenous peoples contest the idea of being identified as members of that state, and insist that their relationship with the state is a nation-to-nation rather than state-subject relationship.

Second, it highlights an ongoing gap in international criminal law. In spite of the field's tremendous growth in the previous 25 years, one persistent problem is the unwillingness of states to support or pursue accountabil-

---

[9] Asad G. Kiyani, "International Crime and the Politics of Criminal Theory: Voices and Conduct of Exclusion", in *NYU Journal of International Law and Politics*, 2015, vol. 48, no. 1, pp. 129–208.

[10] Asad G. Kiyani, "Group-Based Differentiation and Local Repression: The Custom and Curse of Selectivity", in *Journal of International Criminal Justice*, 2016, vol. 14, no. 4, pp. 939–957.

ity for international crimes committed domestically. This usually manifests in the context of civil wars, where governments are reluctant to hold their own troops accountable for crimes committed to preserve that same government. The Canadian example shows a different dimension of this problem: the unwillingness of settler-colonial states to account for their past and present practices of colonial rights violations. Their avoidance of domestic responsibility parallels that of many post-colonial states, and the application of a TWAIL lens draws out these continuities. These continuities are particularly acute with respect to the ongoing marginalization, suppression of, and violence against Indigenous peoples around the world.

Finally, one of the key drivers of these continued violations is their relationship in land acquisition, land control, and economic development. This chapter briefly sketches the impact of Canada's massive mining economy on overseas territories, and draws some tentative parallels to the exploitation of Indigenous lands within Canada, often without appropriate consultation with Indigenous groups.

In this way, TWAIL is a useful tool for illuminating the problem of colonial crimes, and in particular the double standards of Canada's colonial experience with international criminal law. While Canada has been a norm entrepreneur in modern international criminal justice, this has also been juxtaposed against its treatment of Indigenous peoples. More pertinently, the double standard manifests not just in the *commission* of crimes by Canada, but in its legal activity aimed at *defining* its conduct as non-criminal. In other words, the double-standard identified here is one specifically about Canadian norm entrepreneurship that is designed to *expand* liability for overseas and foreign crimes, while insulating liability for Canadian state crimes against domestic Indigenous populations and by Canadian corporations operating overseas.

16.2. Canada and the Indigenous: International Dichotomy

16.2.1. Canada's Reputation

A brief history shows that Canada's reputation as an influential supporter of international criminal justice stems from a variety of sources. Lester B. Pearson's role in both resolving the Suez Crisis and developing the United Nations Emergency Force,[11] along with Canada's long-standing actual

---

[11] Michael K. Carroll, *Pearson's Peacekeepers: Canada and the United Nations Emergency Force, 1956–67*, University of British Columbia Press, Vancouver, 2009.

support of peace-keeping missions around the world,[12] are antecedents showing a commitment to the multilateralism at the idealistic heart of the push for more international criminal law. Similarly, it surely mattered that the international community quickly realized its failure to respond to the calls of General Romeo Dallaire for peace-keeper support in the prelude to the Rwandan genocide. As noted above, Canada supported the development of the *ad hoc* tribunals in the 1990s as well, and Louise Arbour assumed the role of Chief Prosecutor for both the International Criminal Tribunal for the former Yugoslavia and International Criminal Tribunal for Rwanda.[13] Canada also attempted to institute domestic prosecutions for historical overseas crimes, including those committed during the Holocaust and the Rwandan genocide.[14]

From the perspective of modern international criminal law, however, Canada's commitment to international justice is most clearly indicated by its role in the development of the ICC. Along with other states, Canada helped fund the participation of poorer states and NGOs in the Rome Conference negotiations. With Philippe Kirsch at its head, the Canadian delegation played an important role in obtaining broad approval for the position of the Like-Minded Group through the Committee of the Whole during the extended, and often uncertain, negotiations at the Rome Conference.[15] After its role in leading the participants to largely agree on the text of the Court's statute, Canada was then the first country to enact legislation implementing the Rome Statute.[16] It also encouraged other states to ratify the Statute, and Kirsch was later elected as a judge and then as President of the ICC. Combined with a reputation for largely avoiding wars of aggression and the militarism of its close American and British allies, Canada's commitment to international justice was burnished.

---

[12] Greg Hayes, "Canada as a Middle Power: The Case of Peacekeeping", in Andrew F. Cooper (ed.), *Niche Diplomacy*, Palgrave Macmillan, London, 1997, pp. 73–89.

[13] International Criminal Tribunal for the former Yugoslavia ('ICTY'), "Justice Louse Arbour takes up her office", Press Release, 30 September 1996, Doc. No. CC/PIO/180-E.

[14] As outlined in Valerie Oosterveld, "Canada and the Development of International Criminal Law: What Role for the Future?", in *Canada in International Law at 150 and Beyond*, Paper No. 16, 16 March 2018 (available on the Centre for International Governance Innovation's web site).

[15] *Ibid.*

[16] *Ibid.*

16.2.2. Canadian Practices Overseas

Yet, this history glosses over important shifts and underlying inconsistencies in Canadian practices. Canadian participation in UN peace-keeping missions has fallen to historic lows, as Canada reprioritizes joining NATO-led missions rather than UN participation.[17] This shift was itself precipitated by the beating to death of a Somali teen at the hands of two Canadian peace-keepers, which led to questions about whether peace-keeping was as noble an enterprise as it was made out to be.[18]

The ICC itself may now be turning its eyes towards Canada for its role in handing over detainees to the Afghan forces in the knowledge that those detainees would likely be abused or tortured.[19] When those allegations originally arose, and the Canadian parliament sought unredacted documents about the practice, the government of the day took the extraordinary step of proroguing Parliament for the second time in a year, leading to allegations of stifling inquiries into the allegations.[20]

Even with respect to the ICC, which Canada long-championed, questions have been raised about Canada's active attempts to stop a referral of the Syrian civil war to the Court. This was apparently in order to avoid lending legitimacy to the Court's potential investigation into the Israeli-Palestinian conflict, and thus support Israel.[21]

Yet, all of these practices in respect of public conflicts, wars, and international courts obscure the way in which Canadian support of overseas mining ventures and extractive industries has consistently undermined security and the rights of individuals overseas. The mining sector in Canada is domestically significant and globally dominant. Domestically, the industry contributes to 7.8 percent of the country's real GDP, and di-

---

[17] See, for example, Graeme Young, "Political decision-making and the decline of Canadian peacekeeping", in *Canadian Foreign Policy Journal*, 2019, vol. 25, no. 2, pp. 152–171; Stanley R. Barrett, *The Lamb and the Tiger: From Peacekeepers to Peacewarriors in Canada*, University of Toronto Press, Toronto, 2018.

[18] Shereze Razack, *Dark Threats and White Knights: The Somalia Affair, Peacekeeping, and the New Imperialism*, University of Toronto Press, Toronto, 1996.

[19] Omar Sabry, "Torture of Afghan Detainees: Canada's Alleged Complicity and the Need for a Public Inquiry", Canadian Centre for Policy Alternatives – Rideau Institute on International Affairs, September 2015 (available on the Rideau Institute's web site).

[20] "PM shuts down Parliament until March", *CBC News*, 30 December 2009.

[21] David Petrasek, "Why has Canada given up on justice in Syria?", *The Globe & Mail* (Canada), 23 January 2013.

rectly and indirectly employs over 625,000 people.[22] Mining companies are primarily listed in the Toronto Stock Exchange ('TSX') and Toronto Venture Exchange ('TSXV'). Approximately 50 percent of the world's mining companies are listed in these two exchanges.[23] The TSX and TSXV raised over one third of all global equity financing for mining projects in 2018, representing 49 per cent of all such global transactions.[24] The value of Canadian private investment in mining overseas is USD 168.7 billions, with over half of that investment in Latin America and the Caribbean.[25] Canadian mining is thus a major sector of the domestic economy, a commanding presence in the global mining economy, and therefore is profoundly influential in standard-setting for human rights protection (or degradation) in mining projects around the world.

The range of concerns raised by this massive international mining presence was articulated by a mining industry group, which stated that Canadian extractive companies presented concerns in respect of:

> environmental concerns; community relations; human rights; security and armed conflict; labor relations; indigenous peoples' rights; compatibility of resource development with national and local economic priorities; benefit sharing with local communities; ineffective legal systems and the potential for corruption.[26]

In Latin America, Canadian mining projects cause, *inter alia*, forced displacement, violent deaths and injuries, as well as the fraudulent acquisition of property and land, adverse health consequences to peoples living in the areas of the mines, the impoverishment of surrounding communities, and the breakdown of their community bonds.[27] Each of these violations has the potential to disproportionately impact Indigenous communities,

---

[22] The Mining Association of Canada, "The State of Canada's Mining Industry", 2019, p. 12, (available on its web site).

[23] Toronto Stock Exchange and Toronto Venture Exchange, "2020 Guide to Listing", p. 21 (available on the Toronto Stock Exchange's web site).

[24] *Ibid.*, p. 20.

[25] "The State of Canada's Mining Industry", p. 69, see above note 22.

[26] See, for example, National Roundtables on Corporate Social Responsibility (CSR) and the Canadian Extractive Industry in Developing Countries, "Advisory Group Report", 29 March 2007, pp. 4–5, (available on Mining Watch's web site).

[27] *Ibid.*

affecting rights to self-determination and to free, prior and informed consent for mining projects.[28]

Many of these effects amount to violations of international human rights, but little to no redress is available. Successive Canadian governments have deliberately avoided imposing greater accountability mechanisms. This in spite of multiple international bodies – including the Inter-American Commission on Human Rights,[29] the UN Human Rights Committee,[30] the UN Working Group on Business and Human Rights,[31] and the UN Committee on Economic, Social and Cultural Rights[32] – identifying the need for greater regulation of Canadian mining companies and effective mechanisms to prevent violations (and routinely linking these issues to concerns about the domestic treatment of Indigenous persons). Instead, Canada refused to pass a mining regulation bill that would have given effect to the most important recommendations proposed by international and regional bodies,[33] and instead created an Ombudsperson with inadequate powers to investigate overseas mining activity.[34]

---

[28] Canadian Catholic Organization for Development and Peace (Caritas Canada), "Open Letter to Prime Minister Justin Trudeau", 25 April 2016, pp. 2–3 (available on its web site).

[29] See, for example, Working Group on Mining and Human Rights in Latin America, "The Impact of Canadian Mining in Latin America and Canada's Responsibility: Executive Summary of the Report Submitted to the Inter-American Commission on Human Rights", 14 April 2014; and Inter-American Commission on Human Rights, "Report on the 153rd Session of the IACHR", 7 November 2014, p. 10.

[30] Concluding observations on the sixth periodic report of Canada, UN Doc. CCPR/C/CAN/CO/6, 13 August 2015 (recommending, *inter alia*, the establishment of an independent investigatory authority, and legal frameworks for overseas victims of Canadian corporate activity to obtain remedies in Canada).

[31] Report of the Working Group on the issue of human rights and transnational corporations and other business enterprises on its mission to Canada, UN Doc. A/HRC/38/48/Add.1, 23 April 2018 (recommending, *inter alia*, meaningful consultation with Indigenous groups about resource extraction on their lands, limiting public support to those companies that respect human rights, and creating an effective and independent ombudsperson).

[32] Concluding observations on the sixth periodic report of Canada, UN Doc. E/C.12/CAN/CO/6, 23 March 2016 (recommending, *inter alia*, legislative measures to facilitate remedies before Canadian courts for overseas human rights violations committed by Canadian corporations).

[33] Trinh Theresa Do, "MP John McKay resigned to 'glorious death' of mining transparency bill", *CBC News*, 31 January 2014.

[34] See, for example, "Parliament is dissolved and Canada still does not have an ombudsperson with #power2investigate", *Canadian Network on Corporate Accountability*, 17 September 2019 (available on its web site); Emily Dwyer, "Canada's 'toothless' new corporate

Of course, not all of these impacts amount to a violation of international criminal prohibitions. Nonetheless, these activities and the lack of response represent striking parallels with the indifference the Canadian state has shown to Indigenous peoples on its own territories. These groups have suffered similar violations – the dispossession of their land, the exploitation of that land for its resources (including for mining) without adequate consultation and/or compensation, the destruction of social bonds, the forced removal of children, impoverishment, and, at times, the deliberate taking of life. In examining that history, analogous processes of corrosive action are visible, as are the additional steps taken by the Canadian government to limit accountability for these violations.

What emerges from this is a distinct understanding of the colonial dimensions of contemporary Canadian law, and the unwillingness of the Canadian state to seriously confront the idea of accountability for a variety of serious human rights violations (even if those violations do not necessarily rise to the level of international crimes).

16.2.3. The Domestic Treatment of Indigenous Peoples

As with Canadian overseas mining, international bodies have warned of the need to properly protect Indigenous peoples who live in Canada, and to meet their basic needs. The UN Special Rapporteur for Indigenous Peoples noted "[i]t is difficult to reconcile Canada's well-developed legal framework and general prosperity with the human rights problems faced by indigenous peoples in Canada that have reached crisis proportions in many respects."[35] The Special Rapporteur noted important and persistent gaps between Indigenous and non-Indigenous peoples in Canada in respect of key human development indicators: health care, housing (including widespread unsafe water supply), education, welfare and social services.[36] This was complemented by a variety of other problems, including: the continued and growing overrepresentation of indigenous peoples in the criminal justice system, and the disproportionate victimization of indigenous women and girls through violent crime; extremely limited sup-

---

watchdog is a broken promise and a major setback for human rights", *Business & Human Rights Resource Centre*, 15 May 2019 (available on its web site).

[35] James Anaya, Report of the Special Rapporteur on the rights of indigenous peoples, *The situation of indigenous peoples in Canada*, UN Doc. A/HRC/27/52/Add.2, 4 July 2014, para. 14.

[36] *Ibid.*, para. 15.

port for self-government, or indigenous participation in decisions that affect them; limited engagement in, and implementation of, land claim agreements; and, limited participation in economic development.[37] As the Special Rapporteur put it,

> '[o]ne of the most dramatic contradictions indigenous peoples in Canada face is that so many live in abysmal conditions on traditional territories that are full of valuable and plentiful natural resources. These resources are in many cases targeted for extraction and development by non-indigenous interests […]. Perhaps more importantly, indigenous nations' efforts to protect their long-term interests in lands and resources often fit uneasily into the efforts of private non-indigenous companies, with the backing of the federal and provincial governments, to move forward with natural resource projects.[38]

Many of the reports recommending the prevention, investigation, and remediation of overseas human rights violations make similar recommendations in respect of the treatment of Indigenous peoples in Canada.[39] Similar concerns about Canada's exploitation of Indigenous lands were raised by the UN Committee on the Elimination of Racial Discrimination ('CERD') in 2017.[40] CERD also recommended the domestic implementation of the UN Declaration on the Rights of Indigenous Peoples ('UNDRIP'),[41] which requires states to establish – in partnership with Indigenous peoples – effective mechanisms for affirming the rights of Indigenous peoples, including issues identified by CERD and the Special Rapporteur. In June 2019, a bill to implement UNDRIP was not passed by Parliament.[42] And, just as the Canadian state collaborates with the interests of private industry by inadequately regulating overseas mining, it collaborates with those same interests through its shaping of the general legal and specific contractual regimes regulating the exploitation of Indigenous

---

[37] *Ibid.*

[38] *Ibid.*, para. 69.

[39] See, for example, above notes 29–31.

[40] Concluding observations on the twenty-first to twenty-third periodic reports of Canada, UN Doc. CERD/C/CAN/CO/21-23, 25 August 2017.

[41] *Ibid.*, para. 18.

[42] Brenda L. Gunn, "The Senate halts recognition of Indigenous rights on National Indigenous Peoples Day", *Canadian Lawyer*, 24 June 2019.

lands.[43] The continued dispossession, development and exploitation of Indigenous peoples' lands have profound negative impacts on ndigenous political orders, laws, cultures, health, economic well-being and lives.[44] This 'colonial economy'[45] remains at the root of Indigenous impoverishment and loss of culture and life: the 'accumulation by dispossession' of poor health, chronic illness, accidental death, and shorter life expectancies.[46]

These contemporary failings are themselves rooted in extensive practices of suppression of Indigenous people by the Canadian state and non-Indigenous peoples. While Indigenous people now make up 4–5 percent of the Canadian population, hundreds of thousands were killed in the early years of colonization. Some of these deaths happened via direct conflicts, such as the Fraser Canyon Wars, in which thousands of miners faced off against local indigenous groups during the 1858 Gold Rush.[47] Others were the result of the spread of disease by settlers. In British Columbia, 90 to 95 percent of Indigenous peoples (estimated at 180,000 people) were estimated to have been killed through the spread of smallpox.[48] While the spread of disease is often described as accidental or unintentional, in at least some situations there was clear foresight. In 1862 and 1863, smallpox arrived in Victoria, in British Columbia, with an infected miner from San Francisco. At the time, there were approximately 5,000

---

[43] Dayna Nadine Scott, "Extraction Contracting: The Struggle for Control of Indigenous Lands", in *South Atlantic Quarterly*, 2020, vol. 119, no. 2, pp. 269–299.

[44] Chris Hiller and Elizabeth Carson, "These are Indigenous Lands: Foregrounding Settler Colonialism and Indigenous Sovereignty as Primary Contexts for Canadian Environmental Social Work", in *Canadian Social Work Review*, 2018, vol. 35, no. 1, p. 51.

[45] See, for example, Warren Bernauer, "The limits to extraction: mining and colonialism in Nunavut", in *Canadian Journal of Development Studies*, 2019, vol. 40, no. 3, pp. 404–422, and Rebecca Hall, "Diamond Mining in Canada's Northwest Territories: A Colonial Continuity", in *Antipode*, 2012, vol. 45, no. 2, pp. 376–393.

[46] Helen Brown *et al.*, "Our Land, Our Language: Connecting Dispossession and Health Equity in an Indigenous Context", in *Canadian Journal of Nursing Research*, 2012, vol. 44, no. 2, pp. 44–63. See also Arthur Manuel and Ronald Derrickson, *Unsettling Canada: A national wake-up call*, Between the Lines Books, Toronto, 2015, p. 8; Emma LaRocque, *When the other is me: Native resistance discourse, 1850–1990*, University of Manitoba Press, Winnipeg, 2010, pp. 74–76.

[47] Daniel Marshall, *Claiming the Land: British Columbia and the Making of a New El Dorado*, Ronsdale Press, Vancouver, 2018.

[48] Cole Harris, "Voices of Disaster: Smallpox around the Strait of Georgia in 1782", in *Ethnohistory*, 1994, vol. 41, no. 4, pp. 591–626.

colonists and 6,000 Indigenous peoples in the city, with most Indigenous peoples living in camps, and working as traders and labourers. When a lack of general quarantine and vaccination efforts meant that smallpox began to spread, armed police entered the camps and began forcing their occupants to return home – at gunpoint, after burning the camps, or even by towing them in boats – to their traditional territories.[49] This led to the death of approximately 30,000 Indigenous people (60 percent of the remaining Indigenous population) in the province.[50] In forcing this dispersal, settlers acted with knowledge of the devastation to come, which paved the way for greater colonial occupation.[51] As a result of these smallpox epidemics, large areas of the province were "almost completely depopulated", creating space for provincial authorities to claim *terra nullius* and occupy the land without treaties.[52]

In addition, there are documented histories of other forms of Indigenous erosion. Starting in the 1920s and continuing until the 1970s, various local authorities built on eugenics movements to engage in the forced sterilization of women, disproportionately targeting Indigenous women.[53] In 2018, the UN Committee Against Torture expressed concern that there were still numerous contemporary claims of forced sterilization that had not been addressed.[54] The treatment of Indigenous children is as

---

[49] Joshua Ostroff, "How a smallpox epidemic forged modern British Columbia", *Macleans,* 1 August 2017, (quoting Dr John Lutz, "The citizens of Victoria, one could say, panicked. Or, one could say, with a less charitable view, that they deliberately drove the Indigenous people out of town, and that spread the disease back to their home communities up and down the coast.")

[50] *Ibid.*

[51] Robert T. Boyd, *The Coming of the Spirit of Pestilence: Introduced Infectious Diseases and Population Decline among Northwest Coast Indians, 1774 – 1874*, University of Washington Press, Seattle, 1999.

[52] Cole Harris, *The Resettlement of British Columbia: Essays on Colonialism and Geographic Change*, University of British Columbia Press, Vancouver, 2011, p. 147.

[53] See Jana Grekul, Harvey Krahn, and Dave Odynak, "Sterilizing the 'Feeble-minded': Eugenics in Alberta, Canada, 1929–1972", in *Journal of Historical Sociology*, 2004, vol. 17, no. 4, pp. 358–84; Karen Stote, "The Coercive Sterilization of Aboriginal Women in Canada", in *American Indian Culture and Research Journal*, 2012, vol. 36, no. 3, pp. 117–150; and Karen Stote, *An Act of Genocide: Colonialism and the Sterilization of Aboriginal Women*, Fernwood Publishing, Blackpoint, 2015.

[54] Concluding observations of the seventh periodic report of Canada, UN Doc. CAT/C/CAN/CO/7, 21 December 2018, paras. 50–51. See also, for example, Inter-American Commission on Human Rights: "IACHR expresses its deep concern over the claims of forced sterilizations against indigenous women in Canada", Press Release no.

appalling as the treatment of their mothers. Federal agencies intentionally (and without consent) malnourished Indigenous children to study the effects of poor nutrition.[55] The Sixties Scoop saw the removal of Indigenous children from their families and their placement in non-Indigenous families,[56] a practice that appears continues to the present day with the gross over-representation of Indigenous children in the foster system.[57] The federal government has been found to discriminate in its provision of health and education to Indigenous children, and the Canadian Human Rights Tribunal declared that "[t]he Government of Canada willfully and recklessly discriminated against First Nations children [...] taken into out-of-home care since 2006", and that it was only after six non-compliance orders from the tribunal that Canada began to remedy its discrimination against Indigenous children.[58] In respect of education, the federal government spends 30 percent less per student in Aboriginal jurisdictions than provincial governments do.[59] The learning outcomes in these schools are significantly lower than in provincial schools, and the Auditor General noted that Canada has not introduced measurable targets for closing these gaps, does not collect sufficient information to close the gaps, does not

010/19, 18 January 2019; and Yvonne Boyer and Judith Bartlett, "External Review: Tubal Ligation in the Saskatoon Health Region: The Lived Experience of Aboriginal Women", 22 July 2017 (available on the Saskatchewan Health Authority's web site).

[55] Ian Mosby, "Administering Colonial Science: Nutrition Research and Human Biomedical Experimentation in Aboriginal Communities and Residential Schools, 1942–1952", in *Social History*, 2013, vol. 46, no. 91, pp. 145–172.

[56] Patrick Johnston, *Native Children and the Child Welfare System*, Canadian Council on Social Development and James Lorimer Publishing, Toronto, 1983.

[57] See Vandna Sinha and Anna Kozlowski, "The Structure of Aboriginal Child Welfare in Canada", in *International Indigenous Policy Journal*, 2013, vol. 4, no. 2 (Article 2); Nico Trocmé, Della Knoke, and Cindy Blackstock, "Pathways to the Overrepresentation of Aboriginal Children in Canada's Child Welfare System", in *Social Service Review*, 2004, vol. 78, no. 4, pp. 577–600.

[58] Canadian Human Rights Tribunal, *First Nations Child & Family Caring Society of Canada et al. v. Attorney General of Canada*, Judgment, 6 September 2019, File No. T1340/7008, 2019 CHRT 39.

[59] See Don Drummond and Ellen Kachuk Rosenbluth, "The Debate on First Nations Education Funding: Mind the Gap", Policy Studies Working Paper Series no. 49 (2013), Queen's University, Kingston, 2013 (available on its web site) (identifying a disparity in funding, and the difficulties in quantifying it), and Jody Porter, "First Nations students get 30 per cent less funding than other children, economist says", *CBC News*, 14 March 2016 (quantifying the disparity in funding).

use the data it collects to revise programmes,[60] and grossly overstated the graduation rates in these schools.[61]

Of course, the most notorious practice of elimination was the Indian Residential School system, which ran from 1883 to 1996, often in partnership with various churches. At least 150,000 Indigenous students passed through the school system.[62] The end goal was to change behaviour and culture so as to mirror settler society and "to think as 'whites'".[63] Thus, the education in the schools "must consist not merely of the training of the mind, but of a weaning from the habits and feelings of their ancestors, and the acquirements of the language, arts and customs of civilized life".[64] As early as 1913, the government was aware of large numbers of preventable deaths in the schools,[65] and that large numbers of students were either dying in school or shortly after leaving school.[66] Designed to assimilate Indigenous children into settler-colonial mindsets and lifestyles, the schools forcibly removed children from their communities, forbade the use of traditional languages or cultural practices, and became focal points of physical and sexual abuse.[67]

---

[60] Auditor-General of Canada, "2018 Spring Reports: Report 5 – Socio-economic Gaps on First Nations Reserves – Indigenous Services Canada", 11 April 2018, paras. 5.38–5.39.

[61] *Ibid.*, paras. 5.94–5.96.

[62] "Indian Residential Schools Statement of Apology – Prime Minister Stephen Harper", Transcript, 11 June 2008.

[63] Truth and Reconciliation Commission of Canada, "Honouring the Truth, Reconciling for the Future: Summary of the Final Report of the Truth and Reconciliation Commission of Canada", Ottawa, 2015, p. 6.

[64] Superintendent of Education Egerton Ryerson, quoted in Alison L. Prentice and Susan E. Houston, *Family, School and Society in Nineteenth-Century Canada*, Oxford University Press, 1975, p. 220.

[65] In 1907, a lawyer warned that "[d]oing nothing to obviate the preventable causes of death brings the Department within unpleasant nearness to the charge of manslaughter", Frank Oliver, as quoted in John S. Milloy, *A National Crime: The Canadian Government and the Residential School System, 1879 to 1986*, University of Manitoba Press, Winnipeg, 1999, p. 77.

[66] In 1913, Duncan Campbell Scott, Deputy Superintendent General with Indian Affairs noted: "it is quite within the mark to say that fifty percent of the children who passed through these schools did not live to benefit from the education which they had received therein". See Duncan Campbell Scott, quoted in "Indian Affairs, 1867–1912", in Adam Shortt and Arthur G. Doughty (eds.), *Canada and Its Provinces: A History of the Canadian People and their Institutions by One Hundred Associates*, Part II, vol. 7, section 4 Publishers Association of Canada, Toronto, 1914, p. 615.

[67] Truth and Reconciliation Commission of Canada, pp. 3–5, see above note 63.

Along with the other practices and incidents described above, the Indian Residential School system raises the broader question of what international crimes – if any – were committed by the government against Indigenous peoples in Canada. At the same time, the Canadian state has taken important steps to minimize its legal liability for the same. The following section reflects on one particular area – Canadian involvement in the development of the law of genocide. This area is of particular interest because the practices outlined above can all be argued to represent different manifestations of genocidal acts. Well aware of these concerns, the Canadian state deliberately crafted international and domestic law to avoid the possibility of genocide law providing a recourse for state treatment of Indigenous peoples. In doing so, it explicitly connected colonial wrongdoing to colonial self-exculpation.

16.3. The Canadian Legalization of Genocide

The question of the international crimes committed by Canada against Indigenous peoples has been indirectly addressed through careful study of the Indian Residential School system and its association with genocide. The Truth and Reconciliation Commission that investigated the schools declared the system – with its goals of erasing Indigenous spiritual practices, language, and ontologies – to be 'cultural genocide'.[68] The idea of *genocide* is central to debates about the treatment of Indigenous peoples in Canada, and whether it was genocide *proper*, or merely *cultural* genocide. The idea that cultural genocide is somehow a lesser crime is apparent from the internationally recognized definition of genocide, and from the arguments put forward to ensure that cultural genocide did not become part of the international law on genocide. As will be shown, the international definition of genocide suggests two things. First, that, in fact, many of the practices identified in the previous section would amount to acts of genocide. Second, that cultural genocide is not really an international crime, but a political label. As discussed below, this second conclusion is worthy of some skepticism, given the self-interest that became appearent during the negotiations of the definition of genocide.

Under the 1948 Genocide Convention, genocide is defined in Article II in the following terms:

---

[68] *Ibid.*, p. 1.

[…] any of the following acts committed with intent to destroy, in whole or in part, a national, ethnical, racial or religious group, as such:

(a) Killing members of the group;

(b) Causing serious bodily or mental harm to members of the group;

(c) Deliberately inflicting on the group conditions of life calculate to bring about its physical destruction in whole or in part;

(d) Imposing measures intended to prevent births within the group;

(e) Forcibly transferring children of the group to another group.[69]

This definition is repeated in the statutes of various international criminal tribunals, and has been recognized as part of *jus cogens*. [70]

When applied to the treatment of Indigenous peoples in Canada, it can be argued that at least some of these colonial crimes amount to acts of genocide under the international law definition. The direct and indirect killing of Indigenous peoples may amount to "killing members of the group"; forced sterilizations may be "imposing measures intended to prevent births within a group"; residential schools, the Sixties Scoop, and subsequent large numbers of transfers of Indigenous children out of their communities may be "forcibly transferring children of the group to another group"; and, nutritional experimentation, unsafe water provision, discrimination in child welfare and education, and the persistent housing crisis in Indigenous communities may, individually or in totality, equate to the "deliberate infliction on the group of the conditions calculated to bring about the physical destruction of the group". This description is, of course, only partial; it does not assess, for example, the requisite *mens rea* for the offence, which raises a different set of problems. Nonetheless, on their face, these practices seem to satisfy the *actus reus* requirements.

---

[69] Convention on the Prevention and Punishment of the Crime of Genocide, 9 December 1948 ('Genocide Convention') (http://www.legal-tools.org/doc/498c38/).

[70] International Criminal Tribunal for the former Yugoslavia ('ICTY'), *Prosecutor v. Radislav Krstić*, Trial Chamber, Judgment, 2 August 2001, IT-98-33-T, para. 541 ('Krstić Trial Judgement') (https://www.legal-tools.org/doc/440d3a/). See also, for example, International Criminal Tribunal for Rwanda ('ICTR'), *Prosecutor v. Clément Kayishema and Obed Ruzindana*, Trial Chamber, Judgment and Sentence, 21 May 1999, ICTR-95-1-T, para. 88 ('Kayishema Trial Judgement') (https://www.legal-tools.org/doc/0811c9/).

Even if it cannot be definitely declared that these acts amount to genocide, framing these practices as possible genocidal acts helps us to understand a distinct aspect of the Canadian approach to international law: that Canada does not just say one thing (about ending impunity for international crimes) and do another (permit impunity for its own crimes), but that it quite deliberately *legalizes* this impunity both internationally and domestically. Specifically, Canada acted to narrow the definition of genocide currently included in the Genocide Convention, and then similarly sought to narrow the domestic applicability of genocide law. These processes were conditioned by the Canadian state's awareness of its mistreatment of Indigenous peoples, and manifested in two stages.

In the first stage, the Canadian state sought to concretely direct the international definition of genocide by eliminating any reference to 'cultural genocide'. This concern was rooted particularly in the goals of the Indian Residential School system: "to fit the Indian for civilized life in his own environment [...] and the substitution of Christian ideals of conduct and morals for aboriginal conceptions of both".[71] It was in this assimilationist mindset that Canada approached the negotiations over the Genocide Convention with a very specific goal: to guarantee that cultural genocide did not become part of the convention.[72] Canadian delegates were instructed to support any move that would lead to the deletion of the provision, even if that meant jettisoning the entirety of the convention.[73] Aside from that provision, said Canada's lead delegate, "[t]he remaining articles are of no particular concern to Canada".[74] At the negotiations, the Canadian delegate stated that Canada was horrified by the idea of cultural genocide. He then went on to say that Canada mainly consists of a combination of Anglo-Saxon and French elements, and was "opposed to attempts to undermine influence of those two cultures in Canada".[75] Thus,

---

[71] Duncan Campbell Scott, quoted in Shortt and Doughty (eds.), 1914, p. 616, see above note 66.

[72] Report of the Committee and Draft Convention Drawn up by the Committee, UN Doc. E/794, 24 May 1948 (https://www.legal-tools.org/doc/d88e33/).

[73] Ruth Amir, "Cultural Genocide in Canada? It Happened Here", in *Aboriginal Policy Studies*, 2018, vol. 7, no. 1, p. 108.

[74] Hugues Lapointe, "Progress Report on the Work of the Canadian Delegation in Paris", National Archives of Canada, Record Group no. 25, vol. 3699, File 5475-DG-2-40, 1 December 1948.

[75] Hirad Abtahi and Philippa Webb, *The Genocide Convention, Travaux Preparatoires*, vol. 2, 2008 (Hugues Lapointe summarized as saying that the government would reject any at-

in the same utterance, Canada both acknowledged the existence of Indigenous peoples, and then immediately dismissed their value and cultural significance. Canada was supported in its initiative by a number of states, including the United States and France, as well as some new post-colonial states such as India and Peru, and this led to cultural genocide being removed from the draft convention.[76] Having succeeded in its goal of derailing the inclusion of cultural genocide in the Convention, Canada duly ratified the treaty.

In the second stage of this narrowing process, Canada then set about incorporating prohibitions against genocide into domestic law. However, it began reducing the protection of domestic law in two important ways. First, only the advocacy of genocide was criminalized. Second, it was only seen to be a crime to promote some, and not all, of the five enumerated methods of committing genocide. The Parliamentary debates about which methods to include were revealing. The prohibitions against causing serious mental or bodily harm were initially said to be equivalent to a common assault; the prohibition against measures to restrict births was rejected because it might criminalize the use or production of birth control methods (such as condoms or birth control pills); and the prohibition against forcible transfers of children was problematic because it could have criminalized the forcible inclusion of minorities in "boarding schools".[77] When Canada finally did criminalize the promotion of genocide in its domestic Criminal Code in 1969, it only included Article II(a) and Article II(b) – the prohibitions against killing and causing serious mental and bodily harm.[78]

The drafting of the Rome Statute of the International Criminal Court presented another opportunity for Canada to revisit the law of genocide through its domestic legislation. Titled the Crimes Against Humani-

---

tempt to "undermine the influence of those two cultures in Canada", p. 1509). The full preparatory works of the Genocide Convention are freely available in the ICC Legal Tools Database.

[76] See William Schabas, *Genocide in International Law*, 2nd ed., Cambridge University Press, 2009, pp. 209–213.

[77] Senate of Canada, Jean-Paul Deschatelets (Speaker), in *Debates of the Senate: Official Report (Hansard), 1968–1969, First Session Twenty Seventh Parliament* (English translation), Queen's Printer for Canada, Ottawa, 1969, p. 1607. Translated by The Senate of Canada, vol. II, Roger Duhamel F.R.S.C. Queen's Printer for Canada, Ottawa.

[78] Canada, Criminal Code, R.S.C. 1985, c.-46, ss. 318–320 (https://www.legal-tools.org/doc/6b8729/).

ty and War Crimes Act ('CAHWCA')[79], the legislation was trumpeted as the first piece of national law to implement the obligations imposed by the Rome Statute. Two features of the CAHWCA should be pointed out. First, the law permits Canadian courts to interpret that law without recourse to international decisions.[80] To the extent that international law deviates from Canadian judicial understandings of genocide, there is no obligation for Canadian courts to apply the international definition. Instead, there is a real chance that the definition of genocide remains static as interpreted in 2001.

Second, it curiously treats domestic genocides differently than extraterritorial ones. Domestic genocides can only be prosecuted if they took place after the drafting of the Rome Statute in 1998. Overseas genocides, by contrast, can be prosecuted without any statutory temporal limitation.[81] While this temporal range is not unlimited – presumably there cannot be prosecution for alleged genocidal acts that took place prior to the end of World War II, when genocide crystallized as a crime – the distinction between overseas and domestic acts is inexplicable. No normative justification for the difference readily presents itself: genocides are serious international crimes whether they occur domestically or overseas, and if historic overseas genocides are worthy of prosecution, then it seems as though historic domestic ones ought to be as well.

The lack of a clear explanation for this apparent double standard turns the spotlight, instead, to the practical effect of the temporal difference: it effectively forecloses the possibility of legally recognizing as genocide much of the treatment of Indigenous peoples described above. As noted, many of the events described, including the entirety of the Indian Residential School system (and any deaths or assaults that took place in the schools), occurred prior to 1998. While some of those events are arguably continuing in the present day, the vast majority of acts of indigenous elimination had already taken place prior to the enactment of the CAHWCA. Even if the act does not render the state perfectly immune, it is largely insulated. In this way, intentionally or not, the Canadian state

---

[79] Canada, Crimes Against Humanity and War Crimes Act, 22 June 2009, S.C., 2000, c. 24 ('CAHWCA') (https://www.legal-tools.org/doc/0d3078/).

[80] Amir, p. 112, see above note 73.

[81] Contrast the language of s. 4(1) (Offences Committed Within Canada) of the CAHWCA with s. 6(1) (Offences Committed Outside Canada). Only the latter specifies retrospective effect.

has again excluded the applicability of the prohibition against genocide to its own actions through strictly legal means.

16.4. Conclusion

Canada's engagement with international criminal law has and can be lauded as having made many important contributions to the law's development. At the same time, a broader examination of the history of international criminal law, compared with Canada's domestic actions, suggests that there are some double standards at play. While Canada has certainly been a key actor in growing international criminal law and, thus, the scope of potential liability for crimes internationally, it has also been keenly interested in limiting her own liability in important ways.

First, this process of limitation is one that is keenly connected to Canada's domestic experiences rather than to her overseas militarism, although there are still some concerns about Canadian military actions abroad. These concerns may well heighten to the extent that Canada continues to divest from UN peace-keeping and instead participate in NATO-led missions.

Second, this process of limitation is a long-standing one, with roots that extend far beyond Canada's contemporary support for modern international criminal law. The negotiations around international crimes such as genocide extend back to World War II, and the process of domestication of that law began long before modern international criminal law manifested.

Thirdly, this process of limitation is a self-interested, but largely *legalistic* one: that is, it is rooted in the shaping of international and domestic legal norms, rules and institutions in ways that serve Canadian state interests. Thus, the double standards at play here are not so much that Canada flouts the laws it claims to promote globally, but that Canada has intentionally sought to shape those laws so that it cannot be accused of flouting them. In fact, it has shaped those laws in ways that formally – as with the Genocide Convention and CAHWCA – insulate it from accusations of illegality.

Beyond a clearer understanding of the contradictions inherent to Canada's approach to international crimes, this analysis tells us something about the utility of TWAIL as a theory and method. First, it shows that TWAIL has something to offer international criminal law beyond simply denoting that there are double standards at play. Rather, it helps us question the standards that are allegedly being violated, and to understand why those standards might be deficient even if applied evenly. Through TWAIL's recognition of the problematic nature of international law's (in)ability to account for the needs of ordinary peoples *within* states, we can better understand the history of the negotiation of the prohibition against genocide, and why cultural genocide was excluded. It also challenges the idea that the narrow definition of genocide is normatively justified, by pointing to the obvious state interests that shaped the negotiations around the Genocide Convention.

Furthermore, TWAIL suggests that there are some continuities between domestic colonial practices and current international development and resource exploitation practices, including those engaged in by private industry. There is an economic dimension to the practice of genocide: the erasure of Indigenous peoples is what enabled the settlement of Canada by British and French colonizers, and the establishment of Anglo-French social, political and legal structures. Those same forms are now central to human rights violations that are, in a sense, being exported *from* Canada, often to mining sites located in Indigenous communities overseas.

Finally, it gives effect to inherently pluralist sensibilities by pointing to the importance of incorporating Indigenous perspectives and experiences into legal development. As has been noted in the context of resource extraction in Canada, the privatization of lawmaking not only excludes Indigenous interests and understandings, but is designed to benefit private actors and, indirectly, the state.[82]

It goes without saying that Canada is not unique in its inconsistent and self-interested approach to international crimes. Parallels can be drawn with many other states, and the experiences of particular demographic groups in those states. Many of those states are more kinetically violent, both domestically and abroad, than Canada, and that violence should not be ignored or overlooked. Nonetheless, understanding the internal contradictions of Western liberal states, such as Canada, is a way of understanding the challenges that international criminal law continues to face, and the role of the law in limiting accountability and obscuring the

---

[82] For example, Dayna Scott, see above note 43, and Emilie Cameron and Tyler Levitan, "Impact and Benefit Agreements and the Neoliberalization of Resource Governance and Indigenous-State Relations in Northern Canada", in *Studies in Political Economy*, 2014, vol. 93, no. 1, pp. 25–52.

visibility of serious crimes. Moreover, illustrating the double standards employed by these states in respect of allegations of crimes by their agents, armies, and key state-supported industries, suggests an explanation as to why other states may view liberal pontificating as self-serving and hypocritical. These states may undermine international justice more broadly by asking themselves if they should do as Canada does, rather than as she says.

17

Past Wrongdoing Against Romani and Sámi in Norway and the Prism of Modern International Criminal Law and Human Rights

Gunnar M. Ekeløve-Slydal[*]

17.1. Introduction

From the 1850s until the 1980s, Norwegian authorities implemented policies that aimed at assimilation of the Romani ('*Tater*') people, the Sámi people, and minorities of Finnish origin (the '*Kven*' or Norwegian-Finnish people). The assimilation policies were gradually abolished during the period 1960–1990.

Before 1850, policies and negative attitudes towards the groups among authorities and the majority population sometimes resulted in worsened conditions for their way of life. In some cases, serious crimes were conducted against minority persons, including murder, without the culprit being punished.[1] From the 1850s, however, policies and their implementation became more systematic, aiming at assimilating the peoples into the majority Norwegian population.

The policies were motivated by racist, religious and social motives, security considerations regarding Norwegian control of its northernmost territory, as well as by views which maintained that the groups' traditional

---

[*] **Gunnar M. Ekeløve-Slydal** is Director of Policy (Acting Secretary General) of Norwegian Helsinki Committee, and Adjunct Lecturer at the University of South East Norway. He studied philosophy at the University of Oslo and worked for many years for the Norwegian Centre for Human Rights at the University of Oslo and as Editor of the *Nordic Journal on Human Rights*. He has written extensively on human rights, international institutions, and philosophical themes, including textbooks, reports and articles. The author wants to extend his gratitude to Zekeriyya Yahya Karapinar and Anne Hushagen for very useful research assistance and comments.

[1] Thor Gotaas, *Taterne: Livskampen og eventyret [The Taters: Life Struggle and the Adventure]*, Andresen & Butenschøn, Oslo, 2007, p. 92.

economic, cultural or religious practices could not find a place in a modernized and steadily more industrialized Norwegian society.

From 1814 to 1905, Norway was the junior partner in a personal union with Sweden. Previously, it had been ruled by Danish kings for more than 400 years, first as part of the Kalmar Union (1397–1523), and then as the junior partner of the polity of Denmark-Norway. The harsh assimilation policies during the latter part of the 1800s and the 1900s may thus be seen in the context of belated nation-building processes, which led to intolerance towards groups that were seen by political elites and the majority population as alien to and even threatening for Norwegian culture, unity and security.

While it is not common in Norwegian scholarly debate to discuss the expansion of the Norwegian state into Sápmi – the traditional Sámi territory comprising northern parts of present-day Finland, Sweden, Norway and the Kola Peninsula of Russia – in the context of European colonialism, there are important arguments in favour of doing so. In the case of Norway, colonialism may be relevant in two ways: the Norwegian state was formed through quasi-colonial domination by Denmark and Sweden, and Sápmi was "claimed and settled by non-Sámi people while Sámi were assimilated into Norwegian society".[2] Norway was involved in wider colonial endeavours by Denmark-Norway, and ideologies underpinning colonialism were used to legitimize colonizing Sápmi and assimilation of the Sámi.

The aim of the assimilation policies was to make the minorities as similar as possible to the majority population. When applied to the Sámi people and the Kven, they were often named 'Norwegianization' ('fornorsking'), clearly indicating their goal. Assimilation in this context "means that individuals or groups are accepted in mainstream society on the majority's terms. It is a one-way process, where those who are assimilated must change their fundamental cultural values and lifestyles, while the majority makes no adjustments". Assimilation is different from integra-

---

[2] Wilfrid Greaves, "Colonialism, Statehood and the Sámi in Norden and the Norwegian High North", in Kamrul Hussain, José Miguel Roncero Martin and Anna Petrétei (eds.), *Human and Societal Security in the circumpolar Arctic: Local and Indigenous Communities*, Brill Nijhoff, Leiden, 2018, p. 100.

tion processes in that the latter involves a two-way process, both majority and minority adapting to living together.[3]

The use of the Sámi languages in public schools was long restricted, and the Sámi people became socially and economically marginalized in their own homelands due to policies of favouring ethnic Norwegian farmers and developing industrial projects in their traditional territories.

The Romani people experienced harsh policies aimed at eradicating their semi-nomadic culture, including by forced sterilization, removing children from Romani families and placing them in orphanages or ethnic Norwegian foster families, by forced placing of Romani families in a labour colony, and by forced settlement.

These policies were systematized and fully implemented during the 1900s, inflicting widespread harm and frustration among the affected groups, but also resulting in their political and cultural mobilization.

In the post-war period, critical ideas eventually prevailed that were based on human rights, scientific knowledge that refuted ideas that ethnic Norwegians were superior in intelligence and level of civilization compared with the minorities, and a wider recognition of the human suffering caused by the assimilation policies.

In 1958 the Government and the Parliament agreed that Norway should *not* ratify a convention on indigenous populations, since "such groups of people do not exist in our country".[4] A little more than 30 years later, in 1990, Norway became the first state to ratify ILO Convention 169 on indigenous and tribal peoples.[5]

A Constitutional provision had been adopted in 1988 that placed responsibility on state authorities "to create conditions enabling the Sámi

---

[3] Ingvill Thorson Plesner (ed.), *Assimilering og motstand: Norsk politikk overfor taterne/romanifolket fra 1850 til i dag [Assimilation and Resistance: Norwegian Policies Towards Tater/Romani People from 1850 to the Present]*, Norwegian Ministry of Local Government and Modernization, 2015, p. 3 ('NOU 2015:7 English Summary').

[4] Hanne Hagtvedt Vik, "Da samene ble urfolk" ["When the Sámi became Indigenous People"], on Norgeshistorie – fra steinalder til i dag. Fortalt av fagfolk [Norwegian history – from the Stone Age to the Present. Told by professional experts] (available on its web site).

[5] Convention (No. 169) concerning indigenous and tribal peoples in independent countries, 27 June 1989 ('ILO Convention 169') (https://www.legal-tools.org/doc/699b29/), is ratified by 23 states but not by Finland, Sweden and Russia, the other states with Sámi populations.

people to preserve and develop its language, culture and way of life".[6] A Sámi Parliament was opened in 1989, based on the 1987 Sámi Act.[7] The Finnmark Act, pioneering legislation regulating the use of land and natural resources in Finnmark county, was adopted in 2005. A range of other laws and government regulations also have bearing on the situation of the Sámi population.[8]

Today, both national law and international conventions binding on Norway provide legal rights that protect Sámi culture and material interests, including rights to land and natural resources. These rights have also been cemented through case law.[9] Arguments have been presented that Sámi customary law should be fully recognized as law in Norway, and that competence in this law should be strengthened throughout the judiciary.[10]

These developments have, however, not resulted in current relations between Sámi representatives and the Government to be without conflicts. The Sámi Parliament, *inter alia*, complains that the "government are giving permits and authorization to new mines and wind-power industries that effects the use of our lands, territories and resources. This happens at an increasing pace, and in many cases without the Sámi Parliament's will, and without the free, prior and informed consent of concerned Sámi right holders".[11]

The current status of the Sámi is nevertheless considerably stronger than before the shift in policies and adoption of legal rights. Sometimes the Sámi prevails in conflicts with central authorities. Their rights are supported by international human rights bodies, which continuously challenge Norway to redefine policies to protect the Sámi against discrimina-

---

[6] Norway, The Constitution of the Kingdom of Norway, 17 May 1814, Article 108. The Norwegian Sámi Parliament's official web site provides information about its work and organization.

[7] An English translation of the Act is available on the Government's web site.

[8] Government of Norway, "Lover, forskrifter og regelverk i samepolitikken" ["Laws and regulations in Sámi politics"], 20 August 2018 (available on its web site).

[9] Cf. Øyvind Ravna, "The protection of Sámi People's language, culture and way of life in Norwegian Constitution and other legislation", in Øyvind Ravna, *Cahiers d'anthropologie du droit 2011–2012*, Karthala, Paris, 2012, pp. 265–280.

[10] *Ibid*, p. 277.

[11] Eirik Larsen, "Pre-session Universal Periodic Review (UPR) Norway – Thursday, 4 April 2019 – statement by Political Advisor Eirik Larsen", in Sámi Parliament in Norway, 18/5274-8, 11 March 2019.

---

tion and enhance the legal framework protecting Sami land, fishing and
reindeer rights.[12] Sámi culture is widely recognized among ethnic Norwegians and Sámi self-respect is increasing.

While the Sámi is recognised as an indigenous people, and as one of
the two constituent peoples of the Norwegian State,[13] the status of the
Romani people remains weaker. In 1999, Norway ratified the 1994 Council of Europe Framework Convention for the Protection of National Minorities, which together with other relevant international law provisions
have become the basis for Norway's minority policies.[14] Five groups were
identified as national minorities: Forrest Finns, Jews, Kven, Roma
('*Sigøynere*'), and Romani ('*Tater*').

The Convention specifies minimum standards for the states' policies towards national minorities, as well as goals that the states commit
themselves to achieve. State authorities shall facilitate conditions for persons belonging to national minorities to be able to express, hold up and
develop their own identity, their own language and their culture. Minorities shall have the right to full and effective participation in the larger
community.[15]

---

[12] For recent examples of such criticism, see the Concluding observations on the sixth periodic report of Norway, UN Doc. E/C.12/NOR/CO/6, 2 April 2020, paras. 46–47
(https://www.legal-tools.org/doc/ksht2d/); Concluding observations on the combined twenty-third and twenty-fourth periodic reports of Norway, UN Doc. CERD/C/NOR/CO/23-24,
2 January 2019, paras. 21–22 (https://www.legal-tools.org/doc/4bkvmh/); and Consideration of reports submitted by States parties under article 40 of the Covenant pursuant to the
optional reporting procedure – seventh periodic reports of States parties due in 2017 –
Norway, UN Doc. CCPR/C/NOR/7, 7 July 2017, paras. 36–37 (https://www.legal-
tools.org/doc/630blt/).

[13] In his official opening speech of the Sámi Parliament in 1997, King Harald V stated that
the "Norwegian state is founded on the territory of two people - Norwegians and Sami".
See Idar Kintel and others, "Kongens ord betyr mye for samene", on *NRK Sápmi*, 7 October 2014 (available on its web site).

[14] Information about the Convention is available on the web site of the Council of Europe, as
well as the official text of the Convention. The consequences of Norwegian ratification of
the Convention are outlined in Norwegian Ministry of Foreign Affairs, "St.prp. nr. 80
(1997-98) Om samtykke til ratifikasjon av Europarådets rammekonvensjon av 1. februar
1995 om beskyttelse av nasjonale minoriteter" ["Parliament Proposition 80 (1997-98) On
consent to ratification of the Council of Europe's Framework Convention of 1 February
1995 on the Protection of National Minorities"], 18 June 1995 (available on Norwegian
government's web site).

[15] Ministry of Local Government and Modernisation, "Nasjonale minoritetar i Noreg - Om
statleg politikk overfor jødar, kvener, rom, romanifolket og skogfinnar" ["National Minori-

Current policies, based on the Convention, have so far had mixed results. The Convention has not been followed up with national legislation and has neither been incorporated into national law. Romani language and culture are almost invisible in the public domain, and members of the group remain divided on whether to play a more assertive role *vis-à-vis* Norwegian authorities and the wider society. Some fear that this will lead to renewed discrimination and harassment. Others maintain that visibility is necessary to defeat prejudices and discriminatory attitudes. There have been extensive conflicts concerning government support schemes to Romani culture, including with accusations that funds have been misappropriated and that government safeguards against misappropriation have been too weak.[16]

In the 2010s, the Government and the Parliament adopted measures to promote truth and reconciliation. Official truth processes were implemented from 2011 to 2015 for the Romani people,[17] and since 2018 for the Sámi.[18]

17.2. Past Wrongdoing

17.2.1. Government and Private Efforts to Destroy Romani Culture in Norway

> They [the Romani] will no longer be a separate group of people; they will be assimilated into normal everyday life". –

---

ties in Norway – On State Policies towards Jews, Kvens, Roma, Romani, and Forest Finns"], 8 December 2000 (available in Norwegian only).

16. Reporting on Norwegian policies and assessments by the Council of Europe Advisory Committee on the Framework Convention for the Protection of National Minorities is available at the Council of Europe web site. See also Hans Morten Haugen, "Galt samme hva vi gjør? Staten og romanifolket/taterne" ["Wrong no matter what we do? The state and the Romani People/Taters"], in *Kritisk Juss*, 2019, vol. 45, no. 3.

17. The main findings of the Romani Truth Commission (not its official name) are presented in Knut Vollebæk and others, *Assimilering og motstand: Norsk politikk overfor taterne/Romanifolket fra 1850 til i dag* [*Assimilation and resistance: Norwegian policy towards the Roma People from 1850 until today*], Departementenes sikkerhets- og serviceorganisasjon Informasjonsforvaltning, Oslo, 2015 ('NOU 2015:7') (http://www.legal-tools.org/doc/ca4c52/). A separate attachment includes, *inter alia*, reports of 25 research projects on different aspects of past Romani policies and their consequences, see *ibid.*, Vedlegg [Attachments].

18. The Truth and Reconciliation Commission's web site includes information about its mandate and organization.

> 1957 statement by Olav Bjørnstad, Secretary General of the
> Mission among the Homeless[19]

The Romani people – also called 'tater', 'travellers', 'splint', 'vagabonds', 'vagrants' and some other terms – have lived in Norway at least since the beginning of the 1500s. Linguistic and other research indicate that the group originally migrated from North India to Europe. Estimates indicate that the number of Romani people at present may amount to 4–10,000.[20]

The Romani people live and are economically active in different parts of Norway. Historically, some Romani resided parts of the year in neighbouring Sweden, which also have resident Romani. There were numerous inter-marriages between Romani and persons belonging to other ethnic groups, including Norwegians.

In pre-industrial Norway, the Romani people often found work on farms, helping with horses and other animals, functioning as seasonal workers and travelling salespersons. They were active in music, storytelling and crafts, and retained strong family identities and traditions.

Authorities, and sometimes local populations, have been sceptical or had negative attitudes towards Romani people in different degrees since they arrived in Norway.[21] However, from 1850, and increasingly from 1900, they were subject to heavy-handed assimilation policies by the authorities. These policies were expressed through laws and legislative decrees that had clear discriminatory effects.

The Government and the Parliament delegated to a large extent implementation of these policies to a private organization, the Christian philanthropic association *Norwegian Mission among the Homeless* ('The

---

[19] Quoted from Per Haave, "Omstreifer'-politikk på 1900-tallet" ["Vagrant-policies during the 1900s"], on *Norgeshistorie – fra steinalder til i dag. Fortalt av fagfolk*, 25 November 2015 (available on University of Oslo's web site).

[20] Report by Nils Muiznieks, Commissioner for Human Rights of the Council of Europe, following his visit to Norway from 19 to 23 January 2015, CommDH(2015)9, 18 May 2015, p. 15 (https://www.legal-tools.org/doc/whlvgy/). Other estimates indicate that the number could be up to 30,000, see Ole K. Berge, Åsne Dahl Haugsevje og Nanna Løkka, *Kulturell berikelse – politisk besvær: Gennomgang av politikken overfor nasjonale minoriteter 2000–2019 [Cultural enrichment – political problems: Review of policies towards national minorities 2000–2019]*, TF-rapport nr. 490, Telemarksforsking, Bø, 2019, p. 23.

[21] For an overview of Norwegian policies towards Romani people in different periods, see NOU 2015:7, Chapter 4, see above note 17.

Mission').[22] In practice, the Mission was the most prominent organization in this field from 1907 to 1986, and state agencies and local authorities were instructed by the Government and the Parliament to co-operate with it.

These policies made substantial harm and created negative prejudice towards the minority, which has led to fear and distrust between the minority and mainstream society. This has had, and still has, major consequences for many members of the Romani people.

These policies focused on transfer of child custody, forced settlement and forced sterilization of the Romani people. Estimates indicate that about 30 per cent of children were taken from their parents within the group (about 1,500 children) during the first two generations of the 1900s.[23] Research into some of the cases points to families being in difficult situations and needing support to take care of their children. However, there are many examples that the authorities were motivated by illegitimate motives, such as removing the children from a travelling lifestyle. Removing children from their parents was part of the wider efforts of eradicating Romani culture.[24]

Svanviken labour colony was established by the Mission in 1908. From 1949 to 1970, 38 Romani families were placed in the colony, most for five years. Fifteen mothers were sterilized, constituting 40 per cent of the women. The numbers of placed families in other periods are not known.[25]

The purpose of the colony's operation was to prepare families to live in modern Norwegian society and make them "positive and constructive members of society". However, the director of the colony in the peri-

---

[22] The organization was founded in 1897 by a priest, Mr. Jakob Walnum. It had several names until 1935, when it got the name it retained throughout the period it had the role as the main implementer of Norwegian policies towards the Romani people, 'Norsk misjon blant hjemløse' ['Norwegian Mission Among the Homeless']. This period lasted until 1986, when the organization changed name to 'The Church's Social Service' ('Kirkens Sosialtjeneste'). See Hallgeir Elstad, "Norsk Misjon blant Hjemløse", in *Store norske leksikon*, 5 September 2019 (available on its web site).

[23] Gunnar M. Ekeløve-Slydal, *Norsk romani-/taterpolitikk: fortid, nåtid, fremtid [Norwegian Romani/Tater Policies: Past, Present, Future]*, Norwegian Helsinki Committee, Oslo, 2009, p. 21.

[24] NOU 2015:7, p. 75, see above note 17.

[25] The Mission also established a labour colony for unemployed men, Bergfløtt Labour Colony, as well as six orphanages. *Ibid.*

od 1955–69 maintained that many of the 'colonists' were not fit to be parents. Therefore, they should not be permitted to have children.[26]

Svanviken Arbeiderkoloni pr. Kr.sund N.
Smaahjemmene

Picture 1: Svanviken labour colony.

Forced sterilization to reduce the number of children in the group also took place in other contexts, based on a 1934 law on sterilization. Some cases of forced sterilization took place without evaluations based on the law and sometimes conducted illegally, without the women being informed.[27]

The Mission originally considered sterilization a violation of Christian social work. However, it soon changed opinion and came up with a Christian justification for "racial hygiene", arguing for sterilization of

---

[26] For more information about Svanviken labour colony, see: *ibid.*, pp. 16–18.

[27] Per Haave, "Sterilisering av omstreifere" ["Sterilization of vagrants"], in *Norgeshistorie – fra steinalder til i dag. Fortalt av fagfolk*, 25 November 2015 (available on its web site). The following sections are based on Mr. Haave's research, which has been published in NOU 2015:7, Attachment no. 18, see above note 17, and in Per Haave, "Sterilisering av tatere – kirurgi på 'rasemessig grunnlag'" ["Sterilization of taters – surgery based on "racial" foundations"], in Bjørn Hvinden (ed.), *Romanifolket og det norske samfunnet [The Romani People and Norwegian Society]*, Fagbokforlaget, Vigmostad og Bjørke AS, Bergen, 2000, pp. 32–73.

"defective Romani". The Mission estimated that these made up a third of the group, which in 1927 reportedly consisted of about 2,100 people.

During World War II, from the turn of the year 1942–1943, the pro-Nazi regime in Norway introduced a new law which provided even greater access to forced sterilization. In the spring of 1945, a supplement was drawn up with provisions on the *vagrants*. This supplement was however not adopted before the end of the war. From 8 May 1945, the Sterilization Act of 1934 was again in force and remained so until 1977.

In the period 1934–1977, a total of 44,233 persons were sterilized based on the law. It has been documented that 125 of these were Romani. Of these, 109 were sterilized under various provisions of the 1934 Act:

- 50 women and 7 men at their own request (§ 3, first paragraph);
- 18 women and 4 men at their own application with the consent of the guardian or the auxiliary guardian (§ 3, second paragraph);
- 26 women and 4 men at the request of the guardian or the auxiliary guardian, or from others with the consent of the guardian or the auxiliary guardian (section 4);
- the other 16, including one man, were sterilized under the 1942 Act.

Of women that the Mission and authorities believed to be Romani, more than 3.5 per cent were sterilized in the period 1934–1977. The total number of sterilized women was just under 2 per cent of the female population in Norway. Especially from the late 1930s to the late 1940s, Romani women were more subject to forced sterilization than women in general.

More than 230 Romani women may have been sterilized outside the law. Such sterilization was only permitted if pregnancy and childbirth would jeopardize the woman's life and health (so-called medical sterilization). However, many such sterilizations had no medical justification. This also applies to several of the sterilizations performed on women at the Svanviken labour colony.

Norwegian sterilization legislation exemplifies a general trend that legislation was not specifically targeting Romani but was nevertheless

designed to facilitate measures against the group.[28] People belonging to
the group were over-represented among those affected.

A range of legislative acts and official policies were the basis for the
assimilation measures against the Romani. The most important are presented below.[29]

In 1851, the Parliament gave funding to a programme of Mr. Eilert
Sundt (1817–1875, a famous priest and sociologist) providing housing to
Romani families.[30] The programme failed, and funding was eventually
withdrawn. It had, however, a lasting effect and marked the start of practices that entailed forced settlement of Romani families by the Mission in
co-operation with local authorities.

In 1896, the first childcare act (*'vergerådsloven'*) was adopted in
Norway, creating committees to evaluate the situation of children and organize transfer of custody from their family to orphanages or foster families if deemed necessary for the well-being of the child. The law was succeeded in 1953 by a new Child Care Law, but the practice of removing
children from Romani families continued. In some cases, children were
taken from families before official authorization.

In the same year, the Parliament delegated authority to Mr. Jakob
Walnum, a priest, to implement a plan to reduce the number of Romani
people and to initiate other measures to support implementation of the
childcare act.

The Vagrant Act (*'løsgjengerloven'*) was adopted in 1900 and entered into force in 1907. It prohibited "vagrant practices", which were
considered to constitute threats to society, such as extensive traveling
without having permanent residence and occupation and use of alcohol.
The law was repealed only in 2006, but many of its provisions had been
repealed earlier. The measure of forced labour was repealed in 1970. The
law was the legal basis of the programme of forced settlement of Romani
families that was run by the Mission.

In 1907, the government delegated the responsibility for forced settlement of Romani people to the Mission. The main instrument used by

---

[28] NOU 2015:7, p. 49, see above note 17.

[29] The overview is based on *ibid.*, Chapter 4.

[30] Eilert Lund Sundt was a Norwegian theologian, social and cultural scientist. He devoted
his life to the study of ordinary people's lives and history. He is regarded as the founder of
sociology in Norway.

the Mission to facilitate settlement was a five-year stay for Romani families at the Svanviken labour colony, where the parents had to learn to live in a settled way, become financially responsible, speak Norwegian, and to break with their Romani relatives. Women were trained in housework, while men were trained in farming and crafts.

In 1908, the Parliament adopted restrictions on the practices of traveling salespersons, also targeting traveling Romani who were selling tools, art crafts and services ('*omførselshandel*').

In 1927, 1935 and 1948, there were official campaigns to register "vagrants" and report them to the Mission. The Mission also received copies of Criminal Police registration of criminal offences, likely with the purpose to complete its own registration of Romani people.[31]

A 1934 parliamentary law on sterilization was subsequently applied to authorize forced sterilization of Romani women and a few Romani men. In 1937, regulations were put in place by the Government that obliged the police to help transfer custody of Romani children to the Mission.

A 1951 law prohibited Romani to use horse to transport goods or people. The law was repealed only in 1974.

Although the Mission was a driving force in defining the target group and formulating policies, its actions were carried out on behalf of the state, which largely funded its operations. There was close co-operation between the Mission and local authorities on transfer of child custody and forced settlement.

Summing up, both during the first part of the 1900s, when Norway was ruled by the Liberal Party, and after World War II, when the social-democratic Labour Party formed Government, assimilation policies were in place that aimed at destroying Romani culture and way of life. These policies had their origin in 'social reforms' during the late 1800s, which were designed to address negative aspects of travelling lifestyles, abuse of alcohol, and child poverty.

The policies were backed up by legislation that seldom specifically targeted Romani people, but in effect led to discrimination and confirmed popular prejudice that they belonged to a sub-standard group of human beings.

---

[31] NOU 2015:7, p. 61. see above note 17.

The policies were framed by an alliance of the Protestant state church, the emerging bourgeoisie, and the political elite. They were implemented by a missionary organization, that was running six orphanages, two labour colonies, and was well-connected and influential *vis-à-vis* other public institutions that had any impact on the implementation of Romani policies.

The aim of the policies was to remove children from the Romani culture of their families or to change the culture and lifestyle of their parents into mainstream Norwegian culture.

During the 1930s, views were presented by influential members of Norwegian society that assimilation of Romani was impossible due to their inferior biological characteristics.[32] During World War II, when Norway was occupied by Germany, plans for complete sterilization of Romani people were made, but not implemented.

During the post-war period, the assimilation policies lasted for four decades before a gradual shift took place in policies, which recognised that Romani rights and culture should be protected. As late as in the preparatory works for the 1964 Law on Social Protection, a passage is included stating that the "goal is eventually to liquidate the entire vagrant system and adapt both children and adults to orderly social conditions. Most important is to take care of the children while they are still quite small and before they have gotten used to vagrancy".[33]

17.2.2. Stigmatization of Sámi Culture

Sámi (previously often referred to as Lapps or Finns) are descendants of nomadic peoples who inhabited northern Scandinavia for thousands of years. Their traditional occupations were hunting, trapping, fishing and reindeer herding. They have been present in the northernmost Norwegian county, Finnmark, for at least 2,000 years.[34]

When the Finns entered Finland, starting about AD 100, Sámi settlements were probably dispersed over the whole country; today they are confined to its northern extremity. In Sweden and Norway, the Sámi have similarly been pushed north, although today many Sámi also live in the

---

[32] Haave, 2015, see above note 27.
[33] Quoted from NOU 2015:7, p. 75, see above note 17.
[34] Key facts on Sámi history and culture are taken from "Sami People", in *Encyclopedia Britannica*.

bigger cities in the south of the countries. In the late 1900s, there were from 30,000 to 40,000 Sámi in Norway and about 20,000 in Sweden, 6,000 in Finland, and 2,000 in Russia.[35]

During early Norwegian statehood, the main issue with the Sámi was their religion (animism, polytheism, shamanism). The 1025 Christian Law obliged all people on the territory to adhere to Christian doctrines. After the 1536 Reformation, only Protestant Christianity was accepted, excluding also Catholic monastic orders.[36]

The Reformation brought sharper attention to the Sámi in the Nordic countries. The ancient Sámi religion was still strong in Finnmark and other parts of Sápmi. Several of the witchcraft cases in Finnmark during the 1600s were against mainly male Sámi.[37] The Sámi was, however, not targeted more than ethnic Norwegians in these cases. They constituted an estimated 37.5 per cent of the population in Finnmark (1,200 of 3,200 residents), while their share of witchcraft cases was only 21 per cent. However, there was an additional motivation of taking over their land in some of the cases.[38]

The government's acquisition of land within the fjords and in rural areas in the north resulted in stronger integration of Sámi settlement areas into the Danish-Norwegian Kingdom at the time. The Sámi people's use of former common areas was increasingly restricted.

In broad terms, Sámi and non-Sámi people had interacted in the northern regions of today's Norway and Sweden for centuries. From the 1500s, however, these mutual interactions gave gradually way to a system of control of Sámi lands and lives by Denmark-Norway and Sweden. These states "gradually established and enforced a social hierarchy in which they enjoyed cultural superiority and political dominance over Sámi, and in which Sámi were no longer allowed to make decisions governing the course of their collective society or, in many cases, their individual lives.

---

[35] *Ibid.*

[36] Erling Sandmo, "Det flerkulturelle Norge mellom 1500 og 1800" ["The multicultural Norway between 1500 and 1800"], in *Norgeshistorie – fra steinalder til i dag. Fortalt av fagfolk*, 25 November 2015 (available on its web site).

[37] Rune Blix Hagen, "Trolldomsforfølgelse av samer" ["Whitchcraft persecution of Sámi people"], in *Norgeshistorie – fra steinalder til i dag. Fortalt av fagfolk*, 24 August 2016 (available on its web site).

[38] *Ibid.*

This relationship resembles those between Indigenous peoples and colonizing powers elsewhere in the world".[39]

The consolidation of state power in northern Scandinavia and the Kola Peninsula, including by border agreements between Denmark-Norway and Sweden in 1751, and with Russia in 1826, gradually undermined Sámi systems of self-rule in their traditional areas of economic activities.

The old Sámi social order was based on the '*siida* system', in which different hunting teams together formed the basis for larger community units, a Sámi village or a rural unit. The '*siidas*' had a well-established democratic system of governance, where settlement in an area was based on ecological adaptation and relocation according to resources.[40]

Most of the '*siidas*' operated with several seasonal settlements, utilizing the natural resources of different areas. The '*siida*' system may have been one of the reasons that Sámi were able to avoid confrontations with Norwegians at the time of colonization. They simply withdrew to one of their other settlements to avoid conflict, but at the same time their radius of action and access to prey were reduced.

The gradual colonizing of Sámi land thus replaced a flexible system of using the land by different units of Sámi, to a system with state or private ownership of land. Legislation favoured Norwegians acquiring such ownership, in particular the 1902 Land Sale Act, which stated that *only* Norwegian citizens who could speak, read and write Norwegian, and who used Norwegian daily, could buy land. The land property had to be given a Norwegian name. The law was repealed only in 1965, but it was rarely enforced after World War II.[41]

These developments were complemented by measures that stigmatized Sámi culture, religion and language. Such measures facilitated the goal of absorbing "Sámi into the Norwegian nation".[42] Sámi were made to

---

[39] Greaves, 2018, p. 107, see above note 2.

[40] Neil Kent, *The Sámi Peoples of the North*, C. Hurst & Co. (Publishers) Ltd., London, 2018, pp. 21, 37–38; Harald Gaski, "Samenes historie" ["The history of the Sámi"], in *Store Norske Leksikon*, 8 June 2020 (available on its web site).

[41] Steinar Pedersen, "Jordloven for Finnmark – samer måtte ofre språket for å få kjøpe jord" ["The land law for Finnmark – Sámi had to give up their language to be allowed to buy land"], in *Samiske veivisere*, 21 May 2019 (available on its web site).

[42] Statement by Norwegian Prime Minister Johan Sverdrup (1884–1889). Quoted from Laila Susanne Vars, "Samene i Norge: Fra fornorsking til forsoning?" ["Sámi in Norway: From

believe that their own culture was of little worth and that the only way they could be included in the emerging modern state was to give it up and "become Norwegian".

The processes of colonization and assimilation did not take place without conflicts, although these conflicts almost never escalated into violent clashes (the exception being the 1852 Kautokeino Rebellion, which involved religious revivalists and was directed against local government officials).[43]

The conflicts between representatives of Danish-Norwegian authorities who asserted the king's right in Sámi core areas, and Sámi people defending their unwritten customary rights, developed into more severe confrontations during the end of the 1600s than in later times. This was a period when, in addition to Norwegian settlements in Sámi areas close to the coast, mining industry started. Climate was colder during the second half of the 1600s, leading to pressure on limited resources and high mortality rates among the Sámi.

After the witchcraft processes ceased, and especially in the wake of strong Christian Pietist movements in the Nordic countries from about 1700, extensive Christian missionary activities were conducted in the northernmost regions of the kingdom, in Greenland and in Finnmark.

Although many priests and bishops supported teaching religion in native Sámi languages, with some of them learning to speak and write in these languages, the missionary activities may nevertheless have contributed significantly to changing attitudes among local Norwegian authorities and subsequently among central authorities towards Sámi culture.

Many representatives of the Church viewed Sámi as savages, "possessed by the devil", who could only become "viable Norwegians" with the help of the Christian faith. This view formed a formidable motivation for the systematic Norwegianization project, which began in the 1850s. It

---

Norwegianization to Reconciliation?"], in Nik. Brandal, Cora Alexa Døving and Ingvill Thorson Plesner (eds.), *Nasjonale minoriteter og urfolk i norsk politikk fra 1900 til 2016 [National Minorities and Indigenous Peoples in Norwegian Politics from 1900-2016]*, Cappelen Damm Akademisk, Oslo, 2017, p. 177.

43   Kent, 2018, p. 111, see above note 40.

---

provided Norwegianization with a strong rationale for why and how the
Sámi people should be Norwegianized.[44]

Early views on Sámi often underlined their competence as fishermen, boat builders, hunters, navigators in the snowy wilderness of the
Arctic, as well as their hospitality and peaceful ways of organizing society.
The Italian diplomat and traveller Mr. Guiseppe Acerbi (1773–1846) captured these views well: "I have seen very few places where the people live
in so easy and happy a simplicity as in the maritime districts of Lapland."[45] Sámi were perceived as uncorrupted by civilization, as "noble
savages".

In Medieval times and up to the gradual colonization of their lands
from the 1500s, Sámi products such as fur, reindeer skins and martin pelts,
were attractive items in European trade. The Sámi were respected taxpay-
ers; some of them at times had to pay tax both to Russia, Denmark-
Norway, and Sweden due to unclear borders and influence of several
states over the same territory.[46]

Shaping views that were underpinning the later Norwegianization
project, the church missionaries either demonized Sámi culture or described Sámi as childish. As Rector Mr. Andreas Gjølme in Sør-Varanger
in Finnmark wrote in 1886:

> The Lapp people are childlike people in more than one re-
> spect. As people, they have the child's impulsive, naïve, un-
> developed point of view, and it is the goal of Norwegianiza-
> tion that they are brought to the maturity of man, if this is at
> all possible. This is an immense and lasting goal to work to-
> wards.[47]

While some Norwegian practices regarding Sámi language and culture were relatively liberal until the 1850s, policies from that time became
increasingly strict. Norwegianization of Sámi and Kven became the ulti-

---

[44] Bente Persen, "«At bringe dem frem til mands modenhed» – En studie av fornorskingen av
samene i Porsanger 1880–1980" ["«To bring them forth to man's maturity» – A study of
Norwegianization of the Sámi in Porsanger 1880–1980"], Master Thesis, University of Oslo, 2008.

[45] Kent, 2018, p. 5, see above note 40.

[46] *Ibid*, p. 39.

[47] Quoted from Lorenz Khazaleh, "Norwegianization of the Sami was religiously motivated.
Interview with Bente Persen", on *University of Oslo*, 25 May 2011 (available on its web
site).

---

mate goal of Norway's minority policies in the north during the following 130 years. The period may be divided into four main phases.

The first phase started in 1851, when the Parliament allocated money to the so-called Finn or Lapp Fund. This was an item in the national budget to finance measures to change the language and culture of the Sámi. The main focus was on language, and the school became the main "battlefield" with the teachers as "frontline soldiers" in the state's assimilation campaign.[48] As in other states at the time, the school was the cornerstone in nation building.[49] The full range of the assimilation policies came, however, to influence almost all spheres of society and public institutions, including by outlawing or marginalizing Sámi musical instruments, clothing and other cultural items.

This phase, which lasted until the late 1860s, represented a brake with previous policies, which accepted Sámi and Kven languages almost on an equal footing with Norwegian. In line with humanistic and romantic ideas of the first part of the 1800s, to speak one's native tongue had been seen as a right for all peoples. However, this liberal view was opposed by the Norwegian upper class of Finnmark, and in the Norwegian Parliament from 1848.[50]

The measures applied in the first phase focused on the Sámi in so-called "transitional districts", that is, areas that were ethnically mixed with a substantial proportion of Norwegian speakers such as in the coastal areas of Finnmark. The Lapp Fund financed teaching of Norwegian language and culture in these districts.

During the second phase, starting in the late 1860s and lasting until 1905, when Norway became independent from Sweden, the Parliament was concerned by Finnish immigration to East Finnmark. A prevailing view was that assimilation policies so far had not given the desired results. A shift in motivations took place, from 'civilizing' Sámi and Kven so that they could become part of the emerging modern Norwegian society, to

---

[48] Einar Niemi, "Kulturmøte, etnisitet og statlig intervensjon på Nordkalotten" ["Cultural Encounter, Ethnicity and State Intervention in the Northern Hemisphere"], in Rut Boström Andersson (ed.), *Den nordiska mosaiken: språk og kulturmöten i gammal tid och i våra dager [The Nordic Mosaic: Language and Cultural Encounters in Old Times and in Our Days]*, Uppsala University, Uppsala, 1997, p. 268.

[49] Henry Minde, "Assimilation of the Sami – Implementation and Consequences", in *Journal of Indigenous Peoples Rights*, 2005, vol. 3, p. 7.

[50] *Ibid.*, p. 11.

security concerns. The Parliament decided in 1868 that the Lapp Fund should be increased, and finance assimilation measures aimed at the Kven population in addition to the Sámi.[51]

The school instruction for the mixed language districts in Finnmark and Troms (the second northernmost county of Norway) was further sharpened. Up to the 1880s, it was permissible to use Sámi and Kven as the language of instruction in Christianity teaching and otherwise as a language of assistance to facilitate the learning of Norwegian. In practice, this led to pupils also receiving training in their mother tongue.

In 1880, the authorities launched a document entitled "Instructions for teachers in Lappian [Sámi] and Kven transitional districts", introducing a new system for teachers' salaries, differentiating them by how many Sámi and Kven children they could convert to speaking Norwegian, and removing all mother tongue education. The instruction marked "the final breakthrough for the strict Norwegianization policy".[52]

From 1889, the language requirements were further tightened, with intervention in the private sphere as teachers now also had to ensure that children only spoke Norwegian during their breaks.

The school's Norwegianization policy took its final form with the school instruction of 1898, the so-called Wexelsen Decree ('*Wexelsenplakaten*'). Although there was no prohibition against the use of auxiliary language in the school, in reality only Norwegian was used as language of instruction in mixed-language school districts. The exception was in Karasjok and Kautokeino, where it was allowed to use Sámi in Christianity teaching. In other places, Sámi and Kven languages should be limited to what was strictly necessary, "as an aid to explain what is incomprehensible to the children".[53]

There was also increased scepticism against employing Sámi or Kven teachers, as they were "not suited to promote Norwegianization among their fellow countrymen with the desired success", as stated by Director General Mr. Nils Herzberg of the Ministry of Church and Education during discussions in the Parliament in 1877. The Wexelsen Decree

---

[51]   Knut Einar Eriksen and Einar Niemi, *Den finske fare: Sikkerhetsproblemer og minoritetpolitikk i nord 1860–1940 [The Finnish Menace: Boundary Problems and Minority Policy in the North 1860-1940]*, Universitetsforlaget, Oslo, 1981, pp. 30–47.

[52]   Minde, 2005, p. 13, see above note 49.

[53]   *Ibid.*, p. 14.

gave a green light to the proposal, which instituted work prohibition on ethnic grounds.[54]

In order to co-ordinate and control the Norwegianization campaign, Finnmark was the first county in Norway to have its own school director. Mr. Bernt Thomassen, school director from 1902 to 1920, was pushing Norwegianization policies with great vigour. He was at the forefront of the development of the boarding school system in Finnmark and contributed actively to the assimilation policies embracing most aspects of social life. Boarding schools became an important institution for promoting Norwegian language and culture and thus reach the goals of the policies. Up to World War II, 50 boarding schools had been built in Finnmark. Some 2,800 of 7,900 schoolchildren had to leave their families and live at the schools. It was not easy for the children whether they were Sámi, Kven or Norwegian, but it was undoubtedly tougher for those who had to learn a new language as quickly as possible (having no previous knowledge of Norwegian).

The third phase lasted from approximately 1905 to 1950. Measures launched during the second phase were continued, while the political situation changed due to developments after World War I. The 1919 Versailles Treaty of peace resulted in Norway having a common border with both Russia and Finland. The fear of both Finnish intrusion on Norwegian territory and for Sámi mobilization against the education policies led to more secrecy concerning the policies. A secret body, the Finnmark Board, was established in 1931 to strengthen implementation of the policies.

The Lapp Fund was substantially increased during the first part of the 1900s to finance the building of boarding schools, which started as "border fortifications in Kven-dominated areas". Later also other parts of Finnmark were included in the programme.

A new school director for Finnmark, Mr. Christian Brygfjeld, took over in 1923. He rejected demands made by the Sámi to soften Norwegianization measures, expressing clearly racist views:

> The Lapps have had neither the ability nor the will to use their language as written language. [...] The few individuals who are left of the original Lappish tribe are now so degenerated that there is little hope of any change for the better for them. They are hopeless and belong to Finnmark's most

---

[54] *Ibid.*, pp. 14–15.

backward and wretched population and provide the biggest
contingent from these areas to our lunatic asylums and
schools for the mentally retarded.[55]

Mr. Brygfjeld ranked the Sámi well under the Kven, the latter being
a cultured, "industrious and competent" people. While Norwegianization
of the Sámi was an effort to 'civilize' sub-standard people, the Kven
needed to be Norwegianized due to security considerations because of
their Finnish origin and a fear that they would sympathize with Finland if
conflict broke out.

In 1935, a new Labour Party government took over, but no changes
were made in the assimilation policies of the previous non-socialist governments.

The Elementary School Act of 1936 took away the possibility of
even using Finnish as an auxiliary language, which was still the case with
Sámi. The assimilation regime was thus tightened concerning the Kven,
based on security concerns.

The fourth and final phase, the termination or settlement phase,
lasted from 1950 to about 1980. During this period, Norwegianization
continued in the schools as late as in the 1960s, even after the Parliament
had repealed the Wexelsen Decree.

However, due to Sámi political mobilization and international influence, new Sámi policies were developed. In the Parliament, many supported proposals that Sámi languages should be taught in schools. In
Finnmark, however, such proposals were still met by strong resistance.
Some support to Sámi culture and institutions started to be provided by
the state during the 1970s. During the same time, Sámi organizations
started to be active in the international movement of indigenous peoples.[56]

A decisive issue mobilizing Sámi resistance to Norway's disregard
for Sámi interests and rights, was the so-called Alta controversy of 1979–
81. This was a series of protests concerning the construction of a hydro-

---

[55] Quotation from Eriksen and Niemi, 1981, p. 258, see above note 51. The English translation is published in Minde, *op. cit.*, p. 17, see above note 49.

[56] Einar Niemi, "Fornorskingspolitikken overfor samene og kvenene" ["Norwegianization
policies towards the Sámi and the Kven"], in Nik Brandal, Cora Alexa Døving and Ingvill
Thorson Plesner (eds.), *Nasjonale minoriteter og urfolk i norsk politikk fra 1900 til 2016*
[National Minorities and Indigenous Peoples in Norwegian Politics from 1900-2016],
Cappelen Damm Akademisk, Oslo, 2017, p. 147.

electric power plant in the Alta river in Finnmark. Many Norwegians supported Sámi rights to reindeer husbandry as well as ecological considerations that the plant should not be constructed.

The controversy became a symbol of the wider fight for Sámi rights, *against* cultural discrimination and *for* political autonomy and material rights,[57] and led to important legislative and policy changes.

Summing up, based on ideas that stigmatized Sámi culture, as well as security considerations that implied that the Norwegian state could not expect loyalty from in particular the Kven but sometimes also Sámi people living in border areas in Finnmark, the Norwegian state implemented policies that aimed at eradicating Sámi culture, religion and language. The ideas that stigmatized Sámi culture was based on religion, national, Social Darwinist and racist motives.

These policies had profound consequences for Sámi self-esteem and cultural identity. The state efforts may have been made easier by already existing racism against the Sámi, but the efforts in themselves contributed to "a massive downgrading of those who were subjected to the policy".[58] Research indicate that between 1930 and 1950, the proportion of people who identified as Sámi in Kvænangen Municipality was reduced from 44 per cent to 0 per cent. This was not, however, because all Sámi left and never returned. Many of them did return after the war but would not identify themselves as Sámi anymore.[59]

Similar policies of assimilation were conducted in other states, indicated by terms such as "Russification", "Germanification" and "Americanisation". Assimilation policies in Norway were, however, more "determined, continuous and long-lasting" than in most other countries.[60]

17.2.3. Colonization of Sápmi

As has been indicated, an important wider framework for the assimilation policies was the overtaking and securing of Norwegian territorial control over parts of Sápmi, which eventually became the northernmost county of Norway, Finnmark.

---

[57] Minde, 2005, p. 6, see above note 49.
[58] *Ibid.*, p. 20.
[59] *Ibid.*, p. 9.
[60] *Ibid.*, p. 8.

There are traces of ethnic Norwegians settling in Norway's arctic
regions from before the thirteenth century, with not only churches being
established earlier (such as Trondenes Church outside Harstad, which is
considered the world's northernmost surviving medieval building), but
with sources on Viking chieftains based along the coast of Northern-
Norway several centuries earlier (such as Tore or Thorir Hund, whose early eleventh century base was on Bjarkøy, and whose brother was a chief in
Trondenes). The Norwegians mainly settled and created coastal villages to
develop fisheries, which became increasingly important for Norway's exports. Gradually, the influx of Norwegians and other non-Sámi people put
more pressure on the Sámi. There was also pressure on them from Sweden, Finland and Russia. The border agreements between Denmark-
Norway and Sweden in 1751, with Finland in 1809, and with Russia in
1826 were pivotal in securing the states' interests in Sápmi and in undermining Sámi interests. The so-called 'Lappkodicil', an attachment to the
1751 border agreement, obviously helped by providing free access to the
reindeer herding Sámi to cross the border. However, it did not help in all
respects.

Picture 2: The Sápmi area.

Until the border agreement in 1751, Norwegian authorities relied on
alliances with the Sámi to strengthen their influence in the area. Before
the agreement, Finnmark in reality "belonged to no nation and remained
contested grounds. All three powers [Denmark-Norway, Russia and Swe-

den] made opposing demands on the area and used the taxation of the Saamis as grounds for claiming sovereignty".[61]

After the agreement, however, such tactics gave way to restrictive policies that could be implemented without concerns to the need for Sámi support. The Sámi had lost their most effective tool *vis-à-vis* the expanding and competing kingdoms of Denmark-Norway and Sweden.[62] Now the most important goal became to secure loyalty from the Sámi towards the Danish-Norwegian state, as well as to strengthen presence of ethnic Norwegians in the territory.

Immigration from Finland during the eighteenth and nineteenth centuries led to intensified pressure on the Sámi. Norwegianization intensified to strengthen national security and to avoid losing territory to Russia or Finland, which from 1809 became a Russian grand duchy. After Finnish independence in 1917, the so-called 'Finnish menace' remained an important factor. It was considered essential for the territorial integrity of the Norwegian state that Norwegian became the dominant language in all parts of the country.[63]

In understanding the power dynamics of the region and its consequences for the Sámi, one has to look at Sweden's role as a leading Scandinavian state with colonial ambitions. Swedish territory covers the fertile reindeer herding areas across the north-central plateau of Sápmi. Swedish authorities made efforts to colonize Sápmi from the 1600s, by exploiting the natural resources of Sápmi and by populating an area that several states laid claim on.[64]

This process became increasingly strong during the later parts of the 1700s. The 1749 Lapland Regulations resulted in a growing amount of land being granted to Swedish farmers. Sámi efforts to convince "Swedish authorities that their livelihoods would be endangered" failed. At the same time, the territory of Sápmi was "measured, surveyed and mapped, divided into provinces, parishes and tax lands". And this domestication of the

---

[61] Grunlög Fur, *Colonialism in the Margins: Cultural Encounters in New Sweden and Lapland*, Brill, Leiden, 2006, p. 53.

[62] Greaves, 2018, p. 109, see above note 2.

[63] The security motives of Norwegianization has been thoroughly documented by Eriksen and Niemi, 1981, see above note 51.

[64] David Lindmark, "Colonial Encounter in Early Modern Sápmi", in Magdalena Naum and Jonas M. Nordin (eds.), *Scandinavian Colonialism and the Rise of Modernity: Small Agents in a Global Arena*, Springer-Verlag, New York, 2013, p. 131.

---

land went hand in hand with "domestication of its dwellers. Civilizing efforts of Lutheran missionaries and school masters aimed at reforming the minds and bodies of the students and creating obedient subjects".[65]

Terms to describe this intrusion into Sápmi such as "agricultural expansion", "settlement of non-Sámi" or "internal colonization" do not capture the asymmetrical character of the power relationships entailed in the processes. Neither do they recognize that Sámi society and economy were well-organized and well-governed despite the lack of a Sámi nation-state and military defence.

Another important indicator of colonial relationship is the educational system, which offers a restricted curriculum for the colonial subjects "to inculcate knowledge, values and attitudes deemed necessary to controlling the colonized".[66] Lessons were limited to reading, writing and arithmetic, and sometimes vocational skills. "In this manner, the colonized were prepared to enter the labor market equipped with the norms and values essential to creating a loyal, diligent and conscientious working class."[67]

By creating obedient and efficient students, colonial education contributed "to laying the groundwork for political dominance, and economic exploitation". Virtues instilled included "order, precision, punctuality and obedience", preparing the colonized students to fulfil the demands of colonial society. In addition, the students were subject to extensive Christianity lessons, buttressing these norms further.[68]

The root of colonial education of the Sámi in Sweden was a school founded in Lycksele in 1632, through a private donation. However, it was about 100 years later that a public education program for Sápmi was established. In these early years, there were selective enrolment of students and a study period of only two years. The basic tenets of the education model, however, became influential for both Swedish and later, Norwegian Sámi education. Sámi children were isolated from their families and environment and were under constant surveillance of their teacher at the boarding schools. In a Swedish instruction to the headmaster from 1735, the headmaster's surveillance is put in a direct analogy to the omnipres-

---

[65] *Ibid.*, pp. 132–133.
[66] *Ibid.*, p. 133.
[67] *Ibid.*
[68] *Ibid.*

ence of God, who "sees into their souls and hearts and knows how often they transgress his commandments even in the slightest degree".[69]

The aim of the education at the time was thus to reform the students, reshape their will and transform their spirituality, and to achieve a complete "internalisation of Christian philosophy and religiosity". In other words, in addition to facilitating the settling of non-Sámi in Sápmi, taking over and transforming to private ownership the land Sámi had used for centuries, the Scandinavian states also aimed at an "invasion within". The educated Sámi should become a tool for the ruling elites to gradually master and govern the uneducated Sámi.[70]

For the Sámi, the influx of Scandinavian settlers, who were granted tax exemption and other benefits when they moved to Sápmi and farmed its land, as well as the assertion of centralized political authority without taking into account their views and interests "looked suspiciously like an invasion".[71] True, colonization of Sápmi was less violent and more gradual than European colonialism elsewhere. In other aspects, however, the Scandinavian expansion and assertion of power were similar to European colonialism. The purpose was to displace and deny independence to the Sámi, and to 'invade' their minds by educational measures.

Sweden could be seen as the driving force in the colonization of Sápmi, influencing the lives of Sámi but also the policies of its Scandinavian neighbours.

> Swedish expansion into Sápmi thus influenced the political and demographic shape of northern Europe, since it expanded the zone of sovereign control and led to extended boundary disputes between Sweden, Denmark-Norway, and Russia. The borders that resulted brought Sápmi under the control of centralized Christian, European sovereigns.[72]

This taking over of territory and competition between Scandinavian states and Russia to dominate Sápmi played an important role in motivating efforts at eradicating Sámi culture and language. As has been shown, these processes may be seen through the lens of Western colonialism, "a

---

[69] *Ibid.*, p. 134.
[70] *Ibid.*, p. 135.
[71] Fur, 2006, p. 17, see above note 51.
[72] Greaves, 2018, p. 103, see above note 2.

political-economic phenomenon whereby various European nations explored, conquered, settled, and exploited large areas of the world".[73]

Other factors, however, also played a role. Research indicate that while assimilation policies intensified in Norway during the first part of the 1900s, they became more relaxed in Sweden. In Norway, the policies became increasingly a state issue based on security concerns, where the role of the northern Norwegian authorities was reduced. The increasingly harsh policies should probably be understood in the context of society becoming increasingly nationalistic around the establishment of the Norwegian state as independent of Sweden in 1905. "Internal alien people" were deemed to be a threat for the Norwegian statehood. In Sweden, policies seem to have become more relaxed because the state was stronger. It held that the Sámi did not pose a threat and could be accepted as they were.[74]

During World War II, the whole of Norway was occupied by Germany, but the most severe fighting took place in Finnmark, affecting at times the whole civilian population. Pressured to retreat by Soviet troops in the autumn of 1944, German military authorities issued orders that the entire population of 70,000 should be evacuated. Some 23,000 refused and went into hiding in caves and other forms of shelter. Almost all houses and buildings were destroyed by the retreating German army. Many Sámi decided to stay behind.[75]

Nazi Germany's views of the Sámi were complex. Ideologues like Mr. Heinrich Himmler (1900-1945) viewed the Sámi as belonging to non-Germanic peoples who had kept their blood clean. He therefore wanted to create an apartheid state in Finnmark so that the Sámi people would retain their characteristics. The Germans also needed knowledge on how to survive in the harsh climate. Few managed this better than the reindeer-herding Sámi who had a unique knowledge of the conditions in the north. The occupying authorities therefore left the reindeer-herding Sámi industry largely untouched.[76]

---

[73] Charles E. Nowell, Richard A. Webster and Harry Magdoff, "Western Colonialism", in *Encyclopedia Britannia*.

[74] Eriksen and Niemi, 1981, p. 348, see above note 51.

[75] Fredrik Fagertun (ed.), *Krig og frigjøring i nord [War and Liberation in the North]*, Orkana akademisk, Oslo, p. 215.

[76] Bjørg Evjen, "Møter og holdninger mellom samer, norske nazimyndigheter og representanter for okkupasjonsmakten" ["Encounters and attitudes between Sámi, Norwegian Nazi-authorities and representatives of the occupying power"], in *ibid.*, pp. 85–98.

After the war, Finnmark was rebuilt according to Norwegian design with little, if any, consultation with the Sámi. There was, however, a gradual shift in policies as border conflicts with Finland lapsed. In 1948, a breakthrough for more sympathetic views towards the Sámi occurred. Sámi political mobilization became more forceful and state policies started to accept Sámi language and culture in education and society.[77]

However, this was just the beginning of a long process, which has not yet ended, to define the role and rights of the Sámi people on Norwegian territory and in Norwegian politics and society.

17.2.4. The Racist Elements in Past Romani and Sámi Policies

In recognizing that the taking over of Sápmi by the Scandinavian states may be seen through the lens of colonialism, there is an implicit acceptance of the role played by racist elements in its ideological underpinnings. Colonialism represents instrumentalization of territory and human beings, based on assumptions that the people originally living in the colonized territory have less civilization, less rights, or belong to an 'inferior race' compared to the people of the colonizing state.

In general, 'racism' signifies actions, practices or beliefs that in some way reflect the view that humans may be divided into separate and exclusive biological entities. The view holds that there is a causal link between inherited physical traits and traits of personality, intellect, morality and other cultural and behavioural features. In this way, some races are seen as innately superior to others.

Such racist ideas were clearly present in the most prevalent ideological efforts to legitimize assimilation policies towards Norway's minorities, in particular the Romani and the Sámi. The background of these policies was a combination of educational policy ambitions, nation-building ideology, as well as a desire for stronger border security in the north. In the early 1900s, Social Darwinism and racial-biology thoughts became important. These were ideas that most people accepted at the time, and it served both as a defence and a basis for Norwegian policy. According to these ideas, the Sámi and the Romani were 'helped' by getting rid of their languages, religions, dress styles or other cultural features that signalled minority identity. Instead, they were given access to a thriving Norwegian culture. At different times, ideas shifted on whether it was feasible to as-

---

[77] Eriksen and Niemi, 1981, p. 349, see above note 51.

similate the minorities. Some held that the groups were not intellectually
or morally able to adhere to practices of the culture because of their alleged 'inferior biological characteristics'.

During the first part of the 1900s, the Mission thought it possible to
'save' Romani if they were educated. During the period between World
Wars I and II, however, more radical proposals were presented by influential 'experts' and politicians to forcibly sterilize all members of the group.
These proposals were clearly motivated by racist ideas about the inferior
biological nature of the people. Social Darwinism and racial biology became influential among political and scientific elites in Norway, as in several other European states at the time.

Romani people were often portrayed as socially and intellectually
inferior; at times, such characterization was also applied to the Sámi. At
other times, it was their pagan religion and 'uncivilized' lifestyle that was
pointed to as the basis for the policies.

17.2.5. Other Motives

The concentration of Kvens in villages and small towns close to the Finnish border were seen as a security issue from the 1800s and until World
War II. The loyalty of the Kvens, and to a certain degree of the Sámi, to
the Norwegian state was in doubt. In this context, Norwegianization was
seen as a tool to defend Norwegian territory.

Norway chose mainly to defend its territorial integrity by cultural
and religious means, such as erecting churches and symbols of Norwegian
culture to increase visibility and presence in the area. Since some of the
Sámi followed their reindeer across borders, they were not seen as contributing to nation-building and securing the territory of Norway's northernmost province.

During the 1900s, Finnmark's natural resources increasingly drew
investments and modernization of its economy. Building of large hydroelectric power plants, mines and other economic developments increased
pressure on traditional territories for reindeer herding during the post-war
period. Current examples are development of windmill farms, which may
intrude on Sámi reindeer areas. Such conflicts between Sámi and majori-
ty-Norwegian economic interests in the area has a long history and may
also have contributed to efforts to assimilate them.

There were also motives that were not related to security or economy. From the late 1800s, there were strong movements in Norway to increase protection of socially disadvantaged children, including by ensuring their education to become morally upright and hardworking. Norway was among the first states in the world to have a public child welfare system. However, ideas of protecting children, for their own and for the society's good, merged with derogatory beliefs concerning minorities. Like in Australia, Canada and New Zealand, measures targeting children and families became part of policies to facilitate assimilation of minorities.[78]

A view prevailed among elites and large parts of the population that the demography of the nascent state should be as uniform as possible. This conformity ideology aimed at imposing the Protestant faith, Norwegian culture, and strong loyalty towards the Norwegian state. As opposed to the Sámi and the Kven living in the north, the Romani was never seen as a security problem. However, they were seen as a threat towards reaching the goal of conformity.[79]

In this way, taking care of Romani children became a means to repress Romani culture and facilitating assimilation. Similarly, the somewhat less intrusive boarding school system in Finnmark aimed at weakening the bonds between the children and their Sámi family and culture, and transferring them into Norwegian language and culture.

17.3. Norwegian Public Discourse on the Past Wrongdoing

The Norwegian King and several governments have, since the late 1990s, apologized to the Sámi and the Romani for the harm inflicted by the past wrongdoing. As an example, in his official speech at the opening of the Sámi Parliament in 1997, the King stated that the "Norwegian state is founded on the territory of two people – Norwegians and Sámi. Sámi history is closely intertwined with Norwegian history. Today, we must apologize the injustice the Norwegian state has previously inflicted on the Sámi people through a harsh Norwegianization policy".[80]

---

[78] Karen-Sofie Pettersen, "For barnas skyld? Ideologi og praksis i tiltakene rettet mot taternes barn" ["For the sake of the children? Ideology and practice in measures towards Romani children"], in Hvinden (ed.), 2000, pp. 74–75, see above note 27.

[79] *Ibid.*, p. 76.

[80] The speech is available in Norwegian language at the web site of The Norwegian Royal House.

The wording of the King in describing past wrongdoing is telling of the way Norwegian authorities speak. The prevailing political discourse adheres to rather unspecific terms such as "injustices", "failed policies", "assimilation policies" and "Norwegianization". Human rights language and a recognition that the policies represented infringement of core values protected by human rights and international criminal law remains largely absent. This may change in the future due to the influence of the truth commissions.

When the head of the Romani Truth Commission, Mr. Knut Vollebæk (1946-), former Minister of Foreign Affairs and former Organization for Security and Co-operation in Europe Commissioner on National Minorities, presented the Commission's report on 1 June 2015, he said that he was shocked by the way Romani had been treated in Norway:

> State policy has been unsuccessful and disruptive. It has created a fear of authorities that have been inherited. [...] At the Svanviken labour colony, serious interference with the privacy of residents has been revealed. The situation there was characterized by control and directives. Little was up to the individual, and people were often placed there unwillingly.

> Studies show that around 40 per cent of women at Svanviken were sterilized. Previous research has shown that Romani have been sterilized in Norway until the 1970s. Many formally voluntary sterilizations were done under duress, with threats of losing the children you had if you were not sterilized.[81]

The extensive research conducted by the Commission confirmed past wrongdoing against the Romani. It also concluded that parts of the wrongdoing represented violations of human rights as understood today and violations of ethical norms and values that were present in Norwegian society at the time, and which today are protected by human rights.[82] In this way, the Commission introduced more specific ways of describing the past abuses.

---

[81] Quotation translated from Norwegian by the author, based on the author's notes. Facts presented in the quotation are rendered in the official report by the Commission. For an overview of official apologies to the Romani, see NOU 2015:7, pp. 81–88, see above note 17.

[82] *Ibid.*, p. 74.

In particular, the Commission concluded that practices at Svanviken labour colony until the 1970s violated the European Convention on Human Rights Article 8 (right to respect for private and family life) as it is understood today. This also holds for the extensive practice of transferring Romani children to orphanages and to Norwegian foster families.

> The Committee believes that at that time it should have been understood that the practice was contrary to the fundamental considerations which the right to privacy and family life was intended to protect, and which Norway from 1953 was legally obliged to respect. In addition, the Committee finds that several laws and regulations were designed or applied in such a way that they contributed to discrimination or did not provide adequate protection against such behaviour, which today would be a violation of human rights.[83]

The Commission also stated that many cases of sterilization of Romani women represented breaches of national laws. In such cases, women were pressured to accept sterilization, or they were sterilized without fulfilling the legal criteria for forced sterilization. If such sterilization had been conducted today, "it would have constituted a gross violation of integrity which fundamentally breaks with the European Convention on Human Rights [Article 3]". However, the European Court of Human Rights found only in 2011 that "illegitimate forced sterilization constituted a violation of Article 3" of the Convention.

The Commission therefore could not conclude that the practice of forced sterilization of Romani people during the post-war period represented violations of the right to privacy or the right not to be subjected to inhuman or degrading treatment as international human rights were interpreted at the time. According to current interpretations, however, such practices represent "serious violations of human rights".[84]

The Commission did not discuss past practices under international criminal law provisions. Nevertheless, it advanced considerably the way of talking about past abuses by introducing human rights language. Whether the Sámi, Kven and Forrest Finns Truth Commission will introduce similar language remains to be seen. According to its mandate, it shall map former abusive policies, investigate their consequences for in-

---

[83] *Ibid.* (the author's translation).

[84] *Ibid.*, p. 78.

dividuals and the groups, and propose measures to facilitate reconciliation. The mandate does not specifically refer to human rights as a point of reference, but in a meeting with the leader of the Commission, Former Head of the Christian Democrat Party in Norway, Mr. Dagfinn Høybråten (1957-), the author was told that the Commission nevertheless would make such assessments.[85]

The only example of considerations known to the author concerning application of international criminal law norms to the past wrongdoing in Norway, is a report published by the Norwegian Helsinki Committee in 2009, drafted by the author. Chapter six of the report discusses statements by a representative of a Romani organization and by Professor Mr. Knut Aukrust (1953-), a former Head of the Board of the Norwegian Holocaust Centre, that the Romani people in Norway had suffered genocide.[86]

The report concluded that neither legal criteria for crimes against humanity nor for genocide as defined by the Rome Statute of the International Criminal Court was fulfilled. There was not an intent to physically destroy the Romani people or parts of it. Rather, the intention was to assimilate the group and destroy its culture. Proposals were made in the mid-war period for a systematic campaign of sterilizing Romani people, but they were not followed-up. Research indicate that the percentage of Romani women being subject to forced sterilization may have been twice the average, but there was not a practice that constituted a "widespread or systematic attack" directed against a civilian population.

The report concluded that,

> there is a great difference between the Norwegian persecution and situations that have so far led to convictions of genocide and crimes against humanity. But it is still frightening that Norwegian policies contained actions that are elements of such crimes. Prevailing views in Norway was akin to thinking that in other contexts has led to the destruction of a population (genocide) or the execution of widespread and

---

[85] Meeting with Mr. Dagfinn Høybråten, Chair of the Commission, and Ms. Liss-Ellen Ramstad, Head of the Secretariat of the Commission, on 4 December 2019. The Truth and Reconciliation Commission's web site provides further information.

[86] Ekeløve-Slydal, 2009, Chapter 6, see above note 23. The report played an important role in convincing Norwegian authorities to establish the "Romani Truth Commission", see NOU 2015:7, p. 11, see above note 17.

brutal attacks on a group of people (crimes against humanity).

> In particular, in the 1930s and 1940s, it was argued that the Romani people [...] were an inferior race or an inferior mixed race and that one therefore had to prevent childbirth. Fortunately, this line of thinking did not prevail, and the Mission abandoned it in the late 1940s.[87]

Past Wrongdoing as Violations of Core Values Protected by Current International Criminal Law and Human Rights

There are several reasons why it is important to describe and evaluate past wrongs as infringements of core values or generic legal goods protected by current international criminal law and human rights norms.[88]

First, by doing so, the seriousness of the past wrongdoing is underlined. Human rights and international criminal law may be the closest we ever get to a global consensus about norms that can protect individuals and groups against the most harmful practices by states or powerful private organizations. Even if wrongdoing took place before a prohibition of its specific actions was established as an international legal norm, the protected legal good or value may have been present and at least accepted by some segments of the population at the time.

Norwegian assimilation policies breached ethical norms, which were based on values that later came to be protected by international human rights norms. Values protecting private and family life, for instance, have old roots in Norwegian Christian traditions, but were set aside in dealing with minority families. There were also voices at the time, who specifically referred to humanistic values in criticizing parts of the policies. The goal of assimilating the minorities was nevertheless given preference over the adherence to fundamental societal values; values that later were consolidated and confirmed by international laws after World War II.

---

[87] *Ibid.*, p. 41.

[88] For the approach developed in this chapter, I am in debt to Morten Bergsmo, *Myanmar, Colonial Aftermath, and Access to International Law*, Torkel Opsahl Academic EPublisher, Brussels, 2019 (https://www.legal-tools.org/doc/64a8fc/). In particular, I took note of section 2 (pp. 5–14), discussing whether Burma under British rule where subject to colonial practices falling "squarely within the generic legal good or value protected by the prohibition against population transfer into occupied territory? If the answer is in the affirmative, is this not important to recognise if we want to understand the recent situation in Rakhine and the excessive polarisation around accountability?" (p. 11).

Referring to such values and demonstrating how they are protected by modern international criminal and human rights law can be seen as a belated way of providing access to international law. This is not done by a detailed legal analysis, but by defining protected values and then describing how past wrongdoing infringed these values. This is what I mean by *the prism of modern international criminal law and human rights law*, referred to in the title of this chapter. It is a way of applying modern law to shed light on past wrongdoing without resorting to technical legal analysis.

Second, even if there were no large-scale military conflicts or violent attacks involved in Norway's colonizing of Sápmi or the implementation of harsh assimilation policies towards its minorities, the underlying ideas and justifications of these actions and policies were often similar to justifications that motivate atrocious crimes, that is, racist and dehumanizing ideas that belittled dignity and worth of the minority groups, their way of life, their language, and their culture.

Subsuming past wrongdoing as infringements of specific values protected by modern international law points to the need to look beyond the somewhat undramatic and 'peaceful' context of the actions, to the brutal and detrimental aims behind the conduct.

The small size of the minorities in Norway may have been an important factor in reducing the risk of escalation of armed conflict between government and minority-based forces. Confronted with a powerful state, both the Sámi and the Romani chose to avoid confrontations, developing tactics of escaping rather than fighting back.

It is hard to forget a statement by the Swedish Lutheran priest and missionary Samuel Rheen (1615–1680), who arrived in Jokkmokk in Swedish Sápmi to preach to the Sámi (he served from 1666 to 1671), complaining that the "Lapps are a people who, for the major part, are thoroughly unsuited to waging war, for they lack manly courage".[89] However, it was not lack of manly courage, rather a well thought out survival strategy in the Arctic climate and conditions that led the Sámi to avoid fighting.[90]

---

[89] Kent, 2018, p. 31, see above note 40.

[90] As an ironic note, sometimes the Sámi took part in warfare between Russia, Denmark-Norway and Sweden. They were seen as formidable fighters, moving swiftly on skis while shooting their arrows. See *ibid.*, p. 14.

In the following, the author argues that some of the measures implemented by Norwegian authorities to assimilate the Sámi and the Romani clearly represented violations of some of the core values protected by modern international criminal and human rights law, such as territorial and bodily integrity, equal access to the law, and protection of religion, language and culture.

Third, in discussions with members of the groups, the author was often asked what international norms may offer in terms of remedy for past wrongdoing. Not much, the author had to concede, but a determination of the past wrongs as violations of international criminal law and/or human rights may at least point to the state as the responsible party, the violator, and they and their ancestors as the victims.

The next question was often how Norway can be seen by many (both within Norway and internationally) as a champion of human rights and international criminal law when it has not properly dealt with its own past wrongdoing against its small minorities. There were two parts in the author's answer. First, Norway's past wrongs are not so well known, and second, Norway is now trying to remedy its past wrongdoing with a range of measures, including by establishing compensation schemes, establishing schemes to support minority language and culture, and having truth and reconciliation processes.

In this way, Norway has started processes to confront and deal with its past wrongs, and thereby also making genuine efforts to deal with double standard perceptions when it supports accountability mechanisms for contemporary international crimes and human rights violations elsewhere.

The Romani Truth Commission concluded that there is little evidence that Norwegian practices represented clear violations of international legal norms as they were interpreted at the time. They did, however, clearly violate the core values protected by current interpretations of contemporary international norms. "In light of today's values, the objectives and measures of the 20th century assimilation policies towards the Romani appear discriminatory and oppressive".[91] Statements like this by a government appointed Commission clearly represents a step in the right direction.

---

[91] NOU 2015:7, p. 78, see above note 17.

17.3.1. Territorial Integrity of Sámi Land

Norway was, over a protracted period, giving benefits to ethnic Norwegians if they settled in Sápmi, and laws were introduced that discriminated against the Sámi, for example, by requiring Norwegian language skills and citizenship to buy land. There was no military conquest; the territory was not forcedly taken from another state, although there were at times competition between the neighbouring states to dominate, tax and include parts of the territory.

Nevertheless, Norway intruded into an area traditionally used by the Sámi and dominated it. Sápmi was not an empty wilderness but populated by people who had organized themselves and were able to live well from the available resources in this arctic region and trade with other peoples. It is true that the area is "among the most sparsely populated in Europe, and its vast, often snow-covered landscape has long served to attract those enamoured by its natural, unspoiled beauty. Yet such sweeping assertions hardly do justice to the vitality of the Sámi homeland and the rich culture and history of the Sámi people, who have inhabited the region for thousands of years".[92]

The question here is whether Norway's practices represent a violation of values protected by the international criminal law norm that prohibits the "transfer, directly or indirectly, by the Occupying Power of parts of its own civilian population into the territory it occupies". To answer that question, one has to decide on whether the Norwegian part of Sápmi can be seen as "territory under forms of domination similar to occupation" such as "colonial rule".[93]

This constitutes a complex issue, including whether Norway's 'facilitation' of Norwegian settlement in Sápmi amounted to "transfer, directly or indirectly" of its population. It goes beyond the scope of this chapter to deal with this. It is considerably easier to determine whether Norwegian

---

[92] Kent, 2018, p. 1, see above note 40.

[93] See Bergsmo, 2019, p. 9, see above note 88. General Assembly Resolution 1541 (XV), UN Doc. A/RES/1541(XV), Principle IV, puts as a precondition for a colonial situation to exist, that the territory in question must be "geographically separate" and that it is "distinct ethnically and/or culturally from the country administering it" (https://www.legal-tools.org/doc/hqlf9y/). This pre-condition is known as the "salt-water test" of colonialism and excludes integral or adjacent territories that are or may be colonized by a parent State. Norway's colonizing of Sápmi is clearly not an example of salt-water colonization, but nevertheless adheres to other criteria of colonialism.

policies infringed *values* protected by the legal norm. Such values include to avoid undermining the economic survival of the native population or to endanger its separate existence as a distinct ethnic group.[94]

In the case of Sápmi, the criterion could be re-formulated as *preserving the integrity of the land so that the Sámi way of life could be sustained*. Without keeping the vast territory intact, open to reindeer herding or other use which required the territory to be kept without borders or barriers created by private property, vital parts of Sámi economy and culture would suffer. Seen in this perspective, Norwegian settlement practices clearly constituted infringements of such values, as did border regulations with the neighbouring states of Sweden, Finland and Russia. In addition, assimilation policies intended and in practice led to further weakening of Sámi culture and economy.

Some similarities and differences can be observed between what the European colonial powers did in overseas colonies and what the Norwegian state did in Sápmi. I take the British Empire's transfer of Indian citizens to Arakan (now Rakhine State) in colonial Burma as a case of comparison.[95]

The most important similarity between the two cases is the consequences. As a result of the transfer or facilitated immigration of foreigners, the native population faced demographic shifts in their territories detrimental to their economy and culture. The existence of the native populations as distinct groups was undermined.

Although the facilitated immigration of Indian people into Burma under British administration and Norwegian people into Sápmi took place prior to the adoption of the international criminal law norm in question (which was first introduced in the 1949 Geneva Convention IV Article 49 (6)), the value protected by the norm was violated in both cases by changing the demographic structure of the respective regions and threatening the existence of the native populations as separate peoples.

When established, the norm was "intended to prevent a practice adopted during the Second World War by certain Powers, which transferred portions of their own population to occupied territory for political and racial reasons or in order, as they claimed, to colonize those territo-

---

[94] See Bergsmo, 2019, p. 11, see above note 88.

[95] As outlined in *ibid*.

ries".[96] On this background, the Norwegian facilitation of immigration into Sápmi arguably falls more squarely within the concerns behind the norm than the British case because of its seemingly 'political' and 'racial' nature.

The transfer of civilians into Arakan under British administration did not include British people. This was different from Sápmi, where Norwegian authorities facilitated settlement of Norwegians with an aim of ascertaining control and annexing the area into Norwegian jurisdiction. In this respect, the Norwegian practice is arguably more similar to what Turkey has been doing after its 1974 invasion of the northern part of Cyprus.

As mentioned, the Sámi did not defend their land by force. They, however, put up defence in the form of cultural resistance from the early 1900s. That strategy paid off from the 1970s onward, and they have gradually gained respect for their status as an indigenous people with land rights. An important reinforcement of that defence has been Sámi representatives gaining competence in and making use of international law provisions to strengthen their legal position.

17.3.2. Bodily Integrity

Torture and other forms of mistreatment were not part of the assimilation policies.[97] However, bodily integrity as a value was violated through practices of forced sterilization against Romani people, and by placing Romani children in orphanages and Sámi children in boarding schools with little control of adult abuse. The extent of such abuse – in the form of cruel punishment or sexual abuse – is unknown, but it is well-established that it took place.

International criminal law explicitly prohibits "enforced sterilization" as a crime against humanity.[98] The crime of genocide may consist of preventing childbirth in a group, if the intention is to physically destroy the group.[99] In the *Akayesu* case, a Trial Chamber of the International

---

[96] Jean S. Pictet (ed.), *Commentary on IV Geneva Convention*, International Committee of the Red Cross, Geneva, 1958, p. 283 (http://www.legal-tools.org/doc/7d971f/).

[97] Torture or inhuman or degrading treatment is prohibited in a range of international human rights treaties. It is a war crime and can also as part of a systematic or widespread attack on a civilian population, be a crime against humanity.

[98] Rome Statute of the International Criminal Court, 17 July 1998, Article 7(1)(g) ('ICC Statute') (https://www.legal-tools.org/doc/e5faa8/).

[99] *Ibid.*, Article 6(d).

Criminal Tribunal for Rwanda clarified that forced sterilization may be an example of such measures.[100] It also follows from international human rights norms that such practices should be abolished.

Human rights concerns have played an important role in opposing programmes and legislation permitting or promoting forced sterilization of particular groups of the population. Hitler-Germany's programmes of sterilization contributed to a human rights-based resistance, but even before this time, opponents in the United States and Britain argued on the basis of human rights.[101]

After World War II, the Declaration of the World Conference on Human Rights in Teheran in 1968 was important in adapting human rights to reproductive issues. Principle 16 of the Declaration reads:

> The protection of the family and of the child remains the concern of the international community. Parents have a basic human right to determine freely and responsibly the number and the spacing of their children.[102]

Based on this provision, a collective term for a bundle of rights related to conception, pregnancy and childbirth was developed: "reproductive rights".[103] Especially the World Health Organization has promoted these rights, arguing that authorities must have a rights-based approach to population issues. A central provision in this context is prohibition of forced sterilization.

There can be little doubt that values inherent in international criminal law prohibitions and human rights norms were infringed upon by practices of forced sterilization that targeted in particular Romani women

---

[100] International Criminal Tribunal for Rwanda, *The Prosecutor v. Jean-Paul Akayesu*, Trial Chamber, Judgment, 2 September 1998, ICTR-96-4-T, para. 507 (https://www.legal-tools.org/doc/b8d7bd/).

[101] Daniel J. Kevles, "Eugenics and Human Rights", in *British Medical Journal*, 1999, vol. 319, pp. 435–438.

[102] Final Act of the International Conference on Human Rights, UN Doc. A/CONF.32/41, 13 May 1968, p. 4, Principle 16 (https://www.legal-tools.org/doc/46bde6/).

[103] WHO's definition of reproductive rights: "Reproductive rights rest on the recognition of the basic right of all couples and individuals to decide freely and responsibly the number, spacing and timing of their children and to have the information and means to do so, and the right to attain the highest standard of sexual and reproductive health. They also include the right of all to make decisions concerning reproduction free of discrimination, coercion and violence". See "Reproductive Rights", United Nations Department of Economic and Social Affairs (available on its web site).

in Norway. The protected value is that *every woman should be left in control of her fertility, regardless of her ethnicity.*

Research interviews with Romani persons who were placed in the Mission's orphanages during childhood indicate that punishment included "cuff on the ears, pulling by the hair, blows with various implements, such as whip or cane, and confinement over shorter or longer periods of time in small and often dark rooms". The children experienced the use of punishment as unpredictable, disproportionately severe, and often unnecessary and unfair. Some of the interviewees told that they were subject to sexual abuse by adult persons working at the orphanages or connected to it in some way.[104]

Such punishment and abuse clearly represent infringement of values protected by international criminal law and human rights norms that prohibit integrity violations, such as torture and inhuman treatment. Many of the interviewees reported that the abuse they suffered as children had negative consequences for their health and self-respect for the rest of their lives.

17.3.3. Equal Access to the Law[105]

Legislation that did not specifically target Romani but had adverse effects on members of the group due to their way of living, was an important part of the assimilation policies. The laws listed in Section 17.2.1. above, such

---

[104] Anne-Berit Sandvik, "Å være tater i barne- og skolehjem" ["To be Tater (Romani) in orphanages or boarding schools"], in Hvinden (ed.), 2000, pp. 109–113, see above note 27.

[105] This right is guaranteed in several core international human rights instruments, such as (1) Article 7 of the Universal Declaration of Human Rights, 10 December 1948 ('UDHR') (https://www.legal-tools.org/doc/de5d83/), which states: "All are equal before the law and are entitled without any discrimination to equal protection of the law"; (2) Article 1 of the International Convention on the Elimination of All Forms of Racial Discrimination, 21 December 1965 (https://www.legal-tools.org/doc/43a925/), which defines racial discrimination as "any distinction, exclusion, restriction or preference based on race, colour, descent, or national or ethnic origin which has the purpose or effect of nullifying or impairing the recognition, enjoyment or exercise, on an equal footing, of human rights and fundamental freedoms in the political, economic, social, cultural or any other field of public life"; and (3) Article 26 of International Covenant on Civil and Political Rights, 16 December 1966 ('ICCPR') (https://www.legal-tools.org/doc/2838f3/), which states that "[a]ll persons are equal before the law and are entitled without any discrimination to the equal protection of the law. In this respect, the law shall prohibit any discrimination and guarantee to all persons equal and effective protection against discrimination on any ground such as race, colour, sex, language, religion, political or other opinion, national or social origin, property, birth or other status".

as the vagrant law, the child welfare law, as well as laws dealing with trade and animal welfare, were applied in different degrees to target Romani practices.

Legislation and legal practices also played an important role in assimilation policies towards the Sámi, as well as in efforts to take over their land. In particular, legislation that restricted the use of Sámi languages in education and laws that benefited ethnic Norwegians in buying land were instrumental for the Norwegian state to reach its assimilation goals.

Discriminatory attitudes by police was an important effect of the policies. However, the limited research available indicates that police attitudes and actions against minorities varied substantially between police districts. In some districts, the main approach was to hinder 'vagrants' or Romani people from coming and to find ways to expel them as soon as possible. In other districts, the chief of police had more neutral or even accommodating attitudes. In conflicts with non-Romani people, however, the police would often discriminate against the Romani and give the other party (a Norwegian or a person belonging to another nationality) the benefit of the doubt.[106]

In general, constitutional norms of equality before the law and equal access to the law often failed to influence the handling of individual cases. While the police did not systematically persecute Romani, "personal and discretionary application of the law by the police contributed to weakening legal protection of the Romani people at the individual level".[107] Often, police intervention in cases involving Romani people depended on available resources in the police district. If a 'vagrant' left the district, many chiefs of police were eager to close any cases related to that person.[108]

While the police often treated Romani people with discrimination, courts seem in general to have taken a more neutral stance, although ex-

---

[106] For an overview of some of the issues related to police and courts dealing with cases involving Romani people, see Chalak Kaveh, "Taterne/romanifolket i det norske politi- og rettsvesenet 1900–1980: En studie av politiets og domstolenes praktisering av lovverket" ["Romani people in the Norwegian police and courts: A study of police and court application of the legislation"], in NOU 2015:7, pp. 240–308, see above note 17.

[107] *Ibid.*, pp. 305–306.

[108] *Ibid.*

amples of stigmatizing attitudes influencing the outcome of criminal cases do exist.[109]

There are many individual accounts by Sámi and Romani that people were misled, discriminated or otherwise badly treated by the police. Mistrust towards Norwegian authorities remain widespread among Romani people, and for many it remains illusory that the police or courts could provide justice. According to recent research, Sámi women report less frequently than ethnic Norwegian women cases of domestic violence to the police. One of the reasons may be that many Sámi still lack confidence in the larger Norwegian community as a result of the assimilation and Norwegianization policy of the past. This particularly affects meetings between those affected by violence with a Sámi background and non-Sámi employees in health and social services and police.[110]

The lack of trust in police and other public institutions among Sámi and Romani is in stark contrast to average perceptions among Norwegian citizens about these institutions, characterized by high levels of trust.[111]

In conclusion, it is well-documented that Romani and Sámi suffered from legislation that was discriminatory or applied in discriminatory ways, from prejudices among police, and to some degree (but less) from similar negative attitudes in courts. There is, however, also evidence that legislation, courts and even police at times moderated the effects of the assimilation policies.

In general, the groups still have little trust in judicial institutions and legal protection of their rights, confirming that values protected by human rights provisions ensuring equal access to the law and non-discrimination in legal matters were violated during the long period of assimilation policies.

---

[109] *Ibid.*

[110] Norwegian Centre for Violence and Traumatic Stress Studies, *Om du tør å spørre, tør folk å svare: Hjelpeapparatets og politiets erfaringer med vold i nære relasjoner i samiske samfunn [If you dare to ask, people dare to answer: The experiences of the health services and police with violence in close relationships in Sami communities]*, Norwegian Centre for Violence and Traumatic Stress Studies, Oslo, 2017, p. 8.

[111] According to annual surveys, around 80 per cent of the population in Norway has high or very high thrust in the police. See Politidirektoratet [Police Directorate], "Innbyggerundersøkelsen" ["Inhabitant survey"], in *Norwegian Police*, 2014–2019 (available on its web site).

Equality before the laws is a deeply ingrained Norwegian value, with roots in pre-Christian societies. However, this value was not applied to Norway's minorities during a protracted period of assimilation.

17.3.4. Protection of Privacy and Family

Both the Sámi and the Romani experienced widespread disrespect for private and family life as these rights are currently understood.[112]

Sámi children were sent away from their family to boarding schools where only Norwegian was spoken. Many of them only knew a Sámi language when they entered school, and for many of them it took years to fully adapt to a foreign learning environment.

Romani children were taken from their parents and placed in orphanages or Norwegian foster families. In many cases, contact with their biological parents were prohibited and no information about their background were given when they asked.

According to the Romani Truth Commission, taking children away from their parents was among the key measures of the assimilation policy:[113]

> Measures against children were a key instrument in the assimilation of the Tater/Romani people. Children were taken away from their parents and placed in orphanages and foster care, and custody was transferred to the Mission. From 1900, in the course of two generations, almost one third of the children born in Tater/Romani families were taken away by the Child Welfare Services. This had dramatic consequences for the minority as a whole.
>
> The usual justification for separating the children from their parents was that the parents' lifestyle was harmful to

---

[112] The right to privacy and family life is stated in Article 12 of UDHR, see above note 75: "No one shall be subjected to arbitrary interference with his privacy, family, home or correspondence, nor to attacks upon his honour and reputation. Everyone has the right to the protection of the law against such interference or attacks". Similar wording can be found in Article 17 of ICCPR, see above note 105. Moreover, Article 10 (1) of International Covenant on Economic, Social and Cultural Rights, 16 December 1966 (https://www.legal-tools.org/doc/06b87e/), states that the "widest possible protection and assistance should be accorded to the family, which is the natural and fundamental group unit of society, particularly for its establishment and while it is responsible for the care and education of dependent children".

[113] NOU 2015:7 English Summary, p. 3, see above note 3.

the children. The Mission also deliberately severed ties between parents and children. The situation for the children who were taken away, varied. Many children suffered neglect, maltreatment and/or abuse. The consequences for many of the children were unstable, unpredictable and insecure childhoods. The Committee concludes that the widespread practice of separating the children from their families was clearly incompatible with the right to privacy, as this is understood today.

The same applies to several aspects of the treatment at Svanviken labour colony up to the 1970s. At Svanviken, restrictive control was exerted on the residents' daily life. This included for instance controlling the residents' correspondence. In the period 1950-1970, 40% of the women who were placed in Svanviken were sterilised while they were there. The Committee is not aware of any other institution in Norway that has such a high degree of sterilisation.

Fundamental values ingrained in Norwegian traditions, and protected by modern human rights, were disregarded in the context of Norway's assimilation policies during a large part of the twentieth century. The main value places the responsibility for the upbringing and education of the child on its biological parents. Only in exceptional cases can this responsibility be shifted to others, when it is necessary in order to protect the well-being of the child.

In a Norwegian context, the most relevant international human rights provision is to be found in the European Convention on Human Rights, Article 8, which states that "[e]veryone has the right to respect for his private and family life, his home and his correspondence". These rights can only be restricted "in accordance with the law" and if the restriction "is necessary in a democratic society for the sake of national security, public security or the country's economic well-being, to prevent disorder or crime, to protect health or morality, or to protect the rights and freedoms of others". Typically, one will assess whether forced transfer of custody is taken in accordance with a statutory procedure, whether one has adequately taken into account the best interests of the child, whether the parents have been involved in the process, whether their right to meet with the child is being respected, and whether their right to correspondence with the child has been respected.

No cases against Norway for transferring Romani children and breaking all contacts with their biological parents were submitted to the European Court of Human Rights. In a few other Norwegian cases, the first from 1996 (Adele Johansen v. Norway), the Court found that even if the transfer of custody was justified, given the facts of the case, breaking all contacts between the child and its biological parents was not.

Estimates indicate that about 400 transfers of custody of Romani children took place in Norway after the European Convention on Human Rights entered into force and became binding on Norway.[114] How many of these cases would have been found to be in violation of the right to private and family life today is not possible to say. There can be little doubt, however, that many of the cases amounted to violations of values protected by the right to privacy and family.

17.3.5. Protection of Religion, Language and Culture

Both Sámi and Romani peoples were denied freedom of religion or belief.[115] Their traditional believes were repressed, stigmatized and sometimes used to justify assimilation policies and actions. An irony is that for both groups, versions of Christianity later became a mobilizing force against state repression and in building more self-esteem. Some of the priests involved in missionary activities in Sápmi also contributed signifi-

---

[114] Ekeløve-Slydal, 2009, p. 18, see above note 23.

[115] Freedom of religion or belief is protected by several international human rights instruments, such as UDHR Article 18, see above note 75; ICCPR, Article 18, see above note 105; European Convention on Human Rights, 4 November 1950 ('ECHR') (https://www.legal-tools.org/doc/8267cb/), Article 9. ECHR Art. 9 (1) states that "[e]veryone has the right to freedom of thought, conscience and religion; this right includes freedom to change his religion or belief and freedom, either alone or in community with others and in public or private, to manifest his religion or belief, in worship, teaching, practice and observance".

On the other hand, ICCPR Article 18 (2) states that "[n]o one shall be subject to coercion which would impair his freedom to have or to adopt a religion or belief of his choice". The ECtHR recognised that religious freedom includes efforts to "convince" others, but this "does not extend to abusive behaviour such as applying unacceptable pressure, or actual harassment". See Research Division, European Court of Human Rights, "Overview of the Court's case-law on freedom of religion", on *European Court of Human Rights*, 31 October 2013, para. 18 (available on its web site). Also ILO Convention 169, Article 5 (a), see above note 5, states that "[i]n applying the provisions of this Convention: the social, cultural, religious and spiritual values and practices of these peoples shall be recognised and protected, and due account shall be taken of the nature of the problems which face them both as groups and as individuals".

---

cantly to documenting Sámi languages, since they believed that the gospel and the Bible should be available for the Sámi in their mother tongues.

Such positive contributions can, nevertheless, never justify the systematic infringements of values inherent in human rights norms that any individual should be free to choose his own religious or philosophical beliefs. Disregard for such values was at the core of the assimilation policies.

For both groups, Norwegianization meant that they were *pressured* to give up their own language.[116] It was not prohibited to use the languages, but they were marginalized in education and in contact with official institutions. Many Sámi refused to give up their language, while the Romani kept parts of their language as a hidden tool to communicate without Norwegian authorities and society being able to understand it. The status and survival chances of the languages were nevertheless considerably weakened, and while Sámi languages today may have gained a stronger position, it remains an open question whether the Romani language will survive in Norway.[117]

Both Sámi and Romani ways of life were portrayed as uncivilized and repressed by the Norwegian state and the Church.[118] Both cultures

---

[116] A main international human rights reference point is ICCPR, Article 27, see above note 75, which states that "[i]n those States in which ethnic, religious or linguistic minorities exist, persons belonging to such minorities shall not be denied the right, in community with the other members of their group, to enjoy their own culture, to profess and practise their own religion, or to use their own language". Aside from this provision, UDHR, ICCPR and ECHR do not refer to the protection of language and culture as separate rights like the right to privacy and family life or freedom of religion. However, there are provisions that prohibit discrimination based on, *inter alia*, language or culture. The ILO Convention 169, Article 28(1), see above note 5, states that "[c]hildren belonging to the peoples concerned shall, wherever practicable, be taught to read and write in their own indigenous language or in the language most commonly used by the group to which they belong", and Article 28(3) states that "[m]easures shall be taken to preserve and promote the development and practice of the indigenous languages of the peoples concerned". In a European context, the Framework Convention for the Protection of National Minorities and the European Charter for Regional or Minority Languages, 1 February 1998, firmly establishes the right to minority language and culture.

[117] For reporting on and assessment of Norway's minority language policies and the situation of the languages, see Council of Europe, "Reports and Recommendations", on *Council of Europe*, Norway (available on its web site). Norwegian authorities have supported several projects to document Romani language and to write books in Romani. The University of Oslo has created an online Norwegian-Romani dictionary.

[118] ICCPR, Article 27, see above note 75, forms the basis for human rights norms protecting minority cultures. ICESCR also contains provisions that safeguard cultural rights, such as Article 6 and Article 15. ILO Convention 169, see above note 5, includes many provisions

survived to a degree, however, and have influenced Norwegian main-stream culture heavily without many Norwegians being aware of or appreciating it. Recently, Sámi music, craft, and other cultural products have gained more appreciation. Romani culture, however, is still largely invisible in Norwegian society.

17.4. Measures Initiated to Repair Harm Caused by Past Wrongdoing

In the second half of the twentieth century, Norwegian policies started to change. Attention was drawn by media and public discourse to the problems endured by people belonging to the minorities due to the previous policies. In particular, the Sámi people became more assertive in efforts to maintain its culture through the use of Sámi languages in schools and media and by protecting their reindeer pastures.

Norwegian authorities have initiated a range of measures to repair damage caused by past wrongdoing and promote reconciliation, such as compensation schemes and support to Sámi, Kven and Romani cultures and languages. Some 95 per cent of the territory of Norway's northern-most county Finnmark has been transferred to a specialized agency ('*Finnmarkseiendommen*') which takes decisions on natural resources and territorial issues. Three of six members of the board of the agency are appointed by the Sámi Parliament.

Legislation that facilitated the assimilation policies has been repealed, and laws, regulations or ratification of international conventions that protect minority language and culture have been put in place. Norway has strong constitutional and legislative protection of all categories of human rights and has established several national Ombud institutions and a National Human Rights Institution to protect them.[119]

---

on cultural rights such as Articles 4 and 13. Article 4(1) of ILO Convention 169 states that "special measures shall be adopted as appropriate for safeguarding the persons, institutions, property, labour, cultures and environment of the peoples concerned". For Norway's policies regarding minority culture, the European Framework Convention for the Protection of National Minorities plays a particularly important role.

[119] For more information, see the web pages of the Parliamentary Ombudsman, the Equality and anti-Discrimination Ombud, and the Ombud for Children. The National Human Rights Institution has a special focus on Sámi and minority rights, with a separate office in Kao-tokeino, Finnmark.

While a few commentators have argued that justice mechanisms should become part of the restorative process, this has not happened. Some also argue that, while Norway has been a strong supporter internationally of justice mechanisms, it has been reluctant to apply such measures domestically. Instead, the government established an official truth and reconciliation process for the Romani people (2011–2015) and in 2018, Parliament established a similar process for the Sámi, the Kvens and the Forest Finns. The latter process is ongoing at the time of writing, with consultations and interviews with individuals belonging to the minorities, historical research, and other measures. The Commission ends its work on 1 September 2022, when a report with its findings will be submitted to Parliament.

The Romani Truth Commission was established by Royal (that is, governmental) Decree on 3 January 2011.[120] The Commission was mandated to study and describe the policies and measures towards Tater/Romani people since the 1800s, with special emphasis on the objectives, implementation and instruments of these policies.

The Commission was also requested to consider the findings in light of Norwegian legislation and international human rights norms, and whether the findings form a basis to consider new measures that may contribute to justice and reconciliation. The initiative to establish the Commission came from representatives of the Romani people themselves, and was supported, among others, by the Norwegian Helsinki Committee. The mandate was updated in 2013, at the same time as the Commission and its Secretariat changed leadership and composition.[121]

Pursuant to the Commission's interpretation of its mandate, it should "investigate the policies towards Tater/Romani people with emphasis on how these policies have worked, the present situation, and what

---

[120] The official name of the Commission was (in the author's translation) 'The Committee to investigate implementation of the policy towards the Taters/Romani people', referred to in official documents as the Tater/Romani Committee. However, in interviews and private talks, its second leader, Mr. Knut Vollebæk, often referred to it as the Tater/Romani Truth Commission.

[121] NOU 2015:7 English Summary, p. 6, see above note 3. The first leader of the Commission was Mr. Asbjørn Eide (1933-), the former Director of the Norwegian Centre of Human Rights and a former member of the UN Sub-Commission on the Promotion and the Protection of Human Rights (1981–2003), where he was one of the advocates for the establishment of the Working Group on Indigenous Populations. After stepping down as the Commission's leader, Mr. Eide remained a member of the Commission.

can build trust and good relations between the minority and the society at large".[122]

The Commission consisted of 10 members with backgrounds in politics, academic research and law, as well as two representatives of the Romani people. A secretariat was established with three full-time staff, and a resource group with representatives of four Romani organizations and one representative of the Norwegian Helsinki Committee.

The main methods of the Commission were to conduct public meetings with members of the Romani people, individual interviews, undertake or commission archival research, and internal discussions and consultations with the resource group.

In the author's assessment, the Commission presented groundbreaking research and a balanced and well-written report containing topical recommendations for further improvements of Norwegian policies. During its time of functioning, the Commission received some media attention and its leaders (first Mr. Eide and then Mr. Vollebæk) and some of its members published topical articles in some of the most read Norwegian newspapers.

The Ministry responsible for minority policies followed up the report after it was presented on 1 June 2015, with a series of open meetings to further introduce its findings and recommendations to members of the group. It soon became clear, however, that Romani people were in strong disagreement on its content and the wisdom of its recommendations. Some argued that the Commission had failed to reach out to important parts of the Romani people, namely those who were not members of Romani organizations. These were people who preferred to live 'discretely' with their Romani identity, and they did not want to be exposed by the Commission or by Romani organizations funded by the State. There was a fear among some that their children would suffer renewed bullying in schools if their Romani identity became known.

Minorities are seldom monolithic in views and approaches to state authorities and, given the complex composition of the Romani people in Norway, it was to be expected that there would be different views on the truth process in their ranks. The Commission and the ongoing debates about its conclusions nevertheless managed to engage people in discus-

---

[122] *Ibid.*

sions on their priorities and visions for how to develop Romani identity while being fully integrated in modern Norwegian society.

The Sámi, Kven and Forest Finn Truth and Reconciliation Commission also faces similar challenges, tackling differing viewpoints from subgroups and individuals belonging to the minorities. The fact that the Sámi has official status as Norway's indigenous people, while Kven and Forest Finns have status as national minorities may add to these challenges.

There are, however, well-founded hopes that such challenges can be dealt with. The Commission's work represents a unique opportunity to come to terms with some of the darkest chapters of Norwegian history, giving harmed people a chance to speak about their grievances, and to discuss remedies for a better future.

17.5. Conclusions

Norwegian assimilation policies inflicted pain and suffering on large numbers of persons belonging to the Sámi and the Romani peoples. The policies included violations of values protected by modern international criminal law as well as human rights norms.

Norway's intrusion into and efforts to dominate Sápmi may be seen through the lens of European colonialism, even though Norway itself, until independence in 1905, was dominated by its Scandinavian neighbouring states. The colonial logic of instrumentalization of natural resources and humans, designing education with the aim of producing obedient and hard-working subjects, may be detected in Norway's earlier relationship with Sápmi and the Sámi, further underlining the importance of coming to terms with past abuses.

In recent years, Norwegian authorities have shown genuine will to address some of the harms caused by past wrongdoing. Much remains to be done in order to achieve reconciliation and to rebuild minority cultures in Norway. The past assimilation policies were effective in destroying culture, language – and self-esteem. Repairing this harm is easier said than done. Norwegian authorities should nevertheless be given credit for at least trying to do the right thing.

18

Colonial Crime, Environmental Destruction
and Indigenous Peoples:
A Roadmap to Accountability and Protection

Joshua Castellino[*]

18.1. Introduction

The contemporary climate emergency is directly traceable to colonial activities commenced on indigenous territories, continued under post-
colonial regimes, with the active support (material and logistic) of the
former colonial powers.[1] These practices stimulated demand for 'products', treated territories as resource hotbeds,[2] and ignored the human
rights of indigenous peoples[3] who were treated as objects rather than sub-

---

[*] **Joshua Castellino** is the Executive Director of Minority Rights Group (International). He
is a Professor of Law and former Founding Dean of School of Law, Middlesex University
in London, United Kingdom. With special thanks to Lara Dominguez who commented on
a previous draft at short notice and to the editors for facilitating this addition to this body
of work.

[1] For general literature that explore this issue, see Marcie Bianco, "Colonialism Meets Cli-
mate Change", in *Stanford Social Innovation Review*, Winter 2019; Kristina Douglass and
Jago Cooper, "Archaeology, environmental justice, and climate change on islands of the
Caribbean and southwestern Indian Ocean", in *Proceedings of the National Academy of
Sciences*, 2020, vol. 117, no. 15, pp. 8254–8262; Daniel M. Voskoboynik, "To Fix the
Climate Crisis, we must face up to our imperial past", *Open Democracy Net*, 8 October
2018 (available on its web site); and Alex Randall, "When climate change and history
spark violent conflict", *Climate Migration* (available on its web site).

[2] See, for example, Hussein A. Bulhan, "Stages of Colonialism in Africa: From Occupation
of Land to Occupation of Being", in *Journal of Social and Political Psychology*, 2015, vol.
3, no. 1, pp. 239–256, and Stephen Ocheni and Basil C. Nwankwo, "Analysis of Colonialism and Its Impact in Africa", in *Cross-Cultural Communication*, 2012, vol. 8, no. 3, pp.
46–54.

[3] Erin Blakemore, "What is Colonialism?", *National Geographic*, 19 February 2019 (available on its web site).

jects of law,[4] and resulted in the systematic destruction of habitats[5] hastening the breach of planetary boundaries.[6]

The legal norms and techniques for framing, articulating, demanding and seeking just satisfaction for these past crimes is yet to be fully developed. Yet, two contemporary factors lengthen the impact of these crimes, harming the prospect of a climate justice that pays adequate attention to peoples as well as the planet. The first is the determination of the climate lobby to tackle the loss of biodiversity by establishing 'protected areas' further extinguishing native title, and, crucially, removing the environment's traditional guardians from their territories, leaving them in the exclusive possession of sovereign States who have exacerbated their destruction.[7] The second, which directly implicates former colonial powers, is the continued support for protected areas, often funded by development funding pledges (0.7 per cent of Gross Domestic Product) despite lack of evidence that such a route encompasses environmental protection.[8]

This chapter seeks to address these issues, casting light on, first, the correlation between historical colonial activities and planetary destruction; second, emphasizing the regimes and techniques used to dispossess indigenous peoples, replacing them with commercial profit generating ventures in home (rather than host) country. This section will conclude by assessing the contemporary push towards 'protected areas', showing the causal relationship between this and the past practices. The chapter concludes by articulating a roadmap to achieve the twin goals of environmental protection and protection of indigenous peoples' rights. It also seeks to

---

[4] Russel Barsh, "Indigenous Peoples in the 1990s: From Object to Subject in International Law", in *Harvard Human Rights Law Journal*, 1994, vol. 7, pp. 33–86.

[5] Jeremie Gilbert, *Land Grabbing, Investments and Indigenous Peoples' Rights to Land and Natural Resources: Case Studies and Legal Analysis*, International Work Group for Indigenous Affairs Report 26, Copenhagen, 2017.

[6] Johan Rockstrom, Will Steffen, Kevin Noone and Asa Persson, "A Safe Operating Space for Humanity", in *Nature*, 2009, vol. 46, no. 1, pp. 472–475. For a collection of resources developed at the Stockholm Resilience Centre, see "Planetary boundaries research" (available on Stockholm Resilience Centre's web site).

[7] For background reading on 'protected areas', see Bram Büscher and Webster Whande, "Whims of the Winds of Time? Emerging Trends in Biodiversity Conservation and Protected Area Management", in *Conservation Society*, 2007, vol. 5, no. 1, pp. 22–43, and Dan Brockington, "Community Conservation, Inequality and Injustice: Myths of Power in Protected Area Management", in *Conservation Society*, 2004, vol. 2, no. 2, pp. 411–432.

[8] Joseph Murphy, *Environment and Imperialism: Why Colonialism Still Matters*, Sustainability Research Institute, University of Leeds, 2009, pp. 1–27.

highlight the specific duties and obligations upon the international society, commencing with former colonial powers, to achieve this reality, while offering insights into the specific legal tools and norms necessary to support this venture.

18.2. Colonial Crime and Environmental Degradation

In terms of the Law of Nations developed over centuries, the only territory that can be occupied is *terra nullius*.[9] As every scholar of public international law is well aware, unoccupied territory may be acquired via specific avenues. *Oppenheim's International Law* suggests a lack of unanimity among members of the international community *vis-à-vis* the modes of territorial acquisition. Yet standard textbooks often present this subject in definitive terms, despite the fact that the concept of State territory has changed considerably from the times of Grotius, through the Middle Ages, and to contemporary society.[10] Therefore:

> the acquisition of territory by a state normally means the acquisition of *sovereignty* over such territory. In these circumstances the Roman law scheme of "modes" concerning the acquisition of private property are no longer wholly appropriate.[11]

Irrespective of distinction between historical acquisition of territory, often based on private modes of acquisition, and contemporary acquisition of territory, usually occurring under greater international scrutiny, the modes of acquisition are still described in the same way in the annals of public international law, consisting:[12]

1. Cession: State acquisition of territory through transfer of sovereignty by 'owner state';[13]

---

[9] Joshua Castellino, "Territorial Integrity and the 'Right' to Self-determination: An Examination of the Conceptual Tools", in *Brooklyn Journal of International Law*, 2008, vol. 33, no. 2, pp. 503–568.

[10] Robert Jennings and Arthur Watts (eds.), *Oppenheim's International Law*, vol. 1, ninth edition, 1992, pp. 678–79.

[11] *Ibid., p.* 679.

[12] Ian Brownlie, *African Boundaries: A Legal and Diplomatic Encyclopaedia*, Oxford University Press, 1979 (providing a comprehensive view of the theory and practice behind the acquisition of African territory and boundaries in public international law).

[13] Robert Jennings, *The Acquisition of Territory in International Law*, Manchester University Press, 1963, pp. 16–19.

2. occupation: State appropriation of territory over which another is not sovereign;[14]

3. accretion: State acquisition of territory through natural or artificial formations, without violating another State's sovereignty;[15]

4. subjugation: State acquisition of territory through conquest and subsequent annexation, where war-making is a sovereign right, and not illegal;[16] and

5. prescription: State acquisition of territory through continuous and undisturbed exercise of sovereignty over the territory.[17]

Of these modes of acquisition, the two that are fundamental to understanding contemporary boundary disputes are occupation and subjugation, and the impact of this in determining the nexus between self-determination and the post-colonial territorial State. In any case, the underlying premise for this is nonetheless that the territory would have to be blank or unoccupied. When the question of what constitutes a test for this determination, the *Western Sahara Case* is worth quoting, to the effect that:

> It is [...] by reference to the law in force at that period that the legal concept of, *terra nullius* must be interpreted. In law, "occupation" was a means of peaceably acquiring sovereignty over territory otherwise than by cession or succession; it was a cardinal condition of a valid "occupation" that the territory should be *terra nullius*. According to the State practice of that time, territories inhabited by tribes or peoples having a social and political organization were not as *terrae nullius* in their case sovereignty was not generally considered as effected through occupation, but through agreements conclud-

---

[14] See, generally, Arthur S. Keller, Oliver J. Lissitzyn and Frederick J. Mann, *Creation of Rights of Sovereignty through Symbolic Acts 1400–1800*, Columbia University Press, New York, 1938.

[15] Jennings and Watts, 1992, pp. 696–98, see above note 10.

[16] Ian Brownlie, *International Law and the Use of Force by States*, Oxford University Press, 1963, pp. 112–22. See also International Court of Justice, *Application for Revision of the Judgment of 11 September 1992 in the Case Concerning the Land, Island and Maritime Frontier Dispute (El Salvador/Honduras: Nicaragua intervening) (El. Salvador v. Honduras)*, 18 December 2003, 2002 I.C.J. 392 (https://www.legal-tools.org/doc/2f08d7/) (illustrating a modern revision claim based on avulsion).

[17] Jennings and Watts, 1992, pp. 705–08, see above note 10 (reflecting the views of leading international jurists in the historical evolution of this concept).

---

ed with local rulers. The information furnished the court shows [...] that at the time of colonization western Sahara was inhabited by peoples which, if nomadic, were socially and politically organized in tribes and under chiefs competent to represent them.[18]

Thus, it was clearly no longer enough for the territory to be physically bereft of people, in addition, any people that may have inhabited it, ought to have been "socially and politically organised". This blatantly partisan interpretation, which justified *post facto* the spread and lawful (though not legitimate) acquisition of territory, was not a new direction of justification for international law. Ever since Roman law times, the bias has existed which has enabled power to create and interpret norms to suit themselves while offering them up as objective standards.[19] Thus, despite the existence of strong property rights regimes under Roman law, the only territory that could legitimately be acquired by the Roman Empire was territory that was non-Roman.[20] The justification given pertained to racist assumptions about whether non-Romans could be considered 'human enough' to warrant their presence on a territory as 'rights earning'.[21] This trend of course continued well into the colonial era, paving the way for Spanish and Portuguese occupation of 'the New World' legitimised by Papal Bulls and the Treaty or Tordesillas which sought 'equitable' division of land neither possessed between the parties.[22] It was germane to the British Crown's acquisition of territories in the Pacific,[23] with the Treaty

[18] International Court of Justice, Western Sahara, Advisory Opinion, 16 October 1975, 1975 I.C.J. 12, p. 39 (https://www.legal-tools.org/doc/512a2a/).

[19] For a fascinating discussion in a highly cited and well-respected legal text that shows the colonial bias that existed in international law at the time, see Mark F. Lindley, *The Acquisition and Government of Backward Territories in International Law*, Longmans, Green and Co, New York, 1926.

[20] See Mohammed Bedjaoui, *Terra Nullius, 'Droits' Historiques et Autodétermination*, Exposés oraux prononcés devant la Cour Internationale de Justice en l'affaire du Sahara Occidental, La Haye, 1975.

[21] In a Native American context see, for instance, Robert Strausz-Hupé, *Geopolitics: The Struggle for Space and Power*, G.P. Putnam's Sons, New York, 1942; Gregory H. Nobles, "Breaking into the Backcountry: New Approaches to the Early American Frontier, 1750–1800", in *The William and Mary Quarterly*, 1989, vol. 46, no. 4, pp. 641–70.

[22] This is explored in great detail in Cathal Doyle, *Indigenous Peoples, Title to Territory, Rights and Resources: The Transformative Role of Free Prior and Informed Consent*, Routledge, London, 2014.

[23] See Joshua Castellino and David P. Keane, *Minority Rights in the Pacific: A Comparative Legal Analysis*, Oxford University Press, 2009.

of Waitangi as a stand out piece of trickery,[24] even in a playbook littered with dastardly cheating that has never been fully acknowledged to date.

The story of the illegitimate colonial acquisition of land, peoples, resources, wealth and power is only mutedly acknowledged. Consider for instance the extent to which all the great textbooks of public international law reflect on this in their chapters on title to territory. When entertained at all, quick reference is made to the *intertemporal rule of law* considered sufficient in foreclosing further discussion.[25] While that rule may use contemporary legal tenets of dubious value to eliminate questions of reparations, the failure to discuss illegality of acquisitions themselves in educating new international lawyers suggests tacit acceptance of wrongdoing.

Yet while awareness of the illegality of acquisition of territory is known, though ignored or met with knowing glances of 'oh *that* old argument', the nexus between colonial rule and climate change is underexplored. The salience of ignoring this reiterates avoidance of liability ascription for past actions whose tort is being felt most acutely in the present. The rest of this section seeks to highlight five ways in which colonial regimes contributed and continue to contribute to climate change. These are:

1. illegal dispossession of climate guardians;
2. wilful destruction of 'circular economies';
3. facilitation of commercial exploitation;
4. the drive for over-consumption; and
5. sustaining unsustainability.

It could be argued that the starting point for the route to the current climate crisis arose with the treatment of non-Europeans as objects rather than subjects. 'Europeans' did not of course invent colonization or its underlying cruelty, which have existed through history. Indeed, global history is narrated almost exclusively through the process by which one tribe, or 'nation' sought to extend their sovereignty over another, acquiring their lands and spreading their power. In instances as different as the Mongol

---

24 See Nan Seuffert, "Colonising Concepts of the Good Citizen, Law's Deceptions, and the Treaty of Waitangi", in *Law Text Culture*, 1998, vol. 4, no. 2, pp. 69–104.
25 For a detailed discussion of this, see Joshua Castellino and Stephen Allen, *Title to Territory in International Law: An Intertemporal Analysis*, Ashgate, 2005.

invasions,[26] and the rise and spread of the Ottoman Empire,[27] many lives were lost with atrocities perpetrated that were similar to those perpetrated later or simultaneously by European powers.

Yet where European colonization differed from others is captured in the motto of the 'three Cs': Civilization, Christianity and Commerce.[28] While the first two were common – many hegemons used the idea of their cultural superiority as an internal spur to justify brutal subjugation, and many justified actions by the ostensible need to 'save ignorant human beings from their heathen fates'. Though the religion or ideology may have differed, it was in the third 'C' that European colonization differed significantly.

While all empire building processes involve theft, European colonization involved theft on a scale rarely before witnessed. Thus, unlike raids from Persia to India in the twelfth century that took wealth back to Ghazni[29] (today conveniently cited by some in India to justify Islamophobia),[30] European colonization used laws as a weapon to establish sovereignty with a view to establishing a process to systematically extract resources. When indigenous guardians resisted, they were dispossessed through force,[31] captured as indentured labourers to work on plantations elsewhere, or simply incorporated into new economies set up to absorb them as unskilled workers.[32]

---

[26] See, for example, James Chambers, *The Devil's Horsemen: The Mongol's Invasion of Europe*, Phoenix Press, 2001 and more generally John J. Saunders, *The History of the Mongol Conquests*, University of Pennsylvania Press, Pittsburgh, 2001.

[27] Jem Duducu, *The Sultans: The Rise and Fall of the Ottoman Empire and Their World – A 600 Year History*, Amberley Publishing, 2018.

[28] For more, see Henry C. Carey, *Commerce, Christianity and Civilization versus British Free Trade: Letters in Reply to the London Times*, Franklin Classics, 2018.

[29] See Muhammad Nazim, *The Life and Times of Sultan Mahmud of Ghazna*, Cambridge University Press, 1931.

[30] For early propaganda that predates the modern 'debate' on this issue, see this text by a member of the *Rashtriya Sevak Sangh*, Sita Ram Goel, *The Story is Islamic Imperialism in India*, Voice of India, New Delhi, 1982.

[31] See, for instance, Markus B. Heyder, "International Law Commission's Draft Articles on State Responsibility: Draft Article 19 and Native American Self-Determination", in *Columbia Journal of Transnational Law*, 1994, vol. 32, no. 1, pp. 155–178.

[32] Andrei Twibell, "Rethinking Johnson v McIntosh (1823): The Root of the Continued Forced Displacement of American Indians Despite Cobell v. Norton (2001)", in *Georgetown Immigration Law Journal*, 2008, vol. 23, no. 1, pp. 129–200.

This facilitated the second facet that links colonial crime to contemporary environmental destruction. The newly acquired indigenous lands became 'available' for the instigation of a new emerging economy. This involved acquisition of any discernible wealth in the now less occupied territories, and its exploitation for export. Thus, when King Leopold of Belgium saw the untouched Congo Basin,[33] he looked past the indigenous forest dwelling peoples, the *Batwa*, and instead saw vast strands of wood that could change the dimension of Belgian and subsequently European furniture industry.[34] Similarly, the British in an attempt to quell reliance on Chinese tea that was negatively impacting the balance of trade between the Chinese and British Empires,[35] saw fit, after the failure of arguing free trade to justify the sale of opium to China,[36] to turn the Himalayan slopes in what is modern North-Eastern India into a large scale tea garden,[37] destroying the existing fauna and also completely changing the regional lifestyles.[38] That the Democratic Republic of the Congo and India still rely on these activities to sustain their economies shows how long-lasting and continuing the impact of destroying the circular economies was.[39] Equally, as in colonial rule, it shows how this exploitation does not generate wealth for the areas, but creates subsistence economies where the extracted resource was not valued until much higher up in the supply chain, and then only to generate profits for the corporations that exploit it.

That supply chain, and especially the private interests that benefitted from it, were a key component of this form of exploitation. It is not by

---

[33] Deanna M. Wolfire, Jake Brunner and Nigel Sizer, *Forests and the Democratic Republic of Congo: Opportunity in a Time of Crisis*, World Resources Institute, Forest Frontiers Initiative, Washington, DC, 1998.

[34] Adam Hochschild, *King Leopold's Ghost: A Story of Greed, Terror and Heroism in Colonial Africa*, Houghton Mifflin Publishers, 1998.

[35] See Andrew B. Liu, *Tea War: A History of Capitalism in China and India*, Yale University Press, New Haven, 2020.

[36] Stephen R. Platt, *Imperial Twilight: The Opium War and the End of China's Last Golden Age*, Atlantic Books, 2019.

[37] See, for example, Utpal Kumar De, "How Successful is India's Look East Policy Under Globalisation?", in Soumyendra Kishore Datta and Atanu Sengupta (eds.), *Development, Environment and Sustainable Livelihood*, Cambridge Scholars Publishing, 2014, pp. 148–172.

[38] Patrick Oskarsson, *Landlock: Paralysing Dispute over Minerals on Adivasi Land in India*, Australian National University Press, Canberra, 2018.

[39] Bernard Waites, *Europe and the Third World: From Colonisation to Decolonisation, c. 1500-1998*, Palgrave Macmillan Springer, New York, 1999.

accident that a significant part of Britain's global exploitation was under the guise of the East India Company.[40] Irrespective of the other two 'Cs', it was really the pursuit of wealth that remained a common thread through European colonization. Despite the racist rhetoric in its dismissal of other forms of social interaction, the 'civilising' aspect also sought to spread Enlightenment Era ideas concerning the rule of law. These more progressive strands were accompanied but often dominated by the quest for profit, which saw private enterprise ride and often lead the mission with a view to commandeering vast resources that remain at the heart of contemporary European wealth, and especially in its domination of global trade. It has taken two full of centuries of relatively uncontested domination encompassing the growth of multinational firms with long supply chains in a range of industries from sanitary and phytosanitary products to hard engineering. *En route*, Europe pioneered the deadly arms industry that dominated wealth generation creating a private-public partnership that is key to maintaining hegemony while perpetrating injustices and profiting from distance.[41] In the course of this process, Europe, with its ally the United States of America dominated by European immigrants adhering to European values, has been central to the erection of an unfair trading system that pays scant attention to the raw values of materials, ensuring that they start adding value dramatically once they enter jurisdictions of Organisation for Economic Co-operation and Development ('OECD') countries, furthering global inequality. At a macro level, post-colonial States have had little choice but to participate, and within those States this has spurred significant marginalization of indigenous peoples as State-driven or private entities relying on State patronage, have profited in place of former colonial rulers, while indigenous (and other) territories within the State are stripped of resources. Ironically, the significant competition that has emerged from China, and to a lesser extent from Russia, India and Brazil has furthered this model, with Chinese economic ascendance following similar patterns of external domination for resources, without the accompanying missions of Civilisation and Christianization (or its equivalent).[42]

---

[40] See William Dalrymple, *The Anarchy: The Relentless Rise of the East India Company*, Bloomsbury Books, London, 2019.

[41] Paul Cornish, *The Arms Trade and Europe*, Chatham House Papers, Royal Institute of International Affairs, London, 1995.

[42] Elizabeth C. Economy, *The Third Revolution: Xi Jinping and the New Chinese State*, Oxford University Press, 2018.

The fourth factor in this domination is a crucial component to the current environmental crisis. The stimulation of demand 'at home' through a private public partnership that ensured a steady and at times it seemed insatiable thirst for products. With improving technology it was possible to generate longer lasting, sturdier goods, but instead technologies veered towards creating products of lower durability, pursuing a 'use and dispose' idea stimulating bulk exploitation and manufacturing.[43] At the commencement of the industrial revolution in Europe, this brought welcome jobs, spurring economic growth, spreading wealth beyond investors, and then contributing momentum towards economic growth by demand and spending stimulation. However, as technology grew and as the 'worth' of human capital rose, the manufacturing that dominated European economies began to seek cheaper bases for production. This early optimistic phase of globalization appeared to equalise the global economy as formerly poor countries benefitted from external investment into their economies. This trend continues, but two factors are hastening its demise: the improvement of technology which makes human labour too expensive compared to machines, and resistance to jobs leaving OECD shores as unemployment grows. In developing countries, this trend replicates pre-Industrial Revolution inequalities in Europe as a class of entrepreneurs emerge with incredible wealth, who can generate ever greater wealth without having to factor in a return to human labour. The modern global economy can thus be characterised as automated: movement and reinvestment of capital can create high returns, with no trickle down to employment, or where it does exist, to fair wages. The consequence is an angry global politics and a clearer distinction between the haves and have-nots. The significant investment by global oligarchs in media and communication companies enables old-fashioned control of propaganda disguised as 'fact',[44] concerted attack on human rights to undermine calls for accountability and fairness,[45] and a successful quest for political power to maintain hegemony.[46] This stands in sharp contrast and is near diametri-

---

[43] See Nicholas Stern, *The Economics of Climate Change: The Stern Review*, Cambridge University Press, 2014.

[44] Melissa Zimdars and Kembrew McLeod, *Fake News: Understanding Media and Misinformation in a Digital Age*, MIT Press, Ann Arbor, 2020.

[45] Assisted by internal critique which played into the hands of critics. For more, see Elvira Domínguez Redondo, *The Politicization of Human Rights: The UN Special Procedures*, Oxford University Press, 2020.

[46] See Patrick Porter, *The False Promise of Liberal Order*, Polity Press, Cambridge, 2020.

cally opposite to circular indigenous economies that relied on sustainable practices, did not seek to stimulate demand and in particular, had a respect for natural resources and their ability to regenerate, of near spiritual proportions.

Finally, despite the claim that colonial crimes took place long ago and that statutes of limitations put them beyond the realm of contemporary law, the fact is that the tort from these activities has been slower to be realised, and they extend into the current period through maintenance of structures that continue to damage. As the climate justice movement has grown, it has highlighted many of the facets that are being discussed here. At its heart lies the obvious antidote: reduce consumption, generate solutions at scale to specific environmental issues, discourage, reduce, ban or tax the quest for unjustifiable profits and reflect the *real* cost (including of regeneration) of natural resources into product supply chains. The nexus between governance and commerce, so long in the making in European colonization is now 'decentralised', with nearly every country in the globe harnessing its own domesticized creamy layer of wealth, in nearly all cases gained through exploitation of indigenous peoples and their territories. As a consequence, environmental governance has become a useful rhetoric, but in nearly every case the policies implemented remain fig-leaves for what is really needed. Pushed into a corner by civil society about the lack of action, a new drive has emerged which has its essence in an old colonial practice: the creation of strict targets around protected areas, discussed in the next section.

18.3. Decolonizing Law: The Hand-Maiden to Colonization

There is a quote attributed to Martin Luther King (though its origins are older) that "the arc of the moral universe is long but it bends towards justice", replicated in the idea that international law has been the gentle civiliser of nations.[47] The evidence for this seems compelling: the growth of human rights law, especially over the last century has yielded greater freedoms, seen increased inclusivity, eradicated (at least in law) egregious crimes such as genocide, crimes against humanity, torture and slavery. The rule of law has become a cornerstone to legal systems, and equality and non-discrimination have ascended the hierarchy of norms to take centre stage.

---

[47] Martii Koskenniemi, *The Gentle Civilizer of Nations: The Rise and Fall of International Law 1870-1960*, Cambridge University Press, 2009.

From an indigenous peoples' perspective, these developments never had the same reach towards societies, paid mere lip service to destruction of communities, lands and cultures, and seem in large part, with notable exceptions in some courts and jurisdictions, to actively resist calls to design methods to address historical and present injustices.

18.3.1. Legal Reification of Colonial Injustice

The law, legal institutions and structures seem content to articulate and finesse articulation of progressive norms, taking little responsibility for their implementation and realisation (those were questions for politics and policy making to address apparently). There was no awareness or teaching of the extent to which law has been a hand-maiden to legitimization of colonial enterprises or its failure in reigning in absolute power. Rather it appears to have worked as a 'gentleman's agreement' emphasizing values of decency and moderation which had no answers when political power was seized by those unwilling to play within that 'gentleman's agreement'. This section articulates six key legal themes whose violation heightened the impact of colonial regimes, ending with a sub-section on protected areas that epitomises why and how colonization is a current phenomenon.

1. Impact of the global territorial regimes: As emphasized above, the failure to recognise the personhood of indigenous peoples lies at the heart of the colonial project.[48] Not only did the violation of the principle of *terra nullius* dispossess swathes of populations outside Europe, it contributed to the disruption of their legitimacy to exist as autonomous entities. While United Nations ('UN') inspired and sponsored decolonization yielded an optically less 'White' world, the rules, especially *uti possidetis juris*,[49] constrained modification to the emerging territorial entities. The rule, derived from Roman Law, was originally articulated by the Praetor to determine the possession of movable goods contested by rival claimants. Extended to decolonization in Latin America, it sought to foreclose issues of boundary disputes between rival offspring of colonial rulers in a bid to avoid the

---

[48] For an interesting perspective on this in a US context, see Hannah White, "Indigenous Peoples, The International Trend towards Legal Personhood for Nature and the United States", in *American Indian Law Review*, vol. 43, no. 1, 2018, pp. 129–166.

[49] Joshua Castellino, "Territorial Integrity and the 'Right' to Self-Determination: An Examination of the Conceptual Tools", in *Brooklyn Journal of International Law*, 2008, pp. 503–568.

---

spiralling of territorial disputes.[50] Of course even though that decolonization was famed as an extension of Enlightenment Era oriented
principles of consent, it did not factor consent of indigenous peoples,
who were treated as chattel handed from one colonial power to another.[51] When extended to Africa and Asia, the overt racial dimensions appeared better respected, but only at a distance. To local populations the quest for decolonization was instigated, voiced and delivered by communities relatively close to the colonial power. These
communities, usually dominant (in either numbers or proximity to
power) ethnic, linguistic or religious groups, claimed to be legitimate
spokespeople for all the population and in some cases made wide out-
reaches to marginalized communities to support the quest to rid
'White foreigners' from the lands. Externally this legitimized them as
new rulers, welcomed into international society as such, while often
occupying the very palaces and governing seats of the departing rulers. The external rules around the sanctity of borders[52] discouraged
adjustments between different colonial entities, and their ascendance
to notions of sovereignty meant that dissent with regards to their legitimacy could be stemmed.[53] In more 'successful' post-colonial
States the superficial adoption of a multiculturalist unified 'national'
narrative appeased those with historical claims for resumption of
their own sovereignty, previously suppressed by the arrival of colonial rule. The promising notion of self-determination, articulated by the
twin UN declarations in 1960,[54] was reduced to consisting of, at best,

---

[50] Joshua Castellino and Steve Allen, "The Doctrine of *Uti Possidetis*: Crystallisation of
Modern Post-Colonial Identity", in *German Yearbook of International Law*, 2000, vol. 43,
pp. 205–226.

[51] See, more generally, James Anaya, *Indigenous Peoples in International Law*, Oxford University Press, 2004.

[52] Garth Abraham, "Lines upon Maps: Africa and the Sanctity of African Boundaries", in
African Journal of International and Comparative Law, 2007, vol. 15, no. 1, pp. 61–84.

[53] See the work of Robert Jackson which was unfairly criticised at the time, but is particular-
ly salient in examining the track records of post-colonial states: Robert Jackson, *Quasi-
States: Sovereignty, International Relations and the Third World*, Cambridge University
Press, 1990.

[54] As evidenced by two general Assembly Resolutions on the subject, namely Declaration on
the Granting of Independence to Colonial Countries and Peoples, UN Doc.
A/Res/1514(XV), 14 December 1960 (https://www.legal-tools.org/doc/5de655/), and Principles which should guide Members in determining whether or not an obligation exists to
transmit the information called for under Article 73e of the Charter, UN Doc.
A/RES/1541(XV), 15 December 1960 (https://www.legal-tools.org/doc/hqlf9y/). This was

an internal call for autonomy within existing State structures (internal self-determination).[55] This was sold as good for order, highlighted as the best chance for the claimed unity in the colonial struggle to bear real fruits, or simply forcibly enforced against dissenters. The principle of *jus resistendi ac seccionis* (the right to resistance),[56] powerful rhetoric against the White colonial rule, was almost dismissed, a trend that continues to this day accompanied by the widespread use of powerful anti-terrorism laws.

2. Treaty making: The subterfuge of Cecil Rhodes in hoodwinking the Shona King[57] and the unscrupulous officials who deliberately misinterpreted the Treaty of Waitangi[58] English translation are often forgotten footnotes to history. But the notion of unequal treaties – unfair at the outset, imposed through power, based on what today would be called fake facts with only a thin veneer of accountability while being dressed up and celebrated as law worthy of veneration – have remained the norm.[59] Names such as Balfour, Picot, Sykes and Durrand, all key boundary makers of now sovereign States, sit in archives of global history, with little commentary of their impact on modern statehood or the extent to which they effectively sought to maintain European hegemony over lands they felt entitled to. The Black Lives Movement, as a call to consciousness, ought to elicit greater scrutiny

---

subsequently strengthened in the Declaration on the Principles of International law Governing Friendly Relations and Co-operation among States in accordance with the Charter of the United Nations, UN Doc. A/RES/2625(XXV), 24 October 1970 (https://www.legal-tools.org/doc/5039aa/).

[55] Joshua Castellino, "Conceptual Difficulties and the 'Right' to Indigenous Self-Determination", in Nazila Ghanea and Alexandra Xanthaki (eds.), *Minorities, Peoples and Self-Determination*, Martinus Nijhoff, 2004, pp. 55–74.

[56] Gwilym D. Blunt, "Is There a Human Right to Resistance?", in *Human Rights Quarterly*, 2017, vol. 39, no. 4, pp. 860–881.

[57] See Robert I. Rotberg, *The Founder: Cecile Rhodes and the Pursuit of Power*, Oxford University Press, 1988.

[58] Nan Seuffert, "Contract, Consent and Imperialism in New Zealand's Founding Narrative", in *Australia and New Zealand Law and History*, 2015, vol. 2, pp. 1–31; Valmaine Toki, "Tikanga Maori: A Constitutional Right – A Case Study", in *Commonwealth Law Bulletin*, 2014, vol. 40, no. 1, pp. 32–48; Janet McLean, "Crown, Empire and Redressing the Historical Wrongs of Colonisation in New England", in *New Zealand Law Review*, 2015, no. 2, pp. 187–212.

[59] Charles H. Alexandrowicz, "The Role of Treaties in the European-African Confrontation in the Nineteenth Century (1975)", in David Armitage and Jennifer Pitts (eds.), *The Law of Nations in Global History*, Oxford University Press, 2017.

---

not only of these individuals and what drove them, but of the tacit support and effective silence of the entire edifice of international law, in condoning and even celebrating these 'achievements'.

3. Property rights: At macro level, the principle of self-determination, especially as driven by the UN and that led to decolonization, was an attempt to redress colonial violations that stemmed from failures to respect ancestral domain of indigenous peoples in the decision to uni-laterally designate their lands as *terra nullius*. Self-determination has, depending on perspectives, been hailed as a norm of *jus cogens*,[60] or admonished as "a political tenet of uncertain legal value".[61] In any case, at the root of the principle of self-determination lie two en-trenched principles: the legitimacy of the need for people to consent to their fate, and the duty in law, to create mechanisms to respect and implement that decision. Crucial to that first principle was the return of lands and territories, seized without the consent of 'the people' back to them. There are of course several potential contradictions in the doctrine of self-determination that have been highlighted in what is likely to be the most written about area of international law: who are the people, the conflict with territorial autonomy, the modalities of self-determination, whether it is a continuous right, whether it is a right at all, whether it is politics by other means, whether it ought to be crystallised further or left deliberately amorphous. Yet at the heart of this discussion lies the implicit belief that self-determination as achieved against the former colonial State did not extend to discus-sions of how that incoming power ought to respect the property rights that were violated. Discussions of land remain at the heart of the poli-tics of many post-colonial States, with well represented arguments concerning the return of ancestral domain.[62] Yet, the issue of the tort

---

[60] As reviewed in Matthew Saul, "The Normative Status of Self-Determination in Interna-tional Law: A Formula for Uncertainty in the Scope and Content of the Rights", in *Human Rights Law Review*, 2011, vol. 11, no. 4, pp. 609–644.

[61] Steven R. Ratner, "Drawing a Better Line: *Uti Possidetis* and the Borders of New States", in *American Journal of International Law*, 1996, vol. 90, no. 4, p. 590.

[62] See, for example, Valmaine Toki, "Adopting a Maori Property Rights Approach to Fisher-ies", in *New Zealand Journal of Environmental Law*, 2010, vol. 14, pp. 197–222; Ross Levine, "Law, Endowments and Property Rights", in *Journal of Economic Perspectives*, 2005, vol. 19, no. 3, pp. 61–88; Robert Home, "'Culturally Unsuited to Property Rights?' Colonial Land Laws and African Societies", in *Journal of Law and Society*, 2013, vol. 40, no. 3, pp. 403–419; Brian D. Thom, "Reframing Indigenous Territories: Private Property,

of property rights remains in its infancy despite some stirring jurisprudence from courts and tribunals.[63]

4. 'Free trade': Despite an avowed interest driven by the economic ideology that free trade can create benefits for all,[64] the world global
trading system has not been set up on the grounds of equity.[65] Raw
materials extracted in indigenous territory still gain a fraction of the
return due, especially taking into account the opportunity cost they
have in terms of the environment. In addition, while there have been
developments on the free movements of goods and services, this has
been skewed heavily to benefit the richer nations, building their
wealth, ensuring that they have the right to both 'invest' in new ventures in indigenous lands and extract the bulk of the profits that might
result from such a venture. While there have been successful negotiations protecting certain realms of free trade to benefit strong countries,[66] there has been no attempt to regulate spread around harmful
goods and services such as the proliferation of arms (see below).
Even the attempt to prevent nuclear proliferations is heavily skewed
on the basis that the countries that have such weapons will act reasonably.[67] Political motivations of the powerful States have ensured
that the free movement of labour, which would result in significant
migration are severely restricted based on national interest. The con-

---

Human Rights and Overlapping Claims", in *American Indian Cultural Research Journal*,
2014, vol. 38, no. 4, pp. 3–28.

[63] See, for example, High Court of Australia, *Mabo v. Queensland (No 2)*, Judgment, 3 June
1992, (1992) 175 CLR 1; African Commission on Human and Peoples' Rights, *Centre for
Minority Rights Development v. Kenya*, Communication 267/2003, 25 November 2009
(https://www.legal-tools.org/doc/7201ce/); Inter-American Court of Human Rights, *Case
of Xakmok Kasek Indigenous Community v. Paraguay*, Judgment, 24 August 2010
(https://www.legal-tools.org/doc/d50c89/); Inter-American Court of Human Rights, *Kaliña
and Lokono Peoples v. Suriname*, Judgment, 25 November 2015; African Court on Human
and Peoples' Rights, *African Commission on Human and Peoples' Rights v. Republic of
Kenya*, Judgment, 26 May 2017. Also see Supreme Court of India, *Wildlife First v. Union
of India*, Judgment, 12 February 2019, Writ of Petition(s) (Civil) No(s). 109/2008.

[64] See Graham Dunkley, *Free Trade: Myths Realities and Alternatives*, The University Press,
Dhaka, 2004 (Zed Books, London, 2004).

[65] Dani Rodrick, *The Globalization Paradox: Why Global Markets, States and Democracies
Can't Coexist*, Oxford University Press, 2011.

[66] See M. Ataman Aksoy and John C. Beghin, *Global Agricultural Trade and Developing
Countries*, World Bank, Washington, DC, 2005.

[67] See William Potter and Gaukhar Mukhatzhanova, *Nuclear Politics and the Non-Aligned
Movement*, Routledge, London, 2017.

---

sequence of these actions adds to the already significant competitive advantage of corporations from European and allied countries who have been involved in indigenous territories over centuries, operating as near monopolies in those economies.[68]

5. The tacit and explicit support for armed conflict: The world's former colonial countries are overrepresented in the top five producers and exporters of arms.[69] Despite attempts to seek to regulate this trade,[70] their engagement in a bruising battle against each other to manufacture and sell arms has played a significant role in fostering instability and furthering the interests of the former colonial power in the country of their influence. Decolonization left significant existential threats to the fledgling post-independent State, not least because of the failure to pay adequate attention to contestations within the freedom struggles. Many of these were born out of direct colonial actions including the self-interested carving of territories dividing peoples and communities, the agglomeration of antagonistic communities within a single administrative unit,[71] the attempt to use divide and rule policies to maintain their hegemony, the failure to achieve decolonisation through a wide enough dialogue, and the signing of preferential agreements, often with both potential parties to a dispute, to supply weapons to cope with real and imagined foes. This strategy generated significant wealth in former colonial countries, sewed uncertainties and divisions sometimes creating a febrile atmosphere with devastating effects in their former colony that continue as a tort. The failure of any emerging regime to tackle the manufacture, sale and proliferation of all kinds of weapons is not only indicative of the kind of 'free trade' aspired to, as typified in the Opium Wars of the

---

[68] Judy Shelton, "The Case for a New International Monetary System", in *Cato Journal*, 2018, vol. 38, no. 2, pp. 379–390.

[69] Andrew Feinstein, *The Shadow World: Inside the Global Arms Trade*, Farrar, Straus and Giroux, 2011.

[70] See Yasuhito Fukui, "The Arms Trade Treaty: Pursuit for the Effective Control of Arms Transfer", in *Journal of Conflict and Security Law*, 2015, vol. 20, no. 2, pp. 301–322.

[71] Lord Salisbury, speaking to the British House of Lords in 1890, stated: "We have been engaged in drawing lines on maps where no white man's foot ever trod; we have been giving away mountains and rivers and lakes to each, only hindered by the small impediment that we never knew where the mountains and rivers and lakes were". As quoted by Judge Ajibola, International Court of Justice, *Libya v. Chad (Territorial Dispute)*, 3 February 1994, ICJ Reports (1994) 6, p. 53 (https://www.legal-tools.org/doc/054332/).

1800s; it lies at the heart of the abdication of responsibility that the UN Security Council ('UNSC'), responsible for threats to the peace, ought to have had custodianship of, but could not due to the extent to which the permanent members were deeply implicated in generating the threats to the peace.[72]

6. Adjudication of global regimes of law: While the emergence of greater accountability and participation at international level has been significant since the commencement of the UN, two of the former colonial players have retained their pre-eminent role in global regimes of law-making with permanent membership of the UNSC, as mentioned above. This dominance is replicated in key bodies connected with the development and global adjudication of emerging regimes. Thus, the International Court of Justice (until the recent defeat of the UK candidate in an election), the Human Rights Council, the Green Room of the World Trade Organisation, the World Bank, the International Monetary Fund and other leading international organisations are still driven directly and often blatantly by the interests of former colonial powers and their allies. This has not only squeezed out other potentially more progressive European powers who may be keen to develop more equitable global regimes; they have created an environment where the pursuit of national interest continues to drive the agenda forward in the name of the use of expertise thereby weakening both the quality and the legitimacy of global institutions.

18.3.2. The Contemporary Case of 'Protected Areas'

The attempt to seek to protect biodiversity through designating up to thirty per cent of the globe as 'protected areas'[73] is synonymous not only of the continuing legacy of colonial activities, but their ability to generate damage in a contemporary context.

The ostensible justification that drives this objective is uncontested.[74] The proclivity towards profit-making driven by human greed has, mainly in the form of logging of forests and extraction of minerals in bio

---

[72] See Lyndal Rowlands, "UN Security Council Seats Taken by Arms Exporters", *Inter Press Service*, 28 November 2016 (available on its web site).

[73] For the aspiration, explanation and statements on Protected Areas, see "About", *International Union for Conservation of Nature* (available on its web site).

[74] For more on impact of climate change on biodiversity, see "Climate Change", *International Union for Conservation of Nature* (available on its web site).

diverse areas, depleted the globe's flora and fauna to a point of no return for some species.[75] Spiralling human population growth has been a significant contributing factor to this demise with the exponential spread of human settlements into previously untouched areas, signally devastating contact for biodiversity.[76]

In an attempt to seek to bring in much needed protection against the further loss of biodiversity some climate scientists in conjunction with large scale conservation civil society organisations with the support of significant sections of civil society have sought to throw, what in their view is a protective ring around the remaining biodiversity, seeking to safeguard this from further harm.[77] Under this theory ensuring that some parts of the globe can thrive as wilderness is key to off-setting carbon emissions and curbing the widespread destruction that has occurred across the globe from human activity. The proposal currently being considered is that 30 per cent of the globe will consist such 'protected areas'. Expressed against an overt anthroposcenic domination that has assumed that the world's resources should be exclusively available to human consumption, this policy ought to be lauded at face value.

However, significant problems exist with it. First the areas that would immediately come under such protection, which are truly rich in biodiversity are almost exclusively the homes and territories of indigenous peoples.[78] The policy would require and justify their eviction, reducing them to penury on the edges of peri-urban areas. Though many of these communities existed in pre-colonial times, their 'ownership' of the lands has often not been documented according to any colonial or post-

---

[75] Meron Tekalign, Koenraad van Meerbeek, Raf Aerts, Lindsey Norgrove, Jean Poesen, Jan Nyssen, and Bart Muys, "Effects of biodiversity loss and restoration scenarios on tree-related ecosystem services", in *International Journal on Biodiversity Science, Ecosystem Services and Management*, 2017, vol. 13, no. 1, pp. 434–443.

[76] Hannes Weber and Jennifer D. Sciubba, "The Effect of Population Growth on the Environment: Evidence from European Regions", in *European Journal on Population*, 2019, vol. 35, no. 2, pp. 379–402

[77] Jaime R. Garcia Marquez, Tobias Krueger, Carlos A. Paez *et al.*, "Effectiveness of conservation areas for protecting biodiversity and ecosystem services: a multi-criteria approach", in *International Journal of Biodiversity Science, Ecosystem Services and Management*, 2016, vol. 13, no. 1, pp. 1–13.

[78] Dan Brockington, "Community Conservation, Inequality and Injustice: Myths of Power in Protected Area Management", in *Conservation and Society*, 2004, vol. 2, no. 2, pp. 411–432.

colonial lexicon, and they are thus simply treated as illegal settlers who can be removed without compensation.[79] But even this egregious human rights violation is only a small part of the problem.

Indigenous peoples, in their traditions and lifestyles have often acted as the planet's *guardians* over millennia.[80] They have not been responsible for large scale biodiversity loss, but have instead been calling this out regularly over the last century as 'settled' ways of life first visited, (uninvited), before going on to dominate their lands on a permanent basis. They have sought to find ways to continue to live in harmony with nature, including by utilising the benefits of their environs, in a sustainable manner that promotes regeneration. Thus, the second, more crucial problem with this strategy from the perspective of the protection of biodiversity and the environment, is that it removes from the site of its greatest necessity, the traditional knowledge gained from living in close proximity with nature. The rampaging fires in Aboriginal areas in Australia is a clear manifestation of this. Aboriginal Australian knowledge gained over centuries and passed down through generations orally, has always understood the importance of using controlled fires to clear debris from the floor of the forest. Western scientific models preached that fires in the forest would create environmental damage and so they were banned, with the community told that their bushfires were (another) sign of their primitiveness. When the fires flared in January 2020, the flames lived off the forest debris to spread across Australia, destroying 12.1 million hectares and annihilating forest life.[81] The discarding of local knowledge on the basis of a science that has been poorly equipped to seek to understand traditional knowledge, and whose doors have often, through direct and indirect dis-

---

[79] M.D. Madhusudan, "Of Rights and Wrongs: Wildlife Conservation and the Tribal Bill", in *Economic and Political Weekly*, 2005, vol. 40, no. 47, pp. 4893–4895.

[80] Victoria Tauli-Corpuz, Janis Alcorn and Augusta Molnar, "Cornered by Protected Areas: Replacing 'Fortress' Conservation With Rights-Based Approaches Helps Bring Justice for Indigenous Peoples and Local Communities, Reduces Conflict, and Enables Cost-Effective Conservation and Climate Action", *Cornered by Protected Areas*, Rights and Resources Initiative, Washington, DC, 2018 (available on its web site); Alain Frechette, Katie Reytar, S. Saini and Wayne Walker, "Toward a Global Baseline of Carbon Storage in Collective Lands: An Updated Analysis of Indigenous Peoples' and Local Communities' Contributions to Climate Change Mitigation", *Rights and Resources Initiative*, Washington, DC, 2016 (available on its web site); Liz Alden Wily, "Collective Land Ownership in the 21st Century: Overview of Global Trends", in *Land*, 2018, vol. 7, no. 2, p. 68;

[81] Pierre Wiart, "Australia Bushfires: A New Normal?", *RMS*, 10 January 2020 (available on its web site).

crimination, been closed to members of these communities contributed to that devastation. The 'protected areas' scheme regularises this marginalisation at the cost of the environment, in the name of the environment.[82]

A third significant problem looms into the future. As developing countries continue to seek growth while coping with the world's unequal trading systems, they are likely to increasingly rely on their natural resources. With indigenous peoples out of the way (they have presented formidable obstacles to date), the well-established nexus between the State and corporations who it can license to generate national growth will become centre-stage. Many indigenous communities have witnessed this phenomenon at scale, and while the 'protected areas' schemes might create a strong international legislative backdrop against such practice, the lack of enforcement measures against States that exploit these is likely to be as weak as other global governing regimes. The result is a continuation and reification of a colonial practice.[83] This time, the post-colonial State will be in the driving seat; the former colonial economies will access benefits at a price only slightly higher than in the past. For indigenous peoples the outcome will be the same; for biodiversity and the planet it will fatally increase current precarities.

Current research shows that there have been significant actors, with dubious credentials that have been engaged in, and that benefit from the 'protected areas' scheme. Chief among these is the World Wildlife Fund, known across the world for its protection of biodiversity, but less known for its links to organised businesses that have profited out of nature.[84] An ongoing internal investigation into its role in the funding of eco-guards who have been accused of significant violations, including unlawful killings, is ongoing.[85] Global development agencies of powerful countries may also be implicated in these crimes since they may have sought to use their 0.7 per cent of Gross Domestic Product in support of such ventures

---

[82] See Bill Tripp, "Our land was taken. But we still hold knowledge of how to stop mega fires", *The Guardian Newspaper*, 16 September 2020 (available on its web site).

[83] Ngambouk V. Pemunta, "Fortress Conservation, wildlife legislation and the Baka Pygmies of southeast Cameroon", in *GeoJournal*, 2019, vol. 84, pp. 1035–1055.

[84] The organisation is currently subject to a self-commissioned independent review related to killings alleged. See Tripp, "Our land was taken. But we still hold knowledge of how to stop mega fires", see above note 82.

[85] Nils Klawitter, "A Killing in Congo Reveals Human Cost of Conservation", *Der Spiegel*, 1 November 2017 (available on its web site).

that are now evidenced as being fatal for both nature and indigenous communities.

It needs to be stressed that protected areas *per se* are not the problem. Such areas may be significant to planetary regeneration, especially if envisaged as safeguarding territories from commercial exploitation and illegal settlement, and creating zones where flora and fauna may once again flourish. But seeking to create these without indigenous peoples at their very core amounts to no more than dereliction in the hope that damaged nature will be able to heal itself. Many progressive options exist: to have indigenous peoples work hand in hand with conservationists with the latter learning from the former; creating conditionalities for indigenous habitation within protected areas; articulating responsibilities upon tenure holders to regenerate the environment, and providing them with the means and resources necessary to achieve these aims.[86] These tenets are under-explored and inadequately framed in the current protected areas policy. The supreme irony in terms of this chapter is that protected areas were first constructed by colonial rulers, to ensure exclusive zones where they could carry out their pastime of hunting unmolested.[87] At that time, the indigenous peoples were a nuisance that got in the way of 'fun'. Those practices over time depleted resources and dismantled communities. That the world may be stumbling towards this as a solution reflects the collective failure of humanity to understand and appreciate human diversity of lived experience. It could prove fatal to the environment.

---

[86] W. Adams, and M. Mulligan, "Introduction", in William Adams and Martin Mulligan (eds.), *Decolonizing Nature Strategies for Conservation in a Post-Colonial Era*, Routledge, 2012, pp. 1–15; also Val Plumwood, "Decolonizing Relationships with Nature", in Adams and Mulligan (eds.), *Decolonizing Nature Strategies for Conservation in a Post-Colonial Era*, Routledge, 2012, pp. 51–78; Kyle A. Artelle, Janet Stephenson, Merata Kawharu and Nancy Turner, "Values-led management: the guidance of place-based values in environmental relationships of the past, present, and future", in *Ecology and Society*, 2018, vol. 23, no. 3, p. 35; Allen Blackman, Leonardo Corral, Eirivelthon S. Lima and Gregory P. Asner, "Titling indigenous communities protects forests in the Peruvian Amazon", in *Proceedings of the National Academy of Science*, 2017, vol. 114, no. 4, pp. 4123–4128.

[87] For more on the origins of protected areas, see Paul Robbins and Amity A. Doolittle (eds.), "Fortress conservation", *Encyclopaedia of Environment and Society*, Sage Publications, Thousand Oaks, 2012.

18.4. Conclusion

Indigenous peoples have been victimised twice by colonization in the past two centuries. The first, at the often-deadly arrival of colonial rulers;[88] the second, in the manner of their departure, which usually encompassed a lasting legacy of systems that proved harmful to the natural environment, with quasi-colonial rulers trained in the system of continued exploitation and domination.[89]

Today, at the edge of the climate change precipice, it is abundantly clear that the lifestyles fuelled by anthroposcenic domination encompassed a belief that all of nature was an exclusive human legacy to be expended without limit. Worse, the dominant worldview remains one that views profit-making as heroic, and the flow of rewards to such enterprise as admirable. For many parts of the world that view became centre-stage with the arrival and subsequent departure of European colonial rulers, and the global environment they created. Like their predecessors, post-colonial States are equally culpable in maintaining hegemonies, and equally at fault for their continued domination and subjugation of indigenous peoples.[90] However, as awareness of these continuing destructive pathways becomes clear, there are a number of solutions that suggest themselves as ways forward. This chapter ends by articulating six of these.

First, full recognition of the personhood of indigenous peoples and the recognition and full return of all ancestral territories.[91] Courts of law across the world have already been showing the way on this issue, but ensuring full implementation of this remains key to a more sustainable future.

---

[88] Elizabeth Colson, "The Impact of the Colonial Period on the Definition of Land Rights", in Peter Duignan, Lewis H. Gann and Victor Turner (eds.), *Colonialism in Africa, 1870–1960*, vol. 3, Cambridge University Press, 1971.

[89] See Christina Folke Ax, Niels Brimnes, Niklas Thode Jensen and Karen Oslund, *Cultivating the Colonies: Colonial States and Their Environmental Legacies*, Ohio University Press, Athens, 2011, and Yogi Hendlin, "From *Terra Nullius* to *Terra Communis*: Reconsidering Wild Land in an Era of Conservation and Indigenous Rights", in *Environmental Philosophy*, 2014, vol. 11, no. 2, pp. 141–174.

[90] Graham Huggan and Helen Tiffin, "Green Postcolonialism", in *Interventions*, 2007, vol. 9, no. 1, pp. 1–11.

[91] Joshua Castellino, "Righting colonial-era wrongs in land rights", *Place*, Thomson Reuters Foundation, 9 April 2019 (available on its web site).

Second, the installation and equipping of indigenous peoples on the basis of their right to self-determination, with the knowhow gained from modern technology in environmental regeneration.[92] This may still involve throwing a protective ring around such territories, but would restore indigenous knowledge gleaned from the legitimate title holders to their territories, as the key driver to environmental regeneration.[93]

Third, the continued regulation and eventual phasing out of reliance on any natural asset that is exploited without adequate opportunity for regeneration.[94] Indigenous communities have lived for centuries off their environment. This has involved benefitting from nature, but in a manner that pays adequate attention to its regeneration.[95]

Fourth, returning to the debate around reparations, but this time seeking out corporations rather than former colonial States that have historically benefitted from the exploitation of nature and whose current operations continue to deplete it. This goes beyond the *polluter pays* principle, to understanding how the importance of legacy firms with hundreds of years of history who have profited from unfettered access to resources,

---

[92] For an authoritative piece that makes this argument, see Lara Dominguez and Colin Luoma, "Decolonising Conservation Policy: How Colonial Land and Conservation Ideologies Persist and Perpetuate Indigenous Injustices at the Expense of the Environment", in *Land*, 2020, vol. 9, no. 3, p. 65.

[93] There are significant models that are in place around the world that merit significant attention. See Janeth Warden-Fernandez, "Indigenous Communities' Rights and Mineral Development", in *Journal of Energy and Natural Resources Law*, 2005, vol. 23, no. 4, pp. 395–426; Emmanuel Freudenthal, Maurizio F. Ferrari, Justin Kenrick, and Adrian Mylne, "The Whakatane Mechanism: Promoting Justice in Protected Areas", in *Nomadic Peoples*, 2012, vol. 16, no. 2, pp. 84–94; Victoria Tauli-Corpuz, Janis Alcorn and Augusta Molnar, "Violations of Indigenous Peoples' and Local Communities' Rights and Steps Towards Reform in 27 Countries", *Indigenous Peoples' Major Group for Sustainable Development* (available on its web site); Liz Alden Wily, "Could collective title become a new norm?", in *RICS Land Journal*, 2019, pp. 15–17; Ross A. Clarke, "Securing Communal Land Rights to Achieve Sustainable Development in Sub-Saharan Africa: Critical Analysis and Policy Implications", in *Law Environmental Development Journal*, 2009, vol. 5, no. 2, pp. 132–150.

[94] Kyra Bos and Joyeeta Gupta, "Stranded assets and stranded resources: Implications for climate change mitigation and global sustainable development", in *Energy Resource and Social Science*, 2019, vol. 56.

[95] Helen Ding, Peter Veit, Erin Gray and Katie Reytar, *Climate Benefits, Tenure Costs: The Economic Case for Securing Indigenous Land Rights in the Amazon*, World Resources Institute, Washington, DC, 2016.

---

paid negligible return for the resource and sought to generate vast profit edifices off this.

Fifth, to pay significantly more attention to ensuring that product supply chains see monetary value distributed more evenly across the process. These supply chains need to also include replacement costs for natural assets removed, and monetary compensation to the owners of the territory from which it may emanate.

Sixth, active consideration needs to be given to the list of activities that should be proscribed completely. Fossil fuels would be high on such a list, but equal consideration should be given to restricting the extent to which other products are sourced, produced, manufactured, sold and disposed of. Eliminating current consumption cycles is vital to taking the steps towards sustainability.

Public international lawyers and others concerned with questions of order and justice need to take a hard look at ourselves to locate the extent to which we may be implicated in the maintenance of our colonial present. The punishment of individuals for genocide, war crimes and crimes against humanity has dominated recent efforts to secure accountability. These amply demonstrate how lawyers can respond to the need to ensure inter-general justice. Yet these limited instruments of criminal law have fallen significantly short of seeking accountability for crimes perpetrated against entire communities that have also resulted in the erections of endemic structural discrimination. The six points above seek a limited objective: to restore indigenous peoples to the centre of the critical fight for climate justice initially perpetrated by colonial rule that has left a lasting legacy of tort. Along the way, this lens, if adopted without bias, will also enable a review of the role of profiteers and their handmaidens in governance, including international lawyers currently venerated with respect, to the way that indigenous peoples often view them: as armed thieves who came in the dark, tricked their way to profit, used law to justify themselves, and devastated the people and planet.

INDEX

A

accretion
  definition, 580
African Charter on Human and Peoples'
  Rights, 484
African Charter on the Rights and Welfare
  of the Child, 152
African Commission on Human and
  Peoples' Rights, 484
African Union, 41, 152, 435, 440
  fact-finding, 496
  International Conference on the Great
    Lakes Region, 440
  Transitional Justice Policy, 64, 88, 477
Algeria, 22
  French amnesty laws, 22
  Front de Libération Nationale, 12, 22
al-Hussein, Zeid Ra'ad, 231
Allende, Salvador, 6
Anghie, Anthony, 240
Anghie, Antony, 4, 323, 503
Anglo-Burmese War, 109, 345
  First, 111, 186, 212, 265, 289, 291
  Second, 111, 212
  Third, 240, 295, 453
annexation, 108, 111, 115, 116
  Burma, 113
  'premature', 107
Arakan, Kingdom of, 110, 177, 257, 288
Arbenz, Jacobo, 6
Arendt, Hannah, 95
armed conflict
  arms trade, 593
  ethnic, 301, 319, 350, 431, 434, 450,
    487
  international, 153, 159, 162, 233, 414
  non-international, 86, 153, 414, 415
Arusha Peace Agreement, 446, 464, 465
Audin, Maurice, 22
Aung San Suu Kyi, 236, 246, 247, 279,
  355, 356

B

Bandung Conference, 1955, xii, 303
Barbie, Claus, 420
Battle of Plassey, 289
Battle of Syriam, 288
Baumgartner, Elisabeth, 244
Belgium, 413, 417
  Code of Criminal Procedure, 417, 421,
    426
  criminal code. *See* criminal code
    (Belgium)
  *Prosecutor and Lumumba v. Huyghe et
    al.* case (Brussels Court of Appeal),
    416
  Transnuklear case (Antwerp Court of
    Appeal), 424, 425
Benvenisti, Eyal, 239
Bergsmo, Morten, 19, 42, 72, 91, 269, 320,
  451, 495
biodiversity, 595
Black Lives Matter, viii, 3, 590
Boer War, 107
Boxer Protocol, 369
Brandt, Willy, 386
Bretton-Woods System, 5
Burma
  annexation, 116, 117, 187, 345
  Arakan. *See* Arakan, Kingdom of
  Baxter Report on Indian Immigration,
    183, 260, 263, 266
  census (1891), 200
  census (1911), 254
  demographic transformation, 236
  economic exploitation, 348
  Government of Burma Act of 1935, 183
  Indo-Burman Immigration Agreement
    of 1941, 183
  Indo-Burman Immigration Agreement
    of 1947, 201
  reconquest, 119
  re-occupation, 74, 86, 120

legitimacy, 18, 19, 37, 84, 246, *See* also
   international law
International Criminal Tribunal for
   Rwanda, 131, 133, 455, 506
   Akayesu case, 564
   co-operation, 460
   hate speech, 455
   Nahimana et al. case, 137
   Semanza case, 131
International Criminal Tribunal for the
   former Yugoslavia, 416, 506
   Kunarac et al. case, 149
   Kupreškić case, 20
international dispute settlement, 367, 377
international law
   access to international law, v
   access to justice, v
   accountability gap, 432, *See* also
      colonial wrongs
   customary law, 28, 86, 142, 154, 156,
      243, 308, 314, 415, 416, 421, 517,
      591
   decolonization, 3, 7
   double standards, ii, 19, 247, 483
   Eurocentrism, 6, 35
   'gentle civiliser of mankind', 19
   'gentle civiliser of nations', 587
   legitimacy, ii, 72, 362, 394
   weaponisation, 583
International Law Commission, xiv, 17,
   87, 131
   Draft Articles on Responsibility of
      States for Internationally Wrongful
      Acts, 314
   draft code on state responsibility, 173
   draft statute for an international criminal
      court, 168
   transfer of civilian population, 242, 245,
      251
international lawyers, ii, x, 1, 84, 96, 122,
   239, 241, 248, 251, 582, 601
International Military Tribunal for the Far
   East, 79
International Monetary Fund, 5
inter-temporality, doctrine of, 15, 16, 17,
   18, 23, 28, 87

J

Japan
   war reparations, 385
Joinet Principles, 494
joint criminal enterprise, 136, 137, 140
jus ad bellum, 71, 86, 98, 99
jus cogens. *See* international law
   (customary law)
jus in bello, 99
jus resistendi ac seccionis, 590
jus sanguinis, 300
justice, notion of, 44

K

Kellogg-Briand Pact, 79, 118, 305
Kelsen, Hans, 44
Kenya, 12
   Mau-Mau uprising, 12, 22, 60
   transitional justice, 50
   Truth, Justice and Reconciliation
      Commission, 51, 56
Konbaung Dynasty, 288, 295
Koskenniemi, Martti, 5, 20
Kussbach, Erich, 100

L

Lange, Matthew, 51
Langer, Maximo, 13
Las Casas, Bartolomé, 4
League of Nations, xiv, 118, 380, 433,
   434
LEE Yanghee, 232
legality, principle of, 83, 128, 129, 140,
   155, 420
   International Criminal Court, 172
   non-retroactivity, 128, 133, 134, 414,
      429
Liberia
   transitional justice, 50
   Truth and Reconciliation Commission,
      51, 55
Lumumba, Patrice, 413
   assassination, 23, 86, 413, *See* also
      Belgium (*Prosecutor and Lumumba v.
      Huyghe et al.* case)

TOAEP TEAM

OTHER VOLUMES IN THE PUBLICATION SERIES

Morten Bergsmo, Mads Harlem and Nobuo Hayashi (editors):
Importing Core International Crimes into National Law
Torkel Opsahl Academic EPublisher
Oslo, 2010
FICHL Publication Series No. 1 (Second Edition, 2010)
ISBN: 978-82-93081-00-5

Nobuo Hayashi (editor):
National Military Manuals on the Law of Armed Conflict
Torkel Opsahl Academic EPublisher
Oslo, 2010
FICHL Publication Series No. 2 (Second Edition, 2010)
ISBN: 978-82-93081-02-9

Morten Bergsmo, Kjetil Helvig, Ilia Utmelidze and Gorana Žagovec:
The Backlog of Core International Crimes Case Files in Bosnia and Herzegovina
Torkel Opsahl Academic EPublisher
Oslo, 2010
FICHL Publication Series No. 3 (Second Edition, 2010)
ISBN: 978-82-93081-04-3

Morten Bergsmo (editor):
Criteria for Prioritizing and Selecting Core International Crimes Cases
Torkel Opsahl Academic EPublisher
Oslo, 2010
FICHL Publication Series No. 4 (Second Edition, 2010)
ISBN: 978-82-93081-06-7

Morten Bergsmo and Pablo Kalmanovitz (editors):
Law in Peace Negotiations
Torkel Opsahl Academic EPublisher
Oslo, 2010
FICHL Publication Series No. 5 (Second Edition, 2010)
ISBN: 978-82-93081-08-1

Morten Bergsmo, César Rodríguez Garavito, Pablo Kalmanovitz and Maria Paula Saffon (editors):
Distributive Justice in Transitions
Torkel Opsahl Academic EPublisher
Oslo, 2010
FICHL Publication Series No. 6 (2010)
ISBN: 978-82-93081-12-8

Morten Bergsmo, César Rodriguez-Garavito, Pablo Kalmanovitz and Maria Paula Saffon (editors):
Justicia Distributiva en Sociedades en Transición
Torkel Opsahl Academic EPublisher
Oslo, 2012
FICHL Publication Series No. 6 (2012)
ISBN: 978-82-93081-10-4

Morten Bergsmo (editor):
Complementarity and the Exercise of Universal Jurisdiction for Core International Crimes
Torkel Opsahl Academic EPublisher
Oslo, 2010
FICHL Publication Series No. 7 (2010)
ISBN: 978-82-93081-14-2

Morten Bergsmo (editor):
Active Complementarity: Legal Information Transfer
Torkel Opsahl Academic EPublisher
Oslo, 2011
FICHL Publication Series No. 8 (2011)
ISBN print: 978-82-93081-56-2
ISBN e-book: 978-82-93081-55-5

Morten Bergsmo (editor):
Abbreviated Criminal Procedures for Core International Crimes
Torkel Opsahl Academic EPublisher
Brussels, 2017
FICHL Publication Series No. 9 (2018)
ISBN print: 978-82-93081-20-3
ISBN e-book: 978-82-8348-104-4

Sam Muller, Stavros Zouridis, Morly Frishman and Laura Kistemaker (editors):
The Law of the Future and the Future of Law
Torkel Opsahl Academic EPublisher
Oslo, 2010
FICHL Publication Series No. 11 (2011)
ISBN: 978-82-93081-27-2

Morten Bergsmo, Alf Butenschøn Skre and Elisabeth J. Wood (editors):
Understanding and Proving International Sex Crimes
Torkel Opsahl Academic EPublisher
Beijing, 2012
FICHL Publication Series No. 12 (2012)
ISBN: 978-82-93081-29-6

Morten Bergsmo (editor):
Thematic Prosecution of International Sex Crimes
Torkel Opsahl Academic EPublisher
Beijing, 2012
FICHL Publication Series No. 13 (2012)
ISBN: 978-82-93081-31-9

Terje Einarsen:
The Concept of Universal Crimes in International Law
Torkel Opsahl Academic EPublisher
Oslo, 2012
FICHL Publication Series No. 14 (2012)
ISBN: 978-82-93081-33-3

莫滕·伯格斯默 凌岩(主编):
国家主权与国际刑法
Torkel Opsahl Academic EPublisher
Beijing, 2012
FICHL Publication Series No. 15 (2012)
ISBN: 978-82-93081-58-6

Morten Bergsmo and LING Yan (editors):
State Sovereignty and International Criminal Law
Torkel Opsahl Academic EPublisher
Beijing, 2012
FICHL Publication Series No. 15 (2012)
ISBN: 978-82-93081-35-7

Morten Bergsmo and CHEAH Wui Ling (editors):
Old Evidence and Core International Crimes
Torkel Opsahl Academic EPublisher
Beijing, 2012
FICHL Publication Series No. 16 (2012)
ISBN: 978-82-93081-60-9

YI Ping:
戦争と平和の間——発足期日本国際法学における「正しい戦争」の観念とその帰結
Torkel Opsahl Academic EPublisher
Beijing, 2013
FICHL Publication Series No. 17 (2013)
ISBN: 978-82-93081-66-1

Morten Bergsmo and SONG Tianying (editors):
On the Proposed Crimes Against Humanity Convention
Torkel Opsahl Academic EPublisher
Brussels, 2014
FICHL Publication Series No. 18 (2014)
ISBN: 978-82-93081-96-8

Morten Bergsmo, CHEAH Wui Ling and YI Ping (editors):
Historical Origins of International Criminal Law: Volume 1
Torkel Opsahl Academic EPublisher
Brussels, 2014
FICHL Publication Series No. 20 (2014)
ISBN: 978-82-93081-11-1

Morten Bergsmo, CHEAH Wui Ling and YI Ping (editors):
Historical Origins of International Criminal Law: Volume 2
Torkel Opsahl Academic EPublisher
Brussels, 2014
FICHL Publication Series No. 21 (2014)
ISBN: 978-82-93081-13-5

Morten Bergsmo, CHEAH Wui Ling, SONG Tianying and YI Ping (editors):
Historical Origins of International Criminal Law: Volume 3
Torkel Opsahl Academic EPublisher
Brussels, 2015
FICHL Publication Series No. 22 (2015)
ISBN print: 978-82-8348-015-3
ISBN e-book: 978-82-8348-014-6

Morten Bergsmo, CHEAH Wui Ling, SONG Tianying and YI Ping (editors):
Historical Origins of International Criminal Law: Volume 4
Torkel Opsahl Academic EPublisher
Brussels, 2015
FICHL Publication Series No. 23 (2015)
ISBN print: 978-82-8348-017-7
ISBN e-book: 978-82-8348-016-0

Morten Bergsmo, Klaus Rackwitz and SONG Tianying (editors):
Historical Origins of International Criminal Law: Volume 5
Torkel Opsahl Academic EPublisher
Brussels, 2017
FICHL Publication Series No. 24 (2017)
ISBN print: 978-82-8348-106-8
ISBN e-book: 978-82-8348-107-5

Morten Bergsmo and SONG Tianying (editors):
Military Self-Interest in Accountability for Core International Crimes
Torkel Opsahl Academic EPublisher
Brussels, 2015
FICHL Publication Series No. 25 (2015)
ISBN print: 978-82-93081-61-6
ISBN e-book: 978-82-93081-81-4

Wolfgang Kaleck:
Double Standards: International Criminal Law and the West
Torkel Opsahl Academic EPublisher
Brussels, 2015
FICHL Publication Series No. 26 (2015)
ISBN print: 978-82-93081-67-8
ISBN e-book: 978-82-93081-83-8

LIU Daqun and ZHANG Binxin (editors):
Historical War Crimes Trials in Asia
Torkel Opsahl Academic EPublisher
Brussels, 2016
FICHL Publication Series No. 27 (2015)
ISBN print: 978-82-8348-055-9
ISBN e-book: 978-82-8348-056-6

Mark Klamberg (editor):
Commentary on the Law of the International Criminal Court
Torkel Opsahl Academic EPublisher
Brussels, 2017
FICHL Publication Series No. 29 (2017)
ISBN print: 978-82-8348-100-6
ISBN e-book: 978-82-8348-101-3

Stian Nordengen Christensen:
Counterfactual History and Bosnia-Herzegovina
Torkel Opsahl Academic EPublisher
Brussels, 2018
Publication Series No. 30 (2018)
ISBN print: 978-82-8348-102-0
ISBN e-book: 978-82-8348-103-7

Stian Nordengen Christensen:
Possibilities and Impossibilities in a Contradictory Global Order
Torkel Opsahl Academic EPublisher
Brussels, 2018
Publication Series No. 31 (2018)
ISBN print: 978-82-8348-104-4
ISBN e-book: 978-82-8348-105-1

Morten Bergsmo and Carsten Stahn (editors):
Quality Control in Preliminary Examination: Volume 1
Torkel Opsahl Academic EPublisher
Brussels, 2018
Publication Series No. 32 (2018)
ISBN print: 978-82-8348-123-5
ISBN e-book: 978-82-8348-124-2

Morten Bergsmo and Carsten Stahn (editors):
Quality Control in Preliminary Examination: Volume 2
Torkel Opsahl Academic EPublisher
Brussels, 2018
Publication Series No. 33 (2018)
ISBN print: 978-82-8348-111-2
ISBN e-book: 978-82-8348-112-9

Morten Bergsmo and Emiliano J. Buis (editors):
Philosophical Foundations of International Criminal Law: Correlating Thinkers
Torkel Opsahl Academic EPublisher
Brussels, 2018
Publication Series No. 34 (2018)
ISBN print: 978-82-8348-117-4
ISBN e-book: 978-82-8348-118-1

Morten Bergsmo and Emiliano J. Buis (editors):
Philosophical Foundations of International Criminal Law: Foundational Concepts
Torkel Opsahl Academic EPublisher
Brussels, 2019
Publication Series No. 35 (2019)
ISBN print: 978-82-8348-119-8
ISBN e-book: 978-82-8348-120-4

Terje Einarsen and Joseph Rikhof:
A Theory of Punishable Participation in Universal Crimes
Torkel Opsahl Academic EPublisher
Brussels, 2018
Publication Series No. 37 (2018)
ISBN print: 978-82-8348-127-3
ISBN e-book: 978-82-8348-128-0

All volumes are freely available online at http://www.toaep.org/ps/. For printed copies, see http://www.toaep.org/about/distribution/. For reviews of earlier books in this Series in academic journals and yearbooks, see http://www.toaep.org/reviews/.

Lightning Source UK Ltd.
Milton Keynes UK
UKHW021237091120
373077UK00014B/1489/J